THEATRE OF THE BOOK
1480–1880

D1323799

THEATRE OF THE BOOK

1480–1880

Print, Text, and Performance in Europe

JULIE STONE PETERS

OXFORD

UNIVERSITY PRESS

OXFORD
UNIVERSITY PRESS

Great Clarendon Street, Oxford OX2 6DP
Oxford University Press is a department of the University of Oxford.
It furthers the University's objective of excellence in research, scholarship,
and education by publishing worldwide in

Oxford New York

Auckland Bangkok Buenos Aires Cape Town Chennai
Dar es Salaam Delhi Hong Kong Istanbul Karachi Kolkata
Kuala Lumpur Madrid Melbourne Mexico City Mumbai Nairobi
São Paulo Shanghai Taipei Tokyo Toronto

Oxford is a registered trade mark of Oxford University Press
in the UK and in certain other countries

Published in the United States
by Oxford University Press Inc., New York

British Library Cataloguing in Publication Data

Data available

Library of Congress Cataloging in Publication Data

Peters, Julie Stone.
Theatre of the book, 1480–1880 : print, text, and performance in Europe / Julie Stone Peters.
Includes bibliographical references and index.
1. European drama—History and criticism. 2. Printing—Europe—History. 3. Theater—Europe—History.
I. Title.
PN1821 .P48 2000   792'.094'0903—dc21   00-040071
ISBN 0-19-818714-9
ISBN 0-19-926216-0 (pbk.)

1 3 5 7 9 10 8 6 4 2

Typeset by Best-set Typesetter Ltd., Hong Kong
Printed in Great Britain
on acid-free paper by
Biddles Ltd,
Guildford and King's Lynn

Acknowledgements

The convention of an "Acknowledgements" is never adequate thanks for the help one receives on a book dependent on so many. Nonetheless, I would like to offer at least partial thanks to those who have been part of this project's slow emergence. I am indebted first, to my colleagues and students at Columbia University and elsewhere, who continued to encourage me through the manuscript's numerous mutations, to inspire its better ideas, to chasten its excesses, and to suggest many of its forking paths. Nathaniel Berman, Rüdiger Bittner, John Brewer, Douglas Brooks, Marvin Carlson, Roger Chartier, Don Cruickshank, Elizabeth Eisenstein, Jean Howard, David Kastan, Jean Pascal Le Goff, Martin Meisel, Walter Ong, Joseph Roach, Austin Quigley, Jeffrey Ravel, Michael Seidel, Andrew Solomon, and Deborah White read portions of the manuscript (some long ago, some on the brink of publication). James Cain, Abigail Dyer, Rhonda Garelick, Martin Puchner, Elizabeth Ruf, and Emery Snyder offered assistance with difficult translations. April Alliston, Paula Backscheider, Gregory Brown, Ellen Gainor, Angelica Goodden, Mel Gordon, Stephen Lewis, and Alan Nelson provided answers to last-minute queries and ideas for sources. To these I am grateful.

    I count myself lucky to have had extraordinary research assistants: Laura Engel, Lisa Hollibaugh, Victoria Rosner, Mark Sanders, Molly Tambor, Paul West, Eric Wilson, Ellen Wurtzel, and Kristina Zarlengo. I owe special thanks to Darren Gobert, at once my primary research assistant, masterful problem-solver, occasional translator, discussant, and commiserator in the woes of the library. That this book has fewer errors than it might is also due to the work of my editors at Oxford University Press, Sophie Goldsworthy and Frances Whistler, and my copy-editor Mary Worthington, who have been exemplary in both their understanding of the book and their patience. The assistance I have received from the librarians at the Biblioteca Nazionale Centrale in Florence, Biblioteca Nacional in Madrid, Bibliothèque Nationale Française, British Library, Columbia University Libraries, Folger Shakespeare Library, Harvard University Libraries, New York Public Library, and Staatsbibliothek in Berlin, as well as those at the other collections on whose resources I have drawn, has been invaluable. The American Council of Learned Societies, American Philosophical Society, Folger Shakespeare Library, Harvard University, Humboldt Foundation, and National Endowment for the Humanities, as well as Columbia's generous leave policy, gave me the financial support necessary to such a large project. Finally, I am inexpressibly grateful to the friends and family members whose love, conversation, and inspiring disputation have most sustained me in these years.

    For permission to reproduce the illustrations I would like to thank the following institutions: the Houghton Library, Harvard University, for figs. 1, 4, 6–7, 9–10,

15–16, 31–2, 35–8, 40–3, 49, 52–3, 56; the Folger Shakespeare Library for figs. 2, 12, 24, 27, 39; the Bibliothèque Nationale Française for figs. 3, 5, 30; the Henry E. Huntington Library for figs. 8, 22, 45, 47, 60; the Harvard Theatre Collection, Houghton Library, Harvard University, for figs. 11, 57; the General Research Division, New York Public Library, Astor, Lenox and Tilden Foundations, for figs. 13–14, 20, 21, 23, 44, 54; the Rare Book and Manuscript Library, Columbia University, for fig. 17; the British Library for figs. 18, 26, 34, 51; the Billy Rose Theatre Collection, New York Public Library for the Performing Arts, Astor, Lenox and Tilden Foundations, for figs. 19, 25; the Swedish National Museum, Stockholm, for figs. 28, 33; the Rare Books Division, New York Public Library, Astor, Lenox and Tilden Foundations, for fig. 29; the Department of Prints and Drawings, British Museum, for figs. 46, 55; the Cabinet des Estampes, Bibliothèque Nationale Française, for fig. 48; the Fogg Museum, Harvard University, for fig. 50; the Dance Division, New York Public Library for the Performing Arts, Astor, Lenox and Tilden Foundations, for fig. 58; and Widener Library, Harvard University, for fig. 59.

Contents

List of Illustrations

Note: See the Works Cited for full titles of book sources.

THEATRVM

Fig. 1. "Theatrum" illustrated in Johann Grüninger's 1496 Strasbourg edition of Terence.

Introduction

In the late fifteenth century, half-improvised farce, costumed civic festivals, biblical stories enacted on platforms, the songs of court poets, and the dancing of mummers were confronted by print—by a drama conceived in the fixed and silent forms of the text. Commentaries on Aristotle and Terence, solemn Latin dramas, learned architectural disquisitions found themselves in the hands of princes with a taste for fireworks and singing shepherds. Performance had to reconceive its relation to the text. In disseminating volumes of Terence and Plautus and Seneca and identifying them with gesticulating actors on stages, with painted streets and trees, in promoting standards against which the multitude of local performance genres could measure themselves, in textualizing the singing of the *jongleurs*, the dance of acrobats, the playing of *histriones*, in circulating images of "scenes" and "theatres," in supplying performers with playbooks, in identifying "comedy" and "tragedy" as the paradigmatic performance genres, print was at the heart of the Renaissance theatrical revival. It is not mere coincidence that theatre and printing emerged as central forms of cultural communication during the same period, that someone like John Foxe could see "players" and "printers" (along with "preachers") as joining forces in the struggle against the antichrist (a "triple bulwark against the triple crown of the pope").[1] The printing press had an essential role to play in the birth of the modern theatre at the turn of the fifteenth century.[2] As institutions they grew up together.

The new theatres were to provide spaces in which the books of Terence, Plautus, and Seneca could be brought to life. The new books were to enshrine the ancient theatre reborn, to offer it up to princes as models for their own, to interpret it for readers, and (perhaps most important) deliberately to misinterpret it, overlooking the precisions of Horace and Donatus and Vitruvius to serve the needs of the new scenic art. The frontispiece to Johann Grüninger's illustrated edition of Terence, for instance (published in the cosmopolitan city of Strasbourg in 1496) (Fig. 1),[3] offers a version of Vitruvius' amphitheatre, with the audience gathered in the circular risers and elevated above the scene. But the theatre is inside out, with the performers at the margins and the spectators at the centre, crowded on ringed balconies wrapped around a tower rising towards the sky (recalling the medieval iconography of the Tower of Babel and the City of Heaven). The spare fifteenth-century domestic space (the shabby peaked roofs, with their few gawky inhabitants dressed in old-fashioned cap and bonnet, crouching where hell-mouth would once have been) seems suddenly to have burst forth into a great cornucopia of spectacle. The "houses" of the medieval mansion setting are transformed into the rounded classical balconies spilling forth their fruits, filled with fashionable and richly robed onlookers, reigned over by a pot-bellied cherub waving his wand from the theatrical heavens, directing (in the scene below) the dancer and scroll-reading herald, emblem of the union of performance and text. It is, ambiguously, Vitruvius grafted onto Babel turned into the joyous City of Heaven, in a parable of interpretation and epiphany matching the illustrator's attempt to construe and reveal the ancient stage—to understand that thing called "theatre."

The chapters that follow offer an account of the entangled histories of print and the modern stage, addressing the meaning of this relationship for the theatre itself and for the broader cultural understanding of text and performance between the sixteenth and nineteenth centuries. The products of dramatic and theatrical printing, their embodied lives in books and in scripts, in theatres and scenes are at the centre of this study: the dramatic texts, the engravings of theatre architecture, the stage designs, the images of actors in their roles, the posters and playbills, programmes and promptbooks, notation systems for acting, dance, and gesture, theatre calendars, biographies and autobiographies, playlists, scrapbooks, and souvenirs that trace their way through the history of the modern European theatre. But I examine these not in and of themselves but as part of the larger cultural imagination, as objects with complex conceptual genealogies and equally complex roles in the unfolding of theatrical culture. This study is, straightforwardly, a history of the interactions between print and theatre, but more broadly it might be seen as a chapter in the cultural history of communication, in how writing gets turned into action and how action gets recorded in writing, in how people conceive of the relation between them, in how they perform themselves to one another in the mutual mirrors of spectacle and the page. The study of the relationship between theatre and printing is, from this perspective, not a sideline in the history of communication but the paradigmatic instance of the interaction between text and performance.

While this project can be understood as a contribution to the history of the book and theatre history generally (both already inherently interdisciplinary, drawing on the tools of literary criticism, art and architectural history, anthropology, dance and music history), it is also bound up with several intertwined theoretical and historical lines of enquiry: the investigation of the nature of "performance" and "text" (in theatre phenomenology, hermeneutics, and semiotics);[4] the theorization of the relationship between speech and writing;[5] and the history of the relationship between technologies of communication and culture[6] (explored in studies of the "impact" of writing and print, of "literate culture" and "print culture," of the relationships among mass media, politics, and culture, and, not least, in the studies of the early modern dramatic text that have proliferated in the past decade).[7] It owes a debt to each of these projects, but it is a critique of them as well. It is an attempt to offer a history of theatre as phenomenon to the ahistorical characterization of the "nature" of theatrical or textual reception—to offer an archaeology of theatrical effects and a genealogy of ideas of theatrical reception as corrective to the static aesthetic model. It is a contribution to the ongoing revision of the broad-brush characterization of the speech/writing relation—the portrait of the unvarying dominance of European "phonocentrism." And, like a number of recent studies, it is an attempt to offer an alternative to the account of the invariable "impact" of writing or print on thought, or the imperial march of "print culture" across Europe, crushing oral culture in its wake.[8] Perhaps most important, it is an attempt to situate textual studies (historically and geographically narrow, dominated by Shakespeare and his contemporaries as they have been) in the wider European context.

That said, in the chapters that follow I have (out of an aesthetic preference for historical narrative that has fully assimilated its meta-narrative) left out further discussion of the theoretical and methodological concerns that have informed my study. The primary materials have changed my mind on many issues, and I have tried to let them do so as much as possible. If they challenge our habitual ways of thinking about text and performance (the unruly and expressive theatrical text reminding us, for example, of the rich and complex lives of texts generally), they do so in ways that resist easy classification and do not bow to the political lessons for which they are sometimes made to stand. My eclectic, multiplicitous (often *ad hoc*) methodology, eschewing a driving theoretical position and suggested as much as possible by the sources on which I draw, is meant to reflect the multiplicity and contrariness of the materials themselves—the contentious dialogue among and between texts. I have, furthermore, avoided as much as possible the conventional chronological, generic, aesthetic, and socio-economic oppositions on which much theatre history has come to rely ("medieval" *versus* "Renaissance," "Baroque" *versus* "Neo-classical," "court" *versus* "school" or "public," "amateur" *versus* "professional"), finding them inadequately descriptive and ultimately more misleading than illuminating for my arguments. Rather than directly contesting them, however, I have allowed the material itself to proffer alternative, and (I hope) more thickly descriptive categories.

I have, moreover, chosen not to offer extended readings of canonical authors, instead joining the voices of "high-culture" figures like Jonson or Corneille or Goethe to the voices of "marginal" figures like the cantankerously "learned" Renaissance playwright Feliciana Enríquez de Guzmán, or the various makers of obscene *commedia dell'arte lazzi*, or the eighteenth-century actress-autobiographer-puppeteer-sausage-seller Charlotte Charke, treating them as equal (if sometimes deviant) witnesses to their cultures' concerns. I have mixed "high" with "low" where they intersect in the cultural moment: sixteenth-century "morals" with plays by Machiavelli or Ariosto; seventeenth-century German *Trauerspiele* with plays by Molière and Racine; masterpieces with trash. I have tried to honour the peculiar against the background of the tellingly conventional. While attempting, then, to do justice to the expressive diversity of theatrical printing and practice, I have tended to highlight trans-European similarities more than dissimilarities as a corrective to the usual nation-based account of theatre history, with its strong contrasts between north and south, Italy and England—misleading given the variation of traditions within nations and the strong and rapid trafficking in ideas and aesthetics that characterizes European theatrical culture. Despite important differences among national theatrical and printing cultures, I have found more shared cultural concerns across Europe than one might expect and, equally, greater diversity within cultures.

The scope of my project—ranging across four centuries and most of Western

Europe—may seem broad to those accustomed to contemporary academic specialization (though Western Europe is, from another perspective, a very small slice of global geography). But this scope was necessary for situating local claims against the larger European and trans-historical background, necessary for giving context to (and in some cases correcting the overcorrections of) local reading. More than anything, it registers my sense of the inadequacy of the focus on the local alone, my discomfort with the burdening of the single telling instance with a vast historical supernarrative. Like those who have attacked universal models of the impact of literacy and print, I am leery of relying solely on global overviews, with their implicit claims about a purported universality and their colonization of the local. But I am equally leery of relying solely on local accounts, with their implicit claims about phenomena beyond their purview. We need both in a continuing conversation. In taking the broad view, I have been forced to attend to evidence that challenges strong arguments about early modern "epistemic ruptures" or "paradigm shifts" in various periods. This has meant marking persistent topoi across the entire period, implicitly arguing for a degree of conceptual continuity or recurrence (hence what may seem my sometimes rather free movement among periods), and noting conflicting attitudes within a given moment, attending to rhetorical repetitions and contradictions both within and across periods, offering an account that recognizes both change and recurrence (equal and mutually determinative) as significant objects of historical narrative.

My study is not about the rise of print culture in the theatre, then, but about the European theatre's resistance to and continual refashioning of itself in the world of print. Whether one thinks of the general changes brought by the press as a revolution, or as part of a slow evolution from, say, the twelfth century (when Church and State administration began to grow dependent on writing), or as a set of revolutions, or as both revolution and evolution, and whether one thinks of the technologies themselves or the people or the uses of writing and print as agents of change, change there was.[9] But the literate was in no way "displacing" the oral (as the centrality not only of theatre but also of forensic, religious, and political oratory in early—and late—modern culture reminds us). And the significant transformations in the relationship between print and theatre are not best seen as steadily evolutionary or revolutionary, but as something more kaleidoscopic: moving in fits and starts, drawing on pre-existing institutions, conceptual paradigms, and aesthetic forms, and recombining and remaking them in constantly shifting ways. Insofar as there were "developments" in any sense, they were constructed by those looking back on their own history, assemblages that are themselves among the objects of my study. One large and very simple historical claim stands, however: after print, performance was never the same.

✦

In the English-speaking world, Shakespeare's career has helped to produce one of those enduring lies so convenient to the history of progress: that Renaissance dramatists were unconcerned with the circulation of their work on the page; that the press kept aloof from the stage and the early stage kept aloof from the press. But nearly a century before Shakespeare was born, there began, in fact, to develop a relationship that would help create the theatre for which he wrote. Printing, far from being marginal to the Renaissance theatre, was crucial at the outset. Those writing plays during the first century of printing were, in fact, deeply invested in the new technology. Jakob Wimpheling, whose classical play *Stilpho* had been performed in Heidelberg around 1480, encouraged his pupil Peter Attendorn to learn printing (giving him several of his own works to print).[10] Both Juan del Encina and Bartolomé de Torres Naharro, central figures in the Spanish theatrical revival, performed in their own works and saw to their publication (Encina's *Cancionero* in 1496, Torres Naharro's *Propalladia* in 1517).[11] Giangiorgio Trissino, author of the tragedy *Sofonisba* (1524), followed developments in typography closely, and he himself introduced new letter styles for Italian printing.[12] John Rastell printed his own editions of the dramatic *Dialogue of Gentleness and Nobility* and his version of the tragicomedy, *Calisto and Meliboea*, in the same year in which he produced them in the theatre in his garden at Finsbury (around 1527).[13] The prolific playwright Hans Sachs's interest in the printing trade can be seen in the illustrations to his *True Description of All Trades* (1568).[14]

As important, those attempting to re-create ancient performances on stages in academies, universities, and courts across Europe were drawing their inspiration from the Terence editions and the illustrated editions of Vitruvius that began to come out in the first decade of the sixteenth century.[15] At least some of those creating productions in the late fifteenth and early sixteenth centuries were the same people committed to seeing ancient plays or commentaries into print. The images that circulated reflected—even if sometimes in distorted form—what humanists were striving to do on actual stages throughout Europe.[16] The humanist scholar Giovanni Sulpizio, who participated in the classical productions in Rome in the late fifteenth century, edited the first edition of Vitruvius in the 1480s, which he dedicated to Cardinal Raffaele Riario, the theatrical patron: "You were the first to reveal the appearance of a decorated stage when Pomponio's troupe played a comedy."[17] Scholar-dramatists creating reconstructions of the ancient theatre over the next decades drew on the products of the press, their libraries lined with works on classical architecture and the classical drama.[18] People creating theatrical buildings and scenes depended on the modern architectural guides: Andrea Palladio and Vincenzo Scamozzi's Teatro Olimpico in Vicenza used Sebastiano Serlio's *Architettura* (the second book, with a section on theatres, published in Paris in 1545), along with Vitruvius;[19] Serlio's illustrations of tragic, comic, and satyric scenes were widely reproduced in editions of Vitruvius and became a set design staple, along with Leon Battista Alberti's Vitruvian-influenced *De re aedificatoria*, first published in 1485 and often reprinted in the sixteenth century.[20]

The humanist comedies and tragedies played on experimental stages across Europe were starting to be published in the late fifteenth century: Jakob Wimpheling's *Stilpho* in 1495; in 1498, Johannes Reuchlin's *Scenica Progymnasmata* (which had been produced with a chorus and scene changes in Heidelberg the previous year).[21] By the first decade of the sixteenth century the major Greek and Latin dramatists were in print; by the end of the century, most of them had been published in the major European vernaculars, joining the proliferating number of dramatic essays and treatises on theatre architecture.[22] But non-humanist plays were also printed from the beginning: by the late fifteenth century, the presses were producing mysteries like Jean Michel and Arnoul Gréban's the *Mystery of the Passion* (printed in twenty-one editions between 1486 and 1542); saints' plays like Antonia Pulci's *Representation of Saint Guglielma* (printed in Florence in numerous editions from the 1490s on), biblical plays, farces, moralities, interludes.[23] Large collections began to emerge in the first half of the sixteenth century: Nicholas Brylinger's *Comœdiæ ac tragœdiæ* published in Basel in 1540 and John Oporinus' *Dramata sacra* in 1547; a collection of "authentic" saints' lives, along with "histories" of "the acts of the Caesars" and "descriptions of the figures of the apocalypse," with "the cruelties of Nero and Domitian," "played by characters" in Paris and published in two volumes in 1537.[24] Like the treatises, plays could see numerous editions: Encina's works appeared in seven editions between 1496 and 1516 alone; the farce *Maistre Pierre Pathelin* came out in dozens of editions in the fifteenth and sixteenth centuries; Fernando de Rojas' tragi-comedy, the *Comedia of Calisto and Melibea* (*La Celestina*), was printed in various languages over forty times in the sixteenth century. There were at least thirteen Italian editions of Trissino's *Sofonisba* in the sixteenth century, fifteen of Machiavelli's *Mandragola*, twenty-six of Bibbiena's *Calandra*, around forty of Théodore de Bèze's *Abraham sacrifiant*, and, in its first *year* alone, ten editions of Tasso's *Torrismondo*.[25] Terence (viewed as the most performable of the ancients) had appeared in some 650 editions by 1600.[26]

This does not mean that most plays performed actually got printed, that it was normal for a play to be printed as many times as *Pierre Pathelin* or *La Celestina*, or that the production of printed playtexts was particularly large (as compared with that in later periods).[27] There continued to be an important culture of manuscript circulation, sustaining performance well into the seventeenth century and beyond. Travelling troupes and scholars, diplomatic envoys and artists continued to be crucial transporters of theatrical culture. But they now carried printed books with them: presentation copies; production guides. Plays were translated back and forth between vernaculars, distributed by the institutional networks of the developing book trade. If it mattered to dramatic performance that scholars from northern Europe travelled through Italy and France to study with those dedicated to understanding the ancient stage, it mattered equally that illustrated Terences and Plautuses were circulated throughout Europe, their woodcuts copied again and again in dramatic editions.[28] If it was important to recording Renaissance spectacles that the French illustrator Jacques Callot came to Florence for the Medici festivals and the Alsatian engraver Matthias Greuter worked in Rome, it was equally important that their etchings of the festivals were sold throughout Europe. If it was important to the diffusion of classical scenic design that Inigo Jones went to Rome and Vicenza, it was equally important that he carried back to London a copy of Serlio, along with Bernardo Buontalenti's and Giulio Parigi's theatrical prints. In building theatres and designing scenes, architects and scenographers relied on the technical manuals emerging from the press: guides for artists like Giacomo da Vignola's *Two Rules of Perspective Practice* (1583) (with its scene-changing mechanisms). They drew on prints of the new theatres for their own: Serlio's theatre built in Vicenza in 1539, portrayed in the many editions of his *Architettura*; Bernardo Buontalenti's 1586 "*teatro grande*" in Florence, portrayed in Callot's etchings.[29]

With the establishment of professional troupes and theatres over the course of the sixteenth century, actors came to rely on printed editions to fill out their repertoires. By the middle decades of the sixteenth century, publishers were regularly producing texts specifically tailored to amateur players, with smaller casts and shorter speeches: Ulpian Fulwell's *Like Will to Like* (1568), which boasts that "five may easely play this Enterlude," or Nathaniel Woodes's *Conflict of Conscience* (1581), whose title page offers "the Actors names" as "most convenient . . . either to show this Comedie in private houses, or otherwise."[30] Printed editions of plays that had never found a performance venue now could: when Adrien Talmy's troupe was performing in Arras in 1594, it had in its repertoire Garnier's previously unperformed *Les Juives*, *La Troade*, and *Hippolyte*, which had been published between 1573 and 1583.[31] Troupes regularly used printed plays on the road. An official permit allows an unnamed troupe to play in Saint-Omer, France in 1599, representing "several *comedies* and *moralities* of which they have exhibited the printed books."[32] The first quartos of *The White Devil*, *A Looking Glasse for London and England*, *The Travels of the Three English Brothers*, *Pericles*, and *King Lear* were used as working texts by various touring companies in the 1610s,[33] the kind of troupes Aminadab in Middleton's *The Mayor of Queenborough* describes as "country comedians" who "abuse simple people with a printed play or two, which they bought at Canterbury for sixpence."[34]

Print, then, was central to the late fifteenth- and sixteenth-century theatrical revival, and it continued to shape its unfolding history. As the press began to circulate dramatic texts and images of the ancient theatre, as the multiple late-medieval entertainment genres were interwoven with the classical genres in the new plays being circulated by the press, an institution (or, more accurately, a set of institutions) was created. Theatres used exclusively for the production of plays sprang up. Elaborate perspectival views were created in them. There was more money for costumes and machines. Performances no longer had to wait for festivals, or for a wandering troupe, just arrived in town. Professional actors were able to put down roots and enter into complicated financial transactions. Customers paid to watch them. Playbooks circulated, and troupes used them, keeping a collection of scripts for the repertoire. Against these new institutional forms, gathered under the rubric "theatre," the multiplicity of performance forms came to be measured: some amalgamated, some ranked as worthy in this new cultural world, some rejected as archaic, some pushed to the margins. It perhaps bears repeating that generic change did not mean generic—or even institutional—discontinuity, as so much of the scholarship on medieval and Renaissance theatre of the last century has shown.[35] But by the end of the sixteenth century, it became difficult for spectators and readers in most places to think of entertainments with actors and not relate them to "tragedy" and "comedy" in scenic spaces, however rudimentary those spaces might be. By century's end, "theatre" was a trans-European phenomenon, in which performers and those who wrote for them—players, revels masters, dramatic poets—had to find their place. By then (as I will show), the distinction between dramatic text and theatrical performance had displaced the medieval distinction between merely reciting plays and "represent[ing]" them "with [one's] limbs."[36] Drama was understood to play itself out in two arenas—on the stage and on the page. The elaboration of the distinction between text and performance, between the experience of reading and the experience of watching a play—made possible by the proliferation of dramatic texts in the theatre and in the bookstalls—became one of the tasks of commentators and dramatists, actors and spectators in the centuries that followed.

◆

My first three chapters are roughly chronological, offering an overview of the history of European dramatic publication (building on the fragmentary accounts of other scholars but resting primarily on my own work with early editions)[37]—a history that serves as the foundation for the sections that follow (which range across periods but generally move from the early Renaissance towards the nineteenth century). Chapter 1, "Experimenting on the Page, 1480–1630," describes the creation of typographic conventions for the drama and the relations among theatrical troupes, dramatists, and publishers during the period of the establishment of professional theatre in Europe. Chapter 2, "Drama as Institution, 1630–1760," describes the regular publication of drama in conjunction with performance, the interactions of dramatists with the increasingly sophisticated book trade, and the magisterial editions and rough quartos of the high era of dramatic publication. Chapter 3, "Illustrations, Promptbooks, Stage Texts, 1760–1880," describes the mass printing of plays and scenic illustrations, the vogue for published promptbooks and prints of actors, and the problems of theatrical copyright resulting from the expansion of dramatic publishing and of the theatre industry during the period.

The chapters in "Theatre Imprimatur" explore the role of the printed text in the formation and legitimation of Renaissance theatrical culture—its role in shaping the identity of "theatre," the "regular" drama, and the dramatic "author" through the imprimatur of the book. Chapter 4, "Reinventing 'Theatre' via the Printing Press," looks at the impact of printed plays, treatises on poetics, and theatrical images on the performance culture of late fifteenth- and early sixteenth-century Europe—their role in creating, out of the multitude of medieval performance forms, a normative notion of "theatre": a place where comedies and tragedies were to be represented by actors "playing by the book." Chapter 5, "Critical Law, Theatrical Licence," explores the tension between, on the one hand, manuals for the improvement of written and spoken language, norms for scholarly annotation, and "the Rules" (identified with the learned book and reflecting the critical authority of the state) and, on the other, the "licentious" theatre, embracing its own populism and drawing an alternative legitimacy from a spectatorship defined in opposition to the page. Chapter 6, "Accurate Texts, Authoritative Editions," explores the mutual constitution of the "accurate edition," the individuated dramatic author, and the author's "original," monumentalized in the grand collected edition of the seventeenth century.

The chapters in "The Senses of Media" discuss the ways in which Renaissance theatrical aesthetics and the understanding of its particular media were shaped through the contrast between theatrical reception and reading and through the relationship between the book and the stage. Chapter 7, "The Sense of the Senses: Sound, Gesture, and the Body on Stage," examines the role of print in the representation and notation of theatrical media, looking at the shifting positions of the senses identified with them: the disappearance of the tactile and olfactory; the legitimation of stage gesture; the marginalization of metre in the context of anxieties around purely sensuous sound. Chapter 8, "Narrative Form and Theatrical Illusions," examines the Renaissance insistence on the shaping of narrative form to conditions of presentation—the insistence on drama as a performance genre distinct from other literary genres, one reliant on the unities of time and place to defend its illusionism from the spectator's intrusive senses. Chapter 9, "Framing Space: Time, Perspective, and Motion in the Image," looks at dramatic illustrations, theatrical images, and architectural manuals, examining the reciprocal mirroring of page space and stage space: the creation of the focused and single-perspective view, framed by the "frontispiece" (theoretically protected from extra-scenic distraction and stilled in time); the graphic mapping of plot and spectacle; and the problems of translation between the flat and static image and the deep and mobile stage.

The chapters in "The Commerce of Letters" look at the seventeenth- and eighteenth-century dramatist as commercial producer, and at the political and legal culture simultaneously produced by and producing the marketplace of print. Chapter 10, "Dramatists, Poets, and Other Scribblers," discusses the claims of dramatic "poets" and usurping "poetesses," attempting to distinguish themselves from the mass of aspiring scribblers, self-idealizing in distinguished editions, urgently claiming their descent from the ancients, trying to escape the world of commercial production and rapid obsolescence in the merciless economics of both playhouse and Grub Street. Chapter 11, "Who Owns the Play? Pirate, Plagiarist, Imitator, Thief," explores the repudiation of imitation, the identification of piracy and plagiarism as thievery, and the distinction of poetic "original" from copy—crucial to the conceptualization of the playtext as authorial property, by nature owned by the author-creator. Chapter 12, "Making It Public," looks at the interplay between theatrical and print-based constructions of the "public," a public reshaped by print, by changes in patronage, and against shifting notions of the "nation" and the "Republic of Letters."

The chapters in "Theatrical Impressions" look at the effects of the eighteenth- and nineteenth-century celebration of the theatrical, inscribed and reproduced *en masse* in prints, periodicals, promptbooks, and illustrated editions. Chapter 13, "Scenic Pictures," examines the theatre's use of the pictorial image, discussing the dramatist's attempt to harness both the descriptive power of the novel and the emotional power of the picture through the lavish scenic and character indications of the eighteenth- and nineteenth-century text. Chapter 14, "Actor/Author," describes the role of print in the creation of the actor as author of the scene—paradigm of social role-playing, prototype for the changeling self as subject. Chapter 15, "A Theatre Too Much With Us," looks at the renewal of anti-theatricalism in response to the extra-spectacular nineteenth-century theatre, the aversion to the cumbersome palpability of stage bodies and the turn towards the closet, but the simultaneous recognition of the inherent powers of the theatrical (in formal aesthetics as well as stage practice) and the resulting articulation of an idealist aesthetics married to a theatricalism that could be key to the spectator's transcendent imagination.

The Epilogue, finally, looks briefly at the transformation of the theatre in the wake of the late nineteenth- and twentieth-century mass media (from the advent of on-stage photography in the 1880s to the development of gramophone and cinema in the twentieth), marking the beginning of an era in which theatre would live in fraught relation with the performing machine and the end of an era in which theatre was seen through, defined by, and understood in relation to the printed text.

Note on Editions, Spellings, Translations, and Citations

Where visual or bibliographic aspects are material to my argument, I have cited to the relevant early edition. While there is a strong argument to be made for using only early editions,[1] I have (for the convenience of those with limited access) used modern editions where I am not dealing directly with visual or bibliographic aspects of a text. Since my discussion generally focuses on the representation of performance in print rather than on the performances themselves, the dates I give are dates of publication, unless otherwise noted. Like most short-title catalogues, I have generally relied on imprints for dating. While imprints are notoriously unreliable, the bibliographic work involved in investigating precise publication dates would have been over-whelming, and to-the-month dating is rarely material to my arguments. I have generally followed the dating of my sources, not converting dates to the Gregorian calendar (adopted by most Roman Catholic states in 1582 and ten days ahead of the Julian calendar, still used in England until 1752).

Out of deference to English-speaking readers, all material in the text proper is in English, but out of a recognition of the important nuances that are lost in translation I have provided original language quotations and titles in the notes. The majority of the material with which I have dealt has not been translated or has been translated badly, so I have been obliged to do my own, certainly flawed, translations. Where there is no citation to a translation but only to a text in a language other than English, the translation is mine. Otherwise, I cite to the translation I have used, as well as to the original. For reasons of economy, my citations use short titles (full citations are provided in the list of "Works Cited"), with any further identifying information in parentheses. I cite non-consecutively paginated volumes by short title, followed by a bracketed citation to the work within the volume and its page number. Act, scene, and line numbers appear in the form IV.ii.2–7 (Act 4, Scene 2, lines 2–7). I have generally preserved original orthography (in English and other languages), modernizing only consonantal *i*'s and *u*'s, vocalic *v*'s and *j*'s and long *s*'s, unless otherwise noted. I have also reproduced most of the features of typography normally honoured in "original spelling" editions (shifts between italic and roman, the capitalization of individual words). It is, however, difficult for a modern text to mimic the expressive typography of early editions (the variation of typefaces, letter sizes, word breaks, and so on), and would, in any case, be too distracting. Photographs illustrate these features better than any attempt at perfect transcription could. Those I have provided should, in themselves, serve as something of a visual-documentary history of the theatrical text.

PRINTING THE DRAMA

1. *Experimenting on the Page, 1480–1630*

THE PROLIFERATION OF PLAYTEXTS

Before the late fifteenth century, playtexts were hard to find. City officials looking for a script for a major spectacle had to arrange for a copy to be made (an emissary had to go all the way from Abbeville to Paris in 1452 to get a copy of Arnoul Gréban's Passion from Gréban himself) or—not necessarily more difficult—to send for the poet (or "maker") to create the performance from scratch.[1] Travelling entertainers had to invent their material or find it where they could, in stories from the great "authors," in jokes and songs heard along the way, in books like the collections of *sermons joyeux*. Many kinds of texts were usable for performance, but these were not necessarily intended for acting or conceived as theatrical. There were, of course, specifically dramatic texts to be found: of miracles, saints' plays, passion plays, or mysteries (from the early fifteenth century on); of plays like the twelfth-century *Adam* or *The Sacred Resurrection*, with their numerous stage directions. There were ornate presentation copies, like the Arras manuscript of Eustache Mercadé's *Mystery of the Passion* (from c.1470), with its beautifully rendered illustrations of such scenes as the Procès de Paradis.[2] But these were rare. Rare too (before the late fifteenth century) were the working manuscripts of mysteries and pageants, sometimes kept as register copies with a guild, *confrérie*, or city clerk, held in a safe for the next performance. Moreover, many of these were merely performance guides (*abregiés*, *livres de conduite du régisseur*, *Dirigierolle*), made for the director or "ordinary" or *meneur de jeu* (not for readers or actors), indicating no more than the order of appearances, general stage directions, and first lines of speeches and songs.[3]

As theatrical activity increased along with leisure-time reading, as both printers and scriptoria began to produce dramatic texts, more people started describing and documenting theatrical events. Performance records from before the late fifteenth century are scarce. Most of what we know of church plays, of the feast-day processionals, the folk drama, saints' plays, the songs and jokes of minstrels and *jongleurs*, the plays of the mummers, even the later interludes and guild plays, has had to be pieced together from account books and fragmentary comments, or extrapolated from later records.[4] But by the mid-sixteenth century, there was an abundance of documentation: descriptions of dramatic events like those at the 1548 wedding of the Infanta María, for instance; of parades like *The Cavalcade of the Ass . . . in the City of Lyon* (1566); later, of masques and festivals and devices and stage plays.[5]

At the same time, the period produced an abundance of playtexts, printed and manuscript. Like festival descriptions, printed plays could serve as forms of documentation—records of an event—but they served a multitude of other purposes.

They could be, among other things: testimony to the generosity of the performance's patron; instructions to performers on how to put on a play; recollections for the spectator of past performances; libretti or souvenirs; or quite simply (like other forms of literature) books of pleasure or instruction for readers and listeners. Most plays had multiple purposes; most printers and writers attempted to represent the past simultaneously in a variety of ways, and to offer their goods up to a variety of possible future uses and users. Classical dramas intended for learned readers, for instance, might in fact be used as texts for school plays, or by members of the audience who needed help with their Latin, like Queen Elizabeth and several members of her court, who were given five copies of Plautus at the Westminster Boys' performance of the *Miles Gloriosus* in 1565.[6]

I will discuss in greater detail below plays written specifically for the professional theatre and printed from playhouse or author manuscripts. But, while these came to dominate the sense of what drama was, throughout the period there were numerous playtexts that gave no indication of performance: the many cheaply printed fifteenth- and sixteenth-century saints' plays, for instance, farces, religious and polemical plays, plays on classical or biblical subjects, multi-character dialogues of various kinds. The short saints' plays, farces, morals on traditional themes (*Patient Griselda*, *The Prodigal Son*) tended to serve the same purpose as other kinds of entertaining reading. They might be used by the kinds of performers Shakespeare imagines in *A Midsummer Night's Dream*—enthusiastic amateurs—or by travelling troupes without "house" dramatists. But they were also intended for readers: those looking for stories made for reading aloud; those who did not wish to struggle with longer plays, those in search of the comforts of the familiar.

Plays, however, that had already been performed as large-scale, public events tended to identify their performance successes on their title pages, even if their authors and printers hoped for readers outside the limited circle of those who were present. When a late fifteenth-century edition of Jean Michel's version of Arnoul Gréban's *Passion* claims proudly that it "was played with great triumph and sumptuousness in Angers in the year 1486 at the end of August," when subsequent editions note later performances, they are celebrating both the authors' success and that of the city, while offering a record (true or fabricated) of the performance.[7] Some texts were geared specifically towards future performance. Masques, triumphs, and other highly spectacular productions could generate something like programmes explaining the spectacle (expansions of the playbills that were used for advertising, and to be sold at the performance): £197 "paid to Mr Heminge and Mr Thomas Dekker, the Poet," read the accounts of the King's company in 1612, "for the devise of the Land shewes . . . and for the printing of the bookes of the Speeches."[8] We have already seen the use of printed texts by sixteenth-century actors of various sorts. The many texts that offered explanations of how they were to be played were clearly intended for performers, whether travelling troupes or town amateurs of the kind that would have been likely to perform the *Very Excellent and Sacred Mystery of the Old Testament* which explains (in the 1542 Paris edition): "Note that whoever plays the character of God must be at the opening here all alone in paradise until he has created the angels."[9] But, like many such texts, this voluminous Mystery was also intended for readers and connoisseurs of picture books, as the woodcuts, table of contents, and elegant layout show (Fig. 2). The editors of the Terence edition published by Johann Trechsel in Lyon in 1493 specify that they have done their work "so well that even the illiterate can read and understand the comic argument, thanks to the images that we have juxtaposed with each scene."[10] The amateur actor or avid play-goer might also be a lover of books.

TYPOGRAPHY, MISE EN PAGE, AND THE "DRAMATIC"

The attempt to create, in the text of the *Mystery of the Old Testament*, a tool service-able to actors and readers alike reflects the desire on the part of sixteenth-century editors and printers both to make the book as useful to the reader as possible and, at the same time, to clarify the visual semiotics of the dramatic page. Typography was both order and meaning (though it could struggle between conflicting signifying impulses: Jacques Bouchet is uncertain whether he should use "bloody vermillion" to signify "the Fury" in his 1555 edition of Jean de La Péruse's *Médée* or black, to sig-nify his mourning for the recently deceased La Péruse).[11] Printing was central to shaping the look and meaning of the drama. But it was not, of course, instantly trans-formative. While fifteenth-century manuscript producers were already beginning to define the drama through layout and lettering, pre-sixteenth-century manuscript plays look in many ways like non-dramatic texts, and most early printed playtexts look much like the manuscript plays that preceded them.[12] The distinction may, in fact, be an artificial one: books made during this period often combined printed and manuscript elements, and manuscript works and printed works were often bound together.[13] In one copy of the 1476 Venetian Terence, for instance, the large illumi-nated letters beginning each section are hand drawn, as are the smaller initial letters of every line of Terence's text, and spaces have been left in the commentary for Greek words to be entered by hand.[14] Even in books not intended for scholarly readers, printers often left room for scribal completion. In *The Nature of the Four Elements*, printed by John Rastell in 1519, instructions for singers are followed by four blank music bars, which are to be filled in with hand-drawn notes, like those added to one of the songs in several copies: "Tyme to pas with goodly sport our spryte."[15]

Typefaces imitated the variety of scribal hands. In their use of red and black ink, title pages modelled themselves on the work of hand colourists. Even where typo-graphic conveniences had rendered manuscript conventions obsolete, manuscript conventions lingered. The marking of paragraphs by hand, for instance, was dis-placed by paragraph indentation in the early decades of print, but many sixteenth-century books still have paragraph markers, sometimes in combination with indentation. The letters on the page in the earliest printed plays (as in other kinds of books during the period) tend to follow large-scale visual patterns, responding to decorative sensibilities rather than serving ease of reading. Words are often broken randomly to fit visual-spatial designs, for instance in the many funnel-shaped title-page designs (that in Richard Pynson's *Everyman* (*c*.1510–19) or in Henrique Ayres

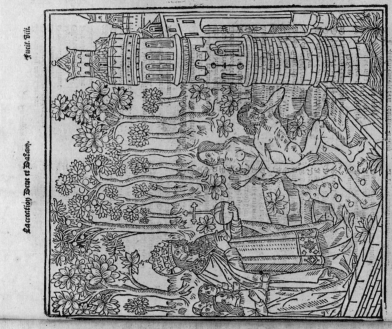

FIG. 2. "The Creation of Eve and Adam" in *The Very Excellent and Sacred Mystery of the Old Testament* (1542 edition).

Victoria's *Tragedy of Revenge* (1555)). While there is often marginal white space in early sixteenth-century plays, there is little use of white space either to differentiate one work from the work that follows, to differentiate separate parts of a work, or even (in some cases) to separate words.[16] Acts and even plays may be run together: a new play may begin on a line on which the preceding play ended, with no visual indication that another play is beginning. A new speaker's line may simply continue on the same line as the last speaker's, with little indication that there has been a change of speaker.

By the beginning of the sixteenth century, however, the shape of the printed page was changing, both in dramatic and non-dramatic books. Publishers were beginning to create distinctive front matter for playbooks (as for other kinds of books), including title pages (becoming conventional in most places, though not universal, from the mid-sixteenth century on) and (often) inviting illustrations which could advertise the book's contents (Fig. 3).[17] Book producers were growing freer with white space: within plays, and at the end of plays, acts, and scenes; at the ends and beginnings of lines. Typefaces were growing lighter and more varied: roman displaced gothic in Italy by the 1530s, and in England and Spain by the end of the century, with front matter and verse often differentiated with italics, and books experimenting with elaborate scripts, as on the title pages for Hans Sachs's works (Fig. 4).[18] By the sixteenth century, new or increasingly conventional features facilitated the identification of the text and its producers, for instance printers' ornaments at the ends of texts or on title pages. Foliation or pagination, indented paragraphs, running titles, catchwords, tables of contents, and indexes contributed to the ease with which the reader could move around in the text: "Indexing table of the first volume of the Actes of the Apostles, for finding, in order, the deeds, acts, miracles, conversions, martyrdoms, and passions of the saint apostles . . . according to the chapters and material one is seeking," declares the table of contents of the 1537 *Mystery of the Acts of the Apostles*.[19]

While utility and beauty were often allied, where they were not, utility tended to win out over beauty even in the early sixteenth century. When Aldus Manutius began experimenting in the early sixteenth century with down-sized octavos of the ancients for school boys to carry, he understood something about the new reading public. The small octavo of Fernando de Rojas' *Celestina* printed in Venice in 1525 explains that it has now been "edited in a more convenient format."[20] Publishers continued to produce large volumes, noble and impressive editions meant to have a certain grandeur and significance in the library: Encina's *Cancionero* (1509); Sachs's five-volume *Gedicht* (1558–79); most famous, Jonson's 1616 folio *Workes* and Shakespeare's 1623 folio *Comedies, Histories, & Tragedies* (a format linking them not only with the early folio editions of the ancients, but also with geographies, law books, and sacred texts, as William Prynne complained).[21] But of the many collections produced in the sixteenth and early seventeenth centuries—dignified works seen as worthy of being published and republished—most came out in smaller formats: Aretino's *Quattro comedie* (1588) was in octavo; Garnier's *Tragédies* appeared repeatedly in duodecimo; even in England plays were most commonly

Comedia de:
calisto ȳ melibẽ
Có sus argumétos nueuaméte añadidos
La ql cótiene ȯ mas ȯ su agradable ȳ dulce estilo muchas sentécias
filosofales: ȳ auisos muy necessarios pa mancebos: mostrádo les los
engaños que estan encerrados en siruientes ȳ alcahuetas.:.

HVGVETANI.

FIG. 3. The title page of the 1501 Seville edition of Fernando de Rojas's *Calisto and Melibea*
(*La Celestina*).

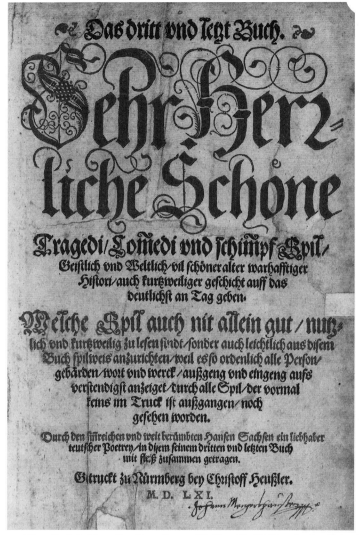

FIG. 4. Hans Sachs's *Tragedies, Comedies, and "schimpf Spil"* ("insult plays") (1561).

published in collections ranging from quarto to duodecimo, not in folio.[22] In England and Spain, individual stage plays in the vernacular were almost always in quarto from the later sixteenth century on, but the most common format for printed drama (as for other kinds of works) was the octavo, small enough to be portable but spacious enough to be easily readable.[23]

If printed drama was, then, from the beginning geared towards the needs of readers, it was not initially geared towards readers accustomed to seeing staged plays. Late fifteenth- and early sixteenth-century drama could be conceptually

indistinguishable from other genres (often meant equally for reading or public recitation, but not necessarily meant for scenic representation with actors). It would be
overstating things to say, on the one hand, that there was no distinctively dramatic
mise en page until the sixteenth century, or that typography created the drama as a distinct genre. One need only look at Pierre Levet's edition of *Pierre Pathelin* (printed
in 1489), with its clear, centred speech-prefixes and vivid illustrations (Fig. 5), to recognize that writers and printers had such conventions available to them. It would also
be misleading to suggest that a single convention came to dominate throughout

FIG. 5.   Pierre Levet's illustrated edition of *Pierre Pathelin* (printed in 1489).

Europe. The Germans and Italians, for instance, continued through the sixteenth and seventeenth centuries to publish prefatory descriptions of the action (often printed separately for use as programmes). If, from the early sixteenth century, Italian dramatic editions modelled themselves on the *mise en page* of the Latin drama, only in the 1630s did the French adopt the Italian style, and the English and Spanish only sporadically followed suit.[24] But it is certainly the case that typography helped to spread and conventionalize particular ways of representing drama on the page: throughout Europe in the first half of the sixteenth century, dramatic *mise en page* looked much like the *mise en page* of other kinds of works; only in the later sixteenth century did it develop conventions that reflected the drama's generic particularity. The majority of fifteenth- and early sixteenth-century dramatic texts (cheaply printed saints' plays, farces, the various kinds of dialogues mentioned above) long continued to be nearly identical to other kinds of works (dialogues, pamphlet tales, devotional exercises), with no *dramatis personae*, no distinctive generic identification, no mention of performance, and (most telling) narrative description rather than stage directions or conventionalized speech-prefixes.

What this last means is that early dramatic texts (manuscript or printed) regularly spelled out descriptively (for the otherwise befuddled reader) the narrative framework that, by the later sixteenth century, would be abbreviated in typographic conventions such as lists of *dramatis personae* or speech-prefixes. Lope de Rueda's *Eufemia* is a play "in which the characters whose names are written below are introduced," explains the text before giving the list of characters.[25] Speech-prefixes may be no different from speech tags in other kinds of narratives, full announcements that the words that follow are those of a character speaking, not those of a narrator. In the late fifteenth-century Brome manuscript of *Abraham and Isaac*, for instance, as Abraham leans over Isaac with the sword, the text explains, "Here Abraham mad hys offryng, knelyng and seyyng thus: . . ."[26] Similarly, the creators of the earliest printed playtexts felt required to explain that a character was about to speak (in *Everyman*, "God speketh . . ."),[27] rather than (as in the texts to which we are accustomed) simply offering an abbreviated version of the name of the character, typographically differentiated from the actual speech. Even in the later sixteenth century, plays simply copied from earlier texts could spell out speech-prefixes as narrative descriptions. An edition of Antonia Pulci's *Representation of Saint Domitilla* (originally *c.*1490–5) instructs: "Domitilla prays, and says . . . ," "Domitilla turning towards her servant says . . . ," followed by the words spoken, with no suggestion that the speech tag and the speech might be different kinds of things.[28]

If such things as style of speech-prefixes or placement of stage directions are "accidentals," they were deliberately accidental—exploratory attempts to use typography meaningfully, not yet bound to printerly protocols. Where texts did typographically differentiate speech-prefixes from the speech itself, the conventions for doing so were, at the least, quite various. In Pamphilus Gengenbach's *The Ten Ages of this World* (*c.*1515) (typical of the religio-moral pamphlet in dialogue form of the period), descriptions of the character speaking at a particular moment in the text run parallel with speech prefixes, and share the margins with biblical citations: "the hermit asks the youth"; "the youth answers," "1.Kings.4.c" (Fig. 6).[29] Different speakers may get different typefaces. Titles, stage directions, speech-prefixes, and dialogue may simply make up a typographic continuum, as do most in Johann Agricola's *Tragedia Johannis Huss* (1537): "Herr Hans von Clum runs angrily to the Pope . . . and says to him in the presence of the Cardinals, Holy Father. . . ."[30] There are speech-prefixes set in a different typeface, or flush left, or in the margins (as in the 1545 *Four Cardynal Vertues*), or centred above speeches; headings with names spelled out in full, abbreviated, or given as single initials mid-line (for instance in many classical texts).[31]

In drama, as in other genres, printers continued to experiment throughout the sixteenth and early seventeenth centuries with page space, lettering types, and colour to differentiate various kinds of material, relating information spatially on the page. Marginal quotations, biblical citations, scholarly notes, descriptions of spectacle continued to create an interchange between text proper and its necessary context; plays continued to be encircled by commentary, writers continued to move freely between narrative description and dramatic dialogue.[32] Classical texts, humanist drama, plays intended for professional troupes, chapbook dialogues, and all the various dramatic forms continued to exert reciprocal influences throughout the period, no single form responsible for determining dramatic *mise en page*.

By the later sixteenth century, however, conventions had begun to harden. At least as important, printers seem to have come to rely on a readership familiar with both the theatre and the typographic conventions of the drama. They seem to have come to rely on the *mise en page*—the visual semiotics of the dramatic text—to explain through visual form what narrative descriptions might do at greater length. As readers grew more accustomed to seeing dramatic texts, printers came to produce plays in increasingly standard formats. Classical plays and those modelled on them began regularly to head each scene with the names of the speakers appearing in it (the first speaker listed first and the speaker's name omitted at the top of the actual speech). Speech-prefixes were not merely scribally contracted like the rest of the text (as they had been in the early dramatic manuscripts), but truncated as typographic signs, their abbreviation serving to identify them *as* dramatic speech-prefixes: "G." could mean, essentially, "God speketh," for those readers who understood how dramatic texts worked. In Chapter 8 I will return to the meaning, for the drama, of the typographic differentiation of narrative elements (stage directions, speech-prefixes) from speeches spoken: of the differentiation of words spoken on the stage from the names of those who spoke them and from descriptions of the places in which they were spoken; of the differentiation of the words a narrator might speak (in explaining the play) from the words of the fictional characters. Suffice it to say, here, that the typographic-visual distinction of the drama from other kinds of writing during the sixteenth century played a crucial role in the representation of drama as a distinct genre.

The growth of the professional theatre, along with the growing play readership that accompanied it, unquestionably exerted a powerful influence on the shape of plays on the page, intensifying the drive towards the conventionalization of dramatic

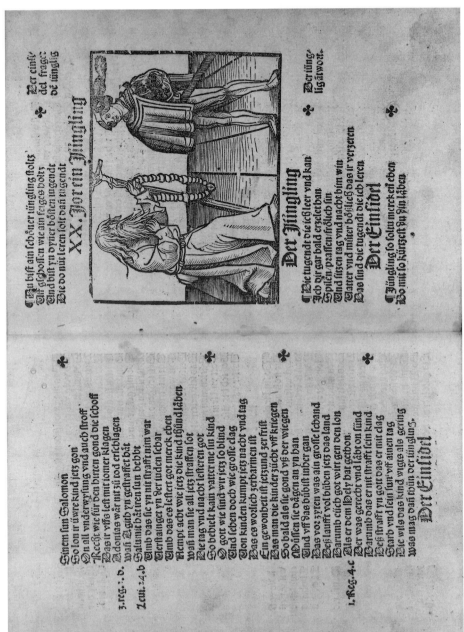

FIG. 6. Scene title, speaker headings, and speech tags in Pamphilus Gengenbach's *The Ten Ages of this World* (c.1516).

form that print had already set in motion. If printers and writers were using (for instance) clearly demarcated speech-prefixes to bring into relief the various characters who peopled the scene, they were also giving readers other tools for organizing their conception of the play as a performance, for instance division into stage scenes.[33] The *dramatis personae* that became conventional, if not universal, in both "classical" and "native" sixteenth-century plays (with the names of the "histrione," "players," "interlocutori," "entreparleurs," or "personaggi," commonly offering tags describing relations among characters—"Vranio, Shepherd in love with Ardelia"; "Mirtilla, Nymph in love with Vranio") simultaneously served those who wished to put on a play and those who wished to imagine the characters on the stage.[34] Plays intended for professional troupes began regularly to announce the number of players required for performance, and to render all stage directions in the vernacular (often in the imperative), with exits and entrances clearly, if irregularly, marked.

With performance in mind, typical early sixteenth-century vernacular plays had tended to offer much of the scenic specificity of their fifteenth-century predecessors, but in a form aimed at ease of production. The stage directions in John Rastell's edition of Skelton's *Magnyfycence* (printed *c.*1530), for instance, are prescriptive, explaining how the play is to be performed: "Here magnyfycence wolde flee hymselfe with a knyfe." Where they do prescribe tone and emotion, they seem to be doing so for actors: "Here magnyfycence dolorously maketh his mone."[35] Rastell's *Four Elements* is more expansive and explicit still. Throughout, it offers production options, even when it is, at the same time, describing action in more ordinary terms: "Then the dancers without the hall sing this wise and they within answer, or else they may say it [if they] need" (presumably if enough singers couldn't be found).[36] On the whole, however, with the greater differentiation of dramatic form from other narrative forms that took hold over the course of the century, there was a decrease rather than an increase in character or scenic description. In the humanist drama, the paucity of stage directions may reflect a self-conscious retreat from the grand fifteenth-century spectacles, with their elaborate descriptions of action. But it also reflects growing professionalization: at once the increase in plays intended for ambulatory troupes whose scenic effects were necessarily limited; and the increase in plays written in haste for professional companies whose staging conventions obviated much of the work of stage directions. Even in plays intended primarily for popular performance, then, directions are usually so spare (if there are any at all) as to be almost invisible: entrances and exits, minimally necessary props, general sound effects such as "music within," special group scenes such as processions, dumb shows, discoveries, costume changes, or necessary actions like that of Hodge in *Gammer Gurton's Needle* ("Here he kysseth Diccons breeche").[37] Influenced by classical conventions, plays work to conceal scenic designations in dialogue: Antoine de Montchrestien's David (in the play of the same name) describes his own make-up in calling attention to his "dull, ghastly yellowish-white complexion"; Montchrestien's Sara and Rachel (in *Aman*) describe Mardochée's physique and attire, "deformed by filth . . . his stomach quivering and completely exposed."[38]

However, there was a parallel tradition in the elaborate descriptions of non- or quasi-textual spectacles, a tradition that was eventually to have an impact on the textual drama. While many of the multi-media performances that kept the great houses entertained—the masques, musical soirées, dance events, and other spectacles— never got recorded at all, those that got published descriptions got elaborate ones. The book of Baltasar de Beaujoyeulx's *Balet comique de la royne* (1581), for instance, has a richly detailed text, with lavish illustrations. The scene shows:

> the god Pan, dressed as a satyr, enveloped in a mantle of cloth of gold, with a golden crown on his head, holding in his left hand a knobby and spiny club, and in his right hand his gilded Pan-pipes. . . . At the other end of the room . . . an artificial garden was created, . . . embellished with a diversity of sorts of flowers, and also strawberries, cucumbers, melons, . . . [with] Circe the enchantress . . . clad in a golden robe of two colors . . . her head, neck and arms being marvellously enriched with precious stones and pearls of inestimable worth. . . [and] a hundred white wax candles . . . shining (as much on the fairy as on the garden). (Fig. 7)[39]

Samuel Daniel's *Vision of the Twelve Goddesses* (1604) "describe[s] the whole forme" of "the late shewe at Court . . . in all points as it was then performed." "These Goddesses [were] thus presented in their proper and severall attyres," offering emblems of their powers to "the Temple of Peace, erected upon foure pillars, representing the foure Vertues that supported a Globe of the earth."[40] Such descriptions offered a model for scenic annotation that was to be crucial to the theatre's sense of itself in the centuries that followed.

PUTTING THE PLAY INTO PRINT

It is easier to identify the dramatic material published and its look on the page than to identify how that material came to be published: who brought it to printers or publishers? Why did those who brought it wish to have it published? What kinds of manuscripts did they bring?[41] In the early sixteenth century, some of those who wrote plays were themselves printer-publishers, Rastell, for instance, who printed his own *Four Elements* and the plays of dramatists like Skelton. Pamphilus Gengenbach, based in Basel, was similarly a scholar-printer, printing, for instance, Reformation plays like his own *Feeder off the Dead* (1521).[42] Even dramatists who were not themselves printers had close friends among the printers and probably took their own plays to the press. Theodore de Bèze almost certainly brought his *Abraham sacrifiant* (written and published in 1550) to his friend the printer Conrad Badius.[43] Patrons might also see that plays got to a printer. An unnamed Duke (probably Norfolk) sponsored the printing of a farce satirizing Cardinal Wolsey. Margaret Beaufort, the patron of Wynken de Worde, may have sponsored De Worde's printing of *The Interlude of Youth* (1530–5), *Hycke Scorner* (1515–16), and *The World and the Child* (1522), all plays sympathetic to her politics and written for noblemen whom she knew.[44] Throughout the century, editions may be explicitly identified as having been paid for by patrons, friends, or family members wishing "to gratulate the love and memory of [a] worthy friend the Author."[45]

FIG. 7. Circe in her garden at the end of the hall in Baltasar de Beaujoyeulx's *Balet comique de la royne* (1582).

While editors and publishers, too, may often have been motivated primarily by the desire to render homage to the author (as so many claimed, in accordance with the literary conventions proper to the ideal sixteenth-century scholar-printer),[46] most such publications were probably generated by a mixture of literary and commercial motives. The publisher Bernardo Giunti, for instance, writes to his dedicatee and potential patron, Giovanni Mocenigo, in his 1585 edition of Gianmaria Cecchi's *Comedie*, that because Cecchi was so "copious of invention, of grace, and of poetic vivacity," Mocenigo will not only be obliging Giunti but doing *himself* honour in "favoring with [his] grace" Cecchi's volume.[47] But patrons were not the only objects. Publishing was a trade enterprise from the beginning and continued to be so, as the sales pitches show, for instance that in the poem, "To the Buyer" that heads Jakob Ayrer's *Opus Thaeatricum* (1618):

> Whoever buys this book will be glad of it,
> The loss of his money nevermore regret.[48]

John Heminge and Henry Condell similarly offer their book of Shakespeare's plays to "the great Variety of Readers" (that is, buyers) in a preface which follows (and supplants?) the dedication:

Read, and censure . . . but buy it first. . . . Judge your sixe-pen'orth, your shillings worth, your five shillings worth at a time, or higher, so you rise to the just rates, and welcome. But, what ever you do, Buy.[49]

Whether or not there was an "illustrious poet" involved (or any identifiable writer at all), there were clearly writers, copyists, printers, and publishers for whom the pecuniary was the primary motive, as the advertising common on title pages suggests.

Routes to the printing house were somewhat different for the growing number of theatrical professionals who emerged, in the later sixteenth century, in conjunction with the new theatres.[50] It was generally assumed, well into the seventeenth century, that the possessors of playtexts had a right to give them to publishers or withhold them from the press, with or without the playwrights' permission. With the rise of professional theatre, this meant that company managers were often the ones who brought plays to the press—perhaps more often than not. But there were still the same variety of potential agents: publishers themselves, who might seek out manuscripts; those in companies who had access to play manuscripts (actors, managers); friends of actors or dramatists (or others who might have access to scripts); or playwrights themselves. The distinctions here are, in some ways, artificial: many of the professional playwrights writing for companies before the 1630s were also actors (even if minor ones), and many of these were also company sharers and managers.[51]

One need not have a particular conception of the dramatic "author" to recognize that, especially after 1600, writers of plays often saw to it that those plays got to the press, some because they hoped they could make money (off patronage from a dedication, sale of the books, or payment from the publisher), some simply because they wished to see their names in print.[52] Cervantes frankly acknowledged that he took his *Eight Plays and Eight Interludes* to a bookseller (in 1615) both because he thought they "deserved to appear from . . . obscurity" and because the bookseller "paid me reasonably for them."[53] Massinger pathetically tells Lady Katherine Stanhope in his dedication for his *Duke of Milan* (1623), "there is no other meanes left mee (my misfortunes having cast me on this course)."[54] Sometimes dramatists would pay for publication themselves, hoping to recoup the initial outlay by selling the books or by the presentation of a copy to the dedicatee. "I have my selfe . . . set forth this Comedie," writes Marston in the preface to *The Malcontent* (1604), indicating that he has not only done the editorial work but also paid for publication.[55] More successful writers might in fact have an ongoing relationship with a publisher, as Samuel Daniel did.

But that there were numerous plays published without the knowledge or consent of their authors (or indeed of the companies that produced them) is equally clear, even if we discount some of the authorial disclaimers of responsibility for publication as disingenuous. We have not only the well-known complaints of Thomas Heywood or the editors of the Shakespeare first folio, but also of many others: Ariosto, Lope de Vega, Guillén de Castro, Jean Mairet.[56] Publishers could acquire dramatic manuscripts from someone other than a playwright in a variety of ways. There were, of course (especially in the early period), anonymous plays simply circulating as reading material that a printer might wish to publish or republish. Company managers or actors might bring a play to a publisher, who would buy it for a small sum, the promise of a number of copies, or future interest in sales. Manuscripts that ended up in printers' hands might be company playtexts, author manuscripts, actors' texts, scribal copies made for individual readers (though to attempt to identify any given manuscript with a single purpose is probably to misconceive the ways in which manuscripts were used, copied, and recopied).[57] The publisher Humphrey Moseley may be referring either to copies the actors made from the company playtext (or other performance texts) or to actors' memorial reconstructions when, reflecting on the origin of various Beaumont and Fletcher quartos, he writes that "when private friends [had] desir'd a Copy," the actors "transcribed what they *Acted*."[58]

By the time there was a developed professional theatre such that plays written for performance were identifiable with a particular company, it was considered wrong not to ask the company's or dramatist's permission to publish (as the many incensed reactions to unauthorized publication show). But there was no general legal requirement that one do so.[59] A reader who had obtained a copy from the actors or the playwright (a friend, for instance, who had admired the play and asked for a copy) might offer the play to a publisher in the hopes of payment or simply because the reader thought the play ought to be printed. If the importance of actors as agents in the publication process has been exaggerated by the romantic mystery tale created to explain the "bad" quartos of Shakespeare (disaffected bit players stealing plays from the company and sneaking off to a stationer to repeat, from memory, the words of the master),[60] "the actors" were, in fact, usually indistinguishable from "the company": it was as actors *and* sharer-managers of the King's Men that Heminge and Condell put together Shakespeare's plays and saw to their publication in 1623. But outside actors also, at least on occasion, brought plays to publishers, since they were simply the people most likely to have copies of play manuscripts. We have no reason to disbelieve Ariosto when, early in the sixteenth century, he blames the actors for the pirated editions of *The Strongbox* and *Supposes*,[61] nor (a century later) Jean Rotrou when he explains that he has been forced to print his *Ring of Forgetting* (performed in 1629) because "all the provincial players have copies of it, and . . . many have bragged that they intend to oblige a printer with it."[62]

Whether or not we can credit the complaints about enterprising audience spies who would memorize or copy plays from performances in order to sell them to troupes or to publishers is unclear.[63] Thomas Heywood refers to plays "copied onely by the eare," and complains that, at his *If You Know Not Me* (*The Play of*

Queen Elizabeth), "some by Stenography drew | The plot: put it in print: (scarce one word trew:)."[64] In Spain, there were two legendary memorizers who would, it was claimed, doctor the texts they produced with their own verses. In *Parte XIII* of his *Comedias* (1620), Lope de Vega complains of "the stealing of comedias by those whom the vulgar call—the one *Memorilla*, and the other *Gran Memoria*," and who, according to Lope, are ultimately responsible for the corrupt texts that appear in print: "With the few verses which they learn, [they] mingle an infinity of their own barbarous lines, whereby they earn a living, selling them to the villages and to distant theatrical managers: base people these, without a calling, and many of whom have been jail-birds."[65] According to Lope and others, in Spain it was common practice to patch together plays partly by memorial reconstruction of plots and verses, partly by writing new verses to fill in the gaps. Chapman seems to be using the threat of such reconstruction and patching as an excuse to publish his *All Fools* (in 1605), writing that he is "expos[ing it] to every common eye . . . least by others stealth it be imprest, | without my pasport, patcht with others wit."[66] There was certainly a gentlemanly habit of copying down choice bits in commonplace books for use when a *bon mot* was required, but it is impossible to know whether this merely gave playwrights and companies the *impression* that their plays were being taken wholesale, or whether in fact the commonplace book served as inspiration for audience thieves.

PRINTED PLAYBOOKS, MANUSCRIPT PLAYBOOKS

Whatever the abundance of sixteenth-century printed drama, whatever competition for playtexts may have developed by the early seventeenth century, there is a good deal of truth to the conventional descriptions of the lackadaisical attitude towards the publication of plays in the Renaissance: the absence of a developed relationship between most playwrights and the printing press; publishers' impassivity towards even theatrically successful plays. Looking backwards from the perspective of the later seventeenth century, the output of printed drama between 1480 and 1630 was small.[67] The difference lay primarily in the fact that publication of even successful plays had simply not become a regular institution. This meant that, even in the late sixteenth and early seventeenth centuries, with a developed professional theatre and a large body of printed drama as model, many plays that had found performance venues still remained unprinted. Only a few of the plays at the Red Bull, Curtain, and Swan performed between 1599 and 1622 were printed, though all three theatres were in full activity during this period.[68] Probably the majority of the 10,000 or so *comedias* and 1,000 or so *autos* written in Spain in the sixteenth and seventeenth centuries were never printed.[69] Of the 800 or so plays Lope de Vega is believed to have written (he claimed to have written over 1,500), almost half were not published during his lifetime.[70] Thomas Heywood claimed that there were 220 plays in which he "had either an entire hand or at least a maine finger," but published only about twenty during his lifetime.[71] Despite the fact that Alexandre Hardy made an effort to see his plays into print in the 1620s, only thirty-four of the 600 he claimed to have written were printed during his lifetime.[72] I have already mentioned (in the

Introduction) some of the many important fifteenth- and early sixteenth-century plays that did not find their way into print. If, even in the earlier sixteenth century, some plays were published almost immediately after performance (Ariosto's first two comedies, for instance, performed and published in 1508 and 1509, or Jacques Grévin's *César*, performed and published in 1561), most were published only after a considerable time lag, often six or seven years, sometimes twenty or more.[73]

That plays often did not get printed at all or did not get printed until long after performance meant they could more easily disappear:[74] Moseley complains that the actors had carelessly lent out Beaumont and Fletcher's *Wilde-Goose Chase* (performed *c.*1621) and it had never been returned so could not be included in the folio: "[It] hath beene long lost, and I feare irrecoverable; for a *Person of Quality* borrowed it from the *Actours* many yeares since, and (by negligence of a Servant) it was never return'd; therefore now I put up this *Si quis*, that whosoever hereafter happily meetes with it, shall be thankfully satisfied if he please to send it home."[75] But plays might still be widely distributed in manuscript, circulated in fair copies reproduced many times over. This could take place on a small scale, as when individuals requested that actor friends or dramatists make copies of popular plays, rather than waiting for them to appear in print: Lord Lisle wrote to Shrewsbury in 1608 that he had tried to get Jonson to make him a copy of the *Masque of Beauty*, but Jonson was too busy working on the *Haddington Masque*; La Calprenède complains of the unauthorized copying of his tragedy *The Death of Mithridate* in 1636, writing that he is publishing it only because, "having imprudently lent my manuscript to persons I could not refuse without incivility, fifteen days later I saw thirty copies of it."[76] Or it could take place on a rather large scale, scribes producing numerous copies of a popular play, working at twice the speed it would take to produce a printer's forme of the same length.[77] Manuscripts might be sold in the same shops and through the same advertising channels as printed books.[78] Manuscript copies of popular plays from the public theatres—plays like Thomas Middleton's *A Game at Chess* (1624)—could circulate in fairly large numbers, belying claims to exclusivity (one manuscript copy of *A Game at Chess*, suppressed by the government, brags: "This, which nor Stage nor Stationer's Stall can showe, | The Common Eye may wish for, but ne're knowe").[79]

Manuscript copying (by one or several hands) was, most often, a pragmatic necessity for theatrical production, more a means of producing usable texts than a means of "publication." Actors often used manuscript copies even of plays available in print, especially if revision was required: we have, for instance, a scribal transcription of *Henry IV* (based on the quartos), which was used for a private production at a country estate in the 1620s.[80] But readers too relied on scribal copying. Manuscript books might be given to eminent spectators or potential patrons as presentation copies, and manuscript libretti or programmes might be made: in Bartolomé de Torres Naharro's *Trophea* (1514), for instance, Apollo gives Fame written copies of the verses he has just sung, which Fame then scatters through the hall.[81] The scrivener Ralph Crane was regularly employed to make presentation copies of plays, and we have one such copy of Fletcher's *Bonduca* made by Edward Knight, the King's Men's bookkeeper.[82]

There were many reasons that publishers did not regularly publish plays in conjunction with performance until some time in the seventeenth century. Probably the three most central were: absence of sufficient readership; authorial reticence or indifference; withholding on the part of companies. I will deal, in other chapters, more extensively with authorial reticence or indifference: aristocratic disdain for the press; anxieties about "self-publication"; the desire to preserve the perceived exclusivity of manuscript circulation; the commercial stigma of print. Suffice it to say, here, that these attitudes had an important role to play in keeping plays in manuscript, particularly in the seventeenth century, though attitudes towards print were by no means uniform. In any case, at least as important was the fact that most printers would not undertake to print what would not sell in fairly large numbers, and playbooks were in limited demand.[83] While there were certainly plenty of play readers (the readers about whom William Prynne was so worried),[84] readers generally seem to have preferred other kinds of books: works of devotion, the ancients, practical management, law, chapbooks, ballads.[85] Terence came out in numerous editions (as Shakespeare does today) because he was considered necessary to the educated person's library.[86] Even Shakespeare (one of the bestselling playwrights of the day) was only a moderate seller.[87] What troupes must have preferred were playbooks they could play, but, since there were only so many troupes, this was a limited market. Those who were rich enough to buy books regularly did not necessarily want to keep playbooks in the most prominent positions on their shelves (even if they might sometimes keep them in their closets).[88] Those who were poor could not necessarily read or, even if they could, could not necessarily afford to buy books.[89] There were books that people felt they needed before they could allow themselves to buy playbooks: books for the carrying out of business (agriculture, domestic economy); books for the care of the soul. In the countryside, readers were more likely to buy books of entertainment better suited to reading aloud: books of dialogue, for instance, not in need of scenic trappings.

Some playbooks, however, were in high demand, as we have already seen. There would not have been some fourteen editions of the anonymous *Mucedorus and Amandine* between 1598 and 1639, or some nine editions of Marlowe's *Doctor Faustus* between 1601 and 1631, or around three dozen editions of Garnier's tragedies between 1580 and 1620, or 20,000 copies of the farces of "Tabarin" sold, if there had not been people willing to buy them.[90] Isabella Andreini's pastoral *Mirtilla* sold out immediately when it was printed in 1588.[91] The Earl of Worcester, writing in 1604, found that although he was able to acquire a copy of *The Twelve Goddesses* for sixpence, the books of another "ballet" were "all called in."[92] That some of the plays most successful on stage remained unpublished (in a world of commercially savvy publishers on the lookout for profit) can be explained only by other factors keeping them from the press.

One such factor was troupe attempts to prevent unauthorized publication, or at least to control publication and its potential profits. We know that there were such attempts from the 1630s onward,[93] and the evidence we have from the last years of the sixteenth century and the first years of the seventeenth suggests similar attempts.

For instance, in 1600 the Admiral's Company gave the stationer Cuthbert Burby £2 to "staye the printing of Patient Gresell," whether to stop a printing not authorized by the company or to invest in publishing rights through the company's chosen stationer or simply to delay printing for a time is unclear.[94] An order in the Stationers' Register, also in 1600 (the same year that four Chamberlain's Men's plays were "to be staied"), may similarly reflect a company-instigated attempt to control or invest in publication (as the King's company did in 1612).[95] More clearly an attempt to control publication, a Whitefriars contract of 1608 (to which several playwrights were party) forbids any company member, acting alone, to publish any of the company's plays.[96] Clearer still, in 1619 the King's Men got the Lord Chamberlain to forbid the publication of their plays without the company's consent, as an order to the Stationers' Company in May of that year shows.[97]

Part of the motivation here may have been to keep playwrights from putting plays into print without the company's say (as a slightly later contract forbidding Richard Brome to do so suggests).[98] It must have seemed clear to company management that, when the company had paid the playwright a significant sum for a new play, the company should receive *all* the potential value of its use. Certainly by the 1620s there was a tension between company control over printing and playwrights' control, in England and elsewhere. In France in 1620, Alexandre Hardy entered into a contract that prohibited him from printing any of the plays he was writing for the troupe headed by Pierre Le Messier ("Bellerose"), signing similar contracts in 1625 and 1627.[99] Whatever Brome or Hardy may have felt about their contracts, Thomas Heywood made it clear that he resented company control over the publication of his plays, writing, in his preface to *The English Traveller* (1633), that some of his plays "are still retained in the hands of some Actors, who thinke it against their peculiar profit to have them come in Print."[100]

There may be insufficient evidence to be certain that it was usual practice for companies to withhold plays from publication. But the plays of many of the professional dramatists who had strong company associations, whether in England, Spain, or France, remained largely unpublished (or published without the playwrights' permission) during most of their professional stage careers: those of Shakespeare, Heywood, Fletcher, Lope de Vega, and Hardy, for instance.[101] That there were frequent unauthorized editions of these playwrights, and that major collections of their plays were published towards the end of their careers (or posthumously), suggest that the demand was there. In some cases there seems to have been no lack of desire on the part of the playwright: a few dramatists saw their plays into print as soon as they had broken relations with a company (James Shirley, for instance, or Brome), suggesting that it was only contract or company loyalty that had kept them from doing so earlier.[102] Heywood was clearly inclined to publish earlier than he did (as his complaint about the profit-seeking actors and his palpably disingenuous disclaimers in the plays he did publish show).

Two explanations have usually been put forth for the fact that English acting companies appear sometimes to have withheld playtexts from the press: the first, that troupes feared that printing made plays "stale"; the second, that the circulation of the text in print allowed rival troupes to mount competitive productions. "New" plays clearly had a certain caché, and printing them could dissipate that caché—or at least some actors felt that it could.[103] "Stale" playbooks were sold off at cut rates: "when they grow stale [plays] must be vented by termers and country chapmen," explains Middleton in the preface to *The Family of Love* (1608).[104] Sometimes publication could be used to vindicate a dramatist after a theatrical failure or in the face of a manager's rejection ("if you find that [the plays] have anything good in them," writes Cervantes to his readers after his interludes were rejected by the theatre, "when you see my cursed theatre manager, tell him to mend his ways").[105] But publication could also stimulate theatrical enthusiasms, and there was usually a relationship between stage success and success in print.[106] The publisher Richard Hawkins (addressing the reader in the third impression of *Philaster* in 1628) assumes that his principal buyers are those who have seen and "approved" the play: "This Play" was "affectionately taken, and approved by the Seeing Auditors, or Hearing Spectators, (of which sort, I take, or conceive you to bee the greatest part)."[107] Printed texts (for instance the masque books which the King's company paid Heminge and Dekker to print, promising a show "on the Morrow next") (Fig. 8) usually served as advertising, souvenir, supplement, not as competitive entertainment in their own right.

The more common explanation for the failure to print plays—that the companies feared that, if a play were printed, a rival company would be able to compete by performing the same play—seems to have been a factor primarily in Spain and (to a lesser extent) in France. Lope de Vega's repeated complaints about play thieves, for instance, go both to the print pirates (who have forced him to produce correct editions) and to performance thieves.[108] For the Italian professional troupes, so long as their emphasis was on virtuoso performance rather than textual originality, guarding dramatic material from competition was of little concern, as the extensive trading in scenarios suggests.[109] In London, there seems to have been an implicit rule against theatrical "theft" that made it unnecessary to guard a text jealously: companies generally kept from treading on the repertories of other companies (no matter how popular the play or how available the manuscript).[110] While touring English troupes regularly used the material owned by London companies, there is (for whatever reason) no evidence that the London companies particularly minded what went on in the provinces or abroad. But in the less stable theatrical climates of Paris or Rouen or Madrid or Valencia, where companies relied on touring far more than did London companies, withholding from publication may have seemed a way of ensuring that one would not arrive in a town after one's "new" play had already got there.

It is clear that there was such withholding, in any case, and that some of the dramatists attached to companies had contracts not to give their plays to other companies. In 1589, for instance, one Alonso del Castillo made an agreement with the manager Gaspar de Porres to work in the company until Shrovetide of 1591, "and the said Alonso del Castillo is to furnish to the said Gaspar de Porres nine comedias composed by him, and amongst them he is to give him the comedia *Las Escuelas de Athenas*, which he is now writing, and he is to give them to no other person, until the four years be past which begin with Shrovetide of 1591."[111] In Spain, actors could go

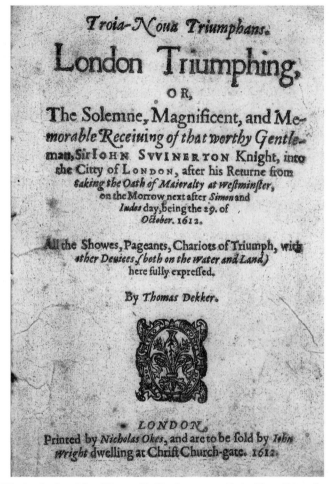

Troia-Nova Triumphans.

London Triumphing,

OR,

The Solemne, Magnificent, and Memorable *Receiuing of that worthy Gentleman,* Sir IOHN SVVINERTON Knight, into the Citty of LONDON, after his Returne from taking the Oath of *Maioralty at Weftminfter,* on the Morrow next after *Simon* and *Iudes* day, being the 29. of *October.* 1612.

All the Showes, Pageants, Chariots of Triumph, with *other Deuices (both on the water and Land)* here fully expreffed.

By *Thomas Dekker.*

LONDON,

Printed by *Nicholas Okes,* and are to be fold by *Iohn Wright* dwelling at Chrift Church-gate. 1612.

FIG. 8. The book advertising Thomas Dekker's masque, *Troia-Nova Triumphans* (1612).

to some length to keep good plays from getting into the hands of rivals, if we are to believe a story told by Cristóbal Suárez de Figueroa. According to him, when Lope de Vega's *El Galan de la Membrilla* was being represented by the Company of Hernan Sanchez de Vargas, Sanchez

began to interrupt the argument and cut short the speeches so obviously that, being questioned as to the cause of this hastening and mutilation of the play, he replied publicly that someone was present in the audience (and he pointed him out) who in three days took down from memory any comedia, and that he recited the comedia thus badly for fear that he might wrongfully get possession of it.[112]

In the absence of the kind of understanding London companies had, managers seem to have felt it important that their material be exclusive and that they secure exclusivity contractually, as did, for instance, the heads of the various troupes of actors who made the contracts with Hardy in the 1620s with clauses forbidding him to give his plays to anyone else.[113] Exclusivity clauses like that in Alonso del Castillo's contract may have been generally understood as non-publishing clauses (as Hardy's were), protecting troupes in a single phrase from all the potential threats to their repertoire that stray copies might pose.

Whether or not managers and dramatists had a defined notion of plays as literary property (an issue I will discuss in Chapter 11), some playtexts were clearly worth money—in the seventeenth century, not just from dedications and not just in the form of copies, but in the form of cash from publishers.[114] When Heywood distinguishes himself from those who have habitually made "a double sale of their labours, first to the Stage, and after to the Presse," he acknowledges the saleability of the play not only to the company but also to the booksellers, even if the latter offered considerably less than the former.[115] If Cervantes assumed that the theatre was the primary venue for his *Comedies and Interludes*, when he was "weary" of petitioning managers and so "sold them to a bookseller who put them into print," the bookseller paid him, after all, "reasonably" for them.[116] When compared to sale of a play to a theatre, sale to a publisher offered scanty rewards: Hardy received only 15 *livres* per play from the publisher Jacques Quesnel in 1625, but 100 *livres* from the manager Pierre Le Messier for his comedy, *The Jealous One* in the same year.[117] When the manager Juan Fernández sold twelve of Lope de Vega's *comedias* to the publisher Francisco de Ávila in 1616, he got only six *reales* per play for them, whereas he had paid Lope around 500 *reales* per script, and, in fact, managers could pay as much as 1,000 *reales* per script.[118] Heywood was probably simply making the wiser financial choice in proclaiming himself ever "faithfull to" the theatre.[119] But sale to a publisher in and of itself would still normally have brought a substantial fee: one and a half to two pounds for an individual play in England, the equivalent of three or four months' wages for the ordinary skilled worker.[120] It must, sometimes, have been clear that a playbook would be worth a good deal more, not to mention a collection. Hardy's 15 *livres* per play totalled 180 *livres* for the twelve plays that made up the Quesnel collection, a significant sum for the sale of plays that had already been "sold" to troupes.[121]

Where troupes were not placing absolute prohibitions on publication, then, they were nonetheless trying to control whatever profits might be had from publication. In preventing dramatists from benefiting from the "double sale" of their plays, they were merely preserving their rights in what they had already bought from the dramatists. If there was money to be made from the sale of a company play to a publisher, it ought to be (or so sharers must have felt) the company's profit. If publication could be used as advertising for a play "as now acted," the company ought to be able to control its timing. If the company did not deem the publication of a play to be profitable immediately after its first performance, the managers nonetheless might wish to preserve the right to publish when publication *would* be most profitable: to capitalize on a highly successful revival or on name recognition from cumulative runs; to present to the public plays "never till now printed" (as one

Spanish collection has it);[122] to advertise a particular production ("as now acted") or a forthcoming revival.

PREPARATION, EDITING, CORRECTION

For most of those sending plays to the press for profit in the context of the professional theatre, the point was to capture readers looking for *a* text of a popular play— hence the messiness of the typical quarto, or of a collection like *The Flower of Spanish Comedias, by Various Authors* (1615), produced for avid play readers or troupes looking for convenient compendia (Fig. 9). Care in the preparation of the printed text must have seemed a waste of time. If, for instance, a revised edition of a play could not be found, most printers were happy to use any available copy, so long as they could convince buyers that it was (for instance) *the Hamlet*. Attributions of author-

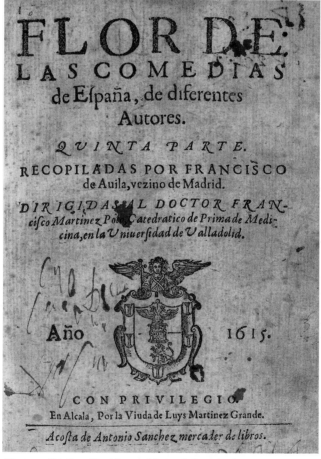

FIG. 9. Quarto collection, *The Flower of Spanish Comedias, by Various Authors* (1615).

ship tended to serve business needs: it was useful to make readers believe that the *Sir John Oldcastle* which William Jaggard and Thomas Pavier dishonestly (or haphazardly) attributed to Shakespeare in their 1619 edition (falsely dated 1600) was in fact *the* work of William Shakespeare, or that most of the plays published in 1603 as *Six Comedias by Lope de Vega* (with the appended phrase "and other authors" added protectively) were actually those of Lope himself.[123] There was, usually, no penalty for being wrong. It is conventional to note that plays were generally less carefully printed than most other genres, and this is generally the case if one is comparing (for instance) poems aimed at patrons with plays from the professional stage, coming to the press either directly from the theatre or after years of manuscript circulation. But the range of quality in both dramatic and non-dramatic printing makes it hard to generalize, and the difference has probably been exaggerated, if one compares the most ephemeral of plays to the most ephemeral of chapbooks, or the most distinguished collected dramatic editions to the most distinguished collections of poems or treatises.[124] Furthermore, "care" is a relative term: Renaissance printers had standards of spelling, capitalization, punctuation, typeface integrity, word and line breaks, layout, and ornamentation different from those of modern printers. It may sometimes be difficult to differentiate expressivity from carelessness. Variation in texts of the same work may mean revision or multiplicity of use, not lack of authority or inattention. It was accepted that different compositors had different styles of punctuation, layout, orthography, that editions usually had multiple compositors, that type might be broken, and that if sufficient type was not available one might well be inventive by turning letters upside down or combining them in new ways.

It is, however, clear that, of the various people responsible for textual production (printers, authors and editors, compositors, correctors), there were many who *were* careless in significant details: in the attribution of speeches, the names of minor characters, press correction; in the things necessary to make sense of a play (hence the notorious haphazardness—at times unintelligibility—of so many early playtexts). "This book has come out with many errors," explains a note appended to the "corrected" 1621 edition of Guillén de Castro's *Primera Parte de las Comedias*: "everywhere it says 'Pandron' it should say 'Pandion' and everywhere it says Frācia it should say Tracia."[125] It was assumed that dramatists who saw their works to the press had the right to do press correction—perhaps often expected that they do such correction.[126] Chapman proof-read *The Revenge of Bussy d'Ambois* (1613),[127] but explained with irritation in the *Memorable Masque* (1613) that the notes were not inserted in their proper places because Chapman had been "prevented by the unexpected haste of the Printer, which he never let me know, and never sending me a proofe, till he had past those speeches."[128] William Sheares, the publisher of Marston's *Workes* in 1633 (an unauthorized edition from which Marston later had his name removed), calls on the author's absence to excuse the errors: "Were it not that [Marston] is so farre distant from this place, hee would have beene more carefull in revising the former Impressions, and more circumspect about this, then I can."[129] But that many playwrights did not in fact correct their works, or did so with little attention to consistency and logic, is apparent from the state of dramatic texts.

Dramatists' frequent complaints about error-ridden printing, however, show that some cared a good deal about the state of the works they were presenting "to the world." "A bookseller who was more impatient than polite . . . printed these twelve Comedias, adding to his errors those of the Printer," writes Guillén de Castro.[130] Hardy registered his exasperation with the publisher of the first three volumes of his *Theatre*, Jacques Quesnel, complaining in the preface to the fourth volume (which he published instead with David du Petit Val): "The volumes that preceded this one make me blush with shame for the Printers, whose greed did treason to my reputation. [The volumes] are so full of errors, as much in the spelling as in the verse, that I wish in good faith I could erase them from memory."[131] That dramatists began to revise for print is a reflection of this concern: Jonson (most notably) often continued to revise deep into the publication process, making stop-press corrections, changing sections on the proofs, and composing on the printers formes, making nearly 700 corrections for his 1616 *Workes*, and still revising months after printing had begun.[132] By the first decades of the seventeenth century, it was not unusual for dramatists to see to editing and visual presentation, as Lope de Vega began to do by around 1617. Chapter 2 will explore, among other things, the increasing role that dramatists played in the printing of their plays.

2. *Drama as Institution, 1630–1760*

PRINT AND MANUSCRIPT

By the middle of the seventeenth century, audiences had come to expect that the texts of performed events—whether plays at the regular playhouses, court masques, royal entrées, or city pageants—would appear in print. Alongside a proliferation of playbooks from the "regular" theatres (with their now-conventionalized formats), there were pageant books, operas, Italian festival books (magnificent volumes with fold-out illustrations recording grand entertainments like *Il Mondo festeggiante*, a horse ballet performed for the wedding of Cosimo III and Marguerita Luisa of Orleans in Florence in 1661), dignified author collections like Corneille's 1664 folio, *Le Theatre de P. Corneille* (Fig. 10), and a vast array of theatrical ephemera. It had become normal, by the 1630s or 1640s, for previously non-publishing professional dramatists to see their work into print, and, by the late seventeenth century, printing seemed the inevitable culmination of the production of a play. "The Impression of Plays, is so much the Practice of the Age," wrote Edward Howard in the "epistle" to his tragedy *The Usurper* (1668), "that few or none have been Acted, which fail to be display'd in Print."[1] To fail to print was to "suppress" or to be suppressed,[2] refusal by the booksellers an embarrassment to be endured only by playwrights as inept as Farquhar's pedant who, cursed by the players and damned by the town, "may bury his Copy in *Pauls*, for not a Bookseller about it will put it in Print."[3]

It is difficult to generalize about theatrical activity and dramatic production across Europe between the seventeenth and mid-eighteenth centuries, given important regional and national differences: in the French and English capitals, the development of a centralized theatrical life and strong dramatic traditions (despite the closure of the theatres in England for eighteen years); in Counter-Reformation Spain, the increase in Church interference in theatrical life and the overwhelming dominance of Lope de Vega and Calderón; in Germany, the absence of a professional theatrical infrastructure comparable to that elsewhere in Europe until well into the eighteenth century, with dramatic production largely confined to school and court milieus; in Italy, the dominance of the "dramma per musica" and its variants (dramatic oratorio and *melodramma*), and the relative ossification of non-musical drama. The differences, however, may be less stark than they seem (particularly with the proliferation of professional theatres throughout Europe in the eighteenth century). Even if theatrical practices cannot be generalized, and even if norms for the printing and circulation of dramatic texts during the period were various, there were trends that exerted their influence throughout Europe.

Manuscript copying was still an important way of circulating plays, certainly in the early seventeenth century and still (in some places) in the eighteenth.[4] Just as Lord Lisle went directly to Jonson to ask for a copy of a masque in 1608, play afficionados still made a practice, in the later seventeenth and eighteenth centuries, of asking their dramatist and actor friends for copies of plays they could not get elsewhere (very new plays, plays performed privately or in the provinces, plays that had been suppressed, plays no longer available in print).[5] At the same time that printed books were distributed as souvenirs, manuscript presentation copies might be made.[6] Although companies generally used printed editions as promptbooks where they were available (the Shakespeare folios, for instance, which the Smock Alley actors used in the 1680s), they continued to copy out new scripts and actor parts by hand.[7] There were still many plays, even in the eighteenth century that remained unpublished: those condemned or suppressed, those determinedly aristocratic, those that had failed in the theatre, those meant for the stage alone. Richard Brome's *The English Moor* (produced in 1637) and James Shirley and the Duke of Newcastle's *Country Captain* (produced in 1639) were disseminated only in manuscript until long after the closure of the theatres.[8] The actors of the Théâtre Italien (the home of the

FIG. 10. Corneille's folio collection, *Le Theatre de P. Corneille* (1664).

commedia dell'arte troupe in Paris), performing in Paris in the last decades of the century, succeeded in withholding their scripts from print for several decades.[9] It was still possible to pose as the aristocratic, non-publishing dramatist, as Calderón did for most of his life, bringing forth collections that he explicitly acknowledged as his only in the 1670s and only (as he claimed) in self-defence against marauding pirates.[10] Even a half century later, when a reading public was essentially guaranteed to the famous, Voltaire kept a dozen or so of his theatrical failures from print.[11] A play as popular on stage as the German *Hamlet* (*The Fratricide Punished*), regularly acted in the later seventeenth century and throughout the eighteenth, was not published until 1781.[12]

However, even where there was good reason to circulate a play in manuscript alone, it could be expensive to have a manuscript made. A manuscript copy of a play probably cost about four to six times what a printed copy cost.[13] When advertising the Beaumont and Fletcher collection of 1647, the (admittedly self-interested) Humphrey Moseley claimed that "Heretofore when Gentlemen desired but a Copy of any of [the *Menuscripts*], the meanest piece here . . . cost them more then foure times the price you pay for the whole Volume."[14] By the time Moseley was vaunting the economic advantages of print, readers had ceased to seek out manuscript copies as a matter of course, counting instead on printed editions. However active seventeenth-century scribal culture may have been, circulation of successful plays in manuscript alone was no longer considered a normal alternative method of circulation. If (with the growth of marginal theatre towards the end of the seventeenth century and beginning of the eighteenth), there was a proliferation of dramatic spectacles, many of whose texts remained unpublished, in the regular theatres there was virtually no such thing as a non-publishing house dramatist. If a play unpopular in the theatre would have difficulty finding a publisher, a play popular in the theatre would invariably find its way into print, as Samuel Chappuzeau suggested in his comment (in 1674) that "a play, however excellent, if it has not been performed, cannot find a Bookseller to undertake its printing; & the least thing scrawled on paper, if it pleased in the Theatre, will immediately find a merchant [among the booksellers in the Palais]."[15] Print publication had come to seem a necessary part of theatrical production, a natural phase in the life cycle of a play.

Changes in literacy certainly created an increased demand, and therefore a stronger impetus to publish.[16] But the presuppositions of dramatists and theatre managers also changed over the course of the seventeenth century. The Venetian theatre manager Girolamo Medebac still considered Goldoni's plays to be the theatre's property in the 1740s and 1750s, refusing to give Goldoni any of the profits from their publication and forcing him to arrange for publication of a rival edition in Florence.[17] But by the later seventeenth century, it was generally assumed that it was dramatists, not companies, who had the right to sell their plays to publishers.[18] This meant that plays were often coming to the press from the dramatists themselves rather than from playhouses, and, as a result, that eighteenth-century printed play-texts were far more likely to be authorial than theatrical versions.[19]

If managers wished to keep plays from the press or reserve publishing rights to the company, they had to contract specifically with dramatists to do so or call on the government for help. In the 1630s and 1640s, the tension between those who wished to publish independently (whether dramatists or publishers) and company managers who wished to retain control of the text seems to have intensified, in London at least. A Salisbury Court company contract of 1635 forbids Richard Brome to publish any of his plays without the company's consent.[20] There were two general orders from the Lord Chamberlain, one in 1637 and one in 1641, forbidding any member of the Stationers' Company to put the King's Men's plays or those of William Beeston's boy actors into print without company consent.[21] Managers clearly still felt print to be a threat to performance.

In France (by the 1630s at the latest), a play was considered the exclusive property of the troupe that had first played it until it was printed, at which point it was available to any troupe wishing to perform it, the rationale presumably being that a troupe yielding a play up to print had exhausted the value of exclusivity. The government did not offer broad protection for exclusive performance rights until the founding of the Comédie-Française in 1680, when the Comédie became the only troupe in Paris and its environs permitted to perform spoken plays in French. But a royal decree in

1674, forbidding the unauthorized performance of Molière's *Imaginary Invalid*, refers to the "time-honoured custom . . . of not undertaking . . . the performance of plays which th[e] other company has prepared for the theatre . . . until [they] shall have been made public by means of a printed text."[22] Clearly troupes saw publication as a threat to exclusive performance rights, valuable as long as the play still had caché but no longer necessary after initial enthusiasms had waned. A letter in an unauthorized 1660 edition of Molière's *Sganarelle* explains (perhaps disingenuously) that the publication of the comedy could do no harm to the troupe, since it had already been played nearly fifty times.[23] As a result, dramatists seem often to have agreed to withhold publication until the first run had exhausted the play's novelty: after all, both actors and dramatists stood to gain financially from success in the first run. Rotrou, for instance, apparently sold his *Florimonde* (acted in 1635) and *Alphrède* (acted in 1636) to Antoine de Sommaville on 17 January 1637 with the proviso that *Alphrède* not be published for six months.[24] As Jean Chapelain wrote to the Seigneur de Balzac, who had requested a copy of Corneille's *Horace* in 1640: "You will not see it yet, because . . . before being published, it must serve six months as breadwinner for the actors. Such are the customs of mercenary poets and such is the destiny of venal plays."[25]

We have testimony about the perceived threat that printing seemed to pose, to the Théâtre Italien at least, from a 1683 warrant forbidding the printing of its scripts, and from a 1694 Paris lawsuit between some members of the troupe trying to print an edition of its plays and other members trying to stop them. When, in 1683, the "Harlequin" Dominique Biancolelli used an agent to publish scenes from the *commedia* scenario titled (ironically enough) *Harlequin Prosecutor*, the troupe was granted protection by the King, who had the printing privilege suppressed and the copies seized because (we are told) printing the scenes "would be highly prejudicial to the supplicants."[26] A decade later (in 1694), when the "Harlequin" Evaristo Gherardi printed over 2,000 copies of a collection of the troupe's scripts, his co-actors secured a judgement against him, and had his privilege withdrawn and the copies destroyed.[27] Here we are given more information about the reason:

> The plays regain all their charm and become, so to say, like new when they have not been performed for several years, since the [public's] memory of them fades with the suspension of performances. Whereas if they were to be published, they would become public and common. The supplicants could no longer dare flatter themselves with any [expectation of] success if they were to perform them, and their theatre would inevitably decline.

According to the complaint, plays "that the vulgar knew by heart . . . would no longer have the least charm."[28]

Perhaps the conflict within the troupe itself indicates an uncertainty about the continuing utility of withholding plays from print, and marks a transition in managerial attitudes towards publication at the turn of the century. Gherardi (at least) discounts the troupe's rationale for non-publication, writing that "it was only envy and not reason which motivated the suppression."[29] Clearly there were somewhat special conditions for a troupe in the *commedia dell'arte* tradition, which had only recently come to rely on written texts. The presupposition that dramatists, not managers, had the right to sell plays to the press obviously did not apply where plays were considered collective products. Moreover, these were short plays, easily learned by heart, performed by a troupe with an improvisational tradition heavily dependent on variety for its audience. But by the early eighteenth century, Luigi Riccoboni could write (with some exaggeration) that the previously extemporizing Italian actors "never acted any Piece that had not before been printed."[30]

In England at the brink of the eighteenth century (and still later in Germany) managers seem still to have held back some plays from immediate publication. A 1696 contract between Christopher Rich and Colley Cibber for Cibber's *Woman's Wit* reads: "And the said Mr Cibber is to have the sole Benefitt of Printing such Play: But he is not to suffer it to bee Printed till a month next after it shall bee first acted."[31] When Richard Steele and Rich entered into a series of lawsuits in 1707 over payment for *The Tender Husband*, Rich's answer refers to a similar contract between Rich and Steele in 1705 specifying that Steele was not to publish the play for a month after the première.[32] Unfortunately, the documents do not tell us why managers contracted to delay publication, but what seems clear is that immediate publication continued to pose some kind of threat either to theatrical exclusivity or to the novelty that an unpublished play purported to offer. Rich apparently did not mind seeing the plays in print after a month's delay, and in fact specified as part of the contract with Steele that "three of the printed Books in Marble paper Covers and Gilt edges [are] to be delivered into the office for the use of the patentees assoone as the same should bee printed."[33] A draft directive for the establishment of the theatre in Drury Lane not only envisioned the replacement of authors' benefits with set fees for plays, but also would have given the managers control over the printing of any of their plays, which, along with prologues, epilogues, and songs were to be published by order of the directors.[34]

The rule, in France, that printing meant an abandonment of exclusive performance rights must have begun to seem an undue constraint in a culture in which printing was so central to the play's circulation. As early as 1643, Corneille sought a royal patent that would allow him to print his *Cinna*, *Polyeucte*, and *The Death of Pompey* and still preserve exclusive acting rights in them (his request was refused).[35] At least one privilege, that which the Sisters of Saint-Louis took out for the 1689 edition of Racine's *Esther* (which Racine wrote specifically for the convent), simply announced that the Sisters were simultaneously declaring exclusive rights both to print and to perform the play.[36] By some time in the eighteenth century, even managers seem no longer to have felt that it was good for business to withhold plays from the press (a notion to be revived only in the nineteenth century in the losing battle against theatrical piracy). The repertoires of the Comédie-Française, the Théâtre Italien, and the Opéra were protected by royal privilege, and the minor theatres prohibited from performing the plays of the regular companies, printed or not (though they repeatedly found ways of evading this prohibition). That Rich, in his long list of complaints against Steele, merely mentions the non-publishing contract clause but does not complain of the fact that Steele breached the contract by allowing the play to be published only sixteen days after it opened may be indicative of a similar change in managerial attitude towards publication. While many of the plays from the Théâtre Italien did not reach the press for some time in the eighteenth century, many were published soon after performance, and there is no evidence of general company withholding. Whether or not some managers still felt that immediate publication might harm performance proceeds, certainly in England they ceased to exert the kinds of constraints on publication in the eighteenth century that they had exerted during the preceding century, a fact evidenced by the near simultaneity of premières and publication dates normal in the eighteenth century. By the eighteenth century, long delays in publication seem due more to something like the lackadaisical attitude that Louis Fuzelier showed in not bothering to print the numerous scripts he hastily wrote for plays performed in the Paris fairground theatres.[37] But it was, in any case, an era in which spectacle was increasingly finding textual form, an era perhaps better exemplified by Alain René Le Sage, who was (like Fuzelier) a prolific writer for the fairground theatres but one dedicated to seeing the plays of the *foire* into print. "What good does it serve to give to the public these miserable poems?" he asks in the preface to the *Theatre of the Foire, or the Comic Opera, Containing the Best Plays Performed at the Saint-German and Saint-Laurent Fairs* (published with his co-editor D'Orneval between 1721 and 1737), responding: "this collection [will] leave a monument to the future."[38]

In England, one might attribute the loosening of managerial constraints on publication to the fact that, after the Restoration, the crown offered strong, formal protection to theatre repertoires, similar to that given to the three main French troupes.[39] Other factors may have been the large number of older, proven plays readily available in printed editions, the rise of opera, and the ascendancy of star actors (which meant that success or failure lay more in performance machinery than in any given text—a rival theatre would do better to steal a star Italian singer than a hit play), along with a recognition on the part of managers that printed plays could be used as theatrical advertising. Managers had, perhaps, come to take seriously the fact that, in Steele's words (writing in 1722), "the greatest Effect of a Play in reading is to excite the Reader to go see it."[40] As managers found, publishing the text of a play currently being performed in fact helped the company capitalize on theatrical success, rather than threatening a run. Probably as important, it had become clear (especially in England after the lapse of publication licensing constraints in the 1690s) that popular plays would, one way or another, find their way into print. For managers, it may have seemed better after all to exert as early as possible whatever control they could over the publication process. For dramatists, it may have seemed better to publish quickly to confirm publication rights than to allow someone else to do so first.

Printing was, of course, being used in the service of theatrical commerce in other ways. Managers were beginning to use newspapers to advertise performances. An advertisement in the *Flying Post* for 2–4 July 1700, reads:

At the Request, and for the Entertainment of several Persons of Quality, at the New Theatre in Lincolns-Inn-Fields, to Morrow, being Friday, the 5th of this instant July, will be acted, The Comical History of Don Quixote, both Parts being made into one by the Author. With a new Entry by the little Boy, being his last time of Dancing before he goes to France. . . . It being for the Benefit of a Gentleman in great distress; and for the Relief of his Wife and three Children.[41]

Companies regularly posted playbills announcing productions (both in the regular theatres and at the fairs) (Fig. 11), passed around hand-bills, had printed tickets made up, and distributed libretti, printed plots, or separately printed prologues and epilogues at the theatre as programmes.[42] "I have printed above a hundred sheets of papyr to insinuate the Plot into the Boxes," explains the poet Bayes in the Duke of Buckingham's *Rehearsal* (1671), famously mocking Dryden's purported distribution of his explanatory *Connexion of the Indian Emperour to the Indian Queen* during the opening run of *The Indian Emperour* in 1665.[43] "Old *Bays* was contented with the Printing a Hundred Sheets, in order to insinuate his Play into the Boxes," writes the unnamed correspondent in John Dennis's *The Characters and Conduct of Sir John Edgar* half a century later, "But you, Sir *John*, upon the like Occasion, have, by way of Lucubration and Speculation, printed a Hundred Thousand Sheets."[44] By the

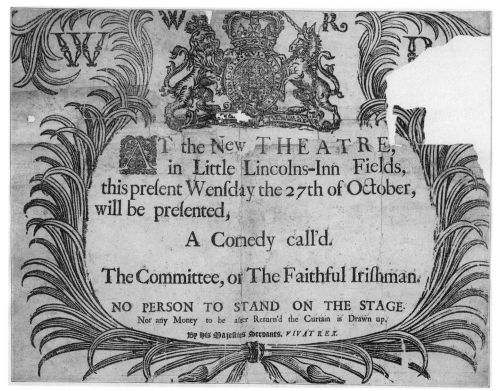

Fig. 11. Playbill for Robert Howard's *The Committee* at Lincoln's Inn Fields (1697).

end of the seventeenth century, the sale of "books" in the theatre—primarily opera and masque libretti (or "livrets"), but sometimes programmes, pamphlet copies of occasional or short pieces, or even full-length texts—was becoming a normal part of theatrical business.[45] A pamphlet of *"Songs and Masques* in the *Tempest,"* for instance, was distributed to the audience in 1674 at the Dorset Garden's spectacular version of *The Tempest*.[46] By the time *The English Stage Italianiz'd, In a New Dramatic Entertainment* (1727) announced parodically that the text would "be sold by the Orange-Women and Door-Keepers, at Six Pence each, during the Time of its Performance," the programmes of even regular plays were sold in the theatre.[47] Sometimes printers made only enough copies of a play for the spectators likely to show up at the performance. "The foregoing Lines," writes Peter Motteux of a masque he later included in *The Novelty* (1697), "were published as a Preface to that Masque [Hercules], some few Copies of which were printed for the use of the Audience, the first day of the *Novelty*'s being Acted."[48] For more prestigious pieces, programmes or livrets might be sold by regular booksellers: in 1682, for instance, Thomas Jolly advertised the availability of the programme for the new version of Corneille's *Andromede: Tragedie en Machines* at his bookshop in the stalls of the Palais de Justice.[49]

With a stronger alliance between printed texts and performances, delay between performance and publication dwindled. It was fairly normal in the first decades of the seventeenth century for a play to be published perhaps two to five years after it had been performed, when a playhouse was ready to get rid of a script, when a printer was looking for material to fill out a list, when a dramatist was looking for a little extra money or to showcase an *œuvre*, or when there was a revival and hence a renewed demand. In England, normal delays dwindled from several years in the pre-Interregnum period, to one year in the 1660s, to three months by the end of the 1670s, to only a month or so in the 1690s.[50] In France, the difference between the time lag normal for the first half of the seventeenth century and that normal for the second half is equally striking.[51] There was a three-year delay between the first performance of Corneille's *Mélite* in 1629–30 and its publication in 1633, but there was only a four-month delay between the first performance of his *Sertorius* in late February 1662 and its publication in early July 1662, and less than a two-month delay between the first performance of his *Pulchérie* in late November 1672 and its publication in late January 1673.[52] When Molière was travelling in the provinces, his plays took four or five years to make it to the press. But by the time he had a relatively stable home in Paris in the 1660s, the average delay between his plays' premières and their publication was generally five or six months.[53] All of Racine's plays (performed between 1664 and 1691) were published in the same year in which they were first performed.[54]

By the 1690s, a play might be held back from the press only by the delay of the licensers or until the first run was over, and a one-month lag (and sometimes less) was common for "regular" plays, with delays of only a few weeks (or sometimes days) common in the first decades of the eighteenth century.[55] Fielding's *Author's Farce* (1730) was printed only a day after its première, and his *Tragedy of Tragedies* (1731) was published the day it opened.[56] Even the plays of the Théâtre Italien could sometimes be published almost instantly: Marivaux's *The Island of Reason* (1727), for instance, was printed only a day after its première.[57] By the middle of the eighteenth century, if publication for premières was uncommon (except for opera), publishers were bringing plays out very close to the première. Goldsmith's *The Good Natur'd Man* (1768) appeared in print a week after it opened.[58] Copies of Goldsmith's *She Stoops to Conquer* were sold in the theatre on its fourth night (ten days after it opened in 1773), as the *Morning Chronicle* reported: "It is very remarkable, that almost every one present had the play in their hands, insomuch that the Orange-women acknowledged they never sold so many of any new piece during its whole run, as they disposed of yesterday evening in less than half an hour."[59]

The general practice of publishing even a moderately successful play relatively soon after performance, along with an increase in theatrical activity, meant, quite simply, that there were more plays being printed. William Prynne's complaint that there were over forty thousand playbooks printed in 1632–3 is actually a fairly close estimate.[60] In any case, there was a clear change in the 1630s, and a surge in the eighteenth century, with the burgeoning of small theatres and the publication of large numbers of farces, pantomimes, and afterpieces along with "regular" plays.[61] The normal number of editions and print runs also increased, notably so in the eighteenth century, when even ordinary plays might be published in several editions. A popular playwright like Voltaire could generally expect to see some dozen editions of any given play.[62] There were generally new editions for revivals, reprints in author collections, and sometimes further reprints in variety collections or in serial collections, which were becoming common a few decades into the eighteenth century.[63]

Author collections had become standard by the middle of the seventeenth century, appearing both *in memorium* and during their authors' lifetimes: in England, Beaumont and Fletcher's in 1647; Richard Brome's in 1653; James Shirley's also in 1653; Thomas Killigrew's in 1664, William Davenant's in 1673, to mention just a few. Editions followed one another with speed: three of Farquhar's *The Constant Couple* during its first season (1699–1700); four of Fielding's *The Author's Farce* in its first year (1730).[64] Even a failure on stage like Addison's *The Drummer* (1716) could go into nine English editions, and sold as many as 10,000 copies, over the course of the eighteenth century.[65] Edition sizes remained fairly stable until the late eighteenth century: Goldoni brags of the fact that the 1,700 copies of the ten-volume edition of his plays (whose publication he oversaw in the 1750s) was fully subscribed by the time the sixth volume was published.[66] But popular hits like Crébillon's tragedy *Catalina* (1749), Jean de La Harpe's *Mélanie* (1770), or Goldsmith's *She Stoops to Conquer* (1773) (which produced a second edition three days after its opening) might sell as many as four or five thousand copies in a few days.[67] Piracy of printed plays was rampant.[68] Voltaire allegedly once commented that a serious book might find forty or fifty readers; a pleasant book might find four or five hundred readers; but there were eleven or twelve hundred readers to be found if the book were a play.[69] True or not, it was clear that there was a population of eager play readers.

BOOKSELLERS AND THE DRAMA

As the book trade developed, publishers grew better at handling material related to the theatre. Alongside such general trade developments as the formation of stock and copy sharing arrangements and joint publishing concerns, wholesaling, subscription publishing, and the gradual distinction of mere bookseller from publisher,[70] new practices specific to drama publication developed. Booksellers began to produce drama catalogues in the middle of the seventeenth century: "An exact and perfect Catalogue of all the Playes, with the Authors Names, and what are Comedies, Tragedies, Histories, Pastoralls, Masks, Interludes" (Fig. 12).[71] Along with catalogues there were booksellers' stock advertisements in newspapers and in playbooks themselves: "In the shop of Joseph Antonio de Hermosilla," reads a typical Spanish

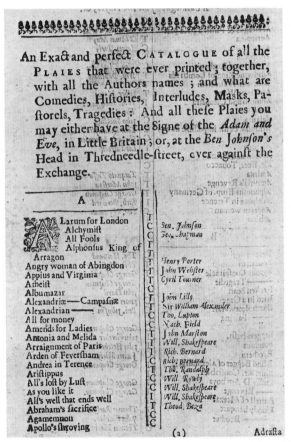

FIG. 12. "An Exact and perfect Catalogue" of plays in the 1656 edition of Massinger, Middleton, and Rowley's *The Old Law*.

title page, "there can be found many Books, Interludes, Ballads, Reports, and Plays, faithfully corrected according to the genuine Originals."[72] To highlight bargains and to allow consumers to compare, publishers began to print prices in advertisements and on title pages, a regular practice in the eighteenth century. Plays got recycled in nonce collections of individual playwrights, and in miscellaneous collections like *The Best English Plays* (1711–12) or *The British Stage* (1752) or in the volumes of *comedias sueltas* compiled in Spanish bookshops from various individually published plays.[73] Publishers created spin-offs and commercial tie-ins: dialogues based on characters in full-length dramas; abbreviated versions of playwrights like Corneille or Calderón (for instance), turned out in chapbook form.[74]

Publishers and booksellers began regularly to advertise old editions and produce new ones in conjunction with revivals, or even with regular stock pieces, noting a current performance venue in the advertisement for the playbook: "On Thursday next will be publish'd, Don Sebastian King of Portugal, a Tragedy, Acted at the Theatre-Royal."[75] Performances and playbooks might be advertised together. The *Daily Courant* for 13 November 1706 informs its readers: "At the Queen's Theatre in the Hay-Market . . . to-morrow will be presented a Comedy (never acted here before) call'd The Recruiting Officer. Most of the Parts being perform'd as they were originally. These Plays are sold by J. Knapton at the Crown in St. Paul's Church-Yard and B. Lintott next Mando's Coffee-House, Temple Bar."[76] Theatres became potential sales venues: instead of mentioning the *bookshop* where copies were "to be sold," the title page of one version of Edward Ravenscroft's *The Anatomist* reads, "London, Printed, and are to be sold at the *New Theatre*, in *Little Lincolns-Inn-fields*."[77] Those producing promotional literature for theatre distribution could plan ahead for the later printing of the play: Jacob Tonson printed the songs of John Dennis's *The Tragedy of Rinaldo and Armida* for distribution at the theatre in 1698, and then kept the type set up for the publication of the play itself after the initial run.[78] In order to assure rapid printing and to reserve potentially popular plays in advance, publishers might secure the rights to plays that looked promising well before production.[79]

Demand could raise prices: a correspondent of Leibniz exclaimed (of the over-priced first copies of Racine's *Phèdre*, hot off the Paris presses), "I don't think there are more than seven sheets and the price is an écu blanc," determining to avoid the "crazy bidding" and wait for "a more reasonable price."[80] Not all publishers, however, were successful with the drama: many, faced with brilliant competitors like Moseley, Henry Herringman, Tonson, or Lintott in London, or Jean Ribou, Claude Barbin, or Antoine de Sommaville in Paris, went out of business. Publishing even a collection likely to sell as well as Moseley's Beaumont and Fletcher could be risky, since costs might be high, as Moseley stressed (in his attempt to justify the price of the volume): " 'Twere vaine to mention the *Chargeablenesse* of this Work; for those who own'd the *Menuscripts*, too well knew their value to make a cheap estimate of any these Pieces, and though another joyn'd with me in the *Purchase* and Printing, yet the *Care & Pains* was wholly mine, which I found to be more then you'l easily imagine."[81]

A publisher like Moseley might attempt, in a magisterial edition, to recapture some of the grandeur he identified with the classical editions of the earliest era of printing. But bigger books were more expensive to produce and hence to buy, a fact that Moseley took into account when he decided not to include previously printed plays in the Beaumont and Fletcher folio: "Those former Pieces had been so long printed and re-printed, that many Gentlemen were already furnished; and I would have none say, they pay twice for the same Booke."[82] While the average labourer probably could not afford such a book, individual English playbooks generally cost less than one-twentieth its price: ordinary playbooks were normally one shilling in late seventeenth-century England (rising to 1s. 6d. in the early eighteenth century), and publishers tried to make them still cheaper.[83] To attract a broader readership in the 1730s, Jacob Tonson Jr. and Andrew Walker entered into a trade war, in which the price of their already cheap Shakespeare editions fell from fourpence to only a penny.[84]

If there was a preference, then, for cheaper playbooks, this encouraged the production of books in smaller formats. Quarto continued to dominate individual play publication throughout the seventeenth century, but there was a general proliferation of octavos and a marked increase in duodecimos, largely displacing quartos throughout Europe in the eighteenth century. Large format certainly seemed to promise distinguished contents, but scale was not necessarily determinate. With multi-volume octavo as the favourite format for collections in the eighteenth century, folios essentially disappeared for drama.[85] Despite a few late seventeenth-century folio reissues, for instance of Shakespeare in 1663–4 and 1685, of Beaumont and Fletcher in 1679, of Dryden in 1701, the grand play folios of the earlier seventeenth century had come to seem impractical, sometimes absurdly pretentious, as the generally satiric eighteenth-century references suggest. In *The Weekly Comedy* of 1708, for instance, a burlesque will grants its beneficiary "Ten of the largest Folio Books in my Study. He shall have . . . 'Tom Thumb' with Annotations and Critical Remarks, two volumes in folio."[86]

If smaller formats were cheaper, they were also easier to handle. Publishers understood how books were used by ordinary people: they kept them in their pockets; they walked with them while they read; they sneaked them into their closets, as so many illustrations of the period show (Fig. 13). Moseley worries about the "Ladies'" inability to handle too weighty a tome.[87] Publishers stressed utility. "To render our work more useful and agreeable, both the Pastoral Drama and the Academic discourses are published in one Volume printed together," writes the publisher of Guidubaldo Bonarelli's one-volume duodecimo *Opere*.[88] The English plays Thomas Johnson issued in the 1710s were "in small volumes fit for the pocket."[89] The editor of the 1711 Beaumont and Fletcher octavo collection writes in his dedication, "It will, My Lord, be the highest Satisfaction to me, if You approve of Publishing these Authors in the same Portable Volume, as *Shakespear* has so successfully appeared in,"[90] naming a Shakespeare edition as precedent in order to reassure his patron that portability was not incompatible with prestige.

FIG. 13. The portable *Theatre Italien* (1700): reading for the ladies, in and out of the closet.

DRAMATISTS ATTEND TO PRINT

Dramatists' own efforts were, to a great extent, responsible both for individual editions and for the dramatist collections appearing in the later seventeenth and eighteenth centuries. Corneille, Calderón, Racine, and Congreve (to name just a few)
were all responsible for collected editions of their works published between the 1640s
and the 1710s. Having published the *School for Husbands* in 1661 (according to him,
the first play which he himself saw into print), Molière not only paid for the initial

printing of several of his plays, but took out a general privilege for the printing of his collected works in 1671 (though he did not live to see it published).[91] William Davenant's bookseller, Henry Herringman, testifies that his 1673 edition includes the plays that Davenant "himself design'd for the Press": "In his Life-time he often express'd to me his great Desire to see them in *One Volume.*"[92] While fantasies of fame must have inspired playwrights to publish, so did greater saleability. Although patronage and performance receipts (sale of a play, authors' benefits, playhouse shares) were still the principal sources of income for playwrights in the seventeenth and early eighteenth centuries, some of the profits made from play publication were passed on to dramatists even in the mid-seventeenth century. In a 1640 commendatory epistle to Thomas Nabbes's *The Unfortunate Mother* (which the theatres had rejected), one "C.G." suggests that play publication might even be *more* profitable than dealing with the ungrateful stage:

> . . . I commend the wisedome of thy Fate,
> To sell thy labours at a better rate,
> Then the contempt of the most squeamish age;
> Or the exactest Roscii of the Stage.[93]

Working with established publishers, well-known dramatists could get many of the benefits that came regularly from non-dramatic writing: contracts granting them long-term shares in a work; payment for revisions.[94] Playwrights distinguished enough to be printed and reprinted were beginning to have a modest but steady income from publication: between 1666 and 1672, Racine probably earned about 1,500 livres a year from the various editions of his plays.[95] According to Juan Pérez de Montalbán, Lope de Vega had earned 1,600 ducats from his printed works by the time of his death in 1635.[96] Calderón's irritation at the incessant piracy of his works was as much for economic as for aesthetic reasons.[97] By the end of the seventeenth century normal payment from a publisher for a play was between 200 and 300 *livres* in France (rising to 700–800 *livres* by the end of the century), and somewhere around £15 to £40 in England. Jacob Tonson paid Dryden 30 guineas (£31 10*s.* 0*d.*) for his *Cleomenes* in 1691.[98] In addition to the £150 in house receipts that Thomas Southerne got for *The Fatal Marriage* (1694) and the 50 guineas he received from nobles who admired the play, he got £36 from the "printer . . . for his copy." (One writer commented: "This kind usage will encourage desponding minor poets, and vex huffing Dryden and Congreve to madness.")[99] Prior proof of saleability usually meant higher contracts: Bernard Lintott paid Farquhar only £16 2*s.* 6*d.* for *The Recruiting Officer* in 1705, but, after it had gone into four editions within two years, Farquhar received £30 from him for *The Beaux Stratagem.*[100]

Payments of £30 and 300 *livres* were substantial,[101] and successful playwrights could get still more. Bernard Lintott paid Nicholas Rowe £50 15*s.* 0*d.* for *Jane Shore* (1714) and raised the payment to £75 5*s.* 0*d.* for *Lady Jane Grey* (1715).[102] Philippe Quinault's publisher paid him 1,650 *livres* for his opera *Thesée* in 1675 and 1,000 for his opera *Isis* in 1677.[103] Voltaire's publisher similarly paid him a thousand for *L'Enfant prodigue* in 1737,[104] and Charles Palissot's publisher paid him an impressive

2,000 *livres* for his comedy *Les Philosophes* in 1760.[105] To be famous, politically hot, and censored was the best combination. Molière eventually made 2,000 *livres* from the publication of *Tartuffe* after the play was suppressed.[106] The publishing contract for *The Beggar's Opera* (with *Fifty Fables*) brought John Gay an already impressive £94 10s. 0d., but after his sequel *Polly* was suppressed, the printing of the play brought him £1,200.[107] For established playwrights, sale outright to a publisher could be a more certain means of income than patronage or the theatre (as Goldoni makes clear in his *Memoirs*): professional dramatists' payments were, by the middle of the seventeenth century, generally keyed to performance takings, and so a theatrical flop could mean a minimal payment, no payment at all, or even a debt to the theatre.[108] As prices for the publication of plays rose, and as successful performance runs signalled to publishers the near guarantee of a successful print run, the gap between performance takings and publication contracts could narrow. Samuel Johnson received £195 17s. 0d. from the three benefit nights in the very respectable nine-night run of his tragedy *Irene* (1749), and then received £100 for the publication of the play, which went into three editions.[109]

Dramatists were not only making a greater effort to sell their work to publishers, but also paying closer attention to *how* their plays were printed: to the preliminary material; to the quality of texts and the look of the page. While a few sixteenth- and early seventeenth-century dramatists, as we have seen, took part in the publication of their plays, it was no longer uncommon in the mid-seventeenth and eighteenth centuries for a dramatist to do the editorial work and oversee publication for an edition. This is not to say that layout normally reflected, to any great extent, the aesthetic choices of the dramatist, or even, for that matter, of the printer. By the first decades of the seventeenth century, standard conventions for the dramatic *mise en page* had set in, and most plays resembled one another more than they resembled the particular *œuvre* of their authors, generally following national norms (italic type in French and Italian plays, for instance, double columns without a separate title page in Spanish plays) (Fig. 14).[110] Moreover, the increase in the numbers of plays in the seventeenth century (along with other factors) meant a proportional decline in quality: cheap paper with bad ink, little ornamentation, inconsistent typography, distorted letter shapes, a general tendency towards the production of works understood as ephemera.[111] Individual printers, compositors, correctors, and dramatists themselves often continued to follow their own orthographic and stylistic peculiarities (as they had in the earlier seventeenth century), which meant inevitable inconsistency.[112] The rush to print soon after performance, or to reprint an edition that sold out more quickly than expected, often meant greater haste than care. While many editions contain stop-press corrections for easily spotted errors (for instance in pagination and running titles), these themselves sometimes contain errors, and errors are usually repeated in later editions.[113]

But dramatists could have an impact on the way their plays were printed, increasingly taking an active part in shaping their texts for print.[114] The disclaimer of authorial involvement in the publication of Robert Davenport's tragedy *King John and Matilda* in 1655 shows how conventional such authorial oversight (with the reward

FIG. 14. Calderón's *The Daughter of Air* (*c*.1680).

of a frontispiece portrait and commendatory poems) had become by the middle of the seventeenth century. "The *Author* of this [book]," says the preface, "had no mind to be a man in Print; nor tooke he any care for a Sculpture to illustrate the Frontispiece by Crowning himselfe with Laurel: Neither did he write his owne *Encomiums* and (to prejudicate the simple) say his friends forc'd them upon him."[115] Whether or not a publication had *in fact* been "perfected, amended and corrected" by the dramatist (as Calderón's brother claimed, apparently spuriously, when he published Calderón's *Primera Parte* in 1636), that the claim had become a convention by the 1630s or so was indicative of the fact that dramatists were not merely engaging in press correction but cleaning up their plays for the press.[116] Corneille oversaw the publication of his works in 1644 and 1648, and again in 1660, 1663–4, and 1682, making revisions and corrections for each edition both in the manuscripts and in the proofs.[117] The general privilege for Molière's works in 1671 explains that, in response to the various unauthorized editions recently published, Molière was in the process of preparing correct texts for publication.[118] Both Racine and Congreve made extensive changes in the plays they included in the later editions of their *Works*.[119] Playwrights regularly commented on the placement of their favourite plays in the collections they were producing, or their editorial decisions to suppress their failed efforts.

This does not mean, however, that dramatists' editorial standards were the same as ours: most tended to overlook textual details that, to a modern author, would seem critical. Molière complained bitterly of the textual distortions that were the result of unauthorized editions, but, when he had *Sganarelle* printed in 1660, he used the precise text that a certain "Sieur de La Neufvillaine" had prepared by means of memorial reconstruction, including in the printed text the "arguments of each scene" that "La Neufvillaine" had added.[120] In the prologue to the *Cuarta Parte* of his plays (1672), Calderón insisted that he was publishing the collection only to protect against the kinds of errors that had plagued earlier unauthorized editions, but the plays whose printing he ostensibly oversaw had numerous missing lines, imperfect strophes, and various bits of incomprehensible verse that had to be corrected in the second edition in 1674.[121] Steele revised *The Funeral* for publication (working closely with Jacob Tonson), but failed to correct a scene in which Campley whispers sweet nothings to his beloved Harriot but, because of a printing error, calls her by the wrong name.[122]

Most publishers and dramatists, however, aspired to a certain level of visual uniformity, consistency of usage, and freedom from obvious error, even if they failed to achieve it. The apology for press errors was a cliché by the middle of the seventeenth century precisely because of such aspirations. Moseley jokes about it in his Beaumont and Fletcher: "For *literall Errours* committed by the Printer, 'tis the fashion to aske pardon, and as much in fashion to take no notice of him that asks it; but in this also I have done my endeavour."[123] The editors of the Beaumont and Fletcher collection apologize for having been forced to farm out the commendatory poems to various printers at the last minute and hence for their mismatched typefaces ("their different Character"), but point out in self-defence that "the *Worke* it selfe is one continued Letter."[124] Those involved in print were conscious of the power of typography as meaning. Black letter, for instance, could evoke the quaint past: *Tom Tyler and his Wife* (reprinted in 1661) is "An Excellent Old Play, As it was Printed and Acted about a hundred Years ago."

Dramatists could, moreover, work closely with printers to establish typographic standards. Dissatisfied with the conventional French spellings that had developed by the middle of the seventeenth century, Corneille tried to create a new orthographic system for his 1663 works, looking to Dutch typographic models (adopting, for instance, "*j*" as the consonantal form of "*i*," and "*v*" as the consonantal form of "*u*") and reforming the use of accents, though he had some trouble getting the printers to follow his instructions: "As the Printers had trouble accustoming themselves [to the new orthography, and as] they did not follow this new order perfectly . . . many errors have slipped through," he writes, begging his readers to "do me the favour of compensating for them."[125] Influenced by Corneille, Congreve accompanied his publisher Jacob Tonson to Holland in 1700 to acquire type, plates, and paper, using a similarly adjusted typography for his 1710 *Works*.[126] By the later eighteenth century, playwrights might become their own (and others') publishers:

Lessing co-founded a printing and publishing house while he was *dramaturg* at the Hamburg National Theatre; Beaumarchais founded his own "Literary and Typographic Society," importing Baskerville type to Kehl, where he set up a printing house for the purpose of publishing Voltaire's complete works, issuing a two-sided sheet, *Notice to Anyone who has Private Writings, Unknown Plays, or Letters by M. de Voltaire*, explaining that the editors were looking for letters from, to, or about Voltaire, which were necessary "for the ordering of the contents, for gathering information on the allusions concealed in the Author's writings, and for the history of his life, . . . no less useful for the annotations and for the choice of variants and fragments."[127] Typographic perfection was fulfilment of biographical reconstruction: "Samples printed with Baskerville types (which the Society has acquired) . . . will show how perfect the Society wishes the typographic aspect of this Edition to be."[128]

PLAYS IN PERFORMANCE, PLAYS IN THE PRESS

Dramatic printing did, on the whole, improve in the eighteenth century, in part thanks to dramatist involvement: there seems to have been more attention to press correction; presses were more accurately adjusted; there had been advances in paper manufacture; lines were no longer crammed into the space of the page; there was better-quality type available, capable of cleaner more consistent printing.[129] More closely involved with the press than ever, more conscious of the impact of the page, dramatists now often revised plays not just for performance but specifically for print. As we have seen, it was unusual for a playwright to do so in the sixteenth and early seventeenth centuries (Jonson or Montchrestien were exceptions), but there was a good deal of such revision from the 1640s on. The revisions of Corneille, Racine, or Congreve—if more extensive than most—were not exceptions but instances of a common practice. Playwrights, for instance, regularly reinserted passages censored or simply left out in performance, advertising the fact on title pages and in prefaces, as Cibber did in his *Richard III* (1700) and in *The Provok'd Husband* (1728) ("the Reader will . . . find here a Scene or two of the lower Humour, that were left out after the first Day's Presentation").[130]

Typography could highlight the differences between performance text and author's text. Thomas Shadwell italicized the passages that had been censored in the performance of *The Lancashire-Witches* when he came to print the play in 1682. "I have in my own vindication Printed it just as I first writ it; and all that was expunged is Printed in the Italick Letter."[131] Molière's editors marked the unperformed passages in *Le Malade imaginaire* with quotation marks (in the posthumous 1682 edition of his works), explaining that even the great Molière himself (in deference to the requirements of the stage) left them out when he acted the play.[132] The 1676 quarto *Hamlet* explains to the reader:

This Play being too long to be conveniently Acted, such places as might be least prejudicial to the Plot or Sense, are left out upon the Stage: but that we may no way wrong the incomparable Author, [they] are here inserted according to the Original Copy with this Mark ".[133]

To publish could be a weapon against censors, interpolating actors, and managers whose "pruning kni[ves]" (as Sheridan's Puff has it) had done violence to the authorial text. "Very well, Sir," cries Puff, "the performers must do as they please, but upon my soul, I'll print it every word . . . I'll print it—egad, I'll print it every word!"[134] But it was also a way of entering the genteel world of the book, unsullied by the vulgar stage. For a collected edition, a playwright or editor might adopt continental scene divisions with their elegant speaker groupings at the head of each scene, regularize spelling, punctuation, and capitalization, and generally "polish" (to use a favourite term), "softening" what was perceived as inappropriate to the dignity of print, sanitizing "coarse jests," banishing obscenities. The Milanese playwright Carlo Maria Maggi explains his struggle in 1698 to keep a Genoese admirer from printing his tragedy *La Griselda*, not yet "polished" for publication.[135] Congreve removed most instances of "pox," "Jesus," and "damnation" from his 1710 *Works* (though he left plenty of "zoons," "demmes," "gadzooks," and their variants).[136] Goldoni notes that, before publishing the first edition of his plays (in 1751), he spent several years in Tuscany so that, "under the eyes and the criticism of the learned," he could "purge them of linguistic faults," continuing self-consciously to shape and reshape his *œuvre* in the various collections of his works.[137]

Those rewriting older plays, of course, "softened" for the stage as well. Nahum Tate's Cordelia is miraculously revived at the end of his 1681 version of *King Lear* to marry Edgar—"Thy bright Example shall convince the World | (Whatever Storms of Fortune are decreed) | That Truth and Vertue shall at last succeed"—while Lear, Kent, and Gloucester cheerfully go off to a retirement home ("some cool Cell [to] gently pass our short reserves of Time").[138] Edmund Waller similarly gave a happy ending to Beaumont and Fletcher's *Maid's Tragedy* "[to] Soften the rigour of the Tragedy."[139] ("'Twas agreeable to the Sweetness of Mr. *Waller*'s Temper . . . ; but whether it be agreeable to the Nature of Tragedy it self, to make every thing come off easily, I leave to the Criticks," commented a contemporary writer acerbically.)[140] In fact, printed authorial editions could actually preserve "harder" endings, endings that might, on the stage, violate the delicate sensibilities of the spectator. Having seen only Tate's version of *Lear*, Samuel Johnson famously attested to the distress he felt on reading a version of the play in which Cordelia actually dies at the end: "I was many years ago so shocked by Cordelia's death, that I know not whether I ever endured to read again the last scenes of the play till I undertook to revise them as an editor."[141] But the edition revised for print, while it could sometimes restore the playwright of an earlier era to "primitive purity,"[142] resisting the theatrical temptation to "ma[k]e every thing come off easily," most often reflected the chastened imagination of a living dramatist's sober maturity.

PERFORMANCE TEXTUALIZED

I will discuss more extensively in Chapter 6 the authorial edition classically conceived: the collection revised to transcend the specificity of individual performance and aspiring towards an idealized, non-theatrical text. But it is important to recognize that, throughout the period, the majority of dramatic texts proudly pointed to their performance venues. It is important to recognize the extent to which even the aspiration to authorial hermeticism (via the printed text) was challenged from the beginning by playbooks that celebrated their provisional theatricality, that insisted on their own currency and implied their own extinction: Betterton's *K. Henry IV. with the humours of Sir John Falstaff. a tragi-comedy. As it is Acted at the theatre in Little-Lincolns-Inn-Fields . . . Revived, with Alterations* (printed in 1700) (Fig. 15); Garrick's *The Lying Valet; In Two Acts. As it is performed Gratis, At the Theatre in Goodman's-Fields* (1742), precursors of the numerous published "promptbooks" of the later eighteenth and nineteenth centuries.

This does not mean that seventeenth- and early eighteenth-century texts

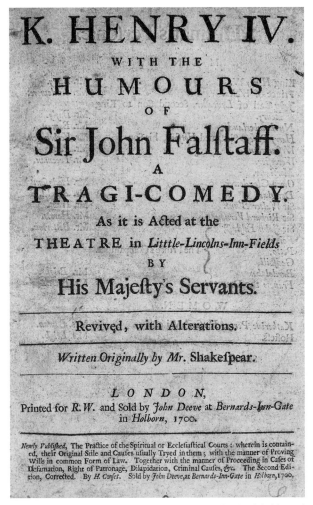

FIG. 15. Thomas Betterton's version of *K. Henry IV* "Revived, with Alterations" (1700).

normally gave much attention to recording performance detail. We have seen some of the extensive prescriptive stage directions that could be included in sixteenth-century performance texts like Rastell's, but we have also seen that, in sixteenth and early seventeenth-century plays, stage directions were usually quite spare. This continued to be the norm throughout the seventeenth century and most of the eighteenth. Despite the fact that, for instance, a play like Daniel Casper von Lohenstein's *Cleopatra* (1661) has half a dozen scene changes in a single act, Lohenstein's descriptions are parsimonious: "The stage represents Cleopatra's room"; "The stage represents the lovely mountain range of Mount Ida in Phrygia."[143] Although there were ornate descriptions for operas, and masques, interludes, and other spectacles throughout the period (sometimes inserted in "regular" plays), even a visual extravaganza like Dryden and Nathaniel Lee's *Oedipus* of 1678 instructs the reader flatly: "The Curtain rises to a plaintive Tune, representing the present condition of *Thebes*; Dead Bodies appear at a distance in the Streets; Some faintly go over the Stage, others drop."[144]

There was, however, a shift. One might think of it as one of tense: from the future tense (instructions for how to perform a piece in the future) or the past tense (descriptions of events now past) to the eternal present tense (descriptions of events happening in the now, on the page and in the reader's imagination). This does not mean that playwrights crafted stage directions with the same care with which they crafted dialogue, or tried to give them the readerly quality that nineteenth-century scenic descriptions would achieve. But the plays of the period are rich in stage directions that bring the performance to the reader—that attempt to make it vividly present in the instant. "After a great Noise of calling Sons of Whores, &c. and bouncing at the Door," we read at the beginning of Act III of *The Debauchee* (1677), "Enter *Careless* drunk, all loose, and without his Perriwig."[145] Events unfold with an ever-present rapidity through expressively punctuated directions (often full of dashes and exclamation points of the kind that Fielding was to parody in *The Author's Farce*).[146] In Aphra Behn's *The Feigned Curtizans* (1679), for instance, we get Sir Signal and Tickletext's typical *commedia* encounter, blow-by-blow:

> They both advance softly, meeting just in the middle of the Stage, and coming close up to each other! both cautiously start back: And stand a tipto in the posture of fear, then gently feeling for each other, (after listening and hearing no noise) draw back their hands at touching each others, and shrinking up their shoulders, make grimases of more fear![147]

There is a similar shift in the use of illustrations. Seventeenth-century plays produced speedily and emerging straight from the theatres are generally unillustrated.[148] If individual plays have illustrations at all, they are usually only title-page woodcuts, most often copied from another book and having no relation to the stage. In grander collected editions, publishers seem to feel that illustration *per se* would interfere with the dignity of the text, linking the dramatist too closely to the indecorums of visual and theatrical culture. They typically offer, instead of illustration, an elegant portrait of the dramatist-as-gentleman (as in the 1685 edition of Calderón, edited by his friend Juan de Vera Tassis), or an abstract architectural or allegorical frontispiece like that in the 1664 Corneille folio, with its presiding angel, its bust of the noble Corneille being crowned by the muses, and its masks and musical instruments harmoniously ranged below. As in earlier periods, engravings may document elements of theatrical (often court) spectacles: they may record an especially lavish setting and the figures in the scene (as in the book for *The Golden Apple* designed by Lodovico Burnacini in 1668), or display the splendid audience in attendance; they may show off a dance configuration or display costumes. But they rarely give intimate portraits of characters in motion.

Most seventeenth-century engravings in play editions are not so much theatrical as (like their predecessors, the woodcuts) more generally narrative and without generic particularity. But, beginning in the later seventeenth century, illustrations start to do more than merely offer iconic or narrative elements of the scene: they *illustrate* the scene theatrically, not just as a particular event (a spectacle for a prince on a given occasion) but as an enduring moment of frozen theatricality, whose narrative power lies in the stilling of the frame. The engravings in Corneille's 1660 *Théâtre* or the 1682 *Les Oeuvres de Monsieur de Moliere*, for instance, try to capture the

FIG. 16. Illustration for Molière's *The Sicilian: or, the Love Painter* in the 1682 edition of his plays.

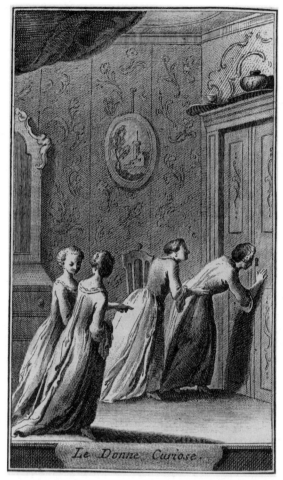

FIG. 17. Illustration for Goldoni's *The Curious Women* in the 1761 edition of his plays.

fleeting instant (the attitude of the characters at an expressive moment) in something of the way that Behn's stage directions do, striving towards theatrical representation. In the illustration for *The Sicilian: or, the Love Painter* in the 1682 edition of Molière's works, for instance, Adraste, disguised as a painter, falls at the feet of Isidore (as the stage directions instruct), while the valet Hali distracts the jealous Dom Pèdre in the background (Fig. 16).[149] Modelling themselves on such editions, eighteenth-century play collections began regularly to include one engraving as the frontispiece to each play.[150] In the edition of Gherardi's *Theatre Italien* published in 1700, each play is illustrated with a convincingly theatrical representation: in *Mezzetin in Hell*, Mezzetin, Columbine, Orpheus, and Euridice plead with Pluto on his throne; in *Harlequin Phaeton*, Harlequin tumbles from his flying chariot, while Columbine, Isabelle, and Pierrot (in their classical guises) raise their arms to try to stop his fall.[151] Domestic scenes preoccupied illustrators: the women, for instance, peering through the keyhole in the illustration for Goldoni's *The Curious Women* in the 1761 edition of his plays (implicitly mirroring the reader's own spying on the play in the closed space of the book) (Fig. 17).[152]

The attempts throughout Europe to explain what actors did when they represented a character, to describe and record non-verbal performance forms (in works like John Weaver's *History of Mimes and Pantomimes* (1728) or Samuel Foote's *A Treatise on the Passions, so far as they regard the Stage* (1747))—or to theorize and offer notation systems for dance—sought similarly to capture the performed moment. Dance manuals and systems of dance notation attempted at once to preserve the work of choreographers and dancers, and to find a form of dance notation as precise as that for words or musical notes.[153] The English translation of Raoul Feuillet's *Choreographie* (1700) explains how to annotate dances ("You must resolve in what part of the *Room* the *Dance* is to begin, and there place the beginning of the *Tract*; then trace out the *Figure*, and mark thereon the *Position*").[154]

All this reflected not only the cultural centrality of theatre but also the interest in recording the non-verbal, reflected similarly in the theatrical histories that proliferated in the later seventeenth and eighteenth centuries (James Wright's *History Histrionica* (1699), Luigi Riccoboni's *Historical and Critical Account of the Theatres in Europe* (1738)) and in calendars like the annual French *Historical and Chronological Theatre Calendar* (1750–78), or as current events, in the newspaper reviews of productions that began to appear in the early eighteenth century (the *Mercure de France*, for instance, began publishing a separate section of drama reviews in 1721).[155] Reviewing, actor biography, scenic illustration, and gestural and dance annotation taught critics, writers, readers, and theatre-goers to pay greater attention to the telling theatrical detail. This kind of attention showed up, in turn, in the long narrative stage directions, the encyclopaedic scenic indications, and the bountiful pictorial records which were essential to the late eighteenth- and nineteenth-century stage. These and other attempts to record and prescribe performance in pictorial and descriptive detail are one of the subjects of the next chapter.

3. *Illustrations, Promptbooks, Stage Texts,*
1760–1880

THE THEATRE INDUSTRY AND THE PRESS

By the early decades of the nineteenth century, theatres had multiplied in the urban capitals: London had over two dozen by the 1830s, and Paris had some thirty (according to one source, more than two hundred had sprouted during the Revolution), to be compared with the two or three that any given city had allowed or been able to support a century earlier.[1] By the middle of the 19th century, theatre was a boom business. "Today in Madrid between Lyceums, Academies, Museums, Circuses, and private home theatres, there are more than forty different places for entertainment!" exclaimed the Madrid newspaper *El Pasatiempo* in 1842.[2] One Paris account estimated that 500,000 Parisians visited the theatre once a week, and that over a million went once a month.[3] Theatres in the capitals were being redesigned and enlarged. New theatres were burgeoning in towns that had before seen only the occasional troupe of strollers: in cities and courts (throughout Germany, for instance) and across the provinces of Europe.[4] Norwich's new "Grand and Magnificent THEATRE," bragged the *Norwich Gazette* in 1758, "is allow'd by all Connoisseurs and Judges to be the most perfect and complete structure of this kind in this Kingdom. . . . The Stage [is] large and lofty;—and the Scenes so highly finish'd and executed . . . that they are accounted far superior to any of the kind."[5] A hit play like Antonio García Gutiérrez's *El trovador* (1836), perpetually sold out in Madrid, might arrive almost immediately after its première in provincial theatres, spreading from there to small towns in which haylofts were converted into *ad hoc* theatres to serve the play-hungry populace.[6]

The new provincial newspapers carried the latest reports on the theatres, bringing urban tastes to the fashionable in the countryside (Fig. 18). The papers (or the "prints") helped also to spread the mania for big stars, along with news of their scandalous lives. The actress Dorothy Jordan, heralded by the press, was awaited by ecstatic crowds when, in the 1780s, she travelled around the provinces—the fact that "the papers have all abused Mrs. Jordan," (as her lover the Duke of Clarence complained in 1791) only adding to her fame.[7] Even those who could not regularly spend money on news could go "to the Library to read the papers," as Jordan did in Bath in search of her own reviews.[8] In the 1770s, London periodicals began regularly to grant space to reports on performances, with more extended reviews developing over time, and by the end of the eighteenth century separate newspaper drama columns, regular reviews, and sheets on theatre like the weekly *Feuilletons* of "Geoffroy" (published in Paris from 1800 on) had become a fixture in the press.[9] Dailies and weeklies

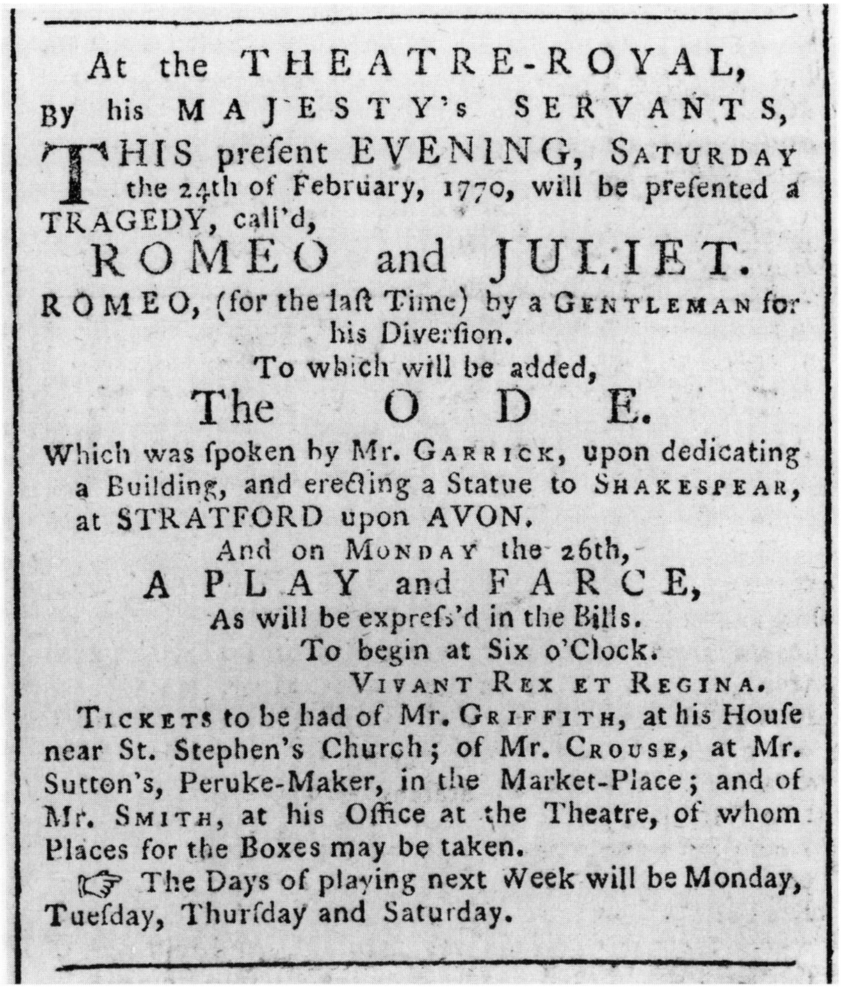

At the T H E A T R E - R O Y A L,
By his M A J E S T Y's S E R V A N T S,
THIS prefent E V E N I N G, Saturday
the 24th of February, 1770, will be prefented a
TRAGEDY, call'd,
R O M E O and J U L I E T.
R O M E O, (for the laft Time) by a Gentleman for
his Diverfion.
To which will be added,
The   O   D   E.
Which was fpoken by Mr. Garrick, upon dedicating
a Building, and erecting a Statue to Shakespear,
at STRATFORD upon AVON.
And on Monday the 26th,
A P L A Y and F A R C E,
As will be exprefs'd in the Bills.
To begin at Six o'Clock.
Vivant Rex et Regina.
Tickets to be had of Mr. Griffith, at his Houfe
near St. Stephen's Church; of Mr. Crouse, at Mr.
Sutton's, Peruke-Maker, in the Market-Place; and of
Mr. Smith, at his Office at the Theatre, of whom
Places for the Boxes may be taken.
☞ The Days of playing next Week will be Monday,
Tuefday, Thurfday and Saturday.

FIG. 18. Advertisement in the *Norwich Mercury* (1770).

specializing in the theatre such as the *Theatrical Guardian* fed an increasingly the-
atre-hungry readership. The Dublin daily, *The Stage*, for instance, announced at the
start of its brief life that the paper would be "written for the most part, about the
solemn hour of twelve; printed in the witching time of night, and published before
the play-loving fold forsake their pillows in the morning . . . demand[ing] our time
at a period when nature calls for rest . . . But . . . THE STAGE must be published every
morning and written every night."[10] In addition to the newspapers there were "posting bills," sometimes used as news and gossip sheets about actors as well as for playhouse advertising.[11]

Even the ordinary papers might track each stage of a production, from pre-production planning through rehearsals to the climactic moment of the première. In the months leading up to the first performance of Cayetano Rosell's *San Fernando's Mother* in 1850, for instance, the Madrid newspapers gave blow-by-blow updates:

Cayetano Rosell, a well-known writer, has just completed a drama called *San Fernando's Mother*, written for the Teatro Español. . . .

Cayetano Rosell has finished his play *San Fernando's Mother*, for the Teatro Español; they are praising it highly.

Last night the Reading Commission of the Teatro Español read and approved the drama entitled *San Fernando's Mother*, written by the well-known author, Cayetano Rosell.

San Fernando's Mother, by Cayetano Rosell, approved by the Reading Commission will be staged shortly. . . .

The first play to be performed at the Teatro Español following the Christmas season will be a new, original verse drama entitled *San Fernando's Mother*, which we have heard is quite successful as a literary work.

On Monday the original verse drama entitled *San Fernando's Mother*, by Cayetano Rosell, will be performed at the Teatro Español.

At the Teatro Español the new, original play in verse by Cayetano Rosell, *San Fernando's Mother*, is in rehearsals. . . .

San Fernando's Mother was a disaster.[12]

Theatre entrepreneurs came to depend on the newspapers for hype. Sheridan, ever the excellent businessman, regularly made arrangements to have favourable reviews of his plays run in the *Morning Chronicle* and *Morning Post*, which he later managed and in which he bought advertisements for the Drury Lane Theatre (as manager and principal owner).[13] Saint-Beuve complained of the regular practice of "paid praises in the newspapers" (along with "tickets given to the claque").[14] If actors like Jordan felt pestered by the "prints," if playwrights carped about the newspaper critics, the newspapers were nonetheless necessary to the competitive business of theatre production.

Along with newspapers and posting bills, there were all the printed forms that served specifically commercial purposes: posters, tickets, playbills, theatre programmes, and guides like Heinrich Reichard's lavishly illustrated calendars—all these counted on as a regular part of theatre-going by the late eighteenth century (Fig. 19). Goethe's *Wilhelm Meister* (1777) describes the playbills that would be passed out as advertising for a show put on by a company of strollers:

A clown was running around in the gathering crowd, handing out playbills as he kissed a girl or smacked a little boy, all the time making jokes, which were so easy to grasp that everybody felt drawn towards him and eager to get to know him better. The printed advertisements extolled the many different skills of the performers, especially those of a Monsieur Narcise and Mademoiselle Landrinette, who, as principals, were wise enough to absent themselves from the procession, in order to give themselves a higher status and arouse more curiosity.[15]

FIG. 19. David Garrick as Hamlet in Heinrich Reichard's *Theater-Kalender* for February 1781.

By the mid-nineteenth century, one could see playbills lavishly describing the scenery and costumes. By later in the nineteenth century, printers could afford to specialize in designs for posters and programmes which managers could copy, producing catalogues like the *Specimens of Theatrical Cuts . . . Suitable for Theatrical, Variety and Circus Business*.[16]

The personal identification with actors (their intimate lives brought home by the newspress), the images of the glamour of the stage reproduced in countless prints, and the general cultural centrality of theatre helped create a vogue for home theatricals: performances like August von Kötzebue's *Lover's Vows* in Jane Austen's *Mansfield Park* (1814).[17] Wilhelm Meister finds the dramatic material for his theatricals in Gottsched's famous collection, *The German Stage*:

After I had several times performed that first play for which theater and actors had been set up, I began to lose interest in it. But among my grandfather's books I found . . . "The German Stage," and texts of several operas in German and Italian, in which I immersed myself, and, having counted up the characters at the beginning of the text, proceeded to perform the play.[18]

The modern circulating libraries,[19] as well as the bookshops and city theatres, could provide amateurs with newer texts, what William Archer referred to later as the "miserable sixpenny pamphlets for the use of amateur clubs" that the nineteenth century had produced.[20] Actors and would-be's in London, along with managers of the provincial theatres, swarmed around the Drury Lane and Covent Garden box offices to buy printed Shakespeare promptbooks based on Kemble's productions ("Kemble copies," only a shilling or two) so that they could take home a guide for the acting of Shakespeare.[21] If both amateur theatricals and provincial productions modelled themselves on performances in major urban theatres, they also modelled themselves on printed editions with detailed scenic descriptions, acting indications, and illustrations—editions like Bell's plays, carefully "Regulated from the Prompt books" (Fig. 20). They copied engravings like those on which the characters in Goethe's *Elective Affinities* (1809) base their home *tableaux vivants*—"copperplates of . . . the Belisarius of Van Dyck," Poussin's Esther, and the "*Instruction paternelle* of Gerald Terborch" ("who does not know Wille's wonderful copperplate of this painting?").[22] Rex (in George Eliot's *Daniel Deronda*) wishes to base his home *tableau vivant* on "Briseis being led away" from Achilles "after the print we have at the Rectory."[23]

More theatres meant more performances (in the nineteenth century, nearly triple what the eighteenth century had produced and ever-increasing).[24] At the same time, the fashion for amateur theatricals and the greater number of theatres (both urban and provincial), along with increases in literacy, created new markets for dramatic material. Variety collections like *The Theatrical Museum* (1776) might be marketed to serve the new play-buying public of amateur actors, as well as urban and provincial actors and ordinary readers: its garrulous title page explains that it offers "some Petite-Pieces, of one Act each . . . properly adapted for all Persons who are Lovers of the Drama, and Ambitious of attaining the Art of Public Declamation," along with interludes and other pieces "which may be now very acceptable to every Comedian, both of Town and Country, who are desirous of entertaining their Friends with Novelty at their *Benefits*."[25] New provincial book distribution networks helped extend play-buying: by the mid-nineteenth century (as the title page of Tomás Rodríguez y Díaz Rubí's *The Daughter of Providence* shows) plays could be distributed in as many as ninety cities and towns in Spain, including such backwaters as Toro, Tuy, Ubeda, Motril, Chiclana, Ecija, and Reus.[26]

Reflecting the theatre mania of the era, there was a profusion of printed drama— the abundance of textual production suggested by the half-impatient entry in one French book catalogue: "a very large number of Plays put on in various Theatres."[27] (James Boaden, presaging the electrical revolution, imagined the relation between theatre and press as one of electrical energy: "The crowd at a manager's door

FIG. 20. Thomas Southerne's *Isabella; or the Fatal Marriage* "Regulated from the Prompt-Book" in *Bell's British Theatre* (1776).

electrically acts upon a publisher's, and a play that *draws* is already destined to the press").[28] Technological changes helped supply to meet demand: the development of machine-made paper and the machine press, most notably, but also such advances as stereotyping, advertised on numerous nineteenth-century title pages.[29] When later nineteenth-century commentators like Shaw noted the difference that "the huge size of modern populations and the development of the press" made, they were noting a real material change.[30] As publishers began to specialize in plays, as publishing houses expanded into publishing empires (with a good deal of their business in printed plays), normal print runs also expanded: from one to two thousand copies throughout the seventeenth and eighteenth centuries to anywhere from one to ten thousand copies in the nineteenth century.[31]

Machine binding, developed from the 1820s onwards, allowed publishers to produce relatively cheap pre-bound editions, sometimes with dozens of volumes (each volume containing several plays).[32] Such collections and dramatic series, expanding the number of printed plays ten or twenty or one hundred fold, began to dominate the drama market, responding to the demand for volumes that could fill library shelves: in England, Bell's *British Theatre* (a collection of old and new plays published between 1776 and 1778), and the many that followed it (*A Collection of Much-Esteemed Dramatic Pieces* (1795) or Tom Dibdin's twenty-six-volume *London Theatre* (1814–18)); in France, the *Fin du répertoire du Théâtre français* (1824), *Collection des théâtres français* (1829), or *Chefs-d'oeuvre du théâtre moderne* (1868); in Spain, the *Colección de Obras Dramáticas y Líricas*, the *Biblioteca Dramática*, or the *Galería Dramática*, with more than 180 titles in print by 1846.[33] Series printing like Kötzebue's *Almanach dramatischer Spiele* (appearing annually between 1803 and 1834) or Bell's Shakespeare ("beginning . . . with Macbeth, and continu[ing] by one play every succeeding Saturday" (*c*.1773))[34] became standard. There was a demand for collections with prefaces by practising playwrights like Johann Ludwig Tieck's *Deutsches Theater* (1817) or Elizabeth Inchbald's twenty-five-volume *British Theatre* (1808), whose sales (according to her) were "prodigious."[35] Publishers began to publish "minor drama" alongside the "chefs-d'œuvres": *Richardson's New Minor Drama* (1828–31); *Cumberland's Minor Theatre* in sixteen volumes (1828–44).[36]

As libraries continued to grow, collections proliferated, the drama's readership expanded, and formats grew more varied. Octavos and duodecimos continued to dominate the market (with octavo as the favoured format for collections), but tiny sizes became quite common: booksellers' catalogues show numerous plays in 16° and 18° editions, and there was even a tiny 64° Molière *Oeuvres* in seven volumes in 1815.[37] Prices had continued to rise during the eighteenth century, but, with mechanization and mass reprinting, they dropped drastically.[38] In France for instance, where normal prices had been between 1½ to 3 francs for a play (depending on length), they declined in the 1820s to 1 to 1½ francs, and publishers like Jean-Nicolas Barba eventually found that they could publish plays for as little as 30 or 40 centimes.[39] In 1776, the editor of *The Theatrical Museum* considered one shilling sewed (the normal price for a play) to be "so small a value" that the book would surely sell well.[40] By the 1820s, John Duncombe and Thomas Hailes Lacy were selling a variety of dramatic texts for 6*d.* a copy. Plays from the minor theatres sold for half that, and by the time John Dicks was publishing his *Standard Plays* in the 1880s he could sell them for only a penny, a price that could not have been matched in an earlier era.[41] There were exceptions: Longman charged an average of two shillings, occasionally half a crown for a play; John Murray charged 4*s.* 6*d.* for his edition of Maturin's highly successful *Bertram; or, the Castle of St Aldobrand* (1816) (a price which Genest considered "a scandalous imposition on the public," though the play had seven editions in a year).[42] But bargain books dominated the dramatic market. Spanish plays were advertised at discount prices, cheaper by the dozen.[43] George Routledge's two-volume collection of James Sheridan Knowles, the leading British playwright, was advertised as at once "elegant" and "extremely cheap."[44]

THE DRAMATIC AUTHOR AND THE THEATRICAL HACK

If lesser printers could achieve better printing standards (working with a larger number of employees with more specialized tasks, producing more uniform products using better quality ink, new machines, and fresh, unworn type), the cheap reprints on deteriorating paper seemed to announce their own ephemerality, their proliferation to point to a decline in dramatic "literature" generally.[45] For Hazlitt, that decline was a direct outcome of the increase in book production and the increase in the number of authors:

As authors multiply in number, books diminish in size; we cannot now, as formerly, swallow libraries whole in a single folio: solid quarto has given place to slender duodecimo, and the dingy letter-press contracts its dimensions, and retreats before the white, unsullied, faultless margin. . . . The staple commodity, the coarse, heavy, dirty, unwieldy bullion of books is driven out of the market of learning, and the intercourse of the literary world is carried on, and the credit of the great capitalists sustained by the flimsy circulating medium of magazines and reviews.[46]

But if "solid quarto" had in fact given place to "slender duodecimo" (in Hazlitt's classic equation between old books and gold bullion, printed ephemera and paper credit), it was not the case that magazines and reviews and dramatic series had displaced the "literary" book. There were more collections of the *œuvres* of living dramatic authors than ever, often in many volumes, placed side by side with the collections of the national drama. It was rare for a serious late eighteenth- or nineteenth-century playwright *not* to see a collection of plays in print, and distinguished playwrights often saw as many as a dozen or more such editions. Eighteen collected editions of Carlo Goldoni's plays were published during his lifetime, twenty-seven of August von Kötzebue's, and fifteen of Victor Hugo's (in addition to the twenty collections of *œuvres* that included his plays).[47] If the popular stage playwright Henry Arthur Jones thought that he could at last become "a real literary man" through the publication of "the library edition of my plays,"[48] if Arthur Wing Pinero hoped that a reading edition of his plays would play their part in "dignify[ing] . . . the craft of the playwright,"[49] such aspirations had been fed during the preceding century by the elevation of the dramatist through the dignified collection.

In fact there was (perhaps for the first time) a substantial body of modern drama with a life independent of the stage. With the mass production and sale of collected editions (both single- and multiple-author), readers were inevitably buying plays they had not seen and would not be likely to see. By the later eighteenth century, publication of a play in advance of performance was no longer uncommon:[50] Schiller, for instance, had *The Robbers* published the summer before its première in 1782; Goethe's verse version of *Iphegenia on Tauris* was not staged until 1800, two years after it had been printed, and he sent the *Helena* section of *Faust* "to Cotta to be printed" (to "meet its fate," as he told Eckermann) in 1827, long before he made any attempt to have it performed.[51] While it continued to be normal to take plays to theatres before publication, the novice playwright of the 1820s might use a printed edition of plays as an entrée to the theatre. Only after Christian Grabbe's publication of *Don Juan and Faust* and a two-volume collection of his "dramatic poems" in 1827–8 made him a celebrity could he finally get a theatre to produce his *Don Juan*.[52] After a number of theatrical rejections, Robert Browning included his unperformed plays in his series of pamphlets, *Bells and Pomegranates* (1841–6), ironically commenting that he "fanc[ied] that the cheap mode in which they appear will for once help me to a sort of Pit audience again."[53]

The coinage of the rubric "closet drama" (as shorthand for what had previously been referred to variously as reading plays, dramas not meant for the stage, plays for the closet, and so on)[54] may have reflected less a literary withdrawal from the commercialized stage than a literary response to the large body of play readers for whom dramatic form on the page was no longer alien. From the later eighteenth century on, playwrights (in England at least) generally took the precaution of making one copy of a play for the playhouse and one for the printer.[55] Even playwrights writing directly for the stage were consciously or unconsciously writing for readers as well. Goethe, while describing precisely the musical and scenic effects he intended *Faust* to convey, repeatedly thinks of the "*reader*" of the poem.[56] When, later in the century, Pinero sent his American producer R. M. Field his play, *The Times*, he stressed that what he was sending was "not a *stage copy*, but the work as prepared for the library [forming] vol:1 of a series of my plays which are being issued monthly to the reading public."[57] Shaw, dedicated man-of-theatre as he was, was writing for readers: "Readers of Ibsen and Maeterlinck, and pianoforte students of Wagner, are rightly warned that they cannot fully appreciate the force of a dramatic masterpiece without the aid of the theatre," he explains. "But," he adds (correcting the overcompensations of nineteenth-century pro-theatricalism—the too-ready truism that only theatrical performance offers a full experience of a text), "I have never found an acquaintance with a dramatist founded on the theatre alone . . . a really intimate and accurate one."[58]

The classic account of the nineteenth-century drama as the product of the alienation of theatre from literary life does not offer a very accurate representation of either drama or theatre during the period, but it is founded in the reality of the simultaneous development of a body of dramatic readers and the explosion of a theatre industry desperately in need of short-order writers. The late eighteenth- and nineteenth-century publishing industry offered a Janus-faced image of the drama-tist: on one side, the theatrical hack, writing up dramatizations published in "miser-able sixpenny pamphlets";[59] on the other, the literary dramatist, penning drama for posterity. Most of those who wrote plays tried to be both stage and literary drama-tists simultaneously, and many succeeded (Goethe and Hugo, for instance, to name only the most notable), but many also failed. Wordsworth (already the famous poet of the *Lyrical Ballads*) took *The Borderers* to the manager of Covent Garden in 1796, but it was (as Wordsworth himself wrote) "*judiciously* returned as not calculated for the stage."[60] The well-known theatrical débâcles of Byron, Browning, and (at the far end of the century) Henry James, despite their interest in things theatrical, suggest the extent to which the talents of "literary" writers in other genres were inadequate to the needs of the contemporary theatre.[61]

The theatre industry had come to rely, instead, on playwright-professionals with expert play-making skills, most of them working in conditions somewhat less grand than Sheridan did (at least as the story has it), locked in the green room of Drury Lane two days before *The Critic* was to open, with several bottles of claret and anchovy sandwiches to sustain him, not allowed to emerge until he had finished the last scene of the play.[62] With the multiplication of theatres, the prototypical stage hack, writing plays at lightning speed to feed the hungry theatres, could become once again a central figure in theatrical life. Translations and the dramatization of novels became theatrical staples. "I . . . tend to translate the first playlet given to me," wrote Mariano José de Larra of his work as a theatrical hack in *The Poor Little Chatterbox* (1832): "because it pays the same and costs much less work: I don't put my name on it, and don't care if the audience brings down the house booing it on opening night. What do you want?"[63]

The theatrical explosion and the rapid-fire production of plays by stage hacks meant that, even while the play-reading public was larger than ever and play publi-cation had increased geometrically, a substantial number of plays performed were not printed at all, or printed only after long delays.[64] By the nineteenth century, although there were bookselling concessions in many theatres, it was no longer standard practice (as it had come to be in the eighteenth century) to sell copies of plays in the theatre during the first run.[65] While many of the scores of plays and playlets performed in the minor theatres did find publishers, at least as many—from the fairs, the gaffs, the booth theatres—never went beyond manuscript (if they were written out at all).[66] There were a number of factors contributing to this situation. The demand for new published plays simply could not keep pace with the demand for new performances. Plays could less and less compete with novels in the literary market-place, still less could dramatizations compete with the novels they drama-tized.[67] "Novels and plays" were no longer classed together as the reading material for frivolous young ladies, but instead "poems and plays" were grouped, identified as the reading material for a slightly narrower (perhaps more refined) literary public than the broad class of novel readers or play-goers. But probably the most important factor was a renewal of deliberate withholding of plays from publication on the part of managers (and sometimes dramatists) in the losing battle against theatrical piracy.

COPYRIGHT

The battle against piracy was a losing one in part because of the proliferation of theatres, which made it hard to keep track of provincial performances, but also because there was little or no effective performance copyright for much of the later eighteenth and nineteenth centuries. The royal protection of repertoires that had existed for most of the eighteenth century had disappeared and not been replaced with anything else, or at least anything effective. Throughout late eighteenth- and nineteenth-century Europe, performance copyright laws lagged behind publication copyright laws.[68] In Spain, for instance, while strong (author-held) publication copyright was firmly entrenched by 1763, there was no formal performance copyright until 1847.[69] In the German and Italian states, the absence of inter-state regulation made performance copyright legislation essentially meaningless until international copyright agreements came into being in the late nineteenth century. As a result of the uncertainties of copyright law, managers and dramatists did what they could to keep scripts out of the hands of theatrical pirates, as they had in the seventeenth century. The 1792 regulations for the Hamburg theatre under the direction of Friedrich Schröder specify, for instance, that it is the prompter's job to guard scripts: the prompter "must not give away any scripts without authorisation at the risk of forfeiting his honour, and he must try to prevent any theft so that neither the author nor the director suffers any damage."[70] An edition of Pierre-Laurent de Belloy's highly successful *Siege of Calais* in 1769 warns feebly that while "this tragedy has been pirated in nearly all the Provinces of the Kingdom, and in foreign countries," the pirated editions were "easy to recognize, as much by the poor quality of the printing as by the errors that have proliferated in them. The Public is thus warned to address itself directly to the bookshop of the *Widow Duchesne, rue St. Jacques*, to have the correct Edition, printed under the eyes of the Author."[71] In 1790, Louis-Abel Beffroy de Reigny ("Cousin Jacques"), author of the wildly popular *Nicomède in the Moon*, declared publicly that, thanks to "highway robbery" on the part of prompters, copyists, and musicians "who are now engaged in furnishing . . . various provincial theatres with the score of *Nicomède dans la lune*," he "will neither print nor engrave any of my plays until there is a new law," but instead will "sell the manuscripts and scores by particular arrangement."[72]

In France, before and in the immediate aftermath of the Revolution, playwrights had complained of the formal monopoly of the principal theatres on spoken drama, the loss of dramatists' privileges after house receipts fell below a certain point, the Comédie-Française's habitual fudging of accounts to limit dramatists' percentages, and the effective prohibition on the printing of plays before or immediately after the première (on pain of loss of performance rights, since the Comédie would generally not perform new plays that had been printed).[73] In an attempt to redress the situation, there were various protests on the part of authors, resulting in (most famously) Beaumarchais's establishment of a Bureau of Dramatic Legislation in 1777 (precursor to the Society of Dramatic Authors). In 1790, in response to long-term agitation on the part of dramatists, the National Assembly formally granted dramatists complete performance copyright for any plays, whether printed or unprinted, declaring that dramatic authors had two distinct rights, that of performance and that of publication, and that selling publication by no means terminated performance rights.[74]

This put French dramatists, at least in Paris after the first decades of the century, in a significantly better position than English dramatists. In England prior to 1833, performance copyright (in so far as it existed) was made up of a set of assumptions, customary practices, and common law rulings, generally contradictory and confused. T. J. Thackeray could protest "the injustice which *now sanctions as a right* the piracy which managers of the theatre commit on dramatic authors" precisely because there was no clearly defined performance copyright.[75] For instance, it was unclear whether the 1710 and 1814 Copyright Acts (which granted authors publication rights for a limited period) also granted dramatists performance rights or whether, on the other hand, managers automatically acquired performance rights when they staged a play.[76] In England more than anywhere else, play publishing practices were affected by the vicissitudes of performance copyright. Some people seemed to believe that once a play was published (by the author or by piracy), it entered a "public domain" temporarily, and was therefore available for production by anyone who could get the copy licensed by the Lord Chamberlain. George Bolwell Davidge (of the Coburg) and David Morris (of the Haymarket), for instance, regularly produced plays that belonged to other theatres but had been published, in the firm belief that the published plays were not protected.[77] When the manager Alfred Bunn appropriated Tom Dibdin's adaptation of Scott's *Kenilworth* "with some little additions" for Drury Lane in 1824 (having obtained it from his wife who was acting Queen Elizabeth in an authorized Bath production), he explained to Dibdin in an attempt at self-justification: "You are, of course, aware that the play, as acted at Bath, is in print by a piracy in Edinburgh."[78] When Elliston (then manager of Drury Lane) succeeded in getting his hands on one of the first copies of Byron's *Marino Faliero* to come off the press (licensing it even before publication), he got a carefully dated receipt for the two copies he bought on the official date of publication so that he could prove that he had produced the play only after publication.[79]

At the same time (and somewhat paradoxically), other managers began regularly to buy publication copyrights along with plays, both in order to prevent premature publication and to advance the equally uncertain argument that performance rights were in fact conferred *with* publication rights, hoarding the copyrights of the most valuable pieces in the repertoire, eventually selling them to a publisher when performance rights were no longer valuable enough to be worth protecting.[80] Thomas Harris, manager of Covent Garden, tried to keep Sheridan's *The Duenna* from publication in 1777, advertising it as not yet published and to be performed only with Harris's permission.[81] William Dimond's comic opera *Brother and Sister* had over seventeen productions from 1815 on, but Dimond could not publish it until

1829 because Henry Harris (successor to his father Thomas as manager of Covent Garden) retained the copyright. Dramatists who wished to publish had no recourse. The managers of Covent Garden bought the publication copyright of Thomas Morton's immensely successful comedy *Speed the Plough* in 1800 and held onto it for more than a year over Morton's protests. The Haymarket was famous for holding onto publication copyrights long after initial productions had run their course. Several of John O'Keeffe's plays had been performed in the late eighteenth century, and both publication and performance copyrights were still owned by the Haymarket in the 1830s.[82]

For managers, this could be a workable safeguard. David Morris of the Haymarket successfully obtained Chancery injunctions prohibiting performance of plays whose copyrights he held. But it was not an infallible one. Morton's *Speed the Plough* was played in numerous provincial theatres despite Covent Garden's sequestering of the copyright. Seeking legal redress was costly and uncertain. As heavily as *Speed the Plough* was pirated, Morton felt (with justification) that legal action would not be worth any recompense he might receive for the piracies. The playwright William Thomas Moncrieff testified that to have sued for an injunction of the unauthorized 1820 Drury Lane production of *Giovanni in London* would have cost him £80, eight times what he made from the play.[83] "We have no protection whatever now," exclaimed Charles Mathews, one of the owners of the Adelphi, in 1832: "For there are four instances before the town of pieces that I have purchased the copyright of, that are acted at Sadler's Wells and the Queen's Theatre."[84] Performance piracy had become big business, often functioning in tandem with print piracy. Unauthorized texts, cobbled together for provincial productions, could be the basis for cobbled together editions; unauthorized editions, by putting texts in the hands of managers, were the basis for new productions.

The proliferation of printed texts helped managers—small and large—avoid having to get texts from dramatists (or pay for them). According to T. J. Thackeray, author of the treatise *On Theatrical Emancipation, and the Rights of Dramatic Authors* (1832), theatrical managers regularly committed "piracy . . . on dramatic authors by the performance, without the consent of the author, of any play as soon as published."[85] In the late eighteenth century, the provincial manager Tate Wilkinson complained that the modern "fashion" of non-publishing dramatists—"the favourite pieces not being printed, but kept under lock and key"—was "of infinite prejudice to us poor devils in the country theatres, as we really cannot afford to pay for the purchase of MSS."[86] But copies were surreptitiously lifted from the theatre, too, to give to both booksellers and managers, with techniques oddly reminiscent of the Renaissance: by shorthand writers, who could take down a play in the course of a few performances; by groups of longhand writers, who would each be assigned one or two characters; or simply by a well-placed agent who could bribe the prompter or house copyist. Charles Mathews testified in 1832 that play profiteers regularly sent "shorthand writers into the pit . . . and instead of the prompter getting that which was formerly considered his perquisite, they steal without ceremony at all, and it has become a kind of property among booksellers and adventurers."[87] The Dublin actor

Thomas Snagg recalled approaching the London shorthand writers about acquiring a copy of Sheridan's *School for Scandal* (withheld from publication precisely in order to keep it out of the hands of the likes of Snagg) and, failing at that,

> going into the two-shilling gallery, a party of five. By sitting together, two on one seat, two behind and two below, we composed a group and with paper and pencils each writing down the direct words of one of the characters in a scene and regulating the whole in a committee after each performance, in four or five nights we completed the whole.[88]

Reproducing and printing a play from memory was perfectly legal and, while reproducing and printing a play from stenographic notes was illegal, this was hard to prove.[89]

Some such copying was informal or *ad hoc*, a one-time event. Thomas Holcroft famously succeeded in taking down, in ten days' time, the entire text of Beaumarchais's unpublished *Marriage of Figaro* in 1784, bringing "away the whole with perfect exactness" so that he could put it on at Covent Garden while it was still a global *cause célèbre*.[90] But perhaps more significant was the new industry of theatrical copyists, Snagg's shorthand writers or "dramatic agents" who advertised their services to willing provincial managers—revitalizing the industry of scribal publication. According to the dramatist Douglas Jerrold, for instance, a certain "Mr Kenneth, at the corner of Bow-street, will supply any gentleman with any manuscript on the lowest terms." As Jerrold and Moncrieff testified, agents like William Kenneth made "a very considerable profit," copying plays for between £2 and £3, "often much more than the author of the piece himself" could make. "I have a letter in my pocket," complained Jerrold in 1832, "in which the manager said he would very willingly have given me 5*l.* for a copy of [my play], had he not before paid 2*l.* for it to a stranger."[91]

The Dramatic Copyright Act ("Bulwer-Lytton's Act"), which went into effect in 1833, remedied the situation to an extent. It granted dramatists "sole liberty" of permitting the representation of any unpublished play, and protected published plays for twenty-eight years after publication or for life (acting retrospectively on any play published seven years prior to the Act).[92] A Dramatic Authors Society was established to collect fees, identify violations, and sponsor publication. Play wrappers began to warn against piracy: "Subject to the | Provisions of the Dramatic Copyright Act," read one series; the publisher would prosecute "in accordance with the laws in force," read another.[93]

Throughout the course of the nineteenth century, both in England and on the Continent, managers and publishers continued to claim copyright, but the position of dramatists continued to be strengthened by legislative reform: in Spain, the *Organic Rules on Theatres and Authors' Rights* was passed in 1847, and plays began regularly to warn potential theatrical pirates that they would be prosecuted for violation of the law (Fig. 21).[94] Dramatists found that they could now sometimes successfully sue to protect performance rights. When, in 1861, Antonio García Gutiérrez sued the owners of the Teatro Real over their performance of Verdi's *El trovador* and *Simón Bocanegra*, which were based on García Gutiérrez's plays of the same name, he was awarded 8,000 *reales* in compensation.[95] When, in 1837, James

Articulos de los Reglamentos orgánicos de Teatros, sobre la propiedad de los autores ó de los editores que la han adquirido.

«El autor de una obra nueva en tres ó mas actos percibirá del Teatro Español, durante el tiempo que la ley de propiedad literaria señalada, el 10 por 100 de la entrada total de cada representacion, incluso el abono. Este derecho será de 3 por 100 si la obra tuviese uno ó dos actos.» *Art.* 10 *del Reglamento del Teatro Español de 7 de febrero de 1849.*

«Las traducciones en verso devengarán la mitad del tanto por ciento señalado respectivamente á las obras originales, y la cuarta parte las traducciones en prosa.» *Idem art 11.*

«Las refundiciones de las comedias del teatro antiguo, devengarán un tanto por ciento igual al señalado á las traducciones en prosa, ó á la mitad de este, segun el mérito de la refundicion.» *Idem art. 12.*

«En las tres primeras representaciones de una obra dramática nueva, percibirá el autor, traductor, ó refundidor, por derechos de estreno, el doble del tanto por ciento que á la misma corresponda.» *Idem art.* 13.

«El autor de una obra dramática tendrá derecho á percibir durante el tiempo que la ley de propiedad literaria señale, y sin perjuicio de lo que en ella se establece, un tanto por ciento de la entrada total de cada representacion, incluso el abono. El máximum de este tanto por ciento será el que pague el Teatro Español, y el minimum la mitad.» *Art.* 59 *del decreto orgánico de Teatros del Reino, de 7 de febrero de 1849.*

«Los autores dispondrán gratis de un palco ó seis asientos de primer órden en la noche del estreno de sus obras, y tendrán derecho á ocupar tambien gratis, uno de los indicados asientos en cada una de las representaciones de aquellas.» *Idem art.* 60.

«Los empresarios ó formadores de Compañias llevarán libros de cuenta y razon, foliado y rubricado por el Gefe Político, á fin de hacer constar en caso necesario los gastos y los ingresos.» *Idem art.* 78.

«Si la empresa careciese del permiso del autor ó dueño para poner en escena la obra, incurrirá en la pena que impone el art. 23 de la ley de propiedad literaria.» *Idem art.* 81.

«Las empresas no podrán cambiar ó alterar en los anuncios de teatro los títulos de las obras dramáticas, ni los nombres de los autores, ni hacer variaciones ó atajos en el testo sin permiso de aquellos; todo bajo la pena de perder, segun los casos, el ingreso total ó parcial de las representaciones de la obra, el cual será adjudicado al autor de la misma, y sin perjuicio de lo que se establece en el artículo antes citado de la ley de propiedad literaria.» *Idem art.* 82.

«Respecto á la publicacion de las obras dramáticas en los teatros, se observarán las reglas siguientes:

1.ª Ninguna composicion dramática podrá representarse en los teatros públicos sin el prévio consentimiento del autor.

2.ª Este derecho de los autores dramáticos durará toda su vida, y se transmitirá por veinte y cinco años mas, contados desde el dia del fallecimiento, á sus herederos legítimos, ó testamentarios, ó á sus derecho-habientes, entrando despues las obras en el dominio público respecto al derecho de representarlas.» *Ley sobre la propiedad literaria de 10 de junio de 1847, art.* 17.

«El empresario de un teatro que haga representar una composicion dramática ó musical, sin prévio consentimiento del autor ó del dueño, pagará á los interesados por via de indemnizacion una multa que no podrá bajar de 1000 reales ni exceder de 3000. Si hubiese ademas cambiado ó ocultar el fraude, se le impondrá doble multa.» *Idem art.* 23.

LA ESCALA DE LA FORTUNA.

COMEDIA EN TRES ACTOS

ORIGINAL Y EN VERSO

por

D. PEDRO CALVO ASENSIO.

MADRID:=1848.

Imprenta de D. L. Cordon; calle del Molino de Viento, número 35.

Robinson Planché sued John Braham, manager of the St James Theatre, for infringement of copyright when Braham used the libretto he had written for Carl Maria von Weber's opera *Oberon*, Braham was forced to pay Planché 40s. per performance.[96] But litigation was expensive and unpleasant ("one of the most disagreeable recollections of my professional life," wrote Planché later).[97] And the new laws had widespread enforcement problems and gaping loopholes, not least the absence of an American copyright law that would protect British published plays.[98]

As a result, copyright laws had only a marginal impact on the fees earned by the mass of writers producing for the nineteenth-century theatre industry. While the Comédie-Française had always paid on a royalty basis, and theatres began increasingly to experiment with per-performance or royalty payments, the largest class of theatre (those that had sprung up in the late eighteenth century and after) offered a straight fee-for-play-deal until the later nineteenth century.[99] The better-known dramatists could normally make substantial fees: Eugène Scribe, for instance, regularly earned between 2,000 and 4,000 francs per play (1,000–1,500 for plays at the Boulevard theatres); Edward Bulwer or James Sheridan Knowles could get £500 or £600 per play even in the depressed London theatre of the 1830s.[100] A few dramatists made fortunes in the theatre: Beaumarchais earned an astonishing 41,500 *livres* from the eight-month run of *Le Marriage de Figaro*;[101] Dion Boucicault made £10,000 out of the London and touring productions of *The Colleen Bawn*.[102] But prices paid to theatrical hacks were minimal: Mariano José de Larra's popular *Leaving on Time* brought him only 240 *reales*, less than half of what Lope de Vega had received for *La hermosa Alfreda* more than 200 years earlier;[103] Beffroy de Reigny's *Nicodème in the Moon* (1790), which had a run of nearly 200 performances to a full house, brought him 400 *livres* in instalment payments.[104] But this was still real money compared with what was paid in the most marginal theatres of Paris and London: in one Paris theatre, 18 *livres* per play (with a limit: playwrights were allowed to write no more than three plays per week); in another, 10 francs per act;[105] in London, two or three pounds for a pantomime, melodrama, or domestic drama in the 1840s; 30 shillings per burletta.[106]

Dramatists' earnings from publication were closely tied to their earnings from the theatre, sometimes inseparable. We have already seen dramatists selling publication rights along with performance rights to theatrical managers. More surprising but more common was the sale of performance rights to publishers. This may sometimes have been an inadvertent product of the uncertainties of performance copyright: the playwright Edward Fitzball was annoyed to find that, having sold his plays to the publisher John Cumberland at discount rates before 1833, Cumberland was found to have the right to the performance fees on the basis of the print copyrights.[107] In Spain until the promulgation of the *Organic Rules on Theatres and Authors' Rights* in 1847, the sale of a play could clearly constitute a grant of both printing and performance rights, as, for instance, in 1844 when José Zorrilla sold *Don Juan Tenorio* to the publisher, Manual Delgado, for 4,200 *reales*: "I hereby create in favor of Don Manuel Delgado an absolute proprietary right, for all time, in the original verse drama in seven acts called *Don Juan Tenorio*, for the amount of 4.200 *reales vellón* . . . in order that . . . he may freely print said drama or have it performed in any theatre."[108] Even where print copyright did not automatically confer performance copyright, publishers seem to have had the bargaining power to contract for performance copyright, or at least a portion thereof.[109] In Paris, theatrical publishers like Jean-Nicolas Barba or Michel Lévy were sufficiently powerful that even immensely successful dramatists like Eugène Scribe or Guilbert de Pixérécourt regularly negotiated contracts in which they turned over large portions of their performance rights.[110]

In any case, earnings from publication were, like earnings from performance, generally small (sometimes non-existent). Print piracy (still a significant problem even in the mid-nineteenth century),[111] the cheap publication of plays, and the large number of dramatists (along with the limited number of readers) meant that improvements in publication copyright had as limited an impact on the majority of theatrical writers as improvements in performance copyright did. Occasionally playwrights would sell only a portion of their publication rights, selling the rights for a certain period only (as Scribe did when he sold Barba publication rights to *The Prison of Edinburgh* for three years), or retaining the rights to reprints in a collection (perhaps in the hope that monetary recompense would come with eventual fame).[112] But they generally sold them outright to publishers.

In the later eighteenth and nineteenth centuries, print could sometimes still bring dramatists with serious reputations or big sellers a nice profit. Sheridan was paid £600 for the copyright of *The School for Scandal* when it was finally published in an authorized edition in 1799, twenty-two years after the première.[113] George Colman got £300 from John Murray for his *John Bull* immediately after its première in 1803.[114] Victor Hugo was dragged into a neighbouring tobacco shop in the middle of the fourth act of *Hernani* and offered 6,000 francs on the spot for publication rights in the play.[115] But payments for print copyrights generally declined in the nineteenth century.[116] While Fanny Kemble got £450 for her *Francis the First* in 1831 ("Only think of it," she exclaimed, "was there ever such publishing munificence!"), probably more common were fees like those that Tom Robertson earned from the sale of his plays: £3 per play, or a few pennies from the publisher T. H. Lacy for revamping West End adaptations from the French for the East End theatres.[117] Even after the huge success of *An Ideal Husband* and *The Importance of Being Earnest* late in the century, Smithers and Co. managed to acquire Wilde's publication copyrights for only £30.[118] "No publisher would offer five hundred, fifty or even five pounds for a play," complained William Archer, looking back at what he saw as the slow impoverishment of nineteenth-century dramatic literature.[119]

PROMPTBOOKS FOR READERS

But if changes in copyright law did not actually mean authorial control of performance or print, if dramatists tended to sell rights off quickly and for little or nothing, if piracy was alive and well, the very centrality of copyright as a concept nonetheless altered dramatists' relationship to their work, contributing to a conception of the playtext as the dramatist's text, not always controllable in production, but to be controlled, as much as possible, from the printed page. The spread of theatres and diffusion of dramatic texts certainly contributed to the loss of the dramatist's power to manage productions: Sheridan kept *The School for Scandal* from being published in part (at least according to a contemporary) to "prevent the play being produced at any theatre where the proper attention could not be paid to its 'getting up.'"[120] If, with the diffusion of dramatic texts and the spread of provincial and amateur performances, the playwright was unlikely to have read the play aloud to the actors and surveyed the production—unlikely to have explained to actors and directors the meaning and look of the scenes—if the dramatist's text had to compete with the "acting play" (with its evocation of the romance of the stage), all the more reason for the dramatist to imitate the promptbook: to attempt to shape the staging through elaborate scenic indications, ornate stage directions, detailed descriptions of setting, costume, and affect.[121]

There were, of course, many factors contributing to the theatre-rich dramatic texts of the nineteenth century: the desire, in competition with the novel, to give readers a thicker and more detailed scenic experience; the increasingly elaborate spectacles produced by the nineteenth-century theatre and the need for dramatists who knew how to work the theatrical machine; a heightened sense of the relation between picture and text, stimulated by the flood of illustrated books and the need for texts that could serve the pictorialism of the age. Certain genres particularly called forth the descriptive talents of the dramatist, melodrama, for instance, which typically offered the delineation of aural effects and their emotional corollaries: "Music to express discontent and alarm" prescribe the stage directions in Thomas Holcroft's *A Tale of Mystery: A Mélo-Drame* (1802), "Music, to express chattering contention," "Music to express pain and disorder," "Confused music," "Music plays alarmingly," "Music loud and discordant," "Music of doubt and terror."[122] Dramatizations of *Robinson Crusoe* give pages to describing the spectacle: the grottos and huge wooden stakes that protect Robinson from cannibals, his long beard and knee-length goatskin breeches and his parrot, which most contemporary illustrations of *Robinson Crusoe* showed (along with the "Faithful, affectionate Friday" and the various other picturesquely adoring savages whom the plays had brought onto the stage) (Fig. 22). Notes offered staging options: managers should, for instance, cast a dog, if an intelligent and docile one was to be found, to carry the dead sea-bird onto the stage.[123]

In shaping playtexts, dramatists were influenced not only by their experience of the live theatre but also by the numerous acting editions and "promptbooks" that came out from the middle of the eighteenth century onwards: variety collections like *The British Stage . . . the Best Modern English Acting Plays* (1752), whose title page captured the new trend, or Bell's plays carefully "Regulated from the Promptbooks"; plays adapted by famous actors (*King Henry VI . . . As adapted by Edmund Kean. Printed from the acting copy*). Such editions not only gave the texts in their edited-down stage versions (cutting speeches too difficult for actors), but also included cast lists (sometimes several), detailed acting and scenic indications, and costume lists ("MACHEATH. First dress: light mixture frock coat; stripe waistcoat; leather breeches.

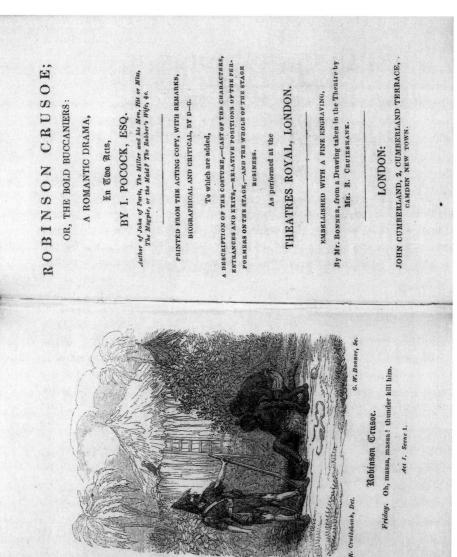

ROBINSON CRUSOE;

OR, THE BOLD BUCCANIERS:

A ROMANTIC DRAMA,

In Two Acts,

BY I. POCOCK, ESQ.

*Author of John of Paris, The Miller and his Men, Hit or Miss,
The Magpie, or the Maid? The Robber's Wife, &c.*

PRINTED FROM THE ACTING COPY, WITH REMARKS,
BIOGRAPHICAL AND CRITICAL, BY D—G.

To which are added,

A DESCRIPTION OF THE COSTUME,—CAST OF THE CHARACTERS,
ENTRANCES AND EXITS,—RELATIVE POSITIONS OF THE PER-
FORMERS ON THE STAGE,—AND THE WHOLE OF THE STAGE
BUSINESS.

As performed at the

THEATRES ROYAL, LONDON.

EMBELLISHED WITH A FINE ENGRAVING,

By Mr. BONNER, from a Drawing taken in the Theatre by
Mr. R. CRUIKSHANK.

LONDON:

JOHN CUMBERLAND, 2, CUMBERLAND TERRACE,
CAMDEN NEW TOWN.

R. Cruikshank, Del.   G. W. Bonner, Sc.

Robinson Crusoe.

Friday. Oh, massa, massa! thunder kill him.

Act I. Scene 1.

Fig. 22. Robinson Crusoe, with his parrot, the "Faithful, affectionate Friday," and the set and costumes prescribed in Isaac Pocock's *Robinson Crusoe; or The Bold Buccaniers* (1817).

Second dress: blue coat; white waistcoat. Third dress: suit of black").[124] William Oxberry's *New English Drama* (1818–25) gave playing time, doors for entrances and exits, occasional blocking: "The first act occupies the space of thirty-two minutes—the second, thirty-five . . ."; "By R. H . . . is meant . . . Right Hand . . . S. E . . . Second Entrance . . . D. F . . . Door in Flat . . ."; "CAPTAIN ABSOLUTE. A scarlet regimental full dress coat . . . LYDIA LANGUISH. White crape frock, festooned up at the bottom, with white silk cord and tassels . . ."; "*Disposition of the Characters when the Curtain falls*" (Fig. 23).[125]

When Shaw came to prepare his texts for publication late in the century, he was self-consciously jettisoning what he saw as the theatrical carpentry of the nineteenth-century promptbook tradition: "I had to make [it a] rule" not to mention stage, proscenium or spectators "to get away from the old 'Stabs her 2 R C; sees ghost up C (biz); and exit R.U.R.' which made plays unreadable and unsaleable."[126] But despite appearances to the contrary, the published "promptbooks" were in fact crafted for the reader, merely a different kind of reader, one hungry for both spectacle and the theatre in a state of undress: bell-and-whistle cues; backstage goings-on. Recognizing the draw of "real" theatrical detail, Kemble included not only cast lists, but scenic prescriptions, cues for music and sound effects, and bits of stage business.[127] While dramatist editions like Malone's 1790 Shakespeare, "Collated Verbatim with the Most Authentick Copies," distanced themselves from the acting versions in the hands of theatrical amateurs, most texts were composites of authorial and acting versions. The practice of using typography to differentiate the dramatist's original from the version acted, sporadic in seventeenth- and eighteenth-century texts, became standard: "All the verses marked with quotation marks in the margin were suppressed in performance because the madness of Elda seemed long to the actress who played the part," explains the text of Gertrudis Gómez de Avellaneda's mid-nineteenth-century tragedy, *Baltasar*.[128] Typical of plays from the period, Oxberry's New English Drama is published "with prefatory remarks, biographical sketches, and notes, critical and explanatory; being the only edition existing which is faithfully marked with the stage business, and stage directions, as performed at the Theatres Royal." If one read "the most esteemed English plays," one read them in Bell's, Kemble's, Inchbald's, Cumberland's, Oxberry's, Hinds's or Lacy's "standard" acting editions, which marked out the boundaries between the Bard and the boards, each displaced by the modernized version that would follow, with its new annotations for actors.[129]

The promptbook could be a different kind of "true and genuine version," rival of the accurate authorial edition. Rochon de Chabannes's *The Jealous One* (1788), for instance, is "the only edition exactly conforming to the representation."[130] The stage arrangements throughout Kemble's promptbooks, writes James Boaden admiringly in his *Memoirs of the Life of John Philip Kemble* (1825), "Were all distinctly marked by him in his own clear exact penmanship, and when he had done his work, his theatre received, in that perfected copy, a principle of exactness, which was of itself sufficient to keep its stage unrivalled for truth of scenic exhibition."[131] Attempting to make their own "perfect copies" of the theatrical experience, captured live from the

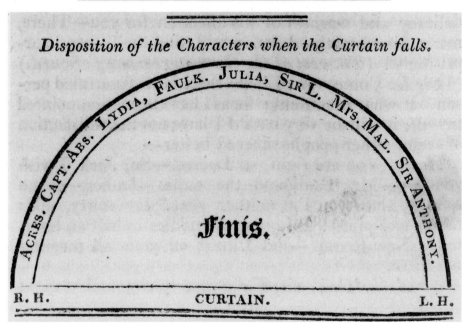

PERSONS REPRESENTED.

————◆————

As originally acted at Covent Garden.

Sir Anthony Absolute	Mr. Shuter.
Captain Absolute	Mr. Woodward.
Sir Lucius O'Trigger	{ Mr. Lee. { Mr. Clinch.
Faulkland	Mr. Lewis.
Acres	Mr. Quick.
Fag	Mr. Lee Lewis.
David	Mr. Dunstall.
Coachman	Mr. Fearon.
Mrs. Malaprop	Mrs. Green.
Lydia Languish	Miss Barsanti.
Julia	Mrs. Bulkley.
Lucy	Mrs. Lessingham.

Disposition of the Characters when the Curtain falls.

ACRES. CAPT. ABS. LYDIA, FAULK. JULIA, SIR L. MRS. MAL. SIR ANTHONY.

Finis.

R. H.   CURTAIN.   L. H.

FIG. 23. Cast list and blocking for Sheridan's *The Rivals* in William Oxberry's *New English Drama* (1818).

theatre itself, theatrical amateurs would bind interleaves in acting editions, or paste pages on larger sheets to allow for annotation on the left-hand page, burrowing in Kemble's library with their "Kemble copies" to be sure to get any "genuine annotations" left out in printed editions.[132] Theatre-lovers commonly pasted pictures of their favourite actors into actor biographies, or interleaved them between the pages of plays in which the actors had appeared in their greatest roles. Sometimes they drew them themselves, copying them from popular prints.[133] Nineteenth-century extra-illustrated editions and theatrical scrapbooks (printed shells to be filled with souvenirs, newspaper clippings, playbills, engravings, and personal memorabilia) abound: *A Collection of Engraved Portraits & Drawings in Illustration of EDMUND KEAN his Life and Theatrical Career 1787–1833* reads the printed title page of the enormous extra-illustrated volume in which the collector's Kean memorabilia are pasted.

ILLUSTRATING THE SCENE

Publishers made efforts to serve the audience of image-hungry theatre lovers: the publishing firm of Fielding and Walker specifically commissioned drawings of actors reciting prologues and epilogues and had them engraved and published as separate prints.[134] Engravers and lithographers created special albums: *The Hundred and One Robert Macaires* reads the title of a French album of lithographs by Daumier documenting the roles of the character played by Frédérick Lemaître.[135] Collections of stage designs were published, both to record the work of famous designers and to offer models for later productions. Periodicals like the *Illustrated London News* regularly showed scenes from plays currently in performance, and these were reproduced in engravings, in etchings, in coloured lithographs. Images, it was felt, could no longer be loosely correlated to text but must directly illustrate the scenic moment, picture linked tightly to stage directions and dialogue. Theatre-goers grew accustomed to correlating pictures to texts, and then relating pictures back to actual performances: "I have found the scene described above among the small pictures that are made of actors here," writes Lichtenberg to a friend, describing a production of *The Beaux Stratagem* he saw in 1775, "only Garrick has not got a red feather, and Weston is wearing a different wig and coat."[136] Engravings or lithographs began to be commonly captioned with dialogue, carefully designating the theatrical moment they were attempting to illustrate: "Defer no more what honour orders you to do; | He demands my head, and I abandon it to you," read the lines under an illustration for *Le Cid* in the 1844 Paris octavo of Corneille's works, showing Rodrigue on his knees offering Chimène his sword, while Chimène clasps her hands before its symbolic target (Fig. 24).[137]

To enrich both staging and images of the stage, designers drew on history, anthropology, and archaeology: the Egypt of Mozart's Magic Flute or the Mexico of Fernando Cortes (in Karl Friedrich Schinkel's stage designs), seen through the eyes of recent excavations (Fig. 25). Theatres had begun advertising performances in the "habit of the times"[138]—with costumes like that which Marie Favart had imported

Fig. 24. "Defer no more what honour orders you to do; | He demands my head, and I abandon it to you." Act III, scene IV of Corneille's *Le Cid* in an 1844 edition.

from Constantinople for her husband's *Soliman II, or the Three Sultans* (1761).[139] Managers turned for inspiration to works like Thomas Jefferey's *The Habits of Other Nations* (1757–72) or Jean Charles Levacher de Charnois's *Investigations into the Costumes and Theatres of All Nations* (1790), whose frontispiece allegorizes the book's role in unveiling the mysteries of the past for the theatre (in the representation of Minerva, protectress of the Arts, shielding Clio as she "lifts the thick veil which covered [father] time").[140] For a production of Alexander Dow's *Sethona* in 1774, Philippe de Loutherbourg studied Bernard de Montfaucon's *Antiquity Explained* in order to create genuinely Egyptian scenes and costumes "much superior to those of

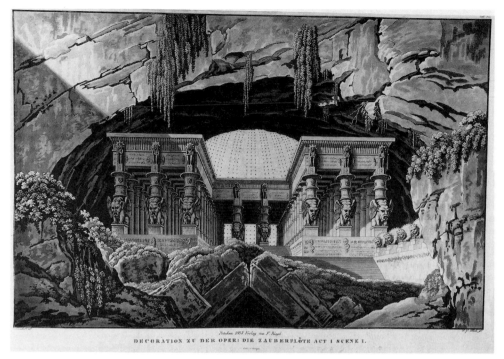

DECORATION ZU DER OPER: DIE ZAUBERFLÖTE ACT 1 SCENE 1.

Fig. 25. Karl Friedrich Schinkel's set for Act 1 Scene 1 of Mozart's *Magic Flute* in an 1849 collection of his stage designs.

any modern Tragedy," as one reviewer exclaimed.[141] Charles Kemble's 1823 production of Shakespeare's *King John*, William Macready's in 1842, and Charles Kean's in 1846 were all modelled on the illustrations in Planché's heavily researched treatise on *Dramatic Costume* (1823), with notes and hand-tinted lithographs.

The work of scholars gave the stage an image of a reciprocal historical task: the stage must bring history to life; recorders and illustrators must capture the theatre's own fleeting history. If medieval history was central to productions like the various *King John*s, the theatre historians' task was critical to preserving the theatrical past and, from that past, creating the theatrical future. The drama of Britain (wrote the dramatic editor John Dicks with alarm) "is sinking fast into oblivion, and if not speedily gathered by friendly hands, must perish irrevocably."[142] Scholars busied themselves digging medieval plays out of the archives and seeing them into print.[143] The exploration of early performance history meant investigating its survival in the countryside: the Oberammergau Passion Play was "discovered," still being performed in the highlands of Bavaria, and at least a dozen illustrated editions of it in various languages followed. In 1874, the text of the Oxfordshire Saint George play was printed, having been "taken down . . . from the lips" of the last of the performers, "now long scattered, and all dead but one," who had handed down the tradition "from time immemorial."[144]

What was spoken was to be written down. What was seen was to be captured in images: all those spectacles whose origin was to be found in the "drama of savage peoples," the "dances of ancient Israel," "the Mahabharata," "African divertissements," those of ancient Mexico, Nepal, the Yucatan (in the list given by Édélestand du Méril in his *History of the Drama* (1864)), passed on in the "popular festivals and gross masquerades of the middle ages," the "bizarres pantomimes of the Peaux-Rouges and the seasonal parades of the South Sea islanders," the "ceremonial madness of the Hindoustan" and the "dramatic orgies of old Europe"—all of them part of a "natural development" in the evolution of the "human spirit."[145] The products of "folk culture"—mummers festivals, morris dances, Punch and Judy shows, farces and moralities—were models of oral culture in the performed present, the essence of theatre itself. And so, as bearers of the unrecorded past, they were precisely to be recorded, inscribed in print so that the purely theatrical—those modes of expression most free of the text—might be textualized, not to be lost altogether in the ruins of time.

THEATRE IMPRIMATUR

4. *Reinventing "Theatre" via the Printing Press*

In writing about dramatic performances and the uses of dramatic texts, early sixteenth-century commentators felt they had to explain themselves at length. In the preface to his morality, *The Condemnation of Feasting* (written 1503–5), Nicolas de la Chesnaye accumulates as many terms as he can to describe his "opuscule," as he calls it, in the hopes that readers will understand what they are supposed to do with it. This is one of those "representations" or "works that we call plays or moralities," he explains. And so one may either "play" it or "represent [it] publicly to the simple people" or "demonstrate [it] to all visibly by actors, gestures, and words on a scaffold or otherwise," or, alternatively, those who prefer to "read it or hear it read," for "study, pastime," or to inculcate "virtuous doctrines," may do so "privately or in solitude."[1] La Chesnaye is not indulging a mere pleasure in copia. He is struggling for the right words. He doesn't quite know what to call this piece or how to explain all the ways it can be experienced. "Play" or "Morality" doesn't seem to do the trick.

At the end of the fifteenth century, few people would have seen a dramatic text. Plays were sometimes circulated for reading and some would have seen a copy of a mystery play meant to be "played by characters," or a part book taken from one.[2] More would have been read to from the many books of dialogues and moral (and not-so-moral) tales to be obtained from booksellers and friends. Some had scholarly editions of ancient authors like Terence. But very few—faced with La Chesnaye's *Condemnation* or one of Terence's plays—would have thought of it primarily as something to be staged with actors in scenic space. There were, of course, plenty of entertainments that one could see in the fifteenth century: the "plays" or "*Spiele*" or "*jeux*," the mummings, and disguisings, the magisterial processions, the newly professional interludes.[3] There were schoolroom readings of classical plays, and isolated productions. But there were no real conventions for reading dramatic texts as theatrical scripts, nothing that would immediately identify a given text as necessarily a performance text. With no regular institutional support for theatre, someone like La Chesnaye could not expect his readers to think of his text as a script for actors.

PERFORMANCE AND THE VERBAL ARTS: BEFORE "THEATRE"

For most early sixteenth-century writers (and many still later) vernacular texts were meant to be read aloud.[4] Since any given narrative might find a variety of venues, presentational circumstances did not determine genre. Both the *lauda lirica* and the *lauda drammatica*, for instance, were to be performed and might be indistinguishable.[5] Vernacular romances were first written down in scripts for jongleurs.

Chronicles were often written for multiple speakers. The dialogues that punctuated third-person narrative in romances were simply vivid ways of presenting material: they could be read silently but were most likely to be read aloud by a reciter, who might well recite from memory, enacting the actions with gestures and dramatic facial and vocal changes. Manuals for various kinds of oration—courtly or legal—often took dramatic form, mingling instruction and entertainment. Lawyers' Year Books and handbooks, or confessors' manuals, written in dialogue form, provided lively models for oral exchange.[6]

Even long after dialogue genres were printed in substantial numbers, there might be little formally to differentiate reading texts from performance texts. Verse *memento mori* like *The Danse Macabre of Women* (Fig. 26), or religious discourses like Hans Sachs's *A Conversation about the False Works and Incantations of the Friars* (1524) were often in dialogue ("to sing and to read").[7] Two-person combat performances like the French *rencontre* or *débat*, the Italian contrasto, or the German *Kampfgespräch* were printed for reading or speaking aloud. Collections of "pleasant devices" were to be "recited," as the title of a 1580 French compendium explains.[8] Monologues, too, might be considered dramatic. The German translation of Erasmus's *Praise of Folly* was "played" (*gespilt*) and "to be read": as the first page explains, "Folly herself speaks to herself through the whole book."[9] Gil Vicente's monologue *Auto of the Visitation* (1502) (which features a cowherd admiring the queen's new baby) or texts for religious occasions like Gómez Manrique's *Representation of the Birth of Our Lord* (*c.*1467–1481) (which was recited at a convent where Manrique's sister was a nun) might or might not include nativity props as part of the representation.[10] Playing and oratory, dialogue and narration, representing and reporting had blurred boundaries. Medieval and Renaissance audiences generally assumed the centrality of performance to verbal arts. Rhetoric was essentially dramatic, as the intertwined institutional histories of rhetoric and drama and their pairing in the iconography of the period remind us.[11] The emphasis on *hearing* as well as reading in the title pages for popular performance genres (Pamphilus Gengenbach's *The Ten Ages of this World* (*c.*1516) is "lovely to read and to hear")[12] reminds us that dialogues, moralities, or cautionary tales were as likely to be read aloud as staged. Even someone as self-conscious about possible receptive conditions as La Chesnaye thinks of reading (the alternative to representation by actors on scaffolds) primarily as reading aloud.[13]

Writers before the late fifteenth century had numerous conventions for classifying literary works, but those classifications rarely invoked specific conditions of reception. In a title, a poet might refer to a work as sacred or secular, a poem or a history, in prose or in a particular verse form, in Latin or in a particular vernacular, but not as a play for performance. For Boccaccio (writing around 1365), Terence, Plautus, Virgil, and Homer belong to the same literary class, since they all wrote fictions that were much like history.[14] For his French translator, Laurent de Premierfait, Boccaccio himself is like Terence, for both wrote "invented fables . . . in comic verse" for the "listener or reader."[15] While generic differentials were important, genres cut across representational lines. When medieval writers talked about tragedy or comedy or

Mors est hic hominis semper cum tempore labi: Et semper quadam condicione mori. Est hominis nudum nasci: nudumque reuerti. Est hominis putrere solo simul quod fateri: Et miseris gradibus in cinerem redigi. Res et opes prestantur ei: famulantur ad horam. Est locuples mane: Vespere pauper erit.

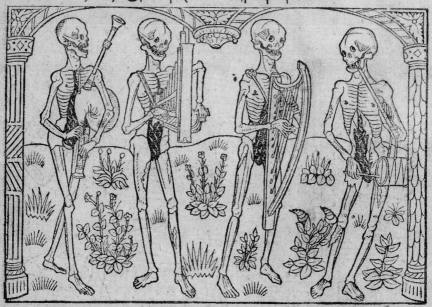

Omnia cesar erat: et gloria cesaris esse desinit. et tumulus vix erat octo pedum

Le premier mort

Vous par diuine sentence
Qui viues en estatz diuers
Tous danseres en ceste danse
Vnefoys. et bons: et peruers
Et si seront menges de vers
Voz corps: helas regardes nous
Mors. pourris, puas, descouuers
Comme sommes: telz seres vous

Le second mort

Dictes nous par quelles raisons
Vous ne penses point a mourir
Quant la mort va en voz maisons
Huy lung: demain lautre querir
Sans quon vous puisse secourir
Cest mal vescu de ny penser
Et trop grant dangier de perir
Force est quil faille ainsi danser.

Le tiers mort

Entendez ce que ie vous dis.
Jeunes et vieulx petis et grans
De iour en iour selon les dis
Des saiges vous alez mourans
Car voz iours vont diminuans
Pour quoy tous seres trespasses
Ceulx qui viuez: deuant cent ans.
Las: cent ans seront tost passes

Le quart mort

Deuant quil soient cent ans passes
Tous les viuans comme tu dis
De ce monde serout passes
En enfer: ou en paradis
Mon compaignon. mais ie te dis
Peu de gens sont qui aient cure
Des trespasses: ne de noz dis.
Le fait deulx: gist en aduenture

FIG. 26. *The Dance Macabre of Women* (1491): *memento mori* as dance and dramatic dialogue.

drama, they almost always described them as species of narrative form with affective and ethical applications, not genres for performance with actors.[16] The Carolingian *Scholia Vindobonensia*, a commentary on Horace's *Ars poetica*, assumes drama to be a form of literary recitation, with a chorus that is simply a group of onlookers. Those few medievals who did not know Donatus on Terence, or Horace or Isidore on theatre, those fewer still who knew Aristotle's *Poetics*, had a very broad notion of theatrical performance.[17] Hermannus Alemannus's thirteenth-century translation of Averroës's commentary on Aristotle's *Poetics*, essentially the only contact Europeans had with the *Poetics* before the fifteenth century, understands tragedy in distinctly non-theatrical terms:[18] tragedy is a "song of praise" which is "based on image-making" and performed by "reciters and enunciators." The tragic poet "does not need to enhance his reputation through extrinsic aids like dramatic gestures and facial expressions. Only those who parade as poets (although they are really not poets) use these devices."[19]

Those writers who referred to theatrical performances with actors felt they had to be very precise about what they meant, often referring to "theatre" in the past tense, as Honorius of Autun or Hugh of St Victor do.[20] John of Salisbury's fourteenth-century French translator Denis Foulechat (elaborating on the *Policraticus*) explains that formerly there were "jugglers and minstrels [who] by facial expressions and movements of their bodies and by the art of words and songs sung with melody in beautiful voices, recounted and recited both histories of actual events and fictional stories, which you can find in Plautus and Menander . . . and Terence."[21] When William of St Thierry writes that the Song of Songs is "written in the mode of a drama and in theatrical style," he feels obliged to specify that this means it is written "as if to be recited by characters and with action."[22] Albertino Mussato similarly feels he must explain that the *fictiones scenicae* is a form in which poetry is not only sung but represented with gestures of the body, a form of spectacle to be avoided (quoting Augustine: "representation is vice if one feigns in words or actions what he says, and at the same time represents it with his limbs").[23] Writing in 1382, John Wycliffe has to gloss "theatre," explaining that a "*teatre*" is a "comune biholdyng place."[24] In Chaucer's translation of Boethius, he tags the term as foreign: the Muses of poetry are "comune strompetes of swich a place that men clepen the theatre."[25] A century later in 1482, Pierre Farget is still using the past tense to refer to the "art that once was called theatrics because of a place in Rome that was called 'theatre' where the people went to play [games] and the others to watch the games."[26]

When medievals referred to a "theatrum," the word covered a broad semantic field. *Theatrica* is one of the seven "mechanical sciences" for Hugh of St Victor and commentators after him, classed with fabric making, weaponry, commerce, agriculture, hunting, and medicine (far from poetry), and including everything from "epics . . . presented . . . by recitals or by acting out dramatic roles or using masks or puppets" to choral processions and dances to spectator sports.[27] While "theatres" might be buildings or performance spaces even in the fourteenth century, they were as often other kinds of spaces for visual representation. "*Comoedia*," "*tragoedia*," and their vernacular cognates similarly covered a broad semantic field for medieval writers.

Dante's divine poem is a "*commedia*" because it has a happy ending. For Chaucer's Monk,

> Tragedie is to seyn a certeyn storie . . .
> Of him that stood in greet prosperitee,
> And is y-fallen out of heigh degree.[28]

Well into the sixteenth century, even those who were generally familiar with Terence and Plautus and with classical stage imitation thought of "comedy" and "tragedy" as terms that could include, for instance, epic and lyric poetry, prose romance, history, and public oration—terms that denoted subject-matter and affect, not representational condition. Comic and tragic poetry was not necessarily linked to theatrics: the primary identity of the classical generic frameworks remained ethical and narrative. Seneca and Terence in the classroom before the sixteenth century were aids for the memorization of Latin sentences, rhetorical and oratorical models, but not theatrical scripts.[29]

TOWARDS "THEATRE"

Like teachers and writers, medieval illustrators do not seem to have thought of the ancient drama as performed by actors, and certainly not as performed on stages with masks or other theatrical paraphernalia. Most late-medieval illustrations of dramatic texts show a single narrator reciting or figures in decorative borders or landscapes, sometimes playing flutes and using the gestures so reviled by treatises on oratory, but without stage trappings or narrative correlation with the scene.[30] The German edition of Terence's *Eunuchus* printed in Ulm in 1486 shows a typical urban scene, the figures labelled and ranged in relation to a perspective of a street, but without any indication that the artist had a performance in mind. But some of the new editions emerging at the end of the fifteenth century were beginning to show actors on what were clearly stages with curtained doors and (sometimes) scaffolding or architectural surroundings. Johann Trechsel's 1493 Lyon edition of Terence, for instance, shows lively figures in hundreds of distinctly theatrical scenes (Fig. 27).[31] Calliopus, who recites most of the prologues and epilogues, appears to be played by a different actor in each of the plays.

These changes point to the central role that printed matter played in shaping the sixteenth-century theatre. In disseminating ancient drama, in producing texts about the Greek and Roman theatre, in identifying comedy and tragedy with gesturing actors, in publicizing the classical rubrics around which theatrical institutions formed themselves, in circulating images of buildings called "theatres," in printing and circulating vernacular playtexts that could be performed in them, in identifying the textual drama as the paradigmatic performance art, print gave the theatre an image of itself. What was printed over the course of the late fifteenth and sixteenth centuries had a profound impact on the way people thought about live performances in scenic spaces: the resurrection of Vitruvius and his popularization through treatises on stage architecture and mechanics; the printing and reprinting of the ancient

FIG. 27. Actors on stage in Terence's *Andria* in Johann Trechsel's 1493 Lyon edition of
Terence's *Comedies*.

dramatists in Greek, Latin, and the vernacular; the abundant editions of humanist comedies and tragedies, mysteries, saints' plays, biblical plays, farces, moralities, interludes; the illustrations of the stage.

Central to the theatre's self-conception were the discussions of the ancient "theatres" shown in books like the Terence editions. Drawing on Vitruvius, Alberti had explicitly identified "theatres" as places for the performance of dramatic texts: "Buildings in which poetry, comedy, tragedy, and so on take place we call theaters, to distinguish them from the others; [circuses] in which noble youths exercise with chariots [or amphitheaters] in which the hunting of caged beasts takes place."[32] Vernacular discussions of the ancient theatres, drawing on Aristotle, Horace, Donatus, and one another, did a good deal to identify comedy and tragedy with actors, sets, and costumes—with performances in scenic space. Charles Estienne's preface to his 1542 translation of Terence's *Andria* is typical in its subsections: "In what places were Tragedies and Comedies first played"; "The ornaments and costumes of scenic players"; "Description of the Theatre."[33] In his *De Poetica* (1579), Giovanni Antonio Viperano gives a detailed description of ancient theatrical conditions, following Horace: of the "Apparatus of the stage," the "makeup of the actors," the "masks, robes, buskins, and other paraphernalia," and the fitting out of the stage "with the erection of walls, towers, and praetorian palaces."[34]

"Tragedy" and "comedy," then, were to be performed in "theatres," not merely to be recited or read. Trissino, for instance, says that not only must each be spoken aloud, but "its gestures seen, and its discourses and melody heard."[35] Viperano explains that the "apparatus" (along with music) is "essential to tragedy, just as memory and delivery are to the orator, since without [it] a tragedy cannot be performed."[36] For Francesco Robortello, writing in the 1540s, tragedy is a scenic art, its audience those "present at performances," the "auditors and spectators of tragedies" who "hear and see people saying and doing things."[37] In fact, if tragedy was an imitation of an action (in Aristotle's famous definition), it was the *actor's* imitation through acting (not only the poet's imitation through words): "Representation . . . is not only poetic but also histrionic"; "imitation" in tragedy refers to "the actor as he acts," who imitates the action.[38] In response to the question, what is dramatic, or "scenic," poetry (as distinguished from epic or lyric), Antonio Minturno explains (in his *Arte poetica* (1563)) that it is "Imitations of things that are represented in the Theatre," and that the stage "apparatus" is necessary to it.[39] Julius Caesar Scaliger (in his 1561 poetics) asserts that the "one and only essential" of tragedy is "acting."[40] According to Lodovico Castelvetro, tragedy requires "a theatre, a stage, costumes, masks, and actors as well as bodily movements and gestures and the use of the voice, not to mention music, singing, and dancing," in short, "a larg[e] financial outlay."[41]

By the mid-sixteenth century the word "theatre" was regularly being used to refer to the spaces in which textual entertainments were given, as in the illustration labelled "The theatre where the Passion of Valenciennes was performed in 1547."[42] The 1541 proclamation against the playing of the *Mystery of the Old Testament* referred to this (like other mysteries) as a "play" ("*jeu*") containing "lascivious farces and mummeries," which is performed in a "theatre," though the ignorant "players" of such spectacles have never been properly trained in "theatres and public places."[43] In England in 1578, John Stockwood might still remark on the unusual use of the word "theatre" for the new playhouse: "I now not how I might . . . more discommende the gorgeous Playing place erected in the fieldes, than to terme it, as they please to have it called, a Theatre, that is even after the maner of the olde heathnish Theatre at Rome, a shew place of al beastly & filthie matters."[44] A few decades later, however, Shakespeare could in *Richard II* assume his audience's familiarity with theatre as institution, using it as a simile for the political scene: "As in a theatre the eyes of men, | After a well-graced actor leaves the stage, | Are idly bent on him that enters next."[45] Although the Germanic languages tended to preserve Germanic forms, the 1561 collection of Hans Sachs's works speaks of "*spilhewsern*" and the "*thäter*" in the same sentence.[46] In the 1573 German-language version of Abraham Ortelius's famous map, the "*Theatrum*" is explicitly the "*Schawplatz*," the place for seeing, metaphorically, the comedies and tragedies that play themselves out on the globe of the world.[47] "Theatre" was becoming, primarily, "a place in which . . . *comedies and tragedies are acted*."[48]

"Theatre" was of course not the only word, or even perhaps the most common, used to refer to theatrical spaces and events: the "stage," the "playhouse," the "scene," or the "commedia" (and their variants) were equally common. But these became associated with the buildings called "theatres." The use of the word "theatre" to denote performance spaces spread metonymically to include the productions in those buildings and the plays that contributed to them, as in Jacques Grévin's 1561 collection of plays: his *Théatre*. When Jean Vauquelin de la Fresnaye writes that "The Theatre" (building and collection of plays) "must never be filled with an argument longer than one whole day," he exploits the semantic overlay.[49] Actual buildings became the referent for the pervasive Renaissance trope of the "theatre of the world." "Theatres" might be amphitheatres for the production of water or animal shows like the 1616 horse ballet described by Jacques Callot as a "Theatre created in Florence during the Equestrian Festival."[50] They might be scenic views or books (Jean Bodin's famous *Universae naturae theatrum* (1596)). They might be memory palaces (mystic encyclopaedic "theatres of memory"). But the word "theatre" used to indicate anything other than the dramas and spaces for actors playing in scenes was understood to be metaphor.

Just as court performance spaces and professional commercial spaces could be called "theatres" and identified with each other even where they housed quite different kinds of performances (masques by the Queen's entourage in one theatre, tragedies by Jonson in another, puppet shows in another), so various performance forms—comedies and tragedies, plays, farces, interludes—could be identified with each other, linked through the institutions developing around the new theatres. That the various kinds of dramas—ancient and modern, secular and sacred, Christian and pagan—were printed beside one another (with similar typographic conventions) suggested that they belonged to the same family. Hans Sachs could print his "*schimpf Spil*" ("insult plays"), "*Faßnacht spil*" (Shrovetide plays) and "sacred" and "worldly Histories" alongside his "*Tragedi*" and "*Comedi*," his "*schawspiel*" along with his Roman plays in a single volume of his works.[51] If "comedy" and "tragedy" were habitually used, in the middle of the sixteenth century, in *opposition* to "farce," "morality," and other popular genres, that very opposition—the very attempt to replace the archaic with the modern classical—tended to link them as part of the same enterprise. In his 1555 *Poetics*, Jacques Peletier du Mans explicitly recognizes the assimilation of old genres into new ones when he expresses the hope that "the Farces that they have played for us for so long will convert themselves into the genre of Comedy, the Martyr Plays into the form of Tragedy."[52] Titles confirmed the identification, not the opposition: John Bale's 1538 *A brefe Comedy or enterlude* (printed

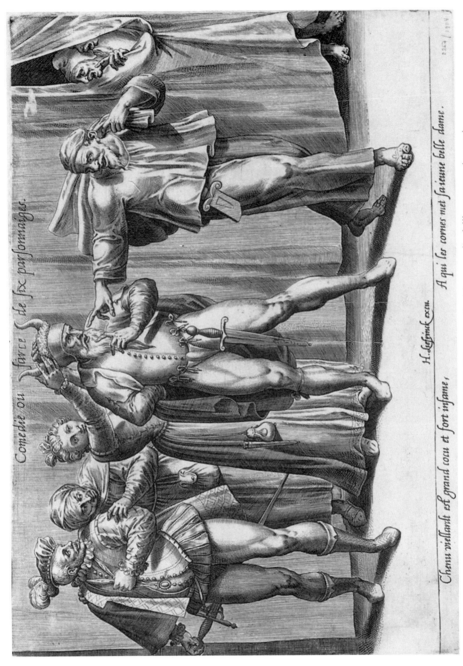

Comedie ou farce de six personnaiges.

Chenu vieillart est grand cocu et fort infame, A qui les cornes met sa ieune belle dame.

H. hondius excu.

FIG. 28. "Comedy or Farce with Six Characters" with *commedia dell'arte* actors (c. 1577).

c.1547); his 1538 *Tragedye or enterlude* (printed *c*.1547); Lucas Fernández's several plays titled *Farce or quasi-comedy* (*c*.1514); the *commedia dell'arte* "Comedy or Farce with Six Characters" of the late 1580s (Fig. 28).[53]

The distinction between farce and comedy, martyr play and tragedy, the ancient and the modern, erudite and popular, pagan and Christian, was, of course, artificial, one on which writers could draw if they wished, but which hardly separated one dramatic genre from another. Writers of morals or *sotties* or farces or *lustspiele* or saints' plays or plays like *Ralph Roister Doister* (printed in 1566) or *Jacke Jugeler* (printed in 1562/3) were inevitably influenced not only by what they had read in school but by the classical material that had become common currency, even when they did not consciously invoke classical forms. Imitators of the ancients just as inevitably drew on native material to make those forms palatable, for instance transforming the satyr play into pastoral via the shepherd's play, or placing very Italian *intermezzi* or Spanish-influenced *moresci* between the acts of a Euripides reconstruction (necessary, thought Isabella d'Este, as relief from the "long and boring" speeches of plays too classically inclined).[54] But the proliferation of mixed genres drawing on ancient dramatic terminology suggests the extent to which playwrights and critics felt a need to fit native forms into Greek and Roman frames: *tragicomedia pastorale*, as Guarini called his *Il pastor fido* (*The Faithful Shepherd*); "pastoral-comical, historical-pastoral, tragical-historical, tragical-comical-historical-pastoral," in Polonius's laborious description of the players' repertoire.[55]

The assimilation of vernacular genres into ancient ones and of regional forms into pan-European ones meant a consolidation of dramatic genres, at the centre of which were "comedy" and "tragedy." Classicizing was one means of making genres more acceptable to a broad European audience, but regional genres generally were translated across the Continent, assimilated with each other under rubrics circulated in print: the Spanish *entremés* and the French *entremets*; the English *mask* and the French *masque* or *mascarade*. This does not, of course, mean that specifically regional or national forms disappeared, but there was a trend to homogenize across Europe: the specifically Neapolitan Pulcinella could become Polichinelle and eventually Punch, losing his dialect as dialect printing disappeared, his local jokes flattening themselves for export. Comedy and tragedy as genres did not, of course, succeed in suppressing the multitude of early modern performance genres. If anything, printing meant the proliferation of marginal and indeterminate performance genres alongside those called "comedies" and "tragedies," of dialogue forms whose conditions of performance were left open to their interpreters. Dramatic genre remained fluid and metamorphic. But by the end of the sixteenth century, there were normative expectations for the drama, generally aligned with norms for comedy and tragedy. If the multitude of spectacular forms continued undiminished in vitality, the idea of "theatre" had a kind of intellectual dominion, subordinating entertainments to an overarching prototype, measuring them against the classical exemplar.

THE PLACE OF THE TEXT

By the middle of the sixteenth century, just as stage directions no longer had to spell out the fact that a speaker was about to speak a line, playbooks no longer had to explain what they were to be used for. Even if Hans Sachs (or his editor) still feels he must indicate his book's place in the array of possible performance texts, he can rely on greater familiarity with dramatic conventions than La Chesnaye could. "These plays are not only useful and amusing to read," the title page to the 1561 volume of his works points out, "but also easy to perform by using this book, because it so neatly shows . . . the gestures, words, and actions, entrances and exits, and there are more comprehensible directions in all the plays than have ever been printed."[56] By the time the 1542 edition of the *Very Excellent and Holy Mystery of the Old Testament, for Characters* was published, readers were used to printed works "arranged for characters" ("*ordonné par personnages*").[57] By the end of the century, most people had a fairly definite idea of what was required for proper dramatic performances, not just "a theatre, a stage, costumes, masks, and actors," but also full-length plays based on dramatic texts. Fynes Moryson complains about the English troupes travelling in Germany and the Netherlands in the 1590s, "having nether a Complete number of Actours, nor any good Apparell, nor any ornament of the Stage . . . and pronowncing peeces and Patches of English playes, which my selfe and some English men there present could not heare without great wearysomenes."[58] If, a century later, Saint-Evremond could pronounce the textless productions of the Italian *commedia dell'arte* troupes to be "not truly Drama" but "nothing but a kind of ill-formed concert among various Actors,"[59] he was reflecting assumptions about the necessary union of text and performance that had been formed over the course of the preceding century.

That theatre built on the classical paradigm required performers to speak more than "peeces and patches" of plays was not only a structural imperative but also a requirement that actors follow texts, that they "play it" (in Jonson's words) "according to the printed booke."[60] As John Earle would write, the "Page" was to be "a patterne for" the "Scene and Stage."[61] While "playing by the book" was not a new concept, medieval and early Renaissance verbal performance commonly stressed *extempore* variation on familiar topoi or the approximation of set speeches in improvised verse, with oral composition subsequently textualized but often recomposed from performance to performance. Many medieval texts reflect the assumption that not all material needs to be textualized, sometimes, for instance, merely pointing to cultural set pieces or offering descriptions of speech or frameworks for the improvisational arts of the performers: "Then let the lover approach, and let Mary greet him; and when they have talked a little, let Mary sing to the young women," directs the Benediktbeuern Passion Play, without specifying what Mary and the lover are to say.[62] Certainly improvisation continued to have a central place in Renaissance culture (theatrical and otherwise). Extempore oratory and poetic composition was taught in schools (its lessons masterfully displayed, for instance, by the young "Phaedra" who extemporized Latin verses when the stage machinery broke down during a performance in Rome in the 1480s).[63] In providing only plot skeletons, the *commedia dell'arte* scenarios self-consciously nurtured, on a professional level, the improvisational art that Italian amateurs continued to cultivate in the academies throughout the early modern period. Certainly, too, there was a good deal of the kind of "play[ing] besyde the booke" to which "John a Kent" refers in Anthony Munday's

John a Kent and John a Cumber (*c*.1590).[64] Thomas Lupton's *All for Money* (1578) comfortably instructs the Vice, Sin, to "turne the proclamation" being read out "to some contrarie sence at everie time All For Money hath read it."[65] But the rarity, in Renaissance dramatic texts, of indications like that in the Benediktbeuern Passion Play suggests the change in assumptions about the kinds of precision the text was to provide. The normative playtext spelled out all the words to be spoken: speeches were to be fully scripted. Even the *commedia dell'arte* actors normally performed fully scripted plays at court and in the academies, specializing in the art of improvisation only in self-conscious competition with the *commedia erudita*.[66] Improvisation, the "liberty" (in Polonius's phrasing), was an exotic alternative to the "law of writ."[67]

Exact memorization of the words in the text, then, took on a new importance. One was playing properly "without book" only when one was, in fact, "playing by the book." Actors were expected to remember the lines of the text and not be in need of a prompter. As Benvolio in *Romeo and Juliet* (*c*.1595) suggests, reflecting on the amateurishness of the old-fashioned theatre:

> We'll have no Cupid hoodwinked with a scarf,
>
> .   .   .   .
>
> Nor no without-book Prologue faintly spoke
> After the prompter for our entrance.[68]

Even the (to Shakespeare) rude mechanicals in *A Midsummer Night's Dream* are supposed to know all their lines: Snug the Joiner is worried that he won't be able to learn the lion's part, "for I am slow of study."[69] Only ignorant amateurs like the Cornish actors Richard Carew describes disdainfully in 1610 had to be prompted in order to speak properly "without booke."[70]

To say this is not to say that early modern performance was itself suddenly transformed into a monolithically literate medium, shrunk into the space of the printed text and contained in its confines. Clearly most entertainments were not reliant on fully developed plays and many had no texts at all. For Fynes Moryson's German audience watching the English actors "speaking English which they understoode not," the actors' "gesture and Action" was enough. That non-textual spectacles, often in "theatres," were central to cultural life throughout the early modern period should go without saying (the numerous special entertainments and festivities; *pompe*, *trionfi*, *tornei*, joustings, tilts, and challenges; stylizations of by-then-archaic medieval warfare; animal shows; water spectacles with floats and boat battles; pageants with fireworks, music, and dance; shows with costumed devils and angels). Performances were composites: of memorized text and oral composition (often founded on memorized text), of verbal art and wordless action. But those who thought of themselves as experienced in modern aesthetics came to feel that a printed dialogue read aloud by one's neighbours was not real drama, that animal shows or gymnastic gags with songs were not really proper plays, but that theatre involved actors in stage space with certain kinds of paraphernalia performing certain kinds of texts.

By the later sixteenth century, the proliferation of theatres (at court, in schools, in the cities and at their edges) meant that many writers in search of a theatre in which their plays could be given full-scale performances had found one. Writing and trying to produce performable plays, writers for the stage grew increasingly conscious of the difference between drama performed by actors and drama on the page. Giraldi, for instance, differentiates dramas created for scenic representation from those "terrible" Aristotelian dramas which may be fine "in writing" but which are "odious in performance."[71] When a "sprite" is sent on stage in "Ruzante's" *La Vacàrria* to explain that the play should not be judged by the standards of the written drama because "many things are fine in writing, which would not work on the stage,"[72] he is echoing the more theoretical contrast between playbook and theatrical representation that obsessed Renaissance commentators. Castelvetro, for instance, notes that "tragedy cannot produce—as epic poetry produces—its proper effect when read": Aristotle (he writes) "is of the opinion that the same pleasure is derived from tragedy through reading it as through seeing it and hearing it recited in action" but (he writes in typical Renaissance pro-theatricalism) "this is false doctrine."[73] In Stephen Gosson's anti-theatrical instruction that "whatsoever such Playes as conteine good matter, are set out in print, may be read with profite, but cannot be playd, without a manifest breach of Gods cōmaundement,"[74] he is reflecting the broader cultural contrast between printing and playing, reading and being a (salacious) spectator. If (until perhaps the eighteenth century) no one referred to plays for reading as "closet drama," if most Renaissance dramas aspired to scenic representation,[75] distinctions between the stage and the page were increasingly central to the Renaissance understanding of theatre.

MEDIUM AND METAPHOR: CONSTRUING TEXT AND PERFORMANCE

In the context of the general spread of print (and the new uses for and economies of the written and printed word—their growing centrality in law and government, in education and religion, in scholarship, commerce, and other kinds of daily life), people were thinking a good deal about what writing was and was not, what speech was and was not, what they could and could not do, exploring the distinct identities of memory, speech, performance, and writing in a variety of arenas: in treatises on the art of letters and on technologies of writing; in books of rhetoric and oratory, speech and pronunciation; in debates on education; in discussions of the likeness of picture and poetry, music and architecture; and (most important) in treatises on the drama. "*Viva vox*" is "the living word," explains Erasmus surrounded by his scholarly editions, "the term used in old times for anything not written, but taken straight from the mouth of the speaker, lifelike, as it were, and effectual."[76] Robert Robinson describes the difference between "voice" and "letters" at length in his *Art of Pronunciation*: "And though the voice be a more lively kind of speech, yet . . . it is no sooner uttered but it is dissolved. . . . But the hand though it give a dumbe and a more dull kind of speech, yet it gives a more durable."[77]

The habitual Renaissance contrast between writing and other things (memory, speech, thought, gesture, action), the chronic metaphoric equations, reflected the concern for the changing status of the written word.[78] Metaphoric equation between, for instance, memory and writing continually challenged the distinct identities of the various forms of record and expression. For Renaissance commentators (following Plato), memory could be a kind of writing or engraving in the soul.[79] The silent word could "speake."[80] To "character" (or write) could mean to remember, as it does for Shakespeare's Polonius, who instructs Laertes: "These few precepts in thy memory | See thou character."[81] Printing itself (having naturalized the metaphoric equation of pressing with letter-press printing) could be metaphor for other kinds of pressing: for the impressions of memory; for the imprint of gender; for the press of bodies in the marital (and nonmarital) bed.[82] To "print" could mean to write, as for Marlowe's Duchess in *The Massacre at Paris* (1593), who prays,

> O would to God this quill that heere doth write,
> Had late been pluckt from out faire *Cupids* wing:
> That it might print these lines within his heart.[83]

Character could be typography: Jonson's Amorphus "is the very mint of comple- ment, all his behaviours are printed, his face is another volume of *essayes*."[84] Trans- posing a painting metaphor into a printing metaphor, Lyly's Apelles understands the heart's memory as a surface for the impression of printed characters:

> O Campaspe, I have painted thee in my heart:—
> painted? nay, contrary to
> mine arte, imprinted; and that in such
> deep characters that nothing can raze it out.[85]

The book of nature could be transposed into the printed book of the urban land- scape: London (wrote one commentator in 1632) was "a great Book-faire Printed, *Cum Privilegio Regis*."[86]

If the performance of the book was central to the arts of the Renaissance—central to medicine in the anatomy theatre, or to the Lord's work on the pulpit—the process of inscribing performance was equally central to Renaissance self-reflection on its media of expression. As the paradigmatic medium for the union of text and perfor- mance, theatre could, in this context, become a locus for the broader discussion of the relation between letters and speech, live presence and inscriptions on the page. Theatre became such a crucial metaphor for the Renaissance not only because of its institutional centrality in narrating history and mirroring culture, but because of its role in relating speech and writing, performance and the book. The Renaissance "theatre of nature" overlaid itself on the medieval "book of nature," the theatre of the world (*theatrum mundi*) on the *theatrum* as panoptic and encyclopaedic book.[87] Title pages whose organizing trope was the architectural portico ringed by animated figures (like that for Ortelius' *Theatrum*) (Fig. 29) habitually reminded readers of the connection between spatial-visual display in scenes and in books. The *theatrum mundi* in printed form could, like the stage, have scene-changing machinery (moving parts with wheels and levers like that in Giovanni Paolo Galluccio's *Theatrum mundi*

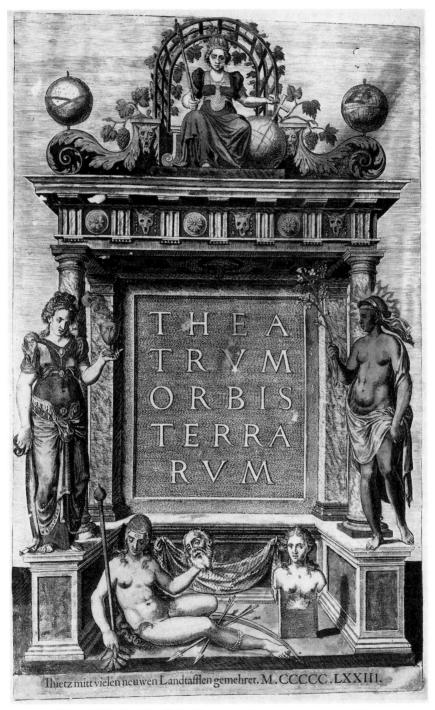

FIG. 29. Abraham Ortelius's *Theatrum orbis terrarum*, in a 1573 edition.

(1588). Renaissance memory theatres like Giulio Camillo's or Robert Fludd's, in theatricalizing knowledge, self-consciously reduplicated the encyclopaedic Renaissance book: both were "theatres," displaying the word in visual form to the eye.[88] In the memory theatres of the mind, the mnemotechnician was (like the actor) to give animate form to the objects of knowledge that had been culled from books: the encyclopaedia was to be bodied forth in lively and impassioned scenes. Both remembering and writing could be theatrics. In their parallel functions and interchangeable uses, the *theatrum* could become a *bibliotheca*, the library a *theatrum*.[89]

But if the likeness between theatre and book was central, the contrast between theatre and book in the treatises of the period most clearly defined them. Translating Aristotle into the world of the Renaissance arts, Trissino, for instance, could understand the distinction between epic and drama as a distinction between text and performance, defining theatre by contrast with the written arts: since tragedy and comedy "must be recited, [their] gestures seen," the *dramatic* poet (unlike other poets) "must take care of those things that of necessity flow from the sensory quality of Poetry, that is from sight and hearing . . . placing before his eyes . . . the gestures and expressions made by those in the throes of passion."[90] For Trissino, theatre uses the senses as a springboard for imagination (unlike writing, which relies primarily on the philosophical faculty of abstraction). For Robortello it is important that, unlike poetry meant for reading, dramatic poetry "joins together with the mind . . . the image of things which are represented, and acts upon the senses almost as if it were the thing itself."[91]

If the treatises attempted to articulate a coherent theatrical aesthetics by contrasting theatre with the book, such discussions drifted into the more commonplace comments on text and performance in prefatory matter to printed playbooks. Playwrights were highly conscious of their double audience, the audience of spectators and of readers. Thomas Heywood explains that he is "commit[ing]" *The Golden Age* "freely to the generall censure of Readers" because it has "already past the approbation of Auditors."[92] The playbook of Middleton's *The Roaring Girl* (1611) "may be allowed," explains Middleton, "both gallery-room at the playhouse, and chamber-room at your lodging."[93] A publishing playwright can only hope that "the grace [plays] had then in the Actings, take not away the expected luster, hoped for in the Reading."[94] For the Seigneur de Racan, plays "are animated only by the representation of several actors" and may not succeed when "read by one person alone": "that which seems excellent in the theatre may be found ridiculous in the study."[95]

Playbooks could, like the treatises, identify the nature of theatre by contrasting it with the book, expressing the differences through the conceptual amplifications of metaphor: a play may, for John Marston, present an "unhansome shape . . . in reading," but may "be pardoned . . . with the soule of lively action."[96] Conversely (for Richard Hawkins), the performed play is merely the raw ore, "that all-tempting Minerall newly digged up," the actors being "onely the labouring Miners," but the readers "the skilfull Triers and Refiners."[97] For Ben Jonson, performance is "soule," the "spirit" opposed to the "shadow" of the letter, which offers only "briefe touches" of that seen on stage.[98] Theatre is live ("lively action"); books are dead. "Action" is "the best life of a Tragedy"[99] or, equally (for André Mareschal), "action is the soul" of comedies: they "languish when they are in writing"; "paper removes much of [their] grace."[100] For George Chapman (as he writes in his dedication to *Caesar and Pompey* in 1631): "Scenicall representation is so farre from giving just cause of any least diminution, that the personall and exact life it gives to any History, or other such delineation of humane actions, ads to them luster, spirit and apprehension."[101] Luster, spirit, soul, life. Books are cold; theatre is hot. "The *Dramaticall* is the most absolute" form of poetry, according to James Shirley, because the dramatic "*Composer*" must "have more then the instruction of Libraries which of it selfe is but a cold contemplative knowledge."[102]

To print is (even in the early sixteenth century) to transcend the requirements of theatrical presence, to draw nearer to incorporeal being, to explode the limits of material space and time and enter the realm of the spirit, as for Guillaume Alabat, who explains that he is publishing his edition of the *Mystery of the Acts of the Apostles* (1537) so that

the reading or hearing of these will come not only to those present but also to the eyes and ears of those who are to come and of those far away, to the delectation of their spirits and edification of their souls. Just as the royal psalmist David prophesied: the sound of them and their words will issue through all the earth and unto the ends of the terrestrial world.[103]

To print is to come close to the presence of the Word. Print is immortal, contrasted with the mortal stage. Plays merely acted are shown "in a conjuring glasse, as suddenly removed as represented," writes James Shirley, but "this volume cannot die."[104] Shakespeare, writes Jonson, is "alive still" while his folio, "thy Booke doth live."[105] If performances dissolve in the instant, "writings and books are immune from such destruction," claims the preface to the German playwright Jakob Ayrer's *Opus Thaeatricum* (1618): "For any that disappear or are destroyed in one country or place are easily found again in countless other places, so that in human experience there is nothing more enduring and immortal than books."[106] "Divested of . . . life," the printed book is, then, at the same time preserver of eternal life, conqueror of time. In a poem and accompanying image (repeated in sixteenth-century dramatic editions and typical of the recurrent trope in which print does battle with time), death destroys the actor, time destroys writings, but immortal print can overcome both time and death: "Man is vanquished by Fate, Death itself by writing. Yet the powerful force of conquering Time vanquishes even writing. PRINT, strongest of all, vanquishes even all-vanquishing Time, in its power grown equal to the immortals" (Fig. 30).[107]

At the same time that such commonplaces hardened the distinction between text and performance, those writing about the dramatic book repeatedly questioned the commonplaces through metaphors of the performing book or the textuality of performance—disruptive figuration that could unveil the paradoxes of medium. Like speech and memory, performance could take the form of inscription: the spectacle could "imprint" itself on the spectator's imagination, the audience's applause be a "stampe" of approval for the play.[108] Actors could be "volumes," appearing

FIG. 30. "PRINT, strongest of all, vanquishes even all-vanquishing Time." Jean de La Péruse's *Medee, tragedie* (1555).

larger than life in "larger print."[109] Theatrical gesture could be a form of writing: in
Titus Andronicus, Marcus will "wrest an alphabet" of the mute Lavinia's "martyred
signs," her "dumb action," her "sigh[s]," "wink[s]," "nod[s]," "kneel[ing]" and
"sign[ing]."[110] In *Dr Faustus*, the body transforms itself magically into script when
Faustus's blood congeals into an "Inscription" on his arm ("What is this Inscription
on mine Arme? | *Homo, fuge*: whether should I flye?").[111] The theatrical face (legible
or otherwise) could be a page for the imprint of character.[112] Conversely, the dramatic
book could be figured as theatrically performing. Playbooks could be animated: the
book "act[s]," "Enter[ing]" the scene of writing, in one early seventeenth-century
conceit;[113] Heywood will print his drama in order "To teach it [to] walke" "upright
upon its feete";[114] for Jasper Maine, the Beaumont and Fletcher folio is "Stage and
Actor" at once.[115] Books could have life breathed into them (in the classic trope of
wind as spirit and animate voice), as in Thomas Peyton's soft-porn fantasy
(addressed to the Beaumont and Fletcher folio), in which he imagines a nun or "some
Novice" who will enter her closet,

> . . . steale a gentle smile
> Upon thy Title, put thee neerer yet,
> Breath on thy Lines a whisper. . . .[116]

Typography could become animate theatrical character, personified, for instance in
the person of the Lord of Misprint who, in festivals in Lyon from the 1570s to the
1590s, tossed printed verses to the crowds,[117] or in the "Text" who comes on stage
with Clorinda and Tancredi in Tasso and Monteverdi's *The Combat of Tancredi and
Clorinda* and narrates their story: "The voice of 'Text' must be clear, firm, and of
good pronunciation."[118]

   By seeming to challenge the conventional characterizations of print and performance but reiterating their terms, metaphor could in fact confirm them ("The
Bookes creepe from the *Presse* to Life, not *Action*," concedes Richard Brome in a half-
hearted attempt to modify the figurative enthusiasms of the usual commendatory
epistle).[119] But while worrying about the limits of metaphor, the commentaries on
print and performance repeatedly draw attention to their own paradoxes, implicitly
recognizing, at the same time that they attempt to define separate media, the limits of
medium distinction. Like theatre, print is fixity and unfixity, it is accuracy and error,
it is enlightenment and obscurity, it is order and chaos, as the drama's conflicting attitudes suggest.[120] For Lope de Vega (speaking through Leonelo in *Fuente Ovejuna*), if
"the art of printing" could "raise up a thousand geniuses from the coarse crowd, and
keep their works sanctified and apart, sheltering them from [the decay of] Time," at
the same time, print could dignify ignorance, sully greatness through false attribution, and produce confusion out of excess.[121] For Jonson, if print could "recover" the
performance "to a part of that *spirit* it had in the gliding by,"[122] the very idea of permanence attached to print could make printed matter seem old, instantly outdated
by its medium, as Cymbal and Fitton in Jonson's *Staple of News* explain: "When
Newes is printed, | It leaves Sir to be *Newes*. While 'tis but written . . . It runnes
Newes still."[123] If print could offer a dignity removed from the stench of the

groundlings, it could at the same time, confer false credibility on unworthy things and render unfairly suspect whatever was not printed (Shakespeare's Mopsa exclaims, "I love a ballad in print, alife, for then we are sure they are true";[124] Jonson's Peni-Boy mocks those who "ha' not the heart to beleeve any thing, | But what they see in print.")[125] If plays "set out in print, may be read with profite" (as Gosson writes) but theatre was "scurrilous wanton [and] prophan,"[126]—if theatre's carnality was opposed to the chastity of print—the playbook could sneak in to seduce the lady in her closet (as the frontispiece to the occasionally naughty *Theatre Italien*, reproduced in Chapter 2, seems to promise its readers).[127]

The contrast between theatre and playbook, text and performance was continually replayed not only in prefaces and treatises on the drama, but also on the stage, in the meta-theatrical reflection on the relation between theatre and playbook. The tropes figuring the relation between performance and text were central to the unconscious of the Renaissance drama—central to its attempts to work out this relationship (thematically, or "tropically," in Hamlet's phrasing).[128] There have been many studies of the ways in which Renaissance and later drama figures book and theatre, text and performance, print, writing, and speech. I will resist attempting to offer my own. My task, instead, is to suggest, in the theatrical context, some of the cultural effects that flowed from the relationship between text and performance in the world of print.

5. *Critical Law, Theatrical Licence*

In a fanciful "Executory Decree" appended to the second edition of Feliciana Enríquez de Guzmán's tragicomedy, *The Sabean Gardens and Fields* (1627), Phoebus Apollo and the nine Muses of the "Royal Council of Poetry" preside over a trial on Mount Parnassus, determining the merits of charges brought against Enríquez de Guzmán's play, the first which "imitated the ancient dramatists" and rigorously "maintained the poetic arts and precepts" prescribed in their treatises, outshining the rest of Spain's dramatic poets and (as their complaint declares, irritably) "notably surpass[ing] us." In order to reach judgement, the counsel engages in a battle of books of sorts, setting Horace's *Ars Poetica* and Enríquez de Guzmán's plays beside a vast pile of books, "all the comedies and tragedies written in romance languages and in Spanish up to the time of the Great Philip IV, King of all Spain," which are brought into the courtroom in "many wagons," laden with the "cargo that filled the archives and warehouses of our Helicon," to be "received into evidence." Having subjected the wagons of books "to our laws and ordinances of poetry," the case is "determined ready for sentencing," and the muses pass judgement: Enríquez de Guzmán has won the laurel wreath, surpassing "all the comic and tragic poets of Spain up to the time of the Great Philip IV." As for the sentence, it is ordered "that from this day forth our Spanish poets . . . adhere to the laws and precepts," "under pain of . . . being erased and thrown out of [the] catalogue of poets and the books of our favours." The new law is publicly declared in the academies, and the edict is duly signed and ratified: "Law passed in the gardens of Mount Parnassus, the first day of March, in the year sixteen hundred and twenty four. Phoebus Apollo, Calliope, Eutrepe, Thalia. By their command, Orpheus of Thrace, Secretary. Registered. Ratified."[1]

Enríquez de Guzmán's judicial trope is a narrative rendering of the period's common figuration of aesthetic judgement in legal terms, reflected in the juridical rhetoric that was conventional for discussing rules of poetic composition, and merging the authority of learned "letters" with the authority of the law. To conform to the Rules was to conform to the "laws of poetry"; to diverge from them was a form of "licence," a charge against which Enríquez de Guzmán defends herself: while (she explains) she permitted herself a degree of "poetic licence" in the first edition, she did so only to "accommodate [herself to] the performance" and did not, in fact, "violate the prohibitions" of Horace's treatise. Moreover, here in the revised edition, she has returned to strictest conformity with the law. In so doing, she is turning from the vulgar "theatres and coliseums," and instead aiming at the audience in the "homes of . . . aficionados of good literature" ("those versed in letters"), "the palaces and halls of princes and great lords, and . . . their cities and kingdoms." Turning her back on the public theatre, then, imagining herself (through the new decree) as the lawgiver of this new cultural nation—made of "cities and kingdoms" linked by "letters" and stretching through "all the provinces of Spain" (as she writes)—Enríquez de Guzmán casts herself as heroic national liberator. She is heir not only to Pallas Minerva (sage lawgiver to Athens), not only to a line of women "learned in letters" whom she proceeds to name ("the most dignified Marquise of Cenete, the celebrated Isabela, jewel of Barcelona, the most erudite Sigea of Toledo, . . . lady Angela Zapata, lady Ana Osorio of Burgos, and lady Catalina de Paz, the glory and honour of Guadalajara), but also to the mythical seven maidens who heroically liberated Spain from paying a tribute each year "to make peace with the pagans." In writing a play whose adherence to aesthetic law is to found a new poetic regime, she hopes—like the seven maidens—to "banish from the nation many comedies unworthy of enjoying the Elysian Fields" and thus "free Spain, and . . . her illustrious and noble poets from the tribute which they have been paying to keep the peace with the barbarous masses."[2]

PEDAGOGY, PERFORMANCE, AND THE SCHOLAR'S BOOK

Renaissance education, like Renaissance theatre, aimed at teaching the proper performance of the book. It should not be a surprise that the schoolroom performance of humanist drama became fashionable at the moment when, at one and the same time, professional theatre was getting an institutional grounding and printed books were becoming an essential tool of a young scholar's education.[3] Throughout the early modern period (and probably well into the twentieth century), the promulgation of classical and other kinds of learning was inseparable from its performance, imbibed through dramatic enactment, rhetorical performance, disputation, grammatical analysis, enunciation, memorization, and scholarly gloss—all essential to an education in genteel comportment. The collections of "sentences" like Nicholas Udall's *Floures for Latine spekynge selected and gathered out of Terence* (1533), the classical and vernacular grammars, the books of rhetoric and poetics that prescribed spoken and written language simultaneously—these remind us that the study of books did not constitute a separate pedagogic sphere but one interwoven with their performance. If pedagogy could at times require an independent relationship to the page—in silent and solitary reading and writing—that pedagogy continued to take the performance of learning as essential to it. Those who could not perform what they knew, but knew it only from books, had no kind of learning at all. At the same time, however, under the influence of printing, there was a shift in the attitude towards books. The ancient metaphor of the book as the sacred symbol of learning (registered in one medieval poem in which Pythagoras appears as a man transformed into a book, astrology shining on his brow, grammar governing his teeth, rhetoric on his tongue, logic spouting from his lips, the mechanical arts drawn on his back)[4] was challenged by the practical realities of dealing with the real books that seemed to be pouring from the presses. Learning was associated ever more strongly with actual texts, and more particularly with printed texts: Shakespeare's Touchstone, for instance, automatically identifies "learned" disputation as "quarrel[ing] in print, by the book."[5]

That in Renaissance satire the pedant's habitat was starting to be extended from the peripatetic schoolroom, where tutors spouted Latin phrases, to the bookshop, where annotators fought among the quartos and the folios, was a sign of the change. The stock pedants with their Latin tags, the warring clergymen, lawyers, and philosophers with their formal phrases, the inflated poets, itching to recite their correctly turned sonnets were surrounded by the paraphernalia of print. Narticoforo and Granchio quibble over spelling in an edition of Cicero in Giambattista della Porta's *La Fantesca* (1592).[6] The pompous "Horace" (representing Jonson in Dekker's *Satiromastix* (1602)) is surrounded in his study by his "bookes lying confusedly" and does his bragging in "Booke-binders shops."[7] Ingenioso in the anonymous *Pilgrimage to Parnassus* and *The Returne from Parnassus* (*c.*1597–1601) has "burnt my [scholar's] bookes" and is now "bounde to the right honourable printing house" as a hack and bookseller, "posted to everie poste in Paules churchyarde *cum gratia et privilegio*."[8] By the seventeenth century, the scholar buried under the weight of learned books was a stock figure. Charles in Fletcher's and Massinger's *The Elder Brother* (written *c.*1625–37), who "eates and digests more Volumes at a meale, | Than there would be Larkes (though the sky should fall) | Devowr'd in a moneth in *Paris*," has his library unloaded on stage: more than a dozen carts worth of books.[9] The emblematic illustration in *Pedantius* (1631) shows the university philosophers Dromodotus and Pedantius arguing learnedly beneath a shelf of books (Fig. 31).[10] Charles Beys's dramatic "Poet" (in his *Illustrious Madmen* (1653)) possesses Aristotle, Horace, and Scaliger, has "read two thousand Authors in various languages," has "reread a thousand times the Commentary of a hundred Translators . . . all in both Latin and Greek."[11]

It may be oversimplification to identify the rebirth of theatre in the Renaissance with the classical revival that followed the rediscovery and dissemination of ancient texts in the late fifteenth century, and hence with print. But (as we saw in Chapter 4) the treatises on ancient dramatic theory, architectural studies, and classical drama were used to produce the distinction between the "theatre" proper and "lascivious farces and mummeries" or "publike shewes [and] interludes" or "peeces and Patches of . . . playes"[12] on which the normative notion of modern theatre was built. Those who wrote for the learned stage, drew on the resources of print and pointed towards the library as the source for theatre's revival, associating their own published works with the "treasures" they found there. Dedicating his tragedy *Aman* (1566) to the Queen of Navarre, a true "friend of the savants," André de Rivaudeau, for instance, advertises his own published commentaries on Euripides' *Electra*, "the rarest sacred books," and "the Greeks' great treasures" (implicitly also the linguistic treasuries or "thesauruses" beginning to emerge from the press), ruing the fact that "the hands of princes are closed to the learned, and letters held in low esteem" and condemning the use of royal finances to support "carnivals, lists, and tournaments."[13] In his 1572 *Art of Tragedy*, Jean de La Taille similarly calls for "kings and great ones" to displace the plays of the popular stage with the kind of drama honoured by "men of letters."[14]

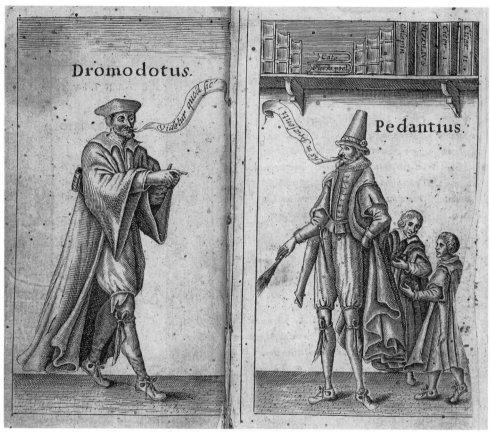

FIG. 31. Dromodotus with Pedantius and his books in *Pedantius* (1631).

Joachim Du Bellay and his co-authors' complaint, in their *Defence and Illustration of the French Language* (1549), that "farces and moralities" had "usurped" the place of "comedies and tragedies" carried with it a gentle directive. "If kings and republics wish to restore these to their ancient dignity," they write to the poetic aspirant, "you would do well to employ yourself in this . . . as an ornament to your language," adding: "you know where to find the archetypes."[15] In the ancient books and those of their modern interpreters, the learned were to find a new aesthetics proper to the new theatre.

For both Du Bellay and La Taille, the reform of the drama on the model of the ancients was, simultaneously, a generic and a linguistic project. Such norms were enforced (to the extent that they were) by the monetary and cultural power of various overlapping institutions and individuals vying for aesthetic prestige, attempting to create an art fit for a newly enlightened aristocracy: academies, formal or informal (the Florentine Accademia della Crusca, the Pléiade, the Madrid Academy, eventually the Académie Française, to name just a few); aristocratic patrons; their beneficiaries (paid, in a sense, to promote linguistic and literary norms in their poems, plays, and treatises); and the state itself, the best patron of all, with its various sinecures.[16] Gentle directives like Du Bellay's or La Taille's could, when taken over by official institutions, become explicit prescriptions for the regulation of both the form and the language of the popular stage along literate lines. For the Paris Procurer General, for instance, issuing an edict against the mysteries in 1541, proper performance was explicitly performance in which diction and pronunciation reflected experience with *letters*, with "A" and "B" (in what was to become the common colloquial phrase for knowledge generally). The players of mysteries, "knowing neither A nor B,"

have neither articulate nor proper language, nor decent accents in pronunciation. . . . They make three words out of one; put a period or pause in the middle of a proposition . . . ; turn an interrogatory into an exclamation, or otherwise make gestures, or place emphases that run counter to what they are saying.[17]

ORTHOGRAPHIES, DICTIONARIES, AND LEARNED ANNOTATION

The Procurer General's view that literate punctuation and word division ought to guide performed speech was consonant with a broader urge towards linguistic regulation, manifest in the dictionaries, handbooks on pronunciation, and grammatical and orthographic manuals and treatises that proliferated during the sixteenth and seventeenth centuries: sponsored by the academies and aristocrats associated with them; promoted by scholars and schoolmasters interested in the diffusion of literate form; condoned by the culture at large and eventually helping to produce, among other things, the standardization of vernacular spelling.[18] Like the Paris Procurer's brief, such manuals urged "learned" standards on oral forms, laying out those standards in specifications for correct written usage, spelling, and punctuation, proposing orthographic reforms that might unify and "purify" the language.[19] Noting that "ignorant people," not "savants," are responsible for the variety of languages, because "the learned would never have created so many monsters," Pierre de Ronsard, for instance, offers detailed instructions on usage and orthography framed to promote proper speech.[20] For John Hart, the ultimate goal of treatises like his *Orthographie* (1569) is the preservation of what "wise and studious men" have written, and therefore what is required for this project is "knowledge of letters."[21] Even those opposed to orthographic reform shared the view that spelling was to reflect the speech of "the learned," and not to match the volubility of the tongue, as the Reformation playwright Theodore de Bèze suggests in his preface to *Abraham sacrifiant* (1550) (mistrustful of those who, in attempting to match pronunciation, would produce a new orthographic chaos to match the chaos of French speech): "As far as the orthography is concerned, I wanted the printer to follow the common [spelling]," he writes—a spelling that reflects the correct speech of the learned—not the "meagre fantasies" of the ignorant:

And I would gladly advise the most opinionated of those who wished to change [conventional spelling] (if they were people who asked advice of anyone but themselves), since they want to match [spelling] to pronunciation, that is to say, since they want there to be almost as many ways of writing as there are, not only regions, but also people in France, that they learn to pronounce before trying to learn to write: . . . he who cannot speak our language is not worthy of handing out rules for writing it.[22]

Setting out such standards in formal terms—regularizing speech and suppressing or stylizing dialects—dictionaries, lexicons, grammars, and rhetorical and orthographic manuals attempted to work out the problem of providing a unified language for the vast territories in the process of becoming (in the case of England, France, and Spain, at least) something like centralized states.[23] Hart's orthographic programme is aimed, importantly, at protecting the gentry from the threat of the rabble: it is "greatly to the increase, noriture, maintenaunce and defence of the few better sort, from the violence of the barbarous multitude." But ultimately it is also a universal, civilizing project (bringing "light" to the "reasonable," in what was to become a classic justificatory trope in literacy projects throughout the early modern period). "Where most of the people doe best know [letters]," he declares, "there is most prosperitie and best assuraunce."

To which ende is this treatise, for the profite of the multitude, and that by opening the windowe whereby is light given to descerne betwixt perfection and barbarousnesse, so as every reasonable creature universally (of what nation soever understanding it) may be a perfite judge howe every language ought to bee written.[24]

Spelling was to reflect not just the speech of the "learned," but the speech of the learned in the increasingly powerful capitals. "He should have a wrong opinion of me," writes Hart defensively, "that should thinke . . . I ment any thing shoulde be printed in London in the maner of Northerne or Westerne speaches," allowing however that one might print in dialect for local readers ("if any one were minded at Newcastell uppon Tine, or Bodman in Cornewale, to write or print his minde there, who could justly blame him for his Orthographie, to serve hys neybours according to their mother speach").[25] In the dedication to his "Abregé de l'Art Poëtique Françoys," Ronsard spells out more definitively an orthographic programme allied with the kind of political programme only implicit in Hart: the unification of the nation under one king and the extension of the "Empire." On the one hand the poet should not suppress the rich vocabulary that dialect has given to French but "appropriate . . . the most meaningful terms," whether from "Gascony, Poitiers, Normandy, Le Mans, Lyon, or from other regions." On the other hand, this appropriation is an imperial venture, ultimately serving a unified France: "Because Princes must not be less eager to enlarge the borders of their Empire than to extend their language through all nations [and] today, because our France obeys only one King, we are compelled, if we wish to achieve any honour, to speak his courtly language."[26]

The drama was seen as working hand in hand with the manuals on the project of improving speech (as Du Bellay's, La Taille's, and Bèze's dual roles as dramatists and reformers suggest), in part through the use of drama for pedagogic purposes in the schools, in part through other kinds of performances (in which the theatre took on its traditional Horatian role as public educator), and in part through dramatic texts like Bèze's, whose lessons in Christian virtue were inextricable from their lessons in proper orthography. Playwrights and their editors took advantage of print as a vehicle for setting forth formal models for correct speech, against which the spoken language of their characters could be measured (as the publication of Jonson's *English Grammar* alongside his plays in the posthumous 1640 edition of his works suggests). The manuals helped to fortify pre-existing stylistic hierarchies: the "lofty" and "learned" language of princes was to be distinguished from the "unlettered" language of peasants "knowing neither A nor B" or the "barbarous speech of your country people"; the speech of "learned or elegantly refined men" was to be distinguished from that of ploughmen, maidservants, and porters.[27] In so doing, they offered a material foundation for the normative model codified in the concept of dramatic "decorum," which acknowledged the range of spoken style to be mirrored on the stage, but advocated nonetheless the purification of each style within its proper range.

If the "polished language" of the standardized vernacular was central to national identity, that language could be promulgated through collections of plays like Robert Garnier's *Tragédies* which (according to Jean Vauquelin de la Fresnaye) demonstrated "that our language surpasses today even the greatest of them"[28] or, several decades later in England, the Beaumont and Fletcher folio which (according to James Shirley) is "not only the *Crowne* and sole *Reputation* of our owne, but the stayne of all other *Nations* and *Languages*,"[29] and from which both the "*Native*" and "*th'Alien*" may learn the correct vernacular.[30] The simultaneous impulse towards linguistic consolidation and expansionism—allied with the project of routing dialects so central to the consolidation of the Renaissance nation-state—was reflected in a change in the way in which linguistic variety was represented on stage. One might generalize this change as a move from the celebration of linguistic abundance in the early Renaissance drama (the fertile mix of competing vernaculars and dialects, the energetic word-coining, the combination and recombination of phonetic possibilities) to the chastening of these by the polite and streamlined national vernaculars mandated by the manuals: from the kind of rich heteroglossia of, for instance, the delirium scene in *Pierre Pathelin* in which Pathelin raves in the Limousin, Picard, Flamand, Normand, and Breton dialects (as well as in flagrantly incorrect Latin); to the kind of self-conscious marking of dialect in Beolco's description of his plays as, for instance, "in rustic language" (i.e. Paduan dialect); to the high-handed mockery of disfavoured dialects in, for instance, the jest-book *A Hundred Merry Tales*, *Gammer Gurton's Needle*, Jonson's *Bartholomew Fair*, Shakespeare's *Henry* plays, or Cyrano de Bergerac's *The Pedant Duped*.[31]

In any case, such standards began to make dramatic writers and editors self-conscious about non-standard vernaculars and "low" speech, even when they understood them as essential to the representation of the range of speech necessarily spoken by a range of characters. In his preface to his collection, *Le Théatre* (1561), Jacques Grévin, who in his prefatory poems excoriates the "vulgar words" of the popular theatre's "farced-up tragedies," feels required to defend his "low" diction, necessary, he explains, to the range of comedy (although he has eliminated rural dialect, in conformity with the purification of the drama):

The freedom of comic poets has always been such that they often use vulgar words, sentences, and manners of speech rejected by the coterie of the better spoken . . . ; which perchance you may find in reading my comedies. Yet you must not scowl, because here it would have been out of the question to paint over the language of a merchant, a servant, or a chambermaid. . . . The comic sets out only to represent the truth and naïveté of the language, as it does the manners, the conditions, and the stations of those it puts in play; without wronging its purity, which is rather of the common sort.[32]

The press corrector of the 1588 edition of Aretino's *Quattro Comedie* is similarly concerned that readers might take Lombard expressions and spellings to be errors, and feels obliged to explain that dialect is, in fact, *part* of decorum: "This Writer has accorded with the nature of the persons he brings on to speak. He has used both the Lombard voice and the foreign, and he has . . . written both in Lombard, and in the foreign manner. One should not take this to be an error on my part or anyone else's."[33]

As heavily annotated historical works proliferated beside the orthographies, dictionaries, and grammars, and as documentary sources became increasingly important to historical authentication, dramatists writing on historical subjects began similarly to register the pressure to adhere to scholarly norms.[34] The "verisimilitude" prescribed by Aristotle was, of course, often interpreted as a requirement for general poetic or moral verisimilitude (with the stress placed on Aristotle's assertion that it was preferable for tragedy to narrate a probable impossibility than an improbable verity), but it was also often interpreted as an injunction to adhere to sources. As Scaliger writes in 1561, "When authors take their plots from history, they must be careful not to depart too widely from the records."[35] Recognition of the power of historical evidence entailed, then, an obligation not to swerve from history as recorded. "Poetry must not and cannot falsify history," explains Castelvetro, especially not "genuine history, the kind that has been received in writing" (though also the fabricated kind) but must "represen[t] what is known to be true precisely as it is known."[36] However often poetry was proclaimed distinct from history, then, the books that proffered the historical record began to seem necessary to the authentication of the dramatist's historical accuracy and scholarly acumen. In Massinger's *Believe as You List*, the prologue might cheerfully disclaim historical or geographical precision: the author is "an English scholler at his best, | a stranger to *Cosmographie*" who "may erre | in the cuntries names, the shape, & character | of the person he presente," and the prologue will not "boast . . . what bookes [the playwright] hath tost | & turnde to make it up."[37] Jonson may apologize for his pretension in providing learned citations for *Sejanus*: "Least in some nice nostrill, the *Quotations* might savour affected, I doe let you know, that I abhor nothing more; and have onely done it to shew my integrity in the *Story*," excusing himself (with a wink to the learned reader) on the grounds that, "Whereas, they are in *Latine* and the worke in *English*, it was presupposd, none but the Learned would take the paynes to conferre them." But if Jonson does mocking tribute to the "nice nostrill" of the ordinary play reader which might recoil from such learned citation, he nonetheless feels that the quotation of Latin sources for *Sejanus* is, in fact, necessary "to shew my integrity in the *Story*," and that even this is incomplete without a further identification of his sources, as testimony to his accuracy: "It may be required, since I have quoted the Page, to name what Edition I follow'd. *Tacit. Lips.* In 4°. *Antuerp. Edt.* 600. *Dio. Folio Hen. Step.* 92. For the rest, as *Sueton. Seneca.* &c. the Chapter doth sufficiently direct, or the Edition is not varied."[38]

If Jonson quotes his Latin sources—if Corneille feels it necessary (in the 1648 edition of his *Oeuvres*) actually to reproduce the texts of his historical sources, "so that [the reader] can thereby see . . . how far I believe poetic licence can go when one is treating of true [historical] subjects"[39]—dramatists' disclaimers about their historical accuracy repeatedly reminded readers of the difficulties of reconciling poetry with history. Samuel Daniel has to excuse himself for swerving from his sources in *The Vision of the Twelve Goddesses* (1604), which (he claims) he must do "or . . . there can be nothing done authenticall, unless we observe all the strict rules of the booke."[40] Insisting on the difference between poetry and history, Marston explains in the preface to his *Sophonisba* (1606): "Know, that I have not labored in this poeme, to tie my selfe to relate any thing as an historian but to inlarge every thing as a Poet, To transcribe Authors, quote authorities, & translate Latin prose orations into English black-verse [*sic*], hath in this subject beene the least aime of my studies."[41] Defending his alteration of history in his own version of *Sophonisbe* in 1635, Jean Mairet points his reader towards the authorities who (alternatives to an authenticating historical record) can vindicate his ahistorical practice:

It is true that I added [some things], and that I even changed two rather important historical incidents. [But] the more refined will see, if they are pleased to take the trouble, the defense of what I have done in Aristotle. . . . As for the moderns, if they have the curiosity they may see me justified in two discourses by Count Prosper Bonarelli . . . on his *Soliman* . . . : they [may be found] in the most recent edition published in M.DC.XXXII.[42]

The protests against the confusion of the scholarly record were at once a sign of defeat in the face of the excess of learned books and a marker of just how powerful the claims of scholarship had become for the drama. "The authors themselves are so irrigular and confused" explains Daniel in the Preface to *The Vision of the Twelve Goddesses*, "as the best Mytheologers, who will make somwhat to seeme any thing, are so unfaithfull to themselves, as they have left us no certaine way at all, but a tract of confusion."[43] If Jonson worries, in *The Masque of Queenes* (1609), about contradictions in the record ("I find" the name of the "*Queene* of *Ægipt* . . . written both *Beronice*, and *Berenice*"),[44] Lope de Vega complains that "[things are] scattered among many books, [and] everything of today is in a state of confusion."[45] The cumulation of commentary on the ancients, "the notes and superficial distinctions that are in our printed editions," as D'Aubignac refers to them disparagingly, are more perplexing than helpful.[46] Andreas Gryphius concludes his *Papinian* (1659), saturated with annotations, with the exhausted sigh: "So much, then, this time. But why so much? For the learned it is all written in vain; for the unlearned it is not enough."[47] But whatever the confusion, insufficiency, or sheer futility of scholarly annotation, the aspiration to accuracy had grown into a norm of literary—and literate—authentication.

THE RULES

The insistence on the "Rules," derived from Aristotle and Horace, prescribing the "regular" drama, and including requirements for "decorum" and historical accuracy but most centrally focused on plot, similarly stressed the importance for the drama of adhering to critical norms capable of validation through printed authorities.[48] While the variety of disputed aesthetic norms that the Rules represented were challenged from the outset (in Italy and France as well as England and Spain), they nonetheless began to exert a powerful normative force over theorists and dramatists, taking a central place in aesthetic discourse in Italy by the early sixteenth century, and, by the later part of the century, spreading to most of the rest of Europe, flowing from the many treatises on the *Poetics* into dramatic prefaces and other commentaries on the dramatist's art. If they remained arenas for fighting a diverse set of aesthetic battles with diverse political meanings, they were nonetheless firmly identified with "letters": derived from the books of the ancients; routinely referred to as the "rules of the booke."

   Associated, then, with the written drama, they could stand in opposition to the values of popular performance (both positively and negatively). Writing in 1543, Giovanni Battista Giraldi, for instance, could contrast the Aristotelian drama, conforming in exemplary fashion to the Rules and admirable on paper, with plays better suited to performance:

> It is better to satisfy . . . the audience with some small excellencies . . . than, with a little more ostentation, to displease those for whom the play is being produced. . . . It serves little to compose a slightly more laudable plot and end up with a repellant performance. Those terrible [Aristotelian] plays (which disgust the feelings of the spectators) can be in writing, the other kind, finally, delight on stage.[49]

From the opposite point of view, Jacques Grévin warns the readers of his *Théatre* (1561) not to expect the kind of "light farces" to which they are accustomed in the playhouse ("unworthy of being put before the eyes of a learned man"). He has instead given them a drama "worthy of being put in writing."[50] However much playbooks and images of the stage may have represented popular performance, in all its multiplicity, the learned drama came to be identified with "the printed book" generally, and the "correct" comedies produced in conformity with the Rules came to be equated with "printed . . . Piece[s]."[51] Jonson, for instance, implicitly opposes the "learned" (printed) book to the unlearned (popular) playing "beside the book" of the puppeteers in *Bartholomew Fair* (1614):

Cokes: But doe you play it according to the printed booke? I have read that.

Lantern Leatherhead: By no meanes, Sir.

Cokes: No? How then?

Lantern Leatherhead: A better way, Sir, that is too learned, and poeticall for our audience; what doe they know what *Hellespont* is? Guilty of true loves blood? or what *Abidos* is? Or the other *Sestos* hight?[52]

The "learned" book is the printed book, from which the popular theatre might declare its liberty.

The contrast between the learned book and the popular stage carried with it, of course, traditional class distinctions between the learned aristocracy and the unlettered rabble. The Paris Procurer General, differentiating "unlettered" pageant masters and actors of mysteries from those who put on classical plays, stresses simultaneously the fact that the pageant masters and their actors are not "knowledgeable in such things" and that they are persons "of ignoble condition, such as a carpenter, a sergeant at arms, an upholsterer, a fish vendor . . . ignorant people, craft artisans."[53] In his *Art of Tragedy* (1572), La Taille offers a classic contrast between "plays that are . . . constructed according to true art and in the mould of the ancients, for instance a Sophocles, Euripides, or Seneca," and those "tragedies and comedies, farces and moralities (where often there is neither sense nor reason, but ridiculous words with a bit of banter)," which "can be nothing but ignorant things, badly made, unworthy of attention, and serv[ing] only as pastimes for domestics and the popular riffraff."[54] Not merely the province of the vulgar masses, popular performance was now the province of the notably "illiterate" masses, as the Paris Procurer General reminds his audience. In prefatory material to printed plays, readers of the drama were repeatedly contrasted with illiterate spectators, in what became a standard insult for audiences that had hissed a play: those who have bought the printed play, explains Beaumont's prefatory poem to Fletcher's *The Faithful Shepherdess* (1609), at least "must have the quallitie | Of reading, which I am affraid is more | Then halfe your shrewdest judges" (the spectators) "had before."[55] Similarly addressing readers of *The New Inn* (1631), Jonson writes tauntingly "If thou canst but spell, and joyne my sense; there is more hope of thee, then of a hundred fastidious *impertinents*, who were there present the first day."[56]

The identity of the popular stage was reshaped, then, even for those playwrights most committed to writing for it, through its contrast with the more refined study. For Lope de Vega (taking on the voice of the Rules-wielding authorities), the popular Spanish drama obeys "the vulgar current" of "the ignorant rabble," ignoring the precepts of the libraries filled with the tomes of "the learned Robortello of Udine," Aristotle, Terence, and Plautus.[57] In his "apologeticall Dialogue" appended to the *Poetaster*, Jonson casts himself as a "learn'd . . . soule" sequestered in his study, persecuted by the ignorant poetasters in "th'abused theaters": "O, this would make a learn'd, and liberall soule, | To rive his stayned quill, up to the back, | And damne his long-watch'd labours to the fire" (a stance Dekker satirizes in *Satiromastix* in his portrait of Jonson as "Horace," scribbling in his study about the Muses' prophecy that baby Horace "*to learned eares should sweetly sing, | But to the vulger and adulterate braine,* | *Should loath to prostitute our Virgin straine*").[58] In the commendatory verses he wrote for Thomas Randolph's *The Jealous Lovers* (1632), Edward Fraunces writes that it is an injustice that the play has been subjected to the "common . . . view" of the public stage, where plays are made "the vulgar peoples sport," rather than confined to the "studie" or the critics' "court," but that now it may at last join the ranks of Plautus, Terence, and Aristophanes ("within the walls of some great librarie").[59]

Such distinctions (clearly more heuristic than descriptive) served a number of functions, among them separating and protecting the status of the amateur literary aristocracy (and those who lived from its direct patronage) from the threat of the professional playwright, whose growing economic importance could be matched by parallel cultural aspirations.[60] As important, the normative aesthetic absolute expressed in the Rules overlapped with a notion of legal normativity (as for Enríquez de Guzmán), both of these registered (literally and metaphorically) in "the book." Treated in the language of jurisprudence, the Rules were "laws" determining which dramas were "legitimate" and which not.[61] Playing by the book meant not only playing "according to the printed [play]booke" but also playing by the lawbook (rendered aesthetically in the Rules), thereby avoiding an accusation of "licence" (or "licentiousness"). For Rivaudeau, to break the Rules laid out in such works as "a great volume by one Scaliger" (Scaliger's 1561 *Poetices libri septem*, to which Rivaudeau refers his readers) is "licentious."[62] In Jonson's 1607 dedication of *Volpone* to "the two famous Universities," the "licence" of the popular theatre is to be chastened by a drama fit for his "learned Arbitresses" (Oxford and Cambridge). "The learned [have] suffer[ed]" by "the too-much licence of *Poetasters*"—the freedom of speech of these "licentious spirits" (his attackers) associated with their generic and linguistic impropriety:

> The increase of . . . lust in liberty, together with the present trade of the stage, in all their misc'line *enter-ludes*, what learned or liberall soule doth not already abhor? where nothing but the filth of the time is utter'd, and that with such impropriety of phrase, such plenty of *solœcismes*, . . . so bold *prolepse's*, so rackt *metaphor's*, with brothelry, able to violate the eare of a pagan, and blasphemy, to turne the bloud of a christian to water.[63]

As Jonson's rhetoric suggests, such concerns over excessive theatrical "liberty" in a sense transferred the old anti-theatricalist objection to the licentious stage into a new sphere, the concern over "licence" displaced (like so much of Renaissance culture) from the sphere of religion into the sphere of secular knowledge. The libertine in poetic matters was to be brought into line with a new set of literate standards, conducing to conformity with a new set of authorities: the ancients and their interpreters. The learned "laws" were seen as properly to be superimposed on the natural "licence" of the popular theatre, taming it for fit consumption. One might think of the academies and universities and those who spoke for them as, in a sense, using the authority of humanist books to displace the religious institutions that had once controlled performance by means of *the* Book. Whether by such institutions as the academies or by the state itself (as under Richelieu, who exerted control over the theatre through control over the press),[64] the book was brought, via the theatre, into the service of politics. The political significance of the Rules was reflected in commentaries that identified the laws of the drama with the laws of the nation, like the orthographic manuals serving the project of forwarding national culture through an aesthetics that would banish "barbarism." Cervantes' Priest (in *Don Quixote*) worries about the damage that the Spanish theatre's violation of the Rules does to the honour of Spain: "All this . . . shames our Spanish wits before foreigners, who observe the rules of drama with great strictness and consider us ignorant barbarians when they see the absurdities and extravagances of the plays we write."[65] Jonson similarly worries about the political dangers inherent in the "barbarism" of theatrical licence, equating the makers of "misc'line *enter-ludes*" with those "licentious spirits" of the stage, who "make . . . a name with the multitude [and] draw their rude, and beastly claps" through libellous attacks. Though patriots may prefer to see "fooles, and devils, and those antique reliques of barbarism" on stage than to "behold the wounds of private men, of princes, and nations," these equally do "hurts . . . in a state."[66]

Both dramatists aspiring towards the prestige of "letters" and dramatists insisting on their alliance with the popular theatre could be defensive about their failure to adhere to the Rules. Reflecting the authoritative and disapproving voice of the Madrid Academy to which he is speaking, Lope de Vega explains: "I was [not] ignorant of the precepts; thank God, even while I was a tyro in grammar, I went through the books which treated the subject," defensively anticipating the Academy's reproaches for his poetic lapses (with a wink to those sympathetic admirers): "Nobody can I call more barbarous than myself, since in defiance of art I . . . allow myself to be borne along in the vulgar current, wherefore Italy and France call me ignorant. . . . [But] since the crowd pays for the comedies, it is fitting to talk foolishly to satisfy its taste."[67] In his dedication for *Volpone*, Jonson asks for lenience from the "learned and charitable critick," admitting that his *catastrophe* does not conform to "the strict rigour of *comick* law," and that he "tooke . . . more liberty" than comedy ordinarily grants so that he could properly punish vice, "though not" (he adds defensively) "without some lines of example, drawne even in the ancients themselves."[68] Claiming (in his preface to *Sejanus* (1605)) that he has failed to write a "true *Poëme*; in the strict Lawes of *Time*" only because it is impossible to reconcile "the ould state, and splendour of *Drammatick Poëmes*" with "preservation of any popular delight" in "these our Times, and to such Auditors, as commonly Things are presented," he promises to make up for this lapse by elaborating further on the true drama "in my Observations upon *Horace* his *Art* of *Poetry*, which (with the Text translated) I intend, shortly to publish."[69]

THE LAW OF LIBERTY

If Jonson, however, feels he must beg indulgence for his poetic licence, there were, from the beginning, more outright apologists for a theatricalist poetics liberated from the Rules. In the prologue to Lodovico Dolce's *Marianna* (1565), for instance, the personification of "Tragedy" embraces the lyric poets over "the great disciple of

Plato" (Aristotle), "who has written rules and laws for me," a great philosopher, declares Tragedy, but "he was not a Poet."[70] While the "laws" of the critical treatises were underwritten by the authorities and identified with the world of the book, those declaring their liberty from the rules regularly asserted that the live theatre had its own principles, underwritten by the public. Pulled one direction by "Terence and Plautus [in] my study," and another by the theatrical "crowd," Lope de Vega defiantly chooses the latter, drawing on the imagery of penal enforcement in which, instead of the Rules locking up the playwright, the playwright locks up the Rules: "When I have to write a comedy I lock in the precepts with six keys . . . and I write in accordance with that art which they devised who aspired to the applause of the crowd."[71] Writing a commendatory epistle for Thomas Killigrew's *The Prisoners* and *Claracilla* (in 1641), "H. Benet" can set "living Rules" in opposition to the Rules found in books, noting that "bookes are dead" and claiming that true dramatic poetry is made "In spight of studied Rules and Arts":

> . . . he who more precisely pennes, and drawes
> His labour'd Scenes true by Dramatique Lawes,
> May well transcribe those Rules perhaps, but then
> The Whole runnes lame and rudely from his pen.[72]

The jurisprudential language that traditionally legitimated the Rules could be used, instead, against the Rules and in the defence of theatrical practice. In his preface to *Theagene et Cariclée* (1623), Alexandre Hardy explains that, if conformity to Horace's *Art of Poetry* "legitimates" dramatic practice, the theatrical public offers an alternative form of legitimation: "I know very well that many . . . will censure [my] direct violation of the laws that Horace prescribed in his *Art of Poetry*," he writes. But, he continues, "all that practice condones and that pleases the public becomes more than legitimate."[73] In his *Countryhouses of Toledo* (1624), contrasting those things produced by the "laws of" the drama's "ancestors" with those things produced by the genuine poet, Tirso de Molina lays claim to the proven authority of praxis, which has the revolutionary power to "repeal the statutes" of the ancients: "If the excellence of Aeschylus and Euripides in Greece (and, among the Latins, Seneca and Terence) is enough to establish the laws so well defended by their professors, the excellence of our Spanish [Lope de] Vega [and] the authority with which he surpasses them [are] sufficient to repeal their statutes."[74]

At once registering the increasingly authoritative rule of the learned book and resisting its sway, the satire of pedantry could emblematize the theatricalist resistance to the "rules of the booke," offering a declaration of "free[dom] from . . . Books, and Book-men" as Walter Charleton would term it (the conjoined coercion of books and of brutal schoolmasters unhappily remembered).[75] Headed a "Comedy by Bruno Nolano, Academician of no Academy," Giordano Bruno's *Il Candelaio* (1582) takes its vengeance on the pedants through Bruno's portrait of Manfurio:

one of those composers of deserving books: margin-fillers, glossators, scissors-and-paste men, analyzers, addition-mongers, riddle-guessers, translators, interpreters, compilers, connoisseurs of obscurities, publicists with a new grammar, a new dictionary, a *lexicon*, a *varia lectio*, . . . a licensed authenticator with epigrams in Greek, Hebrew, Latin, Italian, Spanish, and French *in fronte libri*. . . . Not a page goes by without at least a bit of dictionary vocabulary, a quotation. . . . How they love to show that Saturn pissed wisdom into no one's head but theirs.[76]

Like the staging of the flagellation of Manfurio ("whipped," stripped, and given "fifty blows on the buttocks") in *Il Candelaio*,[77] the mock castration of the Pedant in one *commedia dell'arte* scenario enacts a symbolic chastening of the *commedia erudita*'s misappropriation of authority:

All the men come out, leading Cataldo, the pedant, in a nightshirt, tied with a strong rope. . . . Pedrolino, Arlecchino, and Burattino enter dressed in butchers' aprons and hog gelders' aprons, holding long knives and a large copper tub . . . intend[ing] to castrate him. [Driving] him away as a disgraceful example to all other pedant rogues and rascals like himself, [t]hen they happily discuss marriage preparations for Flaminia . . . and the comedy ends.[78]

After the pedant is chased naked from the city, comic order can be reaffirmed in the marriage of the amorous young couple.

For playwrights embracing the traditional "licence" of the stage (the place of uncontrolled speech, in England located in "the Liberties"),[79] the classic opposition between the scholar's devotion to study and the devotion to amorous pleasures could be a trope for the opposition between the learned book and the theatrical body fully enjoying its licence, for instance in *Love's Labour's Lost*, in the contrast between the pedant Holofernes (with his Latin and his orthographic prescriptions and his turgid drama) and the various courtiers, who quickly turn from books and scholarship to the freedoms of love, played out through the amorous masquerades of the play. *The Pilgrimage to Parnassus* could tease its Cambridge audience (boys in high adolescence, who were to keep to their books and not think of wenching) by showing Amoretto in his study, "*reading . . . verses out of Ovid*" which (paradoxically) inform him that "true learninge" lies not in books ("all books are dull") but in a woman's body:

> Loves cradle is betwixte her rising brest,
> Ther sucking Cupid feedes, and takes his rest:
> Touch not her mount of joy, it is devine,
> There Cupid grazes or els he would pine.
> Expect the world my poesie ere longe
> Where Ile comēnde her daintie quivering thighe,
> Sing of her foot in my sweet minstralsie.[80]

In the intensified satire of the learned woman in the seventeenth century (in plays like Chappuzeau's *Academy of Women* (1653) or Molière's *Learned Women* (1672)), one can read, at once, a bitterness that the "quivering thighe" and "mount of joy" might turn out, after all, to be appended to women who could read and think, and an attempt, more generally, to articulate the claims of the body in a theatre in the grip of the learned book. Molière could gently satirize the scholarly apparatus increasingly requisite in the drama. "The time will come to print my remarks on the plays that I will have written," he threatens, "and I do not despair of one day showing . . . that I can cite Aristotle and Horace," not to mention asking his friends for French or Latin or Greek verses to recommend his play: "for it should not be ignored that praise in Greek is marvellously effective at the front of a book."[81] But for him and his eighteenth-century inheritors, the dictionaries, the critics' commentaries, the glosses of scholars, citations from predecessors, prefaces on prefaces seemed to have overwhelmed the voice of the theatre. In Fielding's *Tragedy of Tragedies; or The Life and Death of Tom Thumb the Great*, the learned annotator H. Scriblerus Secundus has "for ten Years together read nothing" other than the play he is editing, "in which time, I think I may modestly presume, with the help of my *English* Dictionary, to comprehend all the Meanings of every Word in it."[82] The theatre had been, like Tom Thumb himself, swallowed by a great predator, the all-consuming press. Against the Scriblerus Secunduses, however, stood the theatre's declaration of freedom—not licence but a rule of liberty—resisting the "authorities," rejecting "the rule of the booke," embracing the natural and proper freedom of the stage.

6. Accurate Texts, Authoritative Editions

In his preface to the first Beaumont and Fletcher folio (1647), its publisher, Humphrey Moseley, presents his readers with a large volume: the collective product of two authors, well-wishers who contributed many pages of commendatory poems, editors, printers, and, not least, actors, whose participation was crucial to the textual history of the plays. "Now you have both All that was *Acted*, and all that was not; even the perfect full Originalls without the least mutilation," he writes, identifying the "Originalls" as the creations of both actors and authors: the authors' originals un-mutilated by the stage, and actors' originals unmutilated by print (Fig. 32).[1] Poised between two notions of the task of the edition—to bring the plays back to life, ani-mated once again by the printing press, or to offer a shrine to the authors, eternalized in the monumental book—Moseley's rhetorical invocation of the "Originalls" begins to turn him towards the latter. The volume, he explains, includes, in the "perfect full Originalls," "nothing but what is genuine" and "by these Authours," implicitly identifying the "original" creation with the dramatist-authors. Rather than reanimating the once living theatre (temporarily quieted during the Interreg-num), it offers a fixed monument, "now so compleate and finish'd, that the Reader must expect no future Alterations." The plays, once alterable "as occasion led" in the theatre, are now perfected in the folio, its editorial "completeness" measured by the authors' lives: "Here are no *Omissions*; you have not onely All I could get, but All that you must ever expect. For (besides those which were formerly printed) there is not any Piece written by these *Authours*, either Joyntly or Severally, but what are now publish'd to the World in this *Volume*." As if to offer, through the testimony of the authors themselves, a final imprimatur for his now perfected authorial volume, Moseley imagines them returning from the grave to bless the folio with their immor-tal approbation. "Were the *Authours* living (and sure they can never dye) they themselves would challenge neither more nor lesse then what is here published." Uniting end product (that approved in an imaginary future) with "Originall" (that created in an imaginary past), Moseley offers the "Originalls" their temporal other half in the now "finish'd" product, final expression of the immortal authors.

Having isolated the authors from the actors, Moseley continues, however, to worry about his decision to represent the volume as the product not of individual genius (the "*Genius*" represented in so many of the commendatory poems) but of theatrical collaboration:[2] "It was once in my thoughts to have Printed Mr. *Fletcher's* workes by themselves, because single & alone he would make a *Just Volume*," he writes. As it turns out, it is "single & alone" that Fletcher reigns—visually at least—over the vol-ume, for Moseley (as he explains) has been unable, hard as he has tried, to acquire a matching portrait of Beaumont. Its solitude an incarnation of Moseley's only

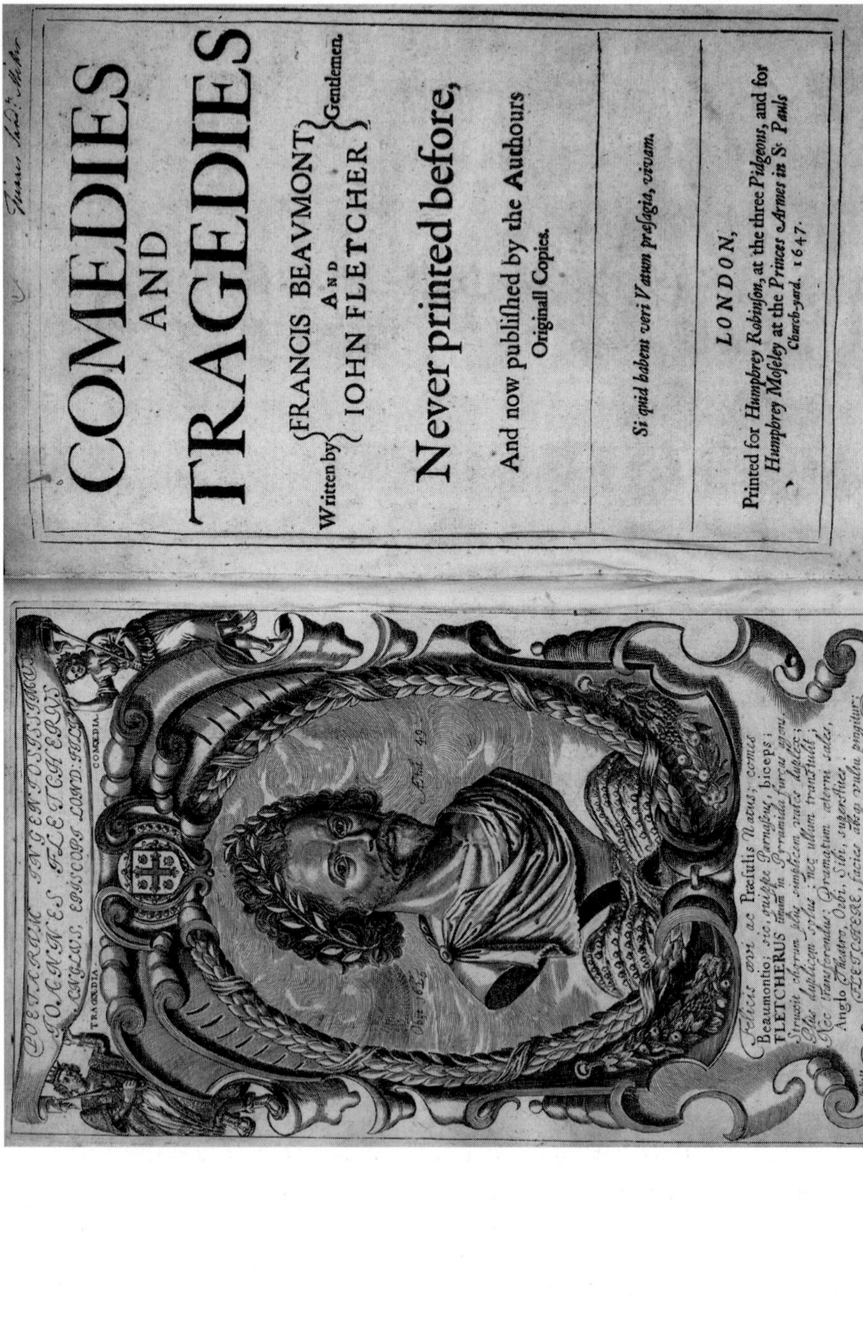

FIG. 32.   Beaumont and Fletcher's *Comedies and Tragedies* (1647), "now published by the Authours Originall Copies."

half-expressed view that the "Author" is not, after all, a plural kind of thing, the portait in turn generates Moseley's matching verbal portrait of the solitary author, Fletcher, at work creating the immutable masterpiece:

What ever I have seene of Mr. *Fletchers* owne hand, is free from interlining; and his friends affirme he never writ any one thing twice: It seemes he had that rare felicity to prepare and perfect all first in his owne braine; to shape and attire his *Notions*, to adde or loppe off, before he committed one word to writing, and never touched pen till all was to stand as firme and imutable as if ingraven in Brasse or Marble.[3]

The writing of the dramatic poem takes place in the private and interior space of the solitary author's "owne braine." The pen (like Fletcher's words standing firm) marks the first moment of externalization, the seminal act that will generate the (masculine) author's text. The use of the future tense ("all was to stand") suggests Moseley's anticipation of his own invisible role in the scene. The moment not of thought's transposition from brain through hand through pen to paper, but of that paper's metaphorical transmutation into "ingraven . . . Brasse or Marble" becomes the telos of the action of the interiorized drama. The "braine"—the space of the "I"—and the "hand"—the infallible mark of the identifiable and singular self—can become lasting only in "ingraven" form, in a folio that is as "firme and imutable as if ingraven in Brasse or Marble." Engraving here, as for so many in mid-seventeenth-century England, brings the theological metaphor (engraving in the book of life, engraving of the Ten Commandments) into the service of the secular, giving quasi-theological authority both to secular printing (here, under the shadow of the Interregnum) and to the secular author who is its first cause. As Moseley's edition transmutes the seminal act into permanent form, the author's mental intention bypasses the fleeting motions of actors to unite, coeternal, with the printed text.

THE TRADITION OF TEXTUAL EDITING

While there were medieval regulations dictating standards for the correction of texts, and while there was a rich discussion of principles of editing long before the sixteenth century, it is generally agreed that certain kinds of textual scholarship developed in late fifteenth- and sixteenth-century Europe in conjunction with the spread of the printing press. Print was driven by the scholarly need for well-edited texts; editing was driven by the commercial possibilities the press provided.[4] Many of the Italian scholars committed to proper textual editing in the sixteenth century could count dramatic editing as part of their work: Robortello, for instance, who produced a scholarly edition of Aeschylus a few years before he published *On the Art or Theory of Correcting Old Authors* (1557);[5] or Ariosto's son Virginio, who made new manuscripts available when Ariosto was being extensively revised and reprinted in the 1540s and 1550s.[6] From their work and the general culture of textual production, principles of textual editing (or at least its claims) filtered into ordinary dramatic publication. The press corrector of a 1588 edition of Aretino's plays advises readers to compare the various editions in order to note the superiority of his own.[7] An edition of Kyd's *Spanish Tragedy* from around 1592 proclaims that it is "Newly corrected and amended of such grosse faults as passed in the first impression."[8] The 1541 Paris edition of the *Catholic Works and Acts of the Apostles* boasts the fact that it is printed "in its entirety, overseen and corrected faithfully and according to the authentic truth" ("*vraye verite*"), and the 1525 Venice edition of Fernando de Rojas's *Celestina* that it is "newly translated," "newly corrected on the basis of all the other editions," "reduced to a more convenient format," and "adorned with things not found in any other edition."[9] The publisher Giorgio Greco explains, in the preface to his 1584 edition of Angelo Beolco's complete works, that he is producing the edition, "newly corrected and enlarged," because "the majority of these works [are] neither in Print nor in Bookstores any longer": "Nor did I . . . forgo any diligence in reprinting such a beautiful thing, correcting it as if no one had previously been inattentive and careless in doing so, [working from texts] that . . . had many important errors, not only on every page but in every line."[10]

If the earliest editors, then, asserted the "accuracy" and "authority" of their editions, they rarely did so with the modern presumption that texts were to follow the author's original intentions or conform to the author's stylistic peculiarities.[11] Sixteenth-century editions of Machiavelli, for instance, progressively stripped him of his Florentine regionalism and Latinism. When Girolamo Ruscelli re-edited the *Mandragola* for his *Commedie elette* in 1554, he altered Machiavelli's now slightly archaic Florentine, arguing that Machiavelli could not have made these "mistakes" himself but must have been corrupted by Florentine printers.[12] Bernardo Zucchetta, in his piracy of Ariosto around 1510, similarly chose to adapt Ariosto's Ferrara dialect to a Florentine vernacular.[13] Certainly, a few early editors of classical (and some vernacular) texts were working on the theory that an unchanging author's *urtext* could be found, transformed into editions that (returning to original manuscripts) would reflect the author's true intentions.[14] There were, unquestionably, claims like that of the 1572 edition of Giraldi's *Orbecche*, which proclaims itself a tragedy "newly corrected according to the original of the author."[15] But "accuracy" generally meant modernization, and most editors continued to correct in accordance with current usage: on the assumption that readers required not archaic language, but exemplary texts; on the assumption that an author's taste would, in any case, have evolved with time; on the assumption that play readers wanted the play "as acted."[16]

"Corrected texts," then, were almost invariably updated texts, altered in conformity with contemporary and local norms for spelling, grammar, usage, propriety, stage currency, and (often) political content. When Richard Jones describes, for instance, what he has done with the text of Marlowe's *Tamburlaine* in his 1590 edition, directing himself towards modern, sophisticated "Gentlemen Readers," he notes the attentiveness of his edition to what is "meet," whether or not Marlowe himself was equally attentive: "I have (purposely) omitted and left out some fond and frivolous Jestures, digressing (and in my poore opinion) far unmeet for the matter, which I thought, might seeme more tedious unto the wise. . . . Now, to be mixtured in print with such matter of worth, it would proove a great disgrace to so honorable and stately a historie."[17] The "*vraye verite*" according to which the *Catholic*

Works and Acts of the Apostles has been corrected denotes simultaneously textual correctness (usage, grammar) and authentic religious truth, eternal and yet, at the same time, cognizant of present controversy. In so far as the text is corrected according to the "*vraye verite*," it has been scoured for any dangerously interpolated Reformation heresies, reflecting the teachings of the true Church. "Veritable" texts may, then, be texts that reflect not the author's particularity, but eternal truth.

If plays were to reflect contemporary expectations about "meet" language, if correction was to perform a (morally) curative function, this often presupposed a collaborative reader, participating in the correction of the text. As in classic scholarly annotation, the reading of plays was a co-operative enterprise of editor and reader: discerning readers were to supply their own amendments.[18] Marston, for instance, calls on his readers' "discretion" in the "corrected" second quarto of *The Fawn* (1606): "Reader, know I have perused this coppy, to make some satisfaction for the first faulty impression: yet so urgent hath been my busines, that some errors have styll passed, which thy discretion may amend."[19] Through the power of correction the reader may displace both printer and author as "Authoritie," as Dekker's instructions in *The Magnificent Entertainment* (1604) suggest: "Some errours wander up and downe in these sheetes, under the Printers warrant: which notwithstanding may by thy Authoritie be brought in, and receive their due Correction."[20] In the ornate conceit that precedes his list of errata in the 1602 quarto of *Satiromastix*, Dekker theatricalizes the convention in order to stress the active role of the reader, present to the reading, which becomes an alternative kind of performance: "In steed of the Trumpets sounding thrice, before the Play begin: it shall not be amisse (for him that will read) first to beholde this short Comedy of Errors, and where the greatest enter, to give them in steed of a hisse, a gentle correction."[21] In the "correction" of dramatic works according to contemporary usage, dramatists and editors could reduplicate the interactive pedagogy or the free-spirited exchange of the theatre. With a tone of genteel negligence, the publisher of the 1607 quarto of Edward Sharpham's *The Fleire* explicitly grants his readers privilege to correct or not, as the spirit moves them: "If you finde anie errors by me committed correct them or neglect them."[22]

The ethical discourse underwriting the calls to the reader as press corrector stresses the way in which the reader's textual corrections may be a formal corollary of the reader's moral correction. For the printer of James Shirley's *The Bird in a Cage* (1633), readers' responses to the mechanics of the text become (in the unforgiving religious climate of the 1630s) a mirror in which they can see both their own sins of judgement and, through that self-reflection, learn mercy towards others. "Many other Errors, (though for the most part literall,) thou shalt meete," claims Shirley's printer, "which thou canst not with safetie of thy owne, interpret a defect in the Authors Judgement, since all bookes are subject to these misfortunes."[23] In his mock-dedication of the play to the anti-theatricalist William Prynne, Shirley himself ironically stresses Prynne's uncharitableness towards error, offering Prynne up as negative exemplar to the true reader (who may, with Shirley, forgivingly recognize the error of Prynne's views): "Many faults have escaped the Presse," writes Shirley to Prynne, "which your Judgement will no sooner find, than your Mercie correct, by which you shall teach others a Charity to your owne Volumes, though they be all *Errata.*"[24] In providing amendment of a linguistic kind, then, the reader could experience metonymically the kind of moral amendment that the work as a whole (in the theatre or in print) was intended to provide: editions called on readers to correct themselves.[25]

Corrective and ongoingly corrigible, the text was not to be driven by the author, but the author created by the text. This is not to say that a conception of authorship at the centre of the work was irrelevant, even in the period before printing: such a concept, in fact, was built into literary culture long before the sixteenth century. The celebrity of late-medieval "poets" like Lydgate or Skelton reminds us that "poet" had long been an important label for certain writers.[26] In the fifteenth century, the semantic field covered by the word "author" and its variants was already starting to spread (from indicating an authority to indicating a more general literary producer).[27] John Rastell could print *Magnificence* in 1533 as *A goodly Interlude and a mery, devysed and made by mayster Skelton poet laureate, late deceasyd* precisely because it had become possible for a "deviser" and "maker" to be, if not yet an author, at least a "poet."

It is, however, equally important, if we are to understand the presuppositions of early dramatic editing, to mark its distance from the modern concept of authorship, to recall that dramatic works were (until perhaps the end of the sixteenth century) generally circulated without dramatists' names, and only sporadically circulated with names after that, to remind ourselves that such naming—and the kind of editorial work that came to follow it—was an after-effect of a certain kind of celebrity, not its precondition.[28] The late medieval *actor* (mere writer of texts) was not the late medieval *auctor* or *author* (authority and creator of works).[29] Whether Rastell was himself the author, compiler, translator, or mere printer of *The Four Elements*, he was (in his view) not quite a poet and so did not identify himself as such. In a culture in which writing and rewriting, inventing and compiling were not clearly distinguished, in which most literary producers were marked as "composers" or "compilers" or "finders" or (most tellingly) "actors" (enacting others' texts by writing them), to identify an individual as author of a work—where there was no identifiable authority on the subject—did not always make sense. The *History of the Destruction of Troy the Great* (1484) may have been "arranged for actors and composed by Jacques Milet," *The Representation of the Prodigal Son* (1500) "composed by Master Castellano Castellani," *A tragedie or enterlude, manifesting the chiefe promises of God unto man* (1577) "compyled by John Bayle."[30] But the naming of the plays seems to displace their composers.

Even where there was an identifiable author, authorship/authority was to be shared: with patrons; with sources; with printers; with other "authors." Fernando de Rojas refers, in the "prologue" to the 1507 revision of his *La Celestina*, to "the first author" of the play (like him, only one in the series who have written versions of *La Celestina*).[31] Playwright-actor-manager ("Actor," "Auctor"), printer, and patron shared title pages, for instance that for the *Farce of the World and Moral* (1524), "by the *Actor* . . . who is Fernan Lopez de Yanguas: which will be dedicated to the Illustrious and thus Magnificant Lady, the Senora Dona Juana d'Cuniga."[32] The most important thing about the comedy *Eutychia* is not that it is by Nicola Grasso but that it is "transcribed from the copy of the magnifico Messer Hieronymo Staccoli, Gentleman of Urbino."[33] We have already seen the collection of saints' plays published in 1541 as:

The First Volume of the Catholic Works and Acts of the Apostles compiled in writing by Saint Luke . . . With several histories inserted in it of the deeds of the Caesars. And the displays of the figures of the Apocalypse seen by Saint John Zebedee . . . under Caesar Domitian, with the cruelties of Nero and those of Domitian. The whole overseen and corrected according to the authentic truth, and performed by actors in Paris. . . . Sold by Arnoul and Charles les Angeliers.[34]

Between the apostles and the Caesars and the actors and the booksellers and the voice of the authentic truth (the maker of makers, the *real* maker of the play), the author is nowhere to be found.

MAKING THE AUTHOR THROUGH PRINT

Conventions for the identification of dramatists in playbooks, where there was any such identification, continued to be in flux throughout the Renaissance and, in various ways, long after. In the fifteenth century, the person responsible for writing or compiling or editing or publishing a text might be identified in the first lines or at the end of a text or in a colophon or not at all; in the sixteenth and seventeenth centuries, on a title page or instead at the end of a dedication (sometimes with initials only), in a preface or a prologue, or again, not at all.[35] Publishers and the names of patrons, troupes, and theatres continued to take a prominent place in title pages, the 1594 quarto of *Titus Andronicus* (for instance) accumulating the names of its distinguished companies: "As it was Plaide by the Right Honourable the Earle of *Darbie*, Earle of *Pembrooke*, and Earle of *Sussex* their Servants."[36] Many individually published plays written for the professional theatres were still published without dramatists' names on their title pages.[37] Where there *was* a title-page designation, a play might be (as in the quarto of Chapman's *Memorable Maske* (1613)) "Supplied, Aplied [*sic*], Digested, and written, By" the playwright.

Nevertheless, whether or not the commerce of print was a necessary precondition for the rise of the modern author (as has often been argued), print became an important vehicle for the representation of the Renaissance dramatist: as writer ("written by . . ."), as poet, as authority, as "author."[38] Dramatic title pages began, in the sixteenth century, to blazon the names of their famous authors in large type, providing labels or portraits in an attempt to infuse literary function with social position: Robert Garnier is (on the title pages to the earliest editions of his *Tragedies*) both tragedian and "Counselor to the King and to Monseigneur, only brother of his Majesty, Lieutenant General Prosecutor" (etc.); Isabella Andreini is (as the portrait accompanying her 1588 *Myrtilla* declares) "comica gelosa," both actor in the Gelosi troupe and (in an attempt to elevate the former) comic pastoralist, academician, winner of literary laurels (as her dedication insists).[39] For playwrights for the professional theatre, title-page identification generally came later but came nonetheless. Where early Shakespeare quartos (the 1594 *Titus Andronicus*, the 1598 *1 Henry IV*) do not carry his name, the 1598 quarto of *Love's Labour's Lost* is "newly corrected and augmented *By W. Shakespere*," and *2 Henry IV* (1598) is "written by William Shakespeare."[40] Where *Edward the Fourth* (1599) does not carry Heywood's name, *A Woman Killed with Kindness* (1607) is "written by Tho: Heywood."[41] On the title page of Jonson's *Comicall Satyre of Every Man Out of His Humor* (1600), "B. J." is "the Author" of the play. Plays could (in Richard Brome's phrase) be "authoriz'd by the Authors name."[42]

The designation "author" for contemporary playwrights (appearing in the sixteenth century but increasing in frequency in the seventeenth)[43] signals a significant conceptual shift. Living dramatists, who (as we have seen) began self-consciously shaping even their theatrically oriented productions for print, could take on the grand demeanour of the dead. To be in print was to be an "author," and to be an author was to dignify the craft of play-making: as Molière was to write (half ironically), his first publication (the *Précieuses ridicules*) brought him into the ranks of "Messieurs the authors."[44] Whether printing could in fact contribute to the canonization of the dramatic poet or merely reflect a reputation constituted by theatrical success, we have seen (in Chapter 2) how seventeenth-century dramatists learned to produce editions in which their *œuvre* was represented as worthy of literary immortality. "Since man cannot be satisfied with the spoken word alone but must, with all industry and art, leave behind a printed memorial of himself and his work," explains the preface to even a collection as collaborative as the *commedia dell'arte* scenarios published by Flaminio Scala in 1611, "so it is that Signor Flavio . . . wished to leave to the world, not simply his words and his beautiful conceits, but his plays which at all times and in all places brought great honor."[45] As the obelisks and laurels on the title page to Jonson's 1616 *Workes* are meant to remind readers, the dramatic edition is legacy, the immortal "Remaines" of the ever-living author.[46] In fashioning a grand edition of his *Théâtre* in folio as vehicle for his new orthography half a century after Jonson (followed by a more portable edition in octavo the following year), Corneille was self-consciously invoking the ancients (Seneca, Sophocles, Terence produced in like format), seeking to consecrate his works in a permanent literary monument.[47]

At the same time, the "correction" of the work was coming to be determined by an attempt to reconstruct the author. Dramatic editions were increasingly advertised as "corrected" or "enlarged" or "reviewed by the Authour": Georg Mauritius' *Comedy of All Trades* (1606) "with great care newly overseen by the Author and variously corrected and prepared for print"; Antoine de Montchrestien's *Tragedies* (1606) in a "new edition augmented by the Author"; Francesco Andreini's *Braveries of Captain Spavento* (1610) "corrected by the Author himself"; John Ford's *The Golden Meane* (1614) "Enlarged by the first Authour" in its second edition.[48] When Jonson proclaims on the title page of the 1600 quarto of *Every Man Out of His Humor* that this edition offers the play "as it was *first* composed by the author B. J.,"[49] he declares the author's primal act, the act of "first compos[ing]," to be the proper basis of textual authority.

That plays were repeatedly advertised as "corrected" or "enlarged" or "reviewed by the Authour" set a standard for textual editing generally. If Richard Jones found it "meet" to erase "some fond and frivolous Jestures" from Marlowe's *Tamburlaine* for the sake of "so honourable and stately a history,"[50] it was now the author's intentions, not abstract linguistic standards, that were to be the basis for the authoritative edition: Lope de Vega's *Twelve Comedias* (1617), for instance, are identified as "taken from his originals by [Lope] himself";[51] in Thomas Nabbes's *Plays* (1640), *Microcosmus* and *The Unfortunate Mother* are printed (as their title pages tell the reader) "according to the intention of the Author."[52] The accompanying change in assumptions about the function of the dramatist's name in the labelling and selling of the play ran counter to the norms which (as we have seen) generally governed dramatic production. Since performed works were (in the professional theatre at least) more often than not the products of collaboration, defining authorship on the page was in some sense unnatural.[53] Even late into the seventeenth century, printed editions could attempt to represent the complexity of collaborative arrangements: linearly (*The Witch of Edmonton* is "By divers well-esteemed Poets; William Rowley, Thomas Dekker, John Ford, &c");[54] or graphically in two dimensions with the brackets that became common in early seventeenth-century English drama (used in the title page for Middleton and Rowley's *A Faire Quarrel*, for instance, in which the woodcut of the quarrelling gentlemen points at once to the play itself and to its bracketed gentlemen authors).[55] But even while title pages continued to represent multiple authorship and multiple authority—to honour patrons and printers and principles alongside playwrights, to represent the play's theatricality—the imperatives of print (the authorial authentication readers seemed to demand and the authorial proprietorship the needs of commerce seemed to require) created a pressure towards individuating authorship. Alongside the theatrical text (and in counterpoint to it) editors and dramatists came to produce editions inspired by the claims to authorial "correctness" and "accuracy" that were so central to the institution of print. The normative (if not the dominant) dramatic text became the individual dramatic author's text, both founded in and reinforcing the early modern notion of the author, unsullied by either the theatre or the prostitute press.

The tendency towards authorial individuation was urged along, gently or not so gently, by dramatists themselves, increasingly (as we have seen) seeing their own plays into print and worrying over the correction of their own editions: "a Printer worthy of his profession is bringing this to you, Dear Reader," writes Alexandre Hardy of the fourth volume of his *Theatre* (1626), promising that it is "as correct as a first edition can be," that it contains "no notable transposition, no perverted meaning . . . no important omissions dismember[ing] the body of the work," and that a second printing "will pass the sponge over" whatever errors might have formerly appeared.[56] In using print to reproduce lines left out in performance—lines "as they should have been delivered, not as they were" (as Dekker writes in his *Magnificent*

Entertainment (1604))[57]—dramatists both drew on and reinforced assumptions about the use of the text to reproduce the author's conception, distinct from theatrical performance or collaboration with other theatre practitioners. When Jonson tells the reader that the "Booke" of his *Sejanus* "is not the same with that which was acted on the publike Stage, wherein a second Pen had good share," and that (pretending reluctance to usurp another's work) he has purged it of the intruder's pen, he is implicitly setting up an individuating norm for the dramatic book in contrast to the collaborative norms of the theatre, reflecting the sense that there is something unnatural in the indiscriminate mingling of authorial hands.[58]

If, then, theatrical production continued to be collaborative, printed editions tended to turn the individual into the basic unit of dramatic production. Moseley, for instance, feels he needs to justify printing Beaumont and Fletcher together in one folio: "It was once in my thoughts to have Printed Mr. *Fletcher's* workes by themselves, because single & alone he would make a *Just Volume*: But since never parted while they lived, I conceived it not equitable to seperate their ashes."[59] In his dedicatory poem to the folio, Jaspar Maine similarly needs to reassure the reader that Beaumont and Fletcher were individually worthy, authors who could equally have been printed separately. Not "out of mutuall want, or emptinesse," writes Maine,

> Did you conspire to go still twins to th'Presse:
> But what thus joyned you wrote, might have come forth
> As good from each, and stored with the same worth
>
> .   .   .   .
>
> For that you could write singly, we may guesse
> By the divided peeces which the Presse
> Hath severally sent forth.[60]

The "worth" of Beaumont and Fletcher's collective *œuvre* can be measured only against the worth of the "divided peeces," measured only against the hypothetical worth of each author's individual *œuvre*. Joint publication might be a stay against generative "want" or "emptinesse" (an association intensified by the homoerotic overtones in the description of the two "joyned," who go "twins to th'-Presse").[61] But against such "want" stands the autonomously generating author, whole and entire.

The representation of singular authorship and theatrical collaboration in print continued to be in flux throughout the seventeenth century. Just as Moseley wavers on the borderline between the collaborative norm and the individuating tendency of seventeenth-century printing (seeming sometimes to treat the volume as Fletcher's, "single & alone," sometimes as the collaborative product that it is), the edition as a whole equivocates between the representation of the collective theatrical enterprise and the recreation of the author as solitary dramatic poet. Moseley promises his readers that he is including only Beaumont and Fletcher's "genuine" works: "here is not any thing *Spurious* or *impos'd*." And yet in a "Postscript" (*sic*), the actors explain that (in a moment of significant repression): "We forgot to tell the *Reader*, that some *Prologues* and *Epilogues* (here inserted) were not written by the *Authours* of this

Volume; but made by others on the *Revivall* of severall *Playes*."[62] The "definitive" 1682 edition of the works of Molière equivocates similarly. The editors are scornful of earlier editions that failed to purge Molière's theatrical collaborationists. The *Imaginary Invalid*, for instance, "was so badly printed in previous Editions that, in addition to several Scenes, the entire third Act was not Monsieur Molière's at all: we are giving it to you here corrected according to the Original of the Author."[63] But, at the same time, they have decided to include Guillaume de Brécourt's *The Shadow of Molière* in *The Works of Molière*:

Even though this play is not written by M. de Molière, we thought that it was appropriate, for the satisfaction of the reader, to put it at the end of his works as was done in previous editions, in order not to suppress a play that is entirely to the credit of this illustrious author, and that has so much to do with several characters in his plays.[64]

If the classic dramatic edition continued to include writings seen as contributing to "the credit of [the] author," it was nonetheless driven by a teleology of the posthumous *œuvre* with a singular author as its organizing principle. The work was identified by reference to the author and the author identified by reference to the work, the *œuvre* that created the author as an entity: the Sieur de la Porteneille's pastoral comedy *Carlina* (1626) is (as the title page announces) "invented by A. Gaillard . . . with several other plays by the same author";[65] plays belonged to "the works of" the "author." With the name of the author on the title page as insignia for the play's place in the social order, the author collection could become the normative vehicle for the drama, conceived of and produced as dignified monument to the *œuvre* of the dramatist. That (for Jaspar Maine) the Beaumont and Fletcher collection is ontologically prior to the individual plays that make it up (plays published are not gathered into a collection, but instead those separately published are "divided" from it, "severally sent forth" in a sort of poetic exile) suggests the new normativity of the authorial collection as organizing principle for the drama.

The drama in the collected edition was an expression, then, not of the actors or even the story represented, but of an "author" conceived as coherent amalgam of body and mind, material product and spirit. In the prefatory poem to Antoine de Montchrestien's *Tragédies* (1601) (on the verso side of the frontispiece portrait), the plays are described as the painted image of the author's "mind": "His Body & his Mind are painted in this work, | One in this portrait, the other in what he wrote."[66] When James Shirley affirms the Beaumont and Fletcher folio to be a direct representation of Beaumont and Fletcher's "Authentick witt," authenticity is proven by the book's purity from actors' interpolations, the "indiscretion[s]" that might have "branded this Paper." Whether at "Blackfriers" or in the book, it is no longer the play (the history) but Beaumont and Fletcher themselves who are "presented" or "set forth."[67] The author's singular "hand" (physiological correlate of mind) becomes central to the understanding of the true text (Shakespeare's "mind and hand went together"; "what ever I have seene of Mr. *Fletchers* owne hand, is free from interlining"),[68] key to the pure trajectory from brain to hand to page. The Accademici

Intrepidi feels it must apologize for publishing Guidubaldo Bonarelli's *Favola pastorale* (1609), "which unfortunately never having been appreciated by the author was not . . . perfected in all its parts by his own hand."[69]

The common trope of authorship as paternity or masculine sexual authority underwrote the normative conception of individuated male literary authorship (as well as marking female authorship as an oxymoron).[70] Heywood classically invokes the trope in his preface to *The English Traveller* (identifying named authorship with acknowledged paternity): "I . . . thought it not fit that it should passe as *filius populi*, a Bastard without a Father to acknowledge it."[71] If the masculine author must restore paternal order by acknowledging his charges, the wayward text may be either bastard or wanton female, to be reclaimed or abandoned to her fate, as Lope de Vega imagines her in his dedication to *The Living Dead* (in the typical figuration of the pirated play as prostitute): "There is no courtesan who has run to Italy, the Indies, or Mecca . . . as disfigured as a poor comedia that has run through villages, servants, and men who live by stealing them and padding them."[72] The stationer's preface to Thomas Sackville and Thomas Norton's *Gorboduc* offers a long narrative describing the fate of the lovely wayward manuscript which (compared with a woman, in an extended simile) was "never intended by the authors thereof to be published" but was violated by a rapacious printer. (The text, "exceedingly corrupted," had been brought back into her own house again and is now ready properly to go abroad publicly, this time escorted by the legitimate authors.)[73]

If, however, mistresses needed escorts and orphans needed fathers, where authorship was figured as patriarchy (the basis for masculine inheritance), too many masters was not a good thing. Most playtexts that came out of the playhouse may have been collaboratively created (multiply fathered *filii populi*), but the individual dramatist collection could offer authenticity (a proper lineage) to the "fatherless" products of the playhouse. If the author-father was necessarily singular, the *œuvre* itself had to be the expression of its singular producer: coherent and total, complete and final, with neither gaps nor intrusions from alien authorial hands. The collected edition was to be a unified book, its plays "cur'd and perfect of their limbes," a means of reconstituting the body of the (usually dead) author in the reconstructive textual corpus.[74] The editor of Jakob Ayrer's posthumous *Opus Thaeatricum* (1618) describes how Ayrer's scattered writings were "found, with care collected, placed in their proper order and gathered into a first volume," re-embodying the author's "profound Spirit" in a lasting monument in place of a "Pyramid" in his memory.[75] The collection is, necessarily, complete: to leave out a work would be (in the words of a late quarto *Hamlet*) to "wrong the incomparable Author."[76] "And as here's nothing but what is genuine and [the Authours']," writes Moseley, "so you will finde here are no *Omissions*; you have not oneley All I could get, but All that you must ever expect."[77] To seal off the tomb containing "the *Ashes* of the Authors"[78]—to say "you have . . . All that you must ever expect"—was to put the authors' ghosts to rest. The poetic body, having been scattered to the winds, disseminated by thieving poets, was to be resurrected:

So shall we joy, when all whom Beasts and Wormes
Had turn'd to their owne substances and formes,
Whom Earth to Earth, or fire hath chang'd to fire,
Wee shall behold more then at first intire
As now we doe, to see all thine, thine owne
In this thy Muses Resurrection.[79]

Permanent and fixed outside of time, the collection implicitly or explicitly repu-diated the temporality of the theatre. If to be "display'd in Print" was (as Edward Howard has it) to "put on the greater formality of Authors," formality required that the drama be "divested of the life of Action."[80] In the classic *mise en page* of the sev-enteenth century, the timeless image or scene echoed and reinforced the timelessness of the dramatic poets' tragedies and comedies, removed from the fleetingness of per-formance, preserved like those of the ancients for centuries to come. The Shake-speare rendered both in the first folio portrait and in Jonson's famous poem accompanying it is no longer player and playhouse writer, but poet, his "wit" frozen by the "Graver" and "writ in brasse," gazing with placid dignity from the pages of the "Book" towards which Jonson directs the reader ("Reader, looke | Not on his Picture, but his Booke").[81]

If "Originall Copies" were generally playhouse copies in the early seventeenth century ("Mr. William Shakespeare's Comedies, Histories, & Tragedies. Published according to the True Originall Copies"),[82] the inclusion of the claim in collections dedicated to the works of a single author began to shift the meaning of the phrase. However much Moseley equivocates in the preface to the Beaumont and Fletcher folio, the title page insists that the plays are "now published by the Authours Origi-nall Copies."[83] Consciousness of the venue and lineage of early editions and empha-sis on the significance of the "original" pervades the prefaces of seventeenth- and eighteenth-century editions. The editor of Guidubaldo Bonarelli's *Opere* (1640), for instance, describes the previous "deformed" editions of Bonarelli's works, and explains that he is using the "ancient originals."[84] Editions stretched to outdo their predecessors: the 1656 edition of Massinger, Middleton, and Rowley's *The Old Law* is (in the hyperbolic phrasing of the title page) "more exactly Printed then ever before." Sir William Davenant's *Works* "Consist[s] of Those which were formerly Printed, and those which he design'd for the Press: Now Published Out of the Authors Originall Copies."[85] In giving the public an edition of the plays of Molière "corrected on the original by the author" himself, the editors of the 1682 *Works of Molière* have (as they explain) "restored" the "comedies of this famous author" to their "purity."[86]

THE GENIUS RESTORED

The author had intervened in the authority of history. Moseley needs to imagine the return of the dead authors to "approve" his edition—to verify that the "Originalls" are indeed "full" and "perfect." When he writes that he "had the Originalls from such as received them from the *Authours* themselves," that "by Those, and none other, I publish this Edition," he invokes the growing identification of "originals" with authors, calling on an authenticating chain that tracks "originals" through intermediaries back to authors: the "legitimate originals" are the authors' (not the collaborative product of actors and playwrights); the "first compos[ition]" is that which sprung "from the *Authours* themselves."[87] In the search for the author at the origin of the edition, the biographical had become the foundation for the biblio-graphical. Dramatist biographies joined dramatist portraits as regular features in author collections, the iconic author "effigy" (traditionally added to collected edi-tions after the death of the author) expanded into the narrative of the life of the liv-ing poet: the 1640 edition of Bonarelli's posthumous *Opere* brags about its inclusion of a "Life of the Author"; the *True Fifth Part of the Comedies* of Calderón is pub-lished (in reaction to a surreptitious *Fifth Part*) with an essay on the "Fame, life and writings of Calderon" in 1682; Shakespeare's works are published by Rowe in 1709 "Revis'd and corrected, with an account of the life and writings of the author."[88] Edi-tors, justifying their work, began to invoke a bibliographical-authenticating chain, linking an edition through earlier editions back to the *ur-edition*, made up of "Authors' Originals." The editor of the 1711 Beaumont and Fletcher, for instance, devotes several pages to describing the history of Beaumont and Fletcher editions, from the conditions surrounding the publication of the early quartos to those sur-rounding the publication of the first and second folios, pointing to the editor's efforts to trace editorial choices back to the authors themselves.[89] By the middle of the eighteenth century, the norm of biographical reconstruction as the basis for biblio-graphical perfection was essentially in place.[90]

None of this is to say that seventeenth- and eighteenth-century dramatic editing inevitably attempted to reconstruct authorial intention or even to note the author's existence. I have already noted that first-run plays often did not carry the dramatist's name on the title page, that most printed plays were very much *theatrical* plays (reflecting what dramatists wrote for specific theatres and actors), that more typical than *The Works of Shakespeare . . . Collated and Corrected by the former Editions* (as Pope's 1725 edition proclaims) was *Macbeth, a Tragedy: with all the Alterations, Amendments, Additions, and New Songs. As it is now acted at the Duke's Theatre*. But a conceptual norm of biographical-bibliographical coherence was established, on which the lively counter-tradition of self-consciously theatrical play publication depended (Vanbrugh has "dealt fairly" in the printed version of *The Relapse* and "not sunk a Sylable" of what was said "upon the Stage";[91] Gozzi is having his plays "printed just as they were performed").[92] Editors either had to conform to that norm or actively to resist it.

In the last chapters, I will discuss the kind of resistance inherent in the eighteenth-and nineteenth-century theatricalist counter-tradition. But theatrical disfigura-tion—as the enemy of authorial editing—became an insistent theme in eighteenth-century discussions of the dramatic edition: the works of the author were to be purified of the temporal exigencies of event and action, preserved in the timeless realm of the authoritative edition. And what remained as a desideratum behind the most literary of dramatic editions from the eighteenth century on was the idea of a single, unitary author, an authoritative genius whose intentions—linguistic or dramatic—the printed text could represent in unadulterated form.

If the typical variorum edition, emerging from the eighteenth-century search for the dramatic "original," presupposed an author who could be found by peeling away the layers of theatrical interpolation, it was, at the same time, a monument to a dramatist who could be extricated from the false and corrupting accumulations of print. Pope is disgusted by the theatrical transcribers, who, "thro' the[ir] ignorance," insert "the notes of direction to the *Property-men* for their *Moveables*, and to the *Players* for their *Entries*," but he is equally disgusted by "the many blunders and illiteracies of the first Publishers of [Shakespeare's] works"—by the "two or more editions" of any given Shakespeare play "by different printers, each of which has whole heaps of trash different from the other."[93] Corrections themselves seemed to breed errors. Texts contradicted one another, refusing to obey unequivocal rules of authenticity. Editions took on their own unstable theatricalism. In the end, the true dramatic author stood alone against the illiterate "Publishers of his works"—as against the illiterate actors—the dramatist's "original" the model of "accuracy" towards which the editor must strive.[94] Despite the layers of multiplying errors, the imaginary original governed more powerfully than ever as a norm, the hypothetical author's existence receding backward in time to the manuscript, in which the true moment of authorship might still be found—an original yet untouched by theatrical and printerly vitiation. The manuscript—free of the corruptions of print—was an expression of the poet's very thoughts, magic instrument which could conjure the evanescent authorial presence, authenticity incarnate, infallible talisman and evidence of the author through the authenticating "hand." The true poet who never "blotted" a line, the genius in the moment of divine inspiration—these could produce the manuscript, born, like Athena, in a flash from the author's brain. What were once "foul sheets" could become authenticating documents: "Autograph Copies," touched by the hand of the author.

THE SENSES OF MEDIA

7. The Sense of the Senses: Sound, Gesture, and the Body on Stage

In one of the "*lazzi*" developed by a *commedia dell'arte* troupe travelling in Bavaria in the mid-sixteenth century, as Pantolone is singing sweet songs to the beautiful Isabella, a servant girl, deaf to music, blithely empties her chamber pot out of the window where its contents land, predictably, on his head. In another, the Doctor administers Arlecchino an enema, which unfortunately leaves him pregnant. As Pantaloon watches Zany tickle the Lady Cornelia between the legs, a flower blooms from his groin (Fig. 33). When a servant girl cries for water for Turchetta who has fainted, Pulcinella comes running, first with rosewater, then with jasmine water, then with orange water, then with mint water, then with lily water and finally, with "the water distilled by our rod," which instantly revives her.[1] Characters are baked into pies, sob into shared bowls of macaroni, chew on their shoes, drink up shavings from their barbers' soapy water, gobble down body parts, from their own feet to their dissociated brains (Arlecchino eats his so he won't lose them).[2] The enema recurs, the giant sausages, the urine poured on wandering minstrels or maidens, which miraculously brings forth children from the earth. Urine is life force. Phalluses have characters all their own. Implicitly opposing the learned and erudite text to the helpless spontaneities of the flesh, the *lazzi* and scenarios invert the hierarchy of the senses, transferring the language of words into the language of gesture, and the language of gesture into the language of expressive sound emitted haplessly by the unconscious body. Whenever Isabella runs mad, the *loci communi* of her mad rants are a frenzied concoction of the erudite and the earthily obscene: the heavenly spheres, Aristotle's sayings, the sighs of Venus, the excretions of the gods. "Jove is going to sneeze, and Saturn is going to break wind," cries the lovely Isabella, playing a Turkish harem girl converted to Christianity: "The soul according to Aristotle is the spirit which was spread by casks of muscatel from Mount Fiascone, and for that reason, the rainbow was seen doing service for the island of England, which could not piss."[3] The free play of the senses ushers in the reign of nonsense, which must run its course through a torrent of tongues before comic closure can be achieved (via the rapid-fire conclusion of half a dozen marriage plots), and Isabella return to her "senses" and her "self."[4] The *commedia* is not just for seeing scenes and hearing words, but a place for all the senses (the tactile, the olfactory, the gustatory, and that sixth sense in the groin). It is the place where "the senses" run riot over "sense" and can promise only the uncertain expulsion of nonsense and the no-more-than-tenuous return to one's senses, properly tamed.

LA DONA CORNELIA.

TIFFIA.

PANTAION.

ZANY.

NODET
LE TAVERNIER.

GRIN-   GOLET.

Fɪɢ. 33. Pantaloon, Donna Cornelia, and Zany in a scene from the *commedia dell'arte*
(*c.*1577).

THEATRE AND THE RENAISSANCE HIERARCHY OF THE SENSES

If Renaissance anti- and pro-theatricalists often held radically opposed views on politics, religion, and aesthetics, they agreed on at least one thing: theatres were places that spoke to the senses. Anti-theatricalists had the traditional complaints: actors were liars and cross-dressers; theatres were hotbeds of lust (or, at the least, places of idleness and drunkenness); God forbade the making of images; spectacle was trickery, exhibitionism, seduction, idolatry.[5] But they were perhaps most of all disturbed by the senses run amok there, the ways in which seeing and hearing and those other dangerously indescribable senses could transform the devout and asensuous reader into a creature of raging sensual consciousness. If "with slovenly talke" plays could "hur[t] the eares of the chast hearers," "with Amorous gesture" they could also "woun[d] the eye."[6] If Isabella could speak scurrilities and bare her lovely breasts in her madness, in so doing she could remind spectators of the diabolical pleasures of touch.

Pro-theatricalists also based their claims for theatre's special place in large part on its sensory power: its pedagogic and aesthetic force seemed to lie in its very sensuousness, in its power to sway the reason through the senses, in the fact that (in Robortello's words) it "acts upon the senses."[7] For Trissino, the pleasures of comedy come "through the senses, that is, from seeing, hearing, touching, tasting, and smelling."[8] For the Abbé D'Aubignac, "the beautiful Representations of the Stage . . . fall more under [the] senses" than those of books, teaching philosophic lessons thus more accessible to the masses.[9] Practitioners knew how to stir all the senses: "On a warm day," explains the German theatrical architect Joseph Furttenbach, the scene might produce "a splendid rain of water perfumed with rose and other odors, dripping through many holes bored through the upper floor but only over the heads of the most prominent ladies and noble youths. . . . Or, instead of rain, a sugared hail can be produced of sugared confections of coriander, almond, cinnamon, etc."[10] Some viewed theatres as festering grounds for the lowest of the senses: the tactile and the gustatory and the poisonous olfactory—"the breath that comes from the uncapable multitude" could "poison . . . the most sententious Tragedy that ever was written," wrote John Webster.[11] But they were also palaces for the higher senses of hearing and seeing. The senses could, after all, serve the faculty of mind, which was, in turn, the agent of moral conscience. "This venture delights the eyes, the ears, and the mind," writes Pierre de Larivey of his comedy, *The Widow* (*c.*1579) (based on Nicolò Buonaparte's *La Vedova*), explaining—with a reminder to the spectators of their own place as spectacular objects in the playhouse—that it delights

the eyes, by the variety of actions and people presented, and by the assemblage of such honorable lords and lovely ladies, such as yourselves, who enrapture the spirit through the contemplation of your perfections; the ears, by the pleasing and sententious speeches that are included in it; and the mind, because, comedy being the mirror of our life, the old learn to keep themselves from that which seems ridiculous in an old man, the young to control themselves in love, the women to preserve their honesty, and fathers and mothers to keep a close eye on the business of their households.[12]

If eyes and ears were the orifices into which "amorous gesture" and "slovenly talk" could enter, only through the eyes and the ears could virtue learn its own defence.

For both pro- and anti-theatricists, the contrast between text and performance served to focus discussions of the use and abuse of the senses in the theatre. In the transformation of action into text, the spectator's senses could be tamed (as anti-theatricalists saw it), or shrunk to a mere shadow of their theatrical selves (as pro-theatricalists saw it). The pro- and anti-theatricalist debate was a response, of course, to the resurgence of secular theatre with the growth of the professional stage generally in the latter half of the sixteenth century. But it was also attributable to the tensions, during the period, between text and spectacular or aural effect. If anti-theatricalists generally feared the incarnate body and honoured the (scriptural) text, the spectacular body was the incarnate body in concentrated form. The dramatic text, by contrast, might offer a rendering of *the* text: numerous plays "were penned only to be . . . read, not acted," writes William Prynne, "their subjects being al serious, sacred, divine, not scurrilous wanton or prophan."[13] Anti-theatricalists classically stressed the differences between reading and going to a spectacle, where an otherwise pure text would be likely to be supplemented by "effeminate amorous, lustfull gestures, complements, kisses, dalliances, or embracements" (as Prynne fretted).[14] But pro-theatricalists classically stressed the same difference: drama was not meant to be dead letters on the page; it was meant to convey "soule," "spirit," "life," and "action" in the "doing" that was the very essence of drama.[15]

The distinctions Renaissance commentators made between text and performance played themselves out against the broader discussion of the differences among aesthetic media generally (their different conditions of production, their different modes of reception, their relative values) and against the discussion of the comparison of the arts. Like the analysis of the difference between text and performance, the analysis of the various arts was often framed in terms of the senses: vision and its objects (pictures, scenes, motion); hearing and its objects (rhythm, metre, language as sound, music, noise); cognition and its objects (plot, discourse, thought). Just as painting, for instance, was both like and unlike poetry (as Renaissance commentators insistently pointed out through Horace's classic comparison, *ut pictura poesis*), so picture and poetry were both like and unlike theatrical performance: performance could be a "speaking Picture" or, in the dumb show for instance, a "mute Poesie" (as Jonson put it, following Plutarch).[16] If the comparison of text and performance informed the comparison of the arts, so the comparison of the arts informed what commentators said about the differences between text and performance, between reading a drama and being present at a stage play. Where performance might be a "picture" with "life [put] into" it, the printed play might be a "dumbe show" (in Robert Armin's metaphor).[17] The transfer from stage to page could be cast as a transfer from ears to eyes: "This Play of *Fletchers* braves the envious light," writes Aston Cokaine of its transfer to the folio, "As wonder of our eares once, now our sight."[18]

The evaluation of the relative merits of the senses and faculties was central, then, not only to the anti- and pro-theatricalist debate, but also to the general discussion of seeing and hearing, discoursing and imagining in the theatre and on the page. Drawing largely on Augustine, Renaissance Neoplatonism postulated a hierarchy of the senses which theatrical commentators inherited (if in vulgarized form). However much the pictorial tradition might dignify the senses of touch, taste, and smell, these ranked lowest (identified with the purely corporeal lower half of the body), with vision as intermediary between body and soul, sound the highest of the senses, ascending through the capacity for language, the faculty of thought, and reaching towards an asensory and non-corporeal divinity. If sound was below cognition and language, sound was nonetheless central to dramatic reception—and to culture generally. Music was not merely a vehicle of emotion but a conveyor of meaning, at the centre of the arts, a fulcrum that linked poetry and dance to cosmological arts like mathematics and astrology (as well as earthly arts like architecture and theatre).[19] In imitating the union of music and poetry in ancient drama (which the opera was intended to reproduce in modern form), Renaissance theatre practitioners insisted on the necessary interpenetration of music and poetry. "I decided it would not be a bad idea to . . . diversify the music with poetry and weave music into the poetry, and most often to merge the two together," explains Baltasar de Beaujoyeulx in his *Balet comique de la royne* (1582): "For in antiquity they never recited poetry without music, and Orpheus never played without words. . . . I have animated and made the Ballet speak, and Comedy sing and resound, and have added many rare and rich scenes and ornaments. I may say that within a single well-proportioned body I have pleased eye, ear, and mind."[20]

Hearing the play was at least as important as watching it. Those who came to the theatre were not only "spectators" but "hearers" or "attentive auditors," "those who watch and listen,"—a notion emblematized in the frontispiece to Alexandre Hardy's *Theatre* (1626), which shows Melpomene holding a banner displaying a varied collection of eyes and ears and reminds the reader, in the caption, of the power of the theatrical voice to bring the dead back to life (Fig. 34).[21] Hearing and watching overlapped in the Renaissance unconscious: for John Dee, the "voyce, of the players sound" must come "cleare & pleasant, to ye eares of the lokers on."[22] Richard Hawkins underlines the way in which the senses worked together in the playhouse when he refers to Beaumont and Fletcher's *Philaster* as a play "approved by the Seeing Auditors, or Hearing Spectators."[23] As we have seen, early Renaissance books were almost invariably "to read and to hear."[24] As important, words themselves were sounded things, whose connection to music was crucial to their function on the stage. For Aristotle and his Renaissance followers, music generally was important to theatre, but melody and rhythm were essential components of the drama because they were aspects of language and part of the meaning of words.[25] As George Puttenham explains, "Poesie is a skill to speake & write harmonically: and verses or rime be a kind of Musicall utterance, by reason of certaine congruitie in sounds pleasing the eare."[26] *How* things sounded was fundamental to what they meant—hence Jonson's concern about "*mis-tuned*" words and the necessary "*tuning* of the voyce" which prevents words from being misunderstood.[27] The intensity of the Renaissance debate on the merits of verse and rhyme, and the attention paid to precise metrical forms and the insistence on their correct use, reflected the centrality of sound to meaning.

If sound was a crucial conveyer of meaning, it could also be dangerously seductive, sensuous, or irrational (in and of itself, even absent "slovenly talke" that might "hur[t] the eares of the chast hearers").[28] Even a defender of the sonorous effects of language like Puttenham can inadvertently reveal a concern about the power of tuneful speech to seduce the auditor from proper attention to the cognitive uses of language: "[Verse] sooner invegleth the judgement of man, and carieth his opinion this way and that, whither soever the heart by impression of the eare shalbe most

FIG. 34. "With the charms of her voice the grave Melpomene | Brings the virtuous back from the Tomb." Alexandre Hardy's *Theatre* (1626).

affectionatly bent and directed."[29] For John Webb, lauding the sonorous powers of poetry with similar ambivalence, Beaumont and Fletcher's

> . . . chiming Muses never fail'd to sing
> A Soule-affecting Musicke; ravishing
> Both Eare and Intellect.[30]

But the ear, closer to the intellect than the eye, was generally perceived as safer than the eye—capable of hearing without danger things that certainly ought not to be shown. Richard Bernard explains that the reason that Terence "brings in here a person" to narrate the "pranke" that Chaerea "hath plaied within" is that "the people might by hearing perceive, that which with honestie could not be beholden with eyes."[31] More commonly than the ears, the susceptible eyes were seen as deluding the spectator's good judgement—one of the reasons that vision was below hearing in the hierarchy of the senses. The sound of verse may, for Puttenham, "invegl[e] the judgement of man, and car[ry] his opinion this way and that," but, more commonly (as for Jonson), images were seen as "orecom[ing] the power of speech, and oratory."[32]

A version of classical anti-ocularism—what might be called the "anti-spectacular prejudice"—could draw both on traditional anti-theatricalism and on the placement of vision below thought and sound, broadening these classic positions into a general challenge to the place of the visual in the theatre. We have already seen, in Chapter 5, the identification of the popular theatre with the "rude multitude" (in Castelvetro's words).[33] The coarseness of the crowd was seen as a product of its sensory susceptibility ("the rough and ignorant crowd of men," writes Robortello, is "led by the senses . . . rather than by prudence and knowledge and wisdom"),[34] and sensory susceptibility was most typically identified as visual susceptibility. Georges de Scudéry gives this position a neo-Platonic twist in his comment that "the common people, who carry their judgement in their eyes, let themselves be tricked by that sense which, of all the senses, is easiest to deceive."[35] Certainly anti-theatricalists like Gosson or Prynne drew on such cultural truisms in their broad attacks on the visual faculty in the theatre. "Vice is learned w[ith] beholding," wrote Gosson, "se[n]se is tickled, desire pricked, & those impressions of mind are secretly co[n]veyed over to [the] gazers, which [the] plaiers do cou[n]terfeit on [the] stage."[36] But dramatists too—even while they recognized the centrality of the visual to the theatre on which they depended—could draw on such anti-ocularist views in fact to *distance* their art (the art of fable and poetry) from the vulgar theatricality of gesture and stage movement, and the cheap thrills of scenery and machines. In the prologue to his *David Combattant* (1582), Louis Des Masures taunts the eager crowd of spectators, who long for a show that will make their "eyes drunk."[37] In contrasting the contemporary "stage," which "the poets" have "purg'd from barbarism," with "the days of Tarlton and Kemp," in which "fools and jesters spent their wits" in ridiculous gestures and bodily contortions, Richard Brome reiterates the usual contrast as progressive history[38] (echoed by Thomas Rymer a half century later: "Carpenters and Coblers" once ruled the drama, but dramatic poets may now sweep them from the stage).[39]

Jonson may assert (echoing Horace) that "Picture is the invention of Heaven: the most ancient, and most a kine to Nature." But he worries about the fact that it "doth so enter, and penetrate the inmost affection (being done by an excellent Artificer) as sometimes it orecomes the power of speech, and oratory," and therefore reason.[40] He may mock the anti-theatricalists' horror of "the concupisence of *Jigges* and *Dances*."[41] But he echoes the more general anti-spectacular prejudice when he scoffs at spectators who value a "*Mountebanke, or Jester*" above "the studie, or studiers of *humanitie*."[42] "Painting & Carpentry" may be for Jonson (echoing Aristotle with some irony) the "Soule of Masque,"[43] but "of the two" "the Pen is more noble then the Pencill," (writing more noble than drawing) "for that can speake to the Understanding; the other but to the Sense."[44] "O Showes! Showes! Mighty Showes!" he writes (putting it somewhat less gently, in his famous attack on Inigo Jones):

> The Eloquence of Masques! What need of prose
> Or Verse, or Sense, t'express Immortall you?[45]

If the masque-maker's art is the senseless art of "Show," the poet's art is, by contrast, verbal, narrative, and conceptual: "the Fable and Fiction is," writes Jonson, "the forme and Soule of any Poeticall worke, or *Poeme*"; "*Language* most shewes a man"; "Words, above action: matter, above words."[46] In the preface to *Hymenaei* (1606), Jonson implicitly links the contrast between the "sense" (or the senses) and understanding (manifest in words and matter) to the contrast between live performance and the printed dramatic book, the one (like sense impressions) fleeting, the other (like thought or soul) enduring. "It is a noble and just advantage, that the things subjected to *understanding* have of those which are objected to *sense*, that the one sort are but momentarie, and meerely taking; the other impressing, and lasting," he writes (with a nod to print in his diction):

Else the glorie of all these *solemnities* had perish'd like a blaze, and gone out, in the *beholders* eyes. So short-liv'd are the *bodies* of all things, in comparison of their *soules*. And, though *bodies* oft-times have the ill luck to be sensually preferr'd, they find afterwards, the good fortune (when *soules* live) to be utterly forgotten.[47]

Offering a lesson to those "royall *Princes*" who may "sensually prefer" "*bodies*" but who ought to recognize the enduring value of "*soules*" (as expressed in language and speaking to the "*understanding*"), Jonson attempts to establish the proper use of "outward celebration, or shew," which must finally turn away from the senses and (like the book itself) be turned to the service of mind. A value for what is enduring

hath made the most royall *Princes*, and the greatest *persons* (who are commonly the *personaters* of these *actions*) not onely studious of riches, and magnificence in the outward celebration, or shew; (which rightly becomes them) but curious after the most high, and heartie *inventions*, to furnish the inward parts: (and those grounded upon *antiquitie*, and solide *learnings*) which, though their *voyce* be taught to sound to present occasions, their *sense*, or doth, or should alwayes lay hold on more remov'd *mysteries*.[48]

Right performance, then, must model itself on the asensuous book: "Grounded upon *antiquitie*, and solide *learnings*," it must convert what the senses perceive into the kind of "*sense*" that is, finally, "impressing, and lasting."

THE LANGUAGE OF GESTURE

Jonson's Neoplatonic views, here, on the possibility of converting the sensory into "sou[l]" echo some of the themes of the *pro-spectacular* positions that developed in response to Renaissance anti-spectacularism. While Renaissance Neoplatonism could offer another rendering of the classical mistrust of vision, it could also offer a means of reclaiming both image and body through a theory of likenesses that, rather than deriding imitation, honoured images as likenesses of the divine. Inigo Jones, for instance (famously in conflict with Jonson over the priority of the scenic image over the text),[49] classically justifies the spectacular focus of his opulent masques in his description of Aurelian Townshend's *Tempe Restored* (1632). He explains that he designed the costume of Henrietta Maria for the masque for the purpose of showing "that Corporeall *Beauty*, consisting in simmetry, colour, and certaine unexpressable Graces, shining in the Queenes Majestie, may draw us to the contemplation of the *Beauty* of the soule, unto which it hath an Analogy."[50] While Jones is still quite close to a comfortable Renaissance Neoplatonism here, a theorist like the Abbé D'Aubignac can move away from such justifications towards an independent foundation for a visualist pro-theatricalism, offering a counter-tradition to the anti-spectacular impulse with only the faintest echoes of Plato. For D'Aubignac, as for Castelvetro, Lope de Vega, and Scudéry, the theatre's populism lies in its visualism. But unlike them, D'Aubignac turns the traditional hierarchies upside down, identifying theatre's visual power as a virtue (aesthetic means which "fall more under [the] senses" can move the ordinarily irrational masses to reason, offering philosophy via effects which "the meanest capacities" may visibly see).[51] In the theatre (if not elsewhere), discourse can cede its ordinarily high status to image and action: "speeches" and "deliberations" are "by nature contrary to Theatre; because the Theatre [is] the place of Actions."[52] Gesture and action might rank with, or even above, discourse; the irrational body, cleansed of its gases and tears and other excretions, might after all be rational.

Much has been written about the role of the printed word in the creation of "graphic space," the legitimation of the visual in late Renaissance and baroque culture, and the marginalization of the other senses.[53] Whether or not print played a part in reshaping attitudes towards the visual, seventeenth-century claims for the legitimacy of stage spectacle seemed to grow less and less reliant on theories that insisted on the dissolution of visual and corporeal being into "soul" or "spirit." Influenced by the proliferation of works on the language of symbols like Giovanni Pierio Valeriano's *Ieroglifici* (1602), as well as by treatises on rhetoric and works on dance like Jean Tabourot's *Orchesographie* (1588),[54] claims for the legitimacy of spectacle instead drew independently on theories of gesture as language. The body could be recharacterized, no longer a mere transit point for the passage towards soul, but now an autonomous signifying agent: "The gesture of a man, is the speache of his bodie," writes Thomas Wilson;[55] the action of the actor is, in John Webster's words, "*signifi-cant*."[56] The body could thus become a vehicle for translating the passions, eventually taxonomized and rendered graphically in such learned works as Charles Le Brun's Academy lectures on painting (1667), with their illustrative "Heads of the Passions." Perhaps with Aristotle's derogation of stage spectacle in mind, Bacon, for instance, offers an exposition of the significance (in both senses) of gesture, criticizing Aristotle for his failure to include a discussion of gesture as signification in his discussion of the body generally:

For Aristotle hath very ingeniously and diligently handled the factures of the body, but not the gestures of the body, which are no less comprehensible by art, and of greater use and advantage. For the Lineaments of the body do disclose the disposition and inclination of the mind in general; but the Motions of the countenance and parts do not only so, but do further disclose the present humour and state of the mind and will.

Explaining himself by quoting James I (with a certain degree of smoothness), he adds: "For as your Majesty saith most aptly and elegantly, *As the tongue speaketh to the ear, so the gesture speaketh to the eye*."[57]

John Bulwer, author of *Chirologia: or, The Natural Language of the Hand* and its companion, *Chironomia: or, The Art of Manual Rhetoric* (both published in 1644), is perhaps the best-known seventeenth-century exponent of a theory of gesture as language. The art of gesturing is the "very palm and crown of eloquence," he explains, the language of the hand "as easily perceived and understood as if man had another mouth or fountain of discourse in his hand," showing, at the back of the volume, an "Alphabet of naturall Gestures of the HAND"[58] (Fig. 35). Bulwer proposes, in the "Alphabet" or the similar "Alphabet of *Action*, or Table of Rhetorical Indigitations," a system purportedly congruent with nature, yet methodized (in a serious version of the purely gestural language that Jonson satirizes in the *Newes from the New World Discover'd in the Moone*).[59] To demonstrate the superiority of his gestural language, he repeatedly sets up a combat between gesture and words, often imagining this combat on a stage, with actors (its ideal examplars) demonstrating that the language of gestures can, in fact, better the language of letters. His *Chirologia*, he explains, will attempt to describe the "two amphitheatres" in which "the speaking motions, or discoursing gestures, and natural language of the body" take place, "to wit, the hand and the head." The pantomime shows this, for the mime's hand and head may translate what the senses experience into sense through the signs of gesture, as clear as "definite letters": "Then the very hand of the senses," he writes, translating Cassiodorus approvingly, "explains the singer's song to the eyes, and by composite signs as though by definite letters, he instructs the watching of the audience; and in this are read the most important facts." Pitting discourse against gesture in *Chironomia*, he imagines a paradigmatic theatrical scene in which Cicero the orator and Roscius the actor compete to see whether words or gestures can best express meaning:

[Cicero] would often contend and strive . . . with Roscius whether he should more often express the same sentence in gesture, or whether he himself by the copiousness of his elo-

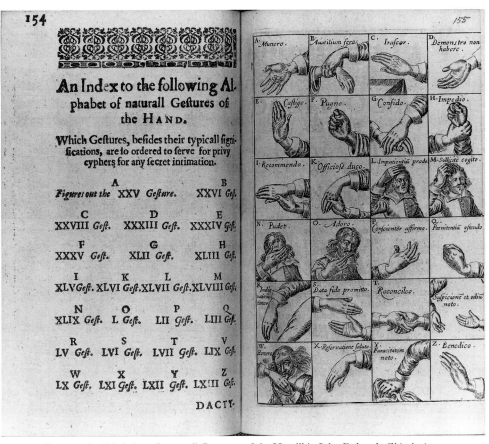

FIG. 35. An "Alphabet of naturall Gestures of the Hand" in John Bulwer's *Chirologia* (1644).

quence in a differing [of] speech and variety of expression pronounced the same; which raised Roscius to that height and perfection of knowledge that he wrote a book wherein he compared eloquence with the art or science of stage-players. . . . Pantomimical Roscius . . . could vary a thing more by gestures than [Cicero] could by phrase, or . . . by his witty speeches.[60]

The contest between actor and orator is replayed in the microcosm of the individual body itself, in which the hand becomes synecdoche for the actor and the tongue for the orator:

The hand is so ready and cunning to expound our intentions, abounding in a sense so copious and so connatural a kind of eloquence, wherein all things are so lively expressed: the hand seems to enter into contestation, and [seems] to vie expresses [*sic*] with the tongue, and to overmatch it in speaking labors and the significant variety of important motions that it almost transcends the faculty of art to enumerate the postures of the hand, and the discoursing gestures which present the interpretation of the mind.

In an anti-lingual diatribe, Bulwer can celebrate that "rich and silent trade by signs whereby," in "commerce with those sa[v]age nations, . . . many a dumb bargain without the crafty brocage of the tongue is advantageously made," declaring, "Hence 'tis apparent, that there's no native law, or absolute necessity, that those thoughts which arise in our pregnant mind must by mediation of our tongue flow out in a vocal stream of words." Stressing the greater proximity of the hand than the tongue to the thoughts (and the senses from which they flow), Bulwer explains that "Whatsoever is perceptible unto sense, and capable of a due and fitting difference; hath a natural competency to express the motives and affections of the mind, in whose labors the hand which is a ready midwife takes oftentimes the thoughts from the forestalled tongue, making a more quick dispatch by gesture."[61]

Bulwer's postulation of gesture not only as "speech" that can displace the tongue but as a "*general* language of human *nature*," is significant. In gesturing, the body is not merely "instructed by nature," but produces out of that instruction a discourse more natural than the sophistications of speech:

And all these motions and habits of the hand are purely natural, not positive; nor in their senses remote from the true nature of the things that are implied. The natural resemblance and congruity of . . . expressions result from the habits of the mind by the effort of an impetuous affection wrought in the invaded hand which is made very pliant for such impressions.

Gesture is creator of a natural and universal language, the only one exempt from the alienation of humanity after Babel:

Nor doth the hand in one speech or kind of language serve to intimate and express our mind; it speaks all languages, and as an universal character of reason, is generally understood and known by all nations among the formal differences of their tongue. And being the only speech that is natural to man, it may well be called the tongue and general language of human nature which without teaching, men in all regions of the habitable world do at the first sight most easily understand.

Drawing an explicit parallel between pantomimes and primitives in a prelinguistic state, he describes

[the] discoursing faculty of the hand in our common jesters who without their voice, speaking only by gestures, can counterfeit the manners, fashions, and significant actions of men. . . . 'Tis parallel to this, what nature's grand inquisitor reports of certain nations that have no other language wherein to impart their minds the common tongue of beasts, who by gestures declare their senses, and dumb affections.[62]

Just as the gesturing hand reunites alienated peoples, so (in Bulwer's extended political trope) it reunites the alienated body itself:

The hand being the substitute and vicegerent [*sic*] of the tongue, in a full, and majestic way of expression, presents the signifying faculties of the soul, and the inward discourse of reason; and as another tongue, which we may justly call the spokesman of the body, it speaks for all the members thereof, denoting their suffrages, and including their votes.

The hand may stand in for the tongue but it is more representative of the body as a whole than the tongue (sequestered as the tongue is in the upper palace). It restores the voice of those parts (vehicles of the senses) long unrepresented in communicative action. The body is producer of signs that may displace both voice and writing, competing with *the* Text by "do[ing] what the Scripture declared," but doing it "without writing." As signifier of a collective soul (that of the reunited individual body and that of the reunited global body), as vehicle of the only language exempt from the desecrations of Babel and hence the one closest to the language of God, the gesturing body manifests in human form, at once divine writing and the divine "signifying voice": "To these signs God attributes a voice. . . . (And as there is in the supernatural, so there is a signifying voice in the natural signs of the hand.)"[63]

THE SPATIAL RENDERING OF SOUND

At least as important to the late Renaissance understanding of the objects of the senses as the re-establishing of gesture was the project of notating sound and analysing its relation to the written and printed word: for instance, in innovations in musical notation;[64] in the various Renaissance manuals on orthography, pronunciation, punctuation, and shorthand; in seventeenth-century proposals for a rational alphabet like that in John Wilkins's *Essay towards a Real Character and a Philosophical Language* (1668); or in treatises on the speaking instrument like Owen Price's *The Vocal Organ* (1665), with its representation of "visible speech" by means of a taxonomy of the human mouth and its various sound-creating positions (Fig. 36).[65] Voice was (like gesture) to be inscribed in the material or graphic sign, translated out of the realm of sound into notation, transferred onto the page: "Words come to life only through writing," wrote Jacques Peletier du Mans in the orthography manual he published in the same year that he published his *Poetics*.[66] We have already seen the importance for dramatists of the work of the orthographic treatises—the way in which the printed text was used as a mechanism for regulating speech. Particularly conscious of the varieties of speech, dramatists could expand the work of orthographers with further innovations in punctuation and other kinds of marks: mapping sound on the page, inventing new means of indicating expression; creating for the voice an adequate graphic language.[67] In the printed text of his *Comedy of Nuptial Fidelity* (1577), for instance, Gérard de Vivre offers a list headed "The meaning of the signs which I will use in all my Plays,"—a list indicating pauses and other variations in tone and tempo: "This sign signifies a pause"; "This two"; "This three, each one equal to an inhalation" (etc.).[68] Concerned that, with even the best orthographic system the sounds of words may be misread, Jonson suggests the creation of a notation system for "the *Accent*," which "hath not yet obtained with us any signe; which notwithstanding were most needfull to be added."[69] Dramatic texts were, with increasing freedom, relying on the expressive use of the em–dash or ellipsis (eventually imitated in non-dramatic works to express the centrality of oral style to meaning).[70] Reshaping writing to conform to and express the sound of words, correlating page with voice, the printed text was (for both dramatists and orthographers) to offer

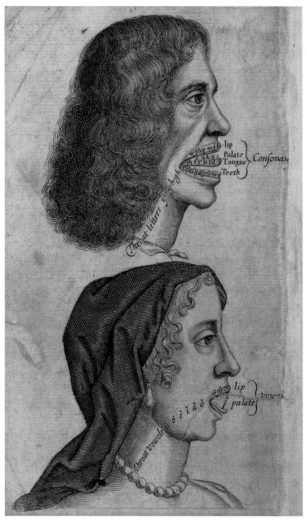

FIG. 36. Speech rendered visible in Owen Price's *The Vocal Organ* (1665).

a notation system for the sound of language and a guide to pronunciation, and thereby to eliminate the ambiguities arising from the indeterminate sound of letters. The subtitle of John Hart's *An Orthographie* (1569), "howe to write or paint th[e] image of mannes voice," is telling: spelling and punctuation were to render voice in graphic or visual form; the expressions of the mouth were to be rendered graphically through "ortho-graphy."

Such technical prescriptions were grounded in an extensive theoretical discussion of the nature of speech and writing. Letters, explains Hart, are the "markes and figures" of the voice: "Seeing then that letters are the figures and colours wherewith the image of mans voice is painted, you are are forced to graunt the writing should have so many letters as the speach hath voyces, and no more nor lesse."[71] Billing itself as describing "divers Characters, by which every part of the voice may be aptly known and severally distinguished," Robert Robinson's *Art of Pronunciation* (1617) similarly explains its project as "appointing for every simple sound in mans voice sundry letters and characters, that the voice being thereunto once commited may by any (who shall know the use of them) without any other expositor or instructor be aptly and truly pronounced upon view of the writing." Robinson's recognition of the ways in which printed texts have already conventionalized English spelling keeps him from trying to create a new spelling system of his graphic rendering of speech.

My intent and purpose herein is not, that I would any waies goe about, or desire to alter the order of letters, which of so long time hath been used and allowed of, wherein so many worthy works have been imprinted, knowing that could not be brought to passe without much difficulty, and greater prejudice then my simple judgement can discerne.

But he champions the project of teaching pronunciation by means of the printed book: "No perfect Dictionary or Grammar hath hitherto been made," he explains, "that the true order of pronunciation might be taught."[72]

For Robinson, as for Bulwer, the translation of sensory expression into specific, graphic signs is a universalist endeavour—an attempt to overcome the babble of languages. To create a true art of pronunciation is to give outsiders the capacity of communicating with one another by properly pronouncing one another's tongues, "how strange soever the language be":

The pronunciation of every different language which hitherto is chiefly taught by word of mouth, might in a more certain manner be deciphered with the pen. . . . The simple and distinct parts, and members of the whole voice . . . being once certainly knowne, and cast into visible letters . . . the eye by it's quicke and sharpe sight doth suddenly apprehend them, and thereby teach the mouth of one altogether ignorant, & unacquainted with such language, as aptly and truly to pronounce it, as any one to whom the same is naturally the speech.[73]

Those alien tongues are now to be learned from a new universal, visible language of signs, necessary because, despite the fact that humans have been given a standardized sound-making instrument (the body, the tongue, and the vocal machinery), there is not only a Babel of languages in the world, but a Babel of pronunciations:

Notwithstanding all nations of the earth came from one root, our first father *Adam*, and that God had given them all the same forme of body, the like sences, and for their voyce all instruments alike: (howsoever he had dispersed them into severall parts and habitations) yet the people of one kingdom in their learning of the language of any other nation have not in many yeers, yea some in the whole course of their life have not attained to . . . exact and perfect pronuntiation therein.

Even in speaking the learned languages, "men of different nations . . . cannot one suddenly understand the other in any argument, or conference had betweene them . . . every one of them inclining to the manner of pronunciation of their owne country speech."

Writing several decades before Robinson, the spelling-master Richard Mulcaster (an opponent of a radically revised orthography but nonetheless similar in many of his views to the reformers) had explained that letters, having once been discovered, "to serve a nedefull turn took the force of expressing everie distinct *sound* in voice." But they took this force "not by them selves or anie vertew in their form (for what likenesse or what affinitie hath the form of anie letter in his own natur, to answer the force or sound in mans voice?) but onelie by consent of those men, which first invented them, and the pretie use therof perceaved by those, which first did receive them."[74] For Robinson, on the other hand, writing in and of itself might be, like the voice, a natural faculty: "God . . . for the further benefit of mankind, as hee hath given us a voice to express the minde unto the eare, so hee hath given us hands to frame letters or markes for the voice to express the minde unto the eyes."[75] But, just as there is no universal oral language, for Robinson (as for Mulcaster) there is no natural relationship between particular sounds and their conventional graphic representations. Writing, as it stands, is the product of a mere consent to agree to an arbitrary set of relationships between oral and graphic signs. This is precisely, however, the reason that a new, more natural, graphic system for representing speech is needed. Such a system, artificial as it still might be, could return the God-given hand to its right use, "to express the minde to the eye."

SENSUAL NONSENSE: MARGINALIZING SOUND

The desire, expressed by orthographers, to repair the disjunction between written and spoken language reflected a more general cultural anxiety about the status of the sounded word after print had come to seem the normative home for language. The typical Renaissance insistence that reason and sound go together, and the books that attempted to legislate this complicity, might be seen as attempts to control the relation between word and sound, where the word seemed to have separated itself from sound and (conversely) where sound seemed dangerously capable of breaking free of the significant word. The voice was marked (increasingly) as an unstable producer of meaning, for sound was a thing that "altereth still," and hence it was an unsatisfactory arbiter of spelling: "No man having anie sense in the right of writing, which experience had commended," writes Mulcaster, "wold yeild the direction to sound alone, which altereth still, and is never like to it self."[76] For Bulwer, the universal, material signs of the body's gestures were to correct "the crafty brocage of the tongue."[77] If a manual like John Willis's *Art of Stenographie* (1602) could teach a "Secret Writing" founded not purely in the voice but also in the silent graphic sign (one largely pictoriographic, inspired by the hieroglyphic),[78] if philosophers like John Wilkins (freed from the notion of a necessary relation between sign and sound) could set about creating rational and universal graphic languages detached from the arbitrary voice, this was symptomatic of the apparent detachment of sign from sound, which the Renaissance orthographies were attempting to redress.

Playwrights often expressed doubts about the ability of the seductive and sensual—but not necessarily rational—voice to communicate meaning. Milton's Lady (in *Comus*) might identify the ear as the only steady guide among the senses,[79] but a Renaissance topos like the figure of Echo could express the period's consciousness of the potential of linguistic sound to engage in free play (even while Echoes might attempt to turn the free play of purely sensuous sound back into meaning—as prophecy, warning, or answer, typically graphically rendered in the margin).[80] The anxieties about sounded language were reflected in the attention to wordplay and phonetic slippage (homonym, pun, malapropism, "wit inflation") and in commonplaces about the unruly voice. The more general dangers of the unruly tongue could be thematized in a play like the anonymous *Lingua: Or The Combat of the Tonge, And the five Senses For Superiority* (1607), or in complaints about the particular unruliness of the actors' tongues. George Chapman, disclaiming responsibility for what the actors said on stage in the production of his *Byron* in 1608, expostulates: "I see not myne owne Plaies; nor carrie the Actors Tongues in my mouthe."[81] In the theatre, noise could seem to displace "sense," language to dissolve into pure sound and leave reason behind ("Verse . . . for Charmes may pass; more Noise than Sense").[82]

Where in the early Renaissance, the "hearing" that took place in the theatre was as important as the "seeing," in the seventeenth century the ear was losing its place to vision: theatre is "*a place where one looks at something*" (insists D'Aubignac), "*not where one listens to something*"; its audience is made up of "*Spectators or Watchers, not Auditors*."[83] The transformation of "hearers" into "spectators" in George Chapman's verse epistle included in Jonson's 1616 *Workes* is emblematic: "Thy *Poëme* perform[s] such a lively evidence | In thy narrations," writes Chapman to Jonson, "that thy hearers still | Thou turn'st to thy spectators."[84] In the analysis of the sensory power of the stage (as in poetics generally) sound was coming to seem less central to poetic meaning. Discussion of metre and rhyme was diminishing in relation to discussion of structure and story, "plot," "fable," and action (conceived both narratively and theatrically). Like many, Jules de La Mesnardière cannot figure out what to do with Aristotle's central placement of rhythm and melody in his definition of tragedy in the *Poetics*, and decides simply to discard them: "We deliberately banish from our definition *Rhythms and Music*, which Aristotle includes in his, since our Tragedy does not make use of such beauties as absolutely necessary things."[85] Identifying the chorus with the musical interlude, rather than thinking of it only in narrative terms, seventeenth-century dramatists were uncertain of how to integrate it into the visually and discursively (or textually) determined play. Alexandre Hardy writes that choruses are "superfluous to the representation," and too troublesome to prepare for publication.[86] John Dennis, writing late in the century, can envision the chorus only as a group of ladies "dancing a *Saraband* to a doleful Ditty."[87]

For most late seventeenth-century dramatists and theorists, music had come to be secondary on the regular stage, the "servant" of poetry, something that "in some measure must calm an Audience which the Episode disturb'd by its Sublimity, and by its Pathetick" (as John Dennis allows) but not an essential component of the drama.[88] As Saint-Evremond writes (in his treatise on opera): "Harmony need be no more than a simple accompaniment, and the grand masters of theatre added it as an agreeable thing, not as a necessary thing, after having worked out everything on the subject."[89] In the opera houses, however, music could find its place as an independent entity. There the figure of Orpheus could, significantly, be transformed from a lyric poet (whose words and music were together central to his art) into a musician, whose harmonies merely happened to be accompanied by words.[90] By putting music at the centre and subordinating text to it, opera and its allied musical forms could offer the music-lover a place for acclaiming the beauties of voice for its purely sensuous qualities. But as such, opera could also become the focus of attacks on the purely sensuous voice, seen as detached from the kind of "reason" invested in verbal discourse and (sometimes) in significant gesture. In opera, "there is a Cup of Enchantment, there is Musick and Machine," writes Rymer in 1693: "'Tis a Debauch the most insinuating, and the most pernicious; none would think an *Opera* and Civil Reason, should be the growth of one and the same Climate."[91] For Saint-Evremond, opera is a "folly stuffed with music, danses, machines, decorations."[92] In Fielding's *The Author's Farce*, it is, notably, Signior Opera who is to be married to the Goddess of Nonsense.[93] "When learning is decried, wit not understood . . . if you must write, write nonsense, write operas," exclaims Witmore in the *Author's Farce*, in the conventional eighteenth-century equation.[94] Commentators were conscious of the tension between, on the one hand, the norm of words as unsounded material signs and, on the other, the musically overburdened word of the opera. "People were wonderfully surprized to hear Generals singing in the Word of Command, and Ladies delivering Messages in Musick," writes Addison, describing an Italian *Recitativo* (in an issue of the *Spectator* in 1711): "Our Country-men could not forbear laughing when they heard a Lover chanting out a Billet-doux, and even the Superscription of a Letter set to a Tune."[95]

Text was meaning, music bereft of text was unmeaning sound, as Colley Cibber suggests when he decries a theatre that—in turning towards opera—had "slavishly giv[en] up . . . language to the despotic power of sound only, reducing the "book" to "little more than the title-page of what it pretends to": "as it now stands, the whole entertainment seems to be dwindled into a concert of instruments; [with] no more meaning than the fiddle that plays to it."[96] The attack on opera (with its exchange of meaningful discourse for sensuous music) could join up with the attack on the various kinds of "nonsense" seen as embodied in the increasingly spectacular eighteenth-century stage: the drowning of "wit" under "noise," and the loss of "reason" in "pantomimes" and "puppet shows," as the revitalized anti-spectacularism of the eighteenth century would have it. The theatre would have to return, it was felt, from the senses to its senses. With a new focus on sound and spectacle in the later eighteenth century, "pure" sound and "pure" gesture were to take a central position both on the stage and in the theoretical analysis of the performing arts, even while there was a self-conscious attempt to redress the theoretical and practical divorce between music and poetry in works like the Marquis de Chastellux's *Essay on the Union of Poetry and Music* (1765) or Laurent Garcin's *Treatise on Melodrama* (1772).[97] But, more determinative for the shaping of the drama throughout the sixteenth and seventeenth centuries (and well into the eighteenth) was the suspicion of the spectator's all-too highly-tuned senses—in a different sense the subject of the next chapter.

8. *Narrative Form and Theatrical Illusions*

"There are three kinds of composition using dialogue," explains Lodovico Castelvetro in his *Poetics* (1570):

> The first kind may be mounted on the stage and may therefore be called dramatic, for the interlocutors actually converse with one another like the characters in tragedies and comedies. . . . A second kind, which may be called historical or narrative, cannot be mounted on the stage because the author writes as a historian and simply quotes what his various interlocutors have said. [In] the third kind, . . . a combination of the other two kinds, the author first speaks in his own person and narrates like a historian and then introduces his interlocutors to speak dramatically.

The third kind is, unfortunately, a confusing and mistaken amalgam of the first two, neither to be mounted on stage nor wholly at home off it: "This kind can and cannot be mounted on stage: it cannot insofar as the author speaks in his own person, and it can insofar as it represents characters speaking." This is because to mix narrative with direct speech is a "self-defeating yoking together of two incompatible elements":

> For if a writer intends to compose drama that will afford the pleasure peculiar to drama, he will surely defeat his own purpose if he treats some of his matter in the narrative mode, which will destroy every trace of verisimilitude. . . . How, indeed, can dramatized matter present the appearance of truth if the dramatist confesses in his own person or in another's that it is a fiction?[1]

If Castelvetro rejects the intermingling of authorial and dialogue voices for their failure of verisimilitude and uncertainty of venue, he similarly rejects philosophical dialogues—those of Plato or Cicero, for instance. Because they are in dialogue form, such philosophical works are clearly meant to be staged, "attain[ing] perfection only in the theatre." But because they are learned, they are unsuited for the stage, frequented by the ignorant rabble as it is. Moreover, because they are in prose, philosophical dialogues must be "true." But things on stage are necessarily "imaginary," merely *appearing* true. One must conclude, sadly, that both philosophical dialogues and mixed narrative forms "sin" against art. They are misshapen hybrids, amphibians belonging neither on stage nor off, with no proper place in the literary order.[2]

LATE MEDIEVAL POETICS: PERFORMING AND READING
DIALOGUE GENRES

To understand Castelvetro's peculiar rejection of philosophical prose dialogue and of hybrid narrative forms, it is worth recalling some of the discussion in earlier chapters of the development of drama as a distinct performance genre in the Renaissance, and the development of distinct Renaissance typographic conventions for the drama. We have already seen that medieval verbal forms were also generally performance forms, and that this meant that medieval theorists did not usually differentiate between drama and other genres on the basis of medium. We have seen, similarly, that Aristotle's emphasis on drama as narrative form (even if it needed a good deal of interpretation) was easier for medievals who had encountered the *Poetics* to understand than his differentiation of reading from performance, and that medieval distinctions on the basis of presentational medium were almost invariably subordinate to distinctions on the basis of narrative form (length, proportion, logical unity). Even for Aristotle, living in a culture with a highly developed theatrical life, genre was not determined by performance conditions, for most genres were performed (epic in recitations like those of Sostratus, songs in singing contests, philosophical texts in public readings, tragedies and comedies in recitations or enactment by actors). There was a continuum of representational possibilities for various verbal arts. Across those representational possibilities, one could identify narrative form, and it was narrative form that distinguished the drama.[3] William of St Thierry's view of dramatic action was probably closer to Aristotle's than that of Renaissance interpreters of the *Poetics*: action was, for him, primarily about narration and fateful event, not about actors gesticulating with their limbs.[4]

The intermingling of direct speech and narrative overlay in medieval and early Renaissance performance reflects an implicit theoretical understanding that verbal genres generally (whatever their performance conditions) combined the functions of representing and reporting events. Certainly medieval verbal arts foregrounded their use of direct speech and indirect speech in combination, their conjoined use of both characters speaking in their own voices and an author's or narrator's voice describing the action, past or present.[5] In Arnoul Gréban's *Mystère de la passion* (*c*.1450), for instance, a narrator named "The Actor" (author and actor at once) both explains what has passed on stage and announces the action to come:

> Now we have given you, in brief,
> the high and fruitful subject
> of the creation of the world
>
> .   .   .   .   .   .
>
> Let us move on, and let it be enough,
> to speed matters, for us to show
> how Cain slew his brother
> out of jealousy; and we will treat of all of this
> as briefly as we can.[6]

Verbal performances—even those by costumed players pretending to be characters—did not have to exclude the author's or narrator's voice speaking to the audience. "Entertainments" might consist of a single long monologue, in which the speaker counselled the spectators, admonished them, narrated an action, explained it, prayed for humankind. Prologues, heraldic announcements, orations, arguments pointed the moral of the tale and served as staged narration. The messenger at the beginning of *Everyman* exhorts the crowd:

> I pray you all gyve your audyence,
> And here this mater with reverence.
>
> .   .   .   .
>
> For ye shall here how our Heven Kynge
> Calleth Everyman to a generall rekenynge.[7]

In most mummings, a herald read a ballad while the mummers mimed the action in accordance with each verse.[8] The "truchman" in court revels complimented the nobles present and provided an explanatory introduction to the show to be performed.[9] Typically even in the early Renaissance, parts of the plot were read out by a performer, for instance in Gil Vicente's *Don Duardos* (1522), in which the action is suddenly telescoped and one of the ladies-in-waiting becomes the narrator.[10] Actors were not to *be* their characters (certainly not to identify with them), but merely to embody the narration of the play—the reason it must have seemed perfectly natural, for instance, to have three different actors taking turns playing Saint John in one 1505 *auto*.[11] The dramatist's voice could be difficult to distinguish from that of the characters, especially when the interpreter, herald, or orator *was* the author, as, for instance, John Lydgate or Juan del Encina often were.[12] Drama reported as much as it represented: it narrated, dictated, commented; it spoke for the dramatist; it addressed the audience.

Speeches or mimed action often reiterated what narrative had already explained or represented what was to come, as in the archaic play-within-a-play in *Hamlet*, in which there is a double version of the "mousetrap" play (first in dumb-show, then in spoken action).[13] Narrative overlay could constitute a similar kind of redoubling, as in Beolco's "comedia" *Anconitana*, which begins with a prologue by "Time," the "Argument," another prologue by Ruzante (all narrative and explanatory variations on a theme), and only then gets to the opening of the first act (a speech by Tancredi).[14] Such prefatory invocations and redoublings could help to make sure that an easily distracted audience (with no eyeglasses or hearing aids) had understood the plot and had leisure to digest its import. But they also deliberately called on multiple narrative modes, the mimetic and the diegetic, narration, gesture, and direct speech, to tell and show the story. Similarly, scenic display could include its own form of narration, reduplicating the kind of explanation that might be spoken by a narrator. The use of "Nuncupations onely in Text Letters," which William Percy recommended as an alternative to elaborate scenery in his *Faery Pastoral*,[15] was a way of describing locale—presenting "narration" textually on stage, as so many early Renaissance dramatic illustrations do.

Medieval and early Renaissance dramatic texts reflected a similar comfort with multiplicity of narrative mode. Stage directions could be full of explanatory and didactic comments intended for the edification of the reader or listener. Instructions for speeches (and actions) were often repeated in several different narrative forms (a reiteration at once serving the practical considerations of part-book distribution and reflecting narrative conventions). Such instructions might first be described in a stage direction, then repeated in lines written to be spoken, as for instance in the Chester *Harrowing of Hell*, in which a stage direction describes Jesus' lines (in Latin) and then repeats them in English dialogue:

Then shall come Jesus, and a clamour shall be made, or a loud sound of things striking together, and let Jesus say: 'Lift of your heads, O ye gates; and be ye lift up, ye everlasting doors; and the King of glory shall come in.'

Jesus

> Open up hell-gates anon,
> ye princes of pain every one,
> that God's Son may in goen,
> and the kinge of bliss.[16]

Both action and speech could be detailed in an undifferentiated narration, at once stage direction and speaker indication. The words to be spoken or sung were not always precisely scripted, because (like other kinds of narratives) the script was a description of an action: "God the father returns to his seat and the angels sing," instructs the text of Gréban's *Mystère de la Passion*, without giving the words they were actually to sing.[17] The playtext of *The Prodigal Son* (*c.*1525–34) instructs: "Here the servant cometh in spekyinge some straunge language." "Ill Will" in *Wealth and Health* (*c.*1557–65) enters "with some jest."[18] The narrative description was to do much of the labour of representing, on the page, what was to happen in the scene (the action, made up of a combination of words spoken and things done).

As we have seen, early printed texts continued to offer narrative descriptions as the equivalent of speech-prefixes (not yet foreshortened by modern convention), mingling narration, stage directions, and speech, descriptively explaining speech as merely a particular kind of action, a kind that could be rendered in words but that was to be introduced by ordinary description: "Here begins the history and legend of Saint Apollonia virgin and martyr of Christ," opens Antonia Pulci's *Representation of Saint Apollonia* (*c.*1485), "And first says an Angel thus: 'O People. . . .'"[19] Similarly, in all the editions of Hans Sachs's sixteenth-century collected works, the title, the argument, a didactic lesson, an explanation of dramatic and book structure, and a speech-prefix appear as a single narrative unit in un-differentiated typography:

In this third part of the second book are brought together comedy | tragedy | and maxims. It contains various secular histories drawn from notable chroniclers, showing both good and evil, as in a mirror so that the righteous may avoid evil misdeeds and instead follow in good and laudable footsteps with honor and uprightness. A Tragedy with thirteen characters, *The Six Fighters* has four acts. The Herald enters and speaks.[20]

As we have seen, the typographic and structural mingling of narrative overlay and direct speech in the *mise en page* of early printed editions mirrored the mingling of instruction, narrative overlay, and direct speech in performance. Such mingling was an expression of the weakness, in the fifteenth century and for much of the sixteenth, of distinctions between dramatic and other kinds of verbal genres, either in theory, on the page, or on the stage. *Everyman* announces itself as "a treatyse."[21] In the early sixteenth century, a scribe could move uncertainly between copying the story of *The Burial and Resurrection* as a "treyte" to be "rede" and "a play to be playede," starting only half-way through the manuscript to underline the narrative elements in red ink (". . . said Holy Joseph," . . . "answered Mary") and eventually—after a note suggesting proper days for it to be "playede" as "a play"—dropping narrative elements altogether.[22] However, a typographic identification of drama as a distinct genre with its own particular *mise en page* began to come into being with the institutionalization of theatre. When printers began typographically distinguishing stage directions from dialogue (breaking lines for speech-prefixes or stage directions, centring them, setting them in the margins), and when writers began to suppress extraneous explanatory information for the reader, they were beginning to establish norms for the immediate visual identification of dramatic genres, at the same time reinforcing the distinction of staged dramatic form from other forms of literate text. Texts like Francesco Andreini's *The Bravery of Captain Spavento Divided in Many Arguments* (1607), a collection of fifty-five *commedia* dialogues translated and reprinted frequently in the seventeenth century, continued to challenge the boundaries between narrative for performance by a lively enactor and drama proper. But, as we have seen, those creating the dramatic page no longer felt they had to spell out, "here beginneth . . ." or "God speketh" because readers were growing accustomed to understanding that particular typographic configurations (speech-prefixes) visually *meant* "here beginneth."

RENAISSANCE POETICS: THE NARRATIVE REQUIREMENTS OF THE STAGE

Sixteenth-century typography both reflected and reinforced a distinction of staged from unstaged literary genres, a distinction that was to grow central to Renaissance generic theory in conjunction with the regular printing of drama and the proliferation of commentaries on the *Poetics*. Aristotle's distinction between the epic and the dramatic ("the difference betwixt reporting and representing," as Philip Sidney phrases it in the *Apology for Poetry*)[23] was at the centre of the discussion of dramatic form. But Renaissance commentators tended to elide Aristotle's insistence that the distinction between the epic and the dramatic was not a distinction of medium but rather one of form. Instead, they used his distinction as a starting-point for a discussion, importantly, of the difference between stage and page, identifying the drama with the theatre (and specifically with Renaissance theatrical conditions), and the epic with the experience of reading. Ignoring Aristotle's insistence that "tragedy does not depend upon public performance and actors," Viperano, for instance, explains in his *Poetics* (1579) that tragedy is superior to epic "because a clearer and more immediate impact is achieved by acting than by reading."[24] The drama must fit into the timeframe of the theatrical event, explains Castelvetro; "an epic poem must not be so long that it cannot be read in a single day."[25] "Representing" was, in this context, representing on stage, as opposed to the kinds of "reporting" that took place in the book.

The "action" that it was tragedy's task to imitate became, from this point of view, not the action narrated (as for Aristotle) but the action of the actor. For Castelvetro, for instance, "the definition of tragedy states that tragedy is the imitation of an action by performers who do not recite it but enact it before an audience," and "hence it follows that the staging of a tragedy requires performers and also a stage, costumes, and other necessary equipment."[26] For Robortello, as he writes in his *Poetics* (1548), action on the part of the actors is the true end of tragedy.[27] Even those who understood Aristotle's narrative distinctions as distinctions of voice could nonetheless insist on the identification of drama with theatrical performance. Minturno, for instance, can explain quite clearly Aristotle's distinction in narrative terms in his *Poetics* (1563):

The Scenic Poet is different from the Lyric Poet and the Epic Poet in his mode of imitation. The Lyric Poet simply narrates, without ridding himself of his own persona. The Epic Poet sometimes retains it, sometimes rids himself of it, in part simply narrating, in part introducing other speakers. But [the Scenic Poet] appears from beginning to end in the guise of others.

But despite his acceptance of Aristotle's narrative distinctions as distinctions of voice rather than medium, Minturno nonetheless tellingly refers to Aristotle's "tragic poet" as the "Scenic Poet," and insists on theatrical performance (the art of the "Scenic Poet") as essential to the identity of dramatic poetry: "What is Scenic Poetry? . . . Imitation of things which are represented in a Theatre with a [theatrical] apparatus."[28] Lope de Vega's editor Don Francisco López de Aguilar feels he must specially explain that *La Dorotea* is merely dramatic, not actually for performance: "What is shown in *La Dorotea* is not characters in costume but actions imitated."[29]

In focusing on the difference between the poetics of the stage and the poetics of the book, the treatises, as we have seen, laid out a theatrical aesthetics, one formulated through the contrast with the experience of reading. As important as the insistent identification of theatrical reception with the senses which we saw in Chapter 7 was the understanding of theatre as presence—as "the thing itself"—which underwrote its claims to the kind of immediacy that could distinguish it from other verbal arts: Renaissance theorists made no apologies for overriding old-fashioned metaphysical notions of presence and absence (divinely determined) with distinctly phenomenal ones. For Guillaume Alabat (offering an early glimpse of such distinctly this-worldly notions of theatrical presence in his 1537 preface to the two-volume *Mystery of the Acts of the Apostles*), theatre is the "live exhibition of speaking characters and spectacles present right in the theatre."[30] Identifying the specifically theatrical by contrast with the verbal-poetic, Robortello differentiates poetic imitation from histrionic imitation by noting that the poet merely "expresses and describes," while the actor produces the object of imitation itself: "The poet . . . makes a kind of mute representation put in words, while the [actor], speaking and expressing through the voice, the mouth, the face, the gesture [creates] the very thing which is to be imitated."[31] As the stage poet says in Gabriel Chappuis's *The Celestial Worlds* (1583), "the thing represented live" in the theatre is represented "exactly as it was done."[32] Because of its connection to the worldly icon, theatre was seen (as it often still is) as a more immediate form of representation than the purely verbal arts of the page: "each one of its constituent parts appears on the stage as it is known to be in the world," writes Castelvetro.[33] Identical with its correlate phenomenon in the world, the stage icon seemed not to require of the spectator the same efforts of translation required of the reader or mere listener. "Who can deny that the performance of a tragedy, in so far as it is a thing seen, is less fatiguing to follow?" asks Castelvetro, since "when the very young, the mute, and the uncultivated undertake to report something they have seen happen they reenact it with words, gestures, signs, bodily movements, and by other means bearing a close resemblance to the things witnessed."[34]

Representing (as opposed to reporting), then, meant showing things happening in the here and now, not telling of things that happened somewhere else at another time—and this was crucial to the definition of the drama. "Scenic Poetry," explains Minturno in his *Arte poetica*, as distinguished from epic, "is not simply narrating; but introducing characters in action[s] and discussion[s]."[35] The difference between showing and telling was understood in theatrical terms. We have already seen Castelvetro's rejection of telling (in the hybrid third kind of dialogue) as a violation of dramatic decorum. When Sidney complains of the player who, "when he cometh in, must ever begin with telling where he is, or else the tale will not be conceived,"[36] he is similarly complaining of the overlay of "telling" on what should be showing, the interpolation of indexical elements or latent stage directions in represented, temporally immediate speech. Such insistence on the narrative decorum of the drama was crucial not only to the initial explorations of the *Poetics*, but also to the seventeenth-century consolidation of the identity of theatre as a distinct art. Dramatic poetry is action represented, asserts the Abbé D'Aubignac in a diatribe against staged récit: it is "called *Drama*, that is, *Action* and not *Narration*; those who represent it are called *Actors* and not *Orators*."[37] Similarly complaining of the excessive reporting in the ancient drama and implicitly insisting on the difference between drama and "simple narrative," François Ogier asks: "What difference is there, I beg you, between *The Persians* of Æschylus," in which "a messenger plays all the characters," and "a simple relation of what occurred between Xerxes and the Greeks? Is there anything so flat or so thin?"[38]

Castelvetro's discussion of dialogue (with which I began this chapter) offers, of course, an even more radical version of the argument that drama equals speech represented, not narrative report (and, in a logical inversion—as we saw—that speech represented equals drama, and hence must be staged)—the kind of extreme argument with which more sober theorists could take issue. Tasso, for instance, responds to Castelvetro by asserting that it is subject-matter, not medium, that distinguishes dramatic poetry from philosophical or historical dialogue. "Tragedies and comedies, properly understood, imitate actions, but dialogues imitate discussions." Distinctions of form here are "accidental rather than essential," for "the essential distinctions between types of dialogues derive from . . . the things discussed." Dialogue is not necessarily drama. However—and here Tasso is in line with Castelvetro and indeed most Renaissance theorists—drama *is* in need of a stage (made up, as it is, of "things represented on the stage," called "actions or acts," and therefore "called plays or dramatic representations"). And—as important—even if dialogue is not necessarily drama, drama *is* necessarily dialogue and dialogue alone, "introducing characters who speak" in their own voices and leaving out the voice of the poet.[39]

The insistence that drama consist only in direct speech certainly had ramifications for theatrical practice. But practice seemed to require something of a compromise, for one could not do altogether without explanation of the action. We might think of the practice of pushing explanatory devices to the margins as just such a compromise. There, prologues and epilogues, announcements of the "orator," entertaining interludes between the acts[40] could become framing devices, bridging the gap between represented illusion and the return to the world. This is not, of course, to suggest that "reporting" in any of its senses ever actually disappeared from the stage. The old narrative devices lingered, developing new manifestations, perpetually transformed through formal experiment. If the poet as narrator was banned from the classical stage, "reporting" through *characters* actually acquired a new importance (formalized in the *récit*, "those long narrations" of which D'Aubignac complains, unfortunately necessary in a theatre shy of the vulgarities of violent spectacle). The norms of "probability" generated, among those with aspirations to modern classical form, a general discomfort with solitary reporting or narrative overlay in the drama proper. But playwrights continued to put long explanatory monologues in the mouths of their actors (narrations, soliloquies, asides, apostrophes), justifying them as unfortunately necessary improbabilities and recommending special provisions. Corneille, for instance, insists that monologue be driven by a special "passion" and not be "a simple narration," but even this exception does not quite cover all the cases where he wishes to use the device, and he must finally fall back on a plea for the spectator's indulgence: "Above all the poet must remember that when an actor is alone on stage, he is understood to be talking to himself alone, and speaks aloud only to let the spectator know what he is speaking of, and what he is thinking about."[41]

Still, dramatists worked hard to marginalize narrative explanations on stage, and they worked equally hard to marginalize them in print, turning them into prefaces meant only for readers, dedications, arguments, stage directions, appendices, all structurally separate from the play proper and clearly distinct from the body of the text. The temporal separation of the narration of the theatrical event in the playhouse was correlated to the spatial separation of the narration of the book's structure on the page. Stage prologues explaining the action and characters could become printed prefaces, no longer to be performed; the printed dedication could displace the stage dedication. Playwrights often explicitly likened front matter to stage prologues: "If you be not reasonably assurde of your knowledge in this kinde of Poeme, lay downe the booke or read this, which I would wish had bene the prologue," John Fletcher advises the readers of *The Faithful Shepherdess* (1609).[42] In his poem accompanying the Beaumont and Fletcher folio, Humphrey Moseley can make a game of attempting to render the stage orator's speech typographically:

> As after th'*Epilogue* there comes some one
> To tell *Spectators* what shall next be shown;
> So here, am I; but though I've toyld and vext,
> 'Cannot devise what to present ye next.[43]

The uncertainty over the identity of the textual apparatus in dramatic editions—the anxiety that perhaps *any* explanation, no matter how marginal, might violate decorum—produced, in France, an extended debate on the use of stage directions. "I know very well," writes D'Aubignac, for instance, "that, to aid the Reader's understanding, several of our Poets have put Notes in their printed Works, which inform the Reader about things the verse fails to indicate." But he views them as a violation of the true nature of the drama: "In these Notes it is the Poet who speaks, and we have said that he may not do so in this sort of Poetry."[44] He is especially annoyed with the fact that, after having read Corneille's *Andromède*, he was "obliged to turn to the explanation printed before each Act, without which I would have had no idea what the Decorators did, because the Poet utterly failed to indicate [in the verse] what they were supposed to do."[45] His solution is the simple and elegant one used by dramatists from time immemorial: playwrights should, for the benefit of both spectators and readers, implant latent scenic indications in the speeches of their characters.

In response to D'Aubignac, Corneille offers a lengthy defence of stage directions as in fact a way of protecting pure dramatic "representing" on stage and, at the same time, giving pleasure to the reader: "To facilitate the pleasure of the reader . . . the poet should take great care to mark in the margins the lesser actions," which otherwise the reader is not able to see. Such directions, if embedded in speeches, would "burden" the poet's verse, and "would even detract from its dignity if he lowered himself to express them."[46] Corneille worries that without such marginalia "in [reading] the book one would often be required to guess at [the action]." This would pose difficulties not only for readers, but for professional actors as well, Corneille notes, differentiating seventeenth-century performance from that of the Ancients: "Printing puts our plays in the hands of actors who tour the provinces, and whom we can alert to what they have to do only by means of these [marginal stage directions], and who would do strange things if we did not help them out with these notes."[47] The conventions of typographically distinct explanation of the action might, on the one hand, violate the classical understanding of drama as dialogue, but printed explanations were necessary to the pragmatics of modern play-making (at least for those playwrights wishing for a measure of control). If they were a form of printed "telling" improper in a genre made of "showing," they nonetheless served the important purpose of allowing *performance* to steer clear of narrative overlay: authors did not have to *speak* for they could, separately, write; speeches did not have to contain instructions for action; stage directions could steer clear of dialogue.

NARRATIVE UNITY AND THE SPECTATOR'S IMAGINATION

If drama was made up of representing rather than reporting, and if representing meant representing on stage, it was the theatrical environment, then, that explained and helped interpret the formal rules for representational genres. That is, theatrical conditions determined dramatic form. Reworking Aristotle in the attempt to define the nature of the dramatic, Renaissance theorists may have been interested in the status of narrative form in and of itself, but their focus was on the relation of narrative form to medium. Whereas for Aristotle, "probability" was a logical term (applied to the sequence of events in the construction of the plot) that both described the formation of beliefs and prescribed aesthetic verisimilitude,[48] for Renaissance theorists, linking Aristotle's epistemological and logical concerns to issues of medium, it was no longer the logic of plot that determined theatrical probability but theatrical conditions. "A tragic or comic plot should contain a single action," writes Castelvetro, "not because it cannot by nature hold more, but because the limitations of [the] time . . . and place under which tragedies and comedies are performed will not permit the representation of many actions."[49] Dramatic probability was theatrical probability, impossible without correct dramatic-narrative form but determined by the constraints of performance. For Robortello, for instance, since tragedy was not reporting but representing in the theatre, there were limits on what it could credibly represent: "The epic admits certain things," he writes,

such as the stories told about Circe, the Sirens, the Cyclops. Tragedy does not receive these because it is not presented through narration, that is, a reporting of events, as is the epic. For in such reporting, many things, however marvelous . . . and against the belief of men, may be recounted, which cannot be acted by actors, on a stage, in the presence of spectators.[50]

In reading, by contrast, imagination was liberated. The conflict between the real world and the reception of the represented object seemed to disappear, in part because words were so different from stage objects. Castelvetro, for instance, argues that, unlike tragedy, "epic, narrating with words alone, can recount an action occurring over many years and in various places, without disturbing anyone." Words, he writes, "present to our minds things distant in space and time; which tragedy cannot do."[51] Words inhabited a zone liberated from space and time, and hence could become free vehicles of the imagination.

For actual stage practitioners developing the poetics of the sixteenth-century, to recognize the limits of imagination in the theatre was crucial to the proper practice of theatrical art. Differentiating the receptive constraints of the stage from the receptive freedom of the page, Jean Mairet, for instance, places at the centre of his defence of the unities an insistence on the contrast between novel (or history) and theatre, where sudden changes of scene invariably disgust and chill the spectator's imagination: "Yes but (someone might say)," he writes (hypothesizing an interlocutor who argues that theatrical imagination is like that involved "in the reading of history and novels"), "why can the imagination [in the theatre] not follow its object everywhere, since it can be stopped neither by mountains nor by seas?" Mairet offers his response:

For the imagination, history and drama are not the same thing. . . . Drama is an active and pathetic representation of things as if they were truly happening in the moment. . . . It is certain that, powerful as the imagination may be, it can never properly imagine that a character has passed from one pole to the other in a quarter of an hour.[52]

Probability might be preserved through proper plot construction. But plot construction was contingent on the limits of the spectator's imagination, bound to real-time experience in the auditorium.

Renaissance theorists acknowledged both implicitly and explicitly the distinction between narrative and "real" theatrical time, between the "three, four, or certainly six hours" of the performance and the somewhat longer narrative time of tragedies.[53] But they had trouble accommodating their own distinction to Aristotle's injunction ("tragedy strives as far as possible to limit itself to a single day")[54] because Aristotle was interested primarily in narrative time. As early as 1518, Machiavelli could joke with his enlightened spectators about their temporal expectations, —their supposed impatience (in *The Mandrake*) with narrative interruptions of real time: "And you, spectators," says Fra' Timoteo, addressing the audience in a moment of commiseration: "don't be impatient with us, because tonight no one will sleep, so that the Acts won't be interrupted by the passage of time."[55] Such teasing reflected a more serious view of the constraints of theatrical time and space on the narrative form of the drama. For Castelvetro,

Tragedy . . . should have as its subject an action occurring in a small space and in a small space of time, that is in whatever place and whatever time where and when the actors remain engaged in acting, and not in another place or time. . . . Nor is it possible to suggest to the audience that more days and nights have passed, when they sensibly know that only a few hours have passed.

For Castelvetro, "the deception" of incongruous narrative and theatrical time "cannot take place, since it is always recognized by the senses."[56] The senses (most prominently sight, but also hearing) determined theatrical probability: "The magnitude of the plot . . . is subject to the senses and taken in by sight and hearing together."[57] Unity of place restricted the scene represented "not only to a single city, village, field, etc., but to as much of any of them as can be seen by the eyes of a single person."[58] Castelvetro can treat unity of action (the most important of the unities for Aristotle) as unnecessary, since it is merely a narrative desideratum unconnected to the spectator's experience of time and place (though it may be a byproduct of the unities of time and place).[59]

If, linking belief to the empirical, Castelvetro understands Aristotle's prescriptions for dramatic time to be determined by the limitations of the senses, it is not merely the senses—conceived of abstractly—that govern, but the very real senses contained in the spectator's wilful body. "Just as the place is restricted to the stage, so the time is restricted to that in which the spectators can comfortably remain seated in the theatre," he writes, "which I cannot see as more than the revolution of the sun, if (as Aristotle says) that is twelve hours, on account of bodily necessities, for instance eating, drinking, excreting the superfluous loads of the stomach and bladder, sleeping, and other necessities."[60] Castelvetro translates the discomfort of one's bladder (having to go to the bathroom in the middle of the second act) into the discomfort of any dissociation between narrative time and real time, narrative space and real space. For him, as for many Renaissance theorists of theatre, the phenomenal resistance of the auditorium to the fiction's attempt to seduce and transform the evidence of the senses necessarily shocks the spectator's sense of probability.

When Sidney complains of narrative excess, he is implicitly asserting, similarly, the dominance of "two hours'" time (the time of the spectators) over expandable and collapsible narrative time: "Now of time they are much more liberal," Sidney explains in discussing the barbarities of non-classical English drama: "For ordinary it is that two young princes fall in love. After many traverses, she is got with child, delivered of a fair boy, he is lost, groweth a man, falls in love, and is ready to get another child, and all this in two hours' space: which, how absurd it is in sense, even sense may imagine."[61] Sidney's conflation of time and space here is telling: unity of time *is* a unity of place of sorts, that of the spectators' environment. The temporal dislocations of such barbaric narrative structures are correlated with their spatial dislocations (the parallelism reinforced in Sidney's rhetoric):

Now ye shall have three ladies walk to gather flowers, and then we must believe the stage to be a garden. By and by we hear news of shipwreck in the same place, and then we are to blame if we accept it not for a rock. Upon the back of that comes out a hideous monster with fire and smoke, and then the miserable beholders are bound to take it for a cave. While in the mean time two armies fly in, represented with four swords and bucklers, and then what hard heart will not receive it for a pitched field?[62]

Scaliger similarly links unity of place to unity of time, and here the stress on the visible as temporal limit is crucial: "as the whole time for Scenic events is only six or eight hours, it is not verisimilar to have a tempest come up and the ship founder in a part of the sea from which no land can be seen."[63] Sceptical vision (questioning what it sees, as it would soon begin to do in natural science) determines narrative time and space. What is invisible is too temporally distant not to strain narrative probability. Whatever the spectators' generosity of heart towards the fictional creation, belief is powerless over visual phenomena—what (in Sidney's words) the "miserable *behold-ers*" see with their own eyes. The senses control imagination and belief (the absurdities which, "in sense, even sense may imagine"): theatrical illusion must be grounded in them. Even for those with the tenderest of sensibilities, even through an effort of will, disbelief cannot be suspended.

However attractive the idea of the congruence of narrative time and space with real time and space may have been to a culture steeping itself in the analysis of sense perceptions (in philosophy as in dramatic aesthetics), the unities posed as many problems as they resolved. What was one to do about the fact that, with permanent theatres and hence shorter performance times, even the "artificial day" of twelve hours (not to mention the natural day of twenty-four hours) was a little too long for nature to bear on a regular basis. If one had to adhere to narrative/phenomenal congruence, how was one to compress even twelve hours, let alone twenty-four, into two?[64] Even if the audience could fall for the two-hours-as-twenty-four trick, problems remained. How was the dramatist to pack enough interesting events into twenty-four hours' narrative to keep impatient spectators satisfied without creating new improbabilities? (a problem Tirso de Molina addressed in terms much like Sidney's).[65]

If audiences required a variety which unity of time did not allow, practising dramatists attempted to develop new theories which would provide for the passage of greater expanses of narrative time but not present too great a conflict between narrative and theatrical time. Addressing seriously the problem that Machiavelli's prologue to *The Mandrake* raised in jest, Lope de Vega recommends that the dramatic plot "take place in as little time as possible, except when the poet is writing history in which some years have to pass; these he can relegate to the space between the acts, wherein, if necessary, he can have a character go on some journey."[66]

Corneille advises similarly that the playwright conceal lost time between the acts or, alternatively that the entire play simply be left temporally indeterminate. If the theatre was a constraint on the spectator's imagination, the playwright's goal was to free the imagination—to leave it (in Corneille's words) the "liberty to let itself flow with the action."[67] If absolute unity of time was a temporal aspiration, it was at the same time a way of allowing narrative to dissolve into the kind of atemporality represented at its absolute by Racine's *Britannicus*, which takes place in "a single day . . . sustained only by the interests, the sentiments, and the passions of the characters."[68] Dramatic-narrative atemporality might, after all, mimic the atemporal realm of those genres in which "words" without theatrical trappings could "present to our minds things distant in space and time," allowing the imagination free reign.[69]

The attempt to provide a bit of eternity can explain the atemporal feeling of much classical drama (however temporally precise its sets and locales may have been).[70] But non-specificity was also the last recourse of a troubled illusionism—one that could not, finally, sustain its own insistence on the distinction between the spectator's imagination and that of the reader. There was a fundamental underlying tension between the insistence that in the theatre only what the spectators "sensibly know" be shown and the recognition of theatre as the place where (in D'Aubignac's words) "all things must become larger, and where there is nothing but enchantment and illusion,"[71] between the insistence that theatre be grounded in the rational senses and the recognition that theatre was a producer of the imaginary—invariably dangerously proximate to unbridled and unwholesome fantasy transposed into action. On the one hand, well-tempered spectators were not to get carried away by imagination, but to be firmly grounded in their material surroundings. (Those not so grounded—Peregrine in Richard Brome's *Antipodes* (1638), who dons a knight's sword and shield and slashes at the "monsters" in the tiring room—were simply mad).[72]

The recognition of the power of the spectator's imagination, understood as analogous to the reader's imagination and trained by reading to imaginative leaps, was definitively to overthrow the unities only in the nineteenth century. But even in the early seventeenth century, practitioners could challenge the unities by imagining theatrical illusion by analogy with, rather than in contradistinction to, the book. Tirso de Molina, for instance, follows his attack on the absurdity of plot compression with a claim for freedom from the unities founded in a *parallel* between the spectator and the reader:

FIG. 37. Peering across narrative time zones in Corneille's *Theatrical Illusion* (1636).

Just as he who reads a story in a few pages without spending many hours informs himself of the things that happen over a long period of time and in distant places, so at the *comedia*, which is an image and a representation of the plot, when [the spectator] takes in the fortunes of the two lovers, since what happens to them is portrayed live and could not plausibly happen in one day, he is obliged to pretend whatever is necessary in order for the action to be perfect.[73]

Corneille more subtly calls on the freedom of romance narrative, with its temporal telescoping, in his 1636 comedy, the *Theatrical Illusion* (Fig. 37). There, he simultaneously obeys and evades the unities by virtue of the powers of the necromancer Alcandre who, through a magical illusion, can show, in the space of roughly two hours, many years in the life of the picaresque actor-hero of the play. In this, Corneille creates in Alcandre a figure for the playwright as conjurer, capable like romance writers of carrying the audience's imagination beyond the limits of space and time, but—more powerful than they—capable of using a theatrical illusion to carry away the spectator's resistant senses as well. "I want to *show* you his brilliant fortune," announces the magician:

The novices in the art with their . . . unknown words, which they pretend are so powerful . . . bring [you] those infinite *longeurs* that are in the end nothing but trickery and a mystery meant to impress and frighten you. My wand in hand, I will do more,

> *He waves his wand and a curtain is drawn . . .*[74]

Behind the curtain is revealed at once a theatrical spectacle (the actors parading in their most splendid costumes) and an alternative reality, the simultaneous space- and time-zone of the hero now become an actor (in Corneille's deliberate telescoping of the real and the theatrical). In calling on the magician's power to leap over time and space, Corneille reminds his own audience that the theatre is, after all, a conjuring glass, a medium "not fixed by [the] boundaries" of the auditorium but, like reading or any other form of aesthetic reception, subject to the imaginative complicity and enhanced by the imaginative freedom of the spectator.

9. *Framing Space: Time, Perspective, and Motion in the Image*

COMPOSING THE IMAGE

The illustration accompanying Terence's *Andria* (*The Woman of Andros*) in the edition of *Six Comedies by Terence* published in Frankfurt in 1568 (Fig. 38) offers a compendium of the plot, one analogous to those offered in narrative form in the "Inhalten" ("arguments") that accompanied many plays of the period. At the front of the image are clustered two scenic groups: Simo (N), turning for a moment from his son Pamphilus (O) to give instructions to his slave Davus (M) and his freedman Sosia (L), who emerges from the house just behind; and Chremes (P) discussing with his daughter Philumena (Q) her impending marriage to Pamphilus, with Pasibula (R) listening in the doorway. Slightly further back stands Crito (K), just arrived from Andros; behind him to the left, Charinus (I) with his slave, Birria (H), bemoaning his beloved Philumena's betrothal to Pamphilus; and behind him to the right, the house where the midwife Lesbia (F) delivers Pamphilus and Glycerium's (E) baby, who is then spirited out of the house by Archylis (D) and Mysis (C). Towards the rear (in an image growing increasingly romantic, as the town recedes into fields which melt into the sea) are scenes not represented in the play but crucial to its plot: Pasibula (B) set naked and adrift at sea after Chremes' brother's shipwreck (which is shown slightly further back in the image); and, at the far edges of the horizon, the distant island of Andros (A). The image represents the action by showing various scenes simultaneously: scenes that appear only sequentially in performance or in the larger narrative background to the play, spanning a decade or so in the life of the characters. As if, however, this simultaneous representation—with its temporal proliferation—is still insufficiently descriptive of the story's narrative richness, the illustrator has added a series of criss-crossing vectors, identifying a complex set of familial, social, and narrative relations among the characters. Pamphilus (O) is Glycerium's (E) lover (consorting with her off-stage, happily reunited with her at the end), and Glycerium *is* (it turns out) Pasibula (B) (the vector informs the viewer), Cremes' lost daughter and hence connected to his household (R) by another vector. Philumena (Q) is Charinus' (I) true love. Crito (K) is just come from Andros (A), and stands at the centre of the vectors of the plot, carrying the secret that is the key to its denouement. Representing the play, then, as at once a structure of status relationships, narrative events, and scenic interactions, the vectors seem also to be attempting to represent the motion of the drama in the still image, suggesting the movement of the narrative action and the (not always synchronized) movement of the characters on stage,

A. Andria infula.   G. Chryfis.   N. Simo.
B. Pafibula.   H.Birrhia.   O.Pamphilus.
C.Myfis.   I.Charinus.   P.Chremes.
D.Archillis.   K.Crito.   Q. Philumena.
F. Glycerium.   L.Sofia.   R.Pafibula.
F.Lesbia.   M.Dauus.   ):(iij

Fig. 38. Diagramming the plot in Terence's *Woman of Andros* (1568).

transferring the old Aristotelian notion of the drama as action into the modern diagrammatic scheme.

The diffusion of images with the spread of Renaissance printing brought a heightened consciousness of the problems of rendering the world, in all its dimensionality, on the page. Conversely, it made theatre practitioners aware of how the stage could import visual renderings of the world from images. "Not in vain is poetry called a *living picture*, imitating the dead picture which, in the small space of a yard and a half of canvas, depicts distant objects and perspectives that persuade the beholder of what they represent," explains Tirso de Molina, identifying the pictorial illusionism at the heart of the dramatic poetics of the period.[1] We have seen, in Chapter 7, the attention that sixteenth- and seventeenth-century writers on theatre paid to the power of the visual, and glanced briefly there at the period's fixation on Horace's comparison of poetry to pictures. The recurrence of the *ut pictura poesis* topos, the invention of the unity of place as a necessary complement to the unity of time, and the revival of visual-spatial mnemonics in Renaissance memory theatres were all manifestations of the fixation on the image, and were—like the images themselves—expressions of the general cultural impulse to match stories, representations of knowledge, and renderings of history to a set of visual and spatial co-ordinates. In an era in which telescopes, microscopes, and personal optical lenses were coming into common use, illustrated playbooks and books about theatre were, of course, only two arenas in which theorists and illustrators could explore the visual and spatial representation of time, motion, and the boundaries of the object, but they were particularly important ones for thinking about the problems of spatial and temporal representation. Through the interaction of theatres (with their scenes) and books (with *their* scenes), Renaissance and baroque practitioners and commentators (whether Sebastiano Serlio providing the definitive architectural guide for European princes or cheap playbook illustrators cutting a block) necessarily explored a variety of medium translation problems: the problem of constructing scenic space (of giving depth to flat surfaces); the problem of relating the time of the stilled frame (whether the page or the painted scene) to a variety of kinds of narrative time; the problem of representing different kinds of sensory impact on the page. The consequent reshaping and accompanying reconceptualization of theatrical space—through printed images, through the discussion of the relationship between the flat unmoving image and deep and mobile theatre, through the doctrine of unity of place, through the framing of the object—is the subject of this chapter.

In representing mutiple moments—theatrical and extra-theatrical—simultaneously, the illustration in the 1568 Terence *Andria* is typical of sixteenth- and early seventeenth-century play illustrations. In the 1615 title-page illustration for Thomas Kyd's *Spanish Tragedy*, for instance, instead of suppressing the narrative movement of the play, the illustrator chooses to represent a series of sequential scenes—the hanging of Horatio in the arbour, Balthazar and Lorenzo dragging Belimperia away (after the murder), and Hieronimo's discovery of the body of his son—composing these in sequence across the image.[2] In many title-page illustrations of the period, rather than merely representing the narrative multiplicity of plot, the illustrator attempts to represent the various temporal dimensions engaged by theatrical production itself. The image serving as illustration for the 1625 London edition of *A Game at Chess* (Fig. 39), for instance, is divided into tiers, each of which points to a different kind of temporal scheme: the top tier offers a verbal description of the play as event ("as it was Acted nine days to gether at the Globe on the banks side") representing the calendar time of the external world; the middle tier offers a theatricalized image of the chess kings, queens, knights, and bishops in the play, representing theatrical time as the spectator might experience it; and the bottom tier offers a series of broadside-style portraits of the real-life figures caricatured in the play (the Spanish Ambassador Count Gondomar as the Black Knight, the Anglican convert Marco Antonio de Dominis as the Fat Bishop, and Prince Charles as the

FIG. 39. Thomas Middleton's *A Game at Chess* (1625 edition).

White Knight), representing the broader political and historical time against which the play is set. Similarly, the frontispiece for the first volume of Alexandre Hardy's *Theatre* (1626) (reproduced in Chapter 7) suggests not only the multiple sensory modes of the drama (seeing and hearing, represented on Melpomene's banner), but also the multiple temporal modes of the drama: theatrical time, represented in the image of Melpomene on a typical platform stage in front of the audience; narrative time, represented in the illustrations to the plays, shown in the landscape behind her throne; and classical-historical time, allegorized in the traditional sculptural figures on either side of the medallion that serves as showcase for the title.

The representation of multiple narrative time in the typical dramatic illustration mirrored the usual linear and additive or circular representation of time on the Renaissance stage: in the "mansion" settings, with their lines of houses across which the action was to unfold, with each of the houses as the locus of a different moment in the narrative (the *décor simultané*, for instance, of a theatre like the Hôtel de Bourgogne); in the perspective stages like that built for Ariosto's *Cassaria* in Ferrara in 1508 showing an elaborate perspective backdrop with a traditional row of houses in front of it, or in Andrea Palladio and Vincenzo Scamozzi's 1585 Teatro Olimpico with its five grand perspective views (the equivalent of the five doors common on the Terence stages), or in Bernardo Buontalenti's set for the 1589 festival production of *La Pellegrina*, with its three perspective streets on which Buontalenti's seven scene changes were played out; in circular theatres like the Globe ("this wooden O") or the spherical "*Microcosme* or *Globe*" "figuring Man['s]" place in cosmic time in Jonson's *Hymenai*; in the dispersed settings of spectacles like Baltasar de Beaujoyeulx's *Balet Comique* (1581) or Samuel Daniel and Inigo Jones's *Vision of the Twelve Goddesses* (1604); in the scenic spaces representing "several apartments" and "several different [outdoor] locales" divided by "diverse frontispieces, posts, columns, or arcades," described by the French theorist Jules de La Mesnardière as late as 1639.[3] In scenic design, as in illustrations, different moments of narrative time could be present simultaneously. The eye of the viewer was free to roam among them, watching the narrative both through time and across space.

FRAMES, ILLUSTRATIONS, GRAPHS

The now conventional categories—medieval and classical, Renaissance and baroque, multiple staging and unified perspective—are clearly inadequate to describe the continually shifting variety of solutions to the representation of dramatic time and movement in theatrical space in the sixteenth and seventeenth centuries. But if there was not a simple, chronological transformation from "old-fashioned" (multiple, simultaneous, decentred) playing spaces to the "modern" (unified, centralized, framed) single-perspective scene—if various kinds of playing spaces and various ways of playing in them continued to coexist—there were certainly shifts in expectations about proper scenic design that expressed a general drive towards scenic unification. This drive was articulated both theoretically and architecturally: in, for instance, the reverent French phrase "*scène à l'italienne*," and in actual theatres, the centralizing tendency arguably represented emblematically in the reduction in the number of perspectives and widening of the central arch in the three Italian theatres probably most influential for the rest of Europe: Palladio and Scamozzi's five-perspective Teatro Olimpico built in Vicenza in 1585; Scamozzi's three-perspective theatre built in Sabbionetta in 1588; and Giovanni Battista Aleotti's single-perspective theatre framed with a single large proscenium arch, built in the Farnese Palace in Parma in 1618.[4] Whatever the significance of the Olimpico, Sabbionetta, and Parma theatres, the new theatres built on the model of the *scène à l'italienne* began to eliminate "houses" and other forms of linear décor, using perspective to place the attention at the centre of the scene. Architects relied on machinery to produce scenic *changes* rather than merely scenic effects, showing new scenes serially rather than simultaneously, and striving for unity and symmetry. Designers used curtains and frames within frames (curtained balconies, curtained interiors, revelations of windows within windows), for instance in the masque *Oberon* (performed 1611), in which the cliff setting of the anti-masque opens to show the stage "frontispiece," and finally the interior palace, or in James Shirley and Inigo Jones's masque, *The Triumph of Peace* (1634), which describes the "border of the front and sides that enclosed all the Sceane."[5] Both visually and thematically, scenes stressed harmonious balance and the triumph of order over division (civil and aesthetic), for instance in William Davenant and Inigo Jones's masque, *Salmacida Spolia* (1639), in which the King and other masquers are "discovered, sitting in the throne of Honour," surrounded by "captives bound in several postures, lying on trophies of armours, shields, and antique weapons," a scene replaced by the next: "buildings in prospective . . . the suburbs of a great city," over which appears a cloud "representing the spheres" and beyond it "a heaven . . . full of deities" and a chorus filling "the whole scene with . . . harmony."[6]

The use of framed, unified perspective encouraged the focusing of the eye and the containment of vision within the borders of the stage. Such containment could be the accomplice of verisimilitude, which (as we have seen) depended, for its illusions, on the erasure of both extra-scenic space and any preceding or subsequent scenes.[7] As Nicola Sabbattini explains in his *Manual for Building Scenes and Machines in Theatres* (1638), the house fronts on stage for the first scene did not always correspond with the dramatically different scenes that followed: "When the scene of the houses has been changed to woods, mountains, and so on, these two house fronts remain alone unchanged, and do not give either a pleasing or realistic [*verisimile*] impression. To obviate this difficulty, you may place at the front of the stage an arch with columns or statues, and build the scene within it."[8] Focus and erasure of extra-scenic space were mutually reinforcing. Since perspective was understood to be best seen along a single line of vision, drawn between an imaginary vanishing point at one end (behind the stage) and an ideal viewing position at the other (the Prince's seat in the hall), there could be only one scene and only one ideal viewing position. Following such treatises as Giacomo da Vignola's *Two Rules of Practical Perspective*, Sabbattini stresses the importance of singularity for proper perspective. "Some designers," he writes, "are in the habit of drawing more than one street on the back shutter, either with a single or with several vanishing points, a practice of which, in truth, I cannot approve very highly."[9] The scene as object and the ideal viewing position had an important relationship: the eye of the person in the ideal viewing position, Sabbattini specifies, "will be as high as the vanishing point, for all the objects in the scene appear better from that position than from any other place."[10]

Unified perspective entailed, ideally, perfect control of the gaze of the spectator. The perspective scene was to amaze, to enrapture, to conquer: "What a lovely, deep and stirring thing . . . is *Perspective* . . . in a *Theatre* or *Theatrical Scene*," writes Joseph Furttenbach in his *Noble Mirror of Art*. "The perspective lines . . . conquer . . . the spectator . . . [who] is seduced and stirred, his senses . . . enraptured."[11] Rather than the spectator creating the scene (focusing on one house or another), the scene created the position of the "astonished and entranced" spectator. The ideal of controlling the spectator's gaze reinforced the sense that the spectacle ought to take place in a space apart, untouched by the noisy audience, the grinding machinery and dripping candles, the disturbances of the auditorium ("the ladies," for instance, whom Filippo Pigafetta found so distracting at the inaugural Olimpico *Oedipus* in 1585).[12] This ideal was not to come fully into its own until the later eighteenth century (as we shall see in Chapter 13), and it was never, of course, actually attainable: when Sabbattini writes that "most of the spectators have thoughts only for . . . the scene,"[13] he is expressing at best a mere desideratum. But there was a general aspiration towards scenic magnificence protected from audience incursion, an aspiration reflected in visual representations of the auditorium, in the images of spectators massed in the hall, an indistinguishable block, faceless and turned motionless towards the imposingly framed stage (Fig. 40).

Such images reflected the more general change in dramatic and theatrical illustrations during the period, which accompanied the new norms for theatrical space. The illustration in the 1644 edition of Corneille's *Death of Pompey*, for instance, represents a single narrative moment, showing the murder of Pompey at sea at the hands of Septime and his henchmen: off-stage action nonetheless rendered, in the image, in scenic terms (Fig. 41). The composition is centred on the prow of the boat, and the lines of the image cause the eye to travel towards the centre of the scene, a movement reinforced by the direction of wind and water, the lines of the spears seeming to descend from the stormy heavens towards the dark events in the boat, and the gesture of the figures watching the scene (who frame the lower left-hand corner, their backs turned from the viewer, pointing towards the boat). Rather than crowding further events into the image, the illustrator has left the stretch of storm clouds and the vastness of the watery horizon open, as a contrast to the compressed scenic action shown in the turbulent event in the boat. Movement is not represented as narrative change over time but by the sea itself, at once suggestively mobile (in the scene) and frozen in time (in the image) at the single, climactic moment of the story. Similarly representing narrative action centred on a single moment in the play, a slightly later image for Corneille's *Horace* (modelled on an earlier illustration) shows the young Horace at the instant in which, with a forward thrust, he stabs Curiace (Fig. 42). Centred on the symmetrical fighting figures and receding into a deep scenic backdrop

FIG. 40.   The audience at a performance of Jean Baptiste Lully's *The Festival of Love and Bacchus* in the theatre at Versailles in 1668.

LA. MORT. DE. POMPEE.
A. PARIS,
Chez. A. De Sommauille. &. A Courbé.
Au palles. 1644.

FiG. 41. The murder of
Pompey in Corneille's
Death of Pompey (1644).

representing the battlefield and the Roman camp rising into the hills, the image is
framed by theatrical curtains at the top and upper edges, at once to evoke an actual
stage and to enforce the image's compositional unity.[14] The scene could not be shown
on stage because of the rule against on-stage violence but, drawing on a theatrical
vocabulary by using curtains to frame the scene, the image suggests (for the viewer)
the theatrical conception of narrative that will come to shape not only illustrations
but also, eventually, non-dramatic storytelling as well: a story is made of individual
scenes, conceived compositionally, the figures' relations to one another spatially representing the deeper narrative relations of the story.

Illustrations representing performances (showing scenes on stage in the theatre)
similarly emphasized not linear progress in time (as, for instance, in the early Terence illustrations, with their stage houses lined up in a row), but overall spatial composition and scenic depth. Those in Pio Enea Obizzi's *Hermione*, for instance, show
a framed stage (with the standard sculptural figures on each side) containing a perspective scene, in which the figures appear fully integrated in the scenic space. In

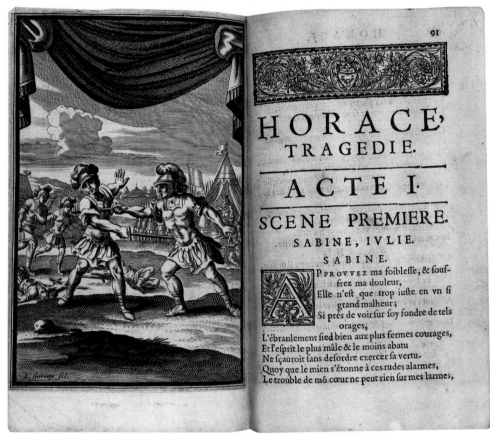

Fig. 42. Horace stabbing Curiace in Corneille's *Horace* (1660 edition).

one, for instance (illustrating a scene in Act III, described by the stage directions), Venus is shown in her shell being pulled by two swans, with a knight (the real-life Paolo Zabarella) entering on his "charger covered with mother-of-pearl" accompanied by "the principal rivers of the Dominion of Venice in the form of robust old men," emerging from the deeps of the watery stage to pour the rivers from their urns (Fig. 43).[15] Images commonly emphasized not merely the unification and enclosure of the scene but also the grandeur of the performance, with the stage figures dwarfed by the massive and imposing architectural frame. The habitual breaching of the framed stage, by figures emerging from the perspective image and (as in the Obizzi illustration) descending the steps of the stage into the auditorium, could serve as an implicit commentary on the relationship between images and performance, pointing to the tension between the image enclosed by the frontispiece and the animation of the performance which, not fully contained by it, spills (like the rivers of Venice themselves) abundantly over its edges.

Fɪɢ. 43. Venus rowed by Neptune, a knight on his charger, and "the principal rivers of . . .
Venice" in the form of "robust old men" in Pio Enea Obizzi's *Hermione* (1638).

Numerous explanations have been given for the fact that unified and framed
scenes came to dominate other spatial arrangements in seventeenth-century theatres, among them: the advent of permanent theatres, which allowed for the use of
increasingly sophisticated set-changing machinery, so that scenes no longer had to
remain together on stage but could be replaced with the pull of a few levers; the
development of perspective painting on stage, which seemed to demand a single
"vanishing point," to be seen from the "ideal viewing position" (the seat of the
Prince); and the centralizing politics of the period, with the body politic ideally to be
subject to the surveillance of the Prince's omniscient eye (just as, in the theatre, the
scene was ideally subject to the surveillance of the Prince, watching from the ideal
viewing position). Clearly the scenic harmony in *Salmacida Spolia* represents the
centralizing authority of the nation state (its violence transformed into the harmony
of the spheres, echoed in the harmonious architecture of the metropolis). But one
might, at the same time, attribute the change in scenic design to an unconscious
absorption of the aesthetics of printed illustrations and graphic designs: necessarily
framed by the edges of the page, conventionally ringed by borders, the focused object

of a particular line of vision, aesthetically protected from the incursions of the viewer or the accidents of time and live bodies, stilled and fixed in a moment of time. Whether the proliferation of illustrations in itself helped to reshape scenic design, it is clear that there was an important reciprocity between stage design and page design. Framed stage settings (stage "frontispieces") and architecturally framed title pages (book "frontispieces") mirrored each other. The space of the decorative page (delimited and ringed in ornamental borders) helped to model the framed and unified space of the scene: theoretically fixed in time; representing a translation of temporal unity into space; ideally protected from audience incursion, aesthetically untouchable and apart. At the same time, baroque theatre architecture was crucial to the aesthetics of the baroque title page (as theatrical space was to book illustration generally).[16] The typical engraved frontispiece, drawing on theatre architecture, arched and framed in columns and ringed with allegorical figures, recalled the theatrical scene, as in the title-page design for Ortelius' collection of maps, the *Theatrum Orbis Terrarum* (1570) (reproduced in Chapter 4), its evocation of the theatrical metaphor merely rendering explicit what other title pages implied visually. If (as one critic has put it) classical drama emerged not only from the "scène à l'italienne" but also from the classical "mise en texte,"[17] the classical "mise en texte" mirrored and, in turn, reshaped the classical "mise en scène."

The rebuilding of Renaissance theatres depended, moreover, on the architectural and scenic designs—the illustrations and graphic representations—both produced by architects (in books) and reproduced by them (in the theatres built on others' models). And these necessarily reshaped those theatres: not merely in their specifics, but in the larger sense, as graphic representations of spatial form *per se*, shifting the ways both architects and those interested in theatre generally thought about space. When Serlio struggles to squeeze Vitruvius' grand theatre into the narrow Renaissance hall, he does so by flattening the theatre's components into a series of vectors and co-ordinates, which can then be reset in the hall (conveniently rectangular, like the page):

Although halls (however large they may be) could not accommodate theatres such as the ancients had, nevertheless in order to follow the ancients as closely as possible, I have included in my plan such parts of the ancient theatre as a great hall might contain. Thus the part D corresponds to the *proscenio*, the circular part marked E corresponds to the *orchestra*, raised one step from the *proscenio*.[18]

Furttenbach, in his *Recreational Architecture* (1640), explains how the painted front curtains are to be used for consecutive disclosures of the perspective stage, illustrating these in a series of images, and orienting them in relation to the graphs in which he explains, like Serlio, how to rebuild old spaces for the new theatres, with a correspondence between the perspective images to be seen by the awe-struck spectator and the logic of space that configures what they see (Fig. 44).[19]

At the same time, the graphic rendering of space on the page contributed to the imaginative reconceptualization of scenic space in graphic terms. While preserving Renaissance pictorial simultaneity, the illustration for the *Andria* in the Frankfurt

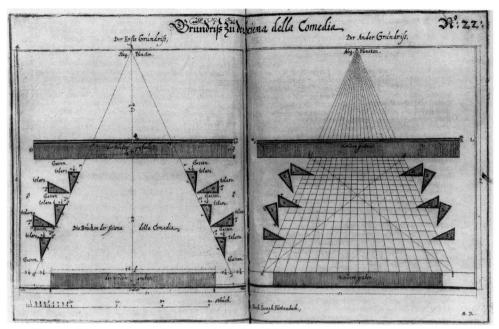

Fig. 44. Diagramming scenic perspective in Joseph Furttenbach's *Recreational Architecture* (1640).

Terence offers a reinterpretation of two kinds of dramatic images with which the illustrator must have been familiar: the traditional early Renaissance play illustration showing characters beside an "argument" or scene (for instance in the 1527 French translation of Fernando de Rojas's *Celestina*, portraying Parmeno and Calisto beside the "argument of the second act");[20] and the specifically theatrical images that attempted to give performance reality and perspectival depth to the drama (those in the Strasbourg or Lyon Terences, for instance, or in manuals like Serlio's). Rather than simply pictorializing character or representing theatrical space through perspective, the Frankfurt illustration provides a rendering that uses the diagram as a tool of analysis, overlaying, by means of its multiple vectors and lettered coordinates (kin to those in architecture manuals of the period), the graphic representation of narrative on the graphic representation of stage space.

If it was the task of a manual of theatre architecture like Furttenbach's *Recreational Architecture* to catch the fleeting moment of performance (as he writes) through its diagrammatic renderings,[21] the diagram in turn influenced ways of imagining scenic space. Both designers and dramatists, whether consciously or unconsciously, conceived of theatrical space in graphic terms: "Sit in a full Theater, and you will thinke you see so many lines drawne from the circumference of so many eares, whiles the *Actor* is the *Center*," writes John Webster.[22] Reflecting the transformed aesthetic of the middle decades of the seventeenth century, Jean Claveret advises the reader of his *Rape of Proserpine* (1640) to reconceive the separate stage spaces ("Heaven," "hell," and "Sicily") as if they were part of a diagram, with a line running between them to create, graphically, a new kind of unity of place: "The scene is in Heaven, in Sicily & in hell. . . . The imagination of the reader can represent to itself a certain kind of unity of place, conceiving of it as a perpendicular line from heaven to hell."[23] The frontispiece for an edition of the Abbé D'Aubignac's *Whole Art of the Theatre* seems to offer itself as an allegory for the graphic rendering of the theatrical, identifying this with the rationalizing of theatrical art: above, Apollo lectures Melpomene and Thalia on the logic of aesthetics as a foundation for practice, while below the philosopher (presumably D'Aubignac) measures out the proper co-ordinates of the art with his compass and squares.

While the unities of time and place served a complex of purposes, one might think of them as, in addition, unconscious extrapolations from the framed, temporally stilled, and logical images that theorists saw in books and prints. We have already seen Sidney's use of the word "space" to describe theatrical time ("all this in two hours' space"),[24] suggesting the importance of spatial and visual co-ordinates to the unity of time. As early as 1539, Antonio Landi had attempted, in his comedy *Il Commodo*, to represent the twenty-four-hour day prescribed by Renaissance poetics through a series of stage images.[25] Certainly, for seventeenth-century illustrators and critics, spatial form could express narrative structure. A play like Wohlfarth Spangenberg's translation of Thomas Naogeorg's "sacred tragedy" *Jeremia* (1603) could experiment with a graphic rendering of biblical and dramatic time, providing a map of the "Names of the Idols in this Tragedy," the acts and scenes in which they appeared, and the biblical passages which referred to them.[26] Georges de Scudéry's explanation of unity of time—"as bodies are objects of the eyes, so the Poem is the object of memory"[27]—calls on a familiar optical model to explain the natural limits of dramatic form (like visual objects, limited by the capacity of the faculty perceiving it). Narrative was the object of vision, in part because the logic of the unities was a visual logic, in part because of the identification of theatres and books—the vehicles for narrative—as themselves the objects of vision. When James Shirley refers to the Beaumont and Fletcher folio as an "optick" and the stage as a "conjuring glasse," he suggests the strong association of the book and stage with tools for the focusing of vision.[28] As objects of the eyes, both the theatre and the illustration could offer places for working out what ought to be seen and the point of view from which it ought to be seen—for shaping the gaze of the viewer.

PROBLEMS OF TRANSLATION: DIMENSION, MOTION, AND MEDIUM

The woodcut accompanying Elizabeth Allde's 1630 quarto of Robert Greene's *Friar Bacon and Friar Bungay*, showing, simultaneously, three moments in the play, depicted in three superimposed images of Friar Bacon (Friar Bacon sitting up to speak, Friar Bacon nodding off at the table, and the moment in which lightning strikes and the inanimate and previously silent "brazen-head" speaks aloud) (Fig. 45), offers not merely one such object, reflecting the period's assumptions about the proper shaping of the viewer's gaze. In its triple typographic speech banners, con-

FIG. 45. Robert Greene's *Friar Bacon and Friar Bungay* (1630 edition).

trolling the image with a triad of tenses ("Time is," "Time was," and "Time is past"), and in its representation of the head (once an inanimate and silent object, now emerging from a pile of books to speak aloud), the woodcut implicitly engages the very problems of time, motion, and medium that the illustrator was facing. Those creating illustrations for popular plays like *Friar Bacon*, those creating treatises on the construction of scenic space in the Italianate court theatres, and those designing actual scenes all had to respond to a similar set of questions. How were illustrators and scenic architects to represent three-dimensional depth on the page and on the stage? How were they to represent the temporal flow and motion of performance and narrative in pictorial and scenic terms? How were they to represent non-visual sensory impact and cognitive content? What were they to treat as the frame of the theatrical event (were spectators—the prince, the commoner, the courtesan, the mob—to be comprehended in the scene, on the page or on the stage?)

The questions went the other direction as well, from the page to the stage: how, for instance, were designers to translate the two-dimensionality of classical architectural manuals into the three-dimensionality and temporality of the stage? When Sabbattini acknowledges, in describing methods of painting the stage parapet, that, because of the crowds of people, an elaborately painted stage parapet "can present a fine appearance only on paper,"[29] he recognizes the difficulty of showing off book images to proper effect on the stage. It was simple to create perspective on the fixed and perfectly flat space of the canvas or page, but how to take such perspectives back out into the scene, with its various spectator points of view and its relation to moving objects, was a different problem. Basic principles of perspective painting taught, for instance, that the stage could be made to look deeper by painting buildings and trees smaller and smaller towards the rear of the stage, so that the eye thought that it was looking far into the distance. The problem was that, as actors moved upstage (particularly frequent in crowd scenes), they grew larger in proportion to the buildings, until a normal-sized actor could dwarf what had before seemed giant towers (a problem which later practitioners solved with the use of children upstage, so that audiences would ostensibly not notice that the buildings were shrinking).[30] Designers were similarly faced with the problem of "living things having motion" (in Serlio's words)[31]—the problem of the relation between immobile painted renderings and the animate representations of the actors. "Some artists," writes Serlio,

are in the habit of painting supposedly living characters in these scenes—such as a woman on a balcony or in a doorway, even a few animals. I do not recommend this practice, however, because although the figures represent living creatures they show no movement. On the other hand, it is quite appropriate to represent some person who sleeps, or some dog or other animal that sleeps, because no movement is expected here.[32]

Despite such recommendations, the pictorial representation of "stilled life" on the stage was perhaps more the rule than the exception: set painters continued to paint, behind ordinary actors, ships immobile on frozen seas, skies filled with clouds stuck half-way through their drifting. In the illustration for Serlio's Satyric Scene, there are a few birds stopped mid-air above the desolate huts. Sabbattini actually shows a clock (raising a different problem for theatre phenomenology, in the incongruity between clock time and the time of the dramatic narrative).[33] But the theory of temporal/pictorial correspondence was important, seen as central to theatrical illusion. Echoing Serlio on the problem of motion, for instance, Sabbattini frames the interdiction against the painting of animate creatures on stage in terms of "verisimilitude." In painting the scene, he writes,

Take care not to depict any men or women at the windows or in the streets, or birds in cages, monkeys, or other domestic pets. These take away from the impression of reality for the authors make their comedies include action which often goes beyond the period of one entire day, and it is impossible that these men and animals should stand immovable entire days. . . . It would be scarcely true to nature that an object would remain motionless through the action of the limits of a day, and for other reasons that need not be mentioned here.[34]

Sabbattini creates, here, an equation between scenic stasis and unity of time: they both protect the credibility of represented narrative from the sceptical attacks of "natural" time and vision, thus underwriting verisimilitude. Invoking a tension between experiential time and representational time similar to Castelvetro's, Sabbattini translates the requirement that narrative time correlate with the spectator's time (the time of bodily needs) into a requirement that pictorial-scenic time correlate with the spectator's time. He may be deliberately echoing Castelvetro on the bodily needs of the spectators (are the "other needs" that prevent Castelvetro's real spectators from being able to endure a long performance—those in addition to eating, drinking, and purging—the same as Sabbattini's painted monkeys' "other reasons" for not remaining mobile?)[35] In any case, he similarly relates phenomenal experience to the performance narrative and these to the frozen scene painting, seeming to take up Castelvetro's anxiety about the spectators' freedom to take care of their needs and to project that anxiety onto the painted figures, as if fearing that the spectators (through empathic identification) might be as anxious about the bodily needs of the monkeys as they are about their own. This time the relationship is triple: phenomenal (spectator) time must not clash with narrative-theatrical time, and these must not clash with the time of the painted scene. The problem with set immobility in a theatre of narrative motion was that, eventually, the set might begin to have "other needs." Things naturally in motion over time, it was felt, should not be made to stand still simply because sets were painted.

Even if animate figures were not painted on sets, a related difficulty remained: stories moved around in space, whereas stages were fixed and sets often immobile. How was the audience to believe that what they saw was real when the scene changed but the stage and set remained behind (the problem, as we saw in Chapter 8, that troubled Sidney when, insisting on the senses as limits on the imagination, he complained of the staccato scenes that the "miserable beholders" were asked to follow on one and the same stage)?[36] There were several methods that dramatists could use to deal with the problem of correlating extended narrative time with set immobility. One was to leave time and place sufficiently imprecise that the audience just might not notice that the set ought to have changed—sufficiently imprecise for the "imagination of the spectator" simply to "flow with the action" (Corneille's solution in the "Discourse on the Unities," as we saw in Chapter 8).[37] Another was to adhere rigorously to unity of place, preserving a setting that represented a precise location, but one location alone. But while these were doctrinally the solutions of choice, they left the drama an extremely narrow range of scenic options. Moreover, certain doctrines meant to enforce verisimilitude by means of unity could, in fact, create new problems for verisimilitude. Like unity of place, the doctrine of *liaison des scènes* ("linkage of scenes") was intended to promote plot and scenic unity (in this case by requiring that at least one character from the preceding scene remain present in the following scene). But "it would have been ridiculous," writes Corneille of his use of place in *Cinna*, "if I had made this Emperor [Augustus] deliberate with Maxime and Cinna over whether or not to give up the empire in exactly the same place where [Cinna] just came from reporting to Emilie about his conspiracy against him, which is the reason I broke the *liaison des scènes* in the fourth act."[38] In the guise of "Neander" (in his *Essay of Dramatic Poesy* (1665)), Dryden similarly describes the awkward results of a rigid adherence to the *liaison des scènes*:

> The Act begins in the Street. There a Gentleman is to meet his Friend; he sees him with his man, coming out from his Father's house; . . . the second, who is a Lover, has made an appointment with his Mistress; she appears at the window, and then we are to imagine the Scene lies under it. This Gentleman is call'd away, and leaves his servant with his Mistress: [when her father is heard within], the young Lady . . . thrusts [the servingman] into . . . her Closet. After this, the Father enters to the Daughter. . . . The Play goes forward, the Stage being never empty all the while: so that the Street, the Window, the two Houses, and the Closet, are made to walk about, and the Persons to stand still.[39]

Writing (not coincidentally) in the years in which permanent public theatres fully rigged with scene-changing machinery were starting to be built in England, Dryden, of course, ironizes what was, in fact, the practitioner's solution of choice to the temporal stasis of the rules. One could preserve the illusion of reality by changing the sets (so that scenes followed one another in sequence) and by attempting to erase extra-scenic space (so that there would no longer be a conflict between theatrical stasis and scenic change). Although immobile things were meant to stay immobile on stage, streets, windows, houses, and closets *could* be "made to walk about" while the persons stood still. While this solution might technically violate unity of place, it might in other ways enforce narrative unity. Just as, through the right use of perspective painting and the proper positioning of actors and stage objects, designers could attempt to correlate the depth of the stage set with the moving objects that came into relation with it, through the right use of machines, designers could attempt to correlate the time of the scenic design with the time of the dramatic narrative. Landi's *Il Commodo*, showing "Act by Act the hour of the fictional day," beginning with Aurora representing the dawn, measured by the new position of the sun in each act, and ending with the figure of Night,[40] offers an explicit rendering of what later playwrights and designers were, similarly, attempting, in their efforts to correlate staging with narrative structure. Just as (a century later) Scudéry imagines the plot structure as the object of the eye, so Landi imagines spectacle as, after all, a proper vehicle for showcasing dramatic-narrative form. When Jules de La Mesnardière insists that the poets must occupy themselves not only with narrative structure but with scenic effect,[41] he is pointing towards the use of stage machinery as a vehicle for, rather than a rival of, dramatic form. In *Andromède* (1650), Corneille attempts precisely this, demonstrating that spectacle need not come into conflict with narrative coherence but may in fact be a means of highlighting the artful construction of the drama. Committed to narrative orthodoxy and at the same time committed to performance pleasures, he insists that in the well-wrought machine play, the tragedy itself and its "represent[ation] with machines" are inseparable: "Each act, as well as the prologue, has its particular décor, and at least one flying machine. . . . [The machines] are not in this tragedy detached embellishments. They create in it . . . the conflict and the dénouement, and are so necessary to it that you could not remove a single one without toppling the entire edifice."[42] The mechanics of plotting hinge on theatrical machines, which Corneille then translates back into textual form in the printed edition of the *Design of the Tragedy of Andromède* (published at his own expense), with its descriptions of the "decorations" and its fold-out illustrations of each act. The structural integrity of the work as a whole—its unity of action—(described by the architectural metaphor, "the entire edifice," and detailed in Corneille's "Examen") is understood at once spatially and textually, its "design" to be seen equally on the stage, in the printed text, and in the engraved images of the *Design*.

Both the static stage tableau so important to the theatre of the period and the machine play that was its mobile form served the era's visual-spatial impulses, each of them offering a different solution to disjunctions among narrative time, scenic motion, and the image. To freeze the stage image, as in a tableau, was to allow space to represent itself as an image, disjoined from the experience of time altogether and thus seemingly not in conflict with narrative-bodily time. The instantaneousness of the pictorial could resolve the problems created by the drama's temporal extension, serving as a model for an alternative theatricality, stopped in the instant. In his "Parallel Betwixt Painting and Poetry," Dryden would identify this as one of the advantages of painting over poetry (politely casting painting's capacity to immobilize time as an "advantage" while delicately suggesting that the painter's task was therefore much easier than the poet's). "I must say this to the advantage of painting, even above tragedy," he writes: "that what this last represents in the space of many Hours, the former shows us in one Moment. The Action, the Passion, and the manners of so many Persons as are contain'd in a Picture, are to be discern'd at once, in the twinkling of an Eye."[43] While the essay reflects Dryden's general interest in the relationship between the "Sister Arts" (which he had explored a year or two earlier in his poem to the painter Sir Godfrey Kneller), it also implicitly reflects his understanding of the way in which the theatrical might imitate the painterly, in the kind of stage painting he himself had used as a theatre professional during the preceding decades: "From the Heavens, (which are opened) fall the rebellious Angels wheeling in the Air, and seeming transfix'd with Thunderbolts," begins his *State of Innocence* (written in 1674 and never, in fact, staged): ". . . Angels discover'd above, brandishing their Swords. . . . Hell: Part of the Scene is a Lake of Brimstone or rowling Fire; the Earth of a burnt colour: The fall'n Angels appear on the Lake, lying prostrate."[44] To transfix the Angels with Thunderbolts, to display them prostrate on the Lake, was to show an action "in the twinkling of an Eye," a means of unifying the mechanical scene in the suggestively stilled moment.

Images—painted and printed—might be contrasted with the mobile and deep space of the stage. But they could also be the model for the stilled scene, framed and protected from the unruly spectators, momentarily stopped in time. If designers and playwrights revelled in the machines that might allow (in Serlio's words) a "horned and lucent moon" to "rise slowly"[45] in harmony with dramatic nightfall, they also aspired to the autonomy of the page,—where designers could bypass the problem of usurpation in the auditorum, where the reader was always the ideal spectator. In the representations of the unifying frontispiece (frame for the stage or frame for the page), in the frozen moment of the scenic tableau, the woman no longer seemed paralysed in the window nor the monkey in need of relief. There, one was no longer troubled by the fact that the real world was filled with birds flying across the sky and wind in the trees and ships drifting across the sea and the ticking hand of the clock.

THE COMMERCE OF LETTERS

10. *Dramatists, Poets, and Other Scribblers*

On the seventeenth- and eighteenth-century stage, the drama is surrounded by the paraphernalia of print. Dramatic poetry lives in a world of quartos, broadsheets, and ballads, the printed pictures of cuckolds "hang'd in Effigy" on the wall of the "necessary Houses,"[1] advertisements for new editions, bills, and posters. In Fielding's *Author's Farce*, Marplay the theatre manager lays out substantial sums on "puffs to cry up our new plays, and one half guinea to Mr. Scribler for a panegyrical essay in the newspaper, with some other such services." "Take this paper and you will be discouraged from writing," says Witmore, waving one of the playbills at the penniless Luckless, whose only capital is his wit and his books. On the stage with Signior Opera, Don Tragedio, Sir Farcical Comic, and Monsieur Pantomime are Curry the Bookseller and Mrs Novel, and (in the main play) the "scribblers" Scarecrow, Dash, Quibble, and Blotpage, and Bookweight the Bookseller, the representative of print as trade and its only beneficiary. "Booksellers grow fat," complains "the Poet" (Luckless's alter ego), and "Grub Street harbors as many pirates as ever Algiers did." Begging the bookseller Bookweight for an "advance [of] fifty guineas on my play," Luckless is told he won't get "fifty shillings," no, nor "fifty farthings." "Writing is the silliest thing a man can undertake," sneers Bookweight. If Luckless kicks Bookweight downstairs, Bookweight has the better of him, for Grub Street is oversupplied with starving playwrights. "*No Lodgings for Poets*" says the sign that Luckless's rapacious landlady Mrs Moneywood wants to hang over her door. Only in his fantasy dramatic confection, in which he turns out to be the Prince of Bantam lost at sea as a child and now rediscovered, is the penniless poet victorious, and little Luckless happy at last:

> *Luckless*: Taught by my fate, let never bard despair,
> Though long he drudge and feed on Grub Street air,
> Since him, at last, 'tis possible to see
> As happy and as great a king as me.[2]

LITERARY FAME AND THE STIGMA OF PRINT

Fielding's Luckless may seem distant from the world of the laurelled classical "author" we saw in Chapter 6: the "dramatic poet," residing in elegant books, separate from the vicissitudes of the theatre, represented in the frontispiece portrait— Ariosto or Garnier or Shakespeare, frozen in time in their beautiful books. But he is, in fact, the mirror image of the dramatic poet at the far end of the period of high drama, equally a product of the press, though a different kind of press: one whose promise of literary honour was elegantly overlaid on its (equally uncertain) promise of cold cash. Humphrey Moseley's Beaumont and Fletcher folio may hold out an image of aristocratic poetry untouched by crass lucre, but he and the poets who fill the dozens of pages that precede the plays cannot help but remind readers repeatedly of their role as consumers ("'Twere vaine to mention the *Chargeablenesse* of this Work," writes Moseley; "The Frontis-piece will satisfie the wise | And good so well, they will not grudge the price," suggests a poem "To the Stationer" hopefully, with a silent question mark at the end).[3] On the one hand, plays could, after all, rise to the dignity of dramatic poetry (or so the apologists insisted). "Tragedies," explains Antoine de Montchrestien in his dedication to Henri de Bourbon, "are worthy be read by Princes, [who are] born and bred to letters and virtue, no less than other books that may carry more dignified titles and appear more serious."[4] The publisher Thomas Creede explains, in a note in Fletcher's *Cupid's Revenge* (1615), that it is now "a custome used by some Writers in this Age to Dedicate their Playes to worthy persons, as well as their other works; and there is reason for it, because they are the best Minervaes of their braine."[5] But, on the other hand, even if dramatists could dissociate from the workaday playhouse, with its treatment of its playwrights as hired help, even if their plays appeared in dignified and ennobling editions, a contradiction remained: genteel poets were not to sell their labour, but genuine poets were monumentalized in printed books, and books were for sale. The image of the dramatist had run up against the commercial world of print.

As the writing of plays grew increasingly professionalized in France, England, and Spain (with the firm establishment of the professional theatre), as playwrights began to earn substantial sums from the printing of plays (recall Lope de Vega's 1,600 ducats from publication or Racine's 1,500 livres a year),[6] publishing plays seemed ever more clearly a commercial enterprise against the background of the general commercialization of letters in the economy of print. William Lombarde could note with alarm "the sundrie bokes, pamfletes, Poesies, ditties, songs, and other woorkes . . . serving . . . to no small or sufferable wast[e] of the treasure of this Realme which is thearby consumed and spent in paper, [a] chargeable commoditie."[7] With literature itself a "chargeable commoditie," there developed a new type of relationship in the seventeenth century, that between hack authors and the booksellers who lived off them, described viscerally by George Wither: "For, many of our moderne book-sellers, are but needelesse excrements, or rather vermine, who beeing ingendred by the sweat of schollers, Printers, and book-binders, doe (as wormes in timber, or like the generation of vipers) devour those that bred them." Over the following century or so, with the growth in readership and the expansion of the press, literary production became a large enterprise, with a cottage industry of hacks labouring in booksellers' shops, real-life versions of Fielding's Scarecrow, Quibble, and Blotpage.[8] By the early eighteenth century, what Lombarde saw as waste, Joseph Addison could see as part of the great industrial expansion of England, observing (with only moderate irony) that great material "Benefits . . . arise to the Publick from" the publication of his own works, "as they consume a considerable quantity of our Paper Manufacture, employ our Artisans in Printing, and find Business for great Numbers of Indigent Persons."[9]

Even early in the seventeenth century, the expansion of the press seemed to have spawned a new crop of dramatic writers writing not just for the stage but for print. "Everyone . . . as soon as he knows how to speak puts his hand to the pen, [and] wants to write books, and muddy paper," complains a commendatory epistle in Montchrestien's *Tragédies*.[10] For those who wished to protect the image of the aristocracy of letters (actual or aspirational) from the growing class of writers perched between desperation and glory, a distinction in terms was necessary. That distinction created two classes of playwrights: on the one hand "poet," "author," "dramatist"; on the other, "versifier," "scribbler," "Jean-de-Lettres," all identified with the "muddied poet" (*"poète crotté"*) described by the Sieur de Saint-Amant, or the "necessitous plumepushers" (*"plumitifs nécessiteux"*) whom Saint-Evremond portrays as hovering about the "Bookseller Camusat, rue Saint-Jacques" in his comedy, *The Academicians* (1637).[11] The distinction between dramatic poet and dramatic hack became an important critical fixture, marking out the genteel literary amateur from the necessitous professional in the writing business. A late fifteenth- or early sixteenth-century court writer like John Skelton might have been a "poet" (in Skelton's line-up of vernacular English "auncient poetis") because he was bearing the English laurel, presenting his poems to the worthy.[12] A playwright like Jonson must mark himself as "poet" in order to "stand off from" the swarm of modern playwrights, to make sure that he will not be taken for a "Poetaster," a scribbler, a labourer falsely claiming poetic title. To justify the cost of his folio, Moseley must protest (as he does a little too insistently, again and again) that his stagewriters are "poets," "authors," the creators of "Dramaticall Workes,"[13] not mere makers of plays.

The distinction was, of course, hard to sustain in the face of the general aspiration to poetry. Despite everything, the name of "Poet," "a Name, so full of authority, antiquity, and all great marke," was (to borrow from Jonson) "through th[e] insolence" of the poetasters "become the lowest scorne of the age."[14] (Even "your dull scribbler," the prologue to Edward Ravenscroft's *The Anatomist* would complain at the other end of the century, "Writes a damn'd Play, and is misnam'd a Poet.")[15] But it was nonetheless important, in an attempt to rebuild class distinctions (seemingly undermined by print) as aesthetic distinctions. The publisher's dedicatory epistle in Francis Beaumont's posthumous *Poems* (1653) stresses the difference between the "Poems" of his poet (stage poet though he may have been) and a "common scribler['s] Rimes," addressing the fear he anticipates on the part of his dedicatee (whose permission for the dedication he apparently failed to secure) that, instead of the dedicatee ennobling the poems, the poems will debase him:

> Were these but worthless Poems, or light Rimes,
> Writ by some common scribler of the Times,
> Without your leave I durst not then engage
> You, to ennoble 'em by your patronage.[16]

The prologues and epilogues for seventeenth-century plays insistently return to the contrast between "legitimate Poets" and what the prologue to the Earl of Rochester's

Valentinian refers to as "spurious Issue" (with perhaps a gentle reproach to Charles II and Rochester for their own, live, spurious issue):

> Let *Grubstreet*-Pens such mean Diversion find,
> But we have Subjects of a nobler kind.
> We of legitimate Poets sing the praise,
> No kin to th' spurious Issue of these days.[17]

Identifying themselves with the ancients—the "legitimate Poets" of yore—was one way in which playwrights could attempt to establish themselves as *genuine* dramatic poets rather than mere aspirants. In his "Stanzas to himself," Montchrestien, for instance, delicately suggests that he himself might be that latter-day Homer who could save "the Muses of our day," who have been "vilely profaned | by so many unworthy hands."[18] The increasingly heated discussion of the relative merits of ancients and moderns in the seventeenth century suggests the anxiety of dramatists to find for themselves a place among the books. They begin compulsively to rank one another in relation to their predecessors, creating and recreating poetic genealogies, clambering for position in the canon wars.[19] Such ranking begins to seem obligatory in laudatory epistles. The poem "In Memory of Mr. John Fletcher" in the Beaumont and Fletcher folio has Fletcher retreat to the Elysian fields, where each of the ancients in turn admits that he was outdone by the modern poet.[20] In the Beaumont and Fletcher folio, George Buck places Fletcher before Shakespeare, Chapman, and Jonson, in a contest between men (with all the homoerotics therein) allusively updating the poetry contest in Aristophanes' *The Frogs* in which Dionysus finally confesses to his embarrassing passion for the more modern Euripides: "Let *Shakespeare, Chapman*, and applauded *Ben*," writes Buck, "Weare the Eternall merit of their Pen, | Here I am love-sicke: and were I to chuse, | A Mistris corrivall 'tis *Fletcher's* Muse."[21]

With their decidedly aristocratic and exclusionary tone, the recurrent comments on the decay of letters or the decline of learning reinforced the distinction between aristocratic amateurs, with their genteel (and decidedly male) educations, and upstart professionals, writing for commercial gain. What has been referred to as "the stigma of print"—the shame that ostensibly accrued to writers who published instead of confining themselves to manuscript circulation in aristocratic circles—was already part of the vocabulary of sixteenth-century literary amateurs who wished to imagine themselves untouched by commerce.[22] Sidney, for instance, explains the aristocratic reluctance to publish as a reaction to the "base men with servile wits" who "no more but setting their names to it, by their own disgracefulness disgrace the most graceful Poesy": in reaction, those like Sidney must be "better content to suppress the outflowing of their wit, than, by publishing them, to be accounted knights of the same order."[23] By the seventeenth century, such attitudes were standard fare. For Corneille, for instance (writing in 1633), "to publish a play is to debase it."[24]

In an economy, however, in which literary fame was cultural capital and printing was a practical prerequisite to such fame, the would-be dramatic poet, wishing to eschew the commercial associations of print, was in a difficult position. For those who wanted to poise themselves above the world of filthy lucre, the hard thing was that fame relied on publishing and publishing seemed incorrigibly commercial. Boileau tries to distinguish between the "legitimate tribute" presumably granted by patrons, or even sometimes a publisher, and the money earned by a bookseller's hack: "I know a noble spirit may, without shame or crime | Earn a legitimate tribute by means of his work. | But I cannot suffer those renowned authors | Who, sick of glory and greedy for money, | Hire out their Apollo to a bookseller for a wage | And make of a divine art a mercenary trade."[25] But the distinction between a "legitimate" monetary tribute and a wage was hard to sustain: "This commerce between the booksellers and the actors spoils good writers every day," writes Gabriel Ghéret in 1669 (pointing to the "commerce" of playwrights as commerce with the press). "You can find almost no one any more who works purely for glory; money is responsible for most of the books around."[26] Writing, says one seventeenth-century commentator disdainfully, had become a mere "métier" for "earning one's bread."[27]

The discussion of the term "Works" in England, as applied to collections of plays, reflected the double face of even the most dignified dramatic printing: the producer of dramatic works might be associated with the producer of the Latinate *Opera*; but one who worked was a labourer. Marston's publisher William Sheares attempts to dignify playbooks by casting them as "Workes" (identified with the Puritan value for work over play): "Yet for my part I cannot perceive wherein [Playes] should apeare so vile and abominable, that they should bee so vehemently inveighed against; Is it because they are Playes? The name it seemes somewhat offends them, whereas if they were styled Workes, they might have their Approbation also."[28] But work was not actually nice. If, in his poem to the Beaumont and Fletcher folio, William Cartwright exclaims that a "piece" may "Come up a glorifi'd Worke,"[29] in the preface to Cartwright's own posthumous *Comedies, Tragi-comedies, With other Poems* (1651), Moseley offers a portrait of the leisured aristocrat writing "Poems" ("scatter'd" about), carefully distancing him from anything resembling work: "You will do him wrong to call [his *Poems*] his *Works*; they were his *Recreation*."[30] It is, similarly, surely no accident that when Thomas Killigrew printed his plays in 1664, he titled the collection *Comedies and Tragedies* (rather than *Works*), stressing in his brief prefatory note that he had written his plays not as labour but in leisure, identifying the enforced leisure of Interregnum exile with loyal (courtly, Royalist) virtue: "If you have as much leasure to Read as I had to Write these *Plays*, you may, as I did, find a diversion; though I wish it you upon better terms then Twenty Years Banishment."[31] In the shaping of literary identity, dramatists who wished to dissociate themselves from the commercial associations of the press were better off choosing to embrace the frivolity of play over the vulgarity of work.

Paradoxically, the very gentility of the dramatic poet represented in the dignified collection as printing "Wit worthy th'Presse"[32] could intensify the stigma of print by marking the publishing poet as a self-serving aspirant to fame with (as one writer put it) "the Vanity of getting a Name."[33] For the playwright to "be in print for making of ill rimes" (as Ralph Eure's commendatory poem for John Ford's *Perkin Warbeck* has it)[34] smacked of "ambition" or "presumption." The concern is registered powerfully in the first decades of the century. "My presumption of coming in print in this kind hath hitherto been unreprovable," writes Ford in his dedication to *The Lover's Melancholy* (1629), "This piece being the first that ever courted Reader."[35] "In publishing this Tragedy, I do but challenge to my selfe that liberty, which other men have tane before mee," explains Webster defensively in his preface to *The White Devil* (1612).[36] Samuel Daniel explains that he is publishing *Tethy's Festivall* "not out of a desire to be seene in pamphlets, or of forwardness to shew my inve[n]tion therin: for I thank God, I labour not with that disease of ostentation . . . having my name already wider in this kind then I desire, and more in the winde then I would."[37] To treat one's own works as worthy of publication was to presuppose not just an interested readership in the present, but an interested posterity. If printing could dignify the unworthy ("we dignify our stupidities when we set them up in type," Montaigne had written),[38] to offer up one's works to print was to risk the kind of self-"Deification by private authority" of which Georges de Scudéry accuses Corneille in having "set down in print his flattering views of himself."[39]

In the *ad nauseum* claim of piracy as an excuse to print throughout the century, one hears the tension between the artificially aristocratic disdain for the press and the recognition, on the part of dramatists, of the power of print to create literary identity (and sometimes fame, with all of its benefits): "To publish these ill-polished drafts which . . . I kept for many years far from censure" writes Calderón in his edition of his *Autos* in 1677, "would suggest a blameworthy arrogance." But he has been forced to publish a corrected edition, not, mind you, "out of arrogance born of self-love," but rather to redress the "injury" done him by the pirates.[40] Corneille similarly explains his publication of his 1644 works as a defensive move against a potential piracy, stressing his own reluctance in the matter:

> It is against my inclination that my booksellers are bringing you this [book]. I would certainly have let [these plays] perish completely had I not recognized that the noise that the last ones made had already caused several curious persons to seek out others, and might well have brought a printer (printing [these plays] without my consent) . . . to add a thousand faults to my own.[41]

POETRY AS COMMERCE AND THE OVERBURDENED PRESS

The "stigma of print" generating such apologies, however, was beginning to fade in a world in which everything seemed to find its way to the press. A 1676 lampoon, *The Session of the Poets*, could still grant the actor Thomas Betterton a laureateship for his restraint in keeping his plays from the press, "the great'st wonder the age ever bore," worthy of the laureateship (despite his status as player):

> For of all the play scribblers that e'er writ before
> His wit had most worth and most modesty in't,
> For he had writ plays, yet ne'er came into print.[42]

But while, on the one hand it was shameful to print, it was equally shameful to *fail* to print. In Molière's *The Misanthrope*, Alceste invokes the traditional opposition to attempt to disuade Oronte from publishing his dreadful sonnet:

> You're under no necessity to compose;
> Why you should wish to publish, heaven knows.
> There's no excuse for printing tedious rot
> Unless one writes for bread, as you do not.
>
> .   .   .   .
>
> Don't give up, on any provocation,
> Your present high and courtly reputation,
> To purchase at a greedy printer's shop
> The name of silly author and scribbling fop.[43]

Yet Molière here implicitly inverts the message of the commonplace: it is not that (as for Sidney) printing has been debased by "base men" writing for bread when it should have been reserved for gentleman amateurs; rather, printing is in danger of being debased by dilettantish amateurs when it should be reserved for professionals (like Molière himself, of course) who know their craft and may claim, by virtue of merit, the honours of authorship.

By the later seventeenth century the critical distinction between the aristocrat circulating manuscripts to friends and the popular writer for the print-reading masses had become far less important than the distinction between the aristocrat of letters publishing in elegant editions and the usurping commercial scribbler, between the Racines or the Congreves and those forebears of the hapless Luckless in Fielding's *Author's Farce*, toiling in the inferno of Grub Street. The genuine author was (according to the definition in Antoine Furetière's *Dictionaire universel*) one who was in print ("Author: . . . All those who have brought out a book, now referring only to those who have had [a book] printed").[44] Complaining of the pirates in the preface to *Les Précieuses ridicules* (1660), instead of giving the usual excuse that he has been forced to publish, Molière jokingly insists that if they had given him time "I would have tempted liberality by a dedicatory epistle, properly florid [and] tried to write a beautiful . . . preface."[45] In both reality and fiction, playwrights worthy and unworthy met at the shops where their books were sold, as the poets Trissotin and Vadius in Molière's *Femmes savantes* do at the shop of Molière's real-life bookseller, Claude Barbin.[46]

Locating the battle between Trissotin and Vadius at the bookseller's shop, Molière emblematizes the period's identification of literary competition with the institutions of print. While, on the one hand, print could bring both prestige and lucre, its very promise of that combination of cultural capital and cold cash seemed to bring forth from the margins an ever-larger crop of scribblers attempting to publish—all those who might once have been (as Thomas Gray would put it romantically a century later) illiterate and "mute inglorious Milton[s]"[47] and who were decidedly no longer mute. "Want of Money" had brought "the scribling Fit"[48] to the masses, and the expanding crop of scribblers overburdened still more the already overburdened press. There was too much of it: the "Presse" was "too pregnant";[49] "bookes and common places" were "so stuffed" that it was "superflous to write any more."[50] Printers were seen as "putting everything into the press."[51] The world was too full of "silly Authors, . . . Books and Booksellers . . . Readers courteous or uncourteous" (as a seventeenth-century stage character puts the familiar categories, in a parody of aristocratic sneering).[52]

In a bit of doggerel published with Thomas Randolph's *The Jealous Lovers*, Edward Hide describes the surfeit of "Stage Poets" "Scatter[ing] their scribbles, and invad[ing] the presse."[53] "Wits Empire" was in trouble, wrote John Denham, with "a thousand lesser Poets sprong | Like petty Princes from the fall of *Rome*."[54] In an unsigned poem prefacing Randolph's 1638 works, the poets whose names regularly show up on the "Frontispice or Titlepage of Playes" are described as drunken desperados, "sack-shop wits" hanging about the tavern in the hope of picking up a line or two, just one step away from begging scraps door to door:

> The sneaking Tribe, that drinke and write by fits,
> As they can steale or borrow coine or wits,
> That Pandars fee for Plots, and then belie
> The paper with—*An excellent Comedie.*
>
> .   .   .   .
>
> These that scrape legges and trenchers to my Lord,
> Had starv'd but for some scraps pickt from thy Bord.
> They'had try'd the Balladiers or Fidlers trade,
> Or a *New Comedie* at Tiburne made.[55]

The metaphoric equations that became increasingly insistent in the later seventeenth century underlined the status of poetry as commerce and wit as capital.[56] In the habitual figurative linkage of the two, words were "coins" (as for Prince *Pretty-man* in Buckingham's *Rehearsal*, who pays *Tom Thimble* "in your own coyn: you give me nothing but words").[57] Literary pamphlets were the equivalent of paper money and credit instruments, reproduced indifferently by the printing press, as the Bricklayer explains in John Crowne's *City Politiques* (1683): "As paper in Holland passes for money, pamphlets with us pass for religion and policy. A bit of paper in Holland, from a man of credit, takes up goods here, pays debts there; so a pamphlet will take up fools here, make fools there."[58] "Stamping" was both printing and coining. Language was to be stored in "bank."[59] Wit was circulated in "bills": in his *Satyr against Wit* (1699), Sir Richard Blackmore proposes the establishment of a "Bank for Wit and Sense" to supply the "want of ready wit" with "Bills" that "Will through *Parnassus* circulate with ease" so that poets will "throng to write | Great Sums of Wit."[60] If print was commerce, poetry had become a "trade" that produced "merchandise," "Wares," or "goods."[61] Turning poet was equated with turning speculator—what those with no fixed estate or inherited capital did in the hope of instant wealth: "Authors . . . writ[e] and act . . . like stockjobbers";[62] "Poet[s]" are "Projector[s]."[63] A decade into the new century, "Isaac Bickerstaff" in *The Tatler* could draw on a well-established trope, figuring poets as bank depositors and investors, with publishers as exchange brokers:

The Bank, will take Epigrams and Epistles as Value received for their Notes, and the *East-India* Company accept of Heroick Poems for their Seal'd Bonds. Upon which Bottom, our Publishers have full Power to treat with the City in Behalf of us Authors, to enable Traders to become Patrons and Fellows of the Royal Society, as well as receive certain Degrees of Skill in the *Latin* and *Greek* Tongues, according to the Quantity of the Commodities which they take off our Hands.[64]

If epigrams and epistles were tradable commodities, glut was figured as producing a consequent depression of the value of literature. For Guillot and Hortense in Samuel Chappuzeau's *Academy of Women* (1661), the glut of literary producers and the venality of printers conspire in the sell-out of poetry to an advertising culture, with the result, an overall impoverishment of letters:

> *Hortense*: You know [that] we're in a time | when everyone has the itch to write, | that . . . we have plenty of | greedy printers who aren't afraid of gaol, | and put everything in the press, and who, looking out just for their own gain, | will soon utterly impoverish it. . . .
> *Guillot*: In fact, when I pass by the Palais, they make me drunk, | "The lovely Book, Monsieur; Monsieur, the new Book."[65]

The unsigned preface to Rochester's *Valentinian* (1685) (drawing on the recurrent metaphor of poetry as stock or coin) describes the "Coyner and Debaser of other men's Bullion," attempting to pass "his light alloy'd Mettle . . . upon the Town for sterling": "Men who have got the *Form* of Poetry without the *Power* . . . despair to put off that sorry stock they have, till by under-rating other men's they have starv'd the Market, by disgracing Commodities of an intrinsick Worth and staple Price, they hope to recommend their Gawze and Tinsel."[66]

Excess and consequent devaluation meant rapid obsolescence. Poetry was ephemera, not after all an undying monument which might keep the poet "alive still, while thy Booke doth live,"[67] closer to the kind of thing Wycherley's Country Wife reads ("sixpenny worth" of ballads, the "*Covent-garden*-Drollery, and a Play or two—Oh here's *Tarugos* Wiles, and the Slighted Maiden")[68] than to the works of Sophocles or Terence. Or worse: in a catty moment of high-authorial commiseration between Racine and Boileau, they agree that the actors would be advised to install themselves near the rubbish dump ("dépôts d'ordures"), where they would be able to find plenty more of the commodity already supplied them in the *œuvres* of Pradon and his fellow scribblers.[69] Similarly, Dryden describes the refuse of the Stationers' shops in *Macflecknoe* (1682) (ambiguously abbreviating the name "Shadwell"):

> From dusty shops neglected Authors come,
> Martyrs of Pies, and Reliques of the Bum.
> Much *Heywood*, *Shirly*, *Ogleby* there lay,
> But loads of *Sh*—almost choakt the way.[70]

Bodily emission was literary production in the conditions of Grub Street. Bayes in Buckingham's *Rehearsal* uses his porous body as medium for verbal waste: "If I am to write familiar things, as sonnets to *Armida*, and the like, I make use of Stew'd Prunes only; but, when I have a grand design in hand, I ever take Phisic, and let blood: for, when you would have pure swiftness of thought, and fiery flights of fancy, you must have a care of the pensive part. In fine, you must purge the Belly."[71] The poet's lower half had displaced the upper regions as the locus of literary activity; Bayes's belly had displaced Shakespeare's or Fletcher's "felicit[ous] . . . braine."[72]

By the eighteenth century, the stigma of print had yielded largely to the more general stigma of commerce (often code for the stigma of poverty). But it no longer seemed possible to preserve an aristocracy of genteel, non-commercial letters from the taint of the Grub Street press. Those who clung to the older model of the non-publishing aristocrat—forced to publish only by the rapacious pirates—sounded decidedly disingenuous. Fielding's "Scriblerus Secundus" could complain (in a parody of the outmoded topos) of a "surreptitious and piratical Copy" of *The Tragedy of Tragedies* "which stole last Year into the World; with what Injustice and Prejudice to our Author, I hope will be acknowledged by every one who shall happily peruse this genuine and original Copy."[73] Towards the end of the century, Sheridan could still spoof the affectation of aristocratic disdain for the press, in the fatuous Sir Benjamin, who protests, " 'tis very vulgar to Print," preferring to circulate his "little Productions" by "giving copies in confidence to . . . Friends" but, nonetheless, still finding a few "love-Elegies" which he "mean[s] to give to the Public." ("Yes Madam," he croons, "I think you will like them—when you shall see them on a beautiful Quarto page where a neat rivulet of Text shall murmur thro' a meadow of margin.—'fore Gad they will be the most elegant Things of their Kind.")[74] But the real Sir Benjamins writing "beautiful Quarto page[s]" and "neat rivulet[s] of Text" had ceased to protest—recognizing that publication was a necessary vehicle for literary recognition. Poetic distinctions would have to be made on the basis of literary merit alone, "genius," measured (at least in part) by its objective correlative—the dignified volumes whose durability marked one's place in the canon. And yet, even these were no guarantee of literary immortality, but, it turned out, were made of mere matter, like their all-too-mortal makers, as Hogarth's print showing the works of Shakespeare, Dryden, Otway, Congreve, and Jonson in a wheelbarrow, labelled "Waste paper for Shops," suggests (Fig. 46). "Had you anything of value buried with you?" Charon asks the Poet crossing the Styx in *The Author's Farce*. "Things of inestimable value," responds the Poet, "six folios of my own works." "Most poets of this age will have their works buried with them," quips Luckless.[75] The more important canonization through publication became to the image of the poet, the closer it seemed to draw to its vivid underside: on the one hand, there was the sublime Shakespeare, enshrined in the folios; on the other, there were the many eighteenth-century Bayes, feeding the *dépôts d'ordures* with their printed pages—or the poet of Pope's *Dunciad*, papers flying, running his race for glory beside the Stationers,

> Renew'd by ordure's sympathetic force,
> As oil'd with magic juices for the course,
> Vig'rous he rises; from the' effluvia strong
> Imbibes new life, and scours and stinks along;
> Re-passes [the publisher] Lintot, vindicates the race,
> Nor heeds the brown dishonours of his face.[76]

Could new dumb Fauftus, to reform the Age,
Conjure up Shakefpear's or Ben Johnfon's Ghost,
They'd blufh for shame, to see the Englifh Stage
Debauch'd by fool'ries, at so great a coft,

What would their Manes say? should they behold
Monfters and Mafquerades, where usefull Plays
Adorn'd the fruitfull Theatre of old,
And Rival Wits contended for the Bays.

Price 1 Shilling 1724

FIG. 46. Shakespeare, Dryden, Otway, Congreve, and Jonson as "Waste paper for Shops"
in Hogarth's Masquerades and Operas, or The Taste of the Town (1723–4).

To attempt to escape inevitable ephemerality was to enter into a struggle for one's
ever-threatened integrity, a life struggle (with booksellers, critics, and other poets).
Poetry was a gon, the commercial and the aesthetic intertwined: "Writing is, (as I may
say,) a sort of warfare," says the upstart scrapman-cum-publisher Puff to Dactyll the
dramatic poet in Samuel Foote's *The Patron*.[77] The more there were who wrote (with
economic or aesthetic aspirations), the more one had to fight—against the taint of
the herd, as well as the rest of the "tribe" of poets—and the more there were
who failed to rise. If the famous made fortunes, there were no longer buyers for
ordinary verses hawked by hacks, the poetic rags and bones sold by starving scribblers like Luckless, hounded by duns and attempting to pay their rent with poems.

Those who failed to distinguish themselves from the aspirants, but who still tried to find compensation for the miseries of poverty in the rewards of cultural prestige, became the regular butt of dramatic satire (in an update of the traditional joke on the impoverished scholar). Poetry meant poverty in the popular imagination (the phonetic slippage between "poverty" and "poetry" exploited with glee).[78] "Could I have looked for a poet under laced clothes?" asks Fielding's landlady Mrs Moneywood incredulously.[79] It meant spoiling the floors of the lodging houses with ink, staining the windows with verses (as Mrs Moneywood complains), begging at the playhouse manager's door, blotting pages in the attics of the booksellers. The scribblers could call themselves "poets," but they were still Lucklesses unable to pay their rent to the Mrs Moneywoods of the world. If Congreve's "worn-out Punk" appears "with Verses in her Hand . . . as if she were carrying her Linnen to the Paper-Mill, to be converted into Folio Books,"[80] this was because verses were wares not far different from those of the lowest street pedlars selling rags and bones in the street. "Your trade! and pray with what stock did you trade?" asks Foote's Dactyl of his upstart publisher, Puff: "Two odd volumes of Swift; the Life of Moll Flanders, with cuts; the Five Senses, printed and coloured by Overton; a few classics, thumb'd and blotted by the boys of the Charterhouse; with the Trial of Dr. Sacheverel."[81]

POETESS AND PUNK

Congreve's identification of poetry with prostitution—his identification of the "Punk['s]" verses with her "Linnen" (like her papers, carrying the imprint of her private "parts")—points to the centrality of the female scribbler in the Grub Street economy and in the larger literary and cultural imagination. Women had classically been seen as challenging male sexual control when they took up the pen (as Aretino's Stablemaster exclaims of his wife-to-be, "she is a poetess? When women begin to write songs, husbands begin to get heavy in the forehead").[82] But as women came more fully into the professional literary arena (both via the theatre and via print), there was new force in the vituperation against female poets: "For *Punk* and *Poetess* agree so Pat," wrote Robert Gould in a famous verse satirizing professional playwrights like Aphra Behn, "You cannot well be *This*, and not be *That*."[83] Feared for her economic usurpation and her transgression of the boundaries of gender decorum, the woman writer was cast as cross-dressing, castrating usurper of male literary dominion. Richard Lovelace's "On *Sanazar*'s being honoured with six hundred Duckets . . . for composing an *Eligiack Hexastick*" (*c*.1656–7) describes how Jonson (the paradigm of the masculine poet) would sweat if he could see how "basely deposed men [are] justled from their bed | Whilst *wives* are per'wig'd with their *husbands head*":

> Each snatches the male quill from his faint hand
> And must both nobler write and understand,
> He to her fury the soft plume doth bow,
> O Pen, nere truely justly slit till now!

The woman writer was a gender hybrid: obscenely exposing the female passions by means of the very masculine pen (both castrating and embodying the newly "slit" pen); prostituting poetry and herself at once (dressing a poem "as her self . . . curl[ing] a Line . . . Powder[ing] a Sonnet . . . Then prostitut[ing] them both to publick Aire").[84] But in this, oddly, she could serve as emblem for the new class of writers generally: surviving by exploiting their private parts; struggling to stay alive in a market in which fame was necessary to success but anonymity seemed their inevitable lot. The female scribbler was not just any scribbler but at once a freakish deviant and the very type of the Grub Street hack.

Susanna Centlivre's account of the reception of her comedy, *The Platonick Lady* (1707),[85] suggests the extent to which gender at once inflected the public's construction of its anonymous author-scribblers and determined marketable literary identity in the linked sectors of playhouse and bookshop. The "Play [is] secretly introduc'd to the House, whilst the Author remains unknown, [and] is approv'd by every Body," she narrates in her dedication to the printed play: "The Actors cry it up, and are in expectation of a great Run; the Bookseller of a Second Edition, and the Scribler of a Sixth Night." A happily interdependent economic community has arisen from the "Scribler['s]" labours, forged in the interplay between theatre and bookseller's shop. "But if," she continues, "by chance the Plot's discover'd, and the Brat found Fatherless, immediately it flags in the Opinion of those that extol-l'd it before, and the Bookseller falls in his Price, with this Reason only, *It is a Woman's*." Centlivre here ironizes the classic topos of writing as literary paternity: anonymous, subsuming the role of father, a woman may be "a man in print";[86] named, she becomes unmarried mother, punished for flouting the laws of female continence.

Anonymity can be liberation, then, for through it one can take on the identity of the normative author-father—a necessary defence in the embattled world of the female scribbler, as she explains in a digression she sets (significantly) in a bookshop: "A Spark . . . had seen my *Gamester* three or four times, and lik'd it extremely: Having bought one of the Books, ask'd who the Author was; and being told, a Woman, threw down the Book, and put up his Money, saying, he had spent too much after it already, and was sure if the Town had known that, it wou'd never have run ten days." Such buyers (along with the faithless "Town"), she writes, "rob us," not only of the rewards of the sixth night and second edition, but—more important to her—"of that which inspires the Poet, Praise." Not only the praise of the moment but the more enduring praise of print. For, she explains, "it is such as these" that made the printer of her comedy, *Love's Contrivance; or Medicin Malgre Lui*—wary of book-buyers like her "Spark"—"put two Letters of a wrong Name to it" without her knowledge: "which tho' it was the height of Injustice to me, yet his imposing on the Town turn'd to account with him; and thus passing for a Man's, it has been play'd at least a hundred times." First scrawled over with "a wrong Name" (her identity put under erasure), then named by another with the worse-than-nameless label, "a Woman" (a "Female Pen"), she is stripped of the financial rewards of both stage and press. Forced into typographic cross-dressing by her printer-pimp, Centlivre is "play'd at least a hundred times"—the "Injustice to [her] . . . turn'd to account with him."

In "Plot[ting]" (both her play and the concealment of her gender), she initially embraced her anonymity. But passing or passed "for a Man," she has been "robb[ed]" of her rightful "Praise" and the inspiration it may carry. In the printed edition of the play, she takes the "discover[y]" of her "Plot" into her own hands. The title page of *The Platonick Lady* announces boldly that the play is "By the Author of the *Gamester*, and *Love's Contrivance*," the very plays that have served in Centlivre's dedication to mark out the paired difficulties of exposure and anonymity. Here, transforming anonymity into identity via the reputation her work has garnered her, she can take control of her own exposure. The dedication that follows and that explains, in a sense, the title page's attribution, is directed, notably, "*To all the Generous Encouragers of* Female Ingenuity, . . . *Gentlemen and Ladies*" (those most unlike the ungenerous Spark). In a model of the egalitarianism that the dedication promotes ("since the Poet is born, why not a Woman as well as a Man?"), she identifies her readers' gender but refuses to discriminate on gender grounds. And, in the pairing of title page and dedication, she reverses the relations so troubling in the playhouse: it is she who is named (by reference to her *œuvre*), her audience anonymous.

Here then, where her generous but invisible readers are gathered, she can exclude the discouragers "of *Female Ingenuity*," recapturing the inspiration of the "Praise" that has been bestowed on her work, and, in the process, renaming herself "Poet." In the closing paragraph of the dedication, she rises to rhetorical heights in defence of "Female Ingenuity" ("Genius"), proffering as evidence a long line of female heroes, ending grandly with her sovereign queen (set in opposition to Louis XIV, the incarnation of the authoritarian "Man"):

What Examples we have had of Women that excell'd in all Arts; in Musick, Painting, Poetry; also in War: Nay, to our immortal Praise, what Empresses and Queens have fill'd the World[.] What cannot *England* boast from Women? The mighty *Romans* felt the Power of *Boadicea*'s Arm; *Eliza* made *Spain* tremble; but ANN, the greatest of the Three, has shook the Man that aim'd at Universal Sway.

As if embarrassed by the ambition which such lofty company suggests, the final lines seem to attempt to undo the implicit claim to poetic greatness, enacting yet another erasure of her name:

This I dare venture to say in [the following Scenes'] behalf, there is a Plot and Story in them, I hope will entertain the Reader; which is the utmost Ambition of,

> *Gentlemen and Ladies,*
>> *Your most obedient humble Servant,*

The page ends there, with no identifying initials, but only the word "Servant" to mark her place. But what remains is not the servant nor the invisible "Female Pen," but the "Praise"-worthy "Poet," modern incarnation of the female hero.

Centlivre ultimately refuses anonymity and chooses the identity of "Poet" fully worthy the "Praise" she has garnered. But one could instead disclaim both anonymity and the title of "Poet," turning to that of scribbler, accepting with irony one's place in the irrational literary market-place. In her autobiography, the actress-playwright-penny-novelist Charlotte Charke playfully teases her reader with her various possible authorial identities, from model for the "Female Pen" to maker of scraps for the "dépôts d'ordures." Writing is a "Hazard," and she "tremble[s]" before a readership quite different from Centlivre's "Generous Encouragers of *Female Ingenuity*." For, "instead of being honour'd with the last Row of a Library," she writes, her pages may be "found guilty of Nonsense and Inconsistencies," fated to "undergo the Indignancy of preserving the syrup of many a choice Tart." Demoted from library to the tradesman's world of the bakeshop, Charke imagines her sullied "Muse" suffering the "Contempt" of a "hasty Child," who "commit[s it] to the Flames, or perhaps cast[s] it to the Ground to be trampled to Death by some Thread-bare Poet, whose Works might possibly have undergone the same Malevolence of Fate." If the "Works" of the now "Thread-bare Poet" have been trampled, he in turn must trample the fallen pages of the "Female Pen" (in an enactment of a classic chain of hierarchical violence).

Rather than (like Centlivre) staging a protest against such "Injustice," Charke offers a tongue-in-cheek apology, suggesting—in her juxtaposition of this passage with a discussion of literary decorum—that she may, after all, have deserved this "Indignancy." For while, in writing her autobiography, she has "paid all due Regard to Decency wherever I have introduc'd the Passion of Love," trying to avoid "fulsomely inflaming the Minds of my young Readers, or shamefully offending those of riper Years" ("a Fault I have often condemn'd, when I was myself but a Girl, in some Female Poets"), the moralist must yield to the narrative of her life such as it has been.[87] If her autobiography is ultimately no more than the now sticky and trampled pages wrapping the "choice Tart" found "guilty of Nonsense and Inconsistencies," she herself must be the "guilty" "Tart" in writing at all. To write is to ask for it by laying out one's wares. If "*Poetess*" equals "*Punk*"—if for a woman to write is a kind of prostitution, where she may, for money, be "play'd at least a hundred times"—"*Poetess*" also equals prototypical scribbler: drudge of commerce, inescapably for sale.

Charke's self-positioning as literary "Tart," like Gould's or Congreve's identification of the poetess-scribbler as "Punk," reflects, then, the more general cultural gendering of the Grub-Street hack that had been developing over the course of the later seventeenth and eighteenth centuries, the feminization not so much of literature as of literary poverty, in which the only commodity available to the desperate poet is—finally—herself. The general position of women as the essential commodity meant an identification of the products of the "Female Pen" as the essential literary commodity. Images of women in the literary market-place (real, represented, and metaphoric) offered a new imaginative space for exploring the broader problem of the saleability of dramatic literature: the saleable products of the conjunction of fantasy and bodily labour; the results of the conversion of flesh into paper. In an early exploration of these relations in Aphra Behn's *The Rover* (1677), in the famous scene in which the courtesan Angellica Bianca ("A. B." like her poetess-creator) advertises and sells herself through the three portraits displayed on her balcony, she herself becomes a "Commodity" "to be sold" to interested "Chapmen," sellers of plays and other print ephemera. The courtesans "with Papers pinn'd on their Breasts" who dance onto the scene and then off again establish the homology among the theatrical, the monetary-sexual, and the literary economies, echoed later in the play when Blunt threatens to fasten "a Paper of scruvy [*sic*] Verses to [Florinda's] breast, in praise of damnable women," and hang her (like Angellica's portraits) out of the window.[88] Papers here act as theatrical metonymy for courtesans, identifying the circulation of women and the attendant uncertainty of sexual possession with the circulation of the text and its uncertain possession. The economy of possession and theft within the plays is trope for the economy of possession and theft in which the plays themselves participate, the economy in which literature is property (owned by the poet through the creation of the original work but unscrupulously stolen by the plagiarist and imitator). This is the subject of the next chapter.

11. *Who Owns the Play?*
Pirate, Plagiarist, Imitator, Thief

In Aphra Behn's famous refutation of the charge of plagiarism in the "Post-script" to her comedy *The Rover* (1677) (Fig. 47),[1] she proudly announces the play's debt to Thomas Killigrew's *Thomaso*, identifying her role as playwright for a professional theatre in which old plays are regularly "peec't" and "mended" to serve the needs of the ever-changing repertory. Killigrew's *Thomaso* "indeed has Wit enough to stock a Poet," she writes, reminding her readers that old plays regularly serve as open "stock" for the poet in need of helps for "Wit," and that indeed those old plays themselves once drew on other plays. In this lies Behn's defence, in what she offers as a *reductio ad absurdam*. For *Thomaso* was itself based on Richard Brome's comedy, *The Novella*, and "if," she writes, "the Play of the *Novella* were as well worth remembring as *Thomaso*, they might . . . have as well said, I took it from thence," and that Brome took his from yet another play, and on and on in a never-ending chain. Dramatic writing is a continual process of literary inheritance, from play to play and to new play in turn, in which everyone borrows, and attribution depends, in the end, not only on origins but on merit, for one remembers (and in the theatre re-members) only what is most "worth remembring."

And yet, it turns out, things are not quite so free as they may seem. For "this Play had been sooner in Print," she explains, "but for a Report . . . that 'twas *Thomaso* alter'd; which made the Book-sellers fear some trouble from the Proprietor of that Admirable Play." The play, it seems, has a legal "Proprietor," Killigrew's publisher Henry Herringman. And, indeed it has two, for the performance rights in the play belong to Killigrew himself, as manager of the King's Theatre (rival to the Duke's where *The Rover* was performed). Beyond these two kinds of proprietorship lies yet another kind that seems to belie Behn's defence: Killigrew's more ephemeral proprietorship as "Author" of the play, a play which (Behn acknowledges with the utmost civility) "is not to be peec't or mended by any but the excellent Author himself." The play as "copy" belongs to the bookseller (the "Proprietor"); the play as theatrical performance belongs to the troupe and its manager; but the play as aesthetic object belongs to "the excellent Author himself," and is not to be "peec't or mended" by any but the author under whose name it appears.[2] The bookseller's and theatre's proprietorship are overlaid protectively on the poet's "stock" of wit, the legal and commercial terms serving as umbrella for the aesthetic.

Participating in the tradition of imitation and inheritance (not to mention in need of poetic "stock" from time to time), what was a professional poetess to do to keep herself from being labelled a thief? Behn's solution (like that of so many of her contemporaries) is to distinguish open theft from the *surreptitious* "appropriat[ion]" of

THE

ROVER:

OR,

𝕿𝖍𝖊 𝕭𝖆𝖓𝖎𝖘𝖍𝖙 𝕮𝖆𝖛𝖆𝖑𝖎𝖊𝖗𝖘.

A

COMEDY:

ACTED AT

𝕳𝖎𝖘 𝕽𝖔𝖞𝖆𝖑 𝕳𝖎𝖌𝖍𝖓𝖊𝖘

THE

Duke's Theatre.

Written by Mrs. *A. Behn.*

Poſt-ſcript.

*T*His Play had been *ſooner in Print, but for a Report about the Town (made by*
    ſome either very Malitious or very Ignorant) that 'twas Thomaſo *alter'd ;*
which made the Book-ſellers fear ſome trouble from the Proprietor of that Admirable
Flay, which indeed has Wit enough to ſtock a Poet, and is not to be peec't or mend-
el by any but the Excellent Author himſelf ; That I have ſtoln ſome hints from it,
nay be a proof, that I valu'd it more than to pretend to alter it , had I had the
Dexterity of ſome Poets, who are not more Expert in ſtealing than in the Art of
Concealing, and who even that way out-do the Spartan-Boyes. *I might have ap-*
propriated all to my ſelf, but I, vainly proud of my Judgment, hang out the Sign
of Angellica, *(the only ſtoln Objeɛt) to give Notice where a great part of the Wit*
dwelt ; tho if the Play of the Novella *were as well worth remembring as* Thomaſo,
they might (bating the Name) have as well ſaid, I took it from thence : I will
only ſay the Plot and Buſ'neſs (not to boaſt on't) is my own : as for the Words
and Charaɛters, I leave the Reader to judge and compare 'em with Thomaſo, *to*
whom I recommend the great Entertainment of reading it, tho had this ſucceeded ill,
I ſhou'd have had no need of imploring that Juſtice from the Criticks, who are na-
turally ſo kind to any that pretend to uſurp their Dominion, eſpecially of our Sex,
they wou'd doubtleſs have given me the whole Honour on't.   Therefore I will only
ſay in Engliſh *what the famous* Virgil *does in* Latin ; *I make Verſes, and others*
have the Fame.

FIG. 47. Title page and Post-script for Aphra Behn's *The Rover* (1677).

literary property. "Had I had the Dexterity of some Poets, who are not more Expert in stealing than in the Art of Concealing," she writes (naming herself thief, and, in so doing, disavowing the name's opprobrium), "I might have appropriated all to my self, but I, vainly proud of my Judgment, hang out the Sign of *Angellica*, (the only stoln Object) to give Notice where a great part of the Wit dwelt." "Hang[ing] out the Sign" of one's inheritances from others (in Behn's case, through the apparatus of Post-script, inserted in self-defence in the course of the play's printing) may, in the end, turn theft into quotation. "That I have stoln some hints from [*Thomaso*] may be a proof, that I valu'd it more than to pretend to alter it," writes Behn, evoking the asso-ciations of "alteration" with disguise. To "steal" openly may, after all, be a form of "Judgment," raising plagiarism to the dignity of literary imitation.

That is fine as far as borrowing goes, but the acknowledgement of another's "Wit" is not enough. To qualify as a true poet, one must still be able, rightfully, to declare something one's "own." "I will only say," explains Behn—carefully demarcating her own work from Killigrew's—"the Plot and Bus'ness (not to boast on't) is my own." Behn cannot, she explains, expect credit for what is her "own" from her presumed accusers, the "Criticks" in the Pit ("tho had [it] succeeded ill" they "wou'd doubtless have given me the whole Honour on't"). For they are jealous proprietors of their masculine theatrical-critical terrain, and naturally "[un]kind to any who pretend to usurp their Dominion, especially of our Sex." But the poetess's literary "Dominion" may be recaptured in the world of the book, there identified by a different kind of "Sign": the label "written by Mrs. *A. Behn*," added only during the printing of the third issue of the play but giving, at last, proper "Notice" of Behn's literary propri-etorship. Having (in the textual space of the Post-script) declared herself sole origin of "the Plot and Bus'ness," Behn leaves to the impartial "Reader to judge," she writes, whether "the Words and Characters" are not also her own, recommending to her public "the great Entertainment of reading" *Thomaso* so that they may make the comparison themselves. There in the space of reading—this territory imagined as free of the unjust "Dominion" of the authoritarian male critical regime—Behn can at last hope for "Justice" from her readers.

As important as signalling that the play is now not Behn's predecessors' but her "own," the "Notice" given by the Post-script becomes a means of recording Behn's future aesthetic rights, as she suggests in the ironic final line. Anticipating that she herself will become the object of poetic theft, she will, for the moment (she writes), "only say in *English* what the famous *Virgil* does in *Latin*; I make Verses, and others have the Fame." In this purported disclaimer of poetic proprietorship (with its pointed oxymoron: it is after all "the famous *Virgil*" not the "others" who "have the Fame"), through the transfer of the great male poet into the female vernacular reg-ister, lies a deeper claim for literary "Dominion." For if poetic theft properly marked may be homage, to be the uncorruptible object of such theft is what, ultimately, makes one a true poet. By showing the play there to be her "own," she may join the ranks of those who do not copy but in fact "make the Verses," ensuring that, through the legacy of the printed book, it is she who will be remembered, and her play, finally, remain inalienable.

PRIVILEGES AND GOODS: TOWARDS LITERARY PROPERTY

The creation of the various systems of book monopoly, licensing, registration, and "privilege" functioning throughout Europe from the late fifteenth century onward were attempts to address, through the law, some of the problems of political and commercial control created by the development of printing.[3] Who was to be responsible for texts circulated independently from those who had produced them? Who was to benefit from the sale of a work when, easily reproducible, it could become a highly commercial commodity? The material products of print (whether printer and author labels on title pages or the privileges required in printed books) at once responded to and reinforced such laws: tying responsible parties to their products; sometimes granting those parties the benefit of their sale. In the broadest sense, the concept of intellectual property (the right to a return on the profits of one's invention) predated printing privileges. There were always controls—at least political if not commercial—on manuscript circulation and on the performance of texts. But the regular institutionalized grant of commercial rights in verbal inventions came with print. If print did not create the notion that ideas expressed in words could be forms of property, it played a central role in the formulation and institutionalization of this idea in early modern Europe.

The privilege or licence systems that developed in the late fifteenth and early sixteenth centuries were not initially focused solely on privileging individual works, but often privileged whole classes of works (law books, royal decrees), technologies and designs, or subject-matter. In England, for instance, a printer might be granted a monopoly on books on a certain subject, not on a particular set of words.[4] As important, book privileges were initially put in place to protect printers and publishers, and applied only incidentally to authors or other kinds of potential proprietors.[5] Since the publisher had invested in acquiring the manuscript, editing it, and bringing it out, it was the publisher who was to have the remuneration. The author presumably had long ago received whatever benefits were to be had—from patrons, the Church, whoever might have sponsored the writing of the work. The long privilege for the *Triumphant Mystery of the Acts of the Apostles* (published in 1537) explains that since the book was "corrected at great cost and outlay," the publisher Guillaume Alabat has the initial right to its exclusive printing.[6] Until well into the seventeenth century, publishers might (as we have seen) produce whatever interesting material they could acquire from whatever hands they could acquire it, often without bothering to ask the author or anyone else who might lay claim to the book. Thomas Creede jauntily explains in a note in Fletcher's *Cupid's Revenge* (1615): "Not having any . . . Epistle from the Authour (in regard I am not acquainted with him) I have made bolde my selfe, without his consent to dedicate this Play to the Juditious in generall."[7] Authors did, sometimes, take out privileges themselves or successfully sue printers who had printed unauthorized editions of their works.[8] But this did not imply any assumption that authors naturally held legal rights in their works: when Pierre Gringore took out a privilege for his *Folles Entreprises* in 1505, he felt it necessary to specify that his right lay in a legal ordinance, not in any inherent right of authorship.[9]

Privileges in early playtexts were, in any case, rare. Further, in the theatre the assumption of company ownership—in addition to the norm of collaborative writing and the absence of clearly defined notions of dramatic authorship—acted as a check on dramatist ownership of copyrights in plays. As we saw in Chapter 1, playtexts written for the early professional theatre were generally considered the property of the company, not the property of the dramatist, belonging to the company in the same way that any books or manuscripts might: like other "props," they were protected as a tool of the trade, not to be carted off on a whim. This was probably the attitude that inspired the lawsuit in the 1520s against a junior actor who, having spent only a few weeks with the King's Players, walked off with a cartload of plays.[10] Even in the late sixteenth century, if play manuscripts were mentioned as troupe property in theatrical contracts they were not differentiated from costumes or scenery.[11] That new plays were not differentiated from old plays in such contracts, or original plays from translations, is indicative of their status: they were tangible goods to be used by the players, not intangible property.

But it was becoming clear, by the first decades of the seventeenth century, that a manuscript could also be the property of the company in the related sense that, as the *exclusive* copy of a play, it could be sold to a publisher who could then secure the sole right to have it printed. At the same time, contracts were beginning to forbid the sale of copies of plays to rival troupes: in a 1627 contract, for instance, Alexandre Hardy's troupe grants him a share in the troupe's profits in return for writing plays "appropriate for the theatre" with the important caveat that he will give "no originals nor copies of the plays" to anyone else.[12] Such specifications opened up new possibilities: the physical possession of *copies* might entail the legal-conceptual possession of *the* "copy" (the right to print the playtext), even if (as in England) only a publisher could bring that right into being. Companies did in fact (as we have already seen in Chapters 1 and 2) attempt to control the publication of plays in their repertories, whether by guarding copies, by contract, or by government order. And they saw these efforts at control as attempts to protect their plays as property. The Lord Chamberlain, for instance, clearly understands company attempts to restrain the unauthorized publication of plays in the late 1630s and early 1640s as property protection measures: the plays are the companies' "proper Goods"; the unauthorized printers and publishers are threatening "unjustly [to] peravay[l] themselves of others' goods."[13] "If any of those Playes shall bee offered to yᵉ Presse," writes the Lord Chamberlain in 1641, "I shall desire yoʳ care that [the actors] may not bee defrauded by that meanes but that they may bee made acquainted wᵗh it . . . & soe have Oportunity to shew their right unto them."[14] The Chamberlain's Men-sponsored staying order in 1600, the 1608 Whitefriars contract forbidding company members to publish the company's plays, the 1619 order forbidding the unauthorized printing of plays belonging to the King's Men—these suggest a developing sense of plays as intangible literary property that serves as prologue to the explicit language of property in the later orders and contracts.[15]

At the same time that companies were beginning to identify plays as intangible literary property, the typical attack on piracy of the period was starting to link commercial claims about damage to literary proprietors with aesthetic claims about damage to authors. Such attacks were beginning to identify piracy not just as a harm to the company- or publisher-owners but also as a harm to the aesthetic property of authors. The Lord Chamberlain protests against the printing of the King's Men's "books of Comædyes. Tragedyes Cronicle Historyes, and the like" (in his 1637 letter) on the grounds that this hurt not only the company but the playwrights as well: "[The actors] had (for the speciall service of his Ma^tye & for their owne use) bought and provided [these] at very Deare & high rates. By meanes wherof, not onely they themselves had much p'judice, but the books much corruption to the injury and disgrace of the Authors."[16] Even if the technical "victim" of the trespass of piracy was the copy-holding company, the discussion of piracy ended up including harms to the author in its purview. That such discussions focused on harms to the author began to help shift the focus from the publisher or company to the author, and to interweave aesthetic issues with commercial claims. This was in part because most of the complaints about piracy that got into print were by authors, and authors generally preferred to present themselves as concerned only with the aesthetic problem of corrupt texts, even if they were equally concerned about the cruder problem of lost profits. In his protest against piracy in the preface to *Theagene and Cariclee* (1623), for instance, Hardy moves quickly from the commercial issue (the greed of the booksellers) to the aesthetic:

Thus Reader, the intolerable greed of certain Booksellers in printing this poem in what was, much to my distress, a completely uncorrected state forced [me] to choose the lesser of two evils [and] allow it to be printed, when I would have much preferred to suppress it. Having made some revisions, I am giving it to you in a slightly more polished form.[17]

The aesthetic problem was beginning to be linked to the commercial problem of possession and appropriation in a new way. If authors had a "right" to have their texts printed pure of corruption, if such texts were central to their poetic reputations (and hence to the value of their work), perhaps authors' commercial rights might flow from authors' aesthetic rights. That licences often praised the excellence of the author, confirming that the book contained nothing dangerous to morals and praising its virtues, reinforced the broader conceptual move from aesthetic claims to legal and commercial claims. "This ingenious book," declares the licence for Guillén de Castro's *Primera Parte de las comedias* (1621) "shows great and varied skill in the disposition of events, [has] excellent verses, [and is] entertaining reading. [Its] Author [is] altogether worthy of the licence he is requesting."[18]

Printed products themselves may have reinforced the sense that the natural rights-bearer was the author: the grand author editions, with authors' names prominent on title pages, author portraits, prefaces and dedications—all of which seemed to identify the author as the one with "title" to the poetic creation. But probably more important to the eventual recasting of plays as the dramatist's literary property was the increasing involvement of dramatists in the publication of their work over the course of the seventeenth century. The development of views tending in this direction can be seen in the French privileges that were, around the middle of the seventeenth century, beginning to be granted regularly to dramatists. In support of their grant of authorial property rights in plays, the privileges often point to the investment of the author's time and "reputation" in the work. The privilege for the 1664 edition of Corneille's *Théâtre*, for instance, explains that it is giving him the right to "print, sell and distribute" his plays "throughout our entire Kingdom." The reason for this is that "Sieur Corneille has corrected many things [in the] Plays," and "he wishes now to have [them] printed with . . . corrections, for the sake of his reputation," the reason he has gone to such expense in putting out the collection.[19] The general privilege for Molière's works similarly attributes the granting of the commercial right to an aesthetic right gained through the dramatist's labours. The 1666 *Oeuvres de M. Molière*, wrongfully published by a cabal of eight booksellers, explains Molière's new privilege, "made a multitude of errors wounding to the reputation of the author." This obliged him "to revise and correct all his works so that the public might have them in their most perfect form," spending a great deal of money on both the printing and the illustrations. And yet he lives in continual fear that "those jealous of his work will form [another] cabal to pirate the plays," which "would prevent him from recovering his expenses and cause him a considerable loss"—a reasonable fear, explains the privilege, given that this had already happened.[20]

As we saw in Chapter 2, such individual grants did not mean that the legal system treated dramatists as having *inherent* commercial rights either in the performance or the publication of their works. In fact, nowhere in Europe was there a legal distinction between a "pirate" who had simply produced an edition by obtaining a privilege without company or dramatist consent and one who had taken the time to get consent. To call the former "dishonest," "corrupt," "scurvy" was an expression of moral opprobrium, not an identification of a legal violation.[21] But the identification of the playwright as a "rights" bearer developing rhetorically and poetically at the end of the sixteenth century suggests an incipient view that authors' property rights in their works might be "natural rights."[22] For instance, just as the Lord Chamberlain wanted to ensure that the actors would "not bee defrauded" by a rogue printer's usurpation of their scripts, so Jonson (invoking the rhetoric of property in his preface to *Sejanus*) wants to ensure that he will not "defraud" his collaborator of "his right, by my lothed usurpation" in the printed edition, labelled with Jonson's name.[23] Such language tracked, consciously or unconsciously, the legal language of publisher copyright. Writing in 1600, the editor of the florilegium, *Englands Helicon*, could challenge the logic of stationer copyright that had grown up in the wake of print on the grounds that, after all, writing was invariably a kind of literary compilation: "Nowe, if any Stationer shall finde faulte, that his Coppies are robd by anything in this Collection, let me aske him this question, Why more in this, then in any Divine or humaine Authour: From whence a man . . . shal gather any saying, sentence, similie, or example." But at the same time, in a flourish of legal rhetoric, he could envision his collection as a means whereby *authors* could publicly reclaim their literary property (his misattribution of their work perversely serving as vehicle for proper attribution): "If any man hath beene defrauded of any thing by him composed, by another mans title put to the same, hee hath this benefit by this collection, freely to challenge his owne in publique, where els he might be robd of his proper due."[24]

From such parallels between publisher's copyright and authors' possessory rights, the modern concept of "plagiarism" was beginning to emerge, via the identification of poetic "theft" inherited from the ancients. In his character of the "Poet-Ape," for instance, "Whose workes are eene the fripperie of wit" and who "From brocage is become so bold a thiefe, | As we, the rob'd, leave rage, and pittie it,"[25] Jonson can evoke the poet of the modern era, cribbing poetic fragments from others' books. Over the course of the next decades, the juridical metaphor began to emerge as an increasingly conventional way of characterizing plagiarism and its remedy. Writing, in his preface to William Cartwright's posthumous *Comedies, Tragi-comedies* (1651), that "Certain *Plagiaries*" began to "plunder" Cartwright after his death, Humphrey Moseley figures the proper recourse against such plundering as a legal one: this "would have forc'd us to an *Action of Trover* for recovery of stollen *Wit*."[26] Here, as elsewhere, the "Author" was—at least rhetorically—a legal "owner" to whom a plagiarist might be liable for poetic theft.[27]

ANXIETIES OF INFLUENCE: IMITATION, TRANSLATION, PLAGIARISM, ORIGINALS

At the same time that commercial control over literary property was changing, attitudes towards poetic imitation and attribution were similarly changing. In the fifteenth and sixteenth centuries, copying, imitating, adapting, translating, transcribing, and inventing could be part of the same process: the "author" was an "actor" (as we have seen), one who, like the performer, produced literary material by reproducing it.[28] If dramatists often worked with compendia—compilations of historical and mythological information, commonplaces, and formulae for the composition of tragedies[29]—these reinforced the view that writing was text-making in the etymological sense: the weaving together, with art and judgement, of the best of the past. We have already seen (in Chapter 5) the sway that "the authorities" still held in dramatic composition, and the view that one could best meet—or surpass—the ancients by copying their subject-matter and learning to imitate their rhetorical style. Invention was derived, first, from imitation, from the ability artfully to vary and multiply what had already been said. For Jean Vauquelin de la Fresnaye, for instance (writing in the 1570s), it is only because Robert Garnier is both "learned" and "copious" (capable of rich rhetorical multiplication) that his verse is able to exceed that of the ancients.[30] Such attitudes, however, had already begun to shift in the sixteenth century, when discussions of poetic art begin to reveal an incipient anxiety about attribution—an uncertainty about the point at which poetic imitation ended and one could, at last, pronounce a work one's own. The printer of William Warner's 1595 translation of Plautus's *Menachmai* explains to the reader that Warner was reluctant to publish his translation because it is "neither so exactly written, as it may carry any name of a Translation, nor such libertie therin used, as that he would notoriously varie from the Poets own order."[31] In his *Poetics*, Castelvetro attempts clearly to identify the limits of borrowing along generic lines: in history, one ought to follow the sources, but in poetry one ought to make something new: "a poet cannot compose a plot composed by another poet, for this would either be history or theft."[32]

By a few decades into the seventeenth century, traditional attitudes about the value of "Imitation" founded in "Studie" (in Jonson's words)[33] were coming under serious pressure. Imitation might still be crucial to the poet, but Georges de Scudéry could write definitively in his *Observations on the Cid* that it was "established as an indisputable maxim that invention is the most important part of both the Poet and the Poem."[34] As writers attempted to demarcate the boundaries between varying levels of literary inheritance, the differences among imitation, translation, and mere copying took on a new importance. Not altogether clear about the distinction between "mere translation" and genuine poetic creation, Corneille is nonetheless indignant that he would be "accused" of being a translator, dependent on his model: "You have attempted to pass me off as a simple Translator, on the basis of seventy-two verses . . . in a work of two thousand," he writes to Scudéry, although "the knowledgeable would never call them simple translations," providing evidence at once of his borrowing and his originality a decade later in a new edition of *Le Cid* (in his 1648 *Works*), in which he italicizes the passages indebted to Guillén de Castro, reproducing the originals at the bottom of the page.[35] Attribution began to seem a necessary defence against the charge of poetic thievery: authors were not to claim credit for the inventions of others. "Since the Subject of *The Cid* is [the] Spanish Author's," sniffs Scudéry, "if the invention is good, the honour belongs to Guillén de Castro,"[36] triggering a petty fight between Corneille and Scudéry over whether or not Corneille named his source and therefore may be exonerated from the charge of plagiarism. "You have attacked me for having suppressed the name of the Spanish Author," cries Corneille defensively, "although you could have learned it only from me, and although you know very well that I have not concealed it from anyone, and that I have even carried the original in [Spanish] to His Eminence Cardinal [Richelieu], your Master and mine."[37]

Behind such defences of imitation, properly attributed, stood, however, the insistent rhetoric of theft, growing louder over the course of the seventeenth century in the world of what seemed an epidemic proliferation of authors and books. The tribe of modern scribblers is made up of "plagiaries,"[38] the town beset by "Purloiners of Wit retail[ing] their stollen Goods to the People,"[39] small poets, "Whose wit is pilfring, and whose veine and wealth | In Poetry lyes meerely in their stealth."[40] Plagiarism was at once an economic violation and a violation of nature: of the poet's work, imagined as a kind of natural "body." In John Denham's vivid imagination, for instance (in a commendatory poem in the Beaumont and Fletcher folio), the corrupting pirates and plagiarists are packs of hounds or teeming worms that feed off the dead poet's body (torn apart in the various quartos, changed into alien forms through poetic borrowing). Fletcher's

> . . . scatter'd parts, from thy owne Race, more wounds
> Hath suffer'd, then *Acteon* from his hounds;
> Which first their Braines, and then their Bellies fed,
> And from their excrements new Poets bred.

New poets are born of the excrement of their cannibalistic predecessors. But (he continues, converting the organic metaphor into a monetary one) the pirates and pla-giarists also, "not content like fellons to purloyne, | Add Treason to it, and debase thy Coyne."[41] Plagiarism is a form of "Treason," a high crime against poetic authority and a corrupter of the natural integrity of the body poetic, as treason is a corrupter of the natural integrity of the body politic.

The figuring of the poet's work as the body natural, torn apart in the work of the plagiarists, had a logical counterpart in the identification of the true poet as a "nat-ural," one whose creations were founded in nature rather than books. In his com-mendatory poem added to the 1638 edition of Thomas Randolph's works, Richard West identifies Randolph as the poet of "Nature" ("Nature and Hee all in an Instant made"), contrasted with the "*Poetasters*" ("but midwives," not "Parents to a Play"), scribbling the words spoken on stage into their "Table-book[s]":

> Their Braines lye all in Notes; Lord! how they'd looke
> If they should chance to loose their Table-book!
> Their Bayes, like Ivy, cannot mount at all
> But by some neighbouring tree, or joyning wall.

West moves easily from the reprobation of the thieving "*Poetasters*" with their Table-books to the idealization of Randolph as literary original, innocent of more formal books (an identity slightly ruffled by Randolph's authorship of several translations):

> With what an extasy shall we behold
> This Book, which is no Ghost of any old
> Wormeaten Authour; heres no jest, or hint,
> But had [Randolph's] Head both for it's Ore an' mint.
> Wer't not for some Translations, none could know
> Whether he had e're look'd in Book or no.[42]

Writing a commendatory epistle for Thomas Killigrew's plays, *The Prisoners* and *Claracilla*, "H. Benet" similarly identifies Killigrew's literary originality as founded in his distance from books. Having "on purpose" declined "th[e] Rules" ("Not trust-ing those which Others Wits design'd"), Killigrew has produced a drama "truely all your owne," not "enrich'd by others cost, or paine, | But like *Minerva*, rais'd from your owne Braine":

> I cannot choose but wonder how your Parts
> Gain'd this perfection without Bookes, or Arts.
> And I may thence conclude, that soules are sent
> Knowing from heaven, Learn'd too and Eloquent
> From their owne Powers within. . . .

Poets who depend on book-learned "Art" are simply revealing their "want of Nature," explains Benet, setting these in opposition to Killigrew, whose freedom from books means that all he writes is "his owne."[43]

Along with claims for unassisted literary invention, the word "original" was taking on a new value: once marking only the oddity, it was beginning to mark literary origination as a value; once a term of derogation (indicating eccentricity, when applied to people, and a similar odd singularity when applied to writings), it was beginning to be a term of approbation.[44] We saw, in Chapter 6, the importance of the "Originall" to the authoritativeness of the authorial edition: the significance, for Jonson, for instance, of the title page claim that an edition was reproducing the play "as it was first composed by the author"; the centrality, for Moseley, of the fact that the Beaumont and Fletcher plays are "now published by the Authours Originall Copies," and of the primal scene of "first" composition linking the author to the finished product.[45] The value for material "originals" ("original copies," author manuscripts, opposed to mere copies) could be extrapolated into a value for linguistic or narrative "originals" (authorial inventions, opposed to mere translations or imitations). Setting the old (negative) usage beside the new (positive usage), the preface to Rochester's *Valentinian* (1685) can mock "*Hudibras* himself, that admirable Original." But it ridicules still more "his little Apers," whose imitations are "so artless" that " 'twere impossible to guess after what Hands they drew, if their Vanity did not take care to inform us in the Title-Page." Having established the opposition between Rochester and his imitative "Apers" with their pedantic citations (with perhaps an ironic nod towards the famous portrait of Rochester nobly crowning his pet monkey with a laurel wreath), the preface can move on to full panegyric for the author as "Original" in the positive sense (drawing, ironically, on a metaphor of print reproduction): "His Poetry, like himself, was all Original, and has a stamp so particular, so unlike any thing that has been writ before, that . . . it disdain'd all servile imitation, and copying from others."[46] As "Original," Rochester himself need not copy.

One could satirize the credo of originality reflected in the preface to *Valentinian*, as those looking anxiously at what they experienced as literary unmooring continued to do in the later seventeenth century and well into the eighteenth. Buckingham ridicules Bayes as much for his fixation on the new (the "new [is what] I aim at. I despise your *Johnson* and *Beaumont*, that borrow'd all they writ from Nature") as for his thefts from his "book of *Drama Common places*."[47] Vanbrugh's *The Relapse* lampoons the mania for originality in wit (along with that for originality in fashion) through Lord Foppington (who dislikes "the inside of a Book" and "think[s] a Man of Quality and Breeding may be much [better] diverted with the Natural Sprauts of his own" brain).[48] One could be a bit too much of a "Natural" (still defined by Johnson in the mid-eighteenth century as an "idiot").[49] Writing in 1697, Swift could portray the Spider (figure for the originating modern) as one who, "spinning out all from [it]self . . . feeding and engendering on it self, turns all into Excrement and Venom; producing nothing at last" (in a trope that identifies the modern's "originality" with the Grub Street imagery of excretion as literary production).[50] But imitation had come to seem all too mechanical in the world of proliferating books (available to any copyist): the world of Dryden's *Macflecknoe* (1682), in which printed detritus lines the streets through which the modern Prince of Nonsense makes his epic journey (peopled with "Bilk't *Stationers*," strewn with "neglected Authors" from "dusty shops"); the world of wholesale theft ("When did [Jonson's] Muse from *Fletcher* scenes purloin," writes Dryden to Shadwell, "As thou whole *Eth'ridg* dost transfuse to thine?")[51] In Buckingham's *Rehearsal*, Bayes's theatrical plagiarism depends on the pamphlets and books which he uses as tools of the trade, composing his plays from his "book of *Drama Common places*," concealing these "helps" to "Art" by means of his "Rules": the rule of "Record, by way of Table Book," for instance, or (more important) the "Rule for invention":

Why, Sir, when I have any thing to invent, I never trouble my head about it, as other men do; but presently turn over this Book, and there I have, at one view, all that *Perseus, Montaigne, Seneca's tragedies, Horace, Juvenal, Claudian, Pliny, Plutarch's lives*, and the rest, have ever thought upon this subject: and so, in a trice, by leaving out a few words, or putting in others of my own, the business is done.[52]

The genuine author, Bayes's mirror image, was not to be a skilful imitator but an originator: in the 1694 edition of Antoine Furetière's *Dictionaire universel*, an "Author" is, pointedly, not merely one who is in print, but one who creates something first (rather than taking it from another):

AUTHOR. One who has created or produced something . . . The *Author* is he who has not taken his work from another. . . . AUTHOR: said especially of those who are the first Inventors of something.[53]

Throughout the century there continued, against the background of the attacks on plagiarism and the growing identification of the author as an originator, to be a good deal of uncertainty about what, exactly, differentiated classic imitation from plagiarism, their differences seeming to blur disconcertingly at the edges. Dryden, for instance, worries regularly about whether dramatic adaptation is, in fact, literary theft, defending his imitation of Shakespeare's *Troilus and Cressida* by noting that the ancients themselves were imitators (in a passage that tautologically justifies imitation through the authority of imitation itself). Since the Athenians held Aeschylus "in the same veneration . . . as Shakespear is by us," he writes, "his Countrymen ordain'd an equal reward to those Poets who could alter his Plays to be Acted on the Theater, with those whose productions were wholly new, and of their own." Attempting more clearly to set apart "imitation" from "theft" by figuring imitation as a wrestling contest with the reigning poet, he explains defensively: "We ought not to regard a good imitation as a theft; but as a beautiful Idea of him who undertakes to imitate, by forming himself on the invention and the work of another man; for he enters into the lists like a new wrestler, to dispute the prize with the former Champion."[54] In his prologue to *Albumazar* (1668), his treatment of Jonson registers similarly a view that strong imitation is the prerogative of poetic greatness: "Like an unrighteous Conquerer [Jonson] raigns," he writes, "Yet" (reinforcing his classic justification with the closure of the couplet) "rules that well, which he unjustly gains." As in the wrestling match of the preface to *Troilus and Cressida*, the might of the poet makes usurpation right. Jonson's powerful classical imitations, then, must be distinguished from the pilfering of the modern hack, a distinction Dryden achieves by recourse to a by-then archaic alchemical metaphor:

> ... *Ben* made nobly his, what he did mould,
> What was another's Lead, becomes his Gold.

Despite, however, Dryden's claim here for the free use of natural resources by the alchemist-poet, his defence of free use is disabled in his conversion of the archaic alchemical metaphor (proper to Jonson as it may have been) into his own era's politicized trope of property and theft, more appropriate to describing his plundering contemporaries:

> But this our age such Authors does afford,
> As make whole Playes, and yet scarce write one word:
> Who in this Anarchy of witt, rob all,
> And what's their Plunder, their Possession call.[55]

ORIGINALITY, PROPERTY, AND THEIR DISCONTENTS

The anxiety about plagiarism and the requirement of originality created, by the eighteenth century, new forms of anxiety about the requirements of authorship, not only in the need to distinguish imitation from translation from plagiarism (as in the seventeenth century), but also in the troubled discussion of poetic mimesis, which was, after all, itself a form of imitation involving the "mere copying" of nature. Writing in 1725 Pope can admiringly cast Shakespeare (already styled the poet of nature) as the prototypical "Original," superior even to the original originals (the Ancients): "If ever any Author deserved the name of an *Original*, it was *Shakespear*. *Homer* himself drew not his art so immediately from the fountains of Nature, it proceeded thro' *Ægyptian* strainers and channels, and came to him not without some tincture of the learning, or some cast of the models, of those before him." Shakespeare is opposed not only to a Homer steeped in Egyptian learning but to the poets who in making "Copies" are "multiplyers of the same image" (in rhetoric identifying their copying with the reproductions of print). But this is not enough, for Pope must further clear him of the opprobrium that might attach even to copying from nature: "His *Characters* are so much Nature her self, that 'tis a sort of injury to call them by so distant a name as Copies of her," he writes, his language reproaching those who might identify Shakespeare's "characters" with the mechanical copying of typographic "characters." "Those of other Poets have a constant resemblance, which shews that they receiv'd them from one another, and were but multiplyers of the same image: each picture like a mock-rainbow is but the reflexion of a reflexion." Shakespeare, however, is (Pope insists) "not so much an Imitator, as an Instrument, of Nature," the poet finally detached from the age-old aim of poetry and inseparable partner of nature herself.[56]

Pope's protest against the "injury" of identifying Shakespeare with the mere copyists (hardly different from the typographic machines unthinkingly churning out printed matter) extols a poetic originality whose negative can be seen in his portrait of Colley Cibber in *The Dunciad*, which he began writing while he was completing his Shakespeare edition and continued to write over the next decades ("Next, o'er his Books his eyes began to roll, | In pleasing memory of all he stole. . . . Here lay poor Fletcher's half-eat scenes, and here | The Frippery of crucify'd Moliere; | There hapless Shakespear . . .").[57] Such portraits, exaggerated as they may have been, reflected a real culture of hackdom (an ever-present threat to middle-class poets like Pope, dependent on print). Fielding could, in the *Author's Farce*, offer a cartoon view of the hack bookseller's standard practices that would have seemed, to contemporaries, all-too realistic. "A translator will be of use to me," explains Fielding's Book-weight, "for my last is in Newgate for shoplifting. The rogue had gotten a trick of translating out of the shops as well as out of the languages." Expert at converting the surplus of literary labour into the hyper-productive machinery required by the expanding book trade, Fielding's enterprising booksellers know how to translate plagiarism (stealing a work and giving it one's name) and misattribution (stealing someone else's name and giving it to a work) into their lucrative commercial forms: piracy and counterfeit. "Sometimes we give a foreign name to our own labor, and sometimes we put our own names to the labor of others," says Bookweight. "The study of book-selling is as difficult as is the law, and there are as many tricks in the one as the other."[58]

Much as they might satirize the plagiarizing hacks, however, playwrights and critics continued to be troubled over the presuppositions of proprietary attribution, legal and otherwise. John Dennis, for instance, registers his culture's chronic ambivalence about the use of the common stock of knowledge and the values of a regime of intellectual property, at once attacking contemporary plagiarists and unconsciously calling into question the coherence of the idea of intellectual property generally. Identifying plagiarism with title-page switching (the rogue bookseller's technique for evading copyright problems), the unnamed correspondent in Dennis's *The Characters and Conduct of Sir John Edgar* (1720) writes of Steele and Cibber:

> You . . . have infinitely surpass'd old *Villers Bays* of *Brentford*! . . . He, poor Mortal, was contented to glean here and there a Sentence, sometimes from *Plutarch*, sometimes from *Seneca*, and sometimes from modern *Montaign*. Whereas you have found a shorter way to *Parnassus*. You and your Viceroy bravely and boldly seize upon other Men's Plays; cause new Title-Pages to be printed; and so, to the Amazement of some few Readers, they pass with the rest for your own.

Excoriating the appropriations of the "brothers" of Bayes, the correspondent continues in sarcastic vein, extending his meditation on the theft of material books to a meditation on theft from the internal realm of "Thoughts": "I was formerly so weak as to think, that nothing was more a Man's own than his Thoughts and Inventions," he writes (extrapolating from the topical issue of freedom of thought to the issue of intellectual property). "Nay, I have been often inclin'd to think, that a Man had absolute Property in his Thoughts and Inventions alone." And yet, Dennis's substantiation of his argument about the inalienability of thought begins to carry him accidentally to a more serious challenge to the foundational conception of property generally. "I have been apt to think, with a great Poet, that every Thing else which the World calls Property, is very improperly nam'd so," he muses. "The Money that is mine, was somebody's else before, and will be hereafter another's." But he quickly turns back from the challenge to property generally to a claim that, after all, one's thoughts really *are* one's own. "My Thoughts are unalterably and unalienably mine, and never can be another's," he writes. "They are out of the Reach of Fortune, that disposes of all Things else. 'Tis not in the Power of Fate it self, to alienate, or transfer them; it can only make them pass for another's, or annihilate them, and cause them to be swallowed and lost in the Abyss of Time." In the course of fate, one's thoughts may be taken and made to pass for another's—there is no legal protection from fate—but to attempt to alienate another's thoughts is a crime, not, perhaps, against "Men," but against what is most "Sacred among Men," Nature herself: "I have more than once observ'd," he writes, "That the impudent Plagiary, who makes it the Business of his Life to seize on [Men's Thoughts and Inventions], and usurp them, has . . . dar'd to violate all that is Sacred among Men."[59]

The continuing figuration of literature as property had come to seem less and less comic metaphor and increasingly necessary—and probable—as legal reality. In Mary Pix's prologue to *Deceiver Deceived* (1698), for instance, in which she attacks George Powell's appropriation of her play after he had rejected it from Drury Lane, she imagines a court for adjudicating literary property claims, "*Apollo*'s Sizes"— though she acknowledges that, for the moment at least, only the audience is available to act as court of justice for the poet:

> Our Authoress, like true Women, shew'd her Play
> To some, who, like true Wits stole't half away.
> We've Fee'd no Councel yet, tho some advise us
> T'indite the Plagiaries at *Apollo*'s Sizes?
>
> .   .   .   .
>
> [However] to you kind Sirs, as to the Laws
> Of Justice she submits her self and Cause,
> For to whom else shou'd a wrong'd Poet sue,
> There's no appeal to any Court but you.[60]

Susanna Centlivre's Bellair (in *Love at a Venture* (1706)) is only partly in jest when he claims that, if "each may claim his share of Wit" at the play, where the "Spungy-Brain'd Poets" have "suck[ed] something from all Companies to squeeze into a Comedy," each "shou'd claim a Share of the Profits too, ha, ha."[61] When Centlivre comments ironically that "our real Estate lies in the Brain," she is formulating what will later be expressed in the phrase "intellectual" or "literary property."[62]

While, then, eighteenth-century playwrights could toy with the figuration of literature as legally cognizable property, at the same time they worried about the ramifications of creating a regime of literary property, one which might produce critics all too ready "with all the reproaches of *plagiarism, pilfering, borrowing, robbing, translating*, &c."[63] but incapable of differentiating legitimate cultural exchange from theft. Plays began to satirize such plagiarism hounds in characters like Sir Tremendous in Gay, Pope, and Arbuthnot's *Three Hours After Marriage* (1717) (progenitor of the more famous Sir Fretful Plagiary in Sheridan's *The Critic* (1779)). Part of the problem was that, since everything had already been written, modern writing was invariably plagiarism, as Monsieur Baliveau attempts to convince his scribbler nephew, Damis, in Alexis Piron's *Versomania, or The Poet* (1738): "The beauties of art are not infinite," he tells Damis, noting that even Damis has admitted that the "geniuses" of the past have already "harvested" whatever modern poets now strain "to glean." Damis does not disagree, but instead turns the usual accusation of plagiarism against his predecessors themselves. It is not that modern poets steal from their forebears but, rather, that their forebears stole (in advance) from them:

> *Damis*: They have, it is true, said all that's been thought;
>   Their writings are thefts, in advance, from our lot;
>   But the remedy is simple: we'll fare as they fared;
>   They've stolen from us; we'll now steal from our heirs;
>   And leaving the sources of poetry dry;
>   We will leave our heirs, finally, with nothing to try.
>   A demon triumphant declares this shall be.
>   Misery to those Writers who come after me![64]

By mid-century, it had become a mocking commonplace that the logic of the regime of literary property, pushed to the extreme, would end up identifying all literary inheritances as theft. Arthur Murphy, for instance, insists that, in "plagiarizing" from Voltaire in his own *Orphan of China* (1759), he is merely following in the footsteps of a great tradition of plagiarists—including Boileau, Corneille, Racine, Milton, Metastasio, Addison, Pope, and no less a figure than Voltaire himself, who, as it turns out, owes everything to Shakespeare. Writing a public letter to Voltaire, Murphy notes that Metastasio was often reproached with having "frequent transfusions of thought" from Voltaire's writings, but (he adds), Voltaire would respond, " 'Ah! le cher voleur! il m'a bien embelli' ['the dear thief! he has in fact embellished me']." Voltaire's own model, then, provides Murphy's defence:

To avail myself of my reading, and to improve my own productions, is all I can pretend to; and this I flatter myself I have done, not only by transplanting from you, but also from many of the writers of antiquity, [on the model of] another very bright example, the example of M. DE VOLTAIRE, whom I have often tracked . . . in the *snow of Shakespear*.[65]

Recognizing the tyranny of a regime of "malic[ious]" plagiarism hounds like Sir Fretful who (out of jealousy of the lustre of rival poets) use the charge of plagiarism as their only remaining weapon, mid-century critics attempted to produce theoretical positions that might detach imitation from its association with plagiarism. In a famous issue of *The Rambler*, Johnson, for instance, explains that it is uncomfortably "certain that whoever attempts any common topick, will find unexpected coincidences of his thoughts with those of other writers; nor can the nicest judgement always distinguish accidental similitude from artful imitation." The distinction, which can be recognized by the quantity of similarities with the source, oddly inverts the traditional terms: "No writer can be fully convicted of imitation, except there is a concurrence of more resemblances than can be imagined to have happened by chance." For Johnson, the plagiarist is the artful (scheming) imitator; the true poet has imitated naïvely and unconsciously, by "chance." Defending the "common stock of images" as public property (particularly in the theatre) and the use of that stock as a form of "liberty," he worries that the logic of rules against plagiarism might require instating a regime of literary "restoration," which would end by punishing the innocent and impoverishing each poet's stock:

> In books which best deserve the name of originals, there is little new beyond the disposition of materials already provided; the same ideas and combinations of ideas have been long in the possession of other hands; and by restoring to every man his own . . . so the most inventive and fertile genius would reduce his folios to a few pages.[66]

The image of Johnson's "inventive and fertile genius," reduced to desperate poverty by a purported restoration of "every man['s] own," was a reaction to the legalistic culture of apportionment that was ultimately, against protests like Johnson's, to prevail. In his comedy, *The Widow'd Wife* (1767), in which Young Melmoth and his servant, Syllogism, discuss whether it is reasonable for Syllogism to quit his present job in order to take up the trade of poet, William Kenrick reminds his audience that the metaphoric identification of literature as property was in the process of becoming legal reality. Identifying the poet's estate as "a freehold on Parnassus," subject however to the critics' provision of favourable "literary legislation" (for the critics have "the privilege of deciding in all money-matters"), Syllogism argues that poetry need no longer mean automatic poverty, since the "man of genius"—even without such a freehold—may now "levy contributions on [the town], whenever his affairs require it." That power was in the process of being strengthened, Young Melmoth suggests (in a reference to the real parliamentary debates of the era, which would lead to the *Donaldson v. Becket* decision in 1774), and Syllogism might safely make his career change, once "the lawyers . . . decide the dispute about literary property."[67] As we saw in Chapter 3, formal conceptions of *theatrical* property were slow in coming, and even the formal copyright laws that emerged during the eighteenth and nineteenth centuries still left ordinary dramatists without easily sustainable legal claims. Moreover, assumptions about the meaning and status of these claims varied. Identifying the plays that dramatists submitted to the Comédie-Française as their "literary property," Beaumarchais, for instance (writing in 1777), understood this property more as a set of personal powers or "honours" due to authors than as a natural commercial right.[68] Referring (in his petition to the Assemblée Nationale in 1790) to dramatic authors as the "natural proprietors" of their works, Jean de La Harpe was asserting, against the "privilege" of the monarchy-identified Comédie-Française, not so much their individual right to exploit their property as their natural interest in using property to serve the "public good"[69] (relying on conceptions of the "public" that I will discuss in the next chapter). But the various rhetorical and theoretical conceptions of authors as owners in the seventeenth and eighteenth centuries had laid the conceptual groundwork for the variety of legal claims that would serve as crucial background to the ultimate dominance of author-held copyright, both in print and in the theatre.

12. *Making it Public*

When the critic, poet, entrepreneur and eventual director of the Hamburg National Theatre Johann Friedrich Löwen printed a manifesto in 1766 announcing to "the public" the opening of a theatre that he hoped would "inspire the nation's authors" to write, at last, true "[German] national dramas," he was addressing at once the "local citizens," the readers of the "public newssheets," and a public that he identified with the fragilely constituted nation as a whole.[1] It has now become conventional to identify the classic "public" of the seventeenth century as having somehow remade itself over the course of the eighteenth century, becoming a newly self-representing, largely bourgeois entity, made up of loosely connected individuals whose sphere was not court or state but such spaces as political and cultural associations, coffee-houses, salons and, not least, the private spaces of the home.[2] Whatever its actual constitution, the public to whom Löwen imagines himself to be speaking—right-minded and engaged citizens, eager patrons of their nation's cultural life, a powerful yet invisible body at once to be enlightened and obeyed—was an entity still in formation in the popular imagination. But it was in part precisely because of such pamphlets as Löwen's that the concept of *the* public took on such significance in political and cultural life during the period. Over the course of the eighteenth century, the body of readers repeatedly addressed in the newspress and in pamphlets like Löwen's came to see itself as, in fact, an entity—a force with which writers putting their work into print would necessarily have to reckon.

This new (or at least newly important) public was, however, constituted not by the newspress alone, but in a number of arenas for collective expression, its life in print emerging, in part, from a species of metonymic transfer: from the concrete public audience gathered in "public places" to that larger public accessible through the printed word; from the public of the noisy pit and boxes to the theatre-loving public of the "public newssheets" scattered across the nation, a public brought back again—conceptually and actually—into the new theatres. Historical accounts often oppose the theatrical baroque court of the seventeenth century, where the monarchy performed its power to a dazzled body politic, to the print-based public sphere, where individuals could engage in rational discourse about the public good from the private space of the bourgeois home.[3] But it is hard to sustain an argument that there was a shift *away* from a theatrically constituted public, given the continuing centrality of the theatrical public (actual and imagined) to the constitution of the general public throughout the eighteenth century. Löwen's identification of this public with the patrons of the new national theatre and that with the nation as a whole is not just a happenstance of German history, the product of the attempt on the part of a cultural backwater to build itself its own national theatrical culture. Rather, the creation of the public generally—theatrical, political, concerned, indifferent, enlightened, despotic, reflecting the civic and national spirit or its underside—was importantly informed throughout Europe by the dialogue between the mutually constituting spheres of the theatre and the press.

"PUBLICATION" IN THE THEATRE AND ON THE PAGE

Print had, from its inception, been conceived of as a way of making writings "public." But "publication" could, across Europe, refer simultaneously to printing and performing: Guillaume Alabat explains that he is printing Simon Gréban's *Mystery of the Acts of the Apostles* (1537) because he wishes it "published and brought to light not only . . . in the theatre . . . but also by [the] public edition of Printed books."[4] In his dedication to *Marc Antoine* (1578), Robert Garnier uses the phrase "emerge in public" ambiguously to refer to both performance and print.[5] The *Engelische Comedien und Tragedien* (1620) uses a single word (*öffentlich*) to indicate the public nature of both acting and printing plays (people have undertaken "publicly to *act* and *recite*" the comedies and tragedies, and those producing the volume now "wish to offer them in public in Print").[6] "To publish" could (throughout the seventeenth century) mean to show something to the public by any one of a number of means, reflecting the range of what it was to make something "public": it could indicate manuscript distribution and sale; it could mean showing something in a public space (in Corneille's *Andromède*, the Sun and Melpomené "publish" the glory of the king to the world) or merely speaking something in company (as when Shakespeare's Troilus asks himself, "Shall I not lie in publishing a truth?"); it could mean either performing or printing it.[7]

The contrast between public and private inflected this usage. "Public" theatres (open to the public for the price of admission) were, of course, contrasted with private theatres in courts and private homes.[8] This contrast was overlaid with the broader contrast between the official world of office holders and administrators (visible to and performing on behalf of the kind of public that might gather in the theatre) and the "private" world, independent of and invisible to the public (the genteel space of private "retirement" from politics, where the public servant might indulge in the leisure of diversion).[9] What was public was the political world visible to the broader population; what was private was what was kept (at least theoretically) between "gentlemen." In an aristocratic gesture, Montchrestien can write in the dedication to the 1604 edition of his *Tragédies* that if it were possible for him to keep his tragedies completely from "the public," he would be very happy, but that unfortunately (in the by now familiar claim) his plays cannot escape the press.[10] It was this public that was, already in the early seventeenth century, *the* public, primarily a political public (beneficiary of "la chose publique" in the classic Renaissance phrasing),[11] but also a theatrical public (Alexandre Hardy writes plays for the "*public*" of the theatre, not the literary critics)[12] and a reading public (as for Montchrestien).

The identity of this public, however, and the significance of the opposition between public and private was changing for writers circulating their work in both manuscript and print. For both professionals and aristocratic amateurs, the distinction between printed works (available to all, "public," for sale) and the works they distributed in manuscript (available to a select few, "private," not for sale) was becoming crucially important. Private *reading* in the private space of the closet might be contrasted with such public experiences as watching a play in the theatre. Gently reminding his readers of his plays' success on stage, Thomas Heywood writes that if his "Comedies . . . prove but as gratious in thy private reading, as they were plausible in the publick acting, I shall not much doubt of their successe."[13] But *printing* a work was understood as a way of making it public, contrasted most commonly with distributing a work to "private" readers in manuscript (an opposition reflected in Jonson's *Poetaster*, in which he figures stamping as public and enduring monument, opposed to the fleeting figure of mere writing: "I could stampe | Their foreheads with those deepe, and publike brands . . . | And these my prints should last, still to be read . . . | when, what they write 'gainst me, | Shall like a figure . . . fleete").[14] Writing in 1637, Henry Lawes can oppose "the often Copying of" Milton's *Comus*, which "hath tired my Pen to give my several friends satisfaction," to "producing it to the public view" by printing it.[15] Print and theatre might be "common," manuscripts uncommon, circulated to "private" and "particular" parties, sometimes in secret, as a poem in a dedicatory manuscript copy of Middleton's *Game at Chess* (whose performance and printing were both forbidden) makes clear: "This, which nor Stage nor Stationers Stall can Showe, | (The Common Eye maye wish for, but ne're knowe)"[16] (the parentheses scribally representing the play's bracketing from the "Common Eye").

By the later seventeenth century, this distinction had firmly taken hold. Poems that were "Deny'd the *Press*," as the rhetoric of Robert Gould's dedication to *The Play-House* suggests, were in effect "forbid the *Publick view*."[17] Publishing inevitably made one "Publick" as Margaret Cavendish explained, extrapolating from the old distinction between public political figures and private individuals in order to identify herself—at once combatively and defensively—with the male world of politics and battle: "It is most certain, That those that perform Publick Actions, expose themselves to Publick Censures; and so do Writers, live they never so privately and retir'd, as soon as they commit their Works to the Press."[18] If publication meant exposure (whether to "Publick Censures" or the vulgarity of the "Common Eye"), print could be seen more positively as a means of reaching a public conceived as broader than that constituted by the generality of spectators, the court, or the town. The public of seventeenth-century readers, for instance, could be the public of a newly conceived "Europe." To publish might be to "publish for the world,"[19] as for John Webb, for instance, for whom the closure of the London theatres is a sort of "fortunate fall" for the drama, for it has triggered the printing of Fletcher's plays and their launching from the circumscribed London theatre into the great theatre of the world:

> What though distempers of the present Age
> Have banish'd your smooth numbers from the Stage?
> You shall be gainers by't; it shall confer
> To th'making the vast world your Theater.[20]

The stage was local, print was global; "the Test of the Stage" was to be contrasted (in Thomas Ravenscroft's phrasing) with "launch[ing] [a play] into the world in Print."[21]

THE CONSTITUTION OF THE COMMERCIAL PUBLIC

The shifting commercial status of writing during the period informed the dramatist's relation to this purportedly broader print-reading public. The patronage system—emanating from the aristocracy but independent of noble households—which had taken shape during the Renaissance, served, throughout the seventeenth and much of the eighteenth centuries, as the only dignified means of support for the genteel person of letters who did not have independent means. Still, even while the patronage system was in the process of formation it was already under attack, challenged in the theatre by the access dramatists had to independent sources of income and, increasingly in the seventeenth and eighteenth centuries (as we have seen), by access to payment from print.[22] In the early seventeenth century, the fissures in the system were already apparent in what could be rather sardonic treatment of the conventional fawning dedications carried by playbooks. Even in his altogether serious dedication of *The Unnatural Combat* to Anthony Sentleger in 1639, for instance, Philip Massinger (somewhat prematurely) dismisses "Dedications, and Inscriptions" in such works as "obsolete, and out of fashion."[23] If dedications were by no means obsolete, the circle of those seen as appropriate dedicatees was nonetheless broadening. After *Cinna*'s theatrical success in 1642, having dedicated *Le Cid* to the Duchess d'Aiguillon (Richelieu's niece) in 1637 and *Horace* to Richelieu himself in 1641, Corneille decided to dedicate *Cinna* to the bourgeois financier Pierre du Pouget de Montauron, who gave him the large sum of 200 *pistoles* for it.[24] This might be thought of as a minor shift, from court circles to financial circles, but it subtly heralded a new recognition of the power of money as the foundation for patronage, irrespective of rank. If a financier could be a patron because he had the money to buy authors, so, presumably, could booksellers or readers.

By the late seventeenth century, writers could identify a real shift towards reliance on payments from booksellers, as one French pamphleteer does:

Once, authors gave money to booksellers to contribute to the cost of printing their works, and this money came to them from pensions and rewards from the King and his ministers, who [thus] engaged them . . . to work for the public. . . . Today, the custom is the opposite and, whether its origin was in the want or the avarice of authors, . . . they are . . . used to it.[25]

If, here, "the public" is not the patron of the work but the beneficiary of the Crown's patronage of the author, in the following decades this public (in its various incarnations, as a theatrical public and a reading public) would come to be seen as capable of displacing more noble patrons. Noting that it was no longer individual patrons who had the power to create dramatic poets or book-producing authors, Charles Gildon could comment in 1714 (quoting Shaftesbury) that "in our Days, the *Audience* makes the *Poet*, and the Bookseller the Author."[26] Writers and publishers were beginning to make the connection between traditional patrons and the public as patron, helped along by such phenomena as subscription publishing, which called attention to the role of book-buyers as a new sort of patron (authors usually sought subscribers in the same way they sought more traditional patronage payments; the names of sub-scribers for expensive books were often, like dedications, printed in the books them-selves). If Charles Coypel's lavish series of engravings illustrating Molière could aspirationally be "Dedicated to the Public," that "highly respectable and formidable judge" (in 1726), Oliver Goldsmith could declare as fact a few decades later that the "poets of England no longer depend on the Great for subsistence," but "have now no other patrons but the public," adding, aspirationally, "and the public . . . is a good and a generous master."[27] By the time Goldsmith was writing, dedications like Coypel's had become a convention in themselves, no longer a peculiar commentary on a surprising transformation in economic power, but a way of acknowledging the democratization of patronage.[28]

It would be a mistake, of course, to imagine that patronage was actually disap-pearing, or that one kind of remuneration necessarily displaced another. Rather, the various forms coexisted: Goldoni notes cheerfully that for his play, *The Surly Bene-factor* (1771), he "received a gratuity of some 150 louis-d'ors from the king, and my right of authorship brought me in a handsome sum at Paris. My bookseller treated me with great liberality, and I was overpowered with honours, pleasure, and joy."[29] But writers were coming to identify themselves as free marketeers, negotiating independently in what was insistently figured as a market-place, in which the economics of consumption (rather than the aesthetics of aristocratic authority) determined "taste." The classic institution of patronage (accompanied by standard dedications to aristocratic patrons) was still an important component of dramatic production, but writers often chose to distance themselves from it. Samuel Foote's comedy *The Patron* (1764) might be taken as emblematic of the change in ethos, offering up for public mockery the modern "patron of the arts" in the figure of Sir Thomas Lofty, described by another character as "the bufo of an illiberal, mercenary tribe," with "neither genius to create, judgement to distinguish, or generosity to reward," one whose "wealth has gain'd him flattery from the indi-gent, and . . . admiration from the ignorant."[30] Sir Thomas, desperate to find writ-ers willing to dedicate works to him, is finally forced to write his own, anonymously, and dedicate them to himself. Foote's own dedication of the play to the Lord Cham-berlain, while surprisingly unironic (a telling indication of the continuing impor-tance of traditional patronage), nonetheless echoes the play's send-up of patronage. Addressing the Lord Chamberlain, Foote writes that it is in fact the *comedy* that is "the Patron, my Lord, who now begs your protection" (playing on the title): the Lord Chamberlain is patron of the play; but the play (already enthusiastically patronized, as it has been, "by the public") is also the patron of the Lord Chamber-lain.[31] Since dedications were necessary to confirming the dedicatee's position as patron of the arts, patrons could actually be as dependent on authors as authors were on them.

Foote's "public," here, is the theatre-going public, that entity represented vividly to theatre-goers in such stage personifications as that in the prologue to Alexis Piron's *Chimeras* (1725), in which a character called "the Public" is set upon by two personifications of Comédie-Française tragedies, or his *The Eight Mariannes* (also 1725), which features an oriental despot called "Sultan-Public."[32] The "public" was still very much a theatrical public, and the theatre was still in some sense identifiable with "the town" (though "the town"—whether Paris, London, or Hamburg—was precipitously moving towards existence as metropolis). But the narrower circle which the seventeenth century envisioned as constituting the public had been abstracted into the expanded sphere of a greater "public." If at the end of the seventeenth century the theatrical public was made up of the highly visible "critics" in the pit, arbiters of taste with the tremendous cultural power of making or breaking a play's fortunes in the theatre through hooting, catcalling, and cabal-creating, a century later the actress Hyppolite Clairon could describe vividly the compelling power of those same critics to control the views of the larger Parisian public: "let one of these cry *Bravo!* without reflection the whole auditorium repeats it," and, "on leaving the theatre, [the audience] circulates through Paris: . . . Whence come you? What was the play? Who were the actors?"[33] This vocalized public opinion—constituted in the theatres where people gathered to "vote" on aesthetics and ideas and spreading to the larger urban public—not only shaped political events (not least, the French Revolution, rehearsed in the auditorium of the Comédie-Française), but was understood in explicitly political terms: the theatrical public had a unified "voice," one that in the revolutionary decades came to be identified with the "voice of the people," akin to that of the ancient agora.[34] Handing down majority decisions, the theatrical public could be figured as a body of legislators, independent of the state, legislating theatrical law and thereby shaping the laws of the broader political arena. "The drama's laws the drama's patrons give," writes Samuel Johnson (overlaying the image of audience as patron on that of audience as lawmaker).[35]

Notions of theatrical public and reading public were in dialogue throughout the century, each reshaping the other against the changing political landscape. The visible, concrete theatre audience of any given performance could be extrapolated into a more general "theatrical public," and that could be extrapolated into a still larger public, which included the reading public in its general purview. If the theatrical public could be opposed to the reading public, the two could also be likened, the print audience conceptually modelled on the more concrete theatrical audience whom poets were in the habit of addressing in prologues and epilogues and whose faces they could watch in response. Printed editions regularly mirrored to readers an image of themselves as play-goers, offering them an understanding of their identity as members of the "reading public" by reference to their identity as members of the "theatrical public," as in Coypel's 1726 collection of scenes from Molière which presents the dedication written on the stage curtain, surrounded by the well-populated pit and boxes of the theatre (Fig. 48). Certainly, at the most concrete level, the theatrical and play-reading publics were more or less made up of the same individuals, and play-going and play-buying were in a symbiotic relationship: playwrights

Fɪɢ. 48.　Charles Coypel's engravings of scenes from Molière, "Dedicated to the Public" (1726).

sold themselves to the book-reading public on the basis of the enthusiasms of the theatre-going public; performances and texts were regularly advertised together. As important, the theatrical and reading publics were understood by mutual reference, the relationship between reader and theatrical public thematized in books and illustrations: "Open the curtain if you wish to see more," declares a French print teasingly, showing Harlequin on a curtained stage.[36]

But if this conception of the "public" was formed in the dialogue between print and theatre, changes in the role and conception of print more generally, independently of the theatre, nonetheless played a crucial role in shaping this new public. "Publication" had come to be identified nearly exclusively with printing in the eighteenth century, losing its association with performance and no longer merely suggestively opposed to manuscript circulation (more private than print) but an actual antonym for it. This is suggested, for instance, by the oppositions in the passage we glanced at in Chapter 10, in which Sheridan's Lady Sneerwell expresses her surprise that Sir Benjamin never "publish[es] any-thing," and Sir Benjamin responds that although "'tis very vulgar to Print," and although he prefers to circulate things in manuscript, he nonetheless has a few pieces which he "mean[s] to give to the Public" by "publish[ing]" them.[37] As important, from the early eighteenth century on, the newspapers were (tellingly) "the Publick Papers" or (in the later eighteenth century) "the Public Prints":[38] pervasive; powerful determinants of theatrical (and attendant economic) success and failure. Whether or not newspapers and journals actually represented widely held views, they represented themselves as organs of the public voice, taking on the authoritatively anonymous editorial voice of the objective observer, a Mr Spectator (or, in a moment of aspiration to such authority, *The Female Spectator*), all-seeing and invisible. Journals were filled with letters from members of "the Publick" writing to "the Publick" about the "Publick" purporting to represent "public opinion." With the extraordinary growth of columns devoted to theatres in the newspress and specialty theatre periodicals, the theatrical public could find its antics, exploits, character, and emotions mirrored back to itself in print—these analysed as closely as were those of the plays and actors on stage. Audiences were given a new arbiter in the form of theatrical reviewing, which could successfully vie with the more traditional arbiter: the critics in the pit. The institution of newspress reviewing was quickly and economically turned into the institution of paid newspress "puffing," which became a crucial part of the advertising machinery of the play—satirized most famously in Sheridan's hack journalist Puff, who offers a rhetoric of newspaper puffing (mimetically rendered in the puffed-up text itself):

Yes Sir,—PUFFING is of various sorts—the principal are, THE PUFF DIRECT—the PUFF PRELIMINARY—the PUFF COLLATERAL—the PUFF COLLUSIVE, and the PUFF OBLIQUE, or PUFF by IMPLICATION.—These all assume, as circumstances require, the various forms of LETTER TO THE EDITOR—OCCASIONAL ANECDOTE—IMPARTIAL CRITIQUE—OBSERVATION from CORRESPONDENT,—or ADVERTISEMENT FROM THE PARTY.[39]

Even in the earlier eighteenth century, commentators were highly conscious of the power of the periodical press over the theatre. When Cibber, for instance, dedicated his tragedy *Ximena* to Steele in 1719, he used the dedication as an occasion for "pub-lick . . . Acknowledgments" of Steele's contributions (in the *Tatler*) to the theatrical public and the public at large, drawing on the tradition of dedicatory machinery to acknowledge the transfer of cultural power from patron to periodical press: "How often have we known the most elegant Audiences drawn together at a Day's Warning, by the Influence or Warrant of a single *Tatler*. . . . I therefore take this Occasion to make our Acknowledgments . . . as publick as our Obligations." Steele's writing had turned the "publick Diversion" that was theatre into the "Improvement" of the "Minds" of the public, writes Cibber, and thus the stage has carried on his amend-ments, "by a kind of substituted Power," translating Steele's work as theatre critic back into the theatre itself. Explicitly identifying "the Stage" as a microcosm of "the Publick" (and of "the World" of the *Tatler*'s readers—retrenching the classical trope of the "theatre of the world" into the tighter sphere of "the World" of the reading "Public"), he explains the links among the periodical press, the theatre, and the larger public good:

While the World was under the daily Correction and Authority of your *Lucubrations*, their Influence on the Publick was not more visible in any one Instance, than the sudden Improve-ment . . . of the Stage, that immediately follow'd them: From whence it is now apparent that many Papers, (which the Grave and Severe then thought were thrown away upon that Subject) were, in your speaking to the *Theatre*, still advancing the same Work, and instructing the same World in Miniature.[40]

If the public was becoming patron, the critic might act as a sort of super-patron, shaping the judgements of that public.

THE CABAL AND THE RATIONAL PUBLIC

However much Cibber may have seen the theatrical audience as itself in need of "Correction" from an esteemed critical "Authority," in the decades that followed there developed an important mythology of the all-powerful public, a body of citi-zens offering "Correction and Authority" to those who benefited from its patronage. One can already see, in the later seventeenth century, the beginnings of the discur-sive constitution of a genteel, rational, nationalist theatrical public in the prefaces of the period—in the routing, on the one hand, of the hideously censorious "Flocks of Critiques" in the pit ("Vultures wait[ing] . . . for their Prey," in the words of Dry-den's prologue to *All for Love* (1678)),[41] and of the equally hideous theatrical mob. In Dryden's prologue to *Cleomenes* (1692), for instance, he calls on the "true Judges" in the audience, "Men of Wit and Sence," to join him in condemnation of "our Bear-Garden Friends," who "bounce with Hands and Feet, and cry *Play, Play*":

> Arise true Judges in your own Defence,
> Controul those Foplings, and declare for Sence.

In distinguishing the "true Judges" from both the "Foplings" in the pit and "our Bear-Garden Friends" standing on the benches with their "dirty Feet" and showing "their Booby Faces" to the disgusted boxes, Dryden's prologue is intended to align him with a newly dignified bourgeoisie, united critically as well as spatially (in the boxes, in town, at the hub of the colonial empire) against both the pseudo-aristocratic "Foplings" and the deportable "Mob":

> Let 'em go people *Ireland*, where there's need
> Of such new Planters to repair the Breed;
> Or to *Virginia* or *Jamaica* Steer,
> But have a care of some *French* Privateer;
> For if they should become the Prize of Battle,
> They'll take 'em Black and White for *Irish* Cattle.[42]

By the later eighteenth century, Dryden's viciously classist distinction between the few "true Judges" and the muddy majority (Irish "Cattle" meant merely for breeding) could be reversed, the enlightenment of the theatrical public generalized to the majority and rhetorically linked to the enlightenment of the more general public and the nation as a whole. The public that developed in the eighteenth century was not, of course, united in its view of what constituted enlightenment and certainly did not actually represent a fixed set of positions, but it was a kind of general authority to which one could appeal, deployed strategically to represent whichever position one happened to hold. Writers often acknowledged the disunity and multiplicity of the actual public—made up of particular individuals and of divisive subgroups ("parties," "cabals"). But "*the* public" was understood as a unified entity, singular rather than plural—in the theatre, the heterogeneous spectators transformed into a united body. If John Home recognized the theatre as "a house in which majorities are common" (a negative assessment of a non-representative tyrannical majority benefiting from political disunity, with overtones recalling the kind of dynastic discord familiar from tragedy), when he describes "the public" in attendance at his tragedy, *Agis* (1758) (in his insanely flattering anonymous puff for his own play), the soul of "public unanimity" takes over, the play's beauties "breath[ing] into" the spectators "all one spirit" and leading "over to the side of Truth those who came determined in the cause of error," drawing "her [singular] voice from the mixed multitude."[43] Anecdotes typically mythologized the unanimity of the oppositional parterre—the ideal reduction of its heterogeneity into the "single voice" of the people—for instance that describing Henri-Louis Lekain's revolutionary performance as Ghenghis-Khan in Voltaire's *Orphan of China* (repeated in endless variants in theatre memoirs of the period): "Public opinion was formed instantaneously," wrote the great actor François-Joseph Talma, "and by an electrical movement it manifested itself in long and loud applause."[44] Advocating a standing pit during the controversy over the placement of benches in the Comédie-Française parterre in the 1770s, Jean-François Marmontel could oppose the "caprice" that ruled the quarrelsome (feminine) boxes to the "judgement" of a free-standing parterre (with a taste "less delicate but also less capricious, and above all more masculine and firm"). Rather than contributing to fragmentation, the free movement of ideas and emotions in the standing pit brought "the public" from discord to unanimity (just as citizens best achieved political unanimity through the free exchange of ideas): "If the parterre . . . did not capture public opinion, and reduce it to unity, bringing it back to its own [views], there would often be as many different views as there are loges at the spectacle, and the success of a play would not be unanimously or firmly decided for a long time."[45]

The portrait of a unified public with a single voice which could determine the success or failure of the play had become central to the collective imagination by the later eighteenth century. If, for Lessing, the public was a "severe master," the public was nonetheless singular, supreme, sovereign, a "tribunal" that was "the sole judge" of works (in Beaumarchais's words, the jurisprudential sense overlaid on the critical).[46] The public determined "the fate" of plays; its judgement offered the final word, proving or disproving a play's worth. The playwright was obliged to yield to its authority: "I had no wish of combatting in any way the public's taste," writes Voltaire in the preface to *Mariamne* (1725). "It is [the public's] sentiments and not my own that I must follow."[47] This authoritative public was sometimes benevolent, sometimes authoritarian, cruel, and tyrannical (as in Piron's figure of the "Sultan-Public"). It had two faces: generally "so respectable," its judgement "enlightened" (as Hyppolite Clairon described it), but capable of transforming itself into "a wild and ferocious beast."[48] Home could evoke vividly this Janus-faced public: on the one hand, a reasonable and benevolent body which could "raise, improve, and perfect" the talents of young playwrights, on the other, beneath this exterior of reason, a body made up of "owls of criticism . . . more hateful than all human beings" who, "if the brightness fade in any part," are awakened by "the gloom, their proper day-break," to "beat down with their broad heavy wings the fearful and weak infant merit," in an image reminiscent of Goya's nightmare *Capricios* to which Goya appended the caption, "the dream of reason produces monsters."[49]

If the public did not always attain to ideals of unity and rationality—if it was not always "one spirit" with a single voice on the "side of Truth," united against error— it was to be educated and united by reference to an objective correlative: canons of judgement akin to the impartial, publicly accessible laws so important to the politics of the period. The critic John Hill, for instance, writing in 1750, argued that he was "publickly" laying down "rules" for acting, not merely in order to improve the actors but as a course for the improvement of public taste, offering lessons in the rational judgement of theatrical art in order to increase "the number of those who judge with knowledge and with candour."[50] In the *Hamburg Dramaturgy* (1767), Lessing suggests that critics have an obligation to draw on a set of objective correlatives for their claims: not to pretend to a specious universality, but to offer a public rationalization of the chaos of individual likes and dislikes. Attacking one French critic for beginning "with a modest 'we should have preferred'" but extrapolating that "we" into "universally binding dicta," Lessing expresses his concern that a critical "we" that purports to speak for universal judgement may be mere individual taste, suggesting the dangerous political consequences in the by-now familiar equation of critical law with the laws of the state (giving "a character of generality" to justifications of one's personal taste "means exceeding the limits permitted to the investigating amateur and instituting oneself an independent lawgiver"). An objective measure is required as corrective, one determined not by any (potentially fallible) authority but by "rules necessitated by . . . nature," the foundation, equally, for "public reason."[51]

Playwrights regularly called on "public reason" as a code phrase for public approbation, contrasting their attackers with the "enlightened" public whose discernment could identify true merit. Assuming a rational public, Lessing could contrast that public to the amateur critics, insisting that "every little criticaster must not deem himself the public."[52] It was crucial to distinguish the genuine public from the critics who had appropriated the public voice. "The public" was not to be confused with the "paid fans," or those in the thrall of "party" or "cabal,"[53] those self-interested persons so harmful to the public good. Sheridan's portrait of such a person in Mr Dangle, "head of a band of critics" who "take upon them to decide" a play's merits "for the whole town," would have resonated with his own public's disapproval of such anti-majoritarian and partisan judgement. His audience could happily congratulate itself in hearing itself described in the justly outraged Mrs Dangle's chastisement of her husband (surely intended by Sheridan as a moment in which the house might rise to its feet in applause for Mrs Dangle's worthy sentiments): "The PUBLIC is [the genuine] CRITIC—without whose fair approbation they know no play can rest on the stage, and with whose applause they welcome such attacks as yours, and laugh at the malice of them."[54]

The opposition between print and performance came to be central to the distinction between the usurping critics and the rational public, the usurping critics identified most strongly with theatrical performances, the rational public identified most strongly as a readership that might come to the theatre but whose real being lay beyond the walls of the theatre. Certainly, the rational public could often be envisioned as the univocal body of *theatre-goers* whose applause might silence the irrational and idiosyncratic critics in *the press*. Arthur Murphy, for instance, could write that he was sometimes attacked by the "libels" of "the small tribe of wits and critics" ("men who cannot think through a dozen connected sentences [but] can spin out a paragraph . . . teem[ing] with virulence"), opposing their attacks to the "favour" the theatrical "Public" has granted him: "I have sometimes the pleasure of hearing that the piece, which is grossly abused in some morning paper, is applauded at the theatre in the evening,"[55] he writes. Sheridan's *The Critic* similarly reflects the concern that the print "public" did not actually represent *the* public—that the ostensible public of the newspapers was manufactured on command, its theatrical views (like its political "news") produced for a fee by the Puffs behind the pseudo-public prints. ("I am, Sir, a Practitioner in Panegyric, or to speak more plainly—a Professor of the Art of Puffing, at your service—or any body else's," exclaims Puff proudly. "Sir, you are very obliging!," responds Sneer, "I have often admired your talents in the daily prints.")[56] But, whatever the scepticism about the genuine representativeness of the "public prints," the *reading* public was generally characterized as a better sort of judge: made up of "those of the most polite Taste among Scholars, the best Breeding among Gentlemen, and the least acquainted with sensual Pleasure among the Ladies," those "vacant . . . from every strong Prepossession,"[57] in Goldsmith's gustatory metaphor a readership of "Epicure[s]"; set in opposition to a public of "Glutton[s],"[58] the theatrical cabal that, with its loud guffaws, could easily sway the assembled crowd.

Playwrights regularly appealed to this reading public, whose judgement they characterized as less interested and more representative than that of party and cabal in the theatre. When, in 1782, the audience hissed Charles Palissot's *The Philosophers* from the stage (in part due to its mocking representation of Rousseau crawling on all fours), Palissot turned to readers of the *Journal de Paris*—members of a general "Public" that had been overwhelmed by the theatrical "Cabal"—referring them to the printed edition to reclaim their hijacked play:

> This ridiculous floundering production is not my work. It belongs (and I dare flatter myself that the Public will not forget it) to the Cabale, which has spoiled the pleasures [rightly belonging to the Public]. [The Public] may . . . find the missing scene in my Collected Works. . . . If it wishes to see it returned to the Theatre, it must see to this itself.[59]

Foote might satirize the failed playwright whom the public has damned and who seeks justice from the "real judges," the print-reading "critics": "I think the public are blockheads; a tasteless, a stupid, ignorant tribe; and a man of genious deserves to be damn'd who writes any thing for them," says Sir Thomas after his play has failed, consoling himself in the thought that "the closet will do . . . that justice the stage has denied. . . . The critics, the real judges, will discover . . . excellent talents [in the printed play]."[60] But only a year later, after the failure of his comedy, *Taste* (in 1765), he could himself sound just like his risible Sir Thomas (with either an astonishing lack of self-awareness or an exceedingly subtle inclination for self-parody). He is, he writes, submitting the play in its printed form ("in the following Sheets") "more generally . . . to the Public," a far worthier public (made up of "the better sort") than the common "tribe" in the theatre: "Tho' I despaire of gratifying the *Populum Tributim* of the *Theatre*, yet I flatter myself the *Primores Populi* will find me no disagreeable Companion in the Closet."[61]

The theatrical public, easily swayed, deluded by the noise of the cabal, could fortunately be overridden by the impartial and rational reading public. Complaining of the reception of *The Barber of Seville* in the preface attached to the second official edition of the play in 1775, Beaumarchais casts the theatre as the space of superstitious religious ritual ("The God of cabals is irritated," he tells the actors, "*Children! a sacrifice is necessary[!]*"), addressing his more enlightened reading public in his "Temperate Letter" to it: "I recognize no other judge than you, not excepting Messieurs the spectators, who—judges only of first resort—often see their sentence overturned by your tribunal."[62] The theatrical public might be a noisy arbiter in the heat of performance, but print was a higher and more final authority regulating the arbitrary spontaneities of the audience: "The success of a Dramatic piece on the Stage, depends . . . upon accidental circumstances," writes Home (quoting Voltaire), "but the day of publication decides its fate."[63] In the discussion between Syllogism and Young Melmoth in William Kenrick's *The Widow'd Wife* (1767) (at which we glanced in Chapter 11), Syllogism suggests that, although poets with "a freehold on Parnassus" may not vote for Members of Parliament (and thereby ensure the passage of literary property legislation beneficial to them), they may "levy contributions" on the town whenever they like:

> *Syllogism*: When poets had no patrons but the great, the poor devils, sure enough, were obliged to live upon little: but since the publick have taken them under their protection, a bard, like another man, may have two coats to his back, and every thing handsome about him.

Young Melmoth expresses his concern that such a system of payments to poets is "too arbitrary," and ought to be regulated by "the convocation of cricks," whose task is "literary legislation." Syllogism agrees that critics may provide legislation in the first instance, but, while the critics in the pit *ought* to rationalize the "arbitrary" distribution of literary rewards, since they themselves are as abitrary as the lawyers debating "literary property," their decisions are subject to the higher authority of "the publick" at large, implicitly, "the upper house":

> *Syllogism*: Yes, Sir, [the critics in the pit] are the lower house, and have the privilege of decid- ing in all money-matters. They hold their sessions in the pit, at the representation of every new play, and proceed directly to the consideration of ways and means.–To be sure, Sir, we cannot raise a shilling without the consent of the house.– But if they approve the bill, they pass it [on to the public].[64]

If the print-reading public was a higher and less arbitrary authority than that in the theatre, it was the "impartiality" of print itself (opposed to the partiality of the all-too impassioned theatre) that allowed for genuine reflection, and hence rational, unprejudiced judgement.[65] For Condorcet, these qualities made of it the medium of enlightenment, truth, and justice:

> We have seen a new species of tribune establish itself, which communicates impressions that are less lively but more profound; which exercises a less tyrannical empire over the passions, but obtains a more certain and durable power over reason; in which all the advantages lie on the side of truth, because what art has lost in means of seduction it has gained in means of enlight- enment. A public opinion has been created, powerful because of the number who share it; energetic, because the motives that determine it act on all the minds of those engaged at once. Thus we have seen, on behalf of reason and justice, a tribunal arise, independent of all human power, from which it is difficult to hide anything and [whose judgements] it is impossible to elude.[66]

Print may communicate with less vivacity, but it communicates with greater depth; it may communicate with less seductive passion, but it communicates with greater reason. The sheer number of participants in this great print-reading public makes of it a new omniscient and all-powerful lawgiver, free of all the old forms of subjection to human tyranny.

THE REPUBLIC OF LETTERS AND THE PATRIOT NATION

This reconstitution of print along political lines offered playwrights at war with the establishment theatre a rhetoric for positioning themselves not as desperate poets rejected by managers, but as dramatists who could circumvent the authoritarian theatres by using print to go straight to the free sphere of the public. When Jean-Jacques Rutlidge published his anonymous dramatic polemics *The Actors* and *The Bureau of Wit* in 1776, protesting against the tyranny of the Comédie-Française, he used them to address directly the "public" to whom he had been denied access in the theatre, highlighting the opposition between the royally dominated theatre and the democratic realm in which his printed plays could travel.[67] In the battle between dramatists and the Comédie-Française in the 1770s, such calls to the public took on distinctly revolutionary overtones, dramatists referring repeatedly, for instance, to the "tribunal of the public," which would "judge" the actions of the royal troupe in the pamphlet press. But the rhetorical opposition between the establishment theatre and the free dramatist communicating directly to the public in print was not exclusive to pre-Revolutionary France. A 1758 letter signed "Severus" and published in the London *Herald*, for instance, protests the monopoly power of the patent theatres, which (given their lack of public regulation) "may be as tyrannical and oppressive as [they] pleas[e]," exerting a power regularly "exercised, at the expence of the general, to partial advantage."[68] Goldsmith could similarly attack the patent theatres, identifying them with "party" (which tyranically rules "our pleasures, as well as more important concerns"), opposing them to a public whose claims he purports to be asserting and which may "at last be taught to vindicate [its] privileges."[69]

The opposition between the government-protected theatres and "the Public" was becoming axiomatic, often cast (in both England and France) in socio-economic terms as an opposition between monopoly (enforced by the police power of the state) and a free market in plays. The increasingly important concept of the "public domain"—in which the public was identified as the owner of cultural property (in a formation linked to new conceptions of intellectual property generally)—was aligned with the concept of the free market: what was public property was freely to be used, not to be monopolized by a few privileged institutions.[70] In their attempts to align themselves with a reading "public" that might join them against the establishment theatres, opposition dramatists commonly drew on conceptions of "public property" or public cultural rights. For instance, a 1775 pamphlet arguing for the production of Palissot's *The Courtesans* at the Comédie-Française describes the right to performance as, in fact, the rights of the "nation" (casting Palissot as the trustee and guardian of those rights), appealing to the reading public to bring justice in the theatre.[71] In *The Actors* (1776), whose title page reads *The Actors . . . performed by the Actors of the city of Paris at the Théâtre du Temple, the 5ᵗʰ of January 2440*, Rutlidge uses the eighteenth-century conceit of the long-lost manuscript (the play has turned up at the Comédie-Française in the year 2440 in an old trunk once belonging to the actor Préville, and is now being printed with a dedication to the "RESPECTABLE PUBLIC!" signed by the enlightened actors of the future) as a device for excoriating the Comédie's monopolistic claim on the heritage of dramatic works. "We still have a number of good manuscripts by the same hand," explain the twenty-fifth-century actors in the dedication they address to the public:

We will return them to you one by one because we firmly believe that they belong to you, and because we certainly do not have the kind of smug complacency that would allow us to think, as [the actors] thought in the old days, that a troupe of players, hired and paid by you, could dispute with you the heritage of the Corneilles and the Racines and the many other illustrious dead [authors].[72]

In the new age, the royal claim on public property (that of the Comédie-Française along with that of the monarchy) would yield to the claims of the public.

That public, constituted by its property (its "heritage"), was strongly identified throughout Europe with "the nation."[73] Certainly the live theatre was central (both actually and conceptually) to the discourse of cultural nationalism gaining strength in the last decades of the eighteenth century, as the calls for national theatres or the noisy patriotism of writers like Sheridan suggest.[74] "We take it for granted that a national theatre can provide great advantages for the entire nation," wrote Löwen, his hypothetical nation extending from the new theatre in Hamburg across the German-speaking lands.[75] The new national theatres were to be responsible for producing national culture, and to address themselves to the nation as a whole. The unified voice especially of the pit or Parisian "parterre" (its populism equating it with "the public" and "the people") could be extrapolated into the larger voice of the "nation," as Louis-Sébastien Mercier suggests when he explains that the parterre "acquits the debt of the nation": what comes "all at once from these assembled men" "is the eruption of a volcano; the acclamations form but a single voice."[76] But conceptually, the nation's culture reached far beyond the bounds of the theatre, and could in some ways be better described by the ancient distopic notion of the "Republic of Letters" that became so central to the eighteenth century's politically inflected conception of its literary life. The "Republic of Letters" could become, in its eighteenth-century incarnation, an extension of the notion of the nation, hypothesizing (like the concept of "public property") a form of popular representation independent of the court and expressing the will of "the people."[77] It offered dramatists a conceptual territory at once as concrete as, and yet more general than, the theatrical auditorium—a territory from which the diffuse and invisible association of writers could direct the rulers for the sake of the populace. In Foote's dedication to *The Patron*, for instance, he evokes a vast territory—the "whole republic of letters" (the theatre constituting merely its "most popular domain")—directing the Lord Chamberlain (who happens to head the "department" with the task of overseeing this "spot") to "cultivat[e]" it "with care."[78] The virtuous theatre, overseen by the broader Republic of Letters, was to be a microcosm of the virtuous nation as a whole.

If the notion of nationhood was to correlate with the conceptual "Republic of Letters," it was being built through letters itself: through, for instance, the representation of the national dramatic heritage in the many national theatre histories and collections of the nation's drama proliferating over the course of the eighteenth and nineteenth centuries. Gottsched's *The German Stage* (1741–5), Pietro Signorelli's, *Critical History of the Ancient and Modern Theatres in Italy* (1762), John Bell's *British Theatre* (1776–8), or (in the next century) Agustín Durán's *General Collection of Plays* (1826–34) were (in Durán's words) "monument[s] to our country's glory," reminding those perusing library shelves that the nation's printed drama *was* the nation.[79] In his 1768 edition of Shakespeare, Edward Capell could describe Shakespeare's plays as "part of the kingdom's riches," "foremost" in the list of her "literary possessions." Such works, he writes, are "talk'd of wherever the name of *Britain* is talk'd of." They are "her estate in fame, that fame which letters confer upon her; the worth of and value of which or sinks or raises her in the opinion of foreign nations, and she takes her rank among them according to the esteem which these are held in."[80] It was, he wrote, "an object of national concern" that Shakespeare's *œuvre* be properly published, casting himself as "a benefactor to his country, and somewhat entitl'd to her good will" in producing his edition for the good of the nation.[81] Just as it could sometimes seem, then, that the genuine public consisted not of theatrical spectators, but instead of enlightened readers, so it could equally seem that the new "nation" lay not in the constricted space of the theatre but out there somewhere in the broader world of print—represented in editions like Capell's, to be addressed by dramatists liberating themselves from the old theatres. "Most dramatists have unfortunately till now worked for only a very small number of men" instead of "the bulk of the nation," explains Mercier in the preface to *Jenneval*. But (he declares) he will submit no more plays to the old theatre, for in printing his play he is now "working for my nation," addressing that vast "multitude in which a crowd of new and sensitive souls resides."[82]

The French Revolution and its aftermath shook Europe's faith in that vast "multitude" of "new and sensitive souls," along with its faith in the virtuous theatre overseen by a virtuous nation. Playwrights could write with horror of "the events" (as Arthur Murphy refers to them in the preface to *Arminius* (1798)) "which in the last seven years have changed the face of Europe, and, under the savage conduct of a Nation of professed Atheists, counteracted the order of Providence in the formation of Civil Society,"—events in which "the fury of a Democratic Faction . . . reduced [a] whole Nation to a state of Slavery."[83] The public, rational judge in the republic of letters, enlightened property-holder of the nation, seemed to have been replaced by something closer to Clairon's "wild and ferocious beast," Home's "owls" awakened by "the gloom, their proper day-break," Goya's "monsters" produced by "the dream of reason." There were those who still embraced the "immense crowd inundating the theatres" (as Victor Hugo would later describe it), a crowd "avid for the pure emotions of art" and possessing "a great and powerful voice."[84] Schiller could exalt the dark side of his Jekyl-and-Hyde version of the "Folk": sometimes a mere "civil polity," an "abstract idea in our minds" whose "living Word" had been driven out by writing; more powerfully, a "sensibly living mass" with all its "brute force," whose "primitive character" the theatre must recapture, for whom dramatists must "restore the gods" and "reproduce every extreme which the artificial frame of . . . life has abolished."[85] But this newly mythologized primitive "Folk" was less a rational actor determining the fate of the cultural republic than the fluid and inchoate spirit of the nation—a turbulent model for a dramatic poetry at once worshipping and chastening the volatility of the masses, whose excesses might more safely be translated into the sphere of the disembodied poetic imagination.

THEATRICAL IMPRESSIONS

13. *Scenic Pictures*

In the "Advertisement" accompanying *The Two Friends, or the Merchant of Lyon*, printed with the play when it was published in 1770, Beaumarchais explains that he is offering, in his text, not only detailed descriptions of the play's "pantomimes" but also specific instructions for blocking: "In order to facilitate the theatrical placement [and movements] of provincial or amateur actors . . . I have printed, at the beginning of each scene, the names of the characters, [listed] in the order in which the Comédie-Française actors were placed, from right to left, from the perspective of the spectators." Given the spread of provincial and amateur theatre, unless the dramatist takes the trouble to give such instructions in the printed text, provincial and amateur players cannot hope to perform the play correctly. For it is with great care that "the actors of the Comédie-Française, the most consummate in their art, test and vary their blocking during rehearsals until they have found the best positions, which are then consecrated, for them and their successors, in the manuscript deposited in their library." Thanks to Beaumarchais's textual specifications, amateur and provincial performers may now have access to the proper *mise-en-scène*, in a printed text that approximates the authoritative promptbook. "This care in specifying everything may appear finicky," he writes, and may cause the play to "los[e] a bit of its warmth in the reading." But it will, thereby, "gain a good deal of reality in the performance"—a result that justifies the minor inconvenience to the reader's pleasure.[1]

A decade and a half later, in a section on the "Placement of the Actors" in the preface to *The Marriage of Figaro*, Beaumarchais's directorial system appears again, with further refinements and without apology to readers. Where, in *The Two Friends*, he left any necessary movements mid-scene "to the discretion of the actors," here, to designate any significant changes in the actors' positions on the stage, he offers notes printed "in the margin at the moment the change occurs." Moreover, he has included a section on the "Character and attire" of those in the play, here expanded from the simpler lists designating the "costumes of the actors" (in *Eugénie* (1767) and *The Barber of Seville* (1775)) to full-fledged descriptions of character:

THE COUNTESS, agitated by two contrary sentiments, must show only a supressed sensibility or a very moderate anger; nothing, above all, that might degrade her amiable and virtuous character in the eyes of the spectator. . . . Her clothing in the first, second and fourth act is a comfortable Levite gown, and no ornament on her head: she is at home and supposed to be indisposed. . . .[2]

As a visual corollary to his carefully prepared editions (both that published in Paris and that published at his printing works in Kehl), he includes five plates showing the sets and the costumes of the characters (the Countess's "comfortable . . . gown," for instance, with an extremely low *décolletage*) (Fig. 49)—plates intended (as one of the many piracies of the play and its plates announces) "to facilitate the fitting out of the scene and the production of th[e] comedy."[3]

Both these and his detailed prefatory instructions not only use the text to shape the disposition of the scene but also give a sense of the overall stage "picture": the kind of careful visual composition, imagined in still form, that recurs throughout his plays. In *Eugénie*, for instance, the scene opens to reveal a salon "in the best taste," with trunks and packages strewn about, a table in the corner laden with a tea cart, the women seated around it, Mme Murer reading an English newspaper near the candle, Eugénie working on her embroidery, the Baron behind the table, Betsy standing next to him holding in one hand a platter with a small glass on it and in the other a straw-covered bottle of maraschino cordial. It closes with the kind of tableau that could typically suggest, in eighteenth-century plays, the harmonious resolution of the plot, with Eugénie's repentant seducer kissing her hand, while her family gathers round her in a picturesque formation.[4] *The Two Friends* opens on another domestic scene, in which the music offers an aural analogue to the scene's pictorial harmony. After the first bars of the orchestra's *andante*, which creates "the illusion of the little concert which the spectacle represents," the curtain rises to show a clavier open and laden with music, Pauline in her dressing gown seated before it playing, and Mélac standing next to her "in light morning attire," his hair held up with a comb, accompanying her on his violin.[5]

In *The Marriage of Figaro*, such scenic pictorialism (its harmony similarly empha-sized by the musical accompaniment that serves as its background) becomes at once more explicit and more referential. In Act II, scene iv, the Page Chérubin has entered the Countess's bedroom, shy and trembling, with a song he has written for her, which Suzanne urges him to sing:

The Countess, seated, holds the paper in order to follow the music. Suzanne is behind her armchair, and warms up by reading the music over her mistress's shoulder. The little Page is before her, his eyes downcast. This tableau is exactly like [Jacques-Firmin Beauvarlet's] beautiful print after Vanloo called *The Spanish Conversation*.*[6] (Fig. 50)

While Beaumarchais, through his marginal notations, repositions the actors to match the line-up in the print (right to left, in accordance with his instructions: "*Chérubin. The Countess. Suzanne"), at the same time he rewrites the image to fit his drama. The virile Spaniard in the print who assumes a theatrical posture to offer himself in courtly fashion to the Countess-figure has been replaced by the Page (in what may be a reference to Chérubin's momentary eclipsing of the Count in the Countess's affections), not theatrically posed but awkward and trembling, his eyes modestly downcast. The open terrace and grand Palladian arches giving onto a stretch of sky with palatial columns in the print have been replaced by the suggestive intimacy of the Countess's bedroom. The little girl who clings, in the print, to the Countess as she looks curiously at the viewer has disappeared. The figures in the scene are now not gazing at their audience, as the girl in the print gazes at hers, but

Dessiné par Sᵗ Quentin ancien Pensionaire du Roy. *Gravé par Halbou*

*Je le tuerai, je le tuerai. Tuez-le donc,
ce méchant Page.*

FIG. 49. Illustration for Act II in Beaumarchais's *The Marriage of Figaro*, published under
his direction at his printing works in Kehl (1785).

CONVERSATION ESPAGNOLE

*Dessiné et Gravé par J. Beauvarlet Graveur du Roy d'après le Tableau peint
par Carle Vanloo Chevalier de l'ordre du Roy et son premier Peintre.*

FIG. 50. Carle Vanloo's "Spanish Conversation," in Jacques-Firmin Beauvarlet's print
(1769).

absorbed in the self-enclosed world of the play, shut off (like the Countess's bedroom) from the public view, their eyes (like Chérubin's) both literally and metaphorically downcast. Rather than transforming the picture into a scene (as the popular
tableaux vivants of the following decades were to do), Beaumarchais has transformed
the scene into a picture, at once removing its model's self-conscious theatricalism
(along with its classicism) and creating of it something closer to that to which both
pictorial and theatrical art would aspire in the decades to come: an image unto itself,
seemingly sequestered from the viewer, domestic, intimate, its figures absorbed in
their world, the picture narrating wordlessly the emotion of the scene.

DIGNIFYING SPECTACLE

Eighteenth-century complaints about the decay of the stage (a stage now, it seemed, devoted to grand-scale spectacle, "the indecent farces of the Italian actors," buffoonish "afterludes," and the opera) ran as counterpoint to the recognition of popular entertainment as art and the general embrace of the visual-theatrical that could conjoin the increasing prestige of the plastic arts to the lively culture of spectacle that was a product of the expanding theatre industry.[7] With the growth of urban populations, the general increase in leisure in the eighteenth century, and the proliferation (and enlargement) of theatres, urban capitals offered a rich variety of scenic art, from such visual spectaculars as Guilbert de Pixérécourt's *Chateau in the Apennines; or, The Living Phantom; Grand Spectacle in Five Acts* (1799) to animal shows, "cabinets" with various kinds of optical displays, rope dancers, and other curiosities. While managers responded to the market for lavish scenic art in the theatre, encouraging it through the large-scale dissemination of advertising (in the newspress, and through playbills and posting bills lengthily detailing the spectacle), publishers responded in print: with descriptions of theatrical display in books on theatre, acting manuals, lives of the actors, *livrets* of various performance genres (the scripts of Pierrot and Punch, the opera, the action-packed pages of melodrama); with visual images in illustrated play editions, engravings, eventually lithographs; with books meant for pictorial interleaving and massive theatrical albums meant to be filled with portraits of one's favourite actors in their most distinguished roles.

The documentation of popular figures in the many illustrations that circulated as separate prints, as well as in books, reviews, prefaces, programmes, and theatre histories gave them at once a wider cultural circulation and a new degree of cultural legitimacy. Such marginal forms as the French *parades* (for which there was an aristocratic vogue in the later eighteenth century) or farce, long reviled but now "greatly relished and applauded" by the knowing in London (or so Tate Wilkinson claimed) were, similarly, growing respectable.[8] Stock clowns like the pig-gelder Hanswurst or *commedia* figures like Pulcinello or Pierrot filled the bins of the print shops, portrayed sometimes as buffoons, but as often as dignified cultural representatives or melancholy souls with romantic gazes. Early in the century, a director like Carolina Neuber might have tried to elevate the theatre by purging it of characters like Hanswurst.[9] In 1721, Alain René Le Sage felt obliged to apologize for publishing the ten-volume *Theatre de la foire*: "The title alone, *Theatre of the Fairground*, carries with it an idea of the low and uncouth, which warns [readers] against the book. Why wish to perpetuate its memory? One cannot too soon forget it." But in attempting "to find a middle way between the high and the low," as Le Sage writes, "to scrape the earth, so to speak, without touching it,"[10] such editors were helping to reposition the "low" so that apology would become unnecessary. With the proliferation of attempts to record gesture and action, of stage directions and printed promptbooks, theatre reviews, gestural maps and physionomic charts, novels that detailed facial and bodily expression, actor biographies and autobiographies, stage histories—with all

FIG. 51. The Muse of Comedy gathers the figures of Music, Poetry and Dance in front of a fair theatre (1730).

these, the spectacular arts seemed not only capable of inscription but also worthy of it. If the spectacular theatre offered a challenge to the printed text, at the same time the printed text honoured it. Some dramatic texts continued to present themselves as purified of the ignominies of the vulgar stage. But print seemed, on the whole, the necessary partner of the spectacular *œuvre*. Engravings like that showing the Muse of Comedy gathering the figures of Music, Poetry, and Dance for her "*divertisemens*" in front of a fair theatre (Fig. 51) suggested that, after all, even rope dancing might rise to the status of dramatic art.

The aesthetics of popular culture were beginning to seep into the official theatre by way of such images and, as important, by way of the revival of the ancient non-verbal theatrical arts. Pantomime and dance might, through their comparison with verbal-narrative arts, become "rational": a story made up of the "connected presentation of Dances in Character" could be "so intelligibly told, by a mute Narration of Gesture," explained Colley Cibber, that "even thinking Spectators" could acknowledge it to be "a rational Entertainment."[11] Pantomime and rope dancing were repeatedly identified with the ancients, in an attempt to use textual scholarship in the service of non-textual spectacle. The 1717 "Loves of Mars and Venus" was billed as "A Dramatick Entertainment of Dancing, Attempted in Imitation of the Pantomimes of the Ancient Greeks and Romans."[12] The "ballet in pantomime action" (performed at the Duchesse du Maine's chateau at Sceaux), which mimed the last act of Corneille's *Horace*, was modelled on the pantomime elements of Greek drama.[13] The anonymous *Letter . . . on the rope dancers and pantomimes that appeared among the Greeks and Romans and in Paris in 1738* cites Terence, Horace, Petronius, Juvenal, and Quintilian in justification of rope-dancing, a lineage reiterated throughout the century.[14]

Such analysis was part of an important re-evaluation of the place of the theatre among the arts, elevated not because it offered a venue for poetry worthy of the ancients, but precisely because it was spectacular, musical, the medium of the live actor. We have already looked (in Chapter 7) at early attempts to legitimize gesture as significant language, to identify the language of signs with the "universal language" of "nature," to celebrate the visual not as a degradation of the ideational but as an autonomous medium of communication. The protheatrical tradition finding early articulation in the Renaissance and seventeenth century began to come into its own in the eighteenth century. "It must be remember'd a Play is to be Seen," writes Richard Steele in 1723, "and is made to be Represented with the Advantage of Action, nor can appear but with half the Spirit, without it."[15] Such particular claims for the life of the play on stage were expanded into the kind of general paean to theatrical art that became more typical as the century wore on: "The enchantments of the theatre enslave the eyes, the ears, the spirit and the heart," writes Pierre Rémond de Sainte-Albine in his essay on *The Actor* (in a comment to which we shall return): "For this reason, its art is one of those which allows us to experience the most complete pleasure. Our imagination is almost always obliged to supply the impotence of the other arts in their imitations of nature. That of the actor requires of us no supplement."[16] Theatre could (by contrast with the arts of the book) achieve that to which all the arts aspired: the universal language of emotion. "Retire, cold moralist, take away your heavy book," wrote Louis-Sébastien Mercier: "What signifies the preserving of your dry maxims, before the eloquent painting that shows the tableau armed with all its colours? . . . Men, approach, look, touch, feel. . . . you weep! Yes, certainly."[17]

Observations like Mercier's were typically expanded from claims for the aesthetic priority of theatrical performance to claims for the historical and ontological priority of its various media: gesture, music, and picture were both the first expressions of humankind, before language, and the most essential. In this priority lay theatre's universalism, key to its power. Unlike words, gestures, for instance, were "not arbitrary," as Rémond de Sainte-Albine's English adaptor John Hill explained in 1755: "they are dictated by nature; they are common to all mankind, and therefore all men understand them."[18] "Gesture is one of the first expressions of feeling given to man by nature," writes Louis Dubroca in his treatise on declamation. It is "the primitive language of the universe in the cradle. . . . [It] will always be the language of all nations . . . understood in all climates."[19] Music, similarly, could call on a universalism founded in its priority to language. "The original language was a song"; "music is a universal language"; "music is a natural language."[20] What music signified was the passions. "Musical sounds," wrote the Abbé Du Bos, have "the power to move us because they are the signs of the passions, instituted by nature."[21] Anteriority to language was crucial to the power of such sounds: "Music . . . imitates sounds prior to all language," wrote Gabriel Bonnot de Mably in his *Letters . . . on the Opera* (1741): "nature has herself given [it] to men to be the signs of their sorrow and of their joy."[22] For the actor Charles Macklin, music (as natural signifier) had in fact been born in the modulations of the human voice, a reminder that the actor's voice was a musical (not merely a word-forming) instrument, imitating the primal music, purest in its formation of significant sound independent of words: "The voice of the Actor must alter in its intonations, according to the qualities that the words express; from this idea Music seems to have taken its birth."[23]

A manifestation of this theatricalist universalism, *Robinson Crusoe* imitations were so popular on stage in the later eighteenth and early nineteenth centuries not because being alone on a desert island with nothing to do for a couple of decades was so inherently dramatic, but precisely because it was so undramatic, and hence allowed the dramatist to concentrate on the articulation of the specifically theatrical: the silent gestures of the sometimes solitary man; the harmony of nature expressed through music; the deep and inherent affectivity of nature's unadorned pictures: "At the rear is a little cheerful hill," the stage directions for Guilbert de Pixérécourt's *Robinson Crusoé* (1805) explain, "whose gentle slope, falling off to the right, reaches out to the edge of the sea."[24] Like pantomime (and sometimes in conjunction with it), the Robinson Crusoe story could strike the theatricalist chord of the universality of nature—a nature that was prior to language—thematized, for instance, in the figure of Pixérécourt's "Vendredi" (Friday), who can speak only a pidgin French, at first meant to stand out as comic butt against the standard French that his once-savage father Iglou learned by means of a good European education:

Vendredi. Me say that father of mine be good also, him well loved in tribe because him know many things.

Iglou. Several commercial interactions between my nation and the Colonists in Trinidad gave me a general familiarity with the customs of Europe: for this reason, [my tribe] appointed me Chief.[25]

But later, when Vendredi addresses the Europeans in the language of gesture alone (as the stage directions explain), the spectator is quietly reminded that beneath linguistic babble lies a deeper shared language, the primitive common language that transcends national particularity and is ultimately nobler than the official languages of the civilized world of letters.[26]

THE PICTORIAL SCENE

If gesture and music were important to the theatre's conception of its special power of signification, the visual image served as the organizing principle of the scene: Mercier's "eloquent painting," the "tableau armed with all its colours." The concern for the scenic image was abstracted in avid discussions of the relation between picture and poetry so important to the period's theatrical aesthetics: in the Abbé Du Bos's *Critical Reflections on Poetry and Painting* (1719), for instance, with "*Ut Pictura Poësis*" as its epigraph and its lengthy discussions of the drama, or, several decades later, in Lessing's *Laokoon* (1766), with its central contrast between painting and dramatic poetry.[27] The theatre-as-picture topos found articulation not only in theoretical works like Lessing's, but also in the theatre itself, in, for instance, the proliferation of picture galleries and portraits on stage, in gallery scenes like those in Sheridan's *School for Scandal* (1777) or Schiller's *The Robbers* (1780). These were indicative not only of the increasing prestige and cultural centrality of the pictorial arts (institutionalized in the museum, salon, and exhibition, reproduced in the grand collections of engravings and lithographs displayed in eighteenth- and nineteenth-century households) but also of the high consciousness of the theatre *as* picture. "Painting, good painting, the great tableaux, there are your models," writes Diderot to the Théâtre Italien actress Mme Riccoboni in 1758, explaining further (in his essay *On Dramatic Poetry*, written in the same year), that the playwright should imagine the spectator in the theatre as if "before a canvas where various paintings follow one another": "apply the laws of picturesque composition" in the theatre "and you will see that they are the same" as those for painting.[28]

The typical scenic indications of the period suggest that playwrights were, in fact, thinking of the stage as a series of unfolding pictorial compositions (as in *Eugénie*, *The Two Friends*, and *The Marriage of Figaro*), creating scenes that could enter into dialogue with the play illustrations that dramatists either imagined or had already seen. The opening stage directions in Arthur Murphy's *The Desert Island* (1760), for instance, describe Constantia dressed in "a romantic habit" and at work on an inscription, perhaps modelling the scene on the illustration in Collet de Messine's version of Metastasio's play published two years earlier (itself a model for the illustration in Murphy's play, though unlike Collet de Messine's, Murphy's turns Constantia away from the viewer, offering the reader an exemplary image of absorption in the text):

The scene represents a vale in the Desert Island, surrounded by rocks, caverns, grottos, flowering shrubs, exotic trees, and plants growing wild. On one side is a cavern in a rock, over the entrance of which appears, in large characters, an unfinished inscription. CONSTANTIA is discovered at work at this inscription, in a romantic habit of skins, leaves and

FIG. 52. "CONSTANTIA . . . in a romantic habit of skins" in Arthur Murphy's
The Desert Island (1760).

flowers; in her hand she holds a broken sword, and stands in act to finish the imperfect inscription. (Fig. 52)[29]

By the late eighteenth or early nineteenth century, pictorialism, formalized in the genre of the theatrical "Tableau" or "Picture Play," was a central trope for the theatre, sufficiently commonplace to be subject to frequent parody, as it is, for instance, in Christian Grabbe's *Jest Satire Irony and Deeper Significance*, in which the Schoolmaster laboriously explains the nature of "the *Picture-Play*": "everything occurring in it is picturesque."[30]

The explicit task of the "picture play" or *tableau vivant* was to model a theatrical image on a well-known painting, but performances generally drew on the common stock of pictorial images circulated *en masse* in print: those engravings and lithographs which (like Beauvarlet's rendering of Vanloo's *Spanish Conversation*) would have been sufficiently familiar to most spectators that they could refer the images they saw on stage to them. An appreciation of Theophilus Cibber's *The Harlot's Progress; or, the Ridotto Al Fresco: A Grotesque Pantomime Entertainment* (1733) (dedicated to Hogarth), or of George Colman's *Ut Pictura Poesis! or, the Enraged Musician* (1789), ending with a tableau "as near as possible to *Hogarth's* Print of *The Enraged Musician*," or of the scene in *The Marriage of Figaro* modelled on Beauvarlet—these relied on the spectator's ability to relate the scenic illustrations to their sources.[31] If printing did not create eighteenth- and nineteenth-century pictorialism, it reinforced it and broadened its reach. Striving to give detail and precision to the historical drama or to such exotic settings as Zaire, Malabar, or the Caribbean, managers and playwrights relied on historical and anthropological illustrations alongside scholarly texts. "A sensible stage manager," advises Johann Christoph Gottsched,

must look to antiquity and study pictures of the costumes of all the nations he intends to put upon the stage. . . . It is absurd when . . . one goes so far as to . . . represent an American princess in a whalebone corset and a fleeing Zaïre in the Orient with a three-ell-long train; nay even the ancient Germans Arminius, Segestes and others dressed like their mortal enemies the Romans, that is to say with wigs, white gloves, dress-sword etc.[32]

Citing its source, "(*) Lafitau's *Customs of the Savage Americans*, 2 vol. in-4° illustrated," a footnote on the cannibalistic ritual in Pixérécourt's *Robinson Crusoé* explains that the playwright has found, in Lafitau, illustrations and "highly interesting and detailed descriptions of the dances and games of the Caribbeans when they put a prisoner to death, and similarly on the peace-pipe dance that I place at the end of the third act." (Fig. 53)[33]

Libraries offered dramatic detail for the pictorial stage, serving the demand for "accuracy": the Count in Goethe's *Wilhelm Meister*, planning to model the pastoral-martial allegory Wilhelm's troupe is to perform on the "innumerable engravings and drawings" that he has collected on his journeys, must consult an entire library to get the representation of Minerva right, using, among other books, Bernard de Montfaucon's illustrated *Antiquity Explained* (1719) (as the real-life Philippe de Loutherbourg did as a basis for his Egyptian set for Alexander Dow's *Sethona*).[34] " 'I approve of the idea of bringing in Minerva,' " says the Count,

"But I have been wondering how she should be costumed so as not to arouse offense. I have therefore asked that all the books in my library which include a picture of her be brought here." And at that very moment in came several servingmen with huge baskets containing books of all shapes and sizes.

Montfaucon's *Antiquity Illustrated*, catalogues of Roman sculptures, gems and coins, together with all kinds of treatises on mythology were consulted and the representations of Minerva compared with each other. But even that did not satisfy the count, whose excellent memory recalled all sorts of Minervas from title pages, vignettes and other places. And so one tome after another had to be fetched from the library, and the count was soon surrounded by piles and piles of books. Finally . . . he exclaimed with a laugh: "I bet there isn't a single Minerva left in my library."[35]

FIG. 53. "Dances and games of the Caribbeans when they put a prisoner to death" in
Joseph-François Lafitau's *Customs of the Savage Americans*, a model for Guilbert de
Pixérécourt's *Robinson Crusoé* (1805).

Reflecting the influence of such pictorially based scenic art, much of the popular
drama developing at the end of the eighteenth century and in the first decades of
the nineteenth strove towards independence from verbal narrative: not just the
tableau or "picture play," but such genres as melodrama, gothic, and historical epic.
When Victor Hugo expressed his dissatisfaction with a theatre whose representations took the form of "narrations" and "descriptions" instead of "scenes" and
"paintings"[36]—he was reflecting the period's general preference for pictorial "narration" (through action and scenery) and its downgrading of verbal recounting and
explanation. Pictures were now to do the talking. Like the illustrated books to which
their audiences were accustomed, the dramas of the period offered striking freeze-

frame images geared towards immediacy of emotional response, even where they were not explicitly modelled on paintings or prints: "A dark night under the Castle Walls;—Bertram appears in a state of the utmost agitation;—he extends his arms towards a spot where the Moon has disappeared," begins Act IV, Scene i of Charles Robert Maturin's *Bertram; or, The Castle of St. Aldobrand* (1816).[37] As important, plays used pictorial metaphors (verbal and visual) to reflect on their theatrical status (as well as on the relationship between pictorial aesthetics and social issues). In Marie Thérèse De Camp Kemble's *Smiles and Tears* (1815), for instance, Lady Emily plans a *tableau vivant* as a means of shocking back to sanity old Fitzharding, who has gone mad and been placed in an asylum after the seduction and abandonment of his daughter Cecil. The scene opens in Lady Emily's uncle's drawing room:

A Room in Stanly's House, hung with Pictures; a full length [portrait] of Cecil, playing upon the Harp occupies the centre: it is covered by a green Curtain.

When Lady Emily draws back the curtain, Cecil is suddenly revealed to her father, "*Rising in the frame,*" playing and singing " '*Tears such as,*' *&c.*"[38] The disarray caused by Cecil's straying can be resolved through the framed picture, which allows the restoration of the paternal family and its harmonization with the bourgeois drawing room. Through the tableau (the flat and frozen image carefully framing the once wild girl, her enclosure replacing her father's unhappy incarceration in the asylum as he is restored to his rightful place as *pater familias*), Cecil may be transformed from actress-errant into an angel producing silent musical harmony—and the theatre's action may cease, displaced by the lingering picture.

In this context, it is no surprise to find the theatrical scene explicitly imagined as "an *animated picture*" "illustrat[ing]" the drama, with the proscenium arch understood as a frame through which moving pictures might pass, in a progression of connected but discrete (proto-cinematic) images.[39] Identifying as a model "those grand night-scenes containing many figures which we admire . . . in painting,—processions by torch-light or in an illuminated street,—crowds gathered to behold a conflagration, &c.," Joanna Baillie proposes that stage boxes be eliminated so that "the front-piece at the top; the boundary of the stage from the orchestra at the bottom; and the pilasters on each side, would then represent the frame of a great moving picture." The purpose of her proposal, she explains, is to keep the stage "entirely separated and distinct from the rest of the theatre; whereas, at present, an unnatural mixture of audience and actors, of house and stage, takes place near the front of the stage, which destroys the general effect in a very great degree."[40] Such comments reflected real changes in scenography: in the vast theatres that had been built in the decades that followed the banishment of spectators from the stages of the major theatres, with advances in lighting techniques (progressively improving from the late eighteenth century on, eventually permitting a darkened auditorium and a better-lighted stage with more suggestive shadows), the aspirations for the kind of control of the pictorial scene already nascent in the framed baroque stage became better capable of realization.[41] Disciplined by an aesthetics mandating the separation of audience and spectacle, modelled on the picture, with the proscenium arch used not only as a framing device but also as a seemingly impermeable boundary, with a darkened auditorium, an illuminated stage, and actors wholly engrossed in the scene, the stage could be a spectacular but dissociated whole. Like the painter or the novelist with their invisible audiences, the actor was (like Murphy's Constantia or the young man with his back turned in the Beauvarlet print) not to look out at the spectators, but to imagine that there was no one there. "Think no more of the spectator than you would if he did not exist," writes Diderot in *On Dramatic Poetry*. "Imagine a great wall at the edge of the stage, separating you from the parterre; perform as if the curtain never rises."[42]

THE DRAMATIST AS NOVELIST OF THE SCENE

Beaumarchais's use of tableaux, or the painterly scenic directions in a play like *Bertram*, or the pictorial trope around which *Smiles and Tears* resolves itself remind us that such pictorialism was driven not just by the demands of audiences raised on pictures, or the market-sense of managers using the technical improvements of the industrial revolution, but by dramatists who were, like managers, envisioning the scene in pictorial terms and, at the same time, approximating the descriptive specificity of the novel. There had always been a good deal of reciprocity between novels and plays, freely passing their plots back and forth. But, by the later eighteenth century, *the* novel had come into its own as a self-conscious genre, plays freely declared their dramatization of the most popular among them (Richardson's *Pamela*, for instance, in its many eighteenth-century stage incarnations), and plays could explicitly mark themselves *as* novels: George Colman's *Polly Honeycombe* (1760), for instance, or Schiller's *The Robbers* (1780) are "Dramatick Novel[s]".[43] If the novel was often contrasted with the drama as a means of identifying the theatre's particular conditions of reception, it was nonetheless a crucial model for it. When eighteenth- or nineteenth-century promptbooks described Shakespeare's heroines throwing roses, meandering through the mazy ways of endlessly shadowed gothic grottos—when they described palpitating hearts, blushes, coy smiles—they were attempting to take back the narrative power of the visual and gestural.

Stage directions attempted to produce externalized renderings of the internal life of the characters in conjunction with narrative description of the scene. In John Thomas Haines's *My Poll and My Partner Joe* (1835), for instance, Harry "tries in vain to speak; at length bursts into a passion of tears," narrate the stage directions. Mary, having seen an account of Harry's death in the paper, enters "in excessive agitation . . . Her manner is wild and hurried in the extreme"; when "she falls insensibly from [a] chair," "*Harry*, overpowered with emotion, leans on the chair, and weeps"; on recovering, Mary "rushes to the paper, holds it up to *Harry*, pointing in agony to the place, and throws herself on her knees," and then it is Harry's turn again to be "overpowered with emotion."[44] Providing something like an emotional score that might suggest the range of human emotion (akin to what the novel had articulated in its detailed psychological portraits), melodrama typically punctuated each speech with an indication of the emotion to be portrayed: "with forced ease," instructs Holcroft's *A Tale of Mystery* (1802), "tenderly . . . haughtily affecting surprise . . . sternly . . . with marked displeasure . . . with courteous resentment . . . retaining himself . . . alarmed . . . eagerly . . . with terror and indignation [h]e then assumes the eye and attitude of menace."[45] By the middle of the nineteenth century, Shakespeare's heroines could be granted imaginary girlhoods (in the famous example of Mary Cowden Clarke's *The Girlhood of Shakespeare's Heroines* (1850)) precisely because heroines in novels always seemed to have had girlhoods.

If, then, the novel was (in Hugo's famous pronouncement) the cathedral of the nineteenth century,[46] the theatre was at once novel and tableau. Rather than choosing to renounce the spectacular stage (as many did in the nineteenth century), dramatists could use the elaborate scenic specifications so common in late eighteenth and nineteenth-century plays at once to provide a more novelistic dramatic text and to shape the theatrical scene. Through these, they could, like Beaumarchais, attempt to "design" the many productions at which (given the proliferation of urban and provincial theatres) they could not be present. In his stage directions for *Robinson Crusoé*, for instance, Pixérécourt specifies that "the observation" of his special scenic instructions on the skin colour of Iglou, Vendredi, and the other Caribbeans ("not black, but merely olive-toned or lightly tanned") "is important, and I wish particular attention to be paid to it wherever this play may be produced."[47] Victor Hugo notes that he is including his own scenic and character specifications for the benefit of "actors who were not able to study the performance of these roles in Paris."[48] In the second part of her *Ethwald* (published in the second volume of her *Plays on the Passions* in 1802), Baillie adds a footnote to the text in which she offers lighting specifications that at once solve the problem that "inferior actors" might pose in a production and describe the painterly cast of the scene:

A scene of this kind, in which so many inferior actors would be put into situations requiring the expression of strong passion, might be a disadvantage to it; I should, therefore, recommend having the front of the stage on which the Thanes are, during the last part of the scene, thrown into deep shade, and the light only to come across the background at the bottom of the stage: this would give to the whole a greater solemnity; and by this means no expression of countenance, but only that of gesture, would be required of them.[49]

In detailing scenery, action, and character, dramatists could vacillate between their roles as invisible directors and set designers and their roles as novelists of the scene, as Schiller does in his description of the scenery for *Wilhelm Tell*, first scenic "painter," then lyric narrator, then stage carpenter worrying about the movable lake on stage:

Act I. I. High bluff above the Lake of Lucerne, the lake forming an inlet, across the lake you clearly see the green meadows, the villages and farms of Schwyz lying in the sunshine. Beyond (to the left of the spectators) the Haken with its two cloud-capped peaks. Still farther off and to the right (of the spectators) shimmer, blue-green, the Glarus mountain glaciers. On the rocks, represented by the wings, are steep paths with railings and ladders on which huntsmen and shepherds are seen climbing down in the course of the action. So the painter must represent the boldness, grandeur and danger of the Swiss mountains. A part of the lake must be movable, because it is shown during a storm.[50]

But, however uncertain they might be about the status of stage directions, dramatists nonetheless relied on them to evoke the descriptive power of both novel and picture, most notably in the wordless (but lavishly described) "illustrations" that punctuated the plays of the period, highlighting points of intense emotion. Towards the end of Maturin's *Bertram*, for instance, Maturin offers a nearly wordless scene (emphasizing the "stupe[faction]" and "speechless[ness]" of the characters) with a descriptive richness worthy of the gothic novel. Bertram must confront his mad beloved Imogine, whose husband he has killed and who has (like Gretchen in *Faust*) done away with her infant child. Maturin tells us that we are in "a dark wood, in the back Scene a Cavern, Rocks and Precipices above":

Bertram turns towards [the Prior] in strong emotion, when a shriek is heard from the cavern, Bertram stands fixed in horror. *Prior.* stretching out his hands towards the cavern. . . . Imogine rushes from it in distraction, bursting from the arms of Clotilda. . . . She rushes forward till she meets Bertram, who stands in speechless horror. . . . He rushes towards her, and first repeats Imogine feebly, as he approaches, he utters her name again passionately, but as he draws nearer and sees her look of madness and desperation, he repeats it once more in despair; and does not dare to approach her, till he perceives her falling into Clotilda's arms, and catches her in his. . . . She dies slowly, with her eyes fixed on Bertram, who continues to gaze on her unconscious of her having expired. . . . A long pause.[51]

Maturin shapes the scene pictorially, centring it visually and symbolically on the cave from which first emerges the unidentifiable cry (invisible sound), then Imogine herself (a silent picture): the image of madness, framed by the cave's edges. The cave is metonymy for the gaping chasm, fallen woman, whose death before it offers tragic closure to the death of her infant, just emerged from the cave of her womb. At the moment of death, her eyes are fixed on Bertram's and his on hers—their gaze immobilized like the picture itself. There the scene freezes, on the eternally stilled woman in the tragic tableau.

Hugo's *Le Roi s'amuse* (*The King Amuses Himself* (1832)) similarly unfolds as a series of scenic tableaux, which Hugo (himself, of course, a visual artist of sorts) clearly envisioned as both scenic and pictorial illustrations: the opening night-time fête, lit by torchlight, where the grotesque hunchbacked Triboulet entertains the splendidly dressed courtiers; the abduction, by moonlight, of his daughter Blanche by ladder from his rooftop garden sanctuary; Blanche peering through the crevices in the open-walled hovel where the gypsy Maguelonne dances for the drunken king; and the final scene, in which Triboulet discovers, against the background of the raging storm, that it is his dying daughter, illuminated by lightning—not the corpse of the king—which he has been carrying away in vengeful triumph (these shown as a series in the various illustrated editions of the play) (Fig. 54). But this scenic pictorialism is also directly engaged with an implicit argument, in the play, about the social place of the popular image and the drama's role as its purveyor. In the opening scene

LE ROI S'AMUSE.   41

TRIBOULET,
. . . Au secours! quelqu'un! personne ici!
Est-ce qu'on va laisser mourir ma fille ainsi?

Di.!
BLANCHE, *mourante.*
Ne me faites pas parler.
TRIBOULET, *la couvrant de baisers.*
Pardonne-moi.
Mais, sans savoir comment, te perdre! Oh! ton front penche!
BLANCHE, *faisant un effort pour se retourner.*
Oh!... de l'autre côté!... J'étouffe!
TRIBOULET, *la soulevant avec angoisse.*
Blanche! Blanche!
Ne meurs pas!....
Se retournant, désespéré.
Au secours! quelqu'un! personne ici!
Est-ce qu'on va laisser mourir ma fille ainsi?
— Ah! la cloche du bac est là, sur la muraille.
Ma pauvre enfant, peux-tu m'attendre un peu que j'aille
Chercher de l'eau, sonner pour qu'on vienne? un instant!
Blanche fait signe que c'est inutile.
Non, tu ne le veux pas! — Il le faudrait pourtant!
Appelant sans la quitter.
Quelqu'un!

Silence partout. La maison demeure impassible dans l'ombre
Cette maison, grand Dieu, c'est une tombe!
BLANCHE agonise.
Oh! ne meurs pas! enfant, mon trésor, ma colombe,
Blanche! si tu t'en vas, moi, je n'aurai plus rien.
Ne meurs pas, je t'en prie!
BLANCHE.
Oh!
TRIBOULET.
Mon bras n'est pas bien,
N'est-ce pas, il te gêne! — Attends, que je me place
Autrement. — Es-tu mieux comme cela? — Par grâce,
Tâche de respirer jusqu'à ce que quelqu'un
Vienne nous assister! — Aucun secours! aucun!
BLANCHE, *d'une voix éteinte et avec effort.*
Pardonnez-lui, mon père... Adieu!
Sa tête retombe.
TRIBOULET, *s'arrachant les cheveux.*
Blanche!... Elle expire!
Il court à la cloche du bac et la secoue avec fureur.
A l'aide! au meurtre! au feu!

6

FIG. 54. "Help! someone! no one here! . . . Is my daughter to be allowed to die thus?" Victor Hugo's *Le Roi s'amuse* (illustrated edition, *c.*1833).

in the Louvre—François I's palace—the king has gathered paintings by the grand masters: "The King as painted by Titian," announces Hugo; "Triboulet is in the dress of the Court Fool, as painted by Bonifacio," he announces a few moments later. The animated paintings within the Louvre—the King by Titian or the Court Fool by Bonifacio—serve as synecdoche for the pictorialism of the unified whole: the "nobles and ladies of the court in full costume"; the "refreshments in vessels of porcelain and gold"; the "architecture, the furniture, and the dresses [in] the style of the Renaissance."[52] Opening the play in the Louvre (not, for instance, at Chambord, François I's chateau, which Hugo had just visited), Hugo identifies the control of pictorial exhibition (in the theatre by analogy with the museum) as central to the role of the poet—the revolutionary Hugo, figured as the vituperative jester Triboulet. By identifying himself with Triboulet, the play's persecuted anti-hero, Hugo suggests a link between this opening scene and the preface in which he protests the censorship of the play: "the French People has *the right to publish*"; theatre is a form of publication, "like the press, like engraving, like lithography." If in the play he implicitly equates the classical drama in the old theatres (the Comédie-Française) with the classical art sequestered in the old palace (the Louvre), in the preface he implicitly equates his own revolutionary and populist drama with "the press, engraving, lithography," and, in general, the free distribution of images to "the French People."[53] The jester-playwright must refuse the King's violative monopoly on beauty: François I's abduction of Triboulet's daughter Blanche from Triboulet's garden in the play; Louis Philippe's suppression of Hugo's drama, itself a form of "violent theft" committed not merely against Hugo but against the French people as a whole.[54] He must use the theatre—a living museum complementing the tasks of "the press, engraving, lithography"—as a place for giving pictures back to the people.

Like so many of his contemporaries, Hugo had, from the beginning of his theatrical career, experimented with dramatic and theatrical form: including novelistic chapter headings for each of the acts of his plays, deploying long stretches of lyric scenic painting, expanding to the edges of the theatrical and beyond (in plays like his 500-page historical drama *Cromwell*). If Hugo eventually turned away from the theatre (perhaps because of the failure of *Les Burgraves*, perhaps because mid-century revolutionary politics seemed to require a change of genre, perhaps because the French theatre could no longer contain his epic-length plays), his experimentation pointed not away from the theatre but, rather, towards its extension, at once through textual, pictorial, and scenic means: towards, for instance, such late Romantic scenography as that in Wagner's vast mythological tableaux, with their conjoined rejection of the traditional constraints of dramatic genre, their painterly sensibility, and their attempted erasure of the spectators in the evocation of mystic ritual; or towards Shaw, with his long, narrative stage directions, each ideally (in his view) to be "expanded into a chapter, or even a series of chapters," transformed into a work "of a mixture of kinds, part narrative, part homily, part description, part dialogue."[55] And, if the richly visual and emotionally detailed plays of the eighteenth and nineteenth centuries (with their lavish scenic indications, their novelistic expatiation on character, and their pictorial supplements) represented a renewed commitment to scenic effect and the actor's art, they also gave actors a new sense of their expressive power, developed in the theatre by means of the verbal and visual texts on which they could draw for instruction, articulated in their self-representation on the page. This is the subject of the next chapter.

14. *Actor/Author*

The 1755 autobiography of Charlotte Charke, actress and the last of eleven children of the actor-playwright-manager and eventually Poet Laureate Colley Cibber, begins with an account of Charke as a cross-dressing 4-year-old who, having stolen her father's legendary periwig, his waistcoat, and a large silver sword, parades through the neighbourhood "in the happy Thought" (as she writes) "of being taken for" Colley Cibber (Fig. 55).[1] The anecdote replicates Charke's repeatedly staged parodies of her oft-ridiculed father, played out later in the theatre. Writing an autobiography becomes another way in which Charke, without hopes for a laureateship, can nonetheless imitate her author-father (his own autobiography published a decade and a half earlier), attempting a more enduring legacy than that which her fallen state as actress-on-the-margins, puppeteer, vagabond, some-time show-woman, transvestite hoodwinking the bailiffs, and Jane-of-all-trades could offer. By writing the memoir of her life, Charke replays Cibber's own reach towards futurity, though with somewhat more irony: he hopes (he writes) to "be read, when the People of this Age shall be Ancestors";[2] her book (she writes) "might justly claim a Right to be transmitted to Posterity," for she (like her father but with a measure of self-knowledge) is one of the "*greatest Curiosities* that ever were the incentives to the most *profound Astonishment*."[3] And indeed, it is in part from "Curiosit[y]" about herself that she writes, using the *Narrative of the Life of Mrs. Charlotte Charke* as an occasion for the kind of authorial distance that will permit her to observe herself with the detached critical judgement with which she herself, as actress, has been observed—at the same time taking on various narrative roles in order to perform her multiple selves on the page. When she dedicates her autobiography to herself, for instance, she becomes at once Author and Patroness of Letters (momentarily erasing the penurious scribbler), splitting herself into observer and observed, ennobled subject and worthy object: "My Choice of you, Madam, to patronize my Works, is an evidential Proof that I am not disinterested in that Point; as the World will easily be convinc'd, from your natural Partiality to all I have hitherto produc'd."[4]

Throughout the *Narrative*, Charke draws her readers' attention to her own "not disinterested" reading not only of her autobiography (of which she is the critic as well as the author) but of another set of texts representing her in print: the London playbills. These offer her a different kind of publicity: pointing to her various theatrical incarnations; presenting her with an objectified rendering of the "Characters" she will play; and giving her occasion to register her "natural Partiality" to the various selves that are posted about town. "I must beg Leave to give the Reader an Idea of that Extasy of Heart I felt, on seeing the Character I was to appear in the Bills," she writes of her début (with a pun on "Character," at once theatrical and

An exact Representation of M.ᵉ Charke walking in the Ditch at four Years of Age, as described by herself in the first Number of the Narrative of her own Life, lately published.

T. Garden Sculpt.   *Published according to Act of Parliament Sep.ᵗ 9.ᵗʰ 1755.*

FIG. 55. Charlotte Charke dressed as her father: print sold in conjunction with the
publication of *The Narrative of the Life of Mrs. Charlotte Charke* (1755).

typographic). At first designated by reference to her characters' names alone, eventually the anonymous actor is given her own name in the playbills: "My name was in Capitals . . . and I dare aver, that the Perusal of it, from one End of the Town to the other . . . was my most immediate and constant Business." And yet this happiness is followed soon after by an anxious fantasy that, having been thus inflated in print, she will be as easily deflated, and the very playbills that registered her theatrical birth will convert themselves into "bills of mortality," pronouncing her dead of hubris for taking on "capital" roles (the wages of too much "natural Partiality" to herself): "DIED ONE, OF CAPITAL CHARACTERS" (the capitals in the autobiographical text themselves theatrically enacting the bills of mortality).[5]

The pleasures of seeing one's name in print, it turns out, are short-lived. Anticipating the "death of character" in her autobiography, the narrative of her lives and selves fragmented among the printed texts, Charke recognizes her "claim . . . to be transmitted to Posterity" for what it is. Named many times over (on the playbills as on the title page of the *Narrative*), reborn again and again as her various selves in bills that, it turns out, are themselves bills of mortality, she must write an autobiography that, instead of staving off death, cheerfully winks at its own temporality. Like the stage, print here offers not fixity or permanence, but simply another medium for the registering and refracting of the actor's multiple and ceaselessly mortal selves— those "characters" that, in fact, ultimately constitute the self. One's "*Narrative of the Life*" may purport to be an account of "what [one] really was when in no body's Shape but [one's] own" (as Cibber described his, in his own autobiography).[6] But it will invariably end up as a correlative of that pretending-to-be-who-one-is that is a fundamental of the actor's profession: a reflexive rendering of the actor's polyphonous and fleeting selves.

THE ACTOR ON THE PAGE

Charke is writing for a readership accustomed to seeing actors' names consecrated in print: in playbills and handbills, in popular engravings and newspaper accounts, in prefaces and treatises on acting, in lists of *dramatis personae* and in the acting editions that were beginning to emerge from the presses. Actors and acting were the focus of the theatre reviews starting to appear regularly in the newspress, the perennial subject of the period's theatre almanacs and collections of anecdotes. In engravings and illustrations, actors were shown in their most characteristic roles: in the midst of a telling gesture; in an evocative scene. In promptbooks, their every move might be recorded. They were becoming figureheads for mass culture (in a premonition of the cult of celebrity), their faces reproduced not only in portraits and theatre prints but on tobacco tins and playing cards.[7] They were immortalized in reference works (Jean-François Marmontel's *Encyclopédie* entry for "*Declamation*" commemorates Adrienne Lecouvreur's "simple, touching, and noble language," "her voice . . . not in the least harmonious" but "fill[ed] with pathos . . . her eyes . . . embellished by tears, & her features by the expression of sentiment . . .").[8] Prints and actor biographies represented them not only in roles but also in their private lives, showing "the actors, actresses, male and female singers, male and female dancers, seen in their boudoirs, on the stage and in the world" (as the title page of the *New Theatrical Biography* proclaimed).[9]

The public hunger for intimate details of actors' lives—the fascination with "performers in their own persons" (with their questionable liaisons, as objects of public display and hence public speculation)—was simultaneously fed and enhanced by such prints and by the gossipy eighteenth- and nineteenth-century newspress (with its "chronicle of the fashionable enterprises of the only realities left on the stage . . . the performers in their own persons," as Shaw would later carp).[10] Actors might be, in themselves "illustrious dramatic characters" (as one writer commented of John Philip Kemble and Sarah Siddons).[11] Fictionalized, romanticized as free spirits, actors were the ideal subjects for plays or novels or those narratives somewhere between fiction and biography like Pietro Chiari's *The Unfortunate Actress, or Memoirs of Madame N. N., Written by Herself* (1755) or the showman George Alexander Stevens's autobiography-à-clef, *The History of Tom Fool* (1760), which Charke identifies as comparable to her own story of life at the theatrical fringes.[12] If the lives of star actors were put on public display in print, actors could themselves use print to control their public images. Writing in journals, treatises, memoirs, and the many autobiographies of the period, they could craft their aesthetics by serving as critics of the histrionic art (their own and others'). Many grew skilful at using the newspapers, the three-penny press, and the posting bills as vehicles for defining their careers and creating images of themselves fit for public consumption. Recognizing the value of manipulating the publicity machine that the press had become, the actress Dorothy Jordan, for instance, enlisted journalists, lawyers, and her powerful lover, the Duke of Clarence in an attempt at publicity and censorship, writing herself to the editors of several London newspapers: "I would not obtrude upon the public an allusion to anything which does not relate to my profession," but "thus called on, in the present instance, there can be no impropriety in my answering those who have so ungenerously attacked me."[13]

Just as actors called on "the prints" for publicity, illustrative prints were called into the service of actors, deemed essential for the study of theatrical art. John Weaver recommends that the actor or stage dancer "make himself acquainted with Paintings, Drawing, and Prints."[14] The illustrations representing the "faces of the passions" printed in Charles Le Brun's Académie lectures on painting (Fig. 56) were taken up by eighteenth-century theorists as a pattern-book for actors, as were the illustrative "figures" printed in Franciscus Lang's *Treatise on Stage Action*, which he directed actors to study, "impressing" such images "on the mind" so that they could recreate their renderings of visual composition and bodily form.[15] We have already seen the ways in which late eighteenth- and nineteenth-century dramatic texts attempted to delineate the details of gesture and facial expression, or tone and attitude. The acting manuals and rhetorical treatises printed in numbers throughout Europe in the eighteenth and nineteenth centuries, similarly attempted to record and prescribe the gestural and expressive: Lang's *Treatise* (1727); Pierre Rémond de Sainte-Albine's *The Actor* (1749); Aaron Hill's "Essay on the Art of Acting" (1746); John

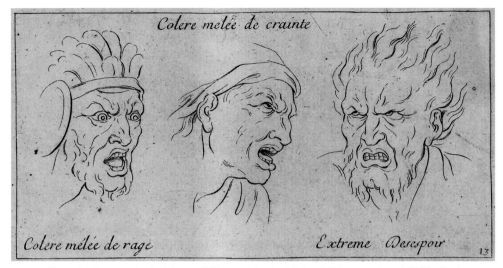

FIG. 56. "Anger mixed with rage," "Anger mixed with fear," "Extreme despair." Charles Le Brun's "heads" for representing the passions (1696).

Hill's adaptation of Rémond de Sainte-Albine (1750); Johann Jakob Engel's *Ideas on the Actor* (1785–6) (to name just a few).[16] Gilbert Austin's *Chironomia, or A Treatise on Rhetorical Delivery* (1806) (titled in self-conscious imitation of John Bulwer's *Chirologia* and *Chironomia*), was, unlike Bulwer's, specifically geared towards actors—towards rendering and prescribing the varieties of theatrical declamation on the page. It is "the dramatic art . . . of all others" that is "most likely to derive improvement" from his notation system, explains Austin, illustrating, for instance, the various "Complex significant Gestures" that he describes with images "after Mrs. Siddons."[17] The *Practical Illustrations of Rhetorical Gesture and Action* (1807) by Henry Siddons (Sarah Siddons' eldest son and himself an actor and theatre manager) is "adapted to the English drama" from Johann Jakob Engel's German *Ideas on the Actor* (1785–6) (as the title page explains) and "embellished with numerous engravings" of actors in their roles.

The titles of the treatises reinforced the identity of acting as "art," not mere craft but aesthetic form, dignified by its association with the other fine arts in the titles of the treatises: Lang's *Treatise* with "Observations on the *Art* of Acting"; François-Joseph Talma's *Reflections on Theatrical Art*; Heinrich Theodor Roetscher's *The Art of Dramatic Representation*.[18] If the plastic and literary arts, however, were their own monuments, the histrionic art seemed tragically evanescent, "one of [its] greatest misfortunes," according to Talma. "Our art," he writes, "dies, as it were, with us, while all other artists leave behind them monuments of their works. The talent of the actor, when he has quitted the stage, exists no longer, except in the recollection of those who have seen and heard him."[19] "We still have Corneille and Racine; [the actors] Baron and Lecouvreur are no more," sighs Marmontel in his *Encyclopédie* essay on "Declamation." "Their lessons were written in the . . . air, their example has disappeared with them."[20] Like Marmontel bemoaning the difference between the poet's glory and the player's ultimate obscurity, Cibber could wish that theatrical action were, like writing, its "own record":

How *Shakepear* [*sic*] wrote, all Men who have a Taste for Nature may read, and know—but with what higher Rapture would he still be *read*, could they conceive how *Betterton play'd* him! . . . Pity it is, that the momentary Beauties flowing from an harmonious Elocution, cannot like those of Poetry, be their own Record! That the animated Graces of the Player can live no longer than the instant Breath and Motion that presents them.[21]

The end of Robert Lloyd's poem, *The Actor* (1760), reiterates Cibber's lament for the mortality of performance, implicitly opposing the "pliant Muscles of the . . . Face" to the "Trace" that is writing (through the echo of the rhyme):

> Relentless Death untwists the mingled Fame,
> And sinks the Player in the Poet's Name.
>   The pliant Muscles of the various Face,
> The Mien that gave each Sentence Strength and Grace,
> The tuneful Voice, the Eye that spoke the Mind
> Are gone, nor leave a single Trace behind.[22]

Such overwrought elegies for the histrionic moment reflected the general sense, on the part of both actors and theatre-lovers, that the actor's art—fleeting as it was—ought not to die with the actor, but instead to be immortalized in print. That the actor's art is so fleeting, Talma argues, "should impart additional weight to the writings, the reflexions, and the lessons which great actors have left."[23] Such writings might serve both future actors and posterity generally: "It is necessary to fix this great art by written tradition and fixed precepts," writes the English translator of Hyppolite Clairon's memoirs.[24] Louis Dubroca could fantasize a sort of theatrical bank, where (as in the new libraries of deposit) theatrical interpretations could be archivally preserved:

How desirable it would be for there to exist a deposit where the great effects of theatrical declamation could be consigned, and where, after having received the well-deserved applause of the public, each actor who was recognized as a model would go to sketch in solitude the history of his soul, of what he intended and the means by which he achieved it in the moments in which he excited the greatest enthusiasm! In this deposit . . . young actors could draw ideas from these sublime movements, which transport the entire assembly and are the triumph of [theatrical] declamation.[25]

The taxonomies of histrionic emotional and gestural expression beginning to accumulate in the eighteenth century, typically rendering gestures both pictorially and verbally, treating them as codes for emotions, attempted to provide something like Dubroca's hypothetic theatrical "deposit." *The Elements of the Art of the Actor* by "Dorfeuille," for instance, explains how the actor is to render a gesture of supplication: "The arms are lifted to chest height and are separated by about one foot. . . . The head [may be] inclined forward, the eye lowered, the hands are brought together and joined when the plea becomes more urgent; the body in this position remains

FIG. 57. "Grief" in Franciscus Lang's *Treatise on Stage Action*, "with Figures Explaining
. . . the Art of Acting" (1727).

immobile after one has made the plea and is awaiting the response."[26] Franciscus
Lang describes with equal precision the proper position for expressing grief
(demonstrated in the figure on the opposing page): "The hands are folded with fin-
gers interlinked and they are usually raised aloft or dropped below the hips. . . .
Decency, however, does not permit the hands to be lowered straight down the front."
(Fig. 57)[27]

The problem with such descriptions, however, was that they did not answer to the
desire (expressed repeatedly throughout the period) for a readable recording
system—one that would be as precise as that for music or the spoken word. "Action
is a sort of language which perhaps one time or other, may come to be taught by a kind
of grammar-rules," writes Hogarth in the *Analysis of Beauty* (in recognition of the
uses of the notation of gesture for both theatre and the visual arts), "but, at present,
it is only got by rote and imitation."[28] The descriptive taxonomies were, moreover,

too verbose and hence cumbersome to be used as notation systems. Austin, for instance, complains that Engel's system takes an entire octavo page to describe a single Italian gesture.[29] But those interested in gesture were beginning to think about notation systems for actors, notably in the various attempts to use notation to mark vocal effects for oratory. The *Course of Lectures on Elocution and the English Language* (1769) by Thomas Sheridan (actor, theatre manager, orator, and father of Richard Brinsley Sheridan), for instance, uses a variety of punctuation symbols to indicate "declamatory" or "elocutionary" units, indicating where the speaker is supposed to pause for effect.[30] We have already glanced at the graphic mapping of movement and blocking in the dance manuals proliferating during the early part of the century: those like Pierre Rameau's *The Dancing Master* (1725), which shows such gestures as the "circle of the arm" in the "Figure ready to do the pirouette" (Fig. 58).[31] Those thinking about the notation of declamation had these in mind in their own attempts to inscribe performance. The Abbé Du Bos, for instance, explicitly compares the notation of pronunciation and gesture to dance notation. "Declamation in the form of notation would be nothing other than the tones and movement of pronunciation written down in notes," writes Du Bos: "As for a method of writing down declamation in notes, it would not be nearly so difficult [to create one] as it was to create a system for notating the steps and figures of an *entrée de ballet* danced by eight people. . . . It is no more difficult to learn gestures from notes than it is to learn steps and figures from them."[32]

If gesture and action could be understood as forms of language legible to the observer ("Gestures have their determinate signification as well as words; and they can no more be misunderstood," writes John Hill),[33] the guides for actors and oratorical manuals offered systematic prescriptions for the articulation of such languages. Dubroca's view that for each emotion there was a perfectly corresponding gesture was somewhat extreme even for an era interested in taxonomizing the passions. But such a view nonetheless indicated the more general sense that gestures ought to be thought of as divisible signs, translatable into written or spoken language. "If it were possible to trace the figures of gestures on paper," writes Dubroca, "one could see their perfect correspondence to the passions of the soul."[34]

The historical argument importantly contributed to the normative one. According to the Abbé de Condillac (drawing on Du Bos), the Greeks must have had an entire system of gestural notation, since they clearly had a rich rhetoric of gesture (naturally accompanying the musicality of their language): in "prescrib[ing] themselves rules," they must have "found the secret of writing them down in notes."[35] What one needed was a complete modern system of gestural notation: precisely what (according to Engel) Lessing set out to produce in a grammar of gesture, to be called *The Eloquence of Gesture* (which unfortunately, Engel explains, Lessing never got around to writing);[36] precisely what Austin takes himself to be perfecting in the system of symbolic letters in his *Chironomia*. In a chapter entitled "Of Notation of Gesture," he reveals his aim: "to produce a language of symbols so simple and so perfect as to render it possible with facility to represent every action . . . of an actor throughout the whole drama, and to record them for posterity, and for repetition and

Figure preste'a faire le piroëte'

FIG. 58. "Circle of the arm . . ." "Figure ready to do the pirouette." Pierre Rameau, *The Dancing Master* (1725).

practice, as well as common language is recorded." Like the Abbé Du Bos, Austin aspires to "trace the figures of gestures on paper," just as one might write down music, illustrating, for instance, an actor performing John Gay's *The Miser and Plutus*, his gestures divided into annotated phrases (Fig. 59). "The language of gesture bears more analogy to that of music than to the language of general ideas: and therefore" (writes Austin of his notation system)

it is named the notation of gesture. As the notation of musical sounds records the melodies and happy harmony of sounds which in their nature endure but for a moment, so the notation of gesture records the beautiful, the dignified, the graceful or expressive actions of the body, by

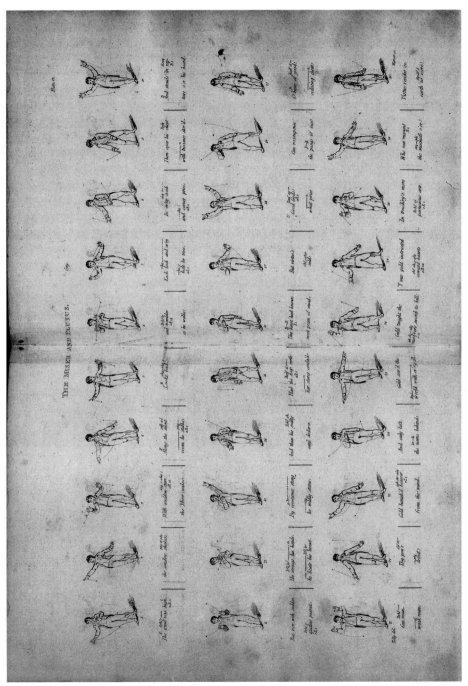

FIG. 59.   Annotating an actor's gestures in Gilbert Austin's *Chironomia* (1806).

which the emotions of the mind are manifested on great and interesting occasions, and which in themselves are no less transitory.

Such a system could serve a number of purposes. It could record the work of individual actors and orators: "A scene of Shakespeare, or a passage of Milton so noted after the manner of a great actor or a great master of recitation; or an oration so noted as delivered by an admired speaker, would prove an incessant study of truth and nature combined with imagination."[37] It could (like Dubroca's theatrical deposit) offer training tools for the neophyte actor.[38] It could promote the cause of historical veracity in the theatre by showing the actor the precise gestures of historical figures (which would prevent actors from creating falsifying fictions), allowing them to work from a record of gestures "as . . . truly represented, as the record of words."[39] Finally and not least, it could serve not only the writer wishing for a new language, but the reader longing to relive the lively action in the quiet of the closet: "To these advantages must be added the extension of the powers of writing, and of the sphere of knowledge and literary enjoyment; by which, in his closet, the lover of the drama may almost contemplate by this aid to his imagination, the actual performance of the most eminent actors."[40]

THE ACTOR'S FREEDOM

If acting was art, worthy of such detailed notation—if as signifier, the actor might be (as Hazlitt writes of John Philip Kemble) a "hieroglyphic of humanity"[41]—the actor could displace the playwright as creative force behind the play. This (along with bullying on the part of actor-managers and the public's newly reverential treatment of star actors) produced a degree of tension between dramatists and actors, reflected in the distinction (developing in the eighteenth century) between the "acting play" and the "reading play," the performer's vehicle and the dramatist's: "Why, sir, your acting play is entirely supported by the merit of the actor, without any regard to the author at all," says the bookseller Bookweight in Fielding's *The Author's Farce*. "Reading plays," he explains, "I call your substantive, as being able to support themselves. [Acting plays] are your adjective, as what requires the buffoonery and gestures of an actor to be joined to them to show their signification."[42] Acting may be supplement (in Bookweight's grammatical metaphor). But Fielding (reflecting his divided views as both author and theatrical manager) inadvertently acknowledges the actor's power: in becoming forms of "signification," the "buffoonery and gestures of [the] actor" transform themselves into the substantive that makes a full sentence of the adjectival acting play.

The old fear of the actor's power to overwhelm or subvert the text (the power to disconcert language through gesture, the power to seduce and to improvise beyond the safe boundaries of the registered text, evading both the censor's and the author's control) was still very much alive for eighteenth-century authors and authorities. But the double view of the actor's supplementations in *The Author's Farce* reflects the culture's ambivalence: improvisation was uncomfortably uncontrollable, giving rein, as it did, to the unpredictable force of the seductive actor-orator; but it was, at the same time, the ultimate expression of theatrical art. If Gottsched tried to rid Germany of the improvisational comedy, Lessing could, not long after, express his admiration for the improvising actors, complaining that Gottsched "put his curse on extemporizing," that "he had harlequin ceremoniously driven from the theatre, which was itself the biggest harlequinade that was ever played."[43] Cibber (writing in 1740) articulates the authorities' anxiety when he writes that acting may "infus[e]" the "dangerous, or offensive" "*acted* scandal" into the "Multitude."[44] The *Historical Calendar of the Opera, the Comedies Française and Italienne, and the Foires* (1751) looks back nostalgically on the early Théâtre Italien: "The plays they performed were impromptu. . . . All the actors had to have a great deal of wit and a lively and fertile imagination."[45]

Honouring the liberation from the text inherent in improvisation, eighteenth- and nineteenth-century writers and actors were paradoxically intent on giving it textual form. Writing in 1695, the *commedia dell'arte* "harlequin" Evaristo Gherardi could warn his readers that they "should not expect to find whole plays in this collection, since we do not know how to print the plays of the Théâtre Italien."[46] But by mid-century, readers were accustomed to textual renderings of the Italian comedy. Goldoni could insist on writing out the *commedia* dialogue, identifying such writing with "liberty" (in an Enlightenment twist on the traditional opposition between "liberty" and "the writ"), quietly proceeding (as he writes) "in making my advances towards the liberty of writing my pieces entirely out."[47] Texts attempted to render with precision what had once been the improvisational scene. While Gozzi, for instance, might insist that even in textualized plays of the *commedia dell'arte* there be left room for improvisation, in *The Raven* (1761), he offers a scene with Truffaldino (played by the great improvisational actor Antonio Sacchi) in which he simultaneously parodies the hyper-literary gothic-heroic verse speeches that his rival playwright, Pietro Chiari, wrote down for his *commedia* actors and offers his own textualization of Truffaldino's stage business and lines:

Truffaldino (*Striking a tragedian's pose, and beginning in a grave tone*). While our attentive and expectant people . . . (*He breaks off his speech, and begs not to be interrupted, since he wishes to do honor to the story, given to him in written verse and, he hopes, memorized. . . . He returns to an affected seriousness, and recites the following narration with tragic emphasis, gesturing pompously*). . . .

> While our attentive and expectant people
> Gather for the wedding beneath the steeple
> . . . but what is afoul? . . . Evil omen! A howl
> From hundreds of invading hounds now sounds,
> Echoing throughout the darkened grounds. . . .
> (*He wipes his forehead and says he's tired of speaking in verse.*)[48]

Improvisational or pantomime actors, whose work might be recorded on the page and in turn serve as prescription for others, were the exemplary actors-as-authors, in so far as their art was utterly independent of the poet's. In a play performed in 1799 at the Théâtre Sans Pretention, the young Sophie must remind her father (who wishes to marry her to the most successful author of a pantomime) that actors, not dramatists, are the "authors" of pantomime.[49] Gozzi explains to advocates of the written *commedia* that "No one will ever be able to write the part of Truffaldino in prose, let alone in verse," for actors like Sacchi can "improvise from the outline of a scene so well that he surpasses any playwright who could try to write it."[50] But even non-improvisational acting could be a form of authorship, as much an art as the writing of dramatic poetry, a means of disputing with dramatists their claim on "genius." Actors could be authors-of-the-stage without actually putting pen to paper, writers of the narrative that gesture and expression entailed.

In pointing to the actor as author, apologists persistently drew analogies between the actor's art and the poet's. The most important quality for the actor, writes Talma, is "sensibility, united with intelligence, which secretly operates on the actor, as on the poet."[51] John Hill, describing the actor Samuel Sandford, could write that "he possessed that sort of genius which had immmortalized the greatest among the dramatick writers."[52] If Hill writes that even such actors do not precisely "disput[e] the laurel" with poets, others were willing to place them on an equal plane: "Between Racine and yourself, you share | . . . the legitimate tribute," writes Pierre-Alexandre Levesque de la Ravaillère of the actress Mlle Duclos (quoting Voltaire).[53]

In adding "finesses" (meaningful gestures or emotional touches that "are not set down in the part," in John Hill's words), the actor could compete with or improve on the dramatist's art. "The writer of a play does not, any more than any other author, say all that could be said upon the subject," writes Hill. "Whatever he has left deficient, the actor may supply, not in words of his own adding, but by the silent eloquence of gestures, looks, and pauses." Thus, rather than detracting from the masterpiece, finesses could elevate the text, filling in the lacunae of "the bare reading": "We frequently see the author's expression raised by these means to an height of which we have not any conception in the bare reading; but that's not all; a look, a gesture, a peculiar attention to what is saying by some other, often does what the author had omitted." A bad actor could not destroy a great play: it "will recover its credit in the reading." But a great actor could permanently transform an ordinary play into a masterpiece, giving it, according to Hill, "new graces in the performance," "beauties the author never thought of, but which the actor of this kind throws in from his own store." Those "beauties" remain with the play: "they shall continue with it, they shall be remembered in the reading, and placed to the account of the author." Having "obtained a character on the stage," the play elevated by the great actor could "preserv[e] it in the closet."[54]

It was in contradistinction to the flat experience of the closet where the poet reigned, then, that the artistry of the stage could be seen in its full force. Great actors in tragedy, explains Hill (describing James Quin in the role of Pyrrhus) "not only convey all the dignity the author meant to give, but more; and raise in us thoughts as we hear them, [t]hat would never have arisen as we read the play in our closets." Quoting a recent version of the *Oresteia*, he writes that "as we read it, we see the sting of the reproach; but as we saw it, it was much more."[55] In doing the masterpieces, one could at once do homage to the great poets and attempt to outdo them. The point was to be master of the masterpiece, to transform the text and, in transforming it, to free oneself of its imperious imperatives: the player's "passion," writes Talma (rebelling at once against the early acting manuals and the specifications of the author's text), "does not follow the rules of grammar; it pays but little respect to colons, and semi-colons, and full stops, which it displaces without any ceremony."[56]

Acting the masterpieces meant engaging in one-upmanship not only of the poet but also of one's predecessors. The practice of "pointing"—presenting a great speech to show off one's virtuosity—gave actors a chance to prove their mastery in interpretation: in acting, one no longer strove to imitate the current "geniuses of the stage" but instead to "create" a role.[57] The actor as creative artist was expected (like the author) to be "original" (in a usage seeping in from literary theory). Referring disparagingly to the actress Maria Rebecca Duncan, for instance, Dorothy Jordan writes privately to the Duke of Clarence: "Her idea of acting does not appear to proceed from any conception or meaning of *her own* but a kind of acting built on the foundation of many other *performers* & *nothing original*."[58] "The actor must not . . . faithfully copy," writes Hill, "he must throw in many strokes that are original," noting of Garrick that "Had imitation alone been the source of good acting, we had lost all that this amazing player has shewn us; nor do we want instances, even among some who are greatly received, how imperfect that playing is, which is derived principally from that source." Copying the passions of another is a kind of "semblance" of acting, explains Hill, describing the neophyte actor who copies a great interpreter in acting "violently moved" in a passionate scene, but whom true connoisseurs will recognize for a counterfeit: "They see that it is semblance of worth, not substance, and despise him; for among all the servile herd of imitators, none are so contemptible as those who would pass upon us a copy for an original, when the affections of the heart are concerned."[59]

ACTING AS CHARACTER

If there was a related dissatisfaction with the "mechanical copying" that the old ora-torical manuals seemed to teach (the actors, with a "pretence of authority," still learned their gestures from Quintilian on oratory, complained Aaron Hill),[60] actors nonetheless needed books, not books of oratory but poetry that would exercise the passions. "Read . . . books besides the plays in which you are concern'd," Garrick advised the actor William Powell, above all, "never let your *Shakespear* be out of your hands, or your pocket."[61] The actor must, writes John Hill, accustom himself to "great and noble sentiments" by "reading attentively and deliberately alone, and abstracted from all other thoughts, the greatest passages in those authors, who have succeeded most in heroic poetry."[62] The great actor must not only read widely in soli-tude, advises Clairon, but must study that reading in depth, "render[ing] it familiar, even to its minutest details."[63] If acting was above all to be "natural," if (as the actor "Préville" writes) "ten volumes on this divine art will not an actor make,"[64] the most natural acting nonetheless came from an acquaintance with books. "If I have ever seemed to have a purely natural manner," writes Clairon, "it is because my studies, joined to some happy gifts which nature has given me, have conducted me to the perfection of art."[65] Accustomed to novelistic detail in the determination of character, actors looked to written descriptions of the passions, which, if they were not already part of the stage directions, would have to be filled in: "I will interleaf your part," writes Aaron Hill to a protégé, "if you send it me, and make room for the necessary notes upon the passions."[66]

If the face, with its conscious and unconscious revelations, suddenly seemed the primary register for the passions, this was not merely because of better lighting and eyeglasses but because of the detailed description of its every expression—in reviews and treatises on acting, in novels, and increasingly in stage directions (as well as the kind of promptbook interleaves Aaron Hill writes out for his protégé). John Hill typically describes the actor Spranger Barry as Othello, glorying in the revenge he will take against Cassio: "we see Mr. Barry redden tro' the very black of his face; his whole visage becomes inflamed, his eyes sparkle with successful vengeance."[67] Unconscious nature was to be viewed at closer range. The rejection of old-fashioned acting in the high style (the "strange shakings of the head, and other antic gesticulations," of Quin, whom Tobias Smollett could mock, imagining "the poor man [to] labour . . . under that paralytical disorder, which is known by the name of St. Vitus's dance")[68] had its flip side in this embrace of novelistic minutiae in acting. The eyes and face had a secret semiosis, figured by Dubroca as "soul" and "fire" that takes the form of alphabetic letters. "The expression of the eyes and of the face is the soul of theatrical performance," he writes. "It is there that the passions must paint themselves in characters of fire."[69] The *commedia* would have to rid itself of masks, insisted Goldoni, so that the actor's face could reveal the emotional vicissitudes that he saw the now-textualized dialogue as delineating.[70]

Where the mask was created for a drama of stock figures, with their stubborn Aristotelian "consistency of character," the unmasked face could reveal the "manifoldness of characters and psychologies" (in the words of Jakob Lenz, writing in 1771), which was so much closer to nature.[71] "All characters are to be considered as mixed, not simple," writes John Hill[72] (perhaps a partial explanation for the proliferation of mad scenes in the drama of the period, which could so aptly thematize fragmentation of character). Helping to establish "manifoldness of characters and psychologies" as an aesthetic norm on stage through acting style, in "real life" actors themselves seemed the exemplary representatives of that norm—by definition multiple, living their many roles all at once. The actor was (to paraphrase Préville) one to whom nature had granted "that which she has granted the cameleon, that is, the power of showing herself in all shapes."[73] Through autobiography and memoir as much as through their stage roles, then—through the poignant delineation of their own struggle between external affect and the mutable passions barely concealed beneath it—actors helped to transform conceptions of character. The doubleness of the actor, paradigm of social performance, could reveal the inherent mutability of character, its contingency as well as its interiority even in the most public of moments. Acting could (metaphorically) imprint the text: comic acting, wrote Cibber, could be a "double Stamp upon the Poet's paper."[74] But the pliant actor was also imprinted by the passions (in a persistently gendered trope that associated the actor with feminine mutability of character). Nature could leave "impressions" on the waxen actor's body; it could "imprin[t] his fancy" (in Aaron Hill's words), or (for Préville) "imprint [its] spirit on [the actor's] face."[75]

It was precisely this seeming mutability of character that had always been so disturbing to anti-theatricalists. One might think of the eighteenth-century mandate calling for identity between actor and role as an aesthetic updating of an ancient disquietude over the actor's doubleness. Certainly commentators had become uncomfortably conscious of discontinuities between character and the person of the actor ("No woman can speak Jane Shore so well as Mrs. Pritchard," writes John Hill, "but a lady so much *en bon point*, makes an odd figure dying of famine").[76] However manifold stage character was to be, the role was ideally to be in harmony with the person and the "real" character of the actor (which usually meant that character represented by the press). "If we ask why Mrs. Cibber" (Colley's daughter-in-law Susannah) "is more herself in Juliet, than in any other character, it is because Mrs. Cibber has an heart more formed for love than any other passion," writes Hill, "and if we approve Miss Bellamy in her declarations of love in the same character, more than in any other, it is because she has an heart also more susceptible of tenderness than of any other passion."[77] In being others, the actor was to be "more" herself, or, rather, she was to become her characters by forgetting herself, "[re]forming" her "susceptible" heart to conform to the passions of her role. In the actress Marie Françoise Dumesnil's view, it was the "spontaneous forgetting of oneself" that was "the basis of theatrical art."[78] The debate about whether actors were to forget themselves and identify fully with their parts or to retain full consciousness of themselves as actors (the argument against identification detailed most famously in Diderot's *Paradoxe sur le comédien*) was not, of course, resolved on one side. But even an advocate of the mastery of art over nature like Clairon (formulating her position in contrast to that of Dumesnil, the advocate of *nature pure*) insists on identification—on an "absorption" in the role. The actor "whose tears constitute his most profound research" and who chooses to "forget his own existence, is certainly a miserable being." But "the actor who does not identify himself with the character he represents is like a schoolchild who repeats his lesson."[79] The actor, the ultimate dissembler, it turned out, was not to "dissemble" the passions—not merely to copy them, but to live them.

The aesthetics of identity that mandated the actor's self-forgetting in the role had a counterpoint, however, in the actor's reclamatory self-remembering in the "memoir," in which actors could recapture their role as subjects resistant to the imprint of character, presenting themselves as now laid bare for the reader, no longer authors of others on stage, but at long last simply themselves in print. While the stage gave actors the opportunity to "create characters," print gave them the opportunity to reflect publicly on the relation between the characters they had played and their real selves, as Cibber does, for instance (in the passage we glanced at in the opening of this chapter): "A Man who has pass'd above Forty Years of his Life upon a Theatre, where he has never appear'd to be Himself," he writes, may have naturally excited the Curiosity of his Spectators to know what he really was when in no body's Shape but his own; and whether he, who by his Profession had so long been ridiculing his Benefactors, might not, when the Coat of his Profession was off, deserve to be laugh'd at himself; or from his being often seen in, the most flagrant, and immoral Characters; whether he might not see as great a Rogue, when he look'd into the Glass himself, as when he held it to others.[80]

The actor who has "never appear'd to be himself," taking every "body's Shape but his own," has turned his spectators' "Curiosity" not towards these histrionic feats, but towards "what he really was"—stripped of the "Coat of his Profession." Here in writing, away from the madding crowd, while the real Cibber gazes unflinching at his own reflection in the Glass, the spectator-reader can invisibly spy on the unaffected man. And yet, peculiarly, Cibber, understanding himself in relation to the various "Shape[s]" he has taken on—reflected as "Rogue" in the "Glass" (eternal trope not for nature but for mimesis) or as an object of ridicule (like his characters, and, indeed like the Cibber he clearly wishes here to disown)—seems to underline not the actor-as-himself but the actor-as-himself-as-others, a self made up merely of its histrionic identity.

In this the *Apology* is much like other actor autobiographies of the period, purportedly contrasting the actor's "real" character with his stage multiplicity, but in the end disclosing the inherent theatricalism of the "real" actor as subject. As actor autobiographies proliferated, the actor's fragmentation of character became a common topos. By the time Talma was writing (in an era more dedicated to "sincerity" and in a more serious vein), he could nonetheless recognize himself as not merely multiple and fragmented but the epitome of dissociated affect, subject to the theatricalism of his emotions even in the privacy of private life:

In my own person, in any circumstance of my life in which I experienced deep sorrow, the passion of the theater was so strong in me that, altho opprest with real sorrow, and disregarding the tears I shed, I made, in spite of myself, a rapid and fugitive observation on the alteration of my voice, and on a certain spasmodic vibration which it contracted as I wept; and, I say it, not without some shame, I even thought of making use of this on the stage.[81]

Clairon's memoirs similarly explore the actor's sense of her own inherent theatricalism, not so much in self-reflective meditation as in the form of compressed *Bildungsroman*. The narrative of her early life begins (midway through the *Memoirs*) with her baptism in Carnival time by a curate dressed as a harlequin and his vicar in pantaloons.[82] This symbolic theatrical baptism is echoed later in the *Memoirs*, in another metaphoric birth in which Clairon's début as an actress (and her fall from the innocence of childhood) takes the form of a scene of initiatory histrionic dissembling. The 12-year-old Hyppolite has learned theatrical deportment by spying on the actress Mlle Dangeville through the window of a neighbouring house, but lies to her mother about the source of her new affectations. "This first falsehood emboldened me to commit others," she writes, teaching her, finally, to "deriv[e] a pleasure from dissimulation" that, she explains, became the foundation for her acting career.[83] In the analysis throughout the memoir of the art of the actor, she stresses her deep identification with her most successful roles: in playing Blanche in Bernard Joseph Saurin's *Blanche and Guiscard*, for instance, "I always thought myself in my own chamber," she writes—"when I played Blanche, I was always myself."[84] And yet, it is in her "own chamber" that she has learned precisely the art of being least "herself," in the originary adolescent moment of imitation and dissimulation. With consciousness, with entry into adulthood, has come theatricalism, the inherent theatricalism of the actor uncontrollably acting in the performance of everyday life, which, in Clairon's narrative, finally overcomes the authenticity of the actor auto-biographically "playing herself" on the revelatory page.

15. *A Theatre Too Much With Us*

In an 1815 essay, William Hazlitt imagines a production of *A Midsummer Night's Dream* "[got] up as a Christmas after-piece," with Kean as Bottom, playing all the parts in mimicry of the most fashionable actors:

There would be two courts, an empire within an empire, the Athenian and the Fairy King and Queen, with their attendants, and with all their finery. What an opportunity for processions, for the sound of trumpets and glittering of spears! What a fluttering of urchins' painted wings; what a delightful profusion of gauze clouds and airy spirits floating on them!

The following year, he appended a paragraph, after having seen a production at Covent Garden: "Alas the experiment has been tried, and has failed."[1] The failure, he explained, lay not so much in the particular production as in the very attempt to stage poetry, for "poetry and the stage do not agree together."[2] "The reading of this play is like wandering in a grove by moonlight," he writes. "The descriptions breathe a sweetness like odours thrown from beds of flowers."[3] But if the play as poetry on the page was a vision of "the ideal," the ideal had no place upon the stage: "That which is merely an airy shape, a dream, a passing thought, immediately becomes an unmanageable reality. . . . Fancy cannot be represented any more than a simile can be painted" (Fig. 60).[4] The problem was that in the theatre the eye retained in unqualified form whatever was given to it: "any offence given to the eye is not to be got rid of by explanation." The eye suffocated the poetic imagination, which might struggle against the coercive power of vision but was powerless in the theatre. There, poetry was incapable of "sufficiently qualify[ing] the impressions of the senses," which rained down upon the spectator: the image of Bottom with ass's ears or of "ye full-grown, well-fed, substantial real fairies" lumbering across the boards at Covent Garden. "The spectacle was fine," writes Hazlitt flatly, "it was that which saved the play." But he cannot contain the anti-theatrical outcry that follows: "Oh, ye scene-shifters, ye scene-painters, ye machinists and dress-makers, ye manufacturers of moon and stars that give no light, ye musical composers, ye men in the orchestra, fiddlers and trumpeters and players on the double drum and loud bassoon, rejoice! This is your triumph; it is not ours."[5] Spectacle had triumphed, and it was an unsightly and cacophonous victory.

   Hazlitt can reconstitute his original experience of "the spirit" and "genius" of the "delightful poem" only by turning back to "the closet," to his copy of the book, whose typography brings some relief: "In turning to Shakespeare to look for [Helena's address to Hermia], the book opened at the *Midsummer Night's Dream*, the title of which half gave us back our old feeling; and in reading this one speech twice over, we have completely forgot all the noise we have heard and the sights we have

FIG. 60. "An airy shape, a dream, a passing thought." Shakespeare's *A Midsummer Night's Dream* in an 1817 edition.

seen." In the closet, the "unmanageable reality" that assaulted the theatre-goer disappeared, for there the imagination was capable of smoothing and softening the "impressions" that the poem evoked: "Where all is left to the imagination, every circumstance has an equal chance of being kept in mind, and tells according to the mixed impression of all that has been suggested." If the "closet and the stage" were finally too "far asunder" to attempt reconciliation, the book could offer "an airy shape, a dream, a passing thought," vision and sound properly mixed in the mind, qualified by the active imagination.[6]

POETIC ANTI-THEATRICALISM

Certainly the late eighteenth- and early nineteenth-century stage—celebrating its liberation from the tyrannies of classical form and from the dull constraints of the unities, embracing the aesthetics of revolution, revelling in the hybrid genres that allowed for multiplicity of effects, unleashing flashes of light and submerging the scene in darkness, filling the theatre with symphonic sound and mesmerizing aria—was not a stage made for the dissociated drama of airy poetry, but for flesh and blood and fiddlers and trumpeters and manufacturers of moon and stars. It was a theatre devoted to bewitching the eyes and ears of the gape-mouthed spectator, overwhelming the imagination with scenes and sounds and lights and motion, serving the taste for plenitude and sensory multiplicity in a conjunction of commercial spectacularism and fantastic dramaturgy. Victor Hugo could sing the praises of his theatre's extravaganza of the fabulous, its orgy of generic and animal hybrids best exemplified in the fused aesthetics of the sublime and the "grotesque": "found everywhere," "free and frank," it "creates the deformed and the horrible . . . the comic and the buffoonish," "sow[ing] liberally in the air, the water, the earth, and the fire these myriads of intermediary beings . . . boldly throw[ing] into relief all those strange forms that earlier periods in timidity had wrapped in swaddling."[7] The aesthetics of the period—glorying in the gothic and the fantastic, the epic and the operatic, the sublime revolution and the surging crowd—was, in the theatre, aggressively sensory.

Attempting like so many of his contemporaries to articulate the difference between the experience of "reading" and the extravagantly sensory representations of the theatre, Hazlitt reflects an ambivalence about theatre-as-medium typical of the era. On the one hand, he recognizes the theatre's special power, drawn by the "finery," "processions," "sound of trumpets," "glittering of spears," "fluttering of . . . painted wings," "delightful profusion of gauze clouds and airy spirits floating on them" that only theatre can provide. On the other hand, his recoil from the "unmanageable reality" and crude materiality of the actors and scenes reflects the revived anti-theatricalism of the era, an anti-theatricalism that, rather than focusing on the religious and ethical issues that had preoccupied Renaissance anti-theatricalists, took the aesthetics of reception as its focus, hypothesizing a normative idealism in contrast to the theatre's troublingly obdurate materialism. Charles Lamb, for instance, recognized the power of "realization" on the stage but (in thinking parallel to Hazlitt's) could at the same time argue that, in producing Shakespeare, "we find to our cost that instead of realizing an idea, we have only materialized and brought down a fine vision to the standard of flesh and blood."[8] Coleridge insisted that the *Sturm* and immediacy of the embodied representation could exercise and train the public's power of imagination, but at the same time feared that the circumstantiality of the theatre would invariably overpower the ideal.[9] For Schiller, theatre was the optimal medium for the elevation of the populace, the medium that the wise lawgiver chooses as a vehicle for giving expression to the feelings and shaping the morals of the Folk, and yet its requirements were an irritation to the dramatic poet: "All of one's poetic sense is stifled by the inevitable and living reality of the actors and all the rest of the conditions of staging. God help me with these *Besogne!*"[10] Goethe's *Wilhelm Meister* can at once celebrate the theatricalism of the theatre (through the happy adventures of the strolling actor-hero) and remind the reader of the superiority of the closet: "You could not employ your time better," the older and wiser Jarno tells Wilhelm, "than by disassociating yourself from everything else and, in the solitude of your own room, peering into the kaleidoscope of this unknown world," a collection of the plays of Shakespeare. "It is a sinful waste of time for you to spend it in dressing up these apes as humans and in teaching these dogs to dance."[11] *Faust* reflects a similar ambivalence in its movement between, on the one hand, a recognition of the value of vision as against dry books and, on the other, a disgust with theatrical "*Besogne*," for instance in the parodic representation of the theatre manager's glee over the marvels he can produce:

> The main thing . . . is having lots of action!
> Spectators come expecting something they can see.
> If you unreel enough before the public's eyes
> to make them marvel open-mouthed,
> a quantitative triumph is already won.[12]

If the theatre was "too much" for Hazlitt or Lamb or Goethe, it had, of course, always been, in some ways, "too much"—too multiple, too sensual, too dangerous, too real in its short-circuiting of the softening that took place in imaginative representation (the mixing of sensory impressions in the mind to which Hazlitt refers)—the reason for the age-old focus of dramatic aesthetics on the *limits* of theatrical representation (limits at once ethical and aesthetic). But, differently conscious of the problem of stage bodies in the spectacular eighteenth- and nineteenth-century theatre, eighteenth- and nineteenth-century dramatists habitually reflected their concerns about the aesthetic "shocks" that the stage could give to the unwary spectator. Elizabeth Inchbald, for instance, explains that, in printing *The Massacre* (1792), she is publishing a play that could not be produced since "the subject is so horrid, that I thought it would shock, rather than give satisfaction, to an audience."[13] Thomas Holcroft notes, in 1781, that the neophyte dramatist "ventures many things, that, perhaps, have their excellencies in reading, but that appear rude, abrupt, or indelicate, when pronounced before a large assembly," adding that, "were the humour of Smollet, which never fails to excite laughter in the closet, spoken upon the stage, it would frequently excite universal disgust."[14] Theorizing the excesses of theatrical representation by contrast with both painting and poetry, Lessing explains that the scream of Sophocles' savage and wretched Philoctetes should not be represented on stage, because "the reporting of someone's scream produces one impression and the scream itself another. . . . In [the theatre], we do not merely believe that we see and hear a screaming Philoctetes, we do actually see and hear him. The closer the actor approaches nature, or reality, the more our eyes and ears must be offended."[15]

While some literary works were too shocking for stage representation and might harm the spectators if put on stage, others were too poetic—too delicate or sublime—and were in danger of themselves being harmed by the stage, in an apparent mirror image that was, in the end, simply the same position reversed: for bodies, grotesque or sublime, enlarged in what Hugo referred to as the "optical glass" of the theatre, were an "unmanageable reality." Unlike "the theatre," writes Hugo, "the page *suffers all*."[16] Like Hugo or Hazlitt, Lamb could contrast the staged body's assault on the spectator's eyes with the literary flow of images through the reader's mind, opposing theatrical corporeality to the fine vagueness of the imagination. "What we see upon a stage is body and bodily action; what we are conscious of in reading is almost exclusively the mind, and its movements," he writes. On the page, Shakespearean tragedy is "a fine abstraction. It presents to the fancy just so much of external appearances as to make us feel that we are among flesh and blood, while by far the greater and better part of our imagination is employed upon the thoughts and internal machinery of the character." In reading *Macbeth*, "some dim images of royalty—a crown and sceptre, may float before our eyes" without durability or clear definition, while staging requires "full and cumbersome" coronation robes and "shiftings and re-reshiftings, like a Romish priest at a mass."[17]

THE PLEASURES OF THE IMAGINATION

In a sense, many of the genres and dramatic techniques that the popular theatre developed in the eighteenth and nineteenth centuries—pantomime, tableau, the forms of musical articulation made specially for melodrama—may be thought of as responses (conscious or unconscious) to the theatrical problem of sensory overload. Their suppressions (of voice in pantomime, for instance, or sound and movement in the fixed tableau) served to control the excesses of a theatre committed to the exploitation of spectacle. The wordless image could smooth over what otherwise seemed too disturbing to be capable of staging. If tableaux or pictorial dances were intended as visual stimuli, they also emblematically silenced what was felt to be "too much," resolving into pleasing pictorial unity the complexities (aesthetic, political) that the union of things too shockingly disparate might convey.[18] Tableau was suppression, but suppression offering a new sort of dramaturgical decorum. Within the purified forms of pantomime or tableau or the darkened stage, grotesque and hybrid figures might maintain an "airy shape." By isolating sensory means, such subgenres not only softened the cacophonies of the hyper-sensory theatre, but also clarified the process of theatrical reception, calling attention to the nature of both the means used and the means excluded. Pantomime made spectators conscious of the power of words by excluding them; the tableau made them conscious of theatrical motion by attempting to suppress it, freezing the living performers into pictorial stillness. Music in melodrama made spectators conscious at once of the communicative power of music by highlighting it and of the nature of verbal means by momentarily over-riding dialogue. Each of these, by highlighting a single aesthetic medium as inter-pretable object with narrative capacities of its own, at the same time occluded the others and allowed the medium to speak in its own terms. Dislocation of means was a way of parsing the various grammars of the theatre in order to examine each more closely, to recognize both their differences and their likenesses, at the same time, allowing for the imaginative supplementation of the spectator.

Writing in 1747, Pierre Rémond de Sainte-Albine had identified theatre as giving us the most "complete pleasure" of all the arts since, alone among the arts, it required no imaginative supplementation ("our imagination is almost always obliged to sup-plement the incapacities of the other arts," whereas theatre "requires of us no sup-plement").[19] But it was precisely such imaginative supplementation that the special genres of the late eighteenth- and nineteenth-century theatre demanded and that commentators identified as the particular source of the pleasure they produced. For Louis-Sébastien Mercier, for instance, pantomime was the most perfect of dramatic arts in that, as with the half-finished sketch, "it is I who create the painting."[20] In pan-tomime, much of the pleasure lay in the process of imagining the words that could make sense of the image—in "hearing" (as one commentator put it) the mime's silent action.[21] For "Mondor" (a character in an anonymous play performed in 1799 at the "Theatre Without Pretension"), the virtue of pantomime was that, "when an actor . . . has fire and there is truth in his gestures, I imagine in my spirit the most beautiful words in the world, in verse, in prose, however I wish."[22] The invention of *pièces à la muette* earlier in the century, in which the audience would read from plac-ards in order to sing the text along with an orchestra, was a pragmatic response to the Ancien Régime's limitation of spoken performance to the official theatres. But it also involved a recognition of the emotional power of interactive performance, a recogni-tion updated in Talma's typically Romantic comment that sensibility allows us "to add the shades that are wanting, or that language cannot express,—to complete, in fine, [the] expression."[23] If Diderot, playing at deafness, liked to plug his ears in the theatre in order to imagine the text that might accompany the action, the marginal theatres similarly understood that audiences liked to fill in the blanks.[24] There, spec-tators were engaged in a continual process of translating one set of signifying or affective means into another: pantomime might be comprehensible by translation into words; tableau might be comprehensible by translation into motion; verbal nar-rative might be comprehensible by translation through expressive gesture; gesture might be comprehensible by translation through music. With the spectator's imagi-native supplementation considered an essential aspect of theatrical reception, the spectator could, in the end, be the creator of the theatrical experience—a creator as important as the poet or actor.

When Hazlitt explains, in his essay on *A Midsummer Night's Dream*, that in read-ing (unlike in the theatre) "every circumstance has an equal chance of being kept in mind," he suggests the reader's freedom by contrast with the spectator's (playing on the liberal overtones of "equal chance" and drawing on the traditional contrast between the freedom of the reader and the enslavement of the spectator).[25] In the closet, "circumstance[s]" could not tyrannize the mind through sensory force but instead, born equal, they could be freely chosen by the autonomous and unfettered mind.[26] But if reading was free and theatrical experience was unfree, imagination could allow the spectator to transcend the limits of the theatre, at once unbinding the drama from the constraints of theatrical time and space that had been mandated by the unities and unbinding the spectator from the tyranny of the senses.[27] Where (as in pantomime or tableau) the recipient of the theatrical experience was central to the aesthetic event, the audience gained (at least conceptually) a new kind of freedom in the theatre—a freedom achieved through the conversion of theatrical experience into a semblance of the reader's experience, in which the spectator could resist the superficial seductions of sensation and transform them, through imagination, into precisely those "airy shape[s]," those "dreams," those "passing thought[s]" that for Hazlitt made up the experience of true poetry.

If popular theatrical arts drew on a recognition of the spectator's free, reconstitutive imagination at the centre of the theatrical moment—on what Mercier refers to as "interior painting"[28]—the theoretical analysis of aesthetic effect could similarly focus on the receptive imagination, modelling its understanding of theatrical imagination on an analysis of the kind of imagining that took place in the reading process. Mid- and late-eighteenth-century dramatists had, in the domestic drama, explored interiors, the unseen spaces of the home. If, for Mercier (equivocally), the "interior of houses" are the "entrails" of empire—if the commonwealth was no longer a body but bodies had instead become intimate commonwealths—the theatre's task (like that of the scientist) was to make manifest those hidden things within.[29] The "within" to be found in the theatre was one repeatedly identified as discovered in reading (that activity that, in fact, took place in those "interior[s] of houses" that were the entrails of empire"). Where the theatre turned the mind's interior activity outward, reading turned the body inward, in a process vividly articulated in the somatic metaphor at the centre of Hazlitt's paean to the virtues of books. Of all the media, he writes, books are "nearest to our thoughts: they wind into the heart; the poet's verse slides into the current of our blood. . . . We breathe but the air of books, . . . we owe every thing to their authors, on this side barbarism."[30] The civilized body politic was formed on the products of the cultural imagination, absorbed back into the interior space of the body through reading.

It was this kind of interiority on which the theatre was to model itself. "The principal and only genuine excitement" in the theatre, writes Coleridge in his notes on *The Tempest*,

ought to come from within,—from the moved and sympathetic imagination; whereas, where so much is addressed to the more external senses of seeing and hearing, the spiritual vision is apt to languish, and the attraction from without will withdraw the mind from the proper and only legitimate interest which is intended to spring from within.[31]

It was not that the imaginative reflex was to displace the sensory—for reflection or reflexivity were deeply sensuous—but that external stimuli were to be mere triggers for the receptive imagination, best if sparingly used, pointing towards the senses within—towards the interior as the location of the sensuous and as the only means of access to the sublime. "The sense of sublimity arises, not from the sight of an outward object," writes Coleridge in his notes on *Hamlet* (notably identifying the experience of the sublime as another kind of "sense"), "but from the beholder's reflection upon it; not from the sensuous impression, but from the imaginative reflex."[32] External phenomena could be liquidated, becoming mere "shadows . . . flit[ting] before you."[33] The body could be volatized; the world could disappear, overwhelmed by the spirit. If imagination was a faculty seen as primarily arising from the experience of the book (for Hazlitt, for instance, only in the closet was "all . . . left to the imagination"),[34] imagination might have the power to transform the theatre into something resembling the disembodied experience of reading.

One could, then, achieve the poetic sublime both through and despite the "unmanageable reality" of theatre. Such paradoxical anti-theatrical theatricalism emerged, in the broader eighteenth-century discussion, in the general insistence (parallel to the claims for pantomime or tableau) that the highest form of theatrical expression actually involved not the articulation of theatrical effects but their suppression. Jean Georges Noverre, for instance, writing in 1760, quotes an actor who claimed that pantomime was the quintessential performance medium because of its "phrases cut short, its suspended meanings, its sighs, its barely articulated sounds."[35] The moment of silence, the telling pause could be more powerful than any verbal articulation or gesture, in a translation of the classic inexpressibility topos into theatrical terms. "We often feel what we cannot express," writes Hyppolite Clairon, and "a noble or sensitive soul has surges of grandeur, moments of refinement, delicacy, to which I do not know what name to give; they are expressed by a look, a gesture, the modulation of the countenance, tempo: these nothings can often express more than words."[36] A "look, a gesture, the modulation of the countenance" might give bodily form to that which was "beyond words," but it was as much the suspension of articulation, the nothingness of "these nothings," that gave access to those depths and heights of feeling that were the essence of art and key to the sublime. If the grotesque was an aggressively sensory aesthetic, the sublime had to constitute itself finally beyond the senses.

The reverence for the half-articulated, the oblique, the "unheard . . . melodies" that were for Keats sweeter than those heard,[37] showed itself in silent, half-lit images like that near the climax of Hugo's *Le Roi s'amuse*:

Maguelonne and Saltabadil are both in the room below. The tempest has struck several moments before. It covers everything in rain and lightning. . . . Both are silent for a time. . . . One can see Blanche appearing, at the rear . . . She advances slowly towards the dilapidated cottage while Saltabadil drinks and Maguelonne, in the attic, gazes with her lamp on the sleeping king.[38]

She is in a black riding habit. As in paintings by Greuze or Eastlake, her pale face is illuminated by the storm's lightning. Here, the picturesque rushes towards the sublime—aided by Romantic natural stage scenery (thunder and lightning, the moon's sudden illumination) and by the play of concealment and revelation. Spectators could see, here, without the distraction of hearing, just as they could hear without the distraction of seeing when the plaintive melody filled a darkened stage. Sensory deprivation made for intensity of experience.

In *Faust*, more abstractly, the negation of the senses could point towards the silent and invisible as the realm of primal meaning. In his study, Faust bemoans the uselessness of words in the struggle to uncover nature's secrets ("Nature, mysterious in day's clear light, | lets none remove her veil").[39] The hero in search of the meaning of the deed must find something that survives the "great mass of books | that worms consume,"[40] something beyond the trivial theatrical languages of gesture and sound (represented by the theatrical manager and actor in the "Prelude in the Theatre"), a new kind of meaning suspended somewhere between the inarticulate "Ach!" which opens the poem and the disembodied song of the maternal voice that closes it. Finally, in "Forest and Cavern" Faust discovers what he has been seeking, not through words or significant signs, but through an interior revelation guided by the Spirit:

> Spirit sublime . . .
> you guide me to the safety of a cave,
> reveal my self to me, and then my heart's
> profound and secret wonders are unveiled.[41]

The deep of the earth's breast and the cavern are the places of knowledge, and knowledge is interior knowledge, the heart in unmediated communion with the Spirit without the need for words or action, free even of the "deed" that is the essence of drama itself (its etymological memory, "drama" as "doing," invoked in Faust's embrace of the "deed" early in the poem, from which he must eventually turn). Like the eternally feminine Mater Gloriosa who, at the end of the poem, effects Faust's apotheosis, the Nature in which he has found truth is more true because formless, just as music may be more musical if unheard or the drama more poetic if unseen. He can know voice best from silence; he can know vision best from the music that comes through darkness or blinding illumination; he can know the senses best in the moments he is bereft of them. If knowledge is self-knowledge (the silent and unseen knowing in one's own breast), there is no need for knowlege founded in the senses, no need for the cumbersome representations of the stage, because what is most importantly to be known may come from the darkness and silence straight to the spectator's purified imagination.

THEATRICALISM UNBOUND: SENSUOUS IDEALISM AND THE COLLECTIVE IMAGINATION OF THE FOLK

In the address, in formal aesthetics, to the nature of the theatrical work of art—processed by the senses and transformed through imagination—theorists were, similarly, attempting to understand the powers of the imagination and to address the limits of the matter-bound stage. While, on the whole, insisting on the power and significance of the theatre's communalism and sensuousness (in a philosophical version of the popular pro-theatricalism at which we glanced in Chapter 13), theorists could (as Goethe does implicitly) hypothesize an idealized stage that might act as a vehicle for collective transcendence of the material world—a means of moving the populace from the enslavement of the senses through subjective imagination towards a higher objectivity. In "The Stage as a Moral Institution" (1784), for instance, Schiller explains how theatre is at once a tool for the education of the populace and the key to the elevation of the senses. Theatre is the concrete manifestation of aesthetics, the optimal vehicle for transposing the sensuous into the ideal and the ideal into the ethical. Thus, the neo-classical unities, insisting on obeisance to the constraints of theatrical space and time "in the most common and empirical sense," deeply misconceive the nature of theatre: "as though" (he writes) "there were any place but the bare ideal one, or any other time than the mere sequence of the incidents."[42] While the senses are, then, for Schiller, necessary to the ascent into the ideal and objective sphere, to remain merely in the senses is to remain enslaved by them: "Whatever fascinates the senses alone is mere matter, and the rude element of a work of art."[43] The theatre, in translating matter into spirit, is not merely free from its own materiality, but can, in fact, actually liberate us from the enslavement of "the sensible world." The aim of theatrical art, like other kinds of art, is "to make us absolutely free," which it accomplishes by "awakening, exercising, and perfecting in us a power to remove to an objective distance the sensible world; (which otherwise only burdens us as rugged matter and presses us down with a brute influence); to transform it into the free working of our spirit, and thus acquire a dominion over the material by means of ideas."[44] In translating the sensual into the ideal, liberating us from a world which otherwise "burdens us as rugged matter and presses us down with brute influence," theatre at the same time liberates us from our individual and subjective experience, carrying us into the realm of the objective. The classical Chorus most perfectly exemplifies, in this, the theatre generally. For, while it is a "palpable body which appeals to the senses," using "the whole sensible influence of melody and rhythm . . . tones and movements," through the Chorus we leave both sensory particularity and the bondage of individuation and enter into the freedom of the "general."[45]

Following Schiller, Hegel too places the theatre theatrical at the centre of his aesthetics, rendering this placement in historical terms. Dramatic poetry is "the highest stage of poetry and of art in general"—the aesthetic form that is most complete, uniting as it does the multitude of artistic forms (gesture, speech, pantomime, picture, sculpture, dance). A material totality, then, it is at the same time "a complete totality of content and form," uniting matter with spirit in its union of sensuous media with the spiritual medium of human speech, and the subjective with the objective through its fusion of lyric and epic. Like lyric poetry, dramatic poetry is immediately present to us: it speaks in the present tense. But at the same time, by manifesting itself in epic action present to the viewer, it turns into collective and historical fact that which was subjective experience. As *action* (both the representation of an action and action on the stage), dramatic poetry "manifest[s] itself objectively" and "reveals at the same time its inner, subjective significance" through speech. In this, like the various theatrical media, it is an agent for the objectification of the subjective.[46] The person of the actor becomes the centre of this activity of objectification. In performance, "the *living* man himself is the material of dramatic expression," expressing at once "his inner life," as in lyric, and "his actual being as a whole subject in relation to others." In its union of the various arts in action with the actor at the centre, performed drama becomes an expression of the union of the multitude of interactions in collective life that come to make up the ideal, a microcosm of the historical moment generally. Theatre is, in a sense, not only the total work of art but a totalizing of the human work of art, rendered as a union of the subjective and the objective, a union effected through the transformation of sensuous matter into spirit. Together, the objectivity of epic (the history of a people) and the subjectivity of lyric (the history of the individual spirit), turned into "action" and made "present" to the observer, become "spirit" realized in the world: "This is spirit in its living totality, which, by being *action*, supplies at once the form and the content of *dramatic* poetry."[47]

Wagner famously translates (via Schopenhauer) Schiller's ethical theatricalist idealism and Hegel's evolutionary and totalizing aesthetic into a vision of the *Gesamtkunstwerk*, a theatre in which "Poetry" does not dominate "Music" and "Dance" but the three are equal and united in a trinity (with all the theological overtones of the word), whose wholeness is the highest expression of the human spirit. Here, he suggests what is implicit in Schiller's and Hegel's idealist pro-theatricalism in the story he positions as key to his evolutionary history of the spirit: its origin in a scene in which Orpheus' mellifluous voice shows its superiority to the "dumb and printed" word. Before the epic was a *literary* form, explains Wagner, the "folk" spun out their "epic songs . . . by voice and gesture, as a bodily enacted Art-work."[48] In this world, Orpheus sang to the savage beasts ready to devour him, and in so doing, tamed them: "The Lyrics of Orpheus would never have been able to turn the savage beasts to silent, placid adoration, if the singer had but given them forsooth some dumb and printed verse to read." Orpheus' choice of song over text becomes a founding moment for civilization, a moment in which the order of eat-or-be-eaten is transformed into the order of mutual recognition through art. The "ears" of the "savage beasts" had to

be enthralled by the sonorous notes that came straight from the heart, their carrion-spying eyes be tamed by the proud and graceful movements of the body,—*in such a way* that they should recognise instinctively in this whole man no longer a mere object for their maw, no mere objective for their feeding-, but for their hearing- and their seeing-powers,—before they could be attuned to duly listen to his moral sentences.[49]

This primal scene presages the actual foundation of the theatre (the next stage in Wagner's evolutionary history), which takes shape and is defined in opposition to the (aristocratic) project of textualizing Homer and, by extension, in opposition to the literate arts generally: "While those pedants and professors in the Prince's castle were labouring at the construction of a *literary Homer . . . Thespis* had already slid his car to Athens, had set it up beside the palace walls, dressed out his *stage* and, stepping from the chorus of the Folk, had *trodden* its planks."[50] But the work of the literary pedants is the beginning of the "shiver[ing] into fragments" of the art of the Folk, "its Religion and primeval Customs . . . pierced and severed by the sophist needles of the egoistic soul of Athenian self-dissection," its spirit desiccated in the translation onto the dry page:

> The professors and the doctors of the literary guilds [took] heritage of the ruins of the fallen edifice, and delved among its beams and stones; to pry, to ponder, and to re-arrange its members. With Aristophanian laughter, the Folk relinquished to these learned insects the refuse of its meal . . . while those scholars cobbled up their tiresome history of Literature. . . . The wintry stem of Speech, stripped of its summer wreath of sounding leaves, shrank to the withered, toneless signs of *Writing*: instead of to the Ear, it dumbly now addressed the *Eye*; the poet's strain became a *written dialect*,—the poet's breath the *penman's scrawl*.[51]

This narrative of the fall from song and gesture to writing echoes the politics Wagner specifically outlines elsewhere in the essay. Orpheus sings to prevent being eaten, and to do so he must enthrall his listeners—mesmerize the eyes and ears of the Folk—so that it will "duly listen to [his] moral sentences." In this moral reconstitution, the Folk comes to recognize its collective hunger as something beyond mere individual want, rising to the level of collective "will" and expressed in the total work of art. The printed sheet is to be rejected not only because it is incapable of quelling the brute cannibalism of the masses, but also because, read in solitude by the "professors" and "doctors," it contributes to the kind of individuation of consciousness that produces modern "*Egoism*" ("the impulse to loose one's self from commonalty, to be free and independent for individual self alone"), and attendant "*Luxury*."[52] If Wagner identifies the egoism, hierarchy, and parasitism of modern life with the egoism of the solitary media and the subordination of music to the word ("where Poetry fain would reign in solitude, as in the spoken play, she took Music into her menial service, for her own convenience"),[53] the printed sheet is a marker of that hierarchy, egoism, and parasitism. Wagner's revolutionary historical science (in line, in many respects, with that of Marx) leads him to a prophecy of the dethroning of the printed text and the restoration of Orpheus' primitive songs and Thespis' primitive gestures to their rightful place in the *Gesamtkunstwerk*—at once an aesthetic and a political prophecy. The political totality towards which the German nation is striving ("Communism," in which the Folk, "all those men *who feel a common and collective Want*," will "no longer be a severed and peculiar class")[54] will arise beside the *Gesamtkunstwerk* with its totalizing aesthetic, founded in music and gesture and set against the text: "in this Art-work we shall all be *one*—heralds and supporters of Necessity, knowers of the unconscious, willers of the unwilful, betokeners of Nature—*blissful men*."[55] For Wagner, a theatre that refuses the atomism of modern life (the atomism of the experience of reading figured in the atomism of the media), a theatre that recognizes its truest expression not in the "dumb and printed verse" but in the primal union of tone, poem, and dance, may unify the Folk in a collectivity that is at once a collective unconscious and a new form of collective self-consciousness.

One might read Wagner's vision of Orpheus before the beasts as an emblem for the philosophical theatricalism of the era, founded in its mythic rejection of the printed text (the original moment in which print intervened in the primal connection between aesthetic expression and the human body), but dissolving specifically theatrical matter into a disembodied collective consciousness. Certainly, the typical identification (in the aesthetics of the period) of each of the art forms as translatable into one another was a way of imagining the disappearance of their separate sensual means in the abstract realm of receptive consciousness. In Schiller's theatre of the ideal, the material differences among the various arts become unimportant, because each of them is striving towards a kind of general beauty. Each art, he writes, as it comes closer to perfection, acquires "a more general character":

At its highest degree of ennobling, music ought to become a form, and act on us with the calm power of an antique statue; in its most elevated perfection the plastic art ought to become music, and move us by the immediate action exercised on the mind by the senses; in its most complete development poetry ought both to stir us powerfully like music, and like plastic art to surround us with peaceful light.[56]

At its most sublime, each somehow transcends the particularity of its sensuous presence. For Wagner, similarly, the various arts emerge from and aspire to a general aesthetic that tends to obviate their specific means: the "tragic Actor of the Future" was "prefigur[ed] in . . . stone and canvas"; the same sense of form drives the "*Mime*" and the sculptor; the same sense of beauty drives the historical painter and "the whole breadth of *actual human show*."[57] Hegel, with his recognition of dramatic poetry as the highest union of form and substance ("sensuous *materia*" expressing "spiritual life"), finally understands genuine poetry not as the audible or visible word but as immaterial spirit:

It serves neither sensual perception, like the plastic arts, nor mere ideal feeling like music. Rather, it offers up . . . spirit (formed in the interior) for the spiritual imagination and perception alone. The material through which it expresses itself has value only as a medium for . . . the expression of the spirit to the spirit, and cannot be taken as a sensual entity to which the spirit corresponds.[58]

If practitioners tended to celebrate the power of the individual spectator to rewrite the spectacle through imagination (with political overtones kindred to those in Hazlitt's liberal vision of reading, in which the impressions on which the spectator's mind may light each have an "equal chance" to come to the fore), German idealist aesthetics tended to envision theatre as directed towards an experience of common consciousness—the consciousness of the masses that was at once subject and object of the total work of art. The whole was to subsume individuation and subjectivity in the spirit of the masses; the individual spectator was to transcend the unfreedom of individuation and enter into the spirit of the collective, in an erasure of the distinctions of producer and recipient, subject and object. By broadening the focus from individual subjectivity to collective subjectivity, imagining the spectator's individual subjectivity finally united with and subsumed in the collective subjectivity (in an aesthetics of mass spectacle that was to re-emerge in the fascist aesthetics of the twentieth century), theorists could still highlight receptive consciousness without necessarily allowing for the freedom of the individual spectator's constructive imagination ("It is a sorry misconception of Freedom," writes Wagner, "that of the being who would fain be free in loneliness").[59] Friedrich Schelling (perhaps following Schiller) describes the vital function of the Chorus, which "anticipat[es] what [goes] on in the spectator, the emotional movement, the participation, the reflection," and, in so doing, importantly "does not allow the spectator to be free, but rather arrests him entirely through art."[60] Genuine art was to arrest the spectator through its union of subject and object, production and reception. Nietzsche (still in the idealist tradition in *The Birth of Tragedy*) could imagine this union as the kind of climactic erasure of boundaries that took place in the "primordial" moment, in which "the genius in the act of artistic creation" found the "eternal essence of art" by becoming "subject and object, at once poet, actor, and spectator . . . like the weird image of the fairy tale [turning] its eyes at will and behold[ing] itself."[61] In this vision of perfect aesthesis, not only might the sensuous *materia* of the theatre be erased, but the theatrical agents and spectators themselves, leaving only the immaterial moment of creation, with pure spirit at the centre. Here, as for Hegel, the stage might not be, after all, the place for objects of the senses. Theatre might not be, after all, so very theatrical. Here, as in the closet, actors in dialogue and bodies in motion might be made, at last, to disappear altogether into a great amorphous and all-consuming consciousness.

Epilogue

In an essay entitled "Mechanization" (1922), discussing the cinema and the phonograph, Adolphe Appia reflects on the new technologies' systematic "violation" of all that the human holds sacred, from the theatre at its most essential (a "Work of Living Art") to "the new Presence": that spirit of collectivity that might, if allowed to thrive, have the power to revive the health of the human spirit through its creation of a newly holistic aesthetics, which would unite producer and consumer into a single, living organism. In the midst of his discussion, he interrupts himself to recount a story. Unacquainted with the phonograph, a musician is invited to the home of a friend to hear a great soprano, who is (he is told) staying there incognito. On arrival, he is received in the corridor and asked to stand with his ear to the wall. Suddenly, a magnificent voice rises from the parlour and fills the air: it is Wagner's death of Isolde. Deeply moved, he enters the room, "burning with desire . . . to accompany this incomparable voice on the piano." What he finds is not the living singer but, at the centre of the parlour, on a small table, a phonograph, "its horrible horn opened wide":

He felt he had been struck a stunning blow. . . . Two sentiments dominated him completely: either he could not bear the suffering any longer and he would have to throw [the machine] out the window; or . . . or what? . . . His body shivered with indignation and [he felt] the need to act. . . . He must at all costs *animate* this monstrous recording, or else he must escape from it.

The musician grows pale, unable to move, but at last seizes the score resting on the piano, leans his ear towards the phonograph horn and begins to accompany what has swelled into the duet, "*O sink hernieder Nacht der Liebe*" ("Oh, sink down upon me, | night of love, | make me forget | I am alive. . . ."). As he grows more and more mesmerized, he begins to whisper softly to the machine: "Ah, that's how you hear it, yes, I understand, I'll be careful there," or simply "Yes! . . . yes! . . ." He plays and plays, growing "firmer" with each bar, until, finally, he is no longer following the voices, but he has, at last, become one with them, their union "consummated." "It was thus," concludes Appia, "that he had to pay his tribute to the infamous instrument": stunned, shivering with rage, ready to flee, finally swallowed up in its voluptuous power.[1] One might attempt valiantly to uphold the theatre, in all its Presence, before the overwhelming and terrifying performing machine. One might attempt to disavow, to escape, to vanquish one's "violation" by modern mechanization—to fight with all one's power the machine's "rape" of the "Work of Living Art." But cinema and phonograph—monstrous mechanical conjurors—are not, ultimately, to be conquered. Betrayed, tricked, violated, certain that he must destroy the infernal instrument, in the end even the maker of music himself grows mesmerized by the machine.

Leaning tenderly towards its dangerously open orifice, in a moment of erotic consummation, he too succumbs, finally, to its irresistible force.

◆

The theatrical spectacles, old and new, that appeared on stages and in showgrounds from the 1880s on celebrated the theatre theatrical, aided by all the mechanical and electrical devices of modern life: the horse or chariot races or train wrecks like the two in *Pluck* (1882) (moved by treadmills and shattering the glass storefronts on the stage); the "automates" and "mechanical games" that Emile Campardon included with other sideshows in his *Spectacles of the Foire*; the dazzling feats of veils and light of a Loie Fuller; the moving Dioramas, Panoramas, Panopticons and all their variations in the ever-more inventive boxes of electric light made for showing moving pictures.[2] The desire for spectacle and its reflection produced a frenzy of images of the scene. With the development of cameras (taking on-stage photos from the 1880s on),[3] the images multiplied: Bernhardt as Théodora (Sardou's whore-cum-Empress-of-Byzantium) in shocking vividness; the crowds flooding the stage in the Meininger *Julius Caesar*; Christ rising heavenward in coloured postcards from the Oberammergau Passion Play. With new technologies for the mechanical reproduction of light, sound, and motion towards the end of the century—the phonograph, vitascope, theatrograph, stéréocinema, biopticon, phototheagraph, cinéma-grapho-théâtre, and other mouvementoscopes (all first feasible in the 1880s, at once made possible by the technical innovations of the era and inspired by the culture of theatricalism itself)—came the ever-faster reproduction of moving images and electric noises, transforming dramatic spectacle into the multitudinous and repeating forms of mass culture.[4]

If the culture of spectacle celebrated the theatre theatrical, so did the high-culture avant-garde in the first decades of the new century, foregrounding its primitive past, its populist present, and the booming beats of its machine-age future. It reached out to the culture of electric entertainment, mass celebration, and ancient rite, creating new performance styles rooted at once in the body mechanic of the machine age and in the rituals of "peoples without writing" (their rhythms and terrors strangely akin to those of the new age). In so doing, it defined itself by declaring its liberation from the text. "The book [is] a wholly passéist means of preserving and communicating thought," proclaimed one Futurist manifesto in 1916. "Static companion of the sedentary," it is "fated to disappear," to be replaced with media that will "smash the boundaries of literature."[5] In destroying the text, the new theatre was to kill the drama of the literary masterpiece: "The Variety Theatre . . . cooperates in the Futurist destruction of immortal masterworks," writes Filippo Marinetti.[6] "Born . . . from electricity," the new theatre was to have "no tradition, no masters, no dogma" but to be "fed by swift actuality."[7] For Artaud (inheriting the Futurists' revolutionary anti-textualism), it was the text that kept the Occidental drama in the realm of petty psychology, stifling the theatricalism of the theatre, and with this, its metaphysical power. "We must get rid of our superstitious valuation of texts and *written* poetry," he writes, excoriating the "Occidental . . . alliance with . . . the written text" and calling for the library at Alexandria to be burnt down ("there are forces above and beyond papyrus"). One had to "let the dead poets make way for others" and return to the essence of theatre, made up of a "pure theatrical language," in which one might rediscover "the ideas of the archetypal, primitive theater"—its "cries, groans, apparitions, surprises, theatricalities of all kinds"—and through this new language come to a theatre reborn for the modern age,[8] a theatre made (in the words of another commentator) for the "Man of the future," living "under [the Machine's] dominion."[9]

The new recording technologies—the motion picture cameras, gramophones, and their variations—took on the age-old romance with the scene in motion, re-enacting the eternal desire to preserve and reproduce motion in time, trying to capture (as dramatists and image-makers had from the beginning) the kinetics of the play. The machine seemed to promise eternity for the theatrical event: "We shall hear no more of the fugitive fame of the actor's art which perishes with himself," writes Shaw. "I shall not be at all surprised if the cinematograph and phonograph turn out to be the most revolutionary inventions since writing and printing, and, indeed, far more revolutionary than either. . . . What a life it will be when all the theatres will be picture theatres, and all the plays immortal."[10] But with the mechanization of performance came the entertainment industry that was to displace the live theatre as the principal venue of mass entertainment. By the 1920s, the theatres were surrounded by the movie houses and picture palaces where the reels ran and the images were projected on screens and the actors were suddenly quite literally larger than life. In towns and cities, the number of cinemas doubled, the number of theatres halved.[11] When he produced *Oedipus Rex* at the Cirque d'Hiver as an "Olympic Spectacle" in 1919–20, the French director Firmin Gémier could declare, "It is not the Circus that we have driven from this auditorium, it is the cinema. Our victory is the first revenge of the theatre against its adversary[!]"[12] But even the mass theatre could not compete with the flashy and cacophonous sights and sounds of the increasingly massive mass media. "*Cinematography triumph[s]*," wrote Fortunato Depero, "it wins" in the contest with theatre "because it is fast, because it moves and transforms rapidly."[13] The "great public," declared Artaud, had abandoned the theatre and "look[ed] to the movies . . . for violent satisfactions."[14] Announcing the death of book and theatre at once, Marinetti's Futurists could joyously embrace the entertainment machines, announcing that the cinema would "tak[e] the place of the literary review (always pedantic), the drama (always predictable) . . . killing the book (always tedious and oppressive)," expressing itself instead through the "mobile illuminated signs" of the screen.[15]

Early twentieth-century aesthetics could treat live theatre as the *ur*-art-form, with its celebration of movement and the body, its sensual apparitions, its necessary transgressions of medium, its festival of forms. Theatre artists could revel in the multiplication of performance tools that the new technologies brought them, using the new media on the stage in an impulse of high-tech spectacularism and as a means of breaking down the distinction between body and machine. The theatre theatrical could embrace its own filmic qualities, drawing near to the cinema, "which enriches it with an incalculable number of visions and otherwise unrealizable spectacles (battles, riots, horse races, automobile and airplane meets . . .)" and all the forms of the "marvelous . . . produced by modern mechanics."[16] "In taking advantage of every possible technical advance," wrote Meyerhold, "let us carry through the 'cinefication' of the theatre to its logical conclusion, let us equip the theatre with all the technical refinements of the cinema . . . and we shall stage productions which will attract just as many spectators as the cinema."[17] But if, in Shaw's view, the high era of print was nearly over so, it seemed, was that of the theatre as the primary medium of popular culture, displaced by the cinematic revolution. Shaw could rejoice in what the film would bring—"Think of the gallops, the sousings in real rivers, the boatings on real salt waves, the flights in real aeroplanes," he wrote, hoping that the cinema's colonization of spectacle might bring about the rebirth of theatre, which (by contrast with the cinema) could become once again the place of the word, following "the path of high human utterance of great thoughts and great wit, of poesy and prophecy," that is ("as some of our more hopelessly prosaic critics call it") the "path of Talk." But when the "talkies" arrived, he saw in them the death of theatre as such: "The poor old theatre is done for!"[18]

The poor old theatre would, of course, refuse to be "done for." But it seemed the end of a particular theatrical moment: the era of a theatre formed in opposition to the page and understood in relation to the written text. The dual-being of text and performance had been displaced by the hybrid recording media (text and performance at once); the definitional opposition between text and performance had been replaced by that between live theatre and machine. Instead of focusing on the difference between the deep and mobile theatre and the flat and stilled page, or that between the sonorous voice and the silent book, practitioners and commentators focused on the difference between human and machine—on the magical yet delusive vividness of the new recording technologies, eerily capable (like Appia's phonograph) of evoking live presence, seemingly made of human body and voice, yet actually made only of vibrations and light, incapable of variation and insensible to response. Instead of focusing on the difference between the presence of live spectators and the remoteness and privacy of the reader in the study, they focused on the theatre's place, on the one hand, in the industry of mass spectatorship and, on the other, in a culture in which one's most intimate relationship might be, in the end, with a machine. Instead of focusing on the disappearance of theatre's sensory richness in the printed text, they focused on the disappearance of the theatre itself into the culture of recorded sound and image that threatened to stifle forever the living work of art. After half a century of electrical recording technologies and mass media, ironically and yet at the same time with a certain pathos, the endlessly repeating reels of Beckett's *Krapp's Last Tape* act out a farewell to a theatre whose longing for a record has produced its own anachronism, and into whose recording devices (listened to by the atomistic spectator sunk into solitude in the darkened den) the theatre as such has finally disappeared:

Past midnight. Never knew such silence. The earth might be uninhabited. . . . *Krapp motionless staring before him. The tape runs on in silence.* CURTAIN.[19]

And yet, the end of one era was the beginning of another, in which the theatre was to continue to transform itself: capturing the crowd with its own mass spectacle, its own mechanized bodies, and its own hypnosis of light and sound; bringing the human organism fully into the electric century, to a "stage . . . amplified in all electrical and mechanical senses";[20] liberating itself into the shock of the new age, discovering new forms of beauty for "a public that shudders at train wrecks, that is familiar with earthquakes, plagues, revolutions, wars," a public (in Artaud's words) living in "the rude and epileptic rhythm of our time."[21]

Notes

INTRODUCTION

1. Foxe, *Acts* VI:57 (Bk. 9, AD 1550).
2. I do not take it for granted that theatre as we know it emerged recognizably in late 15th-
   or 16th-century Europe, and I am certainly not making an argument about print as sole
   cause of the modern theatre as an institution: as David Bevington, Glynne Wickham,
   and others have shown, the development of performance genres and rise of professional
   performers in the 15th century was in itself central to the institutionalization of theatre
   in the following century. Over the past half-century, medievalists have offered an important corrective to the notion of a radical rupture between, for instance, the genres and
   institutional forms unfolding in the 14th and 15th centuries and those that developed in
   the 16th and 17th centuries. But most scholars agree that there were critical changes—
   often understood as constituting the "birth of the modern theatre"—between the late
   15th and 16th centuries: from the classical experimentation of the end of the 15th century to the theatre construction of the end of the 16th (to mention just a few studies,
   Pieri's *Nascita*, Radcliff-Ulmstead's *Birth*; Cruciani's *Teatro*; Mangini's *Alle origini*; the
   essays in Mulryne and Shewring, eds., *Theatre*). While Wickham tends generally to
   stress continuity over change, he divides *Early English Stages* into two parts to reflect the
   importance of the changes in late 16th-century performance practices: "the Elizabethan
   theatrical inheritance" from 1300 to 1576 and "the substitution of a new kind of stage-
   craft" between 1576 and 1660 (*Early* I: pp. vii–viii).

   That said, it is worth listing the features most often identified as differentiating the
   new "modern" theatre of the 16th century from the performance forms that preceded it
   (see, for instance, Andrews, *Scripts* 25; and Anderson, "Changing" 3): fixed scenic
   spaces; buildings used exclusively for the production of plays; performances divorced
   from festivals or specific events; professional actors and acting troupes; customers who
   expected to pay for seats; the regular use of fixed texts; the wide circulation of playbooks;
   dramas modelled on ancient forms; a shift in the primary connotation of the word
   "theatre" from visual displays generally, to scenic representations with actors.

   One further note on my usage of anachronistic designations such as "the theatre"
   (anachronistic as an institutional designation before the mid-16th century) or "publisher" (anachronistic as a designation for the entrepreneurial side of book production
   before the 18th century): when I am stressing a contemporary's view, I generally use the
   word normally used during the period; when I am stressing the function itself, I generally use the modern equivalent.
3. Terence, *Terenti cũ Directorio vocabulorũ Sententiarũ artis Comice* (1496). My discussion,
   here, of late-medieval dress and class draws on Piponnier and Mane, *Se vêtir* 52–117. On
   iconography, see the essays in Davidson, ed., *Iconography*, and Bost, *Babel*. On cultural
   life in Strasbourg, see Chrisman, *Lay*.
4. Discussions of the nature of the text have been influenced not only by structuralist and
   poststructuralist accounts of the text (Barthes's most centrally), but also by such central

texts in hermeneutics as Gadamer's *Wahrheit und Methode* and Ricoeur's *Du texte à l'action*, elaborated in the work of such theorists as Wolfgang Iser and Hans Robert Jauss. For the modern phenomenology of aesthetic media, see most centrally Ingarden's *Literary Work of Art* (esp. 317–23, 377–96); Gadamer's *Truth and Method* (especially "Play as the clue to ontological explanation" 101–34); and, for more recent studies in theatre phenomenology and hermeneutics, Wilshire, *Role Playing and Identity*, and States, *Great Reckonings in Little Rooms*. Important early works in theatre semiotics and the semiotics of the dramatic text by members of the Prague School such as Jiří Veltruský and Jindrich Honzl have been recast in studies by such theatre semioticians as Kier Elam, Anne Ubersfeld, Patrice Pavis, Manfred Pfister, Erika Fischer-Lichte, and Marvin Carlson.

5. For studies of speech and writing taking their inspiration from Derrida's *De la grammatologie* (1967), see, for instance Certeau, *L'Écriture* 215–48; Johnson, *System*; and Krell, *Of Memory*. For correctives to the uniform account of "phonocentrism," and more historical readings of the speech/writing relation nonetheless strongly influenced by Derrida, see Elsky, *Authorizing*; Goldberg, *Writing*; Hudson, *Writing*; Kittler, *Discourse*; and Kroll, *Material*.

6. Studies of technology and culture have been associated most notably with Marshall McLuhan, for instance in his *Gutenberg Galaxy*, *Laws of Media*, *Understanding Media*, and *The Medium is the Massage*. The work of the Frankfurt School might be thought of as the origin of the outpouring of new work on technology and culture, from the general analysis of mass culture, to the theorization of film and television reception, to the analysis of the impact of information technologies, to the querying of the concept of technology itself (for instance, in discussions of "technologies of gender," in Teresa de Lauretis's phrase). The most influential study of the relationship between "oral culture" and "literate culture" is probably Walter J. Ong's *Orality and Literacy*, which took its impetus from early studies of Homeric oral production and the advent of literacy in classical Greece (Milman Parry's *Making of Homeric Verse* and Eric Havelock's *Literate Revolution in Greece*, most notably) and from anthropological studies of the impact of writing such as Lévi-Strauss's famous excursus in *Tristes tropiques* (the basis for Derrida's extended discussion) or Jack Goody's *The Logic of Writing*. The two most influential studies of the advent and impact of printing in Europe, Lucien Febvre and Henri-Jean Martin's *L'Apparition du livre* and Elizabeth Eisenstein's *Printing Press as an Agent of Change*, have generated a rich (and richly contentious) literature on the history of the book and the—highly disputed—consequences of print for early modern culture.

7. Leah Marcus has referred to this as "the newly active field of textual studies" (*Unediting* 3), which emerged in an attempt to address the blind spots of classical bibliography and textual criticism, treating the material text as a rich source for the study of cultural consciousness. What one might refer to as revisionary bibliography—for the drama, most notably the work of Peter W. M. Blayney, Randall McCloud, Laurie McGuire, D. F. McKenzie, Gary Taylor, Steven Urkowitz, and Michael Warren, supplemented by more theoretical studies—has been a source for the many studies of the early modern dramatic text and its relation to the culture of print that have appeared over the past decade or so, most notably those of Douglas Brooks, Roger Chartier, Margreta De Grazia, David Scott Kastan, Frederick Kiefer, Joseph Loewenstein, Leah Marcus, Jeffrey Masten, Timothy Murray, and Stephen Orgel (by no means an exhaustive list, and not mentioning the rich work in early modern non-dramatic texts).

8. Much has been done to modify the grander claims of broad studies of orality, literacy, and print, challenging the unconscious ethnocentrism inherent in universalist accounts of the impact of literacy, questioning as "technologically determinist" the notion that literacy and print *cause* particular cognitive structures or cultural styles in and of themselves (outside their uses and the political relations of their users), describing local variations and the power negotiations that shape them, questioning the existence of "print culture" or "print logic." Such scholars as James Clifford, Jonathan Goldberg, Adrian Johns, Brian Street, and Michael Warner have challenged the traditional anthropological account of a move *from* orality *to* literacy and what they characterize as McLuhan's, Goody's, and Ong's, over-broad account of the impact of writing and print. As Johns puts it, for instance, the identity of print was not a given, but had to be made (*Nature* 2). Brian Stock has characterized the more traditional account as the "strong model" and the critical account as the "weak model" (*Listening* 6), a distinction similar to Street's between "autonomous" theories of literacy and "ideological" theories: the latter (drawing heavily on Foucault), the view that particular locales and particular configurations of power, culture, and ideology interact with and can discursively *create* technologies (Street, ed., *Cross-Cultural* 5–12). The work of the "weak" or "ideological" theorists is given support by recent work in local oralities and literacies, both historical and contemporary (William Harris's, Tony Lenz's, and Rosalind Thomas's studies of ancient literacy, Brian Stock's study of medieval literacy, Street's *Literacy* and *Cross-Cultural*, and Ruth Finnegan's overview in *Oral Tradition*, to name just a few), which have shown the limitations of any theory of "oral composition style" or "oral culture" as such. On the continuing utility of "strong" theories of orality and culture, see Nicolaisen, ed., *Oral*. See the 1992 preface to Finnegan's *Oral Poetry* (pp. ix–xvii), Stock's *Listening* 1–15, and my "Orality," for an evaluation of both the important contribution the critiques have made and the difficulties their own strong claims encounter.

9. On the increasing importance of writing and literacy from the 12th century on, see Stock, *Implications*, and Clanchy, *From Memory*. For discussions of whether the printing of books from movable type in Europe was a "revolution" or an "evolution," see Febvre and Martin, *Coming* (not a revolution, but playing a role in the revolutionary changes of the Renaissance and Reformation (9, 248)); Johns, *Nature* 636 (no single revolution, but many); and Eisenstein, *Printing* ("Unacknowledged Revolution" (3–42)), and Eisenstein, "From Scriptoria" (citing various sources noting the publication norms already in place in the late-medieval manuscript book industry, mass production in late-medieval scriptoria, and the continuity of pre- and post-print culture).

10. Chrisman, *Lay* 23, 100 (on Wimpheling's notion that printing was central to German cultural achievement); citing Wimpheling, *Epithoma Rerum Germanicarum*.

11. On Encina's and Torres Naharro's career and the printing of their plays, see McKendrick, *Theatre* 15, 27–8, 34.

12. The Columbia University Library and Houghton Library (Harvard) have copies of a type-specimen of the alphabet, the Lord's prayer and Ave Maria, and several lines of verse in Trissino's lettering. See Trissino, [Type-specimen]; and Richardson, *Print* 87.

13. Reed, *Early* 17. On the disputed authorship of *Gentleness and Nobility*, see Partridge and Wilson's introduction to Rastell [?], *Gentleness* vii.

14. Sachs, *Eygentliche Beschreibung* (see, for instance, the printer portrayed on sig. Fiiiʳ).

15. By the first decades of the 16th century, there were classical performances and editions across Europe: productions of Terence in Metz in 1502 and Verdun in 1514; a production of Terence's *Eunuchus* in Salzburg in 1516; a production of Plautus in Greenwich in 1519; a Seneca production in Wittenberg in 1525; productions of Plautus and Terence in Salamanca in the 1530s; productions of Terence in Leipzig in 1530 and Halle in 1534, to mention just a few. On the early English public theatres as adaptations of the ancient theatre (based on readings of Vitruvius), see Yates, *Theatre* 112–35, and, on the classical editions as architectural sources in England, Chambers, *Elizabethan* III:2–3. On the classical productions, see: Lazard, *Le Théâtre* 79; Frenzel, *Geschichte* 41; Chambers, *Elizabethan* III:19; Kindermann, *Theatergeschichte* II:250; and Shergold, *History* 169. For general information on the first classical productions and the academic drama, see Cruciani, *Teatro* 184–8, 219–27; Pieri, *Nascita* 54–66; Frenzel, *Geschichte* 39–41; Kindermann, *Theatergeschichte* II:32–44, 204–15, 243–71; Wilson, *English* 85–101; Chambers, *Elizabethan* I:127–9, III:4 ff.; Boas, *University*. On the theatre festivals, see Nagler, *Theatre*; and Blumenthal, *Italian* and *Theater*.

16. The scholar-printer Jodocus Badius Ascensius, for instance, may have been involved in the exploratory productions of ancient plays in Ferrara in the 1480s and in Rome in the 1480s, and was almost certainly involved in the publication of the illustrated edition of Terence that Johann Trechsel published in Lyon in 1493 (see Chambers, *Elizabethan* III:6–7; and the discussion of these illustrations in Chapter 4). As Lawrenson and Purkis point out ("Les Éditions" 5), the theory of Badius's involvement in the edition and his involvement in the productions in Ferrara and Rome is somewhat speculative, but he spent time studying with the Italian humanists in Ferrara and Mantua during the years of the first exploratory classical productions in Italy, moved to Lyon and married Trechsel's daughter just before the publication of the Trechsel Terence, and his description of classical staging in his *Praenotamenta* corresponds precisely with the Trechsel illustrations.

17. Vitruvius, *De architectura* (*c.*1483–90); qtd. and trans. Grafton and Jardine, *From Humanism* 89–90 (and on Sulpizio's work generally see 89–91).

18. Most of the library catalogues of which we have records contain editions of the major Greek dramatists, as well as Vitruvius and some version of the *Poetics*. See, for instance, Dee, *John Dee's Library*, and Yates, *Theatre* 31–3 (citing Dee, *Compendius Rehearsall* in *Autobiographical Tracts* 5–6), on Dee's production of *Pax* and his library's inclusion of Aristophanes, Sophocles, Euripides, Plautus, and Seneca's tragedies.

19. Oosting, *Andrea Palladio's* 28, 133.

20. See Krautheimer, "Alberti," and Gadol, *Leon Battista Alberti*, 98–9. Alberti not only describes how theatres should be built but also explains tragic, comic, and satiric genres and describes rotating machinery that could bring painted backdrops, houses, and woods into sudden view. Alberti, *L'architettura* (1966 edn.) II:739 (Bk. 8, Ch. 7, fol. 150ᵛ), and see II:724–48 generally.

21. See the prefatory material to Wimpheling, *Stilpho* (performed in Heidelberg around 1480) and Reuchlin, *Scenica*. On these productions, see also Kindermann, *Theatergeschichte* II:251.

22. Terence was published first in 1469 or 1470 (it is unclear whether the Italian edition of Vindelinus de Spira of Venice or the German edition of Johann Mentelin of Strasbourg is first: see Rhodes, "La Publication" 285). Plautus was published by Johannes de Colonia in Venice in 1472, Seneca by Andreas Gallicus in Ferrara in 1484, Aristophanes in 1498, Euripides in 1495, Sophocles in 1502, and Aeschylus in 1518 (all by the Aldine

Press). Terence was published in German in 1499 (*Terentius der Hochgalert*), in French around 1500 (*Therence en fra[n]coys*), an edition of the *Andria* alone in English around 1520 (*Terens in Englysh*), in English in full in 1598 (*Terence in English*), in Italian in 1533 (*Comedie di Terentio*), in Dutch in 1555 (*Teretius Comedie nu eerst wt den Latine*), and in Spanish in 1577 (*Las seis comedias de Terencio*). Seneca was published in Italian in 1560 (*Le tragedie di Seneca*) and in English in 1566 (*Eyght Tragedies*). Goff, *Incunabula*, RLIN, and the *National Union Catalogue* list no vernacular collected editions of Aeschylus before 1600, only one of Aristophanes, but eleven of Sophocles, sixteen of Euripides, and a considerable number of Plautus (see also Hirsch, *Printed* VIII (p. 138); and Howard-Hill, "Evolution" 130, on the thirty-nine Plautus editions in the British Library catalogue to 1578; and, generally, Hirsch, "Classics"). This is in addition to the many separately published plays and treatises on the drama, which include Robortello's poetics published in Florence in 1548 and Basel in 1555, Giraldi's in Venice in 1554 and Pavia in 1569, Castelvetro's in Basel in 1566, in Vienna in 1570, and again in Basel in 1576, Scaliger's in ten different editions in the 16th and early 17th centuries. There were over a dozen additional editions of Aristotle's *Poetics* in the 15th and 16th centuries, nearly a dozen of Alberti's *De re aedificatoria*, over two dozen of Vitruvius.

23. The title pages of the many editions of Gréban and Michel's *Mystère de la Passion* record numerous performances in Paris and elsewhere, credibly or not. (Graham Runnals has provided me with edition numbers.) On the many biblical and humanist plays performed and printed in early 16th-century Strasbourg, see Chrisman, *Lay* 215, and generally 213–21. Little is known about Pulci, but during the period in which most of her plays were published she was a member of a convent, one of the most common venues for the performance of *rappresentazioni* (see Toscani, "Antonia Pulci").

24. Gréban [?], *Le Premier ... Volume des ... Actes des Apostres ... Avecques plusieurs Hystoires ... des gestes des Cesars. Et les demonstrances des figures de Lapocalipse ... avecqs les cruaultez tant de Neron que dicelluy Domician ... joue par personnages* (quoted from the 1541 edition; usually, if doubtfully, attributed to Simon Gréban).

25. On the Encina editions, see McKendrick, *Theatre* 15. Holbrook, in the introduction to his facsimile edition of the anonymous *Maistre Pierre Pathelin*, counts forty editions from the first in 1485 (*Maistre Pierre Pathelin* (1953) p. viii). Febvre and Martin claim there were ninety-four editions of *Calisto y Melibea* during the period they evaluate (*Coming* 274, covering 1450–1800). They offer no evidence, but this number does not seem impossible, given my own rough count of forty-two editions-adaptations in various languages between *c.*1499 and 1599. On the Machiavelli and Bibbiena editions, see Andrews, *Scripts* 48. On editions of Bèze's *Abraham*, see Lazard, *Le Théâtre* 97. On the editions of Tasso's *Il re Torrismondo* in 1587, see Clubb, *Italian Drama* 191. Given the imprecision of the sources and the troubled definition of an "edition" or even a work (a translation, for instance, as opposed to a separate work), edition counts are naturally only approximate.

26. Rhodes counts 114 editions of Terence in the 15th century alone ("La Publication" 285); and see Howard-Hill, "Evolution" 130, for a count of 117 in the 15th century, and 533 in the 16th.

27. One might mention, among the numerous early productions whose texts were not printed: large-scale mysteries such as Eustache Mercadé's *Passion d'Arras* (*c.*1415, performed throughout the century), André de la Vigne's *Mystère de Saint Martin* (1496), or nearly 100 others known to have existed (Petit de Julleville, *Les Mystères* II:628–32); Jacques Milet's *Histoire de la destruction de Troie* (*c.*1450, also performed throughout the

century); the nearly two dozen Italian Plautus and Terence productions in Ferrara between 1486 and 1505 (see Andrews, *Scripts* 33, 48, 51; and Clubb, *Italian Plays* p. x); the anonymous dialect comedy *La Venexiana*; plays by Andrea Beolco and such "regular" dramatists as Giovanmaria Cecchi, Donato Giannotti, and Anton Francesco Grazzini.

28. See Lawrenson and Purkis, "Les Éditions" (esp. 14–16) on the extensive copying of woodcuts and imitation of illustrations in late 15th- and early 16th-century Terence and Plautus editions.

29. The Callot prints of Giulio Parigi's set designs for Andrea Salvadori's opera, *La liberazione di Tirreno e d'Arnea* (performed in 1617), are reproduced in Callot, *Callot's Etchings*. On Greuter's and Callot's careers, see Blumenthal, *Theater* pp. xv, 32–7, 93–135. On Jones's journey to Italy with Lord Arundel at the beginning of the 17th century, see Smith, "Italian" 203–4. Jones's copy of Serlio, annotated by his pupil John Webb, is in the Royal Institute of British Architects (reproduced in facsimile: Serlio, *Tutte l'opere*).

30. Fulwell, *Like* 65. Bevington has identified about twenty English plays from the 1530s to the 1570s "which are 'offered for acting,' that is, printed with casting lists to indicate how many actors are required to perform the play" (*'Mankind'* 5). Bevington's appendix (265–73) offers transcripts of the division of parts in these plays.

31. See Lebègue, "Le Répertoire" 15–18; introduction to Garnier, *Two Tragedies* 13; and Faivre, "La 'Profession'" 112. Similarly, when Valleran le Conte's troupe was performing in Rouen, Strasbourg, and Frankfurt in the early 1590s, it had in its repertoire Etienne Jodelle's and Louis Desmasures's plays, along with Garnier's *Les Juives*, Bèze's *Abraham sacrifiant*, and Gabriel Bounin's *La Soltane*, all of which had been printed between the 1550s and 1580s. See Lebègue, "Le Répertoire" 12, 14, and Deierkauf-Holsboer, *Vie* 26. Jodelle's *Cléopâtre captive* was published posthumously in his *Œuvres* in 1574. Bèze's *Abraham sacrifiant* was published in 1550, Desmasures's *Tragédies saintes* in 1563, Bounin's *La Soltane* in 1561, and Garnier's *Les Juives* in 1583.

32. The officials of Saint-Omer accorded "à (*nom laissé en blanc*) et ses compaignons joueurs de *comedies*, de representer au poeuple aulcunes *comedies* et *moralitez* dont ilz ont exhibé les livres imprimés" (qtd. Lebègue, "Le Répertoire" 12–13).

33. See Taylor, "*King Lear*" [Addendum] 485; Baskerville, "Prompt"; Sisson, "Shakespeare"; Mowat, "Theater" 213–14; and Greg, *Shakespeare* 161.

34. Middleton, *Mayor of Queenborough* in Middleton, *Works* II:103 (V.i.267–70) (written *c.*1616–20) (Aminadab's troupe is actually a band of pickpockets).

35. See, for instance, Chambers, *Mediaeval* II:216–17; Wickham, *Early*; Bevington, *'Mankind'*. While one might hesitate to make a strong argument about the impact of print on dramatic genres, it has been plausibly argued that the spread of writing and print had an impact on the decline of the mysteries, and it probably had an impact on genre and style in other ways. Chambers suggests that print may have been responsible for the concomitant decline of minstrelsy and rise of professional acting troupes (*Elizabethan* II:185–6). A. D. Mills argues that the requirement that the guilds deliver playscripts of the mystery cycles, to be recorded in the city "Register" from the 1460s or 1470s on, was a factor in the ultimate decline of the cycles: "the creation of a play-book may well signal the end of a cycle as a living art-form" (Mills, "Chester's" 4).

36. Albertino Mussato, "Ep. 7," col. 45, B; qtd. Greenfield, *Humanist* 85, 93n. (and see my discussion in Chapter 4).

37. My debt to the few studies devoted wholly to the history of dramatic publication is immense, but it has been a surprise to discover just how few these are, in what a frag-

mentary and piecemeal way the subject has been treated, how much dissension there is even among those working with the same theoretical presuppositions, and the extent to which the overarching assumptions of such studies have been (even on the Continent) shaped by the massive body of work on Shakespeare. There are, of course, many bibliographic studies of individual dramatic texts, numerous studies of the publication practices of individual dramatists, and sporadic references to dramatic printing in general histories of the drama or of printing and publishing, on all of which I have gratefully drawn.

NOTE ON EDITIONS, SPELLINGS, TRANSLATIONS, AND CITATIONS

1. As many scholars of the early modern text have noted, modern editions, often composites, tend to efface whatever seems unintelligible to the modern reader. See, for instance, Jeffrey Masten's discussion of his decision to use only early editions (*Textual* 10–11); and Leah Marcus's admonition about the transformations that take place in modern editing and the importance of what we might consider "deviance" in early editions (*Unediting*, esp. 5–19).

1. EXPERIMENTING ON THE PAGE, 1480–1630

1. On the Abbeville emissary, see Gréban, *Mystère de la passion* (1878 edn.) p. ii, and on medieval records and dramatic scribes generally, see Meredith, "Scribes."
2. See the illustrations of this manuscript of the *Mystère de la passion*, reproduced in Cohen, *Le Théâtre*, plates IX–XXXIX (manuscript 697 of the Bibliothèque d'Arras).
3. Examples are: the mid-14th-century Frankfurt Passion Play, for which we have only Baldemar von Peterweil's director's notes; and the directorial guide for the Amiens Passion Play (bought by Mons in 1501), which gives only the first and last lines of verse for each section, but detailed descriptions of movements, scenic effects, and musical interludes (see the *Livre de conduite du régisseur* and Froning, *Das Drama* 340–74). Some early Passion manuscripts contain the full text, with stage directions and other directorial effects and the times and places of performance, and full scripts could be a part of rehearsals. But most often (for the English cycles, for instance) scripts were divided into separate plays, each one given to a guild, and these sometimes divided into actors' parts (*Revels* I:40). Often it is unclear what uses may have been made of a given manuscript, as, for instance, with the *N-Town* manuscripts. On actors' parts, see *Revels* I:40; Greg, *Dramatic* I:173–5; and Runnals, "Actor's." On medieval dramatic texts generally, see Wickham, *Medieval* 55–60, 72–5, 78–84, 183–5.
4. On the spread of recreational and trade literacy in the 12th, 13th, and 14th centuries, and the development of the book trade in the 14th century, see, for instance, Parkes, *Scribes* 275–97; and Olson, *Literature*. Most of the "medieval" stage plans, working playtexts, contracts, and municipal or guild records and accounts that survive are from the late 15th and 16th centuries (see, for instance, those in Meredith and Tailby, eds., *Staging*), and many of the manuscripts that survive were made only in the 16th century, after the plays had ceased to be performed: the earliest extant copy of the Chester Cycle, for instance, is from 1591, sixteen years after its last recorded production.
5. The wedding of the Infanta María is described in Juan Cristóbal Calvete de Estrella's *El*

felicissimo viaje del muy alto y muy poderoso Principe don Philippe (see McKendrick, *Theatre* 39, 274); the *Cavalcade* in the *Recueil faict au vray* (1566).

6. Chambers, *Elizabethan* I:227.

7. "Joué à Angers moult triomphamment et somptueusement en l'an 1486 à la fin d'Août." Qtd. Faivre, "Le Théâtre" 71–2.

8. Robertson and Gordon, eds. *Calendar* 85 (referring to Dekker's 1612 Lord Mayor's pageant, *Troia-Nova Triumphans*; the £197 also covered actors' fees and costumes). See also Chambers, *Elizabethan* I:207, on "programmes" (actually masque descriptions: Chambers notes that there were no programmes in the modern sense in the 16th century, II:548); and II:547 on printed playbills as early as 1564. There is, however, no clear evidence that complete playbooks were sold in the theatre before the late 17th century.

9. "Nota q̃celluy q̃joue le personnage de dieu doit estre a ce cõmencement tout seul en paradis jusq̃s a ce q̃l ait cree les anges." *Le Tres excellẽt & sainct mystere* fol. 2ʳ.

10. Terence, *Comoediae* (1493) sig. Qiiiiᵛ; trans. Lawrenson and Purkis, "Les Éditions" 18.

11. "J'y avais pensé graver ta tragédie | En sanglant vermillon, signe de la furie, | Mais mon deuil n'a permis y mettre que du noir." La Péruse, *La Médée* (1986 edn.) 137.

12. It is difficult to generalize, but most of the pre-print dramatic manuscript facsimiles I have examined (among them: the 10th–15th-century Hroswitha manuscripts; the early 13th-century *Interludium de Clerico et Puella*; Eustache Mercadé's early 15th-century *Mystère de la Passion*; the Cornish *Ordinalia* plays, transcribed in the early 15th century; the *c.*1440 *Castle of Perseverance*; the mid-15th-century *La Passion Nostre Seigneur*; and the *York Plays*, late 1460s or 1470s) have the following features: space for decorative initial letters in the place of clear marking of beginnings and ends of plays (or little clear marking—where several plays have been copied together, a new play usually begins on the same page as the previous play); no title or merely an initial speech-heading indicating that the first speaker is about to speak (though a few early plays have descriptive titles indicating venue and, as in *The Castle of Perseverance*, a *dramatis personae*); no act or scene divisions; extended descriptive indications that a speaker is about to speak in the place of speech-prefixes (some early manuscripts have no speaker indications at all, or mere single initials placed mid-line, although a convention develops in the 15th century for right-margin, scribally contracted speech-prefixes in Latin); spacious margins (for commentary); rhyme brackets at the right and paraphs at the left to mark, primarily, stanza divisions, as in other poetic manuscripts; instead of the kind of prescriptive stage directions that would appear in the 16th century, descriptions of the action in Latin (without indication of entrances or exits); occasional use of "Amen" or "Finis" at the end of a play.

Play manuscripts produced after the spread of printing (the late 15th-century *N-Town Plays*; the *Towneley Cycle*, 1480–1525?; *Wisdom* and *Mankind*, *c.*1490–1500; *The Conversion of St. Paul, Mary Magdalen, Killing of the Children, Christ's Burial* and *Resurrection*, *c.*1510–20; and the *Chester Plays*, 1500–1607) preserve many of these features. But, influenced both by print and by the growth of professional theatre, and reflecting changes in the nature and conception of the dramatic text, they have new or newly emphasized features setting them apart from the earlier plays: clear titles (some have full title pages); strong marking of the beginnings of plays, often followed by a description of venue and performance; the specification of number and names of players required (from the mid-16th century on); the gradual diminishment of metrical or stanzaic markings, and an increase in markings used to differentiate speakers (speech-prefixes regularly set in the left margin and/or strongly marked with rulings; horizontal speech-separating rules; paraphs marking speaker divisions more commonly than stanza divisions); the syllabic abbreviation of speech-prefixes alongside the gradual disappearance of scribal abbreviations in the speeches proper, signifying the conventionalization of speech-prefixes; ruled stage directions, often in the vernacular and centred rather than in the right margin, yielding to a trend towards no stage directions at all in classical and professional plays. For facsimiles and descriptions, see: Haight, *Hroswitha*; *Non-Cycle Plays and the Winchester Dialogues*; Cohen, *Le Théâtre*; Norris, *Ancient*; *Macro Plays*; *La Passion Nostre Seigneur* 17–22; *York Play*; *N-Town Plays*; *Towneley Cycle*; *Digby Plays*; *Chester Mystery*. By the late 16th century, play manuscripts essentially follow the format of printed plays (see the discussion of the many full-length manuscripts copied from printed books in Lutz, *Essays* 129–38). For important discussions confirming many of my own observations, see T. H. Howard-Hill, "Evolution," arguing for the impact of both print and professional theatre on the dramatic *mise en page*; and Graham Runnals' *Études* (pp. 367–89), with its invaluable typology of medieval play manuscripts, classified according to theatrical use.

13. On the continuity between manuscript and print production, see Bühler, *Fifteenth-Century*; Hirsch, *Printing* and *Printed* essay XV; and Blake, "Manuscript" 403–32. Manuscript books were generally, by the 13th century, created in two parts—the principal text written out first and the rubrics and initials written afterwards by specialists. When 15th-century books were printed, many were intended to be hand rubricated. On the separate work of rubricators in the production of late-medieval books, see Saenger, "Books." On Renaissance composite books—in which manuscript sections were bound with printed sections—see Saenger and Heinlen, "Incunable"; and, for some later examples, see Woudhuysen, *Sir Philip Sidney*.

14. Terence, *Comoediae* (1476 edn.) (hand foliation in Folger Library copy, fol. 5^r).

15. Rastell, *Nature* sig. E5^r. See also the four blank music bars on sig. E7^r.

16. Medieval editors had devised methods of punctuation and word division that made the reading of texts significantly easier, but even after conventions for word division and punctuation were in place, punctuation continued to be in flux. Texts continued to conserve space by running words, lines, and works together, in part to conserve paper, which became regularly available only in the first century of print (Rasmuseen, *Transition* 12–13). According to Parkes, however, print created rapid developments in punctuation in the 16th century (*Pause* 50–61, 87–92).

17. As Eisenstein comments, Steinberg and Hirsch may overstate the novelty of title pages in printed books (some humanist quattrocento manuscripts had title pages), but they were regularly used only after print (Eisenstein, *Printing* 52; Steinberg, *Five* 105–16; Hirsch, *Printing* 25 and *Printed* essay XV). Hirsch dates the earliest ones from the 1470s, and says they became a regular feature in the 1520s (*Printed* essay XVII). Very few English plays before the late 16th century have title pages and many 17th-century cheap chapbook-style plays are published without them (in Spain, they are abandoned in the 17th century (Cruickshank, "Editing" 74)), but most larger-than-pamphlet-size plays have separate title pages by the beginning of the 16th century. On the development of the use of printers' ornaments, simplified initial letters, and marginal notes in the English printed drama, see Greg, *Bibliography* I:321. On the development of running heads and tables of contents (as well as marginal identification of arguments) during the shift from monastic to scholastic reading in the 12th and 13th centuries, see Parkes, *Scribes* 19–33. Running heads appear even in some very early editions (Wimpheling's *Stilpho* of 1495, for instance), but grow more common in later editions. Steinberg

identifies the use of catchwords with print (*Five* 107). See Richardson (*Print* 26, 36, 39, 48, 55, 183) on the evolution in the conventional uses of foliation, white space, format, typefaces, annotation, indexes, and appendices in Italian literary books generally from the late 15th- to the mid-16th century.

18. In the early 16th century, some printers in southern Europe and almost all printers in northern Europe used black letter for vernacular works, though even roughly printed works like the first *Everyman* often used roman for Latin passages (in stage directions, for instance). Early 16th-century printers in both northern and southern Europe often used a heavy roman for Latin works, sometimes in combination with italic (for both text and commentary) and with occasional use of black letter (often in red ink) for emphasis, as on the first page of the 1505 Venice *Tragoediae Senecae*. Occasionally Italian printers used black letter alone (as in Dovizi, *Cõmedia* (1521 edn.)), but the norm in Italy was roman for both Latin and vernacular works. Once in a while, italic was used for an entire text, particularly if the editor wished to emphasize its poetic qualities (the 1538 Italian vernacular Terence *Comedie* is an example), but heavy roman tends to dominate. By the third quarter of the 16th century in Spain and the 1590s in England, black letter was outmoded (except for emphasis), though it continued to be used in Germanic countries for vernacular texts, which usually use roman or italic for non-Germanic words. Confirming my own general observations on changes in *mise en page* and typography are: Martin *et al.*, eds., *Histoire* I:480; Howard-Hill, "Evolution"; the visuals in Greg, *Bibliography* (especially I:157–274); Cruickshank, "Editing" 71; and discussions with Peter Blayney.

19. "Table indiciaire du premier volume des Actes des Apostres pour trouver par ordre les faictz | actes | miracles | conversions | martires | y passiõs des sainctz Apostres … selon les chapitres | et la matiere que on vouldra demander." Gréban [?], *Le premier* (1537 edn.) I, sig. Ai^r. Other examples include: Terence, *Terentius comico* (1503); Encina, *Cancionero* (1509); Terence, *P. Terentii Comoediae* (1521); *Le tres excellẽt & sainct mystere* (1542); Sachs, *Gedicht* (1558–78); Cervantes, *Ocho comedias* (1615); and Ayrer, *Opus Thaeatricum* (1618). While some of these features are found in late-medieval manuscripts, they do not become regular features of books until after printing. According to Parkes, "before 1400 foliation was extremely rare in manuscripts, and even after 1450 it was largely limited to a few scriptoria" (*Scribes* 253). Where many editions printed before the 1530s or so have no page numbering at all, most editions after that time have either foliation (often using roman numerals), or (increasingly) pagination.

20. "In piu commoda forma redotta" (Rojas, *Celestina* (1525) title page). See similarly Beolco, *Tutte* (1584) sig. A9^r; and Vitruvius, *I dieci* (1567).

21. Prynne, *Histriomastix* (1633) fol. **7^a ("To the Christian Reader").

22. There are at least fifteen duodecimo editions of Garnier's tragedies between 1580 and 1618. The importance of the printing of major English play collections in folio has become a critical truism (see, for instance, Bentley, *Profession of Dramatist* 251; and Murray, *Theatrical* 53), but English miscellanies that included plays, like their continental counterparts, had varied formats. See, for instance, George Gascoigne's variously titled quarto *Whole Woorkes* of 1587, Samuel Daniel's two quarto, three octavo, one 16mo and three duodecimo collections between 1594 and 1623, the gathering of Shakespeare's plays printed by William Jaggard and Thomas Pavier in 1619 in quarto (on this, see Kastan, *Shakespeare* 84, Greg, "On Certain" and *Shakespeare* 9–14), Lyly's duodecimo *Six Court Comedies* of 1632, the two octavo editions of Marston's *Workes* in 1633, and Nabbes *Plays, Masques, Epigrams, Elegies, and Epithalamiums* in quarto in 1639.

23. This evaluation is based on: Greg, *Bibliography* (about 87 per cent in quarto, but almost all others in octavo and duodecimo); Cruickshank, "Editing" 55 (before 1550, Spanish plays were most commonly in folio, but after that quarto became almost universal); Kirsop, "Le Théâtre" 97 (the normal format for first editions of plays in France was octavo until about 1635); and my own examination of texts (almost twice as many Terence octavos as folios in 16th-century Italy; a strong preponderance of octavos in vernacular Italian plays).

24. See Martin, *Le Livre* 256 on Charles Estienne's role in the French adoption of the *mise en page* of Latin drama around 1630; and, for examples of "arguments," see Bidermann, *Ludi*; and the examples in Franchi, *Drammaturgia*. It is worth recalling here that England and Spain are generally considered to have been printing backwaters from the 15th to the 17th centuries, and that the quality of English and Spanish books is considered to be markedly inferior to those produced in Germany, Italy, France, and the Low Countries during the period, with German books declining in quality in the 17th century (see Febvre and Martin, *Coming* 190–7; and Gaskell, *New* 171). This certainly has some bearing on the printing of the drama: there are, for instance, no 16th-century English dramatic collections comparable to the elegant German, Italian, and French collections of the 16th century, and the Spanish collections appear (even to the untrained eye) inferior in typography and paper quality. But the development of a well-organized and prolific professional theatre in England and Spain in the late 16th century and the strong traditions of scholarly and sacred drama elsewhere, which I will discuss below, probably had more impact on regional differences.

25. *Comedia llamada Eufemia* (written *c*.1542–54, published in 1567) "en la cual se introduzen las personas baxo escriptas." Rueda, *Las Cuatro* 75.

26. *Non-Cycle Plays and Fragments* 54 (*Abraham and Isaac* l. 383). A slightly different example of the same phenomenon can be found in the Digby manuscript of *Mary Magdalen* (*c*.1515–25), in which the stage directions indicating the people's response to the "Inperator's" request for assent are not scribally separated from the people's speech: "Here answerryt all [th]e pepul at onys: [y]a, my lord, [y]a!" (*Mary Magdalen* 25).

27. *Everyman* (1961) 1 (l. 22).

28. "Domitilla fa oratione, e dice …"; "Domitilla voltandosi a' sua servi dice. …" Pulci, *La Rapresentatione di Santa Domitilla* (1594) sig. Av^r.

29. "1. Reg.4.c."; "Der einsidel fraget dẽ jünglĩg"; "Der jünglĩg ãtword." Gengenbach, *Die [Zehn] alter* sig. A3^v–A4^r.

30. "Herr Hans von Clum laufft zornig zum Babst … Und sagt inn gegenwertigkeit der Cardinele. Heilger Vater. …" Agricola, *Tragedia* sig. Ciii^r.

31. For early classical examples of run-on lines with abbreviated speech-prefixes, see Terence, *Comoediae* (1493), Aristophanes, *Aristophanis* (1498), and Terence, *Terence* (1598 edn.).

32. For examples of biblical or scholarly marginal citations in vernacular editions, see Gengenbach's *Die [Zehn] alter*; Terence, *Terence* (1598 edn.); and Spangenberg, *Jeremia*. On dramatic marginalia in Jonson and Dekker, see Tribble *Margins* 130–57; Slights, "Bodies"; and Jowett, "'Fall.'"

33. It is worth noting that while scenic divisions clearly served theatrical functions in the drama, when formal dramatic poetics came to prescribe them, they became identified with act divisions: literary-structural devices seen as necessary to classical form. On the theatricality of scene divisions (as opposed to act divisions), see Greg, *Dramatic* 210–13. Greg argues that playhouse stage plots tended *not* to mark scenes but to mark acts, since

scenes were natural and so would inevitably be recognized by entrances and exits (acts were artificial and so would have to be marked if they were to be recognized by the actors). Whether or not this was the case, the marking of acts and scenes in printed texts is highly variable, but as a rule, texts clearly theatrical in nature or texts that place a strong emphasis on theatrical experience often mark scenes without marking acts, whereas texts highly conscious of their classical inheritances mark both acts and scenes.

34. "Vranio Pastore inamorato di Ardelia"; "Mirtilla Ninfa inamorata di Vranio." Isabella Andreini, *Mirtilla* (1588) sig. *4ᵛ ("Interlocutori"). Unusually, printed editions might give the names of the actual actors, as the 1616 Jonson *Workes*, with its lists of "the principall Comoedians," does. See also, in the Shakespeare first folio, "The Names of the Principall Actors in all these Playes," with Shakespeare at the head (Shakespeare, *Mr. William Shakespeares*, (1623 edn.) sig. *A8ʳ*).

35. Skelton, *Magnyfycence* (1533) fols. xxviiʳ, xxivʳ (misfoliated). It is generally agreed that the edition is Rastell's. It is possible that the stage directions in the play are not Skelton's but the printer's. Skelton died in 1529, but had been a friend of the Rastells. Modern editors treat the *c.*1530 folio as definitive, and do not distinguish the stage directions from the rest of the text. For a helpful discussion, see Johnson, "Stage."

36. Rastell, *Nature* sig. E4ᵛ (slightly modernized). On Bale's attribution of *The Four Elements* to Rastell, see Wilson, *English* 224.

37. *Gammer* (1575) sig. B3ʳ.

38. *David*: "Mon teint terni, livide et jaunastrement blanc | Montre que je nourri du souffre dans le sang. ..." *Sara*: Mardochee is "tout difforme de crasse." *Rachel*: He has "L'estomac pantelant tout à nud découvert." Montchrestien, *Les Tragédies* (1891 edn.) 204, 255.

39. "Le Dieu Pan vestu en Satyre, envelopé d'un mandillet de toile d'or, ayant une couronne d'or sur sa teste, & tenant en sa main gauche un baston noüailleux & espineux, & en la droite ses flageolets ou tuyaux dorez ... A l'autre bout de la salle ... fut faict un jardin artificiel ... embelli de toutes diversitez de fleurs, & aussi de fraizes, concombres, melons [avec] Circé enchanteresse ... vestue d'une robe d'or, de deux couleurs ... ses garnitures de teste, col & bras, estans merveilleusement enrichies de pierreries & perles d'inestimable valeur. ... En ce jardin ... estoyent cent flambeaux de cire blanche, rendans telle lueur & lustre (tant à la fee qu'au jardin)." Beaujoyeulx, *Balet* (1582 edn.) fol. 5ʳ–7ʳ; trans. Beaujoyeulx, *Le Balet* (1971 edn.) 33, 38–40 (trans. modified).

40. Daniel, *Complete* III:187, 189.

41. It is often impossible to identify a single agent responsible for publication, and evidence as to provenance is spare: there are few early contracts involving the publication of plays at all. For one example, see that between the printer Joan Luschner and the bookbinder Luís Palou in Barcelona in 1502 for a book containing the plays *Safira* and *Galatea* (in Madurell and Balaguer, eds., *Documentos* 347–8).

42. Gengenbach printed, in addition to *Totenfresser*, his own *Die Zehn alter* (*c.*1515), *Die Gauchmalt* (*c.*1516), and *Der Nollhart* (*c.*1517). For a discussion of Rastell in this context, see Walker, *Politics* 10, 16–18.

43. See Frankish's introduction in Bèze, *Abraham* (1969 edn.).

44. See Westfall, *Patrons* 122, and White, *Theatre* 72–3 (on printers who specialized in Reformation literature, including plays, and on the role that Tudor theatrical patrons may have played in bringing plays to the press).

45. Preface to John Cooke, *Greene's Tu Quoque* (1614) 3. There were frequent dedications from family members, that of Baccio Cecchi, for instance, in his 1589 dedication of his father Giovanni Maria's *L'Esaltazione della Croce*, "ridotta da lui in atto rappresentativo, (con gl'Intermedi,) ne gli ultimi anni della sua vita" (Cecchi, *L'Esaltazione* sig. a2ᵛ). Francesco Bracciolini dell'Api offers a typical claim, in the preface to his pastoral, *L'amoroso sdegno* (1598), that a friend gave it to the printer (see Clubb, *Italian Plays* 52).

46. See, for instance, the editors' and publishers' prefatory material in: Aretino's *Quattro* (1588); Lope de Rueda's *Las Cuatro* (1567); and La Péruse's *La Médée* (*c*.1554–6).

47. "La prego a compiacermi ... favorendo della sua gratia il presente volume delle comedie del virtuosissimo messer Giovanmaria Cecci, nelle quali ... la vedrà chiaramente, quanto l'Auttor di esse sia stato sempre copioso d'inventione, di gratia, & di vivacità poetica." Cecchi, *Comedie* (1585) sig. +2ʳ.

48. *Ad Emptorem*: "Wer diß Buch kaufft, wird sich drob freuen, | Sein Gelt ihn nimmermehr gereuen." Ayrer, *Ayrers* I:15.

49. Shakespeare, *Mr. William Shakespeares* (1623 edn.) sig. A3ʳ.

50. Due to the fact that most of the material available is from the English theatre, parts of my discussion in this section are skewed towards England, but I have tried, as much as possible, to offer the broader view. In treating the publication of plays from the English professional theatres, I am indebted to Bentley, *Profession of Dramatist* (264–92) and Blayney, "Publication."

51. Shakespeare, Heywood, Jonson, Rowley, Field, Wilson, Munday, and perhaps Webster were simultaneously professional dramatists and at least sometime actors. In France (where there were fewer professional playwrights), Alexandre Hardy and Mathieu Le Febvre ("Laporte") were also similarly simultaneously dramatists and sometime actors. Such *commedia dell'arte* actors as Nicolò Barbieri, Pier Maria Cecchini, Angelo Beolco, Isabella and Francesco Andreini, Silvio Fiorillo, and Marco Napolioni also wrote full-length plays for performance. (Lea, *Italian* II:462–4 lists about sixteen printed plays by *commedia dell'arte* actors before 1630.) In Spain most Renaissance playwrights were clerics, but manager-actors like Andrés de Claramonte could also be company dramatists. The Spanish term for company manager (always also an actor), "autor," suggests the shared and overlapping enterprise of actor and author (see Rennert, *Spanish* 190).

52. A list of English playwrights who oversaw the publication of at least some of their own plays during this period would include Chapman, Daniel, Day, Ford, Heywood, Jonson, Marston, Massinger, Middleton, Shirley, and Webster. A list (not close to exhaustive) of continental dramatists who were writing for the stage and who saw plays to the press between the 1580s and 1630s would include: Cervantes, Lope de Vega, Tirso de Molina, Guillén de Castro, Juan Ruiz de Alarcón, Guarini, Della Porta, Tasso, Isabella Andreini, Prospero Bonarelli, Pescetti, Garnier, Larivey, Montchrestien, Hardy, Bidermann, and Opitz. On payments from publishers, see below.

53. "Mereciesen salir de las tinieblas"; "él me las pagó razonablemente." Cervantes, *Obras* II:159–60 (*Ocho comedias*, Prológo al lector).

54. Massinger, *Plays* I:215.

55. Marston, *Plays* I:139. D. F. McKenzie understands "setting forth" here to refer to "both a financial venture and a careful display of dedication and the text" (McKenzie, "Speech-Manuscript-Print" 103). Marston says that his absence has made it impossible for him to oversee press correction, implying that such "setting forth" would normally

have involved such oversight. See also his preface to a 1606 edition of *The Faune* (1606): "I have been my owne setter out" (Marston, *Plays* II:143).

56. See the prefatory material to: Heywood's *The Rape of Lucrece* (1608), *The Golden Age* (1611), *Four Prentises of London* (1615), and *Play of Queene Elizabeth* (1637); the Shakespeare first folio (1623); Lope de Vega's *El Peregrino en su Patria* (1603), *Doze comedias* (*Novena parte*, 1618), *Trezena parte* (1620), *Décimaquinta parte* (1621), *Décimaséptima parte* (1621), and *La Dorotea* (1632); Guillén de Castro's *La primera parte* (1621). On the unauthorized printing of Ariosto's *La Cassaria* and *I Suppositi* in *c.*1509–10, see Rhodes, "Printer." On the unauthorized printing of Mairet's *Chryséide et Arimand* in 1630, see Bunch, *Jean Mairet* 16. For further examples, see the prefatory material in Marston's *Malcontent* (1604); Middleton's *Family of Love* (1608); Robert Armin's *Two Maids of Moreclack* (1699); Chapman's *Widow's Tears* (1612); Honorat de Bueil Racan's *Bergeries* (1625); and Juan Pérez de Montalvan's *Comedias* (1635).

57. A discussion of manuscript copying in, for, and around the playhouse would require another book, but a few points may clarify the nature of the theatrical texts that ended up in printers' hands, and the continuing centrality of manuscript playtexts long after plays were being regularly printed. Companies relied on professional copyists (along with writers and actors) for fair copies of plays from the author's "foul papers," for new copies from the theatrically annotated fair copy, for licensing or bookkeeper's copies or for actors' parts (like Edward Alleyn's for Orlando in Robert Greene's *Orlando Furioso* (1591), emended by Alleyn himself). Since there might be several versions of the dramatist's foul papers, and several dramatists (working together or working consecutively on revisions), and since a heavily revised playtext might require extensive revision and subsequent recopying, it is a mistake to think of the author's version as completely distinct from the company's working manuscript (as many have in trying to identify the "source" of a printed version for the purposes of producing an authorial edition). When Lope de Vega needed copies of his plays for publication, he got them from the actors (see Morley and Bruerton, "How Many?" 225–6). He also makes it clear that actors and managers were the origin of many of the free-floating copies from which the unauthorized editions of his plays were printed (see the preface to Vega Carpio, *Decima Septima Parte* (1621)). There was extensive copying and recopying in the theatre, by professional scribes, by dramatists, by actors (categories that sometimes overlapped). Since companies often traded working manuscripts (the *commedia dell'arte* troupes regularly swapped their unprinted scenarios), these might be further revised by the new owners to suit their needs. Actors moving to new companies sometimes brought manuscript plays they owned, which became part of the negotiations for their employment, as when Jerónimo Lopez de Sustaya and his wife made a contract in 1602 with the manager Antonio Granado to act in Granado's company for two years and to give Granado "the comedias which he may have, and among them the following four: *San Reymundo*, *Los Caballeros nuevos*, *La Fuensanta de Cordoba*, and *El Trato de la Aldea*," which they had "bought from the poets who had written them, paying ... money for them" (qtd. Rennert, *Spanish* 190). Philip Henslowe similarly bought numerous manuscript plays for the Lord Admiral's company between 1598 and 1602 at about £2 apiece (see Bentley, *Profession of Dramatist* 82–4).

On company playtexts generally, see Long, "'Precious'"; Greg, *Dramatic* 192–221; and Greg, "Prompt." On the *Orlando* part book, see Greg, *Dramatic* 176–87. On *commedia* scenario trading, see Richards and Richards, *Commedia* 93. On the extensive English trade in play manuscripts between the 1580s and 1630s, see Bentley, *Profession of*

Dramatist 82–7. On the manuscript "book" of *Sir Thomas More*, see McMillin, *Elizabethan*, especially 74–84.

58. Beaumont and Fletcher, *Comedies* sig. A3ʳ; and see Chapter 6.

59. In England, one needed only the permission of the Stationers' Company to publish. See Blayney, "Publication" 396–403, on the legal status of unpublished play manuscripts, and Chapter 11.

60. See Pollard, *Shakespeare's Fight*, for the definitive version of this tale. Few scholars still believe Pollard's version of the traitor-actor theory (extrapolated from the preface to the first folio via Jonson, Malone, and others). See, centrally, Blayney, "Publication"; Kastan, "From Manuscript"; and most of the essays in Taylor and Warren, eds., *Division*.

61. See Andrews, *Scripts* 252 on Ariosto's letter to the Duke of Urbino (17 Dec. 1532).

62. "Tous les comédiens de la campagne en ont des copies, et … beaucoup se sont vantés qu'ils en obligeraient un imprimeur." Rotrou, *La Bague* 732.

63. Both Maguire (*Shakespearean* 337) and Jackson ("Fluctuating" 331) offer caveats against extrapolating memorial reconstruction from internal evidence, since memorial reconstruction could produce texts with fewer errors than those of hasty authors revising quickly with a view to performance, and since what seems to be oral reporting may be merely phonetic spelling. According to G. I. Duthie, *Elizabethan*, there is no evidence that stenography was responsible for any of the "bad" quartos. A similar caveat might be offered against extrapolating it from external evidence, since a general *mythology* about memorial reconstruction does not mean it was actually practised. However, several recent discussions offer extensive evidence and convincing arguments in favour of the (still controversial) theory of memorial and shorthand reconstruction by either actors or members of the audience: Davidson, "'Some'" (describing improvements in the technology of shorthand); Chartier, "Publishing" [lecture 2, "Copied onely by the eare"]; and Maguire, *Shakespearean* 101–2 (citing Chapman, the Heywood passage mentioned below, Robert Taylor's *The Hog Hath Lost his Pearl* (1614), in which a character accuses a player of having learned his play by heart in order to pass it on to the playhouse poet, and testimony of theatre-goers who use "table-books" for copying dramatic material).

64. Heywood, *Dramatic* V:163, I:191 (*Rape of Lucrece* and *If You Know Not Me*). It is worth noting that, according to Madeleine Doran, there is no solid internal evidence of stenographic reproduction here (though there is considerable evidence of memorial reconstruction), and it is unlikely that Heywood would, in any case, have known anything of the conditions of the text's reproduction (Heywood, *If You* pp. xv–xvii). The accusation of stenographic reporting may have been a way for Heywood to explain how a "surreptitious" edition got into print without seeming to blame any of the obvious parties (actors, friends for whom copies had been made, or, possibly, the playwright himself).

65. "El hurtar las Comedias estos que llama el vulgo, al uno, *Memorilla*, y al otro, *Gran Memoria*: los quales con algunos versos que aprenden, mezclan infinitos suyos barbaros, con que ganan la vida, vendiendolas a los pueblos, y autores extramuros, gente vil, sinofieio, y que muchas vezes han estado presos." Vega Carpio, *Trezena parte* π4ʳ ("Prologo"); trans. Rennert, *Life* 272. In 1615, Cristobal Suárez de Figueroa similarly describes the practice of one of his contemporaries, Luis Remirez de Arellano: "Este toma de memoria una comedia entera de tres vezes que la oye, sin discrepar un punto en traça y versos. Aplica el primer dia a la disposicion; el segundo a la variedad de la composicion; y el tercero a la puntualidad de las coplas. Deste modo encomienda a

la memoria las comedias que quiere." Suárez de Figueroa, *Plaza Universal* fol. 237ʳ (Discurso 58). See also Schevill, *Dramatic* 126, which mentions a manuscript copy from the first third of the 17th century made by Luis Ramírez de Arellano, Suárez de Figueroa's memorizer.

66. Chapman, *Plays* I:235.

67. To make an accurate count for any country (let alone all countries) would be impossible, given the definitional difficulties alone (the instability of the genre, the instability of the identity of individual plays, the instability of the nature of an "edition"). Most of the dramatic bibliographies that do exist are archaic, and the computerized national catalogues (still incomplete) do not have the capacity to make genre-sensitive counts. But the existing lists of English performed and printed drama nonetheless offer an opportunity for counts that are, if limited, revealing. Greg's *Bibliography* shows 440 plays printed up to 1630 (the number would be larger were Greg to count re-editions and quasi-dramatic pieces). Of these, only twenty-eight were printed in the first four decades of English play publication (*c.*1510–50), seventy-one were printed in the next four decades (1551–90), and 341 were printed in the next four decades (1591–1630), registering a tremendous leap, then, after about 1590. In the decade roughly preceding the closing of the theatres (1631–40), 163 plays were printed, which (if publication had continued steady in the three decades after the closing of the theatres) would have meant the printing of at least 652 plays during the four-decade period 1631–70, approximately double the preceding period. Blayney, "Publication" 384–5 (including only full-length plays written for professional public performance between 1583 and 1642) counts ninety-six plays in the two decades between 1583 and 1602, 115 new plays in the next two decades (1603–22), and 160 new plays in the next two decades (1623–42). Both counts attest to a significant increase in play publication: slow and steady in Blayney's evaluation, substantial in Greg's.

The difference between the percentage of performed plays printed in the approximately forty years before the Interregnum (even assuming many printed plays from this period have been lost) and the percentage of performed plays printed in the approximately forty years after the Restoration (to take these as not-so-arbitrary periods of comparison) is striking. According to an analysis of Harbage, *Annals* (admittedly a flawed source), approximately 41 per cent of all plays produced in England were printed in the four decades between 1601 and 1640, whereas approximately 80 per cent of all plays produced in England to 1700 were printed in the four decades between 1661 and 1700 (a number that includes school plays and counts "lost" plays as unprinted, despite the possibility that some were in fact printed, but that does not include re-editions, which flooded the English book market after the Restoration, substantially increasing the number of printed plays in the later period). For an estimate that 30 per cent of the plays performed in London were printed 1576–1642, see Saeger and Fassler, "London" 67. In most places, edition sizes for general-interest books (including plays) were restricted in the 16th and 17th centuries to 1,000–2,000 copies, and rarely did they go higher, even in the absence of restriction. See Feather, *History* 94; Martin, *Le Livre* 213; Febvre and Martin, *Coming* 219; Bergman, "Calderón." Normal edition sizes throughout the period ranged from about 500 to 2000 copies, with drama probably on the low end. (See, for instance, the estimate that a normal print run for the drama might be 500–600 copies: Walker, *Politics* 13.) But there was a general increase in plays printed paralleling the general (if inconsistent) increase in titles published throughout the 16th century (according to H. S. Bennett a doubling in book production between 1558 and the 1580s, and a steady increase thereafter (Bennett, *English* 269–71)).

68. See Chambers, *Elizabethan* III:106. For a slightly earlier period, see White, *Theatre* 71–2 (noting that comparatively few English Protestant playscripts made it into print).

69. Aubrun, *La Comédie* p. v.

70. Morley and Bruerton ("How Many?") discuss Lope's exaggerated claims, and estimate (on the basis of Lope's *Peregrino* lists and extant plays) a number of about 800. See also their examination of attributions, *Chronology*. Barrera y Leirado (*Catálogo* 424) identifies a total of 608 plays extant or listed in Lope's *Peregrino* lists. My very rough estimate that almost half of Lope's plays remained unpublished during his lifetime, based on a compilation of the sources listed above, may somewhat overcount unpublished plays but it yields a percentage that roughly corresponds to the 40 per cent of plays listed in the *Peregrino* lists but no longer extant, probably never published (see Morley and Bruerton, "How Many?" 232). Murray (*Theatrical* 225) and Willison ("Editorial" 111) stress the uniqueness of the English disjunction between dramatist and publisher, arguing that in the rest of Europe there was a stronger connection between dramatist and publisher. This may be to overstress the differences. Much of the drama being performed by French and Italian troupes in the late 16th and early 17th centuries was printed, but so was its English counterpart. It is true that grand collections of Aretino's plays, Lope de Rueda's, Hans Sachs's, or Garnier's (to mention just a few) appeared in the 16th century, and that Jonson's *Workes* was perceived as an innovation in 1616. But there were dignified English authorial collections that included plays published in the 16th century—Gascoigne's 1587 *Whole Woorkes* (with *Supposes*, *Jocasta*, and the masque at Kenelworth), to name one. Many of the professional playwrights in France, Spain, and Germany did not begin to have their dramatic works published until the 1620s or 1630s (for instance, Hardy, Tirso de Molina, Lope de Vega, Ayrer). Willison, for instance, writes that there was "no ... editorial problem in Corneille" comparable to that in Shakespeare ("Editorial" 111), but Corneille's career began only after Shakespeare's death, and by the time he published his first collection (1644), playwrights were regularly seeing their own work to the press.

71. Heywood, *Dramatic* I:ix. Like Lope de Vega and Tirso de Molina (who claimed to have written 400, though only about eighty are extant (Wilson, *Tirso* 40–1; McKendrick, *Theatre* 72)), Heywood may be exaggerating, but his failure to publish regularly in the early years is typical of "attached" company dramatists like Fletcher, Shakespeare, Massinger, Brome, and Shirley, as has been documented by Bentley (*Profession of Dramatist* 275, 279, 280). Only nine of Fletcher's approximately sixty-nine plays were published during his lifetime, only one with his participation. Only twenty of Shakespeare's thirty-seven plays were published during his lifetime, none unequivocally with his active participation.

72. Deierkauf-Holsboer, *Vie* 139–40 (treating the number 600 as credible).

73. Given the wide variation in practices, it is difficult to generalize, but a six- or seven-year delay between performance and publication was typical of the earlier 16th century (the delay between the performance of Aretino's *Il Marescalco* and its publication, for instance), and a delay of twenty years or more wasn't unusual (the delay between the performance of Jodelle's *Cléopâtre captive* and its publication). I have not done a systematic study and, since delays between performance and publication vary so widely, any average would be meaningless. A few further examples, however, may be helpful. John Heywood's *Playe called the foure P.P.* was performed in 1520 at court and published twenty years later. Giraldi's *Cleopatra tragedia*, written about 1541 for Duke Ercole II d'Este and performed at his court, was published in 1583, forty-two years later. Similar

delays for the later 16th century and early 17th century were not unusual, though delays of a few years were more common for regularly practising playwrights working closely with specific theatres. Some of Lope de Vega's plays from the 1590s and 1610s were not published until 1620 or later, when he began himself to issue the *Partes* of his works, though some were printed in earlier *Partes* not authorized by him. By the time Jean Mairet was writing regularly for the Hôtel de Bourgogne and Théâtre du Marais in the 1620s and 1630s, his plays normally took two or three years to get to the press. Mairet's first play, *Chryséide et Arimand* (performed in 1625 at the Hôtel de Bourgogne) was published without his consent five years later. His second play, *Sylvie* (performed in 1626) was published six years later. The rest of his plays were published between one and four years after their first performance, most often after a two- or three-year delay. On Giraldi's *Cleopatra* and Jodelle's *Cléopâtre captive*, see Hill and Morrison's introduction to: Garnier, *Two Tragedies* 5–6, 14. On Mairet, see Bunch, *Jean Mairet*, "Chronology" (unpaginated).

74. Printed plays, of course, could also eventually be "lost": see Greg, *Bibliography* II:959–1008; IV: pp. viii–x, on the approximately 200 plays printed between about 1510 and 1660 of which no surviving copy exists. See also Lebègue, "Le Répertoire" 21, on the many French farces that were printed and are now lost. Nonetheless, most of the plays listed in Harbage (*Annals*) as lost (about 60 per cent of the plays written between 1576 and 1642) were apparently never printed (Saeger and Fassler, "London" 67).

75. Beaumont and Fletcher, *Comedies* sig. A4ʳ ("Stationer to the Readers"). See also Albright (*Dramatic* 293) on the manuscript of Middleton's unprinted *The Witch*, which he only with difficulty managed to get back from a friend.

76. Jonson, *Ben Jonson* II:274n. La Calprenède, *La Mort* (145): "Ce ne fut jamais mon dessein de faire imprimer des œuvres que jusqu'ici je n'avais avouées qu'à mes particuliers amis. Mais ayant assez imprudemment prêté mon manuscrit à des personnes à qui je ne le pouvais refuser sans incivilité, quinze jours après j'en vis trente copies."

77. According to Love, scribal publication normally operated at a lower volume than print publication, but not always: one 15th-century scriptorium, for instance, got an order for 400 copies of a university text, as compared to the 250 to 500 copies normal for early printed editions (*Scribal* 37–8, and see 128 on scribal efficiency; and, for further details on scribal publication in England in a slightly earlier period, see Woudhuysen, *Sir Philip Sidney*).

78. Love, *Scribal* 75. On the simultaneous and often independent circulation of manuscript and printed copies, see Barker, "Manuscript."

79. Qtd. Middleton, *Works* VII:3. On the scribal publication of Middleton's *A Game at Chess* generally, see Butler, *Theatre* 105; and Love, *Scribal* 68.

80. Shakespeare, *History of King Henry the Fourth as revised by Sir Edward Dering*; cited Orgel, "Acting" 253.

81. Torres Naharro, *Propalladia* II:129; see Shergold, *History* 149.

82. On Crane, see Howard-Hill, "Shakespeare's." On *Bonduca*, see Greg, "Prompt."

83. Blayney shows just how little demand there was for playbooks in England, comparing the yearly number of plays published to the yearly number of total books published in England between 1583 and 1642 (Blayney, "Publication" 385). Even were one to include re-editions (based on Greg's numbers (*Bibliography*)), playbooks still made up only about 2 per cent of the total of printed English books between 1583 and 1642.

84. See Prynne, *Histriomastix* sig. ***2ᵛ, 307, 309 (and throughout); and Hackel, "'Rowme'" 117 (on Prynne's preoccupation with play readers).

85. See the generic classification for early Venetian editions in Richardson, *Print* 28; the figures for European incunabula in Febvre and Martin, *Coming* 220, 249; and the observation that law, theology, and classics dominate early Venetian printing (Lowry, *World* 21–2). Unfortunately, I have been able to base my observations for the 16th and 17th centuries only on my general impressions from the available bibliographies.

86. Febvre and Martin mention that the 1493 Lyons Terence "was alone reissued 31 times" before 1517 (*Coming* 265; see also Pollard and Redgrave, *Short-Title* 390–1; and Lowry, *Nicholas Jenson* 197–8). In the absence of any definite knowledge of edition sizes, it is, of course, impossible to know whether numbers of editions reflect numbers of sales, but it is a likely indicator.

87. Blayney lists the eleven plays that had the greatest number of editions in a span of twenty-five years after their first date of publication. If one includes closet and academic plays, Shakespeare's *Henry IV, part 1* (1598) ranks fourth, with seven editions, his *Richard III* (1597) ranks fifth, with five editions, and his *Richard II* (1597) ranks sixth, with five editions ("Publication" 388), if not impressive, at least quite respectable for a playbook.

88. Jayne, *Library* 54, notes of English catalogues that "they do not generally record the ephemeral literature of the period ... even the immortal ephemera such as Shakespeare's plays. Such materials were all excluded almost as a matter of principle from most large libraries." On the treatment of plays in private libraries as of lower status than other kinds of books, see Hackel, "'Rowme'" 125. The classic citation on the disdain for plays are two letters from Sir Thomas Bodley in 1612, in which he refers to "Almanackes, plaies, & proclamacions" as "idle bookes, & riffe raffes," and instructs his librarian to exclude them from his library (Bodley, *Letters* 219, 222). Hackel, however, notes that many libraries did in fact have extensive play collections (often not mentioned in catalogues).

89. David Cressy estimates that about 80 per cent of the male population and 95 per cent of the female population in England was illiterate in the mid-16th century, and about 70 per cent of the male population and 90 per cent of the female population was still illiterate in the 1630s (see his graph, *Literacy* 177). It has been argued that Cressy substantially underestimates the basic ability to read because he bases his evaluation primarily on the ability to sign one's name (see Thomas, "Meaning" 103; Rappaport, *Worlds* 298; and the review of literacy studies in Kiefer, *Writing* 268–74), but the general outlines of his findings (if not his specific statistics) are confirmed by Furet and Ozouf's study of literacy in France, *Reading*. In any case, a large proportion of even the literate population would not have been able to afford to buy printed plays on a regular basis. The usual (though not invariable) price for an individual playbook in England by the end of the 16th century was six pence, about one-twelfth of a London artisan's weekly wage, six times the price of admission to the cheapest playhouses in London (though the same price as the cheapest seats in the more costly indoor theatres which catered primarily to the wealthy) (Gurr, *Shakespearean* 11–13). The Shakespeare first folio cost a whole pound (Greg, *Shakespeare* 455), forty times the price of a single play and nearly two months' wages for the ordinary skilled worker. See Walker, *Politics*, for an estimate of 2*d.*–6*d.* for a playbook in the earlier part of the century.

90. For *Mucedorus* and *Doctor Faustus*, see Pollard and Redgrave, *Short-Title* 139, 166. On the Garnier editions, see Lazard, *Théâtre* 105. On the Tasso editions, see Clubb, *Italian Drama* 191. Charles Sorel, *Histoire comique de Francion*, is the source for the number of copies of Tabarin's works (cited in Scherer, ed., *Théâtre* I:1200).

91. Clubb, *Italian Drama* 271.
92. Qtd. Chambers, *Elizabethan* I:207n.
93. See Chapter 2, and below (discussing the 1635 contract forbidding Brome to publish his plays, and the 1637 and 1641 letters from the Lord Chamberlain forbidding the Stationers' Company to print the King's Men's or Beeston's plays without the companies' consent).
94. "Lent unto … Robarte shawe the 18 of march 1599 to geve unto the printer to staye the printing of patient gresell the some of … xxxxˢ" (Henslowe, *Henslowe's* I:119). The play was entered in the *Stationers' Register* ten days later to Cuthbert Burby (Arber, ed., *Transcript* III:158 (28 Mar. 1599/1600)). There has been much contradictory discussion of "staying," and there are conflicting explanations for the company payment for the staying of *Patient Griselda*. Pollard, for instance, hypothesized that the payment was the company's way of "buy[ing] off a piractical printer" or revoking a permission granted (Pollard, *Shakespeare's Folios* 12n.), Albright that this was a way to reserve copyright through a favoured stationer (*Dramatic* 244; "'To Be Staied'" 453–4, 468, 483). The money may have been lent to Burby in consideration for what he had already paid when the company changed its mind about publication. The company may have been experimenting in investing in future publication. In any case, the company was in one way or another involving itself in publication. According to Blayney ("Shakespeare's") "staying" entries indicate that a stationer wanted to enter a play but that there was no warden around to do so. In any case, it was one way in which stationers (or companies through stationers) could contingently reserve publication rights.
95. Arber, ed., *Transcript* III:37. On the King's company payment for printing, see Robertson and Gordon, eds., *Calendar* 85. Pollard believed that the four plays listed in the register on 27 May 1600 as "to be staied" were being stayed by James Roberts on behalf of the Chamberlain's Men to prevent an unauthorized publication. But the "staying" order may represent a direct intervention by the Lord Chamberlain on his troupe's behalf, an intervention similar to the interventions of 1619, 1637, and 1641. The language of "staying" is the same as that used in the 10 June 1637 letter from the Lord Chamberlain to the Stationers' Company, which says that the stationers must "take Order for the *stay* of any further Impression of any of the Playes or Interludes of his Maᵗᵉ servante wᵗʰout their consente" (emphasis added) (Boswell and Chambers, ed., "Dramatic" 384). In the similar 1641 letter, the Lord Chamberlain says that such orders for "staying" are an old practice: that "hitherto" the stationers "have beene usually restrained … by the Authority of the Lord Chamberlain" from putting plays belonging to the Chamberlain's Men "in Print wᵗhout their knowledge & consent," and that, in so ordering, he is doing "as formerly my Preecessors have done" (letter reproduced in Chambers, "Plays" 367). It seems quite possible that the 1600 "staying" order in the Register is an earlier instance of the Lord Chamberlain's protection. It and the *Patient Griselda* "staying" may have been unique experiments somehow connected to the sudden rise in play registration in 1600 noted by Blayney (twenty-seven plays registered May 1600–October 1601, as opposed to the norm of about three plays registered per year between 1590 and 1604 ("Publication" 385)). Blayney identifies the entry to James Roberts that precedes the August staying order (headed by the words, "My lord chamberlens mens plaies Entred") with this sudden rise in registration and an expectation on the part of the Stationers' clerk (who may have heard something from the company) that a number of Chamberlain's plays were about to be entered ("Publication" 387), suggesting that the company had something to do with the registrations.

96. The Whitefriars contract reads: "Noe man of the said Company shall at any tyme here-after put into print, or cause to be put in print, any manner of playe booke now in use, or that hereafter shalbe sould unto them, upon the penaltie and forfeiture of ffortie pounds starlinge, or the losse of his place and share of all things amongst them, Except the booke of Torrismount, and that playe not to be printed by any before twelve monthes be fully expired" (qtd. Greenstreet, "Whitefriars" 276, reproducing a later lawsuit between company members quoting the contract). See also Bentley, *Profession of Dramatist* 266–7; and the comments by Albright, *Dramatic* 239–40. Since company plays were entered in the Register only a month later, the clause seems to mean that company members were not to act without the consent of all the sharers. It remains difficult to understand the twelve-month prohibition on the printing of "*Torrismount*" (perhaps a translation of Tasso's very popular 1587 *Torrismondo*): clearly someone was intending to see it into print, but why not simply assume that the requirement of company consent would prevent the printing for a year, and why delay the printing for a year in the first place? Perhaps one company member had agreed to give the play to the company reserving the right to sell the play to a publisher, or perhaps there seemed a special risk of rival productions since this was a translation.

97. The entry in the Stationers' Company Court Book for 3 May 1619 reads: "Hen. Heṁings. upon a lr̃ from the right hoᵇˡᵉ the Lo. Chamberleyne It is thought fitt & so ordered That no playes that his Maᵗʸᵉˢ players do play shalbe printed wᵗʰout consent of soṁe of them" (Jackson, ed., *Records* 110 (fol. 56ᵃ)).

98. The later suit against Brome quotes the 1638 contract as stipulating that Brome "should not suffer any playe made or to bee made or Composed by him for yoʳ subjects or theire successors in the said Companye in Salsbury Courte to bee printed by his Consent or knowledge privitye or dirreccoñ without the License from the said Companie or the Maioʳ *p*te of them" (qtd. Haaker, "Plague" 298, transcribing the suit in full). Whether or not Brome was breaching the contract by publishing *The Antipodes* in 1640 is unclear. The suit (also in 1640) concerned Brome's breach of exclusivity and does not mention unauthorized publication. Bentley speculates that Shirley, Massinger, Fletcher, Shake-speare, and Heywood may have had exclusivity contracts similar to Brome's between the 1590s and 1630s (*Profession of Dramatist* 112–20).

99. The 1620 contract specifies only that Hardy is not to give to anyone else, nor himself to retain, copies of any plays he has written or is contracting to write for the troupe (repro-duced Deierkauf-Holsboer, *Vie* 215–16). But the 1625 contract, which grants the right to print some of the plays, unequivocally recognizes the 1620 contract as having entailed an agreement not to print: "Nonobstant que par le contrat entre eulx faict en l'année mil six cent vingt en la ville de Marseille il ne soyt permis aud. Sr Hardy de faire imprimer les pieces contenues aud. contrat, ils ont consenty et consentent par cesd. presentes que iceluy Sr Hardy fasse imprimer par qui et quand bon luy semblera les pièces que s'ensuivent" (Deierkauf-Holsboer, *Vie* 212). The similarity between the terms in the 1620 contract and terms in the 1625 contract and a contract with a different troupe in 1627 (reproduced in Deierkauf-Holsboer, *Vie* 213–14) suggests that the latter were also understood as non-publishing agreements, which would mean that Hardy had at least three non-publishing agreements with various troupes in the 1620s. On Hardy's attach-ment to the troupes, see Deierkauf-Holsboer, *Le Théatre* I:67–83; and Deierkauf-Holsboer, *Vie*.

100. "True it is," he writes, "that my Playes are not exposed unto the world in Volumes, to beare the title of *Workes*, (as others) one reason is, That many of them by shifting and

change of Companies, have beene negligently lost, Others of them are still retained in the hands of some Actors … and a third, That it never was any great ambition in me, to bee in this kind Volumniously read" (Heywood, *Dramatic* IV:5). Heywood's inveterate inclination to publish makes it clear that his declared "modesty" was no bar: he had in fact announced his intention to publish a collection of his "Ages" plays in "an handsome Volumne" only a year earlier, in the preface to *The Iron Age* (1632). It is also not likely that lack of interest on the part of publishers was a bar. Various publishers *had*, presumably for profit, undertaken the publication of at least thirty-five separate editions of his plays, and the production of a collection of the highly popular Heywood would have seemed a reasonable venture. More to the point, in the preface to *The Iron Age* Heywood claims that he has been promised such a collection: "If the three former Ages (now out of Print,) bee added to these (*as I am promised*) to make up an handsome Volumne; I purpose (*Deo Assistente*,) to illustrate the whole Worke, with an Explanation of all the difficulties, and an Historicall Comment of every hard name" (Heywood, *Dramatic* III:351–2; emphasis added). It seems unlikely that Heywood would lie about the promise in the preface to a play published by Nicholas Okes, who held the rights to the three "Ages" plays and who was the logical person to promise such a collection. Finally, Heywood makes his assertion about the actors' withholding despite the fact that it actually *discredits* his more self-promoting claim (that his modesty is preventing him), suggesting that he is campaigning to get the actors to release the plays or tweaking them for acquisitiveness. Despite his general suspicion of this passage as evidence of withholding, Blayney acknowledges that Heywood "may well be right that some players in 1633 did not want *others* to sell their property to the press" ("Publication" 417), the most likely "other" being Heywood himself.

101. Lope de Vega was regularly selling plays to managers by the mid-1590s (see Rennert, *Life* 93–6), but did not start publishing plays until 1617, despite the fact that others were doing so without his permission (see the discussion of his *Partes* in Barrera y Leirado, *Catálogo* 425–6). Bentley's overwhelming evidence that professional dramatists attached to English companies were not (unlike other playwrights) putting their plays into print (*Profession of Dramatist* 112–16, 264–92) does not amount to proof that companies were actively withholding, nor does the fact that professional dramatists like Lope de Vega (dependent on his dramatic writing) failed to put his plays into print until after the wide circulation of unauthorized editions. But these facts may corroborate the evidence from the contracts and official orders on company withholding.

102. See Bentley, *Profession of Dramatist* 266–71.

103. On the high prices that managers in early 17th-century Spain paid for new playscripts (their "pane quotidiano," necessary to the public demand for "comedias nuevas": a minimum of 300 *reales*, normally 500 to 600 *reales*, and sometimes as much as 1,000 *reales*), and the threat that printing seemed to pose to their value, see Restori, *Saggi* 49. On the value of new plays to London troupes, see Knutson, "Repertory" 467. Whether or not potential spectators were actually less eager to see a play they had read, managers in the later 17th century *thought* this to be the case (see Chapter 2).

104. Middleton, *Works* III:7.

105. "Si hallares que tienen alguna cosa buena, en topando a aquel mi maldiciente autor, dile que se enmiende." Cervantes, *Obras* II:160 (*Ochos comedias*, "Prólogo"). See, similarly, Fletcher's *Faithful Shepherdess* (published in 1609 after it failed in the theatre and the only play which Fletcher himself made efforts to see into print); Webster's *The White*

Devil; and Massinger's *The Emperor of the East* (published in 1632 after it had failed in the theatre).

106. See the discussions in Bentley, *Profession of Dramatist* 268, 274; Chambers, *Elizabethan* I:341; and Blayney, "Publication" 386.

107. Qtd. Beaumont and Fletcher, *Dramatic* I:372.

108. See the prefaces and dedications in his *El Peregrino en su patria* (1603), *Doze comedias* (*Novena parte*, 1618), *Trezena parte* (1620), *Décimaquinta parte* (1621), *Décimaséptima parte* (1621) (including the dedication to *Los Muertos vivos*), and *La Dorotea* (1632); and the discussion of Lope's complaints about managers who steal from one another and actors who sell plays without hesitation in Rennert, *Life* 292–4.

109. Richards and Richards, *Commedia* (but see the discussion in Chapter 2 of *commedia dell'arte* withholding of plays from print once the troupes came to rely on written texts).

110. Wickham, *Early* III:141, offers the traditional view that theatrical rivalry was a reason for withholding ("managers would not release … scripts for publication [and thus for use by other companies] until they were certain that the play had outlived its usefulness in earning money for its owners"), and this may indeed have been a factor before respect for rival repertories became part of the professional code in London. But there were only a few instances of competitive performances by rival companies in London between the 1580s and 1642, most notably the rival *Satiromastixes* of 1601 and the two-way "theft" in 1604 of *Jeronimo* by the Children of the Chapel and *The Malcontent* by the King's Men. On the rival productions (variously interpreted), see Knutson, "Repertory" 470–1 (and 469–70 for her view that there was no withholding from publication to prevent theft); and Chambers, *Elizabethan* III:130. Both Knutson and Blayney ("Publication" 386) argue convincingly that performance piracy was minimal, that there was a protocol of respect for rival repertories, and that as a result rivalry could not have been a rationale for withholding publication. Certainly theatrical "theft" was treated as anomalous, for instance in the induction added to the King's Men's version of *The Malcontent* (Marston, *Plays* I:143).

111. Qtd. Rennert, *Spanish* 170–1.

112. "Estando yo oyendo la del Galan de la Membrilla que representava Sanchez, començò este autor a cortar el argumento y a interrūpir el razonado, tan al descubierto, que obligò le preguntassen de que procedia semejante aceleracion y truncamiento; y respondio publicamente, que de estar delante (y señalole) quien en tres dias tomava de memoria qualquier comedia, y que de temor no le usurpasse aquella, la recitava tan mal." Suárez de Figueroa, *Plaza* fol. 237ʳ (Discurso 58); trans. Rennert, *Spanish* 176.

113. I have mentioned these as non-publishing contracts above, but they are really general exclusivity contracts, with non-publishing as a feature of exclusivity. The 1620 contract between Hardy and Nicolas Prudhomme, Pierre and François Le Messier, Philibert Robin, Philippe Damozeau, Simon Ferreux, and Loys Gallian (reproduced in Deierkauf-Holsboer, *Vie* 214–16) specifies that Hardy must give to the comedians not only all the originals but also all the drafts he has made, and that he must neither give to others, nor himself keep, any copies of the two original plays he has just sold to the troupe. Neither can he claim the right to copies of any of the plays he has written over the previous two years (the contract explains that all the originals and copies he has made, up to the present, belong—like the painted canvasses—to the troupe). He must furthermore swear under oath neither to give away nor to keep any copy or extract of the eleven originals he is contracting to compose over the following two years. The 1625

contract between Hardy and Pierre Le Messier (reproduced in Deierkauf-Holsboer, *Vie* 211) is damaged, but seems to specify that if Hardy gives any of the plays he has contracted to write to anyone else, he must return the 50 *livres* (half the total payment) that he has already received: "L[e Messier a promis] et promect les bailler et payer aud. [Hardy] dedans ung mois prochain venant se trouve que led. Hardy aye reten ... lad. commedie ou qu'il l'aye faict in ... et fourny à aultres personnes en ce cas ... tenu et promect rendre et restituer aud ... les deniers qu'il aura receu de la[d] ... commedie." The 1627 contract between Hardy and Claude Deschamps, Margueritte Begun, and Louis de La Barre (reproduced in Deierkauf-Holsboer, *Vie* 213–14, even more badly damaged) seems to grant Hardy a share in the company in return for writing plays "propres au theatre," with the understanding that "[il] ne ... ra retenir ny bailler aulcuns [origi]naulx ny coppie des pieces." All three of the contracts seem to specify not only that Hardy must not give the originals or copies to anyone else but also that he must not retain the manuscripts, suggesting that, in writing for the troupes, he was yielding up both the material copies and the right to sell or reproduce the plays in any form.

114. Before the 17th century, cash payments to authors were rare, although payment in copies or from patrons was common (see Voet, *Golden* II:284–301; Martin, *Le Livre* 50; Blayney, "Publication" 395–6). The evidence of payments to dramatists in copies is sparse, but we have at least one example, the payment of six vellum-bound copies plus 180 *livres* to Alexandre Hardy for twelve comedies (Deierkauf-Holsboer, *Vie* 210). But, as the examples below should suggest, publishers were beginning to make cash payments to dramatists in the 17th century. According to Blayney, we have no direct evidence of the typical English payment for a publishable playbook, but Blayney creates a hypothetical stationer who (he calculates) can afford to buy an ordinary play manuscript for only 30 shillings ("Publication" 398). However, in France as in England, payments were growing noticeably larger in the 1630s. In 1636, Isaac de Benserade sold his tragedy, *Cléopâtre*, for 75 *livres* (Martin, *Le Livre* 50), and, in the same year, Jean de Rotrou's publishers paid him, in two separate contracts, 1,500 *livres* for ten plays (or 150 *livres* each), and 750 *livres* for four plays, or a little under 200 *livres* each (see Martin, *Le Livre* 50; Pottinger, *French* 100–1, which reproduces one of the Rotrou contracts).

115. Heywood, *Dramatic* V:161 (*Rape of Lucrece*). Company payments to dramatists were relatively generous: between £5 and £7 (usually £6 at the end of the 16th century), rising to £8 in the following years and between £10 and £25 by the 1610s (see the numerous records in Henslowe, *Henslowe's* I). J. W. Saunders notes that a commission for a playwright might be worth between £5 and £30, as much as the whole company would earn for a performance. An average day's takings at the Globe might be only £6, but a performance at court in the early 17th century might bring £35, with a good share of that for the dramatist (Saunders, *Profession* 72). Company payment was certainly more reliable than what one could expect from the press.

116. "Aburríme, y vendíselas al tal librero, que las ha puesto en la estampa" and "él me las pagó razonablemente." Cervantes, *Obras* II:160 (*Ochos comedias*, "Prólogo").

117. See the contracts between Hardy and Le Messier and between Hardy and Quesnel reproduced in Deierkauf-Holsboer, *Vie* 210–11.

118. Díez Borque, *Sociedad* 99; Restori, *Saggi* 49. Cruickshank, "Editing" 54, notes that plays sold for publication probably brought significantly less than plays sold for performance ("a stage manager would pay from 500 to 1000 *reales* [or more] for a play, while a publisher might baulk at 100" ("Editing" 54)).

119. Heywood, *Dramatic* V:161 (*Rape of Lucrece*).

120. The figures should probably not be generalized across too broad a period, but even with inflation in the first half of the 17th century, £2 is a significant sum (see Gurr, *Shakespearean* 12–13, on artisans' wages in the Elizabethan period).

121. Pottinger gives a sense of the value of the French *livre* in the 17th century by comparing it with university professors' salaries (according to Pottinger, relatively unchanging in status and comfort level from medieval to modern times): a normal university or Collège de France salary around the turn of the century might be about 600 *livres* (Pottinger, *French* 351–3). The 180 *livres* (plus six vellum-bound books) that Hardy received for his twelve plays in 1625 would have been nearly one-third of the average professor's salary.

122. *Natividad y Corpus Christi … y nunca hasta aora impresos* (1644). For an earlier example, see Merbury's *Marriage Between Wit and Wisdom* "never before in printed" (title page).

123. See, similarly, the comment on false attribution in Hardy's second volume of his *Theatre* (1625). In a non-dramatic context, see George Wither's complaints about both false attribution and the parallel business practice of printing the same work with a variety of titles that might or might not actually describe the contents (Wither, *Schollers* 29, 121–2). On the Pavier and Jaggard Oldcastle, see Brooks, *From Playhouse* 67–71. The *Seis comedias de Lope de Vega Carpio, y de otros autores* (published in both Lisbon and Madrid in 1603) contains one play certainly by Lope, one play possibly by him, but in any case, five which he disowned. See Rennert, "Bibliography" 4; and Cruickshank, "Editing" 65–6 (and generally on the fact that it was not illegal to publish plays without the author's permission). See also the discussion of similar French practices in Lancaster, *History* I:414.

124. Again, Shakespeare, who paid close attention to the printing of *Venus and Adonis* (1593) and *The Rape of Lucrece* (1594) but not to the publication of his plays, has probably led commentators to exaggerate the differences between the quality of dramatic texts and other kinds of texts. According to Wendy Wall, "editorial practices and typography of printed poetic texts corresponded in striking ways to those of play texts" (*Imprint* 178).

125. "Salio este libro con muchas erratas. … Donde dize Pandron, ha de dezir Pandion: y donde dize Frãcia, ha de dezir Tracia." Castro, *Primera parte* sig. ¶2ʳ.

126. It is hard to distinguish between the right, the custom, and the obligation to proof-read, but non-dramatic authors were clearly expected to do so. According to Pottinger (offering French non-dramatic examples from the 16th to the 18th century), "it was always customary for the author to look over his own proofs" (Pottinger, *French* 51). Dramatists often excuse errors by commenting that they were (unusually) absent during the printing (see, for instance, La Calprenède, *La Mort* (145, 147), in which both La Calprenède and the printer state that errors were due to the fact that the first four acts were printed in the author's absence). Both Simpson, *Proof-Reading* and Albright, *Dramatic* 353, offer numerous English examples from non-dramatic works by writers who were also dramatists, as well as dramatic works. In Fletcher's *The Nice Valour*, the audience gets to see authors in the process of proof correction. "So bring me the last proofe," demands Lapet. "This is corrected. … Look I have perfect Books within this half houre." Somewhat later, the "Clowne" appears with proof sheets, informing Lapet: "Heres your last proof Sir. | You shal have perfect Books now in a twinkling" (Beaumont and Fletcher, *Dramatic* VII:230, 481 (IV.i)).

127. See Lordi, "Proofreading."

128. Chapman, *Plays* I:568 (ll. 144–6).

129. Marston, *Workes* (1633) sig. A4ʳ. According to the British Library catalogue, the title page reading *The Workes of Mr. John Marston* is the second issue. The first issue carries

a title page that reads: *Tragedies and Comedies collected into one volume.* On this edition, which appears in many variants, see Brettle, "Bibliographical"; and Ingram, *John Marston* ("Chronology"; unpaginated). Marston apparently forced Sheares to remove Marston's name from the collection (either because he had gone into the Church or merely because he was annoyed by Sheares's reference to his youthful indiscretions in his dedication) (Ingram, *John Marston* 149, 166n).

130. "Un Mercader de libros, mas curioso que cortes ... imprimiò estas doze Comedias, aña-diendo a sus yerros los del Impressor." Castro, *Primera parte* sig. ¶2ᵛ (dedication). The editors of Castro, *El curioso* 47, argue that Castro must be referring to an edition no longer extant, since the only extant earlier edition of the *Primera parte* (the 1618 edition) was produced by the same publisher as the 1621 edition and is essentially identical to it.

131. "Les precedents [volumes] me font rougir de la honte des Imprimeurs, ausquels l'avarice fist trahir ma reputation, estans si pleins de fautes, tant à l'ortographe qu'aux vers, que je voudrois de bon cœur en pouvoir effacer jusques à la memoire." Hardy, *Theatre* IV sig. ãivʳ. Hardy's complaints had some justification: for instance, when Quesnel reprinted his *Coriolan* in 1632, he set up the type from uncorrected sheets, and managed to introduce new errors as well. See Howe, "Alexandre Hardy" 133.

132. See Bentley, *Profession of Dramatist* 290–1; Simpson, *Proof-Reading* 12; and the notes throughout Herford and Simpson's edition (Jonson, *Ben Jonson*) (though it is worth noting that Jonson did not revise the masques extensively: see Brooks, *From Playhouse* 104–39). There is both internal and external evidence of several other playwrights revising extensively for print, for instance Montchrestien (Griffiths, *Dramatic* 175–213), Massinger (Simpson, *Proof-Reading* 13), and the Spanish playwright Feliciana Enríquez de Guzmán, who revised the 1624 edition of her plays for a second edition in 1627 (Soufas, ed., *Women's* 225–7).

2. DRAMA AS INSTITUTION, 1630–1760

1. Howard, *Usurper* sig. A2ʳ. About sixty plays of English dramatists whose work had essentially never before been published were put in print between 1637 and 1640 (see Bentley, *Profession of Dramatist* 265, 286–8). The playlists in Lancaster, *History*, show the publication of new plays in France increasing only slightly from the 1610s to the 1620s, but more than tripling in the 1630s. Dramatic bibliographies like Saverio Franchi's *Drammaturgia romana*, Louise Clubb's *Italian Plays*, and Cayetano Barrera y Leirado's *Catálogo bibliográfico y biográfico*, as well as perusal of individual careers, suggest similar figures for Italy and Spain. The entries in *The London Stage* and playlists in Lancaster, *History* show that, in London and Paris at least, those plays that remained unpublished were the exceptions. In London, for instance (as Burling, "British Plays" 181, notes), every play performed between 1697 and 1737 was printed, all but one of them within a year of performance.

2. For instance, Molière's *Docteur amoureux* and "quelques autres de cette nature, n'ont point été imprimées" because "il trouva à propos de les supprimer" (preface to the 1682 edition of Molière's *Oeuvres* in Molière, *Œuvres complètes* I:998).

3. Farquhar, *Works* II:369 ("Discourse upon Comedy" (1702)).

4. On the continuing importance of commercial scriptoria in 17th-century England, see Love, *Scribal*; Marotti, *Manuscript*; and McKenzie, "Speech-Manuscript-Print."

5. For Lord Lisle, see Jonson, *Ben Jonson* II:274n. See Love, *Scribal* 67 on the regular circulation of plays in manuscript at mid-century. See also the example of Dryden's *State of Innocence*, "many hundred Copies" of which he claimed to have been "dispers'd abroad" before its publication in 1677 (Dryden, *Works* XII:86). On the manuscript circulation of privately performed or provincial plays in 18th-century France, see Vince, *Neoclassical* 101.

6. See, for instance, the warrant that the Lord Chamberlain sent to the Master of the Great Wardrobe in 1675, two days before the first performance of Crowne's *Calisto*, asking him to provide "a Coppie of the Playe for the Queene … a Copie for the Ladie Marie, and the Ladie Ann. A Copie to Correct upon all occasions, A Copie of the Prologue & all the Songs for Mr Staggins. And Alsoe, … soe many Printed Bookes of the Maske" (qtd. Boswell, *Restoration* 190).

7. On the rarity of manuscript promptbooks in the 17th and 18th centuries, see Shattuck, *Shakespeare* 7; and Langhans, *Eighteenth Century* p. xxii. Shattuck cites the First Folio "Padua" promptbooks dating from the 1630s or 1640s and the Third Folio Smock Alley promptbooks dating from the 1670s or 1680s (*Shakespeare* 7–8). Only two of the twenty promptbooks from London professional theatres that Langhans discusses are manuscripts rather than annotated printed editions (see the facsimiles in Langhans, *Restoration*). Troupes, however, seem to have used manuscript part books throughout the 18th century: see, for instance, John Downes's explanation in *Roscius Anglicanus* of his duty as prompter between 1662 and 1706, "Writing out all the Parts" (Downes, *Roscius* 2); and the prompter's instructions in the 1792 Hamburg Theatre regulations (Brandt, ed., *German* 112–13).

8. See Butler, *Theatre* 105.

9. See Lancaster, *History* IV:602–4, and below.

10. See Calderón's prefaces to the *Cuarta parte* (1672, rev. 1674) and the *Autos sacramentales alegóricos y historiales* (1677), in which he claims that he is publishing only to protect himself against the many error-ridden versions of his plays already published. Scholars unaccountably repeat the truism that Calderón had nothing to do with the printing of his plays, founded on Calderón's own disclaimers and a contemporary's comment that he never sent any of his *comedias* to the press, and that those which were printed were printed against his will (Lara, *Obelisco* [prologue]; qtd. Ticknor, *History* II:416n.). Disclaimers notwithstanding, Everett W. Hesse and George Ticknor both present ample evidence of his involvement in the printing of his plays. In addition to the *Cuarta parte* and *Autos*, there were the two volumes of plays (published in the late 1630s by Calderón's brother) whose publication Calderón never protested; two additional volumes that appear to have been published with his assent; Calderón's own *aprobación* in a volume of *Comedias Escogidas* published in 1652 and including three of his plays; and the plays that he gave to his editor Juan de Vera Tassis to be printed (see Ticknor, *History* II:416–17; and Hesse, "Publication" for an overall account).

11. See the plays in the 1820 collection, Voltaire, *Pièces inédites*; and the entries in Bengesco, *Voltaire* I:1–87 (for instance, *Eriphile*, performed in 1732, whose printing Voltaire interrupted because of the play's failure at the première).

12. On *Der bestrafte Brudermord*, see Brandt, ed., *German* 43.

13. See Blayney for a comparison (6*d.* on average for a printed play, and 2–3*s.* to have a play copied ("Publication" 411, 418 n.19, and 421–2 n.61)); Love, *Scribal* 67; and Moseley (quoted immediately below).

14. Beaumont and Fletcher, *Comedies* sig. A3^v.

15. "Une Piece, quelque excellente qu'elle puisse estre, n'ayant pas esté representée, ne trouvera point de Libraire qui se veuille charger de l'impression; & la moindre bagatelle qui sera fade sur le papier, & que l'action aura fait goûter sur le Theâtre, trouve d'abord marchand dans la Sale du Palais." Chappuzeau, *Le Théatre François* 84 (Bk. 3, Ch. 1). Chappuzeau's identification of performance success with print success is, not surprisingly, substantiated by the available sources from the later 17th and early 18th centuries. Lancaster notes that, of the plays performed in Paris in the 1690s for which there are records, all those that brought the author more than 800 francs from performance takings were published quickly, but only one that brought the author less than 800 francs was published at all (*History* IV:401). In England, a comparison of editions in the short-title catalogues and numbers of performances listed in *The London Stage* gives a general idea. See, for instance, the listings for Dryden's *Indian Emperor* (1667) and *Love Triumphant* (1694), Shadwell's *Squire of Alsatia* (1688) and *Bury Fair* (1689), Southerne's *Fatal Marriage* (1694), and Elkanah Settle's *Ambitious Slave* (1694). A smash hit like Gay's *The Beggar's Opera* (1728) had 395 performances and was published over a hundred times during the 18th century (Stone, "Making of the Repertory" 199).

16. David Cressy identifies a "pronounced improvement in illiteracy levels in the 1630s" in England, and although he identifies a falling off in the later 17th and early 18th centuries, he notes that "by the end of the Stuart period [1714] the English had achieved a level of literacy unknown in the past" (*Literacy* 171, 173, 176, and, on the vicissitudes but overall rise of literacy on the Continent during the 17th and 18th centuries, see 178–82). These findings are confirmed by Furet and Ozouf (*Reading*) who show (with variations) the nobility and gentry across Europe growing literate in the 16th century, the middle classes in the late 17th and 18th, and the labouring classes over the course of the 19th.

17. See Goldoni, *Tutte* I:294–5, 318 (*Mémoires* Pt. 2, Ch. 12, 17).

18. See Lancaster, *History* II:762; Kenny, "Publication" (there were, of course, exceptions: see, for instance, Shergold, *History* 480–1, on the Madrid city authorities' assumption that Calderón's *autos* were its property since it had bought them from him for performance). In my assessment of repertory exclusivity, publication rights, and their relationship, I have worked with the available sources. The details of these intersecting rights throughout Europe between the late 17th and late 18th centuries require further study.

19. The number of English texts set up from promptbooks, for instance, declines notably after the 1680s (see the listings in Langhans, *Restoration*, and his discussion pp. xiv–xvi). In Langhans, ed., *Eighteenth Century* (p. xxii), he notes the absence of traces of prompt copy in all but one 18th-century printed edition, concluding "printers did not normally set copy from promptbooks, as they often did in Restoration times." See also Kenny, "Publication" 316.

20. Haaker, "Plague" 296–300.

21. Malone, "Prolegomena" to Shakespeare, *Plays* (1821) III:160–1; and Chambers, "Plays."

22. "S. M. ayant esté informée que quelques Comédiens de Campagne ont surpris après le décez du Sieur Molière une copie de la Comédie du *Malade Imaginaire*, qu'ils se préparent de donner au Public, contre l'usage de tous tems observé entre tous les Comédiens du Royaume, de n'entreprendre de joüer au préjudice les uns des autres les Pièces qu'ils ont fait accommoder au Théâtre à leurs frais particuliers, pour se récompenser de leurs avances, et en tirer les premiers avantages, Sadite Majesté fait très expresses inhibitions et défenses à tous Comédiens autres que ceux de la Troupe establie à Paris rüe Mazarine

au Faux-bourg Saint-Germain, de joüer et représenter ladite Comédie du *Malade Imaginaire* en quelque manière que ce soit, qu'après qu'elle aura été rendue publique par l'Impression qui en sera faite." Reproduced Mélèse, *Le Théâtre* 422–3; trans. Howarth, ed., *French* 122. See also La Grange's comment on this decree (La Grange, *Le Registre* I:157 (March 1674)); Lancaster's comments in Mahelot, *Le Mémoire* 18; and, for a general description of the prohibition, Bonnassiés, *Les Auteurs* 8–9.

23. "J'ai vu que cela ne vous pouvait apporter aucun dommage, non plus qu'à votre troupe, puisque votre pièce a été jouée près de cinquante fois." Molière, *Œuvres complètes* I:300.

24. See Lancaster, *History* II:103.

25. "Pour le combat des Horaces, ce ne sera pas sitôt encore que vous le verrez, pour ce ... que, devant que d'être publié, il faut qu'il serve six mois de gagne-pain aux comédiens. Telles sont les conventions des poètes mercenaires et tel est le destin des pièces vénales" (9 Mar. 1640); and see the letter of 19 May 1640 from Chapelin to Balzac, qtd. Corneille, *Oeuvres complètes* I:1536.

26. "Une entreprise de cette qualité seroit très-préjudiciable aux supplians." See the warrant and the mention of the incident in the 1694 lawsuit, both reproduced by Campardon, ed., *Les Comédiens* II:111. See also the translations of parts of this and the lawsuit discussed below in Howarth, ed., *French* 321–2.

27. According to the 1694 complaint (reproduced in Campardon, ed., *Les Comédiens* II:109–12), the copies were turned over to the plaintiffs. Of these, the actors who played Cinthio, Scaramouche, Eularia, Isabelle, and Colombine eventually agreed that the copies should be sold for the benefit of the whole troupe. However, the actor who played Mezzetin (Angelo Constantini), his father (who played Gradelin), his brother (who played Octave), Pierrot, the young Scaramouche, and Pulchinello staged a rebellion and determined to burn the copies. The authorities eventually sided with them, arguing that Gherardi had never had a right to the privilege without the troupe's permission, and that the printing would in any case clearly be prejudicial to the troupe. However, apparently Octave, whose responsibility it was to destroy the 900 copies that had been confided to him, burned only a few sheets, selling the copies that survived for 32 *sous* each (the basis for editions in Holland, Brussels, Liège, and provincial France). In 1695, Gherardi did finally bring out an edition (*Le Theatre italien*), with the usual claim that the plays had to be published to defend against spurious editions. For further discussion, see Lancaster, *History* IV:602–4; and Scott, *Commedia* 276–9.

28. "Les pièces de théâtre reprennent tout leur agrément et deviennent pour ainsi dire comme nouvelles lorsqu'elles ont été quelques années sans être jouées, en ce que les idées en sont effacées par la suspension des représentations; au lieu que si cette impression avoit lieu, elles deviendroient publiques et communes, que les supplians n'oseroient plus se flatter d'aucun succès en les jouant sur leur théâtre qui tomberoit infailliblement. ... [Les] supplians ... auroient peine à se résoudre de jouer des pièces que le vulgaire sauroit par cœur et qui n'auroient plus aucun agrément." Complaint reproduced in Campardon, ed., *Les Comédiens* II:110–11. Two years later there is a similar complaint that "au mépris de l'arrêt du Conseil du 17 septembre 1694, qui fait défenses à toutes personnes d'imprimer ou faire imprimer aucune scène ou chanson appartenant aux plaignans, ils viennent d'apprendre que des colporteurs viennent vendre aux portes de l'Hôtel de Bourgogne, les airs qui se chantent sur leur théâtre, composés par Gillier, musicien, sans leur avoir donné avis. Et d'autant qu'ils ont payés ledit Gillier pour avoir composé lesdits airs, ils ont été conseillés de nous rendre la présente plainte de laquelle ledit Constantin, audit nom, nous a requis acte." Campardon, ed., *Les Comédiens* I:137.

29. "Ce n'étoit que par envie, & non pas par raison qu'on en avoit demandé la suppression." Gherardi, *Le Theatre* (1700 edn.) I, sig. eii^v–eiii^r ("Avertissement"). It is worth noting that, in the 1720s, the troupe was still safeguarding its texts and scenarios, and the document that provides for such safeguarding seems to distinguish the unprinted plays (to be kept from colleagues who might lay claim to them) from those that (as it specifies) are printed (to be kept by one member merely for distribution when needed). See the document in the Archives Nationales, O^1 848. 7; reproduced and trans. Howarth, ed., *French* 428.

30. Riccoboni, *Historical* 53. Riccoboni (writing originally in 1738) is clearly wrong or exaggerating: perhaps what he means is that the Italian actors "never acted any Piece that had not before been written out." In any case, he identifies the Italian actors as writing down their texts and circulating them in print.

31. Nicoll, *History* I:381 (reproducing the contract). See the comments by Johann Friedrich Löwen in his *Geschichte des deutschen Theaters* (1766), on Carolina Neuber's withholding of plays from publication in order to prevent their performance by other companies: "Sie war überhaupt wider das Comödiendrucken. Dieser Widerwille war im Grunde nichts anders, als ein Neid, ihre Stücke bey andern Gesellschaften nicht bekannt werden zu lassen." Löwen, *Johann Friedrich Löwens* 31.

32. Aitken, *Life* I:118 (reproducing Rich's answer; and see Aitken's concise discussion of the lawsuit I:111–12).

33. Ibid. I:118.

34. *London Stage* II(i): p. lxxxii (the directive was apparently never issued).

35. "Projet de Lettres Patentes" in Corneille, *Oeuvres complètes* I:1684–5.

36. The "Dames de la Communauté de St-Louis" "[font] défenses à tous libraires ... d[e l']imprimer ... sans le consentement desdites Dames ... Avec pareilles défenses à tous acteurs et autres montant sur les théâtres publics, d'y représenter ni chanter ledit ouvrage." Qtd. Racine, *Oeuvres complètes* I:1154. Racine had similarly attempted to override the theatre's customary rights to repertory control when, in 1665, he gave his *Alexandre le Grand* to the Hôtel de Bourgogne fifteen days after Molière's troupe had first acted it, apparently because he did not like the acting. See Racine, *Oeuvres complètes* I:22, 1071.

37. See David Trott's discussion, estimating that of the more than 200 plays Fuzelier appears to have written, only about seventy-five were published (Trott, "Dramaturgy" 212); and see the discussion of shrinking delays below.

38. "A quoi bon donner au public ces misérables poèmes?" "Ce recueil paraît ... pour laisser à l'avenir un monument qui fasse connaître les diverses formes sous lesquelles on a vu le théâtre de la Foire." Preface to *Le Théâtre de la Foire, ou l'opéra-comique, contenant les meilleurs pièces représentées aux foires de Saint-Germain et de Saint-Laurent*; reproduced in Truchet, ed., *Théâtre* I:161.

39. See Freehafer, "Formation" 24–7; and Hume, "Securing" (noting, however, the early uncertainty over rights to a number of plays, and direct collision in the first season). In the years just preceding the closure of the theatres in 1642, the Lord Chamberlain several times offered protection for company acting rights in particular plays (see the petition of 20 July 1634, requesting that the Lord Chamberlain prevent the performance of a competing play on the Lancashire Witches, and the warrant of 10 Aug. 1639, forbidding the acting of Beeston's boys' plays (Boswell and Chambers, "Dramatic" 389–90, 410)). It is interesting to note that, in the uncertainty over repertory rights that followed the reopening of the theatres in 1660, the publisher Humphrey

Moseley seems to have assumed that, since there were no clear successors to the pre-Interregnum companies, and since he held the *publication* rights to many of the King's Men's plays, he had authority to designate acting rights as well. In a 1660 letter to Sir Henry Herbert, Master of the Revels, Moseley certified, on behalf of the actors of the Red Bull Theatre (led by Michael Mohun), that he had *not* granted John Rhodes (manager of the Cockpit Theatre) permission to act plays in which he had publication rights (Herbert, *Control* 229 (30 Aug. 1660)). Moseley's plea was apparently successful: acting rights in these plays were subsequently formally granted to Thomas Killigrew's King's Men (the successors to Mohun's short-lived troupe and, perhaps due in part to Moseley's certification, recognized as the successors to the pre-Interregnum King's Men).

40. Steele, *Plays* 299 (preface to *Conscious Lovers*).

41. Qtd. *London Stage* I: p. lxxviii. According to Milhous and Hume, London playhouse managers began regularly to buy advertisements in such newspapers as the *Daily Courant* around 1705 ("Dating" 374).

42. On playbills, handbills, and title pages posted as advertisements, see *London Stage* I: pp. lxxv–lxxvi; and Fletcher, "British Playbills." Summers notes that the earliest surviving mention of the theatrical *affiche* in France is in 1556, and in England in 1564, but that they became widespread in the later 17th century, at the same time that the practice of hoisting a flag on the playhouse roof on playing days disappeared (Summers, *Restoration* 4–6, and 4–28 generally). On separately printed prologues and epilogues, for sale during a play's initial run, see Milhous and Hume, "Dating" 389; and on libretti at the fair theatres, see Campardon, *Spectacles* I:90–1. Numerous printed plot summaries (used as programmes) survive from the Continent, particularly for operas and school dramas. For 17th-century examples of the Italian printed "Argomenti" (scenarios, often only a sheet), see Franchi, *Drammaturgia*.

43. Buckingham, *Rehearsal* 9. The editors of the *London Stage* (I:87) note that *The Connexion* was printed with *The Indian Emperour*, and identify it as the target of Bayes's lines.

44. Dennis, *Critical* II:192.

45. See Vince, *Neoclassical* 101, 108; Kenny, "Publication" 323; and Milhous and Hume, "Dating" 402–4. By the middle of the 18th century, the sale of playbills (as programmes) in the theatre seems to have been an established practice: in Samuel Foote's 1748 "Diversions of the Morning," Foote mimics an orange-woman at the playhouse crying "Would you have some oranges?—have some orange-chips, ladies and gentlemen!—Would you have some nonpareils?—Would you have a bill of the play?" (qtd. Summers, *Restoration* 11).

46. Milhous and Hume, "Dating" 402 (noting several early instances).

47. Qtd. Nicoll, *History* II:257–8.

48. Motteux, *Novelty* sig. A4ʳ.

49. Picot, *Bibliographie* 69.

50. Browsing through Harbage, *Annals*, allows one to get a fairly clear idea of the change in the normal delay in England. Two to six years is normal in the first decades of the 17th century (and twenty years not uncommon). My general observations are confirmed by Milhous and Hume's systematic investigation of the years 1660–1700 in London, in which they note the decline in normal delay from one year in the 1660s to only a month or so in the 1690s, observing the "steady drift toward a pattern in which publication follows closely upon performance" ("Dating" 382).

51. For plays performed in Paris, the playlists in Lancaster (*History*) suggest the decrease in normal delay, although the proliferation of marginal genres in the later 1680s and 1690s (not regularly published in the 17th century) complicates the picture. Allowing for the fact that Lancaster rounds most dates to the year so it is impossible to distinguish, for instance, between plays that may have been published nearly a year after performance and plays published a day after performance, the delays between 1610 and 1634 are normally about three to four years, whereas by the 1670s almost all plays are published within two years of performance, and most within a year or less.

52. Corneille, *Oeuvres complètes* I:1143–4, III:1440–1.

53. See Lacroix, *Bibliographie* 1–21; the notes in Molière, *Œuvres complètes*.

54. Picard, *La Carrière* 200.

55. For London plays in the 1690s, see Milhous and Hume, "Dating" 394–404, which offers numerous instances of only a few weeks' delay or less in the 1690s. For the first decade of the 18th century, see Kenny, "Publication" 313–15 (a two-week delay is normal). The playlists in Lancaster, *History* show that, in the 1680s and 1690s, plays performed in Paris seem to be published within a year, if one does not count the plays performed by the Théâtre Italien (generally still withheld from publication) and the numerous marginal plays (not regularly published in the 17th century). According to Picard (*La Carrière* 420), in the last decade of the 17th century publication was normally delayed only until the end of the first run.

56. See Woods's introduction to Fielding, *Author's* xi; and Hume, *Henry Fielding* 91 (according to the *Daily Post* of 22 Mar. 1731, "Books" of the *Tragedy of Tragedies* were sold in the theatre from opening night).

57. "Je l'ai fait imprimer le lendemain de la représentation" (Marivaux, *Théâtre* 485). Normally, Marivaux's plays were published only several years after performance, and he does not appear to have had anything to do with their publication (they are almost invariably anonymous, and he is rarely mentioned as the privilege holder). See the notes in Marivaux, *Théâtre* 1529–64.

58. See Friedman's introduction in Goldsmith, *Collected* V:7.

59. *Morning Chronicle* (26 Mar. 1773); qtd. Goldsmith, *Collected* V:93.

60. Prynne, *Histriomastix* fol. *3ʳ. The thirty-one original and reprinted playbooks printed in 1632–3 (a count based on Greg, *Bibliography*), multiplied by an average edition size of 1,500, equals 46,500 playbooks.

61. See my discussion in Chapter 1 of the difficulties of making a reliable count. It is worth noting, however, the geometric expansion in the number of entries in Greg's *Bibliography*. In England there were probably under a hundred different plays printed before the 17th century. Between 1635 and 1651 alone more than 280 new plays were printed. On the growth in play publication and reading generally, see *London Stage* I: p. cxxii; Wright, "Reading"; Kirsop, "Nouveautés" 218 (referring to "une véritable explosion d'éditions et rééditions de comédies et de tragédies" after the Fronde); Kenny, "Publication" 323; and for Spain, Cruickshank, "On the Stage" 2. Saverio Franchi's *Drammaturgia* shows the number of plays printed in Rome more than doubling over the course of the 17th century (one can compare the sixty-odd plays printed in the first decade of the century with the 226-odd printed in the last decade). While the playlists (for the 17th century) in Lancaster's *History* show a surge in new plays published in the middle decades of the 17th century (reflecting the theatrical vitality and rich patronage of the middle decades and the reliance on revivals in the later years), it is worth comparing the total number of new plays published in France between 1610 and 1699 (slightly over 1,000 according to

the table in Scherer, *La Dramaturgie* 458–9) with the total number of new plays published in France between 1700 and 1789 (5,242, according to Jeffrey Ravel's in-progress census, an increase of over fivefold, not counting re-editions) (Ravel, personal communication).

62. Voltaire's *La Mort de César*, for instance, was published individually ten times in the 18th century, his *Zaïre* and his *Brutus* eleven times each during the 18th century, and this is not to count their reprinting in collections (see Bengesco, *Voltaire* I:10–12, 14–17, 24–7). Where editions of the most successful 16th-century plays can be counted at one or two dozen, both Addison's *Cato* (1713) and Gay's *Beggar's Opera* (1728) were published over a hundred times in the 18th century.

63. What became the most common format for Spanish plays from about 1700 on—their regular reprinting in series with serial numbers (see Cruickshank, "Editing" 74)—was constrained, in England, by the hold of various publishers on copyrights. But Thomas Johnson's pirated series, *A Collection of the Best English Plays* (issued in ten volumes in 1711–12, and in various later versions), and Robert Dodsley's *Select Collection of Old Plays* (published in twelve volumes in 1744, establishing an important precedent) might be thought of as comparable.

64. Farquhar, *Works* I:139 (Kenny's introduction to *Constant Couple*); and Fielding, *Author's Farce* p. xi (Woods's introduction). While there were clearly more editions than in earlier periods, one should be cautious about attributing this to high-volume sales, since later editions were often merely later impressions with new title pages and sometimes the cancellation of a few leaves and the substitution of newly set ones (see Kenny's examples, "Publication" 325–6).

65. William Bowyer published, similarly, a total of 10,500 copies of Gay's *Polly* (Kenny, "Publication" 325), and Hugh Kelly's *False Delicacy* (1768) sold 10,000 copies (Sampson, "Some Bibliographical" 102). I am grateful to Paula Backscheider for the statistic on *The Drummer* (based on the number of copies printed of one edition of *The Drummer*, edition sizes for similar plays, and the number of editions in the ESTC (English Short Title Catalogue)).

66. Goldoni, *Tutte* I:318 (*Mémoires* Pt. 2, Ch. 17). See also Pasta, "Towards" 119 on the Goldoni press runs of 1,500 and 2,000.

67. On *Catalina*, which sold 5,000 copies in the first week, see Pottinger, *French* 204. On *She Stoops to Conquer*, which sold 4,000 copies in a few days, see *The Morning Chronicle* (1 Apr. 1773); qtd. Goldsmith, *Collected* V:93. On *Mélanie*, see La Harpe's preface (4,000 copies sold in twenty-four hours) in Truchet, ed., *Théâtre* II:833. Compare this with a normal edition size of 1,000 for Shakespeare's quartos (Plant, *English* 93). See the discussion of average edition sizes in Sampson, "Some Bibliographical" 101–2 (1,000–1,500 copies of Restoration plays); Martin, *Le Livre* 213 (1,200–1,250 copies of re-editions of Corneille); Mariti, *Commedia* p. L (close to 2,000 copies of late 17th-century *commedia ridicolosa* plays). The existence of a provincial play readership even in the 17th century is attested to, for instance, by the brisk sale in plays in the bookseller Nicolas's bookshop in Grenoble in the 1640s and 1650s (Martin, *Le Livre* 192–3). The 18th-century foreign market is attested to by the large number of English plays in the catalogues of the Leipzig bookseller Weidmann in the 1730s (Fabian and Spieckermann, "House" 308–9).

68. See, for instance, Martin, *Le Livre* 192–3, on the many Avignon piracies of Corneille; Goldoni's complaints about the piracy of his works in Goldoni, *Tutte* I:5–6, 91, 185 (*Mémoires* preface, Pt. 1, Chs. 17, 20, 41).

69. "En fait de livres ... le public est composé de 40 à 50 personnes si le livre est sérieux, de 400 à 500 lorsqu'il est plaisant, et d'environ 1100 à 1200 s'il s'agit d'une pièce de théâtre." Qtd. Avenel, *Les Revenus* 283 (no citation).

70. These were all developments significant for the history of authorship and reading, as well as for the general history of the trade, and they had an impact on dramatic authorship and readership as well. Copy and stock sharing and joint publishing kept literary property ("copies") in the hands of the strongest members of the publishing industry, by suggesting that wholesalers and retailers who bought pirated editions would lose their most important supply sources. Protection against piracy made it possible for publishers to invest in new copies and hence to pay authors significant sums. At the same time, wholesaling developed the reach of the book industry, allowed publishers to specialize in developing authors and lists rather than merely selling books, and made it easier for publishers to make initial investments (again, in authors), since they might realize profits from wholesalers immediately. Subscription publishing (a phenomenon primarily of the 18th century), by raising money before publication, allowed publishers to invest in new authors, risky projects, and expensive books. At the same time, it helped develop a conception of the reading public as patron. For discussions, see Blagden, *Stationers'* 227; Feather, *History* 68–9; Gaskell, *New* 180–1; Plant, *English* 66–8, 219–20, 222–32; Pottinger, *French* 96–7, 198–201; Waquet, "Book"; and Wittmann, *Geschichte* 151–5 (and on the publication by subscription of Voltaire's *La Henriade* in 1728 and Voltaire's edition of Corneille's *Théâtre* in 1764, see Kirsop, "Les Mécanismes" 32).

71. Massinger, Middleton, and Rowley, *Old Law* (1656). See Stratman, *Dramatic*, for a descriptive bibliography of such catalogues. Gaskell (*New* 182–3) writes that booksellers' lists existed from the beginning of print, but were printed in books only after about 1650 (when title pages began to be regularly posted as a form of advertising), and that books were advertised in periodicals only from the 1690s on (when managers began regularly to advertise theatrical productions). See also Feather, *Provincial* 45 and Plant, *English* 248, on the development of regular book advertising in the later 17th century.

72. "... En la Imprenta de Joseph Antonio de Hermosilla ... se hallaràn muchos Libros, Entremeses, Romances, Relaciones, y Comedias, corregidas fielmente por sus legitimos Originales" (Calderón, *Alcalde de Zalamea* (n.d., title page); Bergman and Szmuk, *Catalogue* I:27. Sybil Rosenfeld's "Dramatic Advertisements" shows a distinct increase in newspaper announcements of play publication in London after 1688.

73. See Wiles (*Serial* 15–16) on the nonce collections of Shadwell and Dryden of the 1690s. A German example is Daniel Casper von Lohenstein's *Ibrahim Sultan, Agripppina, Epicharis, Und andere Gedichte* issued in 1685. The plays in such collections as *A Collection of the Best English Plays* (1711–12), *A Select Collection of the Best Modern English Plays* (1750), and *The British Stage* (1752) were issued separately as well as in groups, and the collections bearing these titles vary in contents. *Sueltas* were individually printed and (often) later bound together, but plays were also sometimes printed as part of a collection (with consecutively numbered pages) and subsequently unbound for separate (presumably cheaper) sale (see Restori, *Saggi* 11–35).

74. See Burke, *Popular* 63; and Martin, *Le Livre* 123.

75. *London Gazette*, 2–6 Jan. 1690; qtd. Milhous and Hume, "Dating" 376n. The play was in the active repertory at the Theatre Royal in 1689–90 (*London Stage* I:378).

76. *Daily Courant* (13 Nov. 1706); qtd. Summers, *Restoration* 11.

77. Milhous and Hume, "Dating" 404 (copy at the Huntington Library).

78. *Theatre Miscellany* 99–100 (Davis's introduction); and Milhous and Hume, "Dating" 404.
79. Bernard Lintott, for instance, acquired the rights to most of Farquhar's plays several weeks—and in some cases several months—prior to their premières. See Kenny, "Publication" 315.
80. "Il n'y en a, ce me semble, que sept feuilles, et le prix est un écu blanc. Je permettrai bien que les autres paient la folle enchère; je l'aurai à l'avenir pour un prix plus proportionné" (Leibniz, *Allgemeiner politischer und historischer Briefwechsel*; qtd. Picard, *La Carrière* 259).
81. Beaumont and Fletcher, *Comedies* sig. A3ᵛ.
82. Ibid.
83. The Beaumont and Fletcher collection probably cost about one guinea (Love, *Scribal* 67), more even than the Shakespeare first folio. Writing of the early 18th century, Saunders notes that "schoolmasters earned an average of £12 a year, labouring men 8*d* to 1*s* 6*d* a day, labouring women 4*d* to 1*s* a day, and Johnson calculated that it cost him £30 a year to live" (Saunders, *Profession* 123): for a schoolmaster or a labourer, the Beaumont and Fletcher collection cost more than a month's wages. For contemporaries' concern about the high cost of books, see the prefatory poems to Beaumont and Fletcher, *Comedies*, and Moseley's preface to William Cartwright's *Comedies* (1651). See the listings in the *Term Catalogues* for prices from 1677 onwards ("poems and plays"). By the early decades of the 18th century, booksellers were offering reprints for 4*d*. and less (see Nicoll, *Garrick* 18). On the similarly low cost of Spanish playbooks, see the introduction to Boyer, *Texas* p. xvii. In the later 18th century in France, there were equally wide gaps between expensive dramatic editions and ordinary playbooks: Voltaire's twelve-volume edition of Corneille published in 1764 cost 2 *louis* (or 72 *livres*), an investment of perhaps a month's salary for a university professor, whereas normal playbooks generally cost only 24 to 30 *sols* (Martin *et al.*, eds., *Histoire* II:220).
84. Nicoll, *Garrick* 18.
85. Generalization may be somewhat misleading here, since conventions for dramatic format varied from language to language and genre to genre, and were responsive to such political and economic factors as taxation and paper cost, but there was a trend towards smaller formats. In England, Germany, and Spain, individual first-edition plays were generally printed in quarto throughout the 17th century (with English reprints often in duodecimo or octavo, followed by a shift to duodecimo and then octavo in the early 18th century). In Spain, quarto remained the normal format for both individually and collectively printed *comedias* until the end of the 18th century (though *entremeses* and *sainetes* were printed in octavo). First editions of French plays changed from octavo to quarto around 1635, and in the 1650s from quarto to duodecimo, which remained the most common format for French plays through the 18th century. In Italy, oratorios and *melodramme* were generally in quarto but duodecimo remained the overwhelming preference for regular plays from around the 1630s onward. Folio editions of the drama grew rare after the middle of the 17th century, and throughout Europe there was a proliferation of octavo and duodecimo collections in the 18th century. For English plays, see Sampson, "Some Bibliographical" 103–7; McKenzie, "Typography" 111–12; the late 17th-century listings in Greg, *Bibliography*; and the handlist of plays in Nicoll, *History* II:294–407. For Spanish plays, see the listings in Barrera y Leirado, *Catálogo* and the listings for collections in Simón Díaz, *Bibliografía* IV:146–206. For Italian plays, see the listings in Franchi, *Drammaturgia*; and Clubb, *Italian Plays*. For French plays, see

Kirsop, "Le Théâtre" 97; Lancaster, *History* (discussions of format at the head of each chapter); and Martin *et al.*, eds., *Histoire* II:218–19.

86. *The Weekly Comedy* (22 Jan. 1708); qtd. Fielding, *Tragedy* 7.

87. Beaumont and Fletcher, *Comedies* sig. A3ʳ.

88. "Per render più utile, e dilettevole questa nostra fatica si publicano in un Volume unitamente stampati, e il Drama Pastorale, e i discorsi Accademici" (Bonarelli, *Opere* (1640) sig. *4ᵛ).

89. Qtd. Birrell, "Influence" 166 (with a discussion of playbook formats generally).

90. Beaumont and Fletcher, *Works* sig. A2ʳ–A2ᵛ.

91. *L'Ecole des maris* is "le premier ouvrage que je mets de moi-même au jour" (Molière, *Œuvres complètes* I:415 [dedication]). Molière paid for the publication of both *Tartuffe* and *Le Bourgeois gentilhomme* (see their title pages). For the general privilege, see Molière, *Œuvres de Molière* (1893 edn.) 39–42; and Young and Young, "'Une nouvelle'" (especially 138, 140). And on Molière's relations with his publishers generally, see Caldicott, *La Carrière*. Corneille paid for the publication of *Cinna* (1642) and *Le Dessein de la tragédie d'Andromède* (1650) (see their title pages), and Racine paid for *Bajazet* (1672) (see Picard, *La Carrière* 200, for the extensive evidence of Racine's involvement in the publication of his plays).

92. Davenant, *Works* π4ʳ ("Reader").

93. Nabbes, *Works* II:89 (verses perhaps by Charles Gerbier).

94. See Saunders, *Profession* 82–4; 88–93 for a few specifics. Generally, payments for non-dramatic works exceeded payments for plays, but payments by publishers for plays could be comparable to payments for non-dramatic works. At the end of the 17th century the average price in France for a novel was 300 *livres* (according to Martin, *Le Livre* 51), comparable to the 200 to 300 *livres* paid for a play (according to Viala, *Naissance* 108). The £100 that Samuel Johnson received for the publication of *Irene* in 1749 was not much less than the £125 he received for the publication of *Rasselas* in the same year (Saunders, *Profession* 142; Plant, *English* 77).

95. Picard, *La Carrière* 200.

96. Montalbán, *Fama*; qtd. Díez Borque, *Sociedad* 100 (perhaps an exaggeration, but indicative at least of the *perception* of the lucrativeness of dramatic printing by the 1630s). Payment figures for Spanish plays comparable to those for French or English are difficult to gather (see Cruickshank, "Editing" 54), and those for Italian plays are still more difficult, since the theatres were dominated by the traditions of opera, unscripted drama, and amateur dramatic poetry (see Riccoboni's comment in 1738 that "since the Year 1500 no *Italian* Poet has professed to write for the Theatre, in order to pick up Money; Dramatic Poetry having since that Time been an *Art*, but not a *Trade*" (Riccoboni, *Historical* 53)). Pasta ("Towards" 120) writes that it was not until the late 19th century that Italian writers began to live by their pens, noting the special vulnerability of Italian writers to piracy and citing Goldoni's move to Paris as evidence. But there was a significant trade in published plays (see, for instance, Mariti, *Commedia* pp. XL–LXX); and there were a number of dramatists who, writing for a living, probably earned some of their income from their published works, for instance Giovan Battista Fagiuoli (see Nicastro, *Metastasio* 42). See also, for the 1750s on, Goldoni's discussion of his dependence on his earnings from the publication of his plays (Goldoni, *Tutte* I:294–5 (*Mémoires*) and throughout).

97. See Calderón, *Primera Parte* I, p. xiii (Valbuena Briones's note).

98. Winn, *John Dryden* 451. For the French figures, see Viala, *Naissance* 108; and Brown,

"Field" 417–18 (based on the actor Bellecour's evaluation); and for the English examples, Kenny, "Publication" 310–11 (and below) and, on contemporary perceptions, Kewes, *Authorship* 226–7.

99. Qtd. *London Stage* I:434. For Southerne's earnings, see *London Stage* I: p. lxxxii.
100. Farquhar, *Works* II:18, 148 (Kenny's introductions).
101. Theatre-keepers at court in late 17th-century England made £30 per annum, about the salary of most minor officials, whereas a playwright could make £30 from the sale of a single play to a publisher, and in addition get performance receipts (see Boswell, *Restoration* 276–7, and the salary estimates in Pottinger, *French* 351–3).
102. Mumby and Norrie, *Publishing* 140.
103. Viala, *Naissance* 108. There are further records of payments to French dramatists from publishers recorded for the period: 750 *livres* for four Rotrou tragedies in 1637, and, later, 1,500 for ten Rotrou tragedies; 150 *livres* for Benserade's *Cléopâtre*; 800 *francs* for Crébillon's *Xerxes*, and an astonishing 3,600 francs for his *Catalina* (see Martin, *Le Livre* 50; Pottinger, *French* 99–100).
104. Pottinger, *French* 99–100.
105. Ibid.
106. Martin, *Le Livre* 50.
107. Sutherland, "'Polly'" 291; and Kenny, "Publication" 325. The fact that both *Tartuffe* and *Polly* were published by the dramatists themselves may partly account for these high figures. I am grateful to Robert D. Hume for the *Beggar's Opera* figure.
108. See Goldoni, *Tutte* I:294–5 (on his inability to depend on his theatrical income and his need for payments from print). Arrangements between theatres and dramatists grew complex during this period. Outright payment for plays seems nearly to have disappeared in the stable, urban professional theatres. In Paris, payment to dramatists was normally a set portion (about one-ninth) of performance takings during the first run, so long as takings did not fall below a certain point (Picard, *La Carrière* 199). In London, the principal payment was the author's benefit. A dramatist's takings from theatre productions (an author benefit, a percentage of house receipts, or a company share, depending on the theatre) could range anywhere from nothing to £2,000 or more in London, with the norm about £100 for a third night), and from about 500 francs to nearly 3,000, with 800 francs for a respectable run, substantially less in some cases than what dramatists were paid by publishers (Lancaster, *History* IV:401n.; Picard, *La Carrière* 199, *London Stage* I: pp. lxxx–lxxxiii, II(i): pp. c–ci, III(i): pp. cxi–cxii). Many plays in Paris did not bring in enough to cover house costs, and many London plays did not make it to a third night. On occasion, dramatists actually made the initial outlay for a production, hoping to be repaid from house receipts (Nicoll, *History* II:44; Picard, *La Carrière* 199), or were advanced money dependent on repayment from house receipts which, if the play failed, the playwrights were contractually required to repay.
109. Saunders, *Profession* 142.
110. The extensive literature on play printing during the period can provide a better sense of these conventions than I can, but it is nonetheless worth offering a few general remarks. French and Italian plays are usually printed entirely in italics (with roman for differentiated material), where Spanish and English plays are invariably printed in roman (with italics for differentiated material), and German plays in gothic (with roman or italic for non-German names). Speech-prefixes are generally indented and abbreviated, but sometimes (and almost invariably in French plays) centred and given in full. The classical 17th-century French, Italian, and German play continues throughout the 18th

century to use "continental" scene divisions (a new scene and list of characters each time a character enters or leaves the stage), usually listing the scene number and characters at the head of each scene in larger type than that of the rest of the play. English and Spanish plays rarely divide scenes in this way unless they are self-consciously identifying themselves with the continental (learned) stage. Spanish plays are almost always printed with two columns per page and, since so many were intended to be sold either separately or included in variety collections, normally do not have separate title pages, listing the *dramatis personae* directly under the title, and beginning the play on the same page. While there was a preference, in Spain, for collections of twelve plays each, this was not automatic. Throughout Europe (with the possible exception of Germany), *mise en page* for the ordinary, individually printed play remained fairly stable through the 17th and 18th centuries: the same typefaces; the same title-page designs, with the title, genre (tragedy, comedy, etc.), a note on performance venue, sometimes the author's name or initials and official title, occasionally a mention of the dedicatee, publication information, and (in Spain, France, and Italy) reference to the privilege, often with a printer's ornament but no title-page illustration.

111. See Bowers, *Essays* 135–50; Kenny, "Publication"; Cruickshank, "'Literature'"; and, for general information on the quality of printing during the period, Clair, *History* 131; and Pottinger, *French* 158–9.

112. See, for instance, Bowers (*Essays* 284) on the variants in the first edition (1667) of Dryden's *The Indian Emperour*.

113. For examples, see Kenny, "Publication" 319, 336; Buchanan, "Notes."

114. In the last decades of the 16th century, only a fraction of English or French playbooks contained author dedications or author prefatory material. By the 1630s, over half of English plays and nearly all French plays published appeared with author dedications. The presence of dramatist dedications is, of course, a function also of the patronage system. Still, it can give some indication of dramatist involvement. Blayney has counted the number of English playbooks published between 1583 and 1642 that have dedications: only 5 per cent between 1583 and 1602; 19 per cent between 1603 and 1622; and 58 per cent between 1623 and 1642 ("Publication" 395). Lancaster, *History* I:70 notes that somewhat more than a third of the French plays published 1610–18 have dedications, the majority in the middle decades, with a marked decline in the last decades of the century (Lancaster, *History* IV:486–7), perhaps reflecting the decline in the importance of patronage with the increase in performance and publication payments to dramatists. However, about half of the plays published in England during the later 17th century have dedications (Archer, "Epistle" 8).

115. Davenport, *Works* 3 ("To the knowing Reader"). This note, included in the first edition of the play in 1655, is the only evidence that Davenport was still alive at that date. (The play was originally performed in *c.*1628–9.)

116. "Cabales, enmendadas y corregidas." See Valbuena Briones's preliminary note in Calderón, *Primera parte* I, p. xiii (writing that the edition was corrected neither by Calderón nor his brother). As in the early 17th century, there was at least an expectation that dramatists would correct their own work, and authors continued to read in the printing house (Simpson, *Proof-Reading* 43). Edward Filmer has to make a special point of disclaiming responsibility for the correction of his *Unnatural Brother* (1697): "But one word more to the Reader … and that is, that he would not charge me with any Errors of the Press. The Bookseller in my absence, has undertaken the care of inspecting it, and therefore he only ought to be accountable for all such faults" (sig. A3ʳ). For many later

17th- and 18th-century examples, see Pottinger, *French* 51; and Simpson, *Proof-Reading* 1–45.

117. Corneille, *Oeuvres de Corneille* (*Première partie* 1644; *Seconde partie* 1648); and *Le Theatre de P. Corneille* (1660, 1663, 1664, 1682), all "Reveu & corrigé par l'Autheur." Corneille, *Oeuvres complètes* II:187–8, III:447–51.

118. See the privilege, reproduced in Molière, *Œuvres de Molière* (1893 edn.) 40; and Young and Young, "'Une nouvelle'" 143. There is some debate about whether or not the 1674–5 edition published by Denis Thierry and Claude Barbin was actually the edition prepared by Molière (as is claimed by Picot (*Catalogue* II:73) and Lacroix (*Bibliographie* 74)), or merely a later editorial project which may contain some of Molière's editing (as Young and Young claim ("'Une nouvelle'" 147)).

119. On Racine's extensive revisions for the 1676, 1687, and 1697 editions of his works, see Picard, *La Carrière* 257–8, 353, 513–14. On Congreve's editorial oversight of the publication of his 1710 *Works*, see McKenzie, "When Congreve" and "Typography"; and Peters, *Congreve* 60–2.

120. Molière, *Œuvres complètes* I:291–4, 299–302 (Couton's notes and the letter prefaced to one copy of the play). This is all the more surprising given Molière's efforts to suppress Jean Ribou's unauthorized edition of the La Neufvillaine version of the play (for which Ribou had been granted a privilege for the play under a different name several months after Molière had taken out his own privilege). Molière arranged to have the police raid Ribou's shop, invalidate Ribou's privilege, and ban his edition. See the discussion in Chartier, "Publishing" [lecture 2, "'Copied onely by the eare'" 1].

121. Warner, "First."

122. Steele, *Plays* 8–14 and Farquhar, *Works* I:139–40 (Kenny's introductions).

123. Beaumont and Fletcher, *Comedies* sig. A4^v.

124. Ibid. sig. g2^r.

125. "Comme les Imprimeurs ont eu de la peine à s'y accoutumer, ils n'auront pas suivi ce nouvel ordre si ponctuellement, qu'il ne s'y soit coulé bien des fautes, vous me ferez la grace d'y suppléer." Corneille, *Oeuvres complètes* III:451 (preface to 1663 edition). See Cruickshank, "Editing" 74–5, on the similar influence of the Dutch on the Spanish switch to the consonantal *j* and *u* in Seville in the 1670s and Madrid in the 1690s.

126. Congreve, *Letters* 13–18; and McKenzie, "Typography" 111.

127. Such letters are "nécessaires aux Rédacteurs pour l'ordre des matières, pour l'intelligence des allusions renfermées dans les écrits de l'Auteur, & pour l'histoire de sa vie, elles n'ont pas été moins utiles pour l'application des notes & pour le choix des variantes & des fragments." Beaumarchais, *Avis* (undated two-sided sheet, *c.*1780). On his "Societé Littéraire & Typographique," see Steinberg, *Five* 135–6. On Lessing, see Wittmann, *Geschichte* 149–50. Congreve had similarly done the editorial work on Tonson's edition of Dryden in 1717–18 (Peters, *Congreve* 60); and Voltaire himself produced an edition of Corneille in 1763 (Corneille, *Oeuvres complètes* I: p. lxviii).

128. "Ces modèles imprimés avec les caracteres de Baskerville, dont la Société a acquis les poinçons ... montreront à quel point de perfection la Société veut porter la partie typographique de cette Edition." Beaumarchais, *Avis*.

129. The improvements in English printing generally were more marked than improvements elsewhere (in the view of bibliographers and printing historians), spurred by legal changes—most notably the lapse of the Licensing Act in 1695, with its restrictions on the number of printing houses in England—changes that permitted English printing, inferior to continental printing in the first centuries of print, to surpass its rivals (see

Gaskell, *New* 170–1, Clair, *History* 131, 158). But there were improvements elsewhere as well (see Pottinger, *French* 158–9; Wilhelm, "French" 69, 71–2; Thomas, *Royal* pp. vii, ix). "Pirates" in Amsterdam could do careful printing and proof correction, sometimes turning out editions more consistent and cleaner than those overseen by dramatists (see Kenny, "Publication" 332–5, on the productions of Thomas Johnson in the Hague in the early 18th century). One of the reasons for the textual superiority of 18th-century plays was a change in proof-reading practices. 16th- and 17th-century proofreading was done in-house, often without waiting for a press corrector or author to look over the sheets (the reason for so many variants in early texts). But according to Bowers, some time between the Restoration and the mid-18th century proofs began to be pulled so that authors could correct them at leisure (*Essays* 398).

130. Cibber, *Dramatic* IV:108 (preface).

131. Shadwell, *Lancashire-Witches* sig. A2ʳ. See, similarly, Cibber's preface to his *Tragical History of King Richard III* (1700) (he has printed Shakespeare's text in italics).

132. "Tous les vers qui sont marquez avec deux virgules renversées qu'on nomme ordinaire-ment Guillemets, sont des vers que les Comediens ne recitent point dans leur represen-tations, parce que les Scenes sont trop longues, & que d'ailleurs n'estât pas necessaires, ils refroidissent l'action du Theatre. Monsieur de Moliere a suivy ces observations aussi bien que les autres Acteurs" (Molière, *Les Oeuvres* (1682 edn.) I, sig. a10ʳ–a10ᵛ ("Avis au lecteur")).

133. Shakespeare, *Hamlet* (1676 edn.) sig. A4ʳ. See similarly the marking of additions from revivals with asterisks in Pando's 1717 edition of Calderón's *autos*.

134. Sheridan, *Dramatic* II:537 (*Critic* II.ii).

135. Maggi, *Rime varie di Carlo Maria Maggi* (1700); qtd. Clubb, *Italian Plays* 151.

136. See Eaves and Kimpel, "Text" 336; and compare the Congreve first quartos with the plays as edited in Congreve, *Works* (1710 edn.). In reaction to such print-identified purges, Vanbrugh could publicly resist the convention, promising, in his 1696 edition of *The Relapse*, that "If there was any obscene Expressions upon the Stage, here they are in the Print; for I have dealt fairly, I have not sunk a Sylable, that cou'd (tho' by racking of Mysteries) be rang'd under that head" (Vanbrugh, *Complete* I:11, specifically respond-ing to Jeremy Collier's claim, in *A Short View of the English Stage* (1698), that play-wrights concealed their stage obscenities by revising for print).

137. "Je fis faire à Florence la premiere édition de mes Ouvrages, sous les yeux et sous la cen-sure des savans du pays, pour les purger des défauts de langage." Goldoni, *Tutte* I:383 (Pt. 2, Ch. 32) (and see the *Mémoires* generally for Goldoni's continual editorial oversight of his collections).

138. Tate, *History* 67 (V.v).

139. Waller, *Maid's* 4.

140. Qtd. Beaumont and Fletcher, *Works* (1711 edn.) I: pp. xxxv–xxxvi.

141. Johnson, *Johnson* II:704.

142. John Dennis's prescription for tragedy in Dennis, *Critical* I:30 (*Impartial Critic* (1693)).

143. "Der Schau-Platz bildet ab der Cleopatra Zimmer"; "Der Schauplatz bildet ab das lustiges Gebirge des Berges Ida in Phrygien" (Lohenstein, *Cleopatra* sig. B6ʳ, C5ᵛ (II.i., II.iv.)).

144. Dryden, *Works* XIII:121. I am grateful to Siobhan Kilfeather for, long ago, drawing my attention to this passage.

145. Behn, *Works* V:410 (III.i) (and see Todd's notes on the uncertain attribution to Behn (V:389)).

146. Fielding, *Author's Farce* 30 (II.iv).
147. Behn, *Works* VI:123 (III.i).
148. Of those plays I have examined, nearly half printed before 1580 (counting collections as single plays) have at least one illustration (the typical 16th-century chapbook has several), whereas fewer than a quarter printed 1580–1700 (after the establishment of professional theatres) have any (the typical 17th-century collected edition has only an engraved frontispiece). On the decline of illustration in book production generally in the 17th century and its rise again in the 18th, see Wilhelm, "French" 69–2.
149. Molière, *Les Oeuvres* (1682 edn.) III:276 ("Adraste, aux genoux d'Isidore, pendant que Dom Pèdre parle à Hali" (Molière, *Œuvres complètes* II:340, scene xii)).
150. A few notable examples are the 1709 Shakespeare *Works* (edited by Rowe); the 1711 Beaumont and Fletcher *Works*; *Œuvres de Moliere* (1734) with Laurent Car's engravings of Boucher's illustrations; and Goldoni's *Delle commedie* (1761) with eighty-seven illustrations.
151. Gherardi, *Le Theatre* (1700 ed.) II:362 (*La Descente de Mezzetin aux enfers*); III:440–1 (*Arlequin Phaeton*).
152. Goldoni, *Delle commedie* VI:178.
153. There are a number of pre-18th-century dance manuals: the *Art et instruction de bien dancer* (1488); *The Mayner of Dauncynge of Bace Daunces after the use of Fraunce and Other Places* (1521); Thoinot Arbeau's *Orchesographie: methode et theorie en forme de discours et tablature pour apprendre a danser* (1596). But manuals proliferate in the 18th century: Feuillet's *Choreographie*; Weaver's translation of Feuillet (*Orchesography* 1706); Weaver's own *Anatomical Lectures upon Dancing* (1721); Rameau's *Le Maitre a Danser* (1725) (translated as *The Dancing Master* in 1728); Kellom Tomlinson's *The Art of Dancing* in 1735, to mention just a few. On dance notation during the period generally, see Wynne, "Reviving."
154. Feuillet, *Orchesography* 98–9.
155. Riccoboni, *Réflexions historiques et critiques sur les différents théâtres de l'Europe* (translated into English in 1741); *Les Spectacles de Paris, ou Calendrier Historique & Chronologique des Théatres* (1750–78). On the history of drama reviewing, see Gray, *Theatrical*, noting that it was not until the 1770s that British periodicals regularly began to grant space to theatre reviews (1), but identifying the tremendous growth of specialty theatre periodicals in the 18th century. See also the list in Lagrave, *Le Théâtre* 671–2, which names twenty-four 17th- and 18th-century periodicals carrying dramatic and theatrical criticism.

3. ILLUSTRATIONS, PROMPTBOOKS, STAGE TEXTS, 1760–1880

1. See *Revels* VI: pp. l–lxi; Krakovitch, "Le Théâtre" 147; Brown, *Theater* 41; and Ravel, *Contested* 6. Nicoll lists twelve theatres in London 1750–1800, and some sixty in London and some seventy more in the provinces 1800–50 (*History* III:229–30, IV:222–38). It is worth recalling that in most places the number of theatres allowed was strictly regulated, but that the systems of regulation had already begun to break down in the 18th century and were generally lifted in the 19th century (in London, for instance, after the Theatre Regulation Act of 1843).
2. "¡Hay actualmente en Madrid entre Liceos, Academias, Museos, Circos, y teatros

caseros, más de cuarenta diversiones particulares!" (*El Pasatiempo* (14 Apr. 1842); qtd. Gies, *Theatre* 15).

3. Hemmings, *Theatre* 2.

4. On the multiplication of provincial theatres, see (for instance) Fuchs, *La Vie*; Rosenfeld, *Georgian*. In Germany (beginning to catch up to the rest of Europe) there were fourteen companies in 1774, twenty by 1775, and well over thirty by the 1790s (Patterson, *First* 15).

5. Qtd. Nicoll, *Garrick* 66 (and see 64–5 on the numerous Theatres Royal built outside London in the 1760s and 1770s).

6. Gies, *Theatre* 118–19.

7. Jordan, *Mrs. Jordan* 12 (27th? Nov. 1791). On Jordan's travels in the provinces and her relations with the newspress, see Tomalin, *Mrs Jordan's* 28–40, 93–4. On the role of the Spanish periodical press in creating the modern theatrical celebrity, see Gies, *Theatre* 351.

8. Jordan, *Mrs. Jordan* 80 (13 Apr. 1809).

9. On these, see Pereire, *Le Journal* 144; Gray, *Theatrical* 1; and Carlson, *Places* 23. On Spanish theatrical advertisements and criticism in the newspress during the period, see Cruickshank, "On the Stage" 3.

10. Announcement for *The Stage: A Theatrical Paper Published Daily*; qtd. Myers, "Writing" 123. A list of specialty theatre periodicals in London in the later 18th century alone would include (among others) *The Comedian, The Dramatic Censor, Macaroni and Theatrical Magazine, The Theatre, The Theatrical Guardian, The Theatrical Monitor, The Theatrical Register, The Theatrical Review, Annals of the Drama*.

11. See e.g. Dorothy Jordan's letter to the Duke of Clarence: Jordan, *Mrs. Jordan* 91 (10 June 1809).

12. "Don Cayetano Rosell, conocido escritor, acaba un drama titulado, *La madre de San Fernando*, escrito para el teatro Español" (*La Epoca*, 6 July 1849). "Don Cayetano Rosell ha concluido el drama *La madre de San Fernando*, para el teatro Español, del que se hacen los mayores elogios" (*La Nación*, 7 July 1849). "Anteanoche fue leído y aprobado por la junta de lectura del Teatro Español el drama que con el título de *La madre de San Fernando* ha escrito el conocido literato don Cayetano Rosell" (*La España*, 23 Sept. 1849). "*La madre de San Fernando*, de don Cayetano Rosell, aprobado por la junta de lectura; pronto se pondrá en escena." (*La España*, 4 Nov. 1849). "La primera función que se pondrá en escena en el Teatro Español después de las de Navidad es el drama nuevo, original y en verso, titulado *La madre de San Fernando*, de cuyo éxito como obra literaria tenemos noticias muy ventajosas" (*La Nación*, 25 Dec. 1849). "El lunes se pondrá por primera vez en escena en el Teatro Español el drama original en verso titulado: *La madre de San Fernando*, del señor don Cayetano Rosell" (*La Epoca*, 4 Jan. 1850). "En el Teatro Español se está ensayando el drama nuevo, original del señor Rosell y en verso titulado *La madre de San Fernando*" (*La Epoca*, 17 Feb. 1850). "Desastroso el drama *La madre de San Fernando*" (*La Nación*, 12 Mar. 1850). Gies, *Theatre* 184–5.

13. See O'Toole, *Traitor's* 98–9; Werkmeister, *Newspaper* 36, 42–43; Buckley, "Illusion" 74.

14. "*Des billets donnés à la claque, et des éloges payés dans les journaux*." Sainte-Beuve, *Œuvres* I:288 ("Alexandre Duval" (1828)). Apparently, a more refined form of "purchased praise in the newspapers" developed later in the century, in which a playwright might allow a newspaper editor to be named as co-author and thereby gain part of the royalties, in exchange for the certainty of good publicity in the newspaper (Hemmings, *Theatre* 255–6).

15. "Pagliasso lief unter der andringenden Menge drollig hin und her, und teilte mit sehr begreiflichen Späßen, indem er bald ein Mädchen küßte, bald einen Knaben pritschte, seine Zettel aus, und erweckte unter dem Volke eine unüberwindliche Begierde, ihn näher kennen zu lernen. In den gedruckten Anzeigen waren die mannigfaltigen Künste der Gesellschaft, besonders eines Monsieur Narciß und der Demoiselle Landrinette herausgestrichen, welche beide, als Hauptpersonen, die Klugheit gehabt hatten, sich von dem Zuge zu enthalten, sich dadurch ein vornehmeres Ansehn zu geben, und größere Neugier zu erwecken." Goethe, *Gedenkausgabe* VII:98; Goethe, *Wilhelm Meister* 50–1 (Bk. II, Ch. 4) (trans. modified).

16. According to the modern editor, Appelbaum, the posters and other illustrations in this compilation illustrate the décor and character groupings in the plays they advertise quite faithfully (Appelbaum, ed., *Scenes* ix; pp. vii–viii).

17. See Austen, *Mansfield* (Chs. 13–15, 18). On the more formal "teatros caseros" (home theatres) in Spain, see Cruickshank, "On the Stage" 6–7; and Gies, *Theatre* 17.

18. "Ich hatte kaum das erste Stück, wozu Theater und Schauspieler geschaffen und gestempelt waren, etlichemal aufgeführt, als es mir schon keine Freude mehr machte. Dagegen waren mir unter den Büchern des Großvaters die Deutsche Schaubühne und verschiedene italienisch-deutsche Opern in die Hände gekommen, in die ich mich sehr vertiefte und jedesmal nur erst vorne die Personen überrechnete, und dann sogleich, ohne weiteres, zur Aufführung des Stückes schritt." Goethe, *Gedenkausgabe* VII:24; Goethe, *Wilhelm Meister* 9 (Bk. I, Ch. 6).

19. On the circulating libraries, flourishing from the 1770s on, see Altick, *English* 59–66; and *Buch und Sammler*. According to Roger Chartier ("Book" 120), there were forty-nine lending libraries in France between 1759 and 1789.

20. Archer, *Old* 252.

21. See Shattuck's comments in Kemble, *Kemble* I: p. xiv.

22. "Kupferstiche nach ... de[m] Belisar [von] van Dyck." "Die sogenannte väterliche Ermahnung von Terborch ... und wer kennt nicht den herrlichen Kupferstich unseres Wille von diesem Gemälde?" Goethe, *Gedenkausgabe* IX:170–1 (*Die Wahlverwandtschaften* Pt. 2, Ch. 5); trans. Goethe, *Elective* 190–1.

23. Eliot, *Daniel Deronda* 90 (Bk. 1, Ch. 6). For further 18th- and 19th-century examples, see Meisel, *Realizations* 97–141; and Chapter 13.

24. No fewer than 32,000 new plays were staged in Paris in the 19th century (Hemmings, *Theatre* 2), which one might compare with the 11,662 new plays that Brenner's *Bibliographical List* identifies as having been *written* (though not necessarily performed) in France 1700–89. Nicoll's handlist of English plays for the period 1700–50 takes up 114 pages, that for 1750–1800 131 pages; that for 1800–50 317 pages, and that for 1850–1900 543 pages (*History* II:293–407, III:232–363, IV:249–566, V:229–772).

25. *Theatrical Museum* title page and sig. A2ᵛ.

26. Rodríguez y Díaz Rubí, *La hija de la providencia*; Gies, *Theatre* 175, 225.

27. "Un très-grand nombre de Pièces jouées sur différens Théatres" (library catalogue of "citoyenne Montesquiou" (Paris 1793); qtd. Martin *et al.*, eds., *Histoire* II:222). It is hard to get even approximate numbers of plays printed during the later 18th and 19th centuries, given the enormous numbers involved and the variations in the calculations. Jeffrey Ravel (*Contested* 6) estimates that about 3,000 new French plays were published 1760–89 (and that about half of the new plays published in France 1610–1790 were published 1760–90). Gies comments on the "rather astonishing quantity" of plays printed in 19th-century Spain (*Theatre* 175) but, along with Stephens (*Profession* 117), notes that

bibliographical work has been inadequate to the task of recording the enormous output. While book production generally had risen steadily since the 15th century, it seems to have doubled or tripled over the course of the 18th century, in the first decade of the 19th growing to almost six times what it had been at the beginning of the 18th (Martin, *Le Livre* 117; Chartier, "Book" 120; Cain *et al.*, *Le Livre* 59; Saunders, *Profession* 123–4). In England, the yearly average of under 100 new books a year between 1666 and 1756 rose for the period 1792–1802 to 372, for the period 1802–27 to about 580, and then soared by mid-century to over 2,600 (Plant, *English* 445–6).

28. Boaden, *Memoirs of Mrs Inchbald* II:82 (1833).

29. A paper-making machine was developed in 1803. The machine-press was developed around 1806, but did not come into general usage until around 1840 (though when it did, it was capable of producing about 1,800 impressions an hour, as compared with the 250 per hour of the hand press (Plant, *English* 289)). Composing machines were developed around 1822 but typesetting was not fully mechanized until around 1900. See Plant, *English* 269–81; Clair, *History*; Feather, *History* 131–5; Wittmann, *Geschichte* 201–36. Feather (*History* 142–3) notes the fact that dramatic series like John Murray's made important use of the technological innovations of the period.

30. Shaw, *Shaw on Theatre* 62 ("The Problem Play—A Symposium"). On the growth in the London population from 900,000 at the end of the 18th century to four million by 1880, and the relationship between population size and theatre, see *Revels* VI:3–4.

31. In Spain, specialty theatrical publishers included Antonio Yenes, Repullés, José Rodríguez, and Cipriano López (Gies, *Theatre* 175–6); in England, Longmans, John Murray, Thomas Dolby, John Duncombe, John Cumberland, Thomas Hailes Lacy, Samuel French, and John Dicks ("almost all of whom," according to Stephens (*Profession* 116), "published nothing but cheaply produced plays"); and in France, Jean-Nicolas Barba, Beck, Bézou, Brandus, André Drouot de Charlieu, Heugel, Jonas, Michel Lévy, Marchant, Stock, Christophe and Nicolas Tresse (Mollier, *L'Argent* 319–51). On the expansion of both printing and publishing houses, the final separation of publishing from bookselling functions, and the development of a modern publishing industry, see Feather, *History* 120–5; Gaskell, *New* 175–76, 180; and Plant, *English* 68. According to David Gies, "publishing empires" like Manuel Delgado's "grew up nourished by the production of printed plays" (*Theatre* 351).

   Edition sizes had been restricted in most places throughout the 16th, 17th, and 18th centuries (Merland, "Tirage"; Feather, *History* 94), but the lifting of such restrictions did not automatically mean larger editions. According to Henri-Jean Martin, print runs of one to two thousand copies were still common in the 19th century (depending on subject-matter). Plays could, however, be published in significantly larger editions: Krakovitch ("Le Théâtre" 154) notes that in 1828 normal play editions had print runs of 500 to 1,000 copies, but that in 1829, with the publication of a collection based on the repertory of the Théâtre de Madame, publishers started creating print runs of from 3,000 to 4,000 copies, 5,000 copies in the case of *Théobald*, and 6,000 in the case of the *Manie des places*; Pixérécourt's *Coelina ou l'Enfant du mystère* was published in a special edition of 10,000 copies (Martin, *Le Livre* 223). Furthermore, editions tended to sell out more quickly (Martin, *Le Livre* 219). In a mere three days, 4,000 copies of Goldsmith's *She Stoops to Conquer* (1773) were sold to the public (Kenny, "Publication" 324). In Spain a century later, Rosario de Acuña y Villanueva de la Iglesia's *Rienzi el tribuno* (1876) sold out in two editions of 2,000 copies each within days (Gies, *Theatre* 212).

32. Feather, *History* 134; Plant, *English* 341–53.

33. On 19th-century Spanish and English collections and series printing, see Gies, *Theatre* 90, 175 and Stephens, *Profession* 124–5.

34. Broadsheet advertisement for Bell's Shakespeare, reproduced in the ESTC.

35. Inchbald was rather dismissive of her work as an editor, saying that she earned her 50-guinea fee "in five minutes, by merely looking over a catalogue of fifty farces, drawing my pen across one or two, and writing the names of others in their place." Boaden, *Memoirs of Mrs Inchbald* II:132–3.

36. Stephens, *Profession* 127.

37. See Lacroix, *Bibliographie* 106 on reduced formats in France. It is worth noting that the dominance of the quarto for the publication of *comedias* in Spain loosened at the end of the 18th century, and formats grew more varied and generally smaller.

38. Rising prices between 1780 and 1825 were due in part to the scarcity of paper and growing labour costs. There were attempts to keep prices artificially high in England and France, but reduced formats and the proliferation of cheap reprints in the 1790s, cheap series from the 1830s on, and pocket editions and "railway editions" on sale from the 1850s on, continued to drive prices down. See Martin, *Le Livre* 22; Plant, *English* 414–17; and Thomas Holcroft's comments (Holcroft, *Plays* I [*Love's Frailties* iv]).

39. Krakovitch, "Le Théâtre" 155. On the overall drop in French book prices, see Martin, *Le Livre* 22.

40. *Theatrical Museum* sig. A2ᵛ.

41. Stephens, *Profession* 126, 131.

42. Genest, *Some Account* VIII:533; Stephens, *Profession* 120.

43. Boyer, *Texas* xxi.

44. Stephens, *Profession* 122.

45. On improvements in English and Spanish printing in the later 18th and 19th centuries, see Gaskell, *New* 265; and Thomas, *Royal* ix. On the mass production of cheap ephemera and the apparent decline in the quality of printing, see Plant, *English* 414–15; Feather, *History* 130, 142; and Michel, "French" 88.

46. Hazlitt, *Complete* VI:319 (Lecture VI: "On Miscellaneous Poems").

47. For Goldoni, see Drake's introduction in Goldoni, *Memoirs* p. xv; and Renato Pasta's discussion ("Towards" 119–20), estimating that 20–25,000 complete *sets* of Goldoni's plays (including two 31-volume editions and one 44-volume edition) circulated in Italy before his death in 1793, identifying this, along with similarly impressive publishing statistics for Metastasio ("one of the most successful commercial hits in 18th-century publishing") as indicative of the general broadening of the Italian national market for drama. For Kötzebue, see Meyer, *Bibliographia* I(2):466–7. For Hugo, see the Bibliothèque Nationale, *Catalogue des livres imprimés*.

48. Letter to Frederick Macmillan, qtd. Stephens, *Profession* 142.

49. Pinero, *Times* (1891) ("Introductory Note") p. vii.

50. Examples of plays printed prior to performance in the later 18th and early 19th century include both plays that posed specific problems in performance (or were written initially as closet dramas) and plays clearly intended for the theatre: Diderot's *Le Fils naturel* (1757); Voltaire's *Sophonisbe* (1770); George Colman the elder's *Ut Pictura Poesis!* (1789); Coleridge and Southey's *Death of Robespierre* (1794); and Matthew ('Monk') Lewis's tragedy *Alfonso* (1801). See Diderot, *Oeuvres* 1431; Bengesco, *Voltaire* I:76–7; Langhans, *Eighteenth Century* p. xxii; Southey, *New* I:72–3; and Stephens, *Profession* 120. See also Cruickshank, "On the Stage" 4–5, on the substantial number of Spanish plays published during the period but clearly not intended for the commercial stage, and

Brown, "Field" 179, on the substantial number of French plays printed without prior performance.

51. "Es ist die Helena, die an Cotta zum Druck abgeht. ... Es mag nun seine Schicksale erleben!" Goethe, *Gedenkausgabe* XXIV:222–3 (*Gespräche mit Eckermann* Thu. evening, 29 Jan. 1827). On *Die Räuber* and *Iphegenia*, see Patterson, *First* 37, 92.

52. Grabbe, *Jest* pp. xiv–v (Edwards' introduction). Contrast this with Farquhar's assessment of performance as a necessary precondition for the publication of plays in the 18th century (Farquhar, *Works* II:369).

53. Qtd. Stephens, *Profession* 121 (Browning's unpublished preface).

54. For discussions of the variety and centrality of "closet drama" in the 19th century, see Barish, *Antitheatrical* 334–7, 340; and Mathur, *Closet*.

55. Shirley Strum Kenny speculates that dramatists "probably sent the original version to the printer," and that "frequently two sets of papers were involved, one sent to the playhouse, another to the printer ... a second manuscript ... completed before the play went to rehearsal ("Publication" 317).

56. Goethe, *Gedenkausgabe* XXIV:223 (*Gespräche mit Eckermann* Thu. evening, 29 Jan. 1827).

57. Pinero, *Collected* 131 (27 Oct. 1891).

58. Shaw, *Complete* I:34–5 (preface to *Plays Unpleasant*). Shaw in fact attended not only to such substantive matters as his famously lengthy stage directions and revised orthography when he came to publish *Plays Pleasant and Unpleasant* in 1898, but also to such design details as the use of ugly type and "Egyptian mummy color" paper for *Plays Unpleasant* (to be contrasted with "the best Kelmscott style" type and white paper for *Plays Pleasant*) (Shaw, *Collected* I:740).

59. Archer, *Old* 252.

60. Wordsworth, *Borderers* 814 ("Fenwick Note" (1843)).

61. For a general discussion of the interest of poets like Coleridge, Shelley, Byron, and Tennyson in the theatre and their partial successes and failures, see *Revels* VI:192–202; and Carlson, *In the Theatre*.

62. For the Sheridan story, see Sheridan, *Dramatic* I:2. On dramatic professionals during the period, see Hemmings (*Theatre* 235): Eugène Scribe was the "first to make a fortune out of writing plays and charging the market price for them," but certainly only one of many. As David Gies writes, there was a veritable cottage industry of writers, translators, and *refundidores* to meet the demand for theatrical material (*Theatre* 71).

63. "Suelo traducir ... la primera *piececilla* ... que se me presenta, que lo mismo pagan y cuesta menos: no pongo mi nombre, y ya se puede hundir el teatro a silbidos la noche de la representación. ¿Qué quiere usted?" *El Pobrecito Hablador* (11 Sept. 1832); qtd. Gies, *Theatre* 91 (trans. modified).

64. Stephens writes that a "significant proportion of nineteenth-century plays was never published," noting that only about two-thirds of Francis Burnand's 150 or so plays went into print, only somewhat over half of James Robinson Planché's 180 or so (before the 1879 publication of his five-volume *Extravaganzas*), about the same percentage of John Buckstone's and W. T. Moncrieff's, fewer than half of Edward Fitzball's, only about one quarter of Dion Boucicault's two hundred or so, and perhaps as few as 5 per cent of George Dibdin Pitt's several hundred (*Profession* 118). Even in France, only two-thirds to three-quarters of the new plays that were performed between 1817 and 1830 were published, though after about 1835 over nine-tenths were published (Krakovitch, "Le Théâtre" 149).

65. Stephens, *Profession* 121. On the bookselling concessions in the Comédie Française and the Comédie Italienne, see Ravel, "Printed" 6.

66. Stephens, *Profession* 117.

67. Counts give a general idea. For the year 1829, there were 308 plays published, as against only 267 novels. But Rosa, "'Quot libras in duce?'" 234, shows that in the later 19th century about three times as many copies of novels were printed as copies of plays (and about twice as many copies of poetry collections). See Eliot, *Some Patterns* 43–5, on the decline in the percentage of books classified as "poetry and drama" (in the *Bibliotheca Londinensis* and the *Bookseller*) and the rise in the percentage of books classified as "fiction and juvenile literature." On the contrast between the immense sums that novelists began to make after the first decades of the 19th century and the relatively small sums that dramatists made, see Booth, *Theatre* 143.

68. In most places, author-held copyright was fully established by the last decades of the 18th century: in Spain, as early as 1763 (Thomas, *Royal* 10); in France, in a series of litigations that followed the 1777 promulgation of the "permission simple" (Martin, *Le Livre* 114); in Prussia in 1794, when the *Allgemeines Landrecht* granted inalienable proprietorship to authors (Kittler, *Discourse* 18); in England, only with *Donaldson v. Becket* (1774). On late 18th- and 19th-century copyright legislation and litigation in England, see Feather, *Publishing* 81–96; and Rose, *Authors*. On proposals for German copyright laws in the later 18th century, see Wittmann, *Geschichte* 150–1. While I have pieced together, here, what is known of performance copyright during the period, the relationship between print copyright and performance copyright throughout Europe requires further study.

69. Gies, *Theatre* 18; Thomas, *Royal*.

70. *Annalen des Theaters* 9 (1792) 4–22; reproduced in Brandt, ed., *German* 112. See also Patterson (*First* 17–18) on the general company policy of giving actors only part books to prevent them from giving away or selling scripts that might subsequently be pirated. It is worth noting that the guarding of scripts still sometimes seemed necessary even after significant national copyright protection was in place because of the uncertainty of international copyright until the end of the century: in the 1870s, the D'Oyly Carte company, rehearsing Gilbert and Sullivan's *Pirates of Penzance* in the US, had the score and libretto locked away in a safe to prevent piracy (Stephens, *Profession* 107).

71. "Cette Tragédie [a] été contrefaite dans presque toutes les Provinces du Royaume, & dans les Pays étrangers. ... Ces contrefactions sont aisées à reconnaître, tant par la mauvaise impression, que par les fautes qui y fourmillent. Le Public est donc averti de s'adresser directement chez la *Veuve* DUCHESNE, *Libraire, rue Saint Jacques*, pour avoir l'Édition correcte, & imprimée sous les yeux de l'Auteur." Belloy, *Le Siége* π1ᵛ("Avis Essential"); qtd. Brown, "Field" 173–4.

72. "Le brigandage qui s'exerçait à l'égard des productions des auteurs continue toujours. ... Plusieurs, tant souffleurs et copistes que musiciens de divers théâtres se sont engagés à fournir ... à différents théâtres de province la partition de *Nicomède dans la lune*. ... Je ne fais imprimer ni graver aucune de mes pièces jusqu'à nouvel ordre, et je vends les manuscrits et les partitions, moyennant des arrangements particuliers." Letter reproduced in Lunel, *Le Théâtre* 65.

73. See Boncompain, *Auteurs* 92–144, and Brown, "Field" 98–167, on official Comédie-Française policies, and throughout on the protests against the Comédie-Française policies in the 1760s and 1770s; and Brown, "After," on conceptions of dramatic-literary property (or, rather, "rights") in France in the later 18th century. Unlike late 18th- and

19th-century English theatres, the Comédie-Française apparently never claimed publication rights based on performance rights (Brown, "After" 473) and, according to Brown (personal communication), the revised 1766 Comédie-Française regulations stipulated that a dramatist waiting to have a play performed could print the play after two years, and this would not affect the right to performance.

74. Dramatist copyright was for life plus five years, eventually extended to fifty. There was a good deal of back and forth on the question of the legal effect of publication. The theatres that had formerly held monopolies apparently pretended to believe that the new law concerned only plays that had been printed before it went into effect. In response, the National Assembly promulgated a new, clarificatory decree in 1791 specifying that no plays by authors then living or who had died less than five years earlier were to be performed without the authors' or their heirs' written permission. In 1792, in response to the claims of the former monopoly theatres, the law was modified again, but a year later, under protest from the dramatists, the Convention annulled the modifications of 1792 and revived the decrees of 1791. See Lunel, *Le Théâtre* 72–3; and Carlson, *Theatre* 75.

75. Thackeray, *On Theatrical Emancipation*; qtd. Stephens, *Profession* 85 (emphasis added). Throughout my discussion of British performance copyright, I am heavily indebted to Stephens's analysis in *Profession* 84–115 (drawing extensively on the *Report from the Select Committee on Dramatic Literature* in *British Sessional Papers* (1831–2)).

76. Both William Thomas Moncrieff and Robert William Elliston, for instance, thought they held the rights to Moncrieff's *Giovanni in London*, which Elliston had first staged at the Olympic Theatre in 1817 and which he claimed as his when he moved to Drury Lane in 1820. Moncrieff believed he retained copyright (whatever his arrangements with Elliston had been). The dramatist James Robinson Planché, on the other hand, believed he had too uncertain a legal claim to sue the Theatre Royal in Edinburgh when it produced his *Charles XIIth* without his permission in 1830 (Stephens, *Profession* 85, 89–90). The 1710 Copyright Act (8 Ann. *c*.19, 1709) protected author copyright for fourteen years from the date of publication, with an additional fourteen years added if the author was alive at the expiration of the first period. The 1814 Copyright Act (54 Geo. III *c*.56) protected author copyright for life or for twenty-eight years from the date of publication, whichever was longer. On the history of this legislation, see Feather, *Publishing* 110–21.

77. Stephens, *Profession* 85.

78. Dibdin, *Reminiscences* II:302–4.

79. On the publisher John Murray's suit to enjoin the production of Byron's *Marino Faliero* in 1821 on the grounds that he held the copyright (*Murray* v. *Ellison*), see Stephens, *Profession* 88.

80. Stephens, *Profession* 86–7. Further examples of print copyrights sold to managers with performance rights include: the sale of the libretto of Carl Maria von Weber's *Oberon* in 1836 for £400 (£100 for the copyright); the sale of an unnamed comedy by John Poole (probably *The Wife's Stratagem*) in 1827 for £200 (see Stephens, *Profession* 35, 39).

81. See Cecil Price's introduction to the play in Sheridan, *Dramatic* I:325, describing Harris's attempt to enjoin a 1777 Dublin production based on a pirated text that had been copied by shorthand, and on the advertisement in the *Sussex Weekly Advertiser* (22 June 1778).

82. Stephens, *Profession* 86–7 (and see 31 on Thomas and Henry Harris).

83. Ibid. 85–7, 210n.

84. Qtd. ibid. 87.

85. Thackeray, *On Theatrical Emancipation* 20; qtd. Stephens, *Profession* 85.

86. Wilkinson, *Memoirs* II:230; cited Stephens, *Profession* 85.

87. Qtd. ibid. 86 (and 105 on shorthand writers).

88. Qtd. Sheridan, *Dramatic* I:325. Apparently they had no need to use this version, since the Dublin company had bought a copy of the text which Sheridan had sent to his sister. John Bernard describes his method of "acquiring" the text of *The School for Scandal* for an Exeter production in 1779, recalling the qualms of actors who produced such texts: "I offered to attempt a compilation of the comedy, if Mr. Hughes [the manager of the Exeter company] would give me his word that the manuscript should be destroyed at the end of the season. This was agreed to, and I set about my task in the following manner:—I had played Sir Benjamin at Bath, and Charles at Richmond, and went on for Sir Peter one or two evenings when Edwin was indisposed;—thus I had three parts in my possession. Dimond and Blisset (Joseph and Sir Oliver) transmitted their's by post, on conveying the assurance to them which Mr. Hughes had to me. Old Rowley was in the company, and my wife had played both Lady Teazle and Mrs. Candour. With these materials for a groundwork, my general knowledge of the play, collected in rehearsing and performing in it above forty times, enabled me in a week to construct a comedy in five acts, called, in imitation of the original 'The School for Scandal.'" Bernard, *Retrospections of the Stage* I:208–9; qtd. Sheridan, *Dramatic* I:327–8.

89. See the discussion of various late 18th- and 19th-century cases (most notably *Macklin v. Richardson* (1770) and *Coleman v. Wathen* (1793)) in Albright, "'To Be Staied'" 497–8 and *Dramatic Publication* 313. Several 18th- and 19th-century American cases held similarly that memorial reproduction, without the aid of stenography or other recording instruments, could not be legally enjoined (*Keene v. Wheatley and Clarke*; *Tompkins v. Hallock*).

90. Holcroft, *Life* I:272–3.

91. Qtd. Stephens, *Profession* 89.

92. Ibid. 91.

93. For instance, "The King Incog. | A Farce | Miller's Modern Acting Drama, | Consisting of | The Most Popular Pieces | Produced at the London Theatres ... 1834"; qtd. Stephens, *Profession* 128. There are similar warnings in continental plays, for instance that of the publisher José María Zamora, promising in his *Repertorio Dramático* to prosecute "con arreglo a las leyes vigentes" anyone putting on the plays without permission (qtd. Gies, *Theatre* 225).

94. On the *Reglamentos orgánicos de Teatros, sobre la propriedad de los autores* (seriously enforced only after the creation of the Teatro Español in 1849), see Gies, *Theatre* 18; Thomas, *Royal*. In England, there were reforms under the 1842 Copyright Act (Talfourd's Act (15 & 16 Vict. *c*.12)), which ended the patent monopoly and extended both print and performance copyright to forty-two years or seven years after the death of the author, whichever was longer. But there was also continuing refinement through case law. *Shepherd v. Conquest* (1856), for instance, importantly clarified the position of dramatists (as opposed to managers) as beneficiaries of performance rights, holding that copyright could not be taken from a dramatist (even a house dramatist in the employ of a theatre) except by express transfer in writing in Stationers' Hall (see Stephens, *Profession* 94–5). In France (as in England), agents were appointed for collecting fees from theatres. The French Society of Dramatic Authors (in its various incarnations) continued

to reform the rules over the course of the 19th century to deal in a more satisfactory way with non-compliance and to organize collective bargaining agreements with managers and embargos against non-compliant theatres. For a discussion of the changes in dramatic authors' rights after the Revolution and the organization and rules of the Société des auteurs dramatiques between 1829 and the end of the century, see Hemmings, *Theatre* 233–40; and Boncompain, "Les deux cent."

95. *El Contemporáneo*, 6 Jan. 1861; cited Gies, *Theatre* 18.

96. Braham had apparently taken the precaution of selling books with a different libretto in the theatre. Planché writes that in the performance, "nearly all the vocal portions were given with the original words, and not with those printed in the books sold in the house" (Planché, *Recollections* I:270; see also Stephens, *Profession* 92–3).

97. Planché, *Recollections* I:272.

98. On enforcement problems in France, see Hemmings, *Theatre* 233–4; and in Spain, see Gies, *Theatre* 225. Until the international copyright laws of the 1880s and 1890s, plays first published or performed on foreign soil (including the USA) lost their copyright protection in Britain. The 1852 International Copyright Act (15 & 16 Vict. *c.*12) protected foreign copyrights from piratical publication or performance in Great Britain, but exempted "fair Imitations or Adaptations to the English Stage of any Dramatic Piece … published in any Foreign Country" (qtd. Stephens, *Profession* 102). Since British law treated performance as "publication" for the purposes of the 1852 Act and construed "fair Imitations or Adaptations" broadly, nothing first performed or published elsewhere was protected in Britain. The 1885 Berne Convention (and its British implementing legislation, the 1886 International Copyright Act) secured authors' rights generally in the fourteen countries that signed the convention. In the absence of international copyright protection, dramatists developed a technique, the copyright performance, to secure British rights to plays having an American première (used also to secure rights to dramatizations of novels). As soon as possible after a text was finished, a single poster would be posted, one or two tickets sold to "members of the public" (usually hirelings who would be available as witnesses, should occasion demand), and the full text would be got through with some semblance of staging. US performance copyright legislation, developing from 1856 on, did not protect foreign authors, and when a play was published in Britain, the dramatist gave up US performance rights. Only with the 1891 American Copyright Act were British dramatists protected from unauthorized performance in the USA (Stephens, *Profession* 104–14). As Michael Booth writes, it was only then that "leading dramatists saw their plays through the press as a matter of course" (*Theatre* 145).

99. Fee-for-play arrangements were the norm in France and Spain until the 1840s (Gies, *Theatre* 17; Hemmings, *Theatre* 229–32). In England, with longer runs in the later 18th century, there evolved in the patent theatres a variation on the author-benefit system (individually contracted in the smaller theatres), with payments at regular intervals after a certain number of nights. But fee-for-play arrangements seem to have dominated (certainly in the smaller theatres) well into the 1870s, when some of the most entrepreneurial playwrights were able to benefit from what Stephens refers to as "the profit-sharing revolution." See, generally, Booth, *Theatre* 142–5; and Stephens, *Profession* 26–50 (and 51–83 on the "profit-sharing revolution"). For a useful description of normal performance copyright arrangements in 1866, see Booth, *Theatre* 144.

100. For Scribe, see Krakovitch, "Le Théâtre" 158. For Bulwer and Knowles, see Booth, *Theatre* 143 (and for other examples of payments to dramatists).
101. Larthomas, *Le Théâtre* 36.
102. Stephens, *Profession* 55.
103. Gies, *Theatre* 91.
104. Hemmings, *Theatre* 230–1.
105. Ibid. 230.
106. Stephens, *Profession* 49–50.
107. Fitzball, *Thirty-Five* I:271–2; Stephens, *Profession* 93. See also Booth, *Theatre* 144 on publishers who had bought print copyrights before 1833 and continued to collect performance fees after 1833.
108. "Creo en favor de don Manuel Delgado la propiedad absoluta, y para siempre, del drama original en siete actos y en verso, titulado *Don Juan Tenorio*, por la cantidad de 4.200 reales vellón, … a fin de que … pueda disponer de dicho drama libremente para su impresión y representación en todos los teatros," qtd. Gies, *Theatre* 18.
109. Typically, French playwrights would retain Paris performance rights or performance rights in a particular theatre, or a portion of performance rights (probably because they had already sold them to a Paris manager), but sell provincial performance rights along with publication rights. Krakovitch notes that in contracts of the 1820s and 1830s, dramatists most commonly ceded provincial performance rights to publishers but retained Paris performance rights, but that there were also often arrangements in which dramatists granted publishers a portion of performance rights, most commonly one-third both for known and unknown dramatists, but anywhere from one-quarter to the whole ("Le Théâtre" 156–7).
110. Ibid. 156; Mollier, *L'Argent* 325–6.
111. On the mass pirating of cheap dramatic editions in mid-19th-century Spain, for instance, see Gies, *Theatre* 175.
112. Krakovitch, "Le Théâtre" 157.
113. Sheridan, *Dramatic* I:329.
114. Feather, *History* 170.
115. Hugo, *Théâtre* I:1767 (Thierry and Mélèze's notes).
116. Booth, *Theatre* 142–4.
117. Stephens, *Profession* 119 (Kemble letter, 9 Mar. 1831), 21–2.
118. Wilde, *Letters* 765n.
119. Archer, *Old* 252.
120. Bernard, ed., *Retrospections* I:208–9; qtd. Sheridan, *Dramatic* I:327.
121. Stephens (*Profession* 143–73) notes the *increase* in the author's involvement in production and staging in the latter half of the 19th century, perhaps explicable as a function of the simultaneous expectation that dramatists had production rights and the decline in the dramatist's actual control over performances with the spread of theatres.
122. Holcroft, *Tale* (the English version of Pixérécourt's *Coelina* (1800)) 1, 3, 9, 15, 17.
123. Pocock, *Robinson* 11 (I.i); Pixérécourt, *Robinson Crusoé* 4 (I.ii).
124. Oxberry, ed., *New* II [Gay, *Beggar's Opera* p. vii].
125. Ibid. I [*Rivals* pp. viii–xi, 84].
126. Qtd. Holroyd, *Bernard Shaw* I:403; Stephens, *Profession* 141 (letter to Grant Richards, 1897).
127. Kemble, *Kemble*, ed. Shattuck I: p. xiv.

128. "Todos los versos señalados con comillas al margen se suprimieron en la representación por parecer largo el delirio de Elda a la actriz que desempeñaba el papel de ésta." Qtd. Gies, *Theatre* 203 (IV.vi). Most of the texts in Bell's edition similarly mark lines to be left out in performance: "The lines distinguished by inverted comas [*sic*] are omitted in the Representation, and those printed in Italics are the additions of the Theatre." *Bell's British Theatre* V [Lillo, *London Merchant* 9].

129. See *Bell's British Theatre* (1776–78); Kemble's *Select British Theatre* (1815); Inchbald's *British Theatre* (1808); Cumberland's *The British Drama* (1817); Oxberry's *New English Drama* (1818–25); Hinds' *English Stage* (1838); Lacy's *Acting Edition of Plays, Dramas, Extravaganzas, Farces* (1848–73), and Shattuck's discussion in Shattuck, *Shakespeare* 8.

130. Rochon de Chabannes, *Le Jaloux*, "Nouvelle ed., la seule exactement conforme à la représentation." See similarly, *The Minor* (according to its title page) "Printed under the Inspection of James Wrighten, Prompter, Exactly agreeable to the Representation at the Theatre-Royal in Drury-Lane" (1788).

131. Boaden, *Memoirs of the Life of John Philip Kemble* II:2–3.

132. See Shattuck's comments in Kemble, *Kemble* I: p. xiv.

133. Nicoll, *Garrick* 153.

134. Ibid. 147.

135. Daumier, *Les Cent et un* (1839). On the general vogue for illustrated books in the later 18th and 19th centuries, see Martin, *Le Livre* 120; Michel, "French" 88; and Plant, *English* 269 ff.

136. Lichtenberg, *Lichtenberg's* 70 (to Ernst Gottfried Baldinger, 10 Jan. 1775).

137. "Ne diffère donc plus ce que l'honneur t'ordonne; | Il demande ma tête, et je te l'abandonne." Corneille, *Oeuvres de P. et Th. Corneille* (1844) 30 (III.iv).

138. See, for instance, the title page for the songs from David Mallet and James Thompson's masque adaptation of *Alfred*, "as it is now revived at the Theatre-Royal, Drury-Lane … Dressed in the habit of the times" (1773).

139. Favart, *Mémoires* (1808) I: p. lxxviii; reproduced (with a watercolour portrait of Mme Favart in the costume) in Howarth, ed., *French* 522–3.

140. "Clio, Muse de l'Histoire, assise sur un nuage, préside aux *Recherches sur les Costumes et sur les Théâtres de toutes les Nations de l'Univers.* Minerve comme protectrice des Arts, couvre Clio de son Egide; et de l'autre main, lève le voile épais dont le temps étoit couvert." Levacher de Charnois, *Recherches* π1ᵛ ("Explication du Frontispice"); and see Jefferys, *Recueil des Habilléments des Différents Nations.*

141. Montfaucon's *L'Antiquité expliquée*; qtd. Nicoll, *Garrick* 169.

142. Advertisement for Dicks's Standard Plays (published from 1875 on); qtd. Stephens, *Profession* 131.

143. For a helpful discussion of the 19th- and early 20th-century historiography of the medieval theatre, see Vince, *Ancient* 90–3.

144. Lee, "Oxfordshire" 503.

145. "Les fêtes populaires et les grossières mascarades de notre moyen âge nous aident à comprendre les bizarres pantomimes des Peaux-Rouges et les parades périodiques des insulaires de la mer du Sud. A leur tour, les folies solennelles de l'Hindoustan montrent encore aujourd'hui que les orgies dramatiques de la vieille Europe n'étaient point le caprice fortuit d'imaginations en délire, mais un développement naturel." Du Méril, *Histoire* I:63 (and see I:65–74 for the table of contents listing the other forms of primitive drama).

4. REINVENTING "THEATRE" VIA THE PRINTING PRESS

1. "Pour ce que telles œuvres que nous appellons jeux ou moralitez ne sont tousjours faciles a jouer ou publicquement representer au simple peuple, et aussi que plusieurs ayment autant en avoir ou ouyr la lecture comme veoir la representacion, j'ay voulu ordonner cest opuscule en telle façon qu'il soit propre a demonstrer a tous visiblement par personnages, gestes et parolles sur eschaffault ou autrement, et pareillement qu'il se puisse lyre particulierement ou solitairement par maniere d'estude, de passetemps ou bonne doctrine." La Chesnaye, *La Condamnation* 63.

2. In the Digby *Mary Magdalen*, for instance, the writer addresses the readers (*Mary Magdalen* 95; the surviving manuscript from the early 16th century. See the editors' note, *Mary Magdalen* p. xl). For an early play "joué par personnages," see, for instance, Arnoul Gréban's *Mystere de la Passion* (*c.*1452): "Ce present livre contient le commancement et la creacion du monde en brief par parsonnages." Greban, *Mystere* (1878 edn.) 2.

3. For this history, see Wickham, *Early* I:235–6, I:264–7 ff.; and Bevington, *From "Mankind"* 10–15.

4. Clanchy notes that even Latin works "were generally intended to be read aloud—hence the speeches and frequent use of dramatic dialogue in monastic chronicles" (*From Memory* 216), and Saenger ("Silent" and "Books") provides ample evidence that most people still found silent reading unusual before the 15th century, identifying a definite increase in silent reading in the 15th century and showing that, even then, writers often felt obliged to explain that their works—or parts of them—were to be read silently. Reading aloud was certainly the norm for most literature that served as entertainment or general instruction, even in the 16th and 17th centuries. Chartier describes the many "parades," "recueils," "*plaisants devis*," and similar works printed in the 16th and 17th centuries and "read aloud to the illiterate" ("Culture" 243).

5. See Andrews, *Scripts* 22.

6. See Clanchy, *From Memory* 224–6, on dialogue formats in lawbooks and romances, and on the jongleurs' "stage scripts" (one legal text, the *Play de la courine*, for instance, which contains a dialogue between a steward and his bailiff).

7. Sachs, *Eyn gesprech* (title page and sig. A2ʳ). On *La Danse macabre* as narrated dialogue and drama simultaneously, see Harrison, *Danse Macabre* 12. On the dramatic character of Tudor dialogues and the dialogic character of Tudor drama, see King, *English* 284–318; and see the discussion of generic ambiguity in English plays of the period in Walker, *Politics* 16–25.

8. *Les plaisants devis.*

9. "Die Thorheyt selbst selbst redet durch das gantz Büch hinauß" (Erasmus, *Das Theür* sig. B1ʳ).

10. On Vicente's *Visitaçao* (sometimes entitled *Monólogo de Vaqueiro* or *Auto de la Visitación*) and Manrique's *Representación del Nacimiento de Nuestro Señor* see McKendrick, *Theatre* 10, 19–20.

11. It is worth recalling, for instance, that touring acting companies emerged from the Chambers of Rhetoric in Holland and France. See Enders, *Rhetoric*, for an exploration of the role of rhetoric and oratory in the shaping of medieval drama (with a focus primarily on 15th-century France, but conclusions suggestive for Europe as a whole); and the *Compositions de rhetorique* (*c.*1600–1) illustrated with *commedia dell'arte* figures, reproduced in Beijer and Duchartre, eds., *Recueil* no. XLV.

12. Gengenbach, *Die [Zehn] alter*, "lieplich zü läsen und zü hören" (title page). See similarly the Ulm *Eunuchus* (1486), whose first lines explain that it is "ain Maisterliche und wolgesetzte Comedia zelesen und zehören." Terence, *Eunuchus* sig. a2^r.

13. La Chesnaye's main distinction is between those who will see the representation and those who want to own the book *and* hear the reading ("*en avoir ou ouyr la lecture*"), with reading privately ("*particulierement*": probably aloud to a select group) or, finally, in solitude ("*solitairement*": perhaps aloud) as subordinate options. La Chesnaye, *La Condamnation* 63.

14. See Boccaccio, *Boccaccio* 42 (Genealogia Deorum Gentilium Bk. 14, Ch. 9, fol. 166^r).

15. "En vers comiques ... moult artificieles fables." Prologue to Premierfait's edition of Boccaccio in Hortis, *Studi* 744; and see Olson, *Literature* 224, 225n.

16. For a sketchy summary of definitions of comedy and tragedy from the ancients to the mid-18th century, see McMahon, "Seven." For a summary of the medieval treatment of drama as narrative form and the attention paid to rhetoric, see Carlson, *Theories* 31–6. Carlson writes: "Already by the time of Boethius (*c.*480–524) tragedy was being used to describe a narrative rather than a dramatic genre" (*Theories* 30). "Tragedy" and "comedy" were still terms primarily used to describe non-dramatic genres well into the 16th century. McKendrick notes, for instance, that 15th-century Spanish writers had commented on classical genre division, but "regarded comedy and tragedy as terms applicable to literature at large, using them for such compositions as poetic narratives, addresses and laments" (*Theatre* 18). Armour ("Comedy") gives additional examples of the non-theatrical medieval conception of comedy and tragedy.

17. The principal sources of information on ancient theatres for medieval scholars were Aelius Donatus' commentary on Terence, Horace's description of theatrical conditions in the *Ars poetica*, and Isidore of Seville's mostly anti-theatrical comments in his *Etymologies*. Donatus was known primarily as a grammarian, and his commentary is primarily grammatical and rhetorical. While it refers in some places explicitly to theatres and scenes, to actors with masks and their gestures, it refers as often to readers and reading, implying that literary recitation is the normal mode for the presentation of Terence. Basore notes that Donatus "may have been inclined to annotate [Terence] with stage directions ... for purposes of reading aloud"; the commentary assumes that it is readers, not actors, who will be using the text, frequently referring to "the reader and reading" (Basore, *Scholia* 3–5). Hardison remarks that Evanthius' definition of tragedy and comedy similarly "omits any reference to staging" and "points the way toward the later medieval conception of tragedy and comedy as poems to be recited rather than plays to be acted" ("Medieval" 301). The poet would sing while others mimed the actions. Armour explains: "for Papias *mimi*, 'imitators of human things', would use bodily movements to follow the author's recital of his *fabula*; for Uguccione the *scena* was a tent-like house, shaded and covered with curtains, where, as the reciter spoke ... masked people would come out of hiding to provide gestures; and Giovanni (Balbus) of Genoa actually defined an actor (*histrio*) as a 'gesticulor' or *ioculator* who, wearing a mask, would 'represent the behaviour and gestures of different people' during the recitation of comedies" ("Comedy" 20–1). Nicholas Trevet follows Isidore in understanding the "scene" as a "small edifice in the middle of the theatre in which the poet stood and recited his verses; outside were the actors who mimed the various events, adapting their gestures to suit the characters in whose persons the poet was speaking" (Minnis and Scott, eds, *Medieval Theory* 325–6. On the medieval understanding of classical theatre generally, see Hardison, "Medieval" 287–88; McMahon, "Seven"; and Carlson, *Theories* 32. On

the importance of Donatus and Horace in the medieval and early Renaissance under-standing of drama, see Robbins, *Dramatic* 1–2, 15–37.

18. On the limited medieval knowledge of the *Poetics*, see Weinberg, *History* I:358; Tigerstedt, "Observations"; Boggess, "Aristotle's." On Hermannus Alemannus's Aristotle, see Minnis and Scott, eds., *Medieval Theory* 277–313: "The impressively accurate translation of the *Poetics* which William of Moerbeke made in 1278 was largely ignored by medieval thinkers; they preferred to understand the text within the [non-theatrical] ideological context in which Averroes had located it" (279). Tigerstedt iden-tifies Allessandro Pazzi's translation of the *Poetics* in 1536 and Robortello's commentary of 1548 as entry points to "the high tide of neo-Aristotelianism in Italian and European literary criticism" (21).

19. Hermannus Alemannus, *Rhetorica* sig. f1ʳ, f3ᵛ, f6ʳ; trans. Averroës, "Middle" 349, 355, 359–60.

20. Honorius of Autun, *Gemma* (*c.*1100), Bk. 1, Ch. 83 ("De Tragoediis"); trans. Bevington, *Medieval* 9; and Hugh of St Victor, *Didascalicon* 44 (1939 edn.) (Bk. 2, Ch. 27) (late 1120s). For a discussion of Hugh's understanding of *theatrica* and of those who followed him in the 12th and 13th centuries, see Olson, *Literature* 64–77; and Tatarkiewicz, "Theatrica."

21. "Les jugleurs et menestriex estoient qui, par contenances et manieres de leur corps et par art de paroles et chant de bouche et de belle voix, par melodie racontoient et recitoient en commun les hystoires des faiz advenuz ou des controuvéz que on a faint, les quelz tu trouveras en Plaut et Menandre et ceuls qui ont cognoissance de l'art de nostre Terence." John of Salisbury, *Le Policratique* (trans. 1372) 119 (Bk. 1, Ch. 8).

22. William of St Thierry, *Exposé* 80 (liminaire 8); trans. Minnis, *Medieval Theory* 57 (and see 241 n.78 for a the discussion of similar medieval analyses of the drama).

23. Mussato, "Ep. 7" (col. 45, B); qtd. and trans. Greenfield, *Humanist* 85, 93n. Mussato gave a public reading of his Seneca imitation, the *Ecerinis*, at the University of Padua in 1315, but it is clear that he had no intention that it be performed with actors. See Doglio, *Il teatro* p. xv (Preface); and Braden, *Renaissance* 102 and 99–114 on Mussato's *Ecerinis* generally.

24. Wycliffe *et al.* trans., *Holy Bible* IV:565 (*Acts* 19:29).

25. Chaucer, *Complete* II:2 (*Boethius* (1374) (Bk. I, prose 1, ll. 34–5)).

26. "Art qui jadiz fut appelle theatrique pour respec[t] dune place qui estoyt a romme qui sappelloit theatron ou le peuple aloit jouer [et] les aultres regarder les jeux" (translating Rodrigo Sánchez de Arévalo's *Speculum vitae humanae* (1468)), Farget, *Miroir* sig. h4ʳ–h4ᵛ.

27. Hugh of St Victor, *Didascalicon* (1939 edn.) 38–44 (Bk. 2, Ch. 27); trans. Hugh of St. Victor, *Didascalicon* (1961 edn.) 74–9.

28. Chaucer, *Complete* IV:243 (Monk's Prologue, ll. 85–9).

29. The many Terence phrase books categorizing Latin sentences by topic show the com-mon schoolroom use of Terence. On Giovanni Sulpizio and Pomponio Leto's view that in teaching classical plays as theatre in the 1480s they were doing something novel, see Sulpizio's preface to his 1484 edition of Vitruvius; qtd. Grafton and Jardine, *From Humanism* 89. On the circulation of Seneca in the form of *sententiae* or *flores*, see Braden, *Renaissance* 69.

30. See the images from the Carolingian Terence manuscript reproduced in Bibliothèque Nationale, *Comédies de Térence*; the discussions of various changes in Terence illustra-tions in Herrmann, *Forschungen* 279 ff.; Weston, "Illustrated"; and Lawrenson and

Purkis, "Les Éditions" (on the *Térence des Ducs*, with its representation of epic recitation and mimes). Most 16th-century illustrations continued to show narrative moments, often in complex arrangements (as in the illustration to Seneca's *Thyestes* in the 1512 Paris edition), but without any indication that they involved theatrical space. Printers often simply copied illustrations or used the same woodcuts for a dramatic work they had already used for a non-dramatic work (as with the woodcut in William Myddylton's edition of the *Enterlude of the Four cardynal vertues* (*c.*1545) which also accompanies Wynkyn de Worde's 1517 edition of Sebastian Brant's poem, *Ship of Fools*, or that on the title page of Medwall's *Fulgens and Lucres* (*c.*1512), copied from the colophon woodcut of Michel Toulouze's *L'Art et instruction de bien dancer* (Paris *c.*1488): see Alan Nelson's note in Medwall, *Plays of Henry Medwall*).

31. The illustrations in Trechsel's Terence (Terence, *Comoediae* (1493)) consistently represent a single stage for all the illustrations belonging to an individual play, but the stage changes from play to play, suggesting that the illustrations might represent actual stages rather than the artist's idealized conception of a stage: the *Andria* woodcuts show a platform stage on a scaffold with a flat wall of four curtained and labelled doors, or "houses"; the *Phormionis* woodcuts show a half-hexagon on a hexagonal step; woodcuts for the *Ecyrae* and several other plays show small projecting rounded platforms at the sides for statues of "Liber" and "Phoebus"; the *Adelphorum* woodcuts show a stage with five doors. Lawrenson and Purkis ("Les Éditions") offer a review of the scholarship on the theatricality of the early illustrated Terence editions. They are sceptical of the traditional interpretation of these as illustrating actual performances (Nicoll's view, for instance, that the preservation of backdrops throughout each play but the change from play to play is evidence that the woodcuts represent actual performances (Nicoll, *Development* 82–3)). But they recognize the importance of the Terence illustrations in the general attempt to understand the ancient theatre during the period.

32. Alberti, *L'Architettura* II:729 (Bk. 8, Ch. 7, fol. 149^r); trans. Alberti, *On the Art* 269–70.

33. "En quelz lieux, premierement, se jouoyent les tragedies et comedies"; "Les aornementz et vestementz des joueurs sceniques"; "Description du theatre." *Premiere Comedie de Terence, intitulee l'Andrie* (1542); "Epistre" reproduced Weinberg, *Critical* 92, 97–8.

34. Viperano, *De poetica* 101 (Bk. 2, Ch. 9); trans. Viperano, *On Poetry* 101–2.

35. "La Tragedia ... debbia esser recitata, e veduti i gestis, & uditi i sermoni, e la melodia di essa." Trissino, *La Quinta* (1562) fol. 17^r.

36. Viperano, *De poetica* 102 (Bk. 2, Ch. 9); trans. Viperano, *On Poetry* 102.

37. Robortello, [*De Arte*] 53; trans. Weinberg, "Robortello" 322.

38. Robortello, [*De Arte*] 2–3, 58; trans. Weinberg, "Robortello" 328–9.

39. *Angelo Costanzo*: "Cosa è la Scenica Poesia?" *Minturno*: "Imitatione di cose, che si rappresentino in Theatro. ... Nè senza apparecchiamento." "L'apparecchiamento [è] proprio della Scenica." See also his definition of comedy as "nè senza canto, nè senza ballo, nè senza apparecchiamento." Minturno, *L'arte poetica* 65, 71, 116 (Bk. 2).

40. Scaliger, *Poetices* I:132 (Bk. 1, Ch. 6, "Tragoedia").

41. "La tragedia ... oltre alla spesa, la quale spesa non è miga da patrimonio privato" is different from epic "per lo teatro, per lo palco, per gli abiti, per le maschere, per le persone, per gli movimenti e per li reggimenti del corpo e per la proferenza della voce; io lascio da parte il suono, il canto, il ballo." Castelvetro, *Poetica* II:343 (Pt. 6, Sect. 1); trans. Castelvetro, *Castelvetro* 306.

42. "Le théâtre où fut représentée la Passion de Valenciennes en 1547." MS. in the Bibliothèque Nationale; reproduced in Cohen, *Le Théâtre* I, plate XL. Anderson emphasizes

the endurance of the broader connotation of the Italian word *teatro*—space for any kind of spectacle—but notes the narrowing of its primary connotation, linking that narrowing with work on the text of Vitruvius during the 16th century ("Changing" 7–9).

43. "Ces gens non lettrez … entremettant à la fin ou au commencement du jeu farces lascives et momeries. … Tant les entrepreneurs que les joueurs sont gens ignares … qui oncques ne furent instruicts ni exercez en théâtres et lieux publics. … Souvent advient dérision et clameur publicque dedans le théâtre même, tellement qu'au lieu de tourner à édification leur jeu tourne à scandale et dérision." Requisition of the Paris Parlement against the representation of the *Mystère du Vieil Testament* by the Confrères de la Passion (1541); qtd. Faivre, "Le Théâtre" 84–5.

44. Stockwood, *Sermon* 134–5.

45. Shakespeare, *Complete* 390 (V.ii.23–5).

46. Sachs, *Gedicht* III, π2ᵛ (Georgius Willer's "Vorrede dem volgebornen Hern," and throughout the introductory material to Sachs's works).

47. Ortelius, *Theatrum oder Schawplatz des erdbodems*. Several later examples show the absorption, by the early 17th century, of the classical terms. Many German plays are called "Comedi" or "Tragedi," for instance the anonymous *Comedi vom Crocodilstechen* (*c.*1596). Johann Stainhauser refers to the "schön und groß Theatrum … zu Agieren der Pastoralen zuegerichtet" by the Austrian Prince-Bishop in the early years of the 17th century (qtd. Kindermann, *Theatergeschichte* III:484). The collection of Jakob Ayrer's drama that comes out in 1618 is titled *Opus Thaeatricum*, and the preface refers to it as "dieses Opus Thaeatricum von … Geistlichen und Weltlichen Comedien und Tragedien" (Ayrer, *Ayrers* I:5).

48. Robert Fludd, likening his memory theatre to public theatres, in Fludd, *Utriusque Cosmi … Historia*; qtd. Yates, *Art* 331.

49. "Le Theatre jamais ne doit estre rempli | D'un argument plus long que d'un jour accompli." Vanquelin de la Fresnaye, *L'Art* 78 (Bk. I, ll, 1055–6).

50. "Teatro fatto in Firenze nella Festa a Cavallo." The *Guerre de Beauté*, the equestrian ballet performed on 6 October, 1616 in honour of the entrée of the son of the Duke of Urbino into Florence, was recorded in Andrea Salvadori's *Guerra di Bellezza Festa a cavallo fatta in Firenze per la Venuta del serenissimo Principe d'Urbino* (Florence 1616). See Choné, ed., *Jacques Callot* 192–3.

51. Sachs, *Gedicht* III, title page, π2ᵛ, π4ʳ–π4ᵛ.

52. "Les Farces qu'on nous à si long tans jouees se convertiront au g'anre de la Comedie: les Jeus des Martires, an la forme de Tragedie." Peletier du Mans, *L'Art* 172 (Bk. 2, Ch. 5, "De l'Ode"). See similarly Thomas Sebillet, who identifies "Dialogue, et ses espéces" as "l'Eclogue, la Moralité, la Farce," explaining, for instance, that the morality "represente en quelque chose la Tragédie Gréque et Latine," and that the farce is "ce que lés Latins ont appellé Mimes ou Priapées" (Sebillet, *Art* (1548) 159, 161, 165 (Bk. 2, Ch. 8)).

53. Fernández, *Farsa o cuasi comedia del soldada*; *Farsa o cuasi comedia de una doncella, un pastor y un caballero* (see Shergold, *History* 145).

54. "Si principiò la comedia de la *Bachide*, quale fu tanto longa et fastidiosa e senza balli intramezzi, che piú volte me augurai a Mantua." Letter of 5 Feb. 1502; reproduced in Bonino, ed., *Il teatro* II(1):413.

55. Shakespeare, *Complete* 667 (*Hamlet* (II.ii.399–101)).

56. "Welche Spil auch nit allein gut, nutzlich und kurtzweilig zu lesen sindt, sonder auch leichtlich auß disem Buch spilweiß anzurichten, weil es so ordenlich alle Person gebärden, wort und werck, außgeng und eingeng aufs verstendigst anzeiget, durch alle Spil,

der vormal keins im Truck ist außgangen, noch gesehen worden." Sachs, *Gedicht* III (title page).

57. *Le tres excellẽt & sainct mystere du vieil testament par personnages* (1542). See, similarly, Milet, *L'Istoire de la destruction de Troye* "mise par parsonnages" (1484), the anonymous *Le Mystère de la passion de Jésus-Christ* "par personnages" (*c.*1490), or Simon Gréban, *Le Premier Volume du triumphant mystere des Actes des Apostres* "tout ordonne par personnages" (1537).

58. Moryson, *Shakespeare's* 304.

59. "Ce que nous voions en France sur celui des Italiens, n'est pas proprement Comedie. … Ce n'est ici qu'une espece de concert mal formé entre plusieurs Acteurs." Saint-Evremond, *Œuvres* III:48 ("De la comédie italienne").

60. Jonson, *Ben Jonson* VI:120 (*Bartholomew Fair* V.iii.106–7). The phrase "played according to the printed booke" echoes the normal way of describing what actors were to do with texts that had passed the censor, opposed to the playing beside the book that could sometimes evade the censor's controls. Of course medieval actors also had to speak fixed parts but not necessarily by reading them from books, and many kinds of performances would not have required textual accuracy. Wickham (*Medieval* 84) suggests that medieval actors were required to memorize their parts, but cites as evidence Richard Carew's observation in 1610 (quoted below), hardly evidence for norms in earlier periods. Given what we know of medieval literacy, it is likely that many performers did not memorize fixed parts from texts.

61. Beaumont and Fletcher, *Comedies* sig. C4ʳ ("On Mr Beaumont").

62. *Benediktbeuern Passion Play* ll.63–64; text and trans. Bevington, *Medieval* 208.

63. Tommaso Inghirami, nicknamed "Thomas Phaedra" for his performance in Seneca's *Phaedra*. See Grafton and Jardine, *From Humanism* 91.

64. Munday, *John a Kent* 34.

65. Lupton, *All for Money* (1578); qtd. Walker, *Politics* 25n.

66. Clubb, *Italian Drama* 254.

67. Shakespeare, *Complete* 667 (*Hamlet* (II.ii.402–3)). Chambers, for instance, doubts that the English did complete play improvisations. He cites, as evidence, *The Case is Altered* (1597 (II.vii)), in which Sebastian and Valentine discuss the players in "Utopia" (i.e. England): "*Sebastian*: And how are their plais? as ours are? extemporall? *Valentine*: O no! all premeditated things." Qtd. Chambers, *Elizabethan* II:553.

68. Shakespeare, *Complete* 341 (*Romeo and Juliet* I.iv.4–8).

69. Ibid., 315 (*A Midsummer Night's Dream* I.ii.63).

70. "The Guary miracle, in English, a miracle-play, is a kinde of Enterlude, compiled in *Cornish* out of some scripture history, with that grossenes, which accompanied the *Romanes vetus Comedia*. … The players conne not their parts without booke, but are prompted by one called the Ordinary, who followeth at their back with the booke in his hand, and telleth them softly what they must pronounce aloud" (Carew, *Survey* fol. 72). Wickham argues that the actors here were nonetheless expected to memorize their parts (Wickham, *Medieval* 84), and the exact memorization of parts is clearly the norm for the urbane Carew. But the anecdote that follows, "a mery pranke" in which a "pleasant conceyted gentleman" stepped in for one of the actors and repeated aloud in a stage voice each of the Ordinary's instructions, suggests that the Cornish actors ("Country people," according to Carew) regularly relied on the Ordinary's prompting.

71. "Ho tenuto meglio soddisfare a chi ha ad ascoltare, con qualche minore eccellenza … che con un poco piú di grandezza dispiacere a coloro per piacere dei quali la favola si con-

duce in iscena: che poco gioverebbe compor favola un poco piú lodevole, e che poi ella si avesse a rappresentare odiosamente. Quelle terribile (se gli animi degli spettatori forse le abboriscono) possono essere delle scritture, queste di fin lieto delle rappresentazioni." "Discorso ... intorno al comporre delle comedie e delle tragedie" (1543) in Giraldi, *Scritti* 184.

72. "Molte cose stanno ben nella penna, che nella scena starebben male." Beolco, *Teatro* 1043 (Prologue I for *La Vaccària* ("female cowherd"), spoken by a "spirito folletto").

73. "Non è vero che la tragedia operi quello che è suo proprio per la lettura senza la vista e i movimenti, come fa l'epopea." "Aristotele ... è di questa opinione, che quello diletto si tragga della tragedia in leggendola che si fa in vedendola e in udendola recitare in atto; la qual cosa io reputo falsa." Castelvetro, *Poetica* I:388–9, II:355 (Pt. 3, Sect. 13; Pt. 6, Sect. 2); trans. Castelvetro, *Castelvetro* 149, 312–13.

74. Gosson, *Playes* sig. C6ʳ (1582). See similarly William Prynne's comment that numerous plays "were penned only to be ... read, not acted, their subjects being al serious, sacred, divine, not scurrilous wanton or prophan, as al modern Play poëms are. Thirdly, as it is lawfull to pen, so likewise *to recite, to read such tragicall or comicall poëms as these*, composed onely to be read, not acted on the Stage." Prynne, *Histriomastix* (1633) 834 (and see similarly 928–31). For more examples of the classic Renaissance anti-theatricalist distinction between plays in performance and plays on the page, see Barish, *Antitheatrical* 193, 325.

75. See, for instance, Braden (*Renaissance*) on the theatricality of Senecan imitation and Latin plays generally in the Renaissance. One does not come across a formal distinction between the "reading play" and the "acting play" or the phrase "closet drama" until the 18th or 19th century. The first use of the word "closet" as a modifier (in this context) that I have come across is Richard Steele's comment in his dedication for the second edition of Joseph Addison's *The Drummer* (1722), "here republish'd, and recommended as a Closet-piece, to recreate an intelligent Mind in a vacant Hour" (Addison, *The Drummer* p. xv).

76. Erasmus, *Collected* XXXI:161 (*Adages* I.ii.17).

77. Robinson, *Phonetic* 4.

78. The complex of attitudes towards memory, speech, writing, and print during the early modern period have been discussed extensively from an epistemological and socio-historical point of view in studies like Elsky, *Authorizing*, Goldberg, *Writing*, Hudson, *Writing*, Krell, *Of Memory* (on Descartes, Hobbes, and Locke, see 56–83), Kroll, *Material*, Love, *Scribal*, and McKenzie, "Speech-Manuscript-Print." A list of studies of writing, print, and "inscription" generally as formative trope in Renaissance drama would include Brooks, *From Playhouse*; Kiefer, *Writing*; Knapp, *Shakespeare*; Oriel, *Writing*; Sanders, *Gender*; Smith, *Writing* 127–71; and Williams, *Shakespeare*. All of these studies complicate considerably Derrida's picture of a monolithic "phonocentric" tradition. Hudson, for instance, maps the general move from the "Sacred and occult scripts" of the Renaissance to the "demystification of writing in the seventeenth century" (Chs. 1–2), arguing (against Derrida) that writing serves as central model for authenticity in 17th-century thought.

79. See, for instance, Erasmus ("we have true knowledge onely of suche thynges as we have suerly enprinted & engraven in our memorie" (Erasmus, *Apophthegmes*; qtd. Kiefer, *Writing* 93)); or Suárez de Figueroa, on the reliance of all the arts and sciences on memory ("En confirmacion desto dize Platon, ser la memoria madre de las Musas, y que en ella se imprimen con facilidad, como el sello en la cera, todas las cosas que se veen,

oyen, y piensan" (*Plaza* fol. 236ᵛ, Discurso 58)). On Plato, see Casey, *Remembering* 15–16 (noting that memory is a form of imprinting for both Plato and Freud); and Krell, *Of Memory* (stressing the continuity of traditions in conceptions of memory as inscription, from Plato and Aristotle through Descartes and Locke to Freud, Merleau-Ponty, Heidegger, and Derrida).

80. See, for instance, Samuel Daniel, for whom "the Stage" is now "the mouth of my lines, which before were never heard to speake but in silence" (1604 letter on the publication of *Philotas* in Daniel, *Complete* I: p. xxiii).

81. Shakespeare, *Complete* 659 (*Hamlet* (I.iii.58–9)).

82. Brooks, *From Playhouse*, Sanders, *Gender*, Thompson and Thompson, *Shakespeare* 163–206, Wall, *Imprint*, and Williams, *Shakespeare* all offer extended meditations on the gender identity of writing and print in the Renaissance. Where, for instance, performance is often gendered female, print is often gendered male: if one may be "a man in print," women are "pressed" by the male form(e), in the classic dirty pun of the period (the house to which Phillip urges the "Punke" Doll and her companions, "thy two Compositors," is "this unlawfull printing house" in Dekker and Webster's *Northward Ho*: Dekker, *Dramatic* II:439 (III.i.1–2); and see the discussion of the conventional phrase, "a man in print" in Wall, *Imprint* 1–22 and, throughout, Wall's discussion of the gendered trope of print). What is imprinted takes the male imprint (women are mere vessels for men, who create imprints of themselves in their offspring); to print is to reproduce one's image as a man ("Your mother was most true to wedlock," Leontes tells Florizel, "For she did print your royal father off, | Conceiving you": Shakespeare, *Complete* 1126 (*Winter's Tale* V.i.123–5)). But performance may also be gendered male, print gendered female: "midwife to the muses"; "womb" (Robert Davenport's *King John and Matilda* is "an Infant, newly deliver'd to the world from the wombe of the Press" (Davenport, *Works* 3)). Print is figured by Spenser as the monster "Errour" in *The Faerie Queene* "spew[ing] out of her filthy maw | A floud of poyson horrible and blacke, | Her vomit full of bookes and papers" (Spenser, *Faerie Queene* 97 (Bk. I, canto 1, stanza 20)). Or it may be both at once: the female "muse imprimerie" is also ravisher of poetry, in the printer Jacques Bouchet's homoerotic fantasy about the copulation of the muses, mechanical and spiritual, which he addresses to Jean de La Péruse in his edition of La Péruse's *La Médée* (1555): "la muse mienne, | La muse imprimerie a ravie la tienne" (though La Péruse's masculinity escapes the final pressing: "Tu ne seras pressé de la chargeante pierre, | Ton tombeau volera parmi toute la terre" (137)).

83. Marlowe, *Complete* I:385.

84. Jonson, *Ben Jonson* IV:73 (*Cynthia's Revels* II.iii.88–9).

85. Lyly, *Campaspe* 124 (V.ii.16–19).

86. Lupton, *London* 4; qtd. Mullaney, *Place* 12.

87. See, for instance, Giovanni Porro's characterization of his botanical garden at Padua as "this little Theatre, almost a little world," in which "one will orchestrate the spectacle of all of nature's wonders" (in his *L'orto dei semplici di Padova* (1591)), Federico Cesi's description of his research as a "Theatre of Nature" in a letter of 1622, or L. Legati's characterization of the microscope as "Theatre of the most miraculous Works of Nature" in his *Museo Cospiano* (1677) (qtd. Findlen, "Museum" 64). For a discussion of the medieval metaphor of the book of nature, see Curtius, *European* 319–26. For a discussion of the *theatrum mundi* trope, see Jacquot, "Le Théâtre."

88. On the memory theatres, see (most notably) Yates, *Art*.

89. See generally Paula Findlen's discussion of the crossing of the Renaissance categories, *bibliotheca* and *thesaurus* with visual constructs such as *museum, studio, casino, cabinet/gabinetto, galleria* and *theatro* (Findlen, "Museum").

90. "Il Poeta … dee haver cura di quelle cose che di neceβità segueno alli sensi della Poesia, cioè al vedere, & a l'udire; dico che dee considerare che la Tragedia che scrive debbia esser recitata, e veduti i gesti, … ponendosi quanto li sarà poβibile auanti gli occhi, i gesti, e le figure che fanno quelli che sono nelle paβioni." Trissino, *La Quinta* fol. 16ᵛ–17ʳ.

91. Robortello, [*De Arte*] 3; trans. Weinberg, "Robortello" 324.

92. Heywood, *Dramatic* III:3.

93. Middleton, *Works* IV:8.

94. Heywood, *Dramatic* III:264 (preface to *The Iron Age* (1632)).

95. "Vous savez qu'il est mal aisé que cette sorte de vers, qui ne sont animés que par la représentation de plusieurs acteurs, puissent réussir à n'être lus que d'une seule personne. D'où vient que ce qui semblera excellent sur un théâtre sera trouvé ridicule en un cabinet." Racan, *Les Bergeries* (1625) 288–9 (dedication).

96. Marston, *Plays* I:139 (preface to *The Malcontent* (1604)).

97. The publisher Richard Hawkins's address to the reader in the third impression of *Philaster* (1628); qtd. Beaumont and Fletcher, *Dramatic* I:372.

98. Jonson, *Ben Jonson* VII:229 (*Hymenaei*).

99. Epistle to Thomas Nabbes's *The Unfortunate Mother* (1640) signed "E.B." in Nabbes, *Works* II:88.

100. "Il est vray qu'aux pieces purement Comiques comme est celle cy, le papier ôte beaucoup de leur grace, et que l'action en est l'ame." Mareschal, *Le Railleur ou le satyre du temps* 101; qtd. Murray, *Theatrical* 149. See similarly Marston (the "life" of comedy "rests much in the Actors voice" and is lost in print. "*Comedies* are writ to be spoken, not read: Remember the life of these things consists in action" (Marston, *Plays* II:143–4; preface to *Parasitaster* 1606)); and Edward Howard (when plays are "display'd in Print" they are "divested of the life of Action, which gave no small varnish to their figures" (Edward Howard, *Usurper* sig. A2ʳ)).

101. Chapman, *Plays* II:539.

102. Beaumont and Fletcher, *Comedies* sig. A3ʳ (Shirley, "To the Reader").

103. "La lecture ou audience diceulx | parvient non seulement aux presens | mais aussi aux yeulx et aux oreilles de ceulx qui sont a venir | et des loingtains a la delectation de leurs esperitz | et edification de leurs ames. Tout ainsi que le royal psalmiste David le ayat prophetise. En toute la terre est yssu le son diceulx | y leurs parolles aux fins du monde terrien." Gréban [?], *Le Premier* (1537 edn.) I, sig. +2ᵛ.

104. Beaumont and Fletcher, *Comedies* sig. A4ʳ–A4ᵛ (Shirley, "To the Reader").

105. Jonson, *Ben Jonson* VIII:391 ("To the memory of my beloved, The Author Mr. William Shakespeare").

106. "In bedenckung dessen, das die Pyramides, Seulen und Büldnussen allerhand materien mit der zeit schadhafft oder durch gewalt zerbrochen werden oder wol gar verfallen, … gantze Städt versuncken, untergangen und mit Wasser bedeckt seien, da hergegen die Schrifften und Bücher dergleichen untergang befreyet, dann was irgent in einem Landt oder Ort ab und untergehet, das findet man in vielen andern und unzehlichen orten unschwer wider, also das, Menschlicher weiβ davon zu reden, nichts Tauerhaffters und unsterblichers ist, als eben die Bücher." Ayrer, *Ayrers* I:4; trans. Benjamin, *Origin* 141.

107. "L'homme est forcé par la Parque, la Mort | Par les écris: mais le puissant effort | Du Temps vainqueur, les écris même force. | L'IMPRESSION, plus forte que pas un, | Force le Temps, que forceoit un châcun, | Randant égalle aus immortels sa force." Jean de La Péruse, *La Médée* (1986 edn.) 131. The poem and image are repeated in Caye Jues de Guersens's *Panthée* (1571), also published by Bouchet.

108. Beaumont and Fletcher's *Philaster* has "passed ... currant ... under the infallible stampe of your judicious censure, and applause" (Richard Hawkins's address to the reader in the third impression of *Philaster* (1628); qtd. Beaumont and Fletcher, *Dramatic* I:372).

109. Thomas Randolph "To His Dear Friend," the actor Thomas Riley in Randolph, *Jealous Lovers* (1632) sig. ¶¶1ʳ.

110. Shakespeare, *Complete* 140 (III.ii.36, 40–4).

111. Marlowe, *Complete* II:176 (II.i.465–6).

112. "I read | Strange Comments in those margines of your lookes: | Your cheekes of late are (like bad printed Bookes) | So dimly charactred, I scarce can spell, | One line of love in them." Dekker, *Dramatic* II:169 (*Honest Whore Pt. 2* III.i.127–31); qtd. Kiefer, *Writing* 93.

113. Randolph, *Poems* 56 (Joseph Howe, "To his worthy friend Mr Robert Randolph" (1638)).

114. Heywood, *Dramatic* I:191 (prologue, *If You Know Not Me*).

115. Beaumont and Fletcher, *Comedies* sig. dʳ (Jasper Maine, "On the Workes of *Beaumont* and *Fletcher*, now at length printed").

116. Beaumont and Fletcher, *Comedies* sig. a3ʳ (Peyton, "On Mr Fletchers Works"). And see Cave's discussion of the rhetoric of presence expressed through the trope of wind or breath, imagined as the means of converting script to life (*Cornucopian* 146–9).

117. Davis, *Society* 218.

118. "La voce del Testo doverà essere chiara, ferma e di bona pronuntia." Monteverdi, *Tutte* VIII:132.

119. Beaumont and Fletcher, *Comedies* sig. g1ʳ ("To the memory of the deceased but ever-living *Authour* in these his *Poems*, Mr. JOHN FLETCHER").

120. The concept of print as enlightenment is expressed in the metaphor of print as means of illumination, which becomes naturalized in Italian and French (*dare in luce* is nearly a technical term for printing in Italian, *sacar a luz* in Spanish). Much has been said in the critical literature about the Renaissance perception (and reality) of the simultaneous fixity and mutability of print (see, for instance, Eisenstein, *Printing* 81; Richardson, *Print* 25, 70; McKenzie, "Speech-Manuscript-Print" 99; Elsky, *Authorizing* 219). See the extended discussions in Love, *Scribal* and Kiefer, *Writing* of the similarly contradictory views of script.

121. "*Leonelo*: ... La confusión, con el exceso, | los intentos resuelve en vana espuma; | y aquel que de leer tiene más uso, | de ver letreros sólo está confuso. | No niego yo que de imprimir el arte | mil ingenios sacó de entre la jerga, | y que parece que en sagrada parte | sus obras guarda y contra el tiempo alberga: | éste las destribuye y las reparte. ... | Mas muchos, que opinión tuvieron grave, | por imprimir sus obras la perdieron; | tras esto, con el nombre del que sabe, | muchos sus ignorancias imprimieron. | Otros, en quien la baja envidia cabe, | sus locos desatinos escribieron, | y con nombre de aquel que aborrecían, | impresos por el mundo los envían." Vega Carpio, *Fuente Ovejuna* 44 (II.i.905–13, 917–24).

122. Jonson, *Ben Jonson* VII:229 (*Hymenaei* ll. 578–9).

123. Jonson, *Ben Jonson* VI:295 (ll. 47–50). A Factor expresses a similar sentiment in Jonson's *Newes from the New World Discover'd in the Moone* (1620): "I would have no newes printed; for when they are printed they leave to bee newes; while they are written, though they be false, they remaine newes still" (Jonson, *Ben Jonson* VII:515 (ll. 58–60)).
124. Shakespeare, *Complete* 1120 (*Winter's Tale* (IV.iv.258–9)).
125. Fitton explains in response, "I, that's an Error | Ha's abus'd many." Jonson, *Ben Jonson* VI:295 (*Staple of News* (c.1626) (I.v.53–5)). See similarly Montaigne: "Que ferons nous à ce peuple qui ne fait recepte que de tesmoignages imprimez, qui ne croit les hommes s'ils ne sont en livre" (Montaigne, *Œuvres* 1059).
126. Gosson, *Playes* sig. C6ʳ; Prynne, *Histriomastix* 834.
127. See Peyton's "On Mr Fletchers Works" (above) or John Earle's "On Mr Beaumont (Written thirty yeares since, presently after his death)" (in Beaumont and Fletcher, *Comedies* sig. c4ʳ): plays are actually "more pure, more chaste, more sainted" than other kinds of "Workes" because they are not "with that dull supinenesse to be read, | To passe a fire, or laugh an houre in bed" (identifying the book with whatever one might do in bed, rewriting the standard anti-theatricalist opposition between pure text and "lewd" stage). And see Gherardi, *Le Theatre* (1700 edn.) VI (frontispiece), reproduced in Chapter 2.
128. Shakespeare, *Complete* 673 (III.ii.226).

5 · CRITICAL LAW, THEATRICAL LICENCE

1. "Apolo Febo ... Pallas Minerva, y a las nueve Infantas de nuestro Parnaso, y Consejo Real de Poesía." Enríquez de Guzmán is "la primera, que con toda propiedad y rigor avía imitado a los Cómicos antiguos, y guardado su Arte Poética y preceptos ...: en lo que avía excedido notablemente." "Se recibió a prueva ... todas [las] Comedias y Tragedias fechas en Romance, y lengua Española, hasta estos tiempos del Magno Filipe Quarto, Rey de las Españas; con que vinieron cargadas muchas requas, y carretas, que llevaron los archivos y almazenes de nuestra Elicona." "Y assí se remitían a las leyes, y ordenanças de nuestra Poesía, [y] concluyeron para sentencia." Enríquez de Guzmán "aver ganado nuestra Corona de laurel en la Arte, y preceptos de los Cómicos antiguos a todas las Comedias, y Tragedias Españolas, compuestas hasta los tiempos del Magno Filipe Quarto de las Españas. Y mandamos a nuestros Poetas Españoles, que en las Comedias, que de aquí adelante se hizieren, guarden las leyes, y preceptos ... so pena ... que los mandaremos borrar, y tildar del Catálogo de nuestros Poetas, y de los libros de nuestras mercedes." "Dada en los Jardines de nuestro Monte Parnaso, en primero de Março de mil y seyscientos y veynte y quatro años. Apolo. Febo. Calíope. Euterpe. Talía. Por su mandado Orfeo de Tracia Secretario. Registrada. Anfión." Enríquez de Guzmán, *Dramatic* 258–63 ("Carta Executoria"). For the Spanish cultural context of the "Carta," see Entrambasaguas y Peña, *Una Guerra*.
2. "En la primera impressión dividí licensiosamente [con "la licencia Poética"], cada una de sus dos partes en tres jornadas, ... para sumás cónmoda representación." "Puede salir en público, a ver, no los Teatros, y Coliseos: en los quales no he querido, ni quiero, que parezca: mas los palacios y salas de los Príncipes, y grandes señores, y sus regocijos públicos, y de sus ciudades, y Reynos." If Enríquez de Guzmán "era muger, también lo eran nuestras caríssimas hermanas las nueve Musas. ... Nuestra serenissima hermana Pallas Minerva, era Diosa de las sciencias. ... Y también fueron insignes, en buenas letras, la

digníssima Marquesa de Cenete, la celebrada Ysabella Joya de Barcelona; la eruditíssima Sigea Toledana ... Doña Angela Zapata, doña Ana Osorio, Burgalesa, y doña Catalina de Paz, gloria, y honor de Guadalajara." "Su Tragicomedia era muy útil y provechosa para desterrar de España muchas Comedias, indignas de gozar los Campos Elysios; y para libertarla, y libertar a sus ilustres, y nobles Poetas del tributo, que por tener paz con el bárbaro vulgo, le han pagado hasta su tiempo, como la misma España, y sus perseguidos moradores lo pagaron de cien donzellas en cada un año, por tener treguas con el paganismo, hasta que las siete donzellas mancas, con su valerosa hazaña, dieron causa a su redempción." Enríquez de Guzmán, *Dramatic* 259–63 ("Carta Executoria"; "A los lectores").

3. Books had been central to education in Europe since at least the 13th century when, according to M. T. Clanchy, "gradually formal speech began to be learned by studying books instead of hearing the words of others," noting that "handbooks for this purpose begin in England in the middle of the thirteenth century" (Clanchy, *From Memory* 223). But printed books were first introduced into European classrooms in the late 15th century and student book ownership started to be presumed in the 16th century. On this, see Grafton and Jardine, *From Humanism* 140 (essentially all had Terence and Seneca, and most had Plautus, Sophocles, and Aristophanes, most commonly in editions produced by the Aldine Press). On the role of print in changes in the use of books and writing in Renaissance education, see Orme, *Education* 18; and Petrucci, "Scrittura." That some students were still complaining in the early 16th century about having to copy otherwise unavailable texts (Grafton and Jardine, *From Humanism* 11) suggests the extent to which the norm of student book ownership had already taken hold.

4. Described in Curtius, *European* 317 (and see generally 302–47 on changes in attitudes towards "the book").

5. *Touchstone*: "O sir, we quarrel in print, by the book" (listing the formal degrees of quarrelling, as if from a catalogue of rhetoric). Shakespeare, *Complete* 651 (*As You Like It* (V.iv.88–94)). On the Renaissance identification of learning with the printed book (and on the relationships among the classical revival, Renaissance scholarship, and the rise of print), see Eisenstein, *Printing* 163–302.

6. Porta, *Le Commedie* I:248–9 (*La Fantesca* III.viii).

7. Dekker, *Dramatic* I:316, 382 (*Satiromastix* I.ii.1; V.ii.313).

8. *Three Parnassus Plays* 125, 143–4 (*Pilgrimage to Parnassus* V.i.607–8; *Return from Parnassus*, Pt. One, I.i.153–8).

9. Beaumont and Fletcher, *Dramatic* IX:475 (I.ii.1–2, 15–17).

10. Forsett, *Pedantius* (1631 edn.) (illustrating Act I, scene iii of the play, preceding signatures). For attribution of the play to Edward Forsett, see Tucker's introduction in Forsett, *Pedantius* 1–3. See, similarly, the illustration in George Ruggle's *Ignoramus* (1630).

11. "J'ay leu deux mille Autheurs en langages divers ... | J'ay releu mille fois sur les Autheurs austeres, | Ce que cent Traducteurs ont fait de Commentaires; | Je possede Aristote, Horace, Scaliger ... | Et je les ay tous leus en Latin comme en Grec." Beys, *Les illustres* 149–50 (V.i.1598–1609). See, similarly, the learned books in Molière's *Femmes savantes* and Chappuzeau's *L'Academie des femmes* (especially I.ii).

12. Requisition of the Paris Parlement (1541) (qtd. Faivre, "Le théâtre" 84–5); Ford, *Fancies* 139 (III.ii.68); Moryson, *Shakespeare's* 304.

13. "Amie des sçavans, sçavante et vertueuse." He has devoted himself to "commenter

l'Electre d'Euripide, | ... eclarcir les grans thesors des Grœcs, | ... des livres saintz les plus rares secrets" (represented by the various works included in the *Oeuvres*). But "de ce temps les mains des Princes sont fermees | Aux sçavans, et sont peu les lettres estimees. | Barbare chicheté! les finances des Roys | Servent aux carnevaux, aux lices, aux tournois." Rivaudeau, *Les Oeuvres* 39, 41, 38.

14. La Taille, *Saül* 209–10 (*Art de la tragédie*).

15. "Quant aux comedies et tragedies si les roys et les republiques les vouloyent restituer en leur ancienne dignité, qu'ont usurpée les farces et moralités, je seroy' bien d'opinion que tu t'y employasses, et si tu le veux faire pour l'ornement de ta langue, tu sçais où tu en dois trouver les archetypes." Du Bellay, *La Défense* (1549) 87.

16. For detailed studies of the French, Italian, and Spanish academies, see Yates, *French*; the essays in Chambers and Quiviger, eds., *Italian Academies*; and Sánchez, *Academias*.

17. "Ne sachant ni A ni B," the players "n'ont langue diserte, ni langage propre, ni les accens de prononciation décente. ... D'un mot ils en font trois; font point ou pause au milieu d'une proposition, ... fond d'un interrogant un admirant, ou autre gest, prolation ou accent contraires à ce qu'ils dient." Qtd. Jomaron, ed., *Théâtre* 85.

18. The impact of printing on regularization of spelling in the 17th century has been discussed extensively (see e.g. Marotti, *Manuscript* 284; and Masten, "Pressing"). Printing in itself, along with the dominance of centralized vernaculars that accompanied it, helped trigger the interest in spelling reform in the 16th century (see Catach, *L'Orthographe*; and Chartier, "Texts" 22–5), but there were also practical reasons for increased uniformity. Identity between manuscript spelling and the compositor's habitual spellings meant much quicker typesetting, as well as somewhat less confusion when it came to proof correction. According to Peter Blayney (personal communication), compositors (held responsible for keeping their letter trays clean on their own time, making sure, for instance, that trays were not fouled by "S"s in the "T"s) found it much easier to replace type correctly in the first place if spelling was regular, because they could read an entire word, rather than having to look at each letter. There was a real change by the later 17th century, reflected in Moxon's famous explanation, for instance, that despite the rule that a compositor was to follow the copy, it was generally necessary to amend the author's "bad spelling" (Moxon, *Mechanick* 192).

19. See the related discussion in Chartier, "Publishing" ("Text as Performance" 21–5); and the material on the graphic representation of speech in Chapter 7. On the dictionaries and other manuals, see Landau, *Dictionaries* 35–43; Meschonnic, *Des mots* 131–8; and Van Hoof, *Petite* 18–21, 40–6, 67–8.

20. "Le peuple ignorant a fait les langages, et non les sçavans, car les doctes n'eussent jamais tant creé des monstres." Ronsard, *Œuvres* II:1006 ("Abregé de l'Art Poëtique François" (1565)).

21. Hart, *Orthographie* fol. 1ᵛ.

22. "Quant à l'orthographie, j'ay voulu que l'imprimeur suyvit la commune," not "quelques maigres fantaisies qu'on ait mis en ava[n]t depuis trois ou quatre ans en ca: & co[n]seillerois volontiers aux plus opiniastres de ceux qui l'ont changée, (s'ils estoyent gens qui demandassent conseil à autres qu'à eux mesmes) puis qu'ils la veulent ranger selon la prononciatio[n], c'estadire puis qu'ils veulent faire qu'il y ait quasi autant de manieres d'escrire, qu'il y a non seulement de co[n]trées, mais aussi de personnes en France, ils apprennent à prononcer devant que vouloir apprendre à escrire: car ... celuy

n'est pas dinne de balher les regles d'escrire noutre langue, qui ne la peut parler." Bèze, *Abraham* 6–7 ("Aux lecteurs").

23. On the politics of the suppression of vernaculars in Renaissance England, see Blank, *Broken*; and, on Europe generally, see Eisenstein, *Printing* 117.

24. Hart, *Orthographie* fols. 1ᵛ–2ʳ.

25. Ibid. fols. 20ᵛ–21ʳ.

26. "Tu sçauras ... approprier ... les vocables plus significatifs des dialectes de nostre France ... et ne se fault soucier si'ils sont *Gascons, Poitevins, Normans, Manceaux, Lionnois*, ou d'autre pays. ... Car les Princes ne doivent estre moins curieux d'agrandir les bornes de leur Seigneurie ["Empire" in the first edition], que d'estendre ... le langage de leur pays par toutes nations. Mais aujourd'hui, pource que nostre France n'obeist qu'à un seul Roy, sommes contraints, si nous voulons parvenir à quelque honneur, parler son langage courtizan." Ronsard, *Œuvres* II:998.

27. See Paris Procurer (quoted above); Edmund Coote, *English Schoole-Master* (1597) (qtd. Dobson, *English* I:34), and Alexander Gil, *Logonomia* (1619) (paraphrased by Dobson, *English* I:136).

28. Garnier has demonstrated "par son parler assez doucement grave, | Que nostre langue passe aujourd'huy la plus brave." Vauquelin de la Fresnaye, *L'Art* 121 (Bk. I, ll. 1055–6); qtd. Reiss, *Tragedy* 43. On the representation of "poli langage" in the vernacular drama, see, for instance, the subtitle to Mellin de Saint-Gelais' *Sophonisba* (1559).

29. Beaumont and Fletcher, *Comedies* sig. A4ʳ.

30. "The *Native* may learne English from [Fletcher's] lines, | And *th'Alien* if he can but construe it, | May here be made free *Denison* of wit." Beaumont and Fletcher, *Comedies* sig. a4ᵛ (Robert Stapylton, "On the Works of the most excellent Dramatick Poet, Mr. *John Fletcher*, never before Printed").

31. *Maistre Pierre Pathelin* sig. cviᵛ–diiᵛ (on the dialects, see Taylor, "Typography" 116); Beolco, *Due dialogi di Ruzzante in lingua rustica* (1551); Blank, *Broken*, esp. 34–6, 69, 126–68 (on the mockery of south-western and northern dialects, Welsh, Irish, Scottish, and the languages of inner London); and Cyrano de Bergerac, *Œuvres* 163 (on the peasant Gareau in *Le Pédant joué*, who speaks only the patois of Chevreuse, see Jacques Prévot's introduction).

32. "Tragedies farcées/Ou ... farces moralisées," with "gros mots qu'on ne peult entendre." "La liberté des Poëtes Comiques a tousjours esté telle, que souventes fois ils ont usé de mots assez grossiers, de sentences et manières de parler rejectées de la boutique des mieux disans ... ; ce que par aventure lon pourra trouver lisant mes comedies. Mais pourtant il ne se fault renfrogner, car il n'est pas icy question de farder la langue d'un mercadant, d'un serviteur ou d'une chambrière. ... Seulement le Comique se propose de représenter la vérité et naïveté de sa langue, comme les mœurs, les conditions et les estats de ceux qu'il met en jeu: sans toutesfois faire tort à sa pureté, laquelle est plustost entre le vulgaire (je dy si lon change quelques mots qui resentent leur terroir)." Grévin, *Théâtre* 116 , 49 ("La Trésorière" and "Les Esbahis").

33. "Questo Scrittore ha di maniera servato la natura della persona, che introduce a parlare che non pure ha usate le voci lombarde, & le straniere, ma quelle ha ... scritte alla lombarda, & alla straniere maniera, che ne a me, ne ad altri doverai attribute per errore." Aretino, *Quattro* sig. Oo8ᵛ.

34. For those following Aristotle, these included all tragedies, since Renaissance interpreters of Aristotle took his suggestion that tragic plots were best drawn from history as an imperative. See, for instance, Castelvetro's explanation of this requirement: "Non ci

possiamo imaginare un re che non sia stato, né attribuirgli alcuna azzione." Castelvetro, *Poetica* 252 (Pt. 3, Sect. 7). On the importance of documentation generally to historical authentication in the 17th century, see Shapiro, *Probability* 142–6; Kroll, *Material*; and McKeon, *Origins* (arguing convincingly for a 17th-century shift towards a habit of thinking about documentary authority as written and printed); and Johns, *Nature*, especially 187–265 (describing the work of 17th- and 18th-century printers and booksellers in creating a trustworthy realm of printed knowledge). Such views might usefully be modified by Joseph Levine's identification of the centrality of anti-textual antiquarianism and natural history to Renaissance historiography, stressing the continuity of 17th-century historiography with that developed in the early Renaissance (Levine, *Humanism* 73–106, 123–55); by Barbara J. Shapiro's discussion of 17th-century historians' ambivalence about the ultimate value of documentary research (*Probability* 144, and 119–62 for a general discussion of the impact of scepticism about documentary sources on 17th-century historical scholarship); and by D. F. McKenzie's identification, in the legal context, of the simultaneous endurance of faith in the oral testimony of witnesses during the 17th century, and the continuing competition between the authority of the literate record and the authority of oral testimony by people of "known character" ("Speech-Manuscript-Print").

35. Scaliger, *Poetices* III:26 (Bk. 3, Ch. 96, "Tragoedia, comoedia, mimus"); trans. Scaliger, *Select* 59.

36. "La terza materia soggetta alla poetica nella quale si può commettere errore ... s'è l'istoria ... non pure la vera o la scritta ... Poetica ... non dee né può falsificare l'istoria ... presentando quello che si sa esser vero come apunto sta." Castelvetro, *Poetica* II:232–3 (Pt. 5, Sect. 1); trans. Castelvetro, *Castelvetro* 280.

37. Massinger, *Plays* III:305.

38. Jonson, *Ben Jonson* IV:350–1.

39. "Comme les tragédies de cette seconde partie sont prises de l'Histoire, j'ai cru qu'il ne serait pas hors de propos de vous donner au-devant de chacune le texte ou l'abrégé des auteurs dont je les ai tirées, afin qu'on puisse voir par là ... jusques où je me suis persuadé que peut aller la licence poétique en traitant des sujets véritables." Corneille, *Oeuvres complètes* II:189.

40. Daniel, *Complete* III:189.

41. Marston, *Plays* II:5.

42. "Il est vrai que j'ai voulu ajouter ... et que j'ai même changé deux incidents de l'histoire assez considérables. ... Les plus délicats verront, s'il leur plaît en prendre la peine, la défense de mon procédé dans Aristote. ... Et pour les modernes, qu'ils aient la curiosité de me voir justifier dans les deux discours [du] comte Prosper Bonarelli ... pour son Soliman ...: c'est en la dernière impression de l'année M.DC.XXXII." Mairet, *La Sophonisbe* 670 ("Au Lecteur").

43. Daniel, *Complete* III:188 (and see the discusssion of this passage in Loewenstein, "Printing" 177).

44. Jonson, *Ben Jonson* VII:308.

45. One can see that "por muchos libros hay difuso; que todo lo de agora está confuso." Vega Carpio, *El arte* 14; trans. Vega Carpio, *New* 28 (stanza 13).

46. "Il ne faut pas prendre la connoissance exacte des Piéces anciennes par les notes et les distinctions apparentes qui sont dans nos imprimez, mais par une lecture exacte de ces excellens Ouvrages." D'Aubignac, *Pratique* 270 (Bk. 4, Ch. I).

47. "Und so vil vor dieses mal. Warumb aber so vil? Gelehreten wird dises umbsonst

geschriben | Ungelehrten ist es noch zu wenig." Gryphius, *Großmütiger* 134; trans. Benjamin, *Origin* 63.

48. There are references to plays that conform to the Rules, or "regular plays," as early as the beginning of the 16th century in Italy, but the discussion gets under way only in the later part of the 16th century, with the proliferation of commentaries on the *Poetics*. The constitution of the Rules was fluid and contested, but the following is an (oversimplified) list of the central tenets. Dramas are to follow the unities of time, place, and action: the narrative is to take place in no more than the space of a day, variously defined, in locations no further apart than what might be traversed in a day; the action is to be one whole (without subplots). Dramas are to have a five-act structure with division into scenes in "the Terentian manner" (whenever a character leaves the stage or a new character arrives). Genres are to remain pure: comedies are not to have tragic elements and tragedies are not to have comic elements. Linguistic decorum is to be preserved: characters are to speak in accord with their class; in tragedies, there should be no low diction, in comedies, no overly elevated diction. The number of actors is to be limited to those strictly necessary. There should be no on-stage violence. The action must conform to the rules of verisimilitude, variously interpreted as conformity to the unities, moral plausibility (consistent with character and genre), or consistency with tradition.

49. "Ho tenuto meglio soddisfare a chi ha ad ascoltare, con qualche minore eccellenza … che con un poco piú di grandezza dispiacere a coloro per piacere dei quali la favola si conduce in iscena: che poco gioverebbe compor favola un poco piú lodevole, e che poi ella si avesse a rappresentare odiosamente. Quelle terribile (se gli animi degli spettatori forse le abboriscono) possono essere delle scritture, queste di fin lieto delle rappresentazioni." Giraldi, *Scritti* 184 ("Discorso … intorno al comporre delle comedie e delle tragedie").

50. "N'attendez donc en ce Théâtre | Ne farce, ne moralité: | Mais seulement l'antiquité." "Tout' ces farces badines | Me semblent estre trop indignes | Pour estre mises au devant | Des yeux d'un homme plus sçavant." "La gentille Poësie | Veult une matière choisie | Digne d'estre mise aux escrits." Grévin, *Théâtre* 51–3 ("La Trésorière").

51. Riccoboni, *Historical* 53.

52. Jonson, *Ben Jonson* VI:120 (V.iii.106–13). For a discussion of the period's opposition between rules and performance as the fundamental criterion for the evaluation of plays, see Chartier, "Texts" 11–12.

53. "Ces gens non lettrez ni entenduz en telles affaires, de condition infame, comme un menuisier, un sergent à verge, un tapissier, un vendeur de poisson … gens ignares, artisans mécaniques." Qtd. Jomaron, ed., *Théâtre* 84–5.

54. "Jeux qui … sont faits selon le vrai art, et au moule des vieux, comme d'un Sophocle, Euripide, et Sénèque," opposed to "tragédies et comédies, … farces, et moralités (où bien souvent n'y a sens ni raison, mais des paroles ridicules avec quelque badinage)" which "ne peuvent être que choses ignorantes, mal faites, indignes d'en faire cas, et que ne dussent servir de passe-temps qu'aux valets et menu populaire." La Taille, *Saül* 209 (*Art de la tragédie*).

55. Beaumont and Fletcher, *Dramatic* III:491 ("To my Maister *John Fletcher* upon his faithfull Shepheardesse").

56. Jonson, *Ben Jonson* VI:397.

57. In writing for the popular theatre, he writes, "me dejo llevar de la vulgar corriente" of "el ignorante vulgo," ignoring the "doctísimo Utinense | Robortelo," "Aristóteles," "Terencio y Plauto." Vega Carpio, *El arte* 12, 14, 18 (stanzas 5, 12, 13, 28).

58. Jonson, *Ben Jonson* IV:323; Dekker, *Dramatic* I:336–7 (II.ii.57–9).
59. Randolph, *Jealous Lovers* sig. ¶¶2ʳ–¶¶2ᵛ.
60. The artificial distinction between the learned *commedia erudita* and the "unlearned" *commedia dell'arte* in which an actress like Isabella Andreini was honoured by the academies, could quote Aristotle on *anagnorisis* and *peripeteia* in Greek and recommended imitating Aristophanes, Plautus, Terence, Piccolomini, and Trissino (see Clubb, *Italian Drama* 31; citing Andreini, *Fragmenti di alcune scritture* 60) is only one instance of the more general interpenetration of early modern "popular" and learned culture generally. Peter Burke notes that Lorenzo de' Medici and Machiavelli both composed songs for Carnival, the 16th-century nobleman Gian Giorgio Alione wrote dialect farces, the confessor to Queen Isabella of Spain (Fra Ambrosio Montesino), Marvell, and Swift all wrote broadsheet ballads, Elkanah Settle, an Oxford graduate with Shaftesbury as his patron, "worked for Mrs Mynn, a show-woman at Bartholomew Fair, and in one play was said to have been reduced to playing the dragon" (Burke, *Popular* 96, 104). For a classic example of the typical alignment of distinctions—between the learned and unlearned, regular ("proper") and irregular, high and low, public and private, gentlemanly and vulgarly professional—see Georg Philipp Harsdörfer's *Frauenzimmer* (1646): "D. Ein rechtes poetisches Gedicht gehöret nicht für den gemeinen Pövel sondern für Gelehrte und mehr verständige Leute. C. Die Trauer-und Freudenspiele aber werden dem gemeinen Mann zu Lieb vorstellig gemachet. D. Hierunter ist ein Unterschied zu halten zwischen den Freudenspielen welche von etlichen darzu von Jugend auf angewehnten Schauspielern (Comoedianten) üm Gewinns willen gehalten und denen Lustspielen welche von vornemen Herren zu sonderer Ergetzlichkeit nach Italiänischer Art … angestellet werden. In jenen mag man mit Possenspielen dem Pövelvolk zu Gefallen seyn in diesen aber von welchē wir reden hat man auf die höchste Kunst dieser Spielhändel zu sehen." Harsdörfer, *Frauenzimmer* VI:163–4 (Ch. 229, "Der Schauplatz"). On amateurs and the new class of literary professionals, see Helgerson, *Self-Crowned* (especially 22–5).
61. In addition to Enríquez de Guzmán, see e.g. Annibal Caro, *Gli Straccioni* (1556) 205 (prologue); Jonson's common usage (the dedication to *Volpone*, and the prefaces to *Sejanus* and *Cataline* (Jonson, *Ben Jonson* V:24, IV:350, V:431)); Webster, *Complete* I:107 (preface to *the White Devil*); Hardy, *Theatre* VI sig. ãiiiʳ (*Les Chastes et loyales amours*, "Epistre"); and Cervantes, *Obras* I:497 (*Don Quixote* Pt. I, Ch. 48).
62. "Il ne faut imiter leur licencieuse façon, que nous pouvons blasmer comme Horace tenaille franchement celle de Plaute en son Art Poétique, ou je renvoy aussi ceux qui voudront lire quelque chose de la tragedie, et à un gros volume qu'en a faict un Scaliger." Rivaudeau, *Les Oeuvres* 46 ("Avant-Parler").
63. Jonson, *Ben Jonson* V:17–20.
64. On the relationship between Richelieu's literary programme, his founding of the Académie, and his programme of constructing the model state, see Thuau, *Raison* 219–20; and Fumaroli, *L'Age*. On his control of the theatre, see Couton, *Richelieu*. And see the discussion of the Académie's formal statement on *Le Cid*, whose printing was prompted by and closely overseen by Richelieu, in the notes in Corneille, *Oeuvres complètes* I:1458–60.
65. "Todo esto es … en oprobio de los ingenios españoles, porque los extranjeros, que con mucha puntualidad guardan las leyes de la comedia, nos tienen por bárbaros e ignorantes, viendo los absurdos y disparates de las que hacemos." Cervantes, *Obras* I:497 (*Don Quixote* Pt. I, Ch. 48); trans. Cervantes, *Don Quixote* 429.

66. Jonson, *Ben Jonson* V:19 (dedication for *Volpone*).
67. "No porque yo ignorase los preceptos, | gracias a Dios, que ya tirón gramático | pasé los libros que trataban desto" (stanzas 3) ... Mas ninguno de todos llamar puedo más bárbaro que yo, pues contra el arte | ... me dejo llevar de la vulgar corriente, adonde | me llamen ignorante Italia y Francia. | ... Como las paga el vulgo, es justo hablarle en necio para darle gusto." Vega Carpio, *El arte* 11–12, 18; trans. Vega Carpio, *New* 24–5, 37 (stanzas 3, 5, 28). On the Madrid Academy's demand that Lope make a statement on the Rules and defend his own "art," see Juana de José Prades' introduction to Vega Carpio, *El Arte* 1–29.
68. Jonson, *Ben Jonson* V:20.
69. Ibid. IV:350.
70. "Si lasciò in tutto e Pindaro et Alceo, | E non al gran discepol di Platone, | Il quale ha di me scritto ordini e leggi. | Che se ben fu Filosofo di tanto | Sonoro grido, egli non fu Poeta." Dolce, *Marianna* 749.
71. "Cuando he de escribir una comedia, | encierro los preceptos con seis llaves; | saco a Terencio y Plauto de mi estudio ... | y escribo por el arte que inventaron | los que el vulgar aplauso pretendieron." Vega Carpio, *El arte* 12; trans. Vega Carpio, *New* 24–5 (stanza 5).
72. Killigrew, *Prisoners* sig. A2ᵛ ("To his Most Honour'd Uncle").
73. "Je sçay bien que beaucoup ... trouveront à censurer" the enchainment of plots, "directement contraire aux loix qu'Horace prescrit en son art poëtique, mais ... tout ce qu'aprouve l'usage & qui plait au public devient plus que legitime." Hardy, *Theatre* VI sig. ãiiiʳ (*Les Chastes et loyales amours*, "Epistre").
74. "¿Qué mucho que la comedia, a imitación de entrambas cosas, varíe las leyes de sus antepasados?. ... Si el ser tan excelentes en Grecia Esquilo y Eurípides, como entre los latinos, Séneca y Terencia, bastó para establecer las leyes tan defendidas de sus profesores, la excelencia de nuestra española Vega" and "la autoridad con que se les adelanta" are "suficiente para derogar sus estatutos." Molina, *Obras* I:233 (*Cigarrales de Toledo*, Cigarral Primero).
75. Charleton, *Letters and Poems in Honour of the Incomparable Princess, Margaret, Dutchess of Newcastle* (1676); qtd. Rosenthal, *Playwrights* 58.
76. "Eccovi un di compositor di libri bene meriti di republica, postillatori, glosatori, construttori, metodici, additori, scoliatori, traduttori, interpreti, compendiarii, dialetticarii novelli, appositori con una grammatica nova, un dizionario novo, un *lexicon*, una *varia lectio*. ... un approvato autentico, con epigrammi greci, ebrei, latini, italiani, spagnoli, francesi, posti *in fronte libri*. ... Non lasciar passar un foglio di carta dove non appaia al meno una dizionetta, un versetto. ... Quanto ben dimostrano che essi son quelli soli a' quai Saturno ha pisciato il giudizio in testa." Bruno, *Opere* III:26–7; trans. Bentley, ed., *Genius* 208–9 (trans. modified).
77. Manfurio gets "cinquanta staffilate alle natiche. ... Spalmate, staffilate ... vi lasciò il mantello che non era suo." Bruno, *Opere* III:18 ("Manfurio").
78. "Escono fuora conducono Cataldo Pedante in camicia legato con buona corda. ... Pedrolino Arlecchino e Burattino di nuovo entrano ... vestiti da beccari e da castraporci, con cortelacci grandi in mano et una conca di rame ... vogliono castrar[lo]. ... Lo discacciano come uomo infame e vituperoso, ad essempio de gli altri pedanti manigoldi e furfanti come lui; poi dicono di preparar le nozze di Flaminia, invitano il Capitano, e finisce la comedia." Scala, *Il teatro* 326 ("Il Pedante," 31st day); Italian; trans. Scala, *Scenarios* 233–4.

79. On the importance of the location of Elizabethan and Jacobean theatres in "the Liberties" (those areas around London free from manorial rule and the ordinary legal constraints of city and Crown—in some senses outside the law), see Mullaney, *Place*, esp. 20–59.

80. *Three Parnassus Plays* 116–17 (IV.i.383–5, 396–402). And see Berowne (or "Biron") in *Love's Labour's Lost*: women's eyes "are the books, the arts, the academes | That show, contain, and nourish all the world" (Shakespeare, *Complete* 296 (IV.iii.328–9)).

81. "Le temps viendra de faire imprimer mes remarques sur les pièces que j'aurai faites, et je ne désespère pas de faire voir un jour … que je puis citer Aristote et Horace." "J'aurais parlé … à mes amis, qui pour la recommandation de ma pièce ne m'auraient pas refusé ou des vers français, ou des vers latins. J'en ai même qui m'auraient loué en grec, et l'on n'ignore pas qu'une louange en grec est d'une merveilleuse efficace à la tête d'un livre." Molière, *Œuvres complètes* I:483, I:264 ("Avertissement" for *Les Fâcheux* (1662); preface to *Les Précieuses ridicules*).

82. Fielding, *Tragedy* (1731) 80.

6. ACCURATE TEXTS, AUTHORITATIVE EDITIONS

1. Beaumont and Fletcher, *Comedies* (1647) sig. A3ʳ–A4ᵛ. There has been much discussion of this passage. Greg ("Prompt") identifies it as evidence of the playhouse production of private transcripts. Barker ("Manuscript" 9) and Orgel ("Acting") stress the status of Moseley's "Originalls" as combinations of authorial and theatrical transcriptions. Blayney claims that Moseley is talking about texts actors produced purely from memory, not texts that actors copied from the main company playtext or other theatrical texts ("Publication" 393–4; "Shakespeare's," in which he points out that in 1647 "transcribe" didn't necessarily mean from another text). See also Masten, *Textual* 121–55, for an extended reading of the editorial apparatus and choices of the Beaumont and Fletcher folio, similar in many respects to my own but stressing the centrality of the shift from a model of homoerotic collaboration toward singular authorship on a patriarchal-absolutist model.

2. See, for instance, Richard Lovelace's poem "To FLETCHER Reviv'd" and William Cartwright's "Upon the report of the printing of the Dramaticall Poems of Master *John Fletcher*." Beaumont and Fletcher, *Comedies* sig. b3ʳ, d4ᵛ.

3. See, similarly, Heminge and Condell (what Shakespeare "thought, he uttered with that easiness, that wee have scarse received from him a blot in his papers" (Shakespeare, *Mr. William Shakespeares* (1623 edn.) sig. A3ʳ)); and, a less well-known example, Richard West's "To the pious Memory of my deare Brother in-Law, Mr Thomas Randolph" ("Hee was not like those costive Wits, who blot | A quire of paper to contrive a plot, | And e're they name it, crosse it, till it look | Rased with wounds like an old Mercers Book. | What pleas'd this yeare, is next in peices torne, | It suffers many deaths e're it be borne" (Randolph, *Poems* 60)). See also the discussion of this commonplace in the classical tradition in Honigman, *Stability* 23–5; and De Grazia, *Shakespeare* 44.

4. See Clanchy, *From Memory* 223, on medieval linguistic manuals, Pottinger, *French* 55–6 on medieval and Renaissance regulation of the correction of French texts, and Madurell and Balaguer, eds., *Documentos* 347–8, on early Spanish contracts mandating the correction of texts. Some of the earliest printed editions carry lists of errata and corrections,

for instance Servius' commentary on Virgil, printed by Bernardo Cennini and his son
Domenico (1471–2), which has a colophon explaining the book's emendation, collation,
and careful editorial work. On Renaissance vernacular textual editing, see Trovato, *Con
ogni diligenza*; and Richardson, *Print*. Martin Lowry writes that the process of criticism
and emendation advanced with printing (*World* 238–40), and Lowry, Richardson, and
Trovato all see textual criticism and printing as historically interdependent.

5. Richardson, *Print* 110.

6. Virgino provided previously unpublished verse redactions of *La Cassaria* and *I Suppositi*, an unpublished second version of *Il Negromante*, and a version of *La Lena* different from that printed in 1535. In addition to the editions of the 1540s, there was an
anonymous stylistic revision of *La Cassaria* in 1546 (following Bembo's rules on the
correct number of syllables in the verse), and there were linguistic revisions of *Il
Negromante* and *La Lena* in 1551. Richardson, *Print* 121.

7. In "questa ultima della stampa del valente Mercolino in ottavo stampata nel XLII.
[1542] ... ho trovato le linee intiere di piu. ... Si prendra piacere di confrontare i detti
testi insieme." Aretino, *Quattro* ("Il Correttore al benigno Lettore," end of volume, no
signature).

8. Kyd, *Spanish* (1592 edn.) (title page).

9. Gréban [?], *Le Premier* (1541), "le tout veu et corrige bien ... selon la vraye verite."
Rojas, *Celestina* (Venice, 1525 edn.), "Dopoi ogni altra impressione novissimamente corretta, distinta, ordinata, e in piu commoda forma redotta, adornata lequal cose nelle altre
impressione non si trova." Other examples of early 16th-century reprintings vaunting
the fact that they were "newly printed" and corrected include Gréban and Michel, *Mistere de la passiõ nostre seigñr Jhesucrist ... nouvellemẽt imprimee* (c.1517); Dovizi, *Calandra
... nuovamente corretta & con ogni diligenza stampata* (1530); *Le tres excellẽt & sainct mystere du vieil testament ... Reueu et corrige de nouveau et ... nouvellement imprime a Paris*
(1542); and Antonia Pulci, *La rapresentatione di santa Guglielma. Nuovamente ristampata*
(1554).

10. "La quantità di esse opere, non ritrovandose-ne piu alle Stampe, ne alle Librarie ... ho
voluto restamparlo. ... Ne in cosa cosi bella ho voluto mancar di ogni diligenza in farlo
restampare, si come non ha mancato altrui di sollecitudine, & cura in correggerlo, &
ampliarlo da quello ... che era dianzi, come quello che haveva non solamente in ogni
faccia, ma in ogni riga molti, & importanti errori." Beolco, *Tutte* sig. A9^r–A9^v.

11. On the medieval conception of *intentio auctoris* or *intentio scribentis* as didactic or edify-
ing purpose, see Minnis, *Medieval Theory* 20. A great deal has been written on the idea
of authorial intention as background to early 20th-century textual studies and post-war
New Bibliography (most centrally represented by the work of Alfred Pollard, W. W.
Greg, and Fredson Bowers), and its conception of "the author." For discussions
of authorial intention and Renaissance dramatic texts, see, for instance, Kastan,
"Mechanics" (esp. 33–5); Maguire, *Shakespearean* 38–41; Marcus, *Unediting* (through-
out); Murray, *Theatrical* 62 (discussing authorial intention by way of Derrida); Orgel,
"Authentic" and "What is a Text?," the essays in Maguire and Berger, eds., *Textual*, and
(generally) the revisionist bibliography and textual criticism of such scholars as Jerome
J. McGann, D. F. McKenzie, Randall McLeod, Gary Taylor, and Steven Urkowitz.

12. See Richardson, *Print* 123–4, 197 on Ruscelli's *Delle comedie*, the Aldine editions of 1540
and 1546, and Giolito's edition of 1550. One might read the archaic English that
Fletcher and Shakespeare give Chaucer and Gower (the narrators of *The Two Noble
Kinsmen* and *Pericles*) as standing in for the problem of archaic speech generally in

dramatic editions (Masten offers a useful reading of these narrators as figures for the author (*Textual* 56–64, 75–93); and see Kiefer on the association of Gower with the book (*Writing* 211–12)). Both Chaucer and Gower as narrators point to the tension between the archaic oral style of the ancient book and the necessities of dramatic speech. The "ancient" author (now notably identified with the book in the representation of Gower on the title page of George Wilkins's *The Painful Adventures of Pericles Prince of Tyre* (1608)) may be bodied forth in the stage representation, but the representation must reduplicate the book's archaism.

13. See Richardson, *Print* 79; and Rhodes, "Printer" 13–18.

14. There are early examples of claims that authorial textual authority trumps other editorial values: the 1482/3 edition of Luigi Pulci's *Morgante*, whose colophon says (tellingly of the still living Pulci) that it is "ritracto dallo originale vero e riveduto e corrective dal proprio auctore" (qtd. Richardson, *Print* 105). But Richardson describes a progression: from the kind of editing Aldus did (apparently using multiple sources arbitrarily and eclectically for his 1502 Sophocles and 1503 Euripides); to arguments like those of Vettori that one had to preserve an author's original language, including archaic or unusual spellings; to the treatment (particularly in Florentine Latin editions of the 1550s) of a single source as invariably authoritative; to textual comparison, exemplified in a letter signed by Giolito on the importance of restoring the text not through the editor's taste but through comparison of "various old books" (*Print* 21, 27, 111, 129–30). In a letter in his 1516 edition of the *Decameron*, Filippo di Giunta explains that he is offering newly printed material copied from the originals, edited "using the judgment of several learned Florentines," and brought back to the state in which they left the author's hands. In a Petrarch edition of 1500, the editor complains about previous corruptions and claims to be bringing them back to their "first style" (Richardson, *Print* 33; see also 4, 24–5, 43, 51).

15. Giraldi, *Orbecche, tragedia … Di Nuovo corretta secondo l'originale dell'autore* (1572). See similarly Ariosto's *La Cassaria … Da Lui Medesimo Riformata, Et Ridotta In Versi* (1560).

16. See Richardson, *Print* 135 on, for instance, the editorial work of the playwright Anton Francesco Grazzini, working in the 1540s and 1550s. Rather than calling on "original copies" as sources (in the classic 17th-century phrase), 16th-century editors tended instead to cite, for instance, "un libro antico." A typical attitude is that of the critic who found it exceedingly peculiar that (as he wrote) "Poliziano is wont to judge codices like wines, by age rather than by reason" (qtd. Richardson, *Print* 23).

17. Marlowe, *Complete* I:77. See similarly Henry Chettle's comments in *Kind-Hartes Dreame* (1592), in which he explains that, in editing Robert Greene, he "stroke out what then in conscience I thought he in some displeasure writ: or had it beene true, yet to publish it, was intollerable" (Chettle and Kemp, *Kind-Hartes* 6).

18. The instruction of an early printer to the reader suggests the typical attitude: "Collate with other copies, please, if anything in the text puzzles you" (qtd. Simpson, *Proof-Reading* 18).

19. Marston, *Plays* II:144 ("Written By John Marston. And now corrected of many faults, which by reason of the Authors absence, were let slip in the first edition," published the same year as the first quarto). See similarly the note in Nabbes's *Hannibal and Scipio* (1637): "I desire thee Reader to take notice that some escapes have past the Presse … which notwithstanding are corrected in divers of the copies: where they are not, let thine owne judgement rectifie them, before thy rashness condemne me" (Nabbes, *Works*

I:192). Richard Hawkins's preface to Beaumont and Fletcher's *Philaster* notes that the play "hath received (as appears by the copious vent of two Editions,) no lesse acceptance with improovement of you likewise the Readers, albeit the first Impression swarm'd with Errors" (qtd. Beaumont and Fletcher, *Dramatic* I:372). John Day invokes the kindness of the patron, "Signior No-Body," in *Humour Out of Breath* (1608): "Worthless Sir, I present you with these my imperfect labours, knowing that what defect in me or neglect in the printer hath left imperfect, judgment in you will wink at, if not think absolute" (Day, *Nero* 271).

20. Dekker, *Dramatic* II:303 (note following play).
21. Ibid. I:306 ("Ad Lectorem").
22. Sharpham, *Critical* 246.
23. Shirley, *Bird* sig. K4ʳ ("Printer to the Reader").
24. Ibid. sig. A2ᵛ.
25. A still clearer example is provided in the 1623 edition of Mateo Alemán's novel, *Guzman de Alfarache*, in which the publisher Edward Blount identifies the errors in his work with the errors of the hero whose example he is offering up to the corrective (and corrigible) readers: "It were a hard taske and rarely to be performed, for any Printer to undertake the printing of a Booke of this bulke and nature, without some faults; yea, were his Copy never so fayre, or his Apprehension so quicke. It is a *decorum* in *Guzman* to commit many Solaecismes, whose life was so full of disorders. This life of his being 26. severall Times printed in the Spanish Tongue in a few years, did never appeare to the world, but with *Errata's*: which makes me the more presuming on your humane courtesie: And as in the first, so in this Second part, vouchsafe with your pen, the amendment of these few faults, before you begin to read the rest of his life." Alemán, *Guzman* sig. **7ᵛ.
26. On Lydgate, see Pearsall, *John Lydgate* 1–2; and Wickham, *Early* II:191–7. On Skelton's self-identification as a "poet," in a lineage descending from Chaucer and Gower, see Westfall, *Patrons* 119. On the developing conception of the author, generally, in late medieval England, see Lerer, *Chaucer*.
27. See the useful discussions of the Renaissance semantic shift in the label "author" (and its associations with father and deity) in Masten, *Textual* 64–6.
28. Wickham reminds us that many late-medieval and early Renaissance manuscripts and records mentioned the names of writers for performance (see *Medieval*, especially 74). As playwrights began to get distinguished from copyists (as in the records for the *Mystère des Trois Doms* performed at Romans in 1509 (Wickham, *Medieval* 184)), names were increasingly entering the records: a few in the 10th and 11th and 12th centuries, more in the 13th and 14th centuries, many more in the 15th and 16th centuries. Individuals might be named as the sole "inventors" of dramatic manuscripts: the mid-15th-century manuscripts of Arnoul Gréban's *Mystère de la passion* say that "Maistre" Gréban "made this creation" (Gréban, *Mystère* (1878 edn.) 2); *Die Grablegung Christi* (1494) names Mathias Gundelfinger as its author. However, although many early dramatic texts (manuscript or printed) were circulated with names, many more were circulated without them. The Wakefield Master and his associates or the writers of the Cornish *Ordinalia* were, as Wickham writes, essentially "artists in the service of the Church" (*Medieval* 74). Those identified as having "compiled" the text of the early printed "morals" in England, the writers (in Italy) of the many anonymous *sacre*, the person who wrote down *Pierre Pathelin* were generally "learned clerkes" or "ministers" or other kinds of household servants. One can get a sense of the large number of 16th-century printed plays that do not carry author names from: Clubb, *Italian Plays* 5–14;

Lewicka, *Bibliographie*; and the lists in Brooks, *From Playhouse* 173–77. See also Lazard, *Le Théâtre* 17 (100 of the 130 extant mysteries are anonymous).

29. See Chenu, "Auctor," and Minnis, *Medieval Theory* 10–12 (and throughout), on the medieval distinction between the "author" or "auctor" (ancient creator/authority) and "actor" (non-authoritative writer), with "auctor" sometimes used for "actor"; and the very useful, more general discussion of changes in late-medieval authorial authority in Brown, *Poets*. The distinction between "author" and "actor" was still current at the beginning of the 16th century: Pierre Gringore, for instance, identifies himself, in the acrostic that gives his name in *Chasteau d'amours* (1500), as "l'acteur qui a fait at composé ce livre" (qtd. Brown, "Confrontation" 110). There are numerous early 16th-century instances of the word "auctor": the Messenger in Rastell's *Four Elements* (*c.*1520) refers to "the auctour" of the play (Rastell, *Nature* sig. A2ʳ); Bartolomé de Torres Naharro refers to himself (in his *Propalladia* (1517)) as his readers' "Auctor" (which may incorporate into "auctor" and "actor" the sense of "autor": head of an acting troupe).

30. Jacques Milet's *L'Istoire de la destruction de Troye* is *mise par parsonnages et composée par Jacques Milet*; Castellano Castellani's *Rappresentatione del figliuolo prodigo* is *composta per messer Castellano Castellani*; John Bale's *A tragedie or enterlude, manifesting the chiefe promises of God unto man* is *Compyled by John Bayle*.

31. "El primer autor ["auctor" in several editions] quiso darle denominación del principio, que fue plazer, y llamola comedia." Rojas, *Celestina* (1985 edn., based on the 1507 Saragossa edition) II:13. Rojas's comment on the printers' additions to the various prior editions, while registering a certain annoyance, assumes the legitimacy of the participation of the scholar-printer in the creation of the text, and instead expends its rhetorical energy ambivalently justifying the printer's addition of summary "arguments": "Que aun los impressores an dado sus punturas, poniendo rubrícas o sumarios al principio de cada auto, narrando en breve lo que dentro contenía: una cosa bien escusada, según lo que los antigos escritores usaron." Rojas, *Celestina* (1985 edn.) II:12. See the discussion of Rojas's "prologue" in Chartier, "Texts" 160.

32. Lopez de Yanguas, *Farsa del mundo y moral del actor* ["auctor" in the 1528 edition] ... *que es Fernan Lopez de Yanguas: la qual va dirgida a la yllustre y ansi magnifica senora, la senora dona Juana d'Cuniga*. On Fernán (or Hernán) López de Yanguas, see Crawford, *Spanish* 38–9, 46–8, 60.

33. "Trascritta dallo exemplare del magnifico Messer Hieronymo Staccoli, gentiluomo urbinate" (qtd. Andrews, "Written" 79).

34. Gréban [?], *Le Premier Volume des Catholicques oeuvres et Actes des Apostres* "redigez en escript par sainct Luc ... Avecques plusieurs Hystoires en icelluy inserez des gestes des Cesars. Et les demonstrances des figures de Lapocalipse veues par sainct Jehã Zebedee ... soubz Dominician cesar, avecqs les cruaultez tant de Neron que dicelluy Domician. Le tout veu et corrige bien et devemẽt selon la vraye verite, Et joue par personnages a Paris ... On les vend par Arnoul et Charles les Angeliers" (title page, 1541 edn.).

35. See, as a typical 15th-century instance, the colophon for Jakob Wimpheling's *Stilpho* (1494), whose text closes with the salutation: "Valete et plaudite Jacobus Vympfelingius" (sig. B2ʳ). On signing with initials only, see Sturgess, "Early" 93. See Murray on the significance of signatures at the end of dedications in 17th-century French plays (*Theatrical* 150).

36. Shakespeare, *Titus* p. xi. According to Gurr, 150 of the 500 or so extant plays published during the reign of Charles I carry a playhouse name on the title page (*Playgoing* 77).

37. A large number of first-run English, Spanish, German, and Italian plays were published

without dramatists' names on the title page. In France, however, a 1547 law required that the name of the author and the name and address of the printer be included at the beginning of every book on religion, and this was soon extended to all other kinds of books and repeated in regulations over the following centuries (see Pottinger, *French* 151).

38. "*Tragoedia … Pammachius, autore Thoma Naogeorgo*" (1539). The general view of the birth of authorship from print is summarized in Elizabeth Eisenstein's claim that "the modern game of books and authors" could be played only once print technology was in place (Eisenstein, *Printing* 121). Seth Lerer (*Chaucer*) identifies the establishment of a modern conception of authorship (involving authorial naming and the projection of conceptions of style onto a persona with a history) with the later 15th century, coincident with (and related to) the spread of printing. While stressing the distance between the Renaissance and 20th-century conceptions, scholars such as Martin Elsky (*Authorizing*), Kevin Pask (*Emergence*), Cynthia Brown (*Poets*), Jeffrey Masten (*Textual*), and Timothy Murray (*Theatrical*) similarly identify the consolidation of the modern idea of authorship in early modern Europe with the spread of printing: with the regular use of title pages, the attempt to assign works to readily identifiable authors and to identify an author's corpus in collected editions, author portraits, and the rise of modern conceptions of intellectual property (issues which I will discuss more extensively in Chapters 10 and 11). See especially Murray and Masten on the individuation of the normally collaborative dramatic author, and his representation (as decidedly male author/authority) by and through print; and Brooks, *From Playhouse* 169–71, for a discussion of the significance of the advent of the words "written by" on the title pages of English plays in the last years of the 16th-century. See also Marotti, *Manuscript* 136, 230 ("The manuscript system was far less author-centered than print culture and not at all interested in correcting, perfecting, or fixing texts in authorially sanctioned forms"; "Print cultivated the notion of an 'authorized' text—with or without the cooperation of authors").

39. Garnier, *Les Tragedies de Rob. Garnier Conseiller du Roy et de Monseigneur frere unique de sa Majeste, Lieutenāt general Criminel au siege Presidial & Senechaussee du Maine*. Andreini, *Mirtilla Pastorale d'Isabella Andreini Comica Gelosa*. Different versions of the Garnier engraving (its design copied with slight variations) appear in the 1583 Rouen edition by Raphaël du Petit Val, the 1604 edition by Théodore Reinsart, the 1605 Rouen edition by Raphaël du Petit Val (in another form), and the 1673 Paris edition by Mathieu Guillemot. See the title-page reproductions in Tchemerzine, *Bibliographie* V:426, 432, 436.

40. Shakespeare, *Love's Labour's Lost* p. xvi; Shakespeare, *King Henry IV Part II* p. xii. For a discussion of this change, see Brooks, *From Playhouse* 70–5, and Kastan, *Shakespeare* 80–1.

41. Heywood, *Dramatic* II:89.

42. Brome, "In prayse of the Authour, and his following Poeme" (Beaumont and Fletcher's *Monsieur Thomas*), asserting that the author's name shows the reader the worth of the play. Beaumont and Fletcher, *Dramatic* IV:425; qtd. Masten, *Textual* 117.

43. While in the prologue to Machiavelli's *Mandragola* (1518) he refers to himself as the "componitor" ("Non è il componitor di molta fama" (Machiavelli, *Tutte* 868)), Italian title pages and prefaces commonly refer to the dramatist as the "auttore" after the first decades of the century. The title page of the Latin *Pammachius* (1539) by the German Thomas Naogeorg states that it is by "autore Thoma Naogeorgo," and the Latin *Dramata Sacra Comoediae* (1547) refers to each of the dramatists it lists as "autore." Henrique Ayres Victoria's Portuguese *Tragedia da vingança* (1555) is "ēmendada &

anhadida pello mesmo autor." It is worth noting that none of the 16th-century plays reprinted in Balmas and Dassonville, ed., *La Tragédie*, refer to the dramatist as "auteur" except Jean de La Taille's *Saul le furieux* (1572), which does not mention La Taille on the title page by name and refers to the play in large type as "faicte selon l'art & à la mode des vieux Autheurs Tragiques"(La Taille, *Saül* 201). The 1606 edition of Montchrestien's *Tragédies*, however, is (in large letters) "reveüe et augmentée par l'autheur" (in large letters in the title page). Georg Mauritius's *Comoedia von allerley Ständen* (1606) is "Von dem Autore mit fleiß von newem durchsehen." The 1600 edition of Jonson's *Every Man Out of His Humor* is famously printed "As it was first composed by the Author," and the second edition of Marston's *Parasitaster* (1606) is "corrected of many faults, which by reason of the Authors absence, were let slip in the first edition" (title page). See the discussion of the English use of the term in Masten, *Textual* 64–6, 70–1, and throughout.

44. "Messieurs les auteurs, à présent mes confrères." Molière, *Œuvres complètes* I:264 (preface to *Les Précieuses ridicules* (1660)).

45. "E perché l'uomo non debbe solamente contentarsi dell'uso del parlare, ma debbe con ogni industria e arte lasciar di se medesimo e delle sue fatiche qualche memoria alle stampe ... quindi è ch'el Signor Flavio ... ha poi voluto lasciar al mondo (non le sue parole, non i suoi bellissimi concetti) ma le sue Comedie, le quali in ogni tempo et in ogni luogo gli hanno dato grandissimo onore." Scala, *Il teatro* 12; trans. Scala, *Scenarios* p. xxxi (trans. modified).

46. On the Jonson frontispiece, see Jonson, *Workes*; Corbett and Lightbown, *Comely Frontispiece* 150; and for discussions of the central place of Jonson's *Workes* in establishing norms of authority and "textual sovereignty" through print, see Newton, "Jonson"; Loewenstein, "Script"; Murray, *Theatrical* 51–6 (and throughout). For challenges to the standard view, see Brooks, *From Playhouse* 104–39; and Walker, *Politics* 8. For works as "Remaines," see (for instance) Shirley's poem in Beaumont and Fletcher, *Comedies* sig. A4ᵛ.

47. Corneille, *Le Théâtre de P. Corneille. Revu et corrigé par l'Auteur* (Rouen and Paris: Guillaume de Luyne, Thomas Jolly, and Louis Billaine, 1663 and 1664) (frontispiece reproduced in Chapter 2). The folio itself was preceded by a three-volume octavo in 1660 (published by de Luyne and Augustin Courbé).

48. Mauritius, *Comoedia* "Von dem Autore mit fleiß von newem durchsehen | und männiglich zu gut in den Druck verfertiget"; Montchrestien, *Les Tragédies*, "Dernière édition reveüe et augmentée par l'autheur"; Andreini, *Le bravure* "in questa Seconda impressione dal proprio Autore ricorrette"; Ford, *Golden Meane* "Enlarged by the first Authour."

49. Jonson, *Comicall* (title page; emphasis added).

50. Marlowe, *Complete* I:77.

51. Vega Carpio, *Doze comedias de Lope de Vega, Sacadas de sus originales por el mismo. ... Novena parte* (title page).

52. Nabbes, *Works* II:83, 159.

53. Bentley estimates that perhaps half of the plays of the English professional theatre (up to the Interregnum) were the products of collaboration (*Profession of Dramatist* 199). See also Masten, *Textual* 14 (nearly two-thirds of Henslowe's were collaborative); and Brooks, *From Playhouse* 140–188 (in facing the problems of attribution on title pages and division of texts into authorial editions, printed editions result in the taming of the Elizabethan norm of collaborative dramatic authorship).

54. Rowley, Dekker, and Ford, *Witch* (1658) (title page).

55. See the discussion of collaborative authorship represented variously on the page and of the significance of brackets (and the reproduction of the title page of *A Faire Quarrel*), in Brooks, *From Playhouse* 168–72.

56. "Un Imprimeur digne de sa profeßion te le rend, Amy Lecteur ... außi correct que le peut souffrir la premiere presse. ... Nulle transposition notable, nul sens perverty, & nulles obmissions d'importance, ne démembreront le corps de l'ouvrage." Hardy, *Theatre* IV sig. ãiv^r–ãiv^v. Writing of his *Theagene et Cariclee*: "Une seconde Impression ... passera l'esponge sur tous les deffauts precedens." Hardy, *Theatre* VI sig. aiiii^v ("Au Lecteur").

57. Dekker, *Magnificent* 24.

58. Jonson, *Ben Jonson* IV:351. On the *Sejanus* revisions, see Wikander, *Play* 52; Murray, *Theatrical* 73;.and Orgel, "What is a Text?" 84.

59. Beaumont and Fletcher, *Comedies* sig. A3^v.

60. Ibid. sig. d1^v.

61. On this poem, see Masten, *Textual* 133, and throughout, on the larger homoerotic figuration of Beaumont and Fletcher's relationship.

62. Beaumont and Fletcher, *Comedies* sig. g2^r.

63. *Le Malade imaginaire* "avoit esté si mal imprimée dans les Editions precedentes, qu'outre plusieurs Scenes, tout le troisiéme Acte n'estoit point de Monsieur de Moliere: On vous la donne icy corrigée sur l'Original de l'Autheur." Molière, *Les Oeuvres* (1682 edn.) I, sig. ax^r ("Avis au lecteur").

64. "Quoy que cette Comedie ne soit pas de Monsieur de Moliere, on a crû qu'il estoit à propos, pour la satisfaction du Lecteur, de la mettre à la fin de ses Oeuvres, comme on a fait dans les Editions precedentes, pour ne pas supprimer une Piece de Theatre, qui est toute à l'avantage de cet illustre Autheur, & qui a tant de rapport avec plusieurs Personnages de ses Comedies." Molière, *Les Oeuvres* (1682 edn.) VIII:265.

65. Gaillard, *La Carline ... De l'invention d'A. Gaillard. ... Avec quelques autres pieces du mesme autheur.*

66. "Son Corps & son Esprit sont peints en cest ouvrage; | L'un dedans ce tableau, l'autre en ce qu'il escrit." Montchrestien, *Les Tragédies* (1601 edn.) sig. ai^v (poem signed Bosquet).

67. "It may be boldly averred, not one indiscretion hath branded this Paper in all the Lines, this being the Authentick witt that made Blackfriers an Academy ... while *Beaumont* and *Fletcher* were presented." Beaumont and Fletcher, *Comedies* sig. A3^r.

68. Shakespeare, *Mr. William Shakespeares* (1623 edn.) sig. A3^r. Beaumont and Fletcher, *Comedies* sig. A3^v. On the centrality of the singular "hand" to Renaissance conceptions of writing and the individual, see Goldberg, *Writing*.

69. "Per sua malaventura, non essendo mai dall'autore stata gradita, non hà ... potuto dalla mano di lui in tutte le sue parti ricevere ... perfezzione." Bonarelli, *Filli* sig. A2^r.

70. On the trope of printing as paternity, and Dekker's use of the phrase "man in print," see Wall, *Imprint* 1–22 (and Chapter 4). On the prototype of the singular author-father as marking a crucial moment in the history of the subject, see Masten, *Textual* 44.

71. Heywood, *Dramatic* IV:5 ("To the Reader").

72. "No hay cortesana que haya corrido a Italia, las Indias, y la casa de Meca, que vuelva tan desfigurada como una pobre comedia, que ha corrido por aldeas, criados y hombres que viven de hurtarlas y de añadirlas." Vega Carpio, *Obras* VII:595 (dedication of *Los Muertos vivos*).

73. Sackville and Norton, *Gorboduc* 4–5. For an extended analysis of the cultural significance of the rape metaphor in this passage, see Wall, *Imprint* 182–4.

74. Shakespeare, *Mr. William Shakespeares* (1623 edn.) sig. A3^r.

75. His works have been "gefunden, mit fleiß colligirt unnd in ein richtige Ordnung und gegenwertigen Ersten Tomum … zusammengetragen," For the sake of "sein Sinnreicher geist," his editors are producing this book "an statt eines Pyramidis." Ayrer, *Ayrers* I:6.

76. Shakespeare, *Tragedy of Hamlet* (1676 edn.) π2^r ("To the Reader").

77. Beaumont and Fletcher, *Comedies* sig. A4^r.

78. Ibid. sig. A2^r ("Epistle Dedicatorie").

79. Ibid. sig. b1^v (John Denham, "On Mr. John Fletcher's Workes").

80. Howard, *Usurper* sig. A2^r.

81. Shakespeare, *Mr. William Shakespeares* (1623 edn.) sig. A1^r and π2^v.

82. Shakespeare, *Mr. William Shakespeares* (1623 edn.) (title page). The view that playhouse texts represented the "true" texts was similarly reflected in the playhouse scribe Edward Knight's apology that the basis for his copy of Fletcher's *Bonduca* (made for a private patron) was the author's "foul papers" instead of the promptbook: "The booke where by it was first Acted from is lost: and this hath beene transcrib'd from the fowle papers of the Authors wch were found" (qtd. Greg, *Shakespeare* 107).

83. Beaumont and Fletcher, *Comedies* (title page).

84. The text, writes the editor, is "deformata," and "è paruto necessario di ristampar gli antichi originali di essa." Bonarelli, *Opere* (1640) sig. *4^r–*4^v.

85. Davenant, *Works* (title page).

86. Re the "Comedies de ce fameux Auteur": "On les trouvera rétablis" and the reader can now "les avoir dans leur pureté." Molière, *Les Oeuvres* (1682 edn.) I, sig. aii^r ("Preface").

87. Beaumont and Fletcher, *Comedies* sig. A4^r; Jonson, *Every Man Out of His Humor* (title page). On "originals" and "originality" as a literary value, see the discussion in Chapter 11.

88. See Bonarelli, *Opere* sig. *4^v; Calderón, *Verdadera quinta parte* ("Fama, Vida, y Escritos de D. Pedro Calderon de la Barca" sig. ¶7^r–¶¶3^r); Shakespeare, *Works* (Rowe edn., 1709). 16th- and 17th-century editions generally add author portraits only after the death of the author. On frontispiece portraits, dramatic authorship, and print generally, see Murray, *Theatrical* (especially 16–17, on the way in which "historical figures … memorialize themselves as 'textual figures'" (17)).

89. Beaumont and Fletcher, *Works* I: pp. vi–viii.

90. For helpful discussions of these and other issues in the context of 18th-century Shakespeare editing and textual criticism, see De Grazia, *Shakespeare*; and Jarvis, *Scholars*. On the significance of the biography in Rowe's edition for the 18th-century authorship (and more generally on the significance of Shakespearean biographical reconstruction and canonization to 18th-century notions of dramatic author and text), see Dobson, *Making* 1–2, and throughout.

91. Vanbrugh, *Complete Works* I:11 (preface to *Relapse*).

92. "Io le dò alle stampe tali, e quali furono recitate." Gozzi, *Opere* I:109 (preface to *Il Corvo*); trans. Gozzi, *Five* 23.

93. Shakespeare, *Works* (Pope edn., 1725) I: pp. xviii, xiv, xvi. Pope is echoing Dryden's similar comment about *Troilus and Cressida* in 1679 ("that heap of Rubbish, under which many excellent thoughts lay wholly bury'd" (Dryden, *Works* XIII:226)) and Edward Ravenscroft's about *Titus Andronicus* in 1687 ("rather a heap of Rubbish then a Structure" (Ravenscroft, *Titus* sig. A2^r)).

94. Shakespeare, *Works* (Pope edn., 1725) I: pp. xiv–xv.

7. THE SENSE OF THE SENSES: SOUND, GESTURE, AND
THE BODY ON STAGE

1. I have based these descriptions on the illustrations in Beijer and Duchartre, eds., *Recueil* and on those in Mel Gordon's collection of *lazzi* (*Lazzi* 32–33). They are, respectively: the lazzo of the chamber-pot (Bavaria 1568, and "Le Disgrazie di Flavio," Giornata 35 (Scala, *Il teatro* II:360)); Beijer and Duchartre, eds., *Recueil* plate XXXVIII; the "Lazzo of the Enema" ("Commeda in the Commedia" in the 1618 Basilio Locatelli, a manu-script in the Biblioteca Casanatense in Rome, and Beijer and Duchartre, eds., *Receuil* plate XL; and the "Lazzi of Water" ("Trappolaria" from the 1622 Basilio Locatelli, also in Adriani di Lucca, *Selva overo zibaldone di concetti comici*).

2. See Gordon, *Lazzi* 21–3, describing: the lazzo of the pie (Ferrara 1580); the "Lazzo of Kissing the Hand" (Scala, *Il Teatro* 320 ("Il Pedante")); the "Lazzi of Hunger" (Basilio Locatelli, "Madness of Filandro" and "Great Magician"); the lazzo of the barber's water ("Cruauté du Dr.," notes of Giovan Domenico Biancolelli in the Bibliothèque de l'Opéra, Paris, no. 26); the lazzo of eating oneself ("Arlecchino Cru. Prince," Paris 1716); and the lazzo of being brained ("Arlecchino Soldat," Paris 1716).

3. "Giove vuol stranutare e Saturno vuol tirar una coreggia. ... Anima secondo Aristotele è spirito, che si diffonde per le botte del moscatello di Monte Fiascone, e che per ciò fu veduto l'arco baleno far un serviziale all'Isola d'Inghilterra, che non poteva pisciare." Scala, *Il teatro* II:396 ("La pazzia d'Isabella," Giornata 38); trans. Scala, *Scenarios* 290 (trans. modified).

4. "Poi, seguitando altri spropositi. ..." "Poco a poco, si risente e torna in sé." Scala, *Il teatro* II:396 ("La pazzia d'Isabella," Giornata 38).

5. For instances of such claims, see Barish, *Antitheatrical* 80–154.

6. Gosson, *Schoole* (1579) fol. 23ᵛ.

7. Robortello, [*De Arte*] 3; trans. Weinberg, "Robortello" 324.

8. "Piacere non puo venirli da altro che da i sensi, cioè dal vedere, udire, toccare, gustare, & odorare." Trissino, *La Quinta* fol. 37ʳ.

9. "Les belles representations de Theatre ... tombent sous les sens. ... [Dans] le Theatre, ... quels enseignemens la Philosophie peut-elle avoir qui n'y deviennent sensibles?" D'Aubignac, *Pratique* 8–9; D'Aubignac, *Whole* 5 (Bk. I, Ch. 1 (trans. modified)). See, similarly, Thomas Rymer (1693): "*Aristotle* tells us of *Two Senses* that must be pleas'd, our *Sight*, and our *Ears*: And it is in vain for a *Poet* (with *Bays* in the Rehearsal) to complain of Injustice, and the wrong Judgment in his *Audience*, unless these *Two senses* be gratified" (Rymer, *Critical* 85 (*Short View of Tragedy*, Ch. 1)).

10. "In währendem Wetter ... so thäte man oben in der Bühne (jedoch nur ob den vornembsten *Dames* und junger Herrschafften Häuptern) vil kleine Löchlin bohren dardurch Rosen-und ander wolriechendes Wasser als ein herrlicher Regen herunder tröpffelte. Neben disem daß es auch von verzuckerten Confect Coriander Mandel Zimmet & c. ein Zuckerhagel. ..." Furttenbach, [*Mannhaffter*] 131; trans. Hewitt, ed., *Renaissance* 231 (trans. modified). See similarly the description of the perfumed mist in the performance of Jonson's *Hymenaei* (1606): "There appeared, at the lower end of the *Hall*, a Mist made of delicate perfumes" (Jonson, *Ben Jonson* VII:232–3).

11. Webster, *Complete* I:107 (preface to *White Devil* (1612)).

12. "Cestuy cy delecte les yeux les oreilles & l'entendement. Les yeux per la varieté des gestes & personnages y representez & par l'assemblee de ta[n]t honorables Seigneurs &

belles Dames comme vous qui ravissez l'esprit d'un chacun en la contemplation du parfaict de vos perfections. Les oreilles, par les plaisans & sentencieux discours qui y sont meslez. Et l'entendement, par ce que la Comedie estant le mirouer de nostre vie, les vieillards aprennent à se garder de ce qui paroist ridicule en un homme d'aage [*sic*]. Les jeunes à se gouverner en l'amour, les dames à conserver leur honesteté, & les peres & meres de famille à soigner aux affaires de leur mesnage." Larivey, *Les Six* fol. 54^v (*La Vefve*); trans. Larivey, *Widow* 25 (trans. modified).

13. Prynne, *Histriomastix* (1633) 834 (and see 928–31, and the similar passage in Gosson, *Playes* sig. C6^r).

14. Prynne, *Histriomastix* 930; qtd. Murray, *Theatrical* 35.

15. Marston, *Plays* I:139 (preface to *The Malcontent*: "the soule of lively action"); Jonson, *Ben Jonson* VII:229 (*Hymenaei*: "that *spirit* it had in the gliding by"); Marston, *Plays* II:143–4 (preface to *Parasitaster*: "the life of these things consists in action").

16. Jonson, *Ben Jonson* VIII:609 (*Timber* (1620–5)). For 17th-century examples of the *ut pictura* topos, see D'Aubignac (like the painter who makes "peintures diverses," "quand ["le Poëte dramatique"] entreprend la composition d'une Piéce de Theatre, il doit penser qu'il entreprend de faire une peinture agissante et parlante" (D'Aubignac, *Pratique* 84, Bk. 2, Ch. 3)); Rymer, "Tragedies of the Last Age" (1677) ("Like good Painters [tragic dramatists] must design their Images like the Life, but yet better and more beautiful then the Life" (Rymer, *Critical* 32; qtd. Reiss, *Tragedy* 7)).

17. Armin, *History* (1609) sig. ¶2^r (preface).

18. Cokaine, "On the Deceased Authour, Mr John Fletcher, his Plays; and especially, *The Mad Lover*," in Beaumont and Fletcher, *Comedies* sig. a3^v.

19. On the changing medieval and Renaissance system of the arts, see Kristeller, "Modern." On the centrality of music to architecture for Renaissance theorists (following Vitruvius), as well as to mathematics, astrology, and theatre, see Yates, *Theatre* 25–6, 193–4.

20. "Ainsi que l'antiquité ne recitoit point ses vers sans musique, & Orphee ne sonnoit jamais sans vers … j'ay animé & fait parler le Balet, & chanter & resonner la Comedie: & y adjoutant plusieurs rares & riches representations & ornements, je puis dire avoir contenté en un corps bien proportionné, l'œil, l'oreille, & l'entendement." Beaujoyeulx, *Balet* (1582 edn.) sig. ciii^v; trans. Beaujoyeulx, *Le Balet* (1971 edn.) 33. On the Renaissance relationship between word and sound, and the modelling of early opera on the ancient union of poetry and music, see Katz, *Divining* (esp. 135–75); Winn, *Unsuspected* 122–93; and (for the 17th century) McColley, *Poetry*.

21. "Aux charmes de sa voix la grave Melpomœne | De l'obscur du Tombeau les vertueux rameine." Hardy, *Theatre* I (title page). For "*Spectators* or *Hearers*," see Jonson's induction to *Bartholomew Fair*, and "attentive auditors," see Jonson's induction to *Every Man Out of His Humor*) (Jonson, *Ben Jonson* VI:15, III:435). For "Ceux qui le regardent, et qui l'écoutent," see D'Aubignac, *Pratique* 348 (Bk. 3, Ch. 8).

22. Euclid, *Elements* sig. diii^v (Dee's preface, referring to Vitruvius's theatrical-musical palace); qtd. Yates, *Theatre* 25–6.

23. Qtd. Beaumont and Fletcher, *Dramatic* I:372.

24. See, for instance, Gengenbach, *Die* [*Zehn*] *alter dyser welt*, "lieplich zü läsen und zü hören" (title page); Terence, *Eunuchus* (1486), "ain Maisterliche und wolgesetzte Comedia zelesen und zehören" (sig. a2^r); and La Chesnaye, *La Condamnation* 63 ("en avoir ou ouyr la lecture").

25. See, for instance, Viperano, *De poetica* 102 (Bk. 2, Ch. 9); and Trissino, *La Quinta* fol. 30ᵛ; and see Aristotle, *Poetics* 31–2 (Ch. 1, and throughout).

26. Puttenham, *Arte* (1589) 64 (Bk. 2, Ch. 1); qtd. Winn, *Unsuspected* 161 (and see the discussion of the "Auricular" and the "Sensible" in Renaissance rhetorical theory in Winn, *Unsuspected* 156–63).

27. Jonson, *Ben Jonson* VIII:502 (*English Grammar*).

28. Gosson, *Schoole* fol. 23ᵛ. On music as "pugnacious" and "seductive" in Elizabethan theatre, see Jorgens, "Singer's."

29. Puttenham, *Arte* 8 (Bk. 1, Ch. 3).

30. Beaumont and Fletcher, *Comedies* sig. c2ᵛ (Web, "To the *Manes* of the celebrated Poets and Fellow-writers, *Francis Beaumont* and *John Fletcher*").

31. Terence, *Terence* (1598 edn.) 147.

32. Jonson, *Ben Jonson* VIII:610 (*Timber*).

33. Castelvetro, *Poetica* I:37, 46 (Pt. 1, Sect. 4); trans. Castelvetro, *Castelvetro* 13, 19.

34. Robortello, [*De Arte*] 142; trans. Weinberg, "Robortello" 339.

35. "Le people, qui porte le jugement dans les yeux, se laisse tromper par celui de tous les sens le plus facile à décevoir." Scudéry, "Observations sur Le Cid" (1637) in Corneille, *Oeuvres complètes* I:782.

36. Gosson, *Playes* sig. G4ʳ.

37. "Je vois deçà delà beaucoup de gens ensemble | Dont la plupart, à voir leur contenance, semble | Désirer plus d'ouïr et voir un cas nouveau | Dont les yeux soient saoulés et rempli le cerveau | De fable et vanité qu'apprendre d'autre sorte." Des Masures, *David* 251.

38. Brome, *Antipodes* 40 (II.ii.48–53).

39. Rymer, *Critical* 145 ("Short View of Tragedy").

40. Jonson, *Ben Jonson* VIII:610 (*Timber*). It has been pointed out that Jonson, like many throughout the century, vacillates between two positions. He attempts to legitimize the pictorial arts which in turn further legitimize his work in the artful book; he accepts the spectacle in so far as it can promote his work in the theatre, but jealously safeguards the prerogatives of his text over, say, Jones's scenic plans (whose most notable elements he may leave out of the printed version altogether, as he does in *Pleasure Reconciled to Virtue*). On Jonson's position, see, for instance, Orgel, "Poetics" especially 371; and Orgel, *Jonsonian* 150.

41. Jonson, *Ben Jonson* VI:16 (induction to *Bartholomew Fair*).

42. Ibid. VIII:26 (dedication to *Epigrammes*).

43. Ibid. 404 (*Expostulačon*).

44. Ibid. 610 (*Timber*).

45. Ibid. 403 (*Expostulačon*).

46. Ibid. 635, 625 (*Timber*); VI:43 (prologue to *Cynthia's Revels*).

47. Ibid. VII:209.

48. Ibid. (and see the discussion of this passage in Loewenstein, "Printing" 179, challenging a purely anti-theatrical interpretation).

49. On this, see Gordon, "Poet."

50. Townshend, *Aurelian Townshend's* 99; qtd. Strong, *Splendour* 216.

51. D'Aubignac, *Pratique* 8–9; trans. D'Aubignac, *Whole* 5 (Bk. I, Ch. 1) (trans. modified).

52. "Les Discours ne sont au Theatre que les accessoires de l'Action"; "Deliberations … sont de leur nature contraire au Theatre; parce que le Theatre [est] le lieu des Actions." D'Aubignac, *Pratique* 282–3, 304 (Bk. 4, Ch. 2; Bk. 4, Ch. 4).

53. It is by now a truism that pictorial space was central to the Renaissance "world-view,"

that a new "episteme" conceived in spatial terms came into being in the 17th century (Foucault, *Les mots et les choses*), and that print was essential to Renaissance "topical and spatial logics," to visual thinking, and to the spatial co-ordination of knowledge generally during the period. See, for instance, Ong, *Ramus*; Yates, *Art* 234 ff.; Elsky, *Authorizing* 110–46; and Murray, *Theatrical* 59, 71, 133. For broad arguments about the general shift from a preoccupation with hearing to a preoccupation with seeing, see Chaytor, *From Script* 5–21; Reiss, *Tragedy* 154; and Wall, *Imprint* 190n., 191n. ("the Renaissance was a time in which sight and visibility had an uncertain and less central place in the culture," but the later Renaissance marks "a shift to an era in which plays are seen and reading is a private visual act"). Foucault offers a sweeping argument for the marginalization of the senses of hearing, touch, smelling, and tasting in the face of the new dominance of sight: "Observation, from the seventeenth century onward, is a perceptible knowledge furnished with a series of systematically negative conditions. Hearsay is excluded, that goes without saying; but so are taste and smell, because their lack of certainty and their variability render impossible any analysis into distinct elements that could be universally acceptable. The sense of touch is very narrowly limited to the designation of a few fairly evident distinctions (such as that between smooth and rough); which leaves sight with an almost exclusive privilege, being the sense by which we perceive extent and establish proof" (Foucault, *Order* 132–3). Such an account may be overgeneralized (see, for instance, Nicholas Hudson's qualifications (*Writing* p. xi)). But there is certainly an insistent emphasis on vision accompanied by a decline in interest in the other senses, reflected in such plays as Garnier's *Les Juives* (as Timothy Reiss observes: "a preoccupation with speaking is indeed being replaced by a preoccupation with vision, which will be characteristic of the neoclassical episteme" (Reiss, *Tragedy* 154)).

54. On the importance of hieroglyphics and pictorially or symbolically based notions of language and thought, see Hudson, *Writing* 10–21; Elsky, *Authorizing* 174 ff.; and (for the later 17th century) Kroll, *Material* 63, 67, 238 (and throughout). On Valeriano's *Ieroglifici overo commentarii delle oculte significationi de gl'Egittii, & altre nationi* and its influence on John Bulwer's work on gesture, see James W. Cleary's introduction to Bulwer, *Chirologia* p. xxii. For a discussion of dance manuals of the period (and the conception of dancing itself as a form of writing), see Franko, *Dance* (esp. 15–31).

55. Wilson, *Arte* fol. 118ᵛ.

56. Webster, *Complete* IV:42 (*Characters*, "An Excellent Actor" (1615)).

57. Bacon, *Works* VI:238 ("Advancement of Learning" Bk. 2).

58. Bulwer, *Chirologia* 153, 15.

59. In *Newes*, the Herald describes the world in the moon, where the inhabitants converse "Onely by signes and gestures, for they have no articulate voyces there, but certaine motions to musicke." Jonson, *Ben Jonson* VII:519. For a general discussion of theories of gesture as a universal language during the period, see Knowlson, "Idea."

60. Bulwer, *Chirologia* 6, 161–2.

61. Ibid. 19, 16–17.

62. Ibid. 6, 15–16, 17–18. See, similarly, Michel Le Faucher in 1657: "Mesme le Geste à cét avantage par dessus la parole, qu'au lieu que par la parole nous nous faisons entendre seulement à ceux de nostre Nation, par le Geste nous faisons connoistre nos pensées & nos passions à toutes les Nations indifferemment. C'est comme un langage commun de tout le Genre humain." Le Faucher, *Traicté* 188–9.

63. Bulwer, *Chirologia* 15, 162 (*Chironomia*).

64. On 16th-century innovations in musical notation, see Rastall, *Notation* 97–117.

65. For a discussion of these manuals, see Dobson, *English* (and on "visible speech," esp. I:259, 339, 378); and Roach, *Player's* 32–56 (especially on Bulwer). On the English Renaissance orthography debate generally and efforts to reform orthography to accord with oral enunciation rather than ancient custom, see Elsky, *Authorizing* 44 ff. As Elsky notes, "ironically, humanist orthographers such as Hart and Mulcaster stress language as speech for a reading public that was increasingly encountering language in print" (*Authorizing* 46).

66. "Les paroles n'ont vie que par l'Ecriture." Peletier du Mans, *Dialogue* 4.

67. See Hammond, "Noisy" 231: "Authors, who regarded themselves primarily as the first term in the production of a collaborative 'Play', were coming to realize that deictic punctuation offered them a means of signalling their preferred expression of the dialogue to the performers, and thereby of becoming more actively a part of the entire collaboration." See also the discussions in Chartier, "Texts" 25–8, and Hall, "Ponctuation," of the way in which the individual editions of Molière's plays published in 1666 were innovatively punctuated to evoke the breaths and pauses of the actors.

68. "La signification des signes, desquels j'useray en toutes mes Comedies": "Ce signe signifie une pause"; "Cestuy deux"; "Cestuy trois, chascune pause vaut une reprise d'haleine"; "Un pourmenemét par tout le Theatre"; "Ceci signifie parler bas"; "Ceci signifie, de parler plus viste que le reste." De Vivre, *Comedie* 7.

69. Jonson, *Ben Jonson* VIII:502 (*English Grammar*).

70. For a discussion, see Parkes, *Pause* 59.

71. Hart, *Orthographie* fol. 9ʳ.

72. Robinson, *Phonetic* 1, 7, 5.

73. Ibid. 7–8.

74. Mulcaster, *Mulcaster's* (1582) 72–3.

75. Robinson, *Phonetic* 6, 4.

76. Mulcaster, *Mulcaster's* 75.

77. Bulwer, *Chirologia* 16–17.

78. On this, see Dobson (*English* I:385), who notes that 17th-century shorthand manuals were largely unphonetic, based often on ordinary spelling but sometimes on pictoriographic signs.

79. "*Lady*: This way the noise was, if mine ear be true, | My best guide now. ..." Milton, *Complete* 94 (ll. 170–1).

80. See, for instance, Echo in the various versions of *Daphne* after Rinuccini's. On the 17th-century figure of Echo, see Hollander, *Figure*; and Benjamin, *Origin* 210.

81. Qtd. Albright, *Dramatic* 162.

82. Cartwright, *Comedies* sig. *7ᵛ (R. Waring, "To the Memory of his deceased Friend. Mr William Cartwright").

83. "Ceux-là méme qui s'y trouvent presens s'appellent (*a*) *Spectateurs* ou *Regardans*, et non pas *Auditeurs*; Enfin le Lieu qui sert à ses (I) Representations, est dit *Theatre*, et non pas *Auditoire*, c'est à dire, *un Lieu où on regarde ce qui s'y fait*, et non pas où l'*on Ecoute ce qui s'y dit*." D'Aubignac, *Pratique* 282 (Bk. 4, Ch. 2); qtd. Murray, *Theatrical* 180.

84. Jonson, *Workes* (1616) sig. ¶5ʳ–¶5ᵛ.

85. "Nous bannissons à dessein de nôtre Définition *les Rythmes & la Musique*, qu'Aristote met dans la sienne, d'autant que nôtre Tragédie ne se sert pas de ces beautez comme de choses necessaires." La Mesnardière, *La Poétique* I:10; qtd. Murray, *Theatrical* 148.

86. "Les Chœurs y sont obmis, cóme superflus à la representatió[n], & de trop de fatigue à refó[n]dre." Hardy, *Theatre* I, sig. A5ᵛ.

87. Dennis, *Critical* I:11 ("Impartial Critic" (1693)); qtd. Reiss, *Tragedy* 38. See similarly Dennis's comments (in the same essay) on the chorus as a musical archaism, a remnant of religious ceremonial, a sign of Greek "Superstition" and "bigot[ry]" (Dennis, *Critical* I:34).

88. Dennis, *Critical* I:33 (*Impartial Critic*).

89. "L'harmonie ne doit être qu'un simple accompagnement, et les grands maîtres du Théâtre l'ont ajoutée comme agréable, non pas comme nécessaire, après avoir réglé tout ce qui regarde le sujet et le discours." Saint-Evremond, *Œuvres* III:151–2 (*Sur les opéra*).

90. See Cannone, *Philosophies* 70. On the separation of music from language in the 18th century, and the emergence of classical instrumental music and the phenomenon of public musical performance generally (as separate from church, on the one hand, and from dance and text, on the other), see Neubauer, *Emancipation*. Certainly late 17th- and 18th-century commentators perceived opera mania as an important—and in many ways new—cultural phenomenon, one worthy of comment precisely because it subordinated text to music.

91. Rymer, *Critical* 88 ("Short View of Tragedy"); qtd. Kroll, *Material* 300.

92. Opera is a "sottise chargée de Musique, de Danses, de Machines, de Décorations." Saint-Evremond, *Œuvres* III:151 (*Sur les opéra*).

93. Fielding, *Author's Farce* 48 (III.i.199–201).

94. Ibid. 16 (I.v.29–32).

95. *Spectator* I:20 (No. 29, 3 Apr. 1711).

96. Cibber, *Dramatic* V:213 (preface to *Venus and Adonis*).

97. Chastellux, *Essai sur l'union de la poésie et de la musique*; Garcin, *Traité du mélodrame ou, Réflexions sur la musique dramatique* (describing the "melodrama" (Italian musical theatre), as it was transforming itself into what was to be the 19th-century melodrama, with its use of music as communicative stage language).

8. NARRATIVE FORM AND THEATRICAL ILLUSIONS

1. "Ragionamenti [using dialogue] sono di tre maniere, l'una delle quali può montare in palco e si può nominare rappresentativa, percioché in essi vi sono persone introdotte a ragionare [dramatikos], cioè in atto, come è usanza di farsi nelle tragedie e nelle comedie. ... Ma un'altra ce n'è che non può montare in palco, percioché, conservando l'autore la sua persona, come istorico narra quello che disse il tale e il cotale: e questi ragionamenti si possono dinominare istorici o narrativi. ... E ci è ancora la terza maniera, e è di quelli che sono mescolati della prima e della seconda maniera, conservando l'autore da prima la sua persona e narrando come istorico, e poi introducendo le persone a favellare [dramatikos], come s'usa pur di fare nelle tragedie e nelle comedie, in guisa che questa ultima maniera può e non può montare in palco: cioè non può montarvi in quanto l'autore conserva da prima la sua persona e è come istorico, e può montarvi in quanto s'introducono le persone rappresentativamente a favellare." The third mode of imitation, combining narrative and dramatic, is "mescolata [e] di contrarietà; percioché, se la rappresentativa dee aver luogo e porger diletto, non si dee fare una azzione contraria, che è la narrativa, la quale distrugge e annulla ogni verisimilitudine della rappresentativa. E come vogliamo noi far parere la cosa vera in rappresentando, se confessiamo tuttavia, ragionando noi in nostra persona, che non è vera ma imaginata, o facciamo che altri dica ciò?" Castelvetro,

Poetica I:36, 38 (Pt. 1, Sect. 4); trans. Castelvetro, *Castelvetro* 13–15 (trans. modified). For an extended discussion of Renaissance conceptions of dialogue, see Snyder, *Writing*, on which I have drawn for my discussion of Castelvetro and Tasso.

2. "Senza la qual montata non hanno la loro perfezzione." "Come il verso è fermissimo argomento a darci ad intendere che il soggetto compreso in lui è imaginato e non vero ... così la prosa debba essere non meno fermo argomento a dimostrare che il soggetto a lei sottoposto sia verità, e non cosa imaginata." "In ciò pecca gravemente Platone e Cicerone e molti altri." Castelvetro, *Poetica* I:36–7 (Pt. 1, Sect. 4); trans. Castelvetro, *Castelvetro* 13 (trans. supplemented).

3. Aristotle, following Plato, distinguishes three narrative forms, or modes. In non-dramatic modes (like epic) the poet may either speak in his own voice and then in the voices of the characters (as Homer does by combining his own narrative voice with dialogue) or maintain a single narrative reporting voice. Drama, on the other hand, always represents characters directly acting or speaking in character; dramatic *mimesis* represents people in action, not narrative or descriptive (*diegetic*) reports on people in action. See, similarly, Plato: "There is one kind of poetry and taletelling which works wholly through imitation ... tragedy and comedy, and another which employs the recital of the poet himself, best exemplified ... in the dithyramb, and there is again that which employs both, in epic poetry" (Plato, *Collected* 639 (*Republic* Bk. 3, 394b–c)). Drama is not, then, defined by its performability. While "one element of tragedy" may be "the adornment of visual spectacle," explains Aristotle, tragedy does not require actors and full-scale theatrical machinery: "the potential of tragedy does not depend upon public performance and actors"; "tragedy, just like epic, achieves its aim even without enactment"; "it can achieve vividness either in a reading or in performance." Moreover, epic and other non-dramatic verbal forms may be performed, with visual effects and kinetic activity: "It is equally possible to use excessive gestures in an epic recitation, like Sostratus, or in a singing contest, which Mnasitheos the Opountian used to do." See Aristotle, *Poetics* 33, 37–9, 64 (Chs. 3, 6, 26).

4. On William of St Thierry's view of drama, see Minnis, *Medieval Theory* 57; and Chapter 4.

5. One might well view the Aristotelian/modern distinction between direct speech (representation) and narrative overlay (reporting) as peculiar: direct speech may be a form of reporting (as so often on the classical stage), and narrative overlay is implicitly or explicitly a form of direct speech (that of the narrator or author). For helpful comments on medieval dramatic telling versus showing, see Knapp, *Shakespeare* 17–18.

6. *L'Acteur*: "Or vous avons en brief comprise | la matiere haulte et feconde | de la creacion du monde. ... | [P]asserons oultre, et nous souffit | monstrer, pour depescher matiere, comment Cayn occist son frere | par envye; et le traicterons | tout le plus brief que nous pourrons." Gréban, *Le Mystère* 14–15 (1878 edn., compiled from several mid-15th-century manuscripts). See similarly Lope de Rueda's *Comedia llamada Eufemia* (written *c.*1542–54), in which the prologue is headed "Autor que haze el introito" who, addressing the audience directly, describes the action of the play (Rueda, *Las Cuatro* 77).

7. *Everyman* (1961 edn.) 1 (ll. 1–2, 19–20).

8. See Wickham, *Medieval* 162, 167.

9. See Chambers, *Elizabethan* I:190.

10. McKendrick, *Theatre* 24–5. Similarly typical of early Renaissance interludes, the prologue of Encina's *Egloga de Plácida y Victoriano* (performed in 1513) addresses the audi-

ence, introduces the characters, and summarizes the plot (Encina, *Obra* 917–19). Torres Naharro offered an *introito* to each of his plays, spoken by a comic rustic or (in at least one instance) by Torres Naharro playing himself (McKendrick, *Theatre* 29).

11. See McKendrick, *Theatre* 9. On the medieval exploitation (rather than suppression) of the "make-believe character of the performance," see Knapp, *Shakespeare* 43; and Wickham, *Medieval* 102.

12. On Lydgate, see Westfall, *Patrons* 35; and Wickham, *Early* III:191–7. On Encina, see McKendrick, *Theatre* 10–15.

13. Shakespeare, *Complete* 672 (*Hamlet* (III.ii.129–48)).

14. Beolco, *Tutte* (1584) sig. A1^r–A6^v.

15. Qtd. Chambers, *Elizabethan* III:137 (and see III:464–5 on its uncertain dating and performance history). Many of the early printed editions of Terence show labels for stage doors that may represent the actual use of stage labels in theatres in Italy, France, and Germany. There is further evidence for the use of such labels in England in Elizabethan account books, which list payments for paper and "gold for large letters" (qtd. Chambers, *Elizabethan* III:41), and in plays such as Percy's *Cuck-Queanes and Cuckoldes Errant* (*c*.1601), Jonson's *Poetaster* and *Cynthia's Revels*, Beaumont's *Knight of the Burning Pestle*, and the anonymous *Wily Beguiled* (Chambers, *Elizabethan* III:154).

16. *Chester Mystery* 331 (Play 17, ll. 152–6); trans. Cawley, ed., *Everyman* 163 (English modernized).

17. "Dieu le pere se revient en son siege et chantent les anges." Gréban, *Le Mystère* (1878 edn.) 11.

18. *Prodigal Son* 29 (ll, 52–3); *Wealth and Health* sig. Bii^r; qtd. Walker, *Politics* 25 (and see his discussion; and Lois Potter's in *Revels* 204–5).

19. Pulci and Pulci, *Rappresentazioni* (*c*.1485) sig. A1^v.

20. "In diesem dritten theil des andern Buchs sind zusamen getragen Comedi | Tragedi | uñ[d] sprüch Auß namhafften Geschichtschreibern mancherley Weltlich Histori inhaltent | Beide der guten und der bösen zu einem Spiegel dem Rechsten | der bösen schendtlichen missethat zu vermeiden | Aber der guten löblichen Fußstapffen nach zufolgen in einem Ehrlichen und affrichtigen wandel. Ein Tragedi | Mit dreyzehen Personen | Die sechs Kempffer | hat vier Actus. Der Ehrenhold tritt ein und spricht. ..." Sachs, [*Gedicht*] II(3), fol. 1^r.

21. *Everyman* (1961 edn.) 1.

22. See Baker, "When?" 35–7 (for an extended discussion of the two *Burial and Resurrection* plays).

23. Sidney, *Apology* 135.

24. Aristotle, *Poetics* 39 (Ch. 6); Viperano, *De poetica* 111 (Bk. 2, Ch. 10); trans. Viperano, *On Poetry* 112.

25. "La lunghezza della constituzione dell'epopea non dee passare in leggendola lo spazio d'un dì." Castelvetro, *Poetica* II:147–8 (Pt. 4, Sect. 2); trans. Castelvetro, *Castelvetro* 239.

26. "Nella diffinizione s'è detto che la tragedia è rassomiglianza d'azzione di rappresentatori che operino, e non che narrino: adunque seguita di necessità che ci sieno le persone, gli abiti e 'l palco e ogni cosa convenevole al rappresentamento." Castelvetro, *Poetica* I:168 (Pt. 3, Sect. 2); trans. Castelvetro, *Castelvetro* 60. Recall, similarly, Robortello: Aristotle's "imitation of an action" belongs to "the histrionic art," not the poetic art (Weinberg, "Robortello" 330).

27. Robortello, [*De Arte*] 58, 240; and Weinberg, "Robortello" 329.

28. "[I]l Poeta Scenico è differente dal Lyrico, e dall'Epico nel modo dell'imitare. Percioche il Lyrico narra semplicemen[t]e, e senze deporre la sua propria persona: e l' Epico hor la ritiene, hor la depone, parte semplicemente narrando, parte introducendo altrui à ragionare. Ma questi, del quale hora parliamo, dal principio insin' all'estremo è vestito dell'altrui." "Cosa è la Scenica Poesia? … Imitatione di cose, che si rappresentino in Theatro [con] apparecchiamento." Minturno, *L'arte* 65 (Bk. 2).

29. "En la *Dorotea* no se ven las personas vestidas, sino las acciones imitadas" (Vega Carpio, *Obras* XXXIV:563); trans. Vega Carpio, *La Dorotea* 4.

30. "Vive exhibition de personnages parlans et spectacles presens en plain theatre." Gréban [?], *Le premier* (1537 edn.) I, sig. +2ᵛ.

31. Robortello, [*De Arte*] 3; trans. Weinberg, "Robortello" 328.

32. "La chose representée au vif ainsi qu'elle ha esté faite." Chappuis, *Les Mondes* 666 ("Le Monde des Cornuz").

33. As contrasted with epic, tragedy, "apparendo ogni cosa nella sua propria forma, è meno gravosa." Castelvetro, *Poetica* II:344 (Pt. 6, Sect. 1); trans. Castelvetro, *Castelvetro* 307.

34. "Laonde i fanciulli, i mutoli e le genti grosse, se vogliono manifestare altrui alcuno avenimento, il dimostrano con parole, con atti, con segni, con movimenti e con cose simili all'avenute … chi potrà negare che la rassomiglianza tragica non sia meno gravosa che l'epopeica in quanto si fa vedere?" Castelvetro, *Poetica* II:344 (Pt. 6, Sect. 1); trans. Castelvetro, *Castelvetro* 307.

35. "La Scenica Poesia" is "non semplicemĕte narrando; ma introducĕdo persone in atto et in ragionamento." Minturno, *L'arte* 65 (Bk. 2).

36. Sidney, *Apology* 134.

37. "Ce poëme est nommé *Drama*, c'est à dire, *Action* et non pas *Récit*; Ceux qui le representent se nomment *Acteurs*, et non pas *Orateurs*." D'Aubignac, *Pratique* 282 (Bk. 4, Ch. 2).

38. "Quelle difference y a-il [sic], je vous prie, entre les Perses d'Æschyle, & une simple relatio[n] de ce qui s'est passé entre Xerxes & les Grecs? y a-il rien de si plat & de si maigre?" Schelandre, *Tyr* (1628) sig. aviᵛ (Ogier preface).

39. "Le tragedie e le comedie propriamente sono l'imitazioni dell'azioni; ma 'l dialogo è imitazione di ragionameno." "Queste differenze sono accidentali più tosto ch'altramente; ma le proprie si toranno … dalle cose ragionate." "Avegnachè nella scena si rappresenti l'azione, o atto, dal quale son denominate le favole e le rappresentazioni drammatice." Tasso, *Tasso's* 20–3 ("Discorso dell'arte del dialogo" (text and trans.)).

40. Benjamin comments on choruses suggestively in this light: "The choruses of the baroque drama are not so much interludes, like those of ancient drama, as frames enclosing the act, which bear the same relationship to it as the ornamental borders in Renaissance printing to the type area. They serve to emphasize the nature of the act as part of a mere spectacle" (Benjamin, *Origin* 121).

41. "Quand un acteur parle seul … il faut que ce soit par les sentiments d'une passion qui l'agite, et non pas par une simple narration. … Surtout le poète se doit souvenir, que quand un acteur est seul sur le théâtre, il est présumé ne faire que s'entretenir en lui-même, et ne parle qu'afin que le spectateur sache de quoi il s'entretient, et à quoi il pense." Corneille, *Oeuvres complètes* III:137–8 ("Discours du poème dramatique"). See, similarly, Congreve: "When a man in Soliloquy reasons with himself, and *Pro's* and *Con's*, and weighs all his Designs: We ought not to imagine that this Man either talks to us, or to himself; he is only thinking. … But because we are conceal'd Spectators of the Plot in agitation, and the Poet finds it necessary to let us know the whole Mystery of his Contrivance he is willing to inform us of this Person's Thoughts; and to that end is

forced to make use of the expedient of Speech, no other better way being yet invented for the Communication of Thought." Congreve, *Complete* 120 (dedication to *Double Dealer*).

42. Beamont and Fletcher, *Dramatic* III:497.

43. Beaumont and Fletcher, *Comedies* sig. g2ʳ ("The Stationer").

44. "Je sçay bien aussi que pour secourir l'intelligence des Lecteurs, plusieurs de nos Poëtes ont mis dans l'impression de leurs Ouvrages des Nottes qui apprennent ce que les vers ne disent point. ... En ces Nottes c'est le Poëte qui parle, et nous avons dit qu'il ne le peut faire en cette sorte de Poësie." D'Aubignac, *Pratique* 55–6 (Bk. 1, Ch. 8).

45. "Je fus obligé de recourir à l'explication qui est imprimée au devant de chacun Acte, sans laquelle je n'aurois point sceu ce que les Decorateurs avoient fait, parce que le Poëte ne m'avoit point appris ce qu'ils devoient faire." Ibid. 62 (Bk. 1, Ch. 8).

46. "Pour faciliter ce plaisir au lecteur ... je serais d'avis que le poète prît grand soin de marquer à la marge les menues actions, qui ne méritent pas qu'il en charge ses vers, et qui leur ôteraient même quelque chose de leur dignité, s'il se ravalait à les exprimer." Corneille, *Oeuvres complètes* III:182 ("Discours des trois unités").

47. "Sur le livre on serait assez souvent réduit à deviner [l'action]." "L'impression met nos pièces entre les mains des comédiens, qui courent les provinces, que nous ne pouvons avertir que par là de ce qu'ils ont à faire, et qui feraient d'étranges contretemps, si nous ne leur aidions par ces notes." Corneille, *Oeuvres complètes* III:182 ("Discours des trois unités").

48. "Events which are impossible but plausible [probable] should be preferred to those which are possible but implausible." Aristotle, *Poetics* 60 (Ch. 24). Aristotle makes it clear elsewhere that he is thinking in terms of the logic of narrative form: "I call an 'episodic' plot-structure" (the worst kind, according to Aristotle) "one in which the episodes follow in a succession which is neither probable nor necessary." Aristotle, *Poetics* 41 (Ch. 9). For helpful discussions of Aristotelian logic and dramatic plot (for Aristotle and Renaissance theorists), see Ricoeur, *Time* 31–35; and Eden, *Poetic*.

49. "Nella tragedia e nella comedia la favola contiene una azzione sola ... non perché la favola non sia atta a contenere più azzioni, ma perché lo spazio del tempo, al più di dodici ore, nel quale si rappresenta l'azzione, e la strettezza del luogo nel quale si rappresenta l'azzione, non permettono moltitudine d'azzioni." Castelvetro, *Poetica* I:240–41 (Pt. 3, Sect. 6); trans. Castelvetro, *Castelvetro* 89. See similarly Robortello in Weinberg, "Robortello" 347.

50. Robortello, [*De Arte*] 87; trans., Weinberg, "Robortello" 341.

51. "L'epopea, narrando con parole sole, può raccontare una azzione avenuta in molti anni e in diversi luoghi, senza sconvenevolezza niuna, presentando le parole allo 'ntelletto nostro le cose distanti di luogo e di tempo; la qual cosa non può fare la tragedia." Castelvetro, *Poetica* I:148–9 (Pt. 2, Sect. 7).

52. "Oui mais, dira quelqu'un ... quel plaisir pourra-t-elle [l'imagination] prendre à la lecture des histoires et des romans? ... Ou pourquoi ne suivra-t-elle pas son objet partout, puisqu'elle ne peut être arrêtée ni par les montagnes ni par les mers? À cela je fais réponse que l'histoire et la comédie pour le regard de l'imagination ne sont pas la même chose: ... La comédie est une active et pathétique représentation des choses comme si véritablement elles arrivaient sur le temps. ... Il est assuré que si puissante qu'elle soit, [l'imagination] ne s'imaginera jamais bien qu'un acteur ait passé d'un pôle à l'autre dans un quart d'heure." Mairet, *La Silvanire* 484–5 (preface).

53. On Castelvetro's distinction between the time of the senses (*il sensibile*, that experienced

by the spectator) and intellectual time (*lo'intellettuale*, that conveived by the mind), see Weinberg, "Castelvetro's" 365. See also D'Aubignac's comment on the difference between the two kinds of time: "Le Poëme Dramatique a deux sortes de durée, dont chacune a son Temps propre et convenable. La première est la durée veritable de la representation; ... C'est-à-dire depuis que le Theatre s'ouvre, jusqu'à ce qu'il se ferme. ... L'autre durée du Poëme Dramatique est celle de l'Action representée." D'Aubignac, *Pratique* 113, 116 (Bk. 2, Ch. 7).

54. Aristotle, *Poetics* 36 (Ch. 5).

55. "E voi, spettatori, non ci appuntate, perché in questa notte non ci dormirà persona, sì che gli Atti non sono interrotti dal tempo." Machiavelli, *Tutte* 887 (*Mandragola* IV.xi).

56. "La tragedia ... conviene avere per soggetto un'azzione avenuta in picciolo spazio di luogo e in picciolo spazio di tempo, cioè in quel luogo e in quel tempo dove e quando i rappresentatori dimorano occupati in operazione, e non altrove né in altro tempo. ... Né è possibile a dargli ad intendere che sieno passati più dì e notti, quando essi sensibilmente sanno che non sono passate se non poche ore, non potendo lo 'nganno in loro avere luogo, il quale è tuttavia riconosciuto dal senso." Castelvetro, *Poetica* I:149 (Pt. 2, Sect. 7).

57. "La grandezza della favola ... è sottoposta a' sensi ... e comprendesi con la vista e con l'udita insieme." Castelvetro, *Poetica* I:220 (Pt. 3, Sect. 5).

58. The scene "è ristretto non solamente ad una città o villa o campagna o simile sito, ma ancora a quella vista che sola può apparere agli occhi d'una persona." Castelvetro, *Poetica* II:151 (Pt. 4, Sect. 2); trans. Castelvetro, *Castelvetro* 242. See similarly Jean Chapelain: "l'oeil qui ne sçauroit bien voir qu'une chose d'un regard et duquel l'action est limitée à certain espace" (Chapelain, "Démonstration de la règle des vingt-quatre heures" in Arnaud, *Étude* 339). The discussion of unity of place originates with Scaliger's *Poetices libri septem* (1561) (see, for instance, Bk. 3, Ch. 96, "Tragoedia, comoedia, mimus"), and is reiterated in Castelvetro, the Pléiade writers, and most 17th-century neo-classical critics. Unity of place sometimes (as with Castelvetro and Chapelain) designated what one person could see at any given time, but sometimes included any places within travelling distance in the course of the day prescribed by unity of time.

59. See Castelvetro, *Poetica* I:239–42 (Pt. 3, Sect. 6); trans. Castelvetro, *Castelvetro* 88–90.

60. "Ma così come il luogo stretto è il palco, così il tempo stretto è quello che i veditori possono a suo agio dimorare sedendo in theatro, il quale io non veggo che possa passare il giro del sole, sì come dice Aristotele, cioè ore dodici, conciosia cosa che per le necessità del corpo, come è mangiare, bere, diporre i superflui pesi del ventre e della vesica, dormire, e per altre necessità." Castelvetro, *Poetica* I:149 (Pt. 2, Sect. 7).

61. Sidney, *Apology* 134.

62. Sidney, *Apology* 134. See, similarly, the Priest's comments in *Don Quixote* in Cervantes, *Obras* I:496 (Pt. I, Ch. 48).

63. Scaliger, *Poetices* III:30 (Bk. 3, Ch. 96, "Trageodia, comoedia, mimus").

64. See, for instance, Scudéry's exclamation against the actors: "La piece qu'ils representent, ne sçauroit durer qu'une heure & demie, mais ces insensez asseurent, qu'elle en dure vingt & quatre & ces esprits dereglez, appellent cela suivre les regles. Mais s'ils estoient veritables, vous devriez envoyez querir à disner, à souper & des licts; jugez si

vous ne seriez pas couchez bien chaudement, de dormir dans un jeu de Paume." Scudéry, *La Comédie* (1975 edn.) 8 (Prologue).

65. "¿Cuánto mayor inconveniente será que en tan breve tiempo un galán discreto se enamore de una dama cuerda, la solicite, regale y festeje, y que sin pasar siquiera un día la obligue y disponga de suerte sus amores, que, comenzando a pretenderla por la mañana, se case con ella a la noche? ¿Qué lugar tiene para fundar celos, encarecer desesperaciones, consolarse con esperanzas y pintar los demás afectos y accidentes sin los cuales el amor no es de ninguna estima? Ni ¿cómo se podrá preciar un amante de firme y leal si no pasan algunos días, meses y aun años en que se haga prueba de su constancia? Estos inconvenientes, mayores son en el juicio de cualquier mediano entendimiento que el que se sigue de que los oyentes, sin levantarse de un lugar, vean y oigan cosas sucedidas en muchos días." Tirso de Molina, *Obras* I:231 (*Cigarrales de Toledo*, Cigarral Primero). See similarly Ogier's preface to Schelandre's *Tyr et Sidon* (1628) and Lope de Vega's *El arte nuevo* (1609).

66. "Pase en el menos tiempo que ser pueda, | si no es cuando el poeta escriba historia, | en que hayan de pasar algunos años, | que esto podrá poner en las distancias | de los dos actos, o si fuere fuerza | hacer algún camino una figura, cosa | que tanto ofende a quien lo entiende; | pero no vaya a verlas quien se ofende." Vega Carpio, *El arte* 15; trans. Vega Carpio, *New* 30–1 (stanza 18).

67. The author is advised "de ne marquer aucun temps préfix dans son poème, ni aucun lieu déterminé où il pose ses acteurs. L'imagination de l'auditeur aurait plus de liberté de se laisser aller au courant de l'action, si elle n'était point fixée par ces marques, et il pourrait ne s'apercevoir pas de cette précipitation, si elles ne l'en faisaient souvenir, et n'y appliquaient son esprit malgré lui." Corneille, *Oeuvres complètes* III:171 ("Discours de la tragédie"); and see, on lost time between the acts, Corneille, *Oeuvres complètes* III:185 ("Discours des trois unités").

68. "Une action qui se passe en un seul jour, et qui … n'est soutenue que par les intérêts, les sentiments et les passions des personnages." Racine, *Oeuvres complètes* I:387 (first preface).

69. Castelvetro, *Poetica* I:148–9 (Pt. 2, Sect. 7).

70. On the historically and spatially precise sets for late 17th-century Racine productions, see Herzel, "Racine."

71. "Theatre, où toutes les choses doivent devenir plus grandes, et où il n'y a qu'enchantement et illusion." D'Aubignac, *Pratique* 353 (Bk. 4, Ch. 8).

72. Brome, *Antipodes* 70 (III.iv).

73. "Pues ansí como el que lee una historia en breves planas, sin pasar muchas horas, se informa de casos sucedidos en largos tiempos y distintos lugares, la comedia, que es una imagen y representación de su argumento, es fuerza que cuando le toma de los sucesos de dos amantes, retrate al vivo lo que les pudo acaecer y no siendo esto verosímil en un día, tiene obligación de fingir pasan los necesarios para que la tal acción sea perfecta." Molina, *Obras* I:231 (*Cigarrales de Toledo*, Cigarral Primero).

74. "Je veux vous faire voir sa fortune éclatante. | Les novices de l'art avecques leurs encens | Et leurs mots inconnus qu'ils feignent tous puissants, | … Apportent au métier des longueurs infinies, | Qui ne sont après tout qu'un mystère pipeur | Pour les faire valoir et pour vous faire peur, | Ma baguette à la main, j'en ferai davantage, | *Il donne un coup de baguette et on tire un rideau.* …" Corneille, *Oeuvres complètes* I:621 (*Illusion comique* I.ii).

9.   FRAMING SPACE: TIME, PERSPECTIVE, AND MOTION IN THE IMAGE

1. "No en vano se llamó la poesía *pintura viva*, pues imitando a la muerta, ésta, en el breve espacio de vara y media de lienzo, pinta lejos y distancias que persuaden a la vista a lo que significan." Tirso de Molina, *Obras* I:231 (*Cigarrales de Toledo*, Cigarral Primero).

2. For discussion and reproductions of this image, and the *Game at Chess* and *Friar Bacon* images I discuss below, see Foakes, *Illustrations* 104–5, 118–19, 122–37.

3. Shakespeare, *Complete* 569 (*Henry V* (prologue l. 13)). Jonson, *Ben Jonson* VII:213. La Mesnardière, *La Poétique* 412–13 ("Si l'Aventure s'est passée ... en plusieurs apparte-mens, & ... hors de [la] Maison en beaucoup d'endroits différens, il faut que ... les Ren-fondremens soient diviséz en plusieurs Chambres, par les divers Frontispices, Porteaux, Colonnes, ou Arcades"). On the *Cassaria* set (designed by Pellegrino da Udine), see the letter from Bernardino Prosperi to Isabella d'Este, reproduced in Bonino, ed., *Il teatro* II(1):414; qtd. Andrews, *Scripts* 36. See Rosenfeld, *Short* 16 (on the Buontalenti set). On perspective scenery in Renaissance stage designs generally, see Kernodle, *From Art* 212–14; and Schöne, *Die Entwicklung*.

4. The truism that there is a shift from multiple and simultaneous décor to Italian unified scenic space in 17th-century Europe (carried to northern Europe in the early 17th cen-tury by architects who had studied in Italy) certainly needs a good deal of qualification. The Hôtel de Bourgogne's *Mémoire pour la décoration* (1633), for instance, suggests that the system of houses, or "maisons," was still in use in Paris in the 1630s (Mahelot, *Le Mémoire*). Spanish *corrales* continued to be, through the 18th century, very like those of the late 16th century (Shergold, *History* 413). The numerous travelling players per-forming in *ad hoc* theatres and the growth of informal theatres in the late 17th and 18th centuries should remind us that—if one looks at performance broadly—unified, framed scenic space was probably the exception rather than the rule. That said, there is certainly a drive towards unified and framed theatrical spaces in permanent, indoor theatres in the 17th century, a drive which has been well documented in such accounts of the advent of classical stage design as Pirrotta and Povoledo, *Music* 281–334; Deierkauf-Holsboer, *L'Histoire* (esp. 124–34); Lawrenson, *French* (especially 21–48, 73–107, and 136–40, qualifying accounts of but essentially confirming the Italian influence on French stag-ing); Leacroft, *Development* 51–88; and Wickham, *Early* II:3–12, 153–205. On the Olimpico, Sabbionetta, and Parma theatres, see the discussions in Kernodle, *From Art* 166–71 (esp. 167); Magagnato, *Teatri* 62–6, and Lawrenson, *French* 36, rejecting the notion that the Olimpico was the first in a line of theatres whose central arches were gradually widened (the single proscenium arch was in use before the Teatro Olimpico was built).

5. Jonson, *Ben Jonson* VII:337–56 (*Oberon*); Shirley, *Triumph* 6. On the use of curtains, see Nicoll, *Stuart* 39–44. On the classical *Scena Ductilis* (scene revealing another scene behind) and its use in baroque staging, see Lawrenson, *French* 41–5. On the use of the proscenium arch as frame (partial or whole), see Nicoll, *Stuart* 44–53; and Hewitt, ed., *Renaissance* 4–5. Hewitt notes that there is an engraving of a complete theatrical frame as early as 1560.

6. Davenant, *Dramatic* II:321, 325–6.

7. On the importance of perspective in non-dramatic book illustration, see McKenzie, "Typography" 104–5 (for a discussion of Sir John Harington's 1591 translation of

Ariosto and the perspective illustrations that accompanied it, under Harington's direction).

8. "Essendosi alle volte mutate le Scene delle Case in Selve, in Monti, od altro, non pare c'habbia molto del buono, ne del verisimile, che restino quei due pezzi di Case soli, senza transmutarsi anch'essi: Onde per remediare à tali inconvenienti si potrà in testa al Palco fare un'Arco con Colonne, e Statue, e dentro fabricarvi la Scena." Sabbattini, *Pratica* 73 (Bk. II, Ch. 3); trans. Hewitt, *Renaissance* 100.

9. "Sogliono alcuni nella Prospettiva di mezo far fingere più di una Strada, sì con un solo Punto, come con diversi, cosa nel vero, che non sô finire di approvare." Sabbattini, *Pratica* 46 (Bk. I, Ch. 28); trans. Hewitt, ed., *Renaissance* 80 (trans. modified).

10. "Tanto alto dal piano della Sala, che stando à sedere, la vista sia nel medesimo piano del Punto del concorso, che cosi tutte le cose segnate nella Scena appariranno meglio, che in alcuno altro luogo." Sabbattini, *Pratica* 55 (Bk. I, Ch. 34); trans. Hewitt, ed., *Renaissance* 88.

11. "Was es für ein holdseelig tieff nach sinnendes ... Anschawen umb die *Prospectiva* ... eines *Theatri* oder *Scenæ di Comœdi* [ist]. Sintemahlen der also hinein lauffende Augpuncten ... den Meister selbsten ... dermassen verführet ja solcher massen bestürtzet das der so unvollkommene Mensch gleichsam darüber erstummet und sein Sinnligkeit entzucket wird." Furttenbach, [*Mannhaffter*] (1663) 111; trans. Hewitt, ed., *Renaissance* 203 (trans. modified).

12. On the prince's seat and the "ladies," see Sabbattini, *Pratica* 52, 55 (Bk. I, Ch. 31, 34). On Pigafetta, see Lawrenson, *French* 46n.

13. "Quasi tutti gli Spettatori ... havendo solo il pensiero, & il guardo intento a mirare la Scena." Sabbattini, *Pratica* 52 (Bk. I, Ch. 31).

14. Corneille, *Le Theatre* (1660 edn.) II:90–1. Although the scene could not have been staged, the illustration represents camp backdrops of the sort that were used in the theatre (described in the Hôtel de Bourgogne's register of stage designs). We know, further, that *Horace* was in the active repertory of the Hôtel de Bourgogne in the early 1660s, because in Molière's *Impromptu de Versailles*, he imitates Mlle de Beauchâteau as Camille in *Horace* (Molière, *Œuvres complètes* I:680–1, 1299 (scene i); Corneille, *Oeuvres complètes* I:1538). Unfortunately, the only scenic indication that the Hôtel de Bourgogne *Mémoire* gives for a production of *Horace* (in early 1640) is "Theatres estes un palais a volonté," but for a production of Du Ryer's *Scevole* during the same period at the Hôtel de Bourgogne, we have the description, "Theatre est des tante et pavillons de guerre," a similar description for Pradon's *La Troade* in 1679, also at the Hôtel de Bourgogne (Mahelot, *Le Mémoire* 110, 115, 121), and, from 1666, testimony of the actual use of such a set for Molière's production of Racine's *Alexandre* (see Herzel, "Decor" 92; and Herzel, "Racine" 1067–9 (photographs of a late 18th-century stage set with tents and pavilions, which Herzel argues may have been similar to the set used for *Alexandre*)).

15. "Si vidde Venere in una Conchiglia tirata da due Cigni. ... Dalla banda sinistra del Mare comparve ... uno scoglio, e sopra d'esso un Cavaliere. ... Il suo corsiere era coperto di matriperla, e nella fronte un ramo di corallo accompagnato dai Fiumi principali del Dominio Veneto che in forma di robusti vecchi versavano dall'Urne sotto'l braccio copiosissimo umore." Obizzi, *L'Ermiona* 93–4 (III.vii).

16. On the importance of theatrical space to baroque book illustration generally, see Martin, *French* 91 (and the accompanying illustration to Jean Desmarets de Saint-Sorlin's novel *Ariane*); and the reproductions of the frontispieces and title pages for August Bohse's romantic novels, *Schauplatz der Unglückselig-Verliebten* and *Amor an Hofe oder Das*

spielende Liebes Glück hoher Standes-Personen, Cavalliere und Damen der galanden Welt in Hardin, ed., *German* 59.

17. Laufer, "L'Espace" 480.

18. "Et perche le sale (per grandi che siano) non son capaci di Teatri: io nondimeno per accostarmi quanto io posso à gli antichi, ho voluto di esso Teatro farne quella parte che in una gran sala possi capire. [P]erò la parte D, servirà per la piazza della Scena, la parte circolare segnata E, sarà la piazza del Teatro rilevata un grado dalla piazza della Scena. ..." Serlio, *I sette* I, fol. 48ᵛ; trans. Hewitt, ed., *Renaissance* 27.

19. Furttenbach, *Architectura* 60 ("Das Kupfferblatt No. 20) (for the curtains, and throughout for his architectural designs).

20. Rojas, *Celestine* (1527 edn.) sig. D2ʳ.

21. Furttenbach, *Architectura* 61.

22. Webster, *Complete* IV:42 (*Characters*, "An excellent Actor" (1615)).

23. "La scene est au Ciel, en la Sicile & aux enfers, on L'imagination du Lecteur se peut representer une certaine espece d'unité de lieu, Les concevant comme une lique perpendiculaire du ciel aux enfers." Claveret, *Le Ravissement* π4ᵛ ("Acteurs").

24. Sidney, *Apology* 134.

25. Giambullari, *Apparato* 66.

26. "Die Nahmen der Abgœtter deren in dieser Tragœdien gedacht wirdt." Spangenberg, *Jeremia* sig. A6ʳ–A6ᵛ.

27. "Le Poeme ... est l'objet de la memoire, comme tous les corps le sont des yeux" (explaining Aristotle's comments on magnitude). Gasté, ed., *La Querelle* 78 (Scudéry, "Observations sur Le Cid" (1637)).

28. "These inimitable Playes ... were only shewd our Fathers in a conjuring glasse, as suddenly removed as represented, [but] the Landscrap is now brought home by this optick ... the Presse." Beaumont and Fletcher, *Comedies* sig. A4ʳ (Shirley, "To the Reader").

29. "Come si deve colorire il Parapetto del Palco": "E ben vero che suol dare grande ornamento à i disegni in carta." Sabbattini, *Pratica* 51–2 (Bk. I, Ch. 50); trans. Hewitt, ed., *Renaissance* 85.

30. See Schiller's argument that for *Wilhelm Tell*, "Die Werkleute auf dem Gerüste mässen der Perspective wegen, durch Kinder dargestellt werden" (Schiller, *Schillers Werke* XXXII:90 (letter, 5 Dec. 1803)); and the discussion of 19th-century practice in Brewster and Jacobs, *Theatre* 155.

31. "Cose vive, lequali habbino il moto." Serlio, *I sette* I, fol. 50ᵛ; trans. Hewitt, ed., *Renaissance* 32.

32. "Alcuni hanno dipinto alcuni personaggi, che rappresentano il vivo, come saria una femina ad un balcone, ò dentro d'una porta, etiandio qualche animale: queste cose non consiglio che si faccino, perche non hanno il moto & pure rappresentano il vivo: ma qualche persona che dorma à buon proposito, overo qualche cane, ò altro animale che dorma, perche non hanno il moto." Serlio, *I sette* I, fol. 50ʳ–50ᵛ; trans. Hewitt, ed., *Renaissance* 31–2.

33. Sabbattini, *Pratica* 22 (Bk. I, Ch. 16). On the problem of the clock on stage, see States, *Great* 30 (discussing Benjamin's "Work of Art in the Age of Mechanical Reproduction").

34. "Ghardasi attentamente ... di non fingere Huomini, ne Donne alle Fenestre, ò nelle Strade, od Ucelli in gabbia, Scimie, od altri animali da piacere, che non havrebbe del verisimile, perche da gli Autori si fanno le comedie di attione táto lunga tal'hora, che

trascendono il termine di una giornata, onde saria impossibile, che gli detti Huomini, & Animali stessero li giorni intieri immobili. … Fuggasi dunque le sudette inverisimilitudini, e fingasi solamente quello che mostra di essere stabile." "Non si devono rappresentare nè persone, nè altre cose mobili, ne in altre parti della Scena, poiche sarebbe cosa poco verisimile, per trappassare tal'hora l'attione il termine di un giorno, e per altre cagioni, c'hora non fà luogo di rammemorare." Sabbattini, *Pratica* 50–1, 41 (Bk. I, Ch. 30, 25); trans. Hewitt, ed., *Renaissance* 84, 76.

35. "Le necessità del corpo, come è mangiare, bere, diporre i superflui pesi del ventre e della vesica, dormire e per altre necessità." Castelvetro, *Poetica* I:149 (Pt. 2, Sect. 7).

36. Sidney, *Apology* 134.

37. Corneille, *Oeuvres complètes* III:171 ("Discours de la tragédie").

38. "J'aurais été ridicule si j'avais prétendu que cet Empereur délibérât avec Maxime et Cinna, s'il quitterait l'Empire, ou non, précisément dans la même place, où ce dernier vient de rendre compte à Émilie de la conspiration qu'il a formée contre lui. C'est ce qui m'a fait rompre la liaison des Scènes au quatrième Acte." Corneille, *Oeuvres complètes* I:911 (*Cinna*, "Examen").

39. Dryden, *Works* XVII:52–3.

40. "Dopo le spalle della Aurora, si vide à poco à poco surgere un Sole nel Cielo della Prospettiva: il quale soavemente caminãdo ne fece Atto per Atto conoscere l'hora del finto giorno: Et cosi poi si nascose ultimamente circa alla fine del quinto Atto: poco prima che la Notte cõparissi." Giambullari, *Apparato* 66.

41. "D'abord il faut donc apprendre à nos Poëtes Dramatiques, que cét Appareil de la Scéne dont la pluspart de ces Messieurs laissent tout le soin à l'Acteur, est une Partie de leur Art; & qu'il n'est pas moins nécessaire aux Ecrivains de Théatre d'en sçavoir la disposition." La Mesnardière, *La Poétique* 410.

42. "Chaque acte aussi bien que le prologue a sa décoration particulière, et du moins une machine volante. … [L]es machines … ne sont pas dans cette tragédie comme des agréments détachés, elles en font en quelque sorte le nœud et le dénouement, et y sont si nécessaires, que vous n'en sauriez retrancher aucune, que vous ne fassiez tomber tout l'édifice." Corneille, *Oeuvres complètes* II:452 (*Andromède*, "Examen").

43. Dryden, *Works* XX:54. On the Kneller poem and this essay, see Winn, *John Dryden* 464–70, 478–80.

44. Dryden, *Works* XII:98–9 (I.i).

45. "Si vede la cornuta, & lucida Luna, levarsi pian piano." Serlio, *I sette* I, fol. 48ʳ; trans. Hewitt, ed., *Renaissance* 24.

10. DRAMATISTS, POETS, AND OTHER SCRIBBLERS

1. Congreve, *Complete* 63 (*Old Batchelor* III.i.83–4).

2. Fielding, *Author's* 26–7, 35, 48, 19, 9, 77 (II.i.11–14; II.ix.1–2; III.i.205–6; I.vi.47–54; I.ii.15; III.i.899–902).

3. Beaumont and Fletcher, *Comedies* sig. A3ᵛ, a1ʳ.

4. "Les Tragédies … ne meritent moins d'estre leües des Princes, nés & nourris aux lettres & à la vertu, que d'autres livres, qui portent des tiltres plus specieux, et plus serieux en apparence." Montchrestien, *Les Tragédies* (1601 edn.) sig. a2ᵛ.

5. Beaumont and Fletcher, *Dramatic* II:334 ("The Printer to the Reader"). See similarly Massinger's dedications, calling on the prestigious Italian drama as model, in *The Duke*

of Millan ("Workes of this nature, have found both patronage, and protection, amongst the greatest Princesses of *Italie*") and *A New Way to Pay Old Debts* ("All I can alleage is, that divers *Italian* Princes, and Lords of eminent rancke in *England*, have not disdain'd to receave, and read Poems of this Nature" (Massinger, *Plays* I:215; II:294)); and Chapman's dedications in *The Revenge of Bussy d'Ambois* ("Workes of this kinde have beene lately esteemed worthy the Patronage of some of our worthiest Nobles") and *Widdowes Teares* ("Other Countrie men have thought the like worthie of dukes and Princes acceptations" so the dedicatee should "accept acceptable matter, as well in Plaies; as in many lesse materialls, masking in more serious Titles" (Chapman, *Plays* I:479; II:442)).

6. Diez Borque, *Sociedad* 100; Picard, *La Carrière* 200; and see the discussion in Chapter 2.

7. Qtd. Marotti, *Manuscript* 228.

8. Wither, *Schollers* 10. One can certainly identify a "profession of letters" of sorts long before print, made up of scribes, those who sold copies of verses, the historians and chroniclers with court positions, and many others, and an early version of the hack existed in the *poligrafi* of 16th-century Italy (see Richardson, *Print* 90–1). But most historians agree that the professional author making a living from the printing and sale of books alone is a figure of the later 17th and 18th centuries (for instance, Saunders, *Profession*, Viala, *Naissance*, and Pottinger, *French* 95–103). Richard Helgerson notes the change between the era of Spenser, in which Spenser's fellow poets were all essentially amateurs, to the era in which Jonson started writing, when "the expansion of the literary market, particularly the market for plays, had brought into existence a small but active group of true professionals" (*Self-Crowned* 22). Over the course of the 17th century, there was a significant change not only in the scale of publication, and the size of publishing houses, but also in the relation of the professional writer to the publishing industry. By the 18th century, literary hackdom was a real phenomenon. See Rogers, *Grub*, on the real existence of the Grub Street sub-culture; Hammond, *Professional*, for an analysis of the literature emerging from it; and Kewes, *Authorship*, on the general commercialization of letters during the period. John Feather notes that authors writing to order were sources of almost all new books published in the 18th century (*History* 103). Michael McKeon summarizes succinctly the relation between the growth of the printing industry and the "profession of letters" in England: "By the close of the seventeenth century England had become a major producer of paper, type and various kinds of publication, a development that could not have occurred without the abolition of protectionist printing legislation. By the middle of the eighteenth, licensing laws had been replaced by copyright laws; the commodification of the book market as a massproduction industry had become organized around the mediating figure of the bookseller; and the idea that a writer should get paid for his work was gaining currency on the strength of the perception that there was a growing mass of consumers willing to foot the bill." McKeon, *Origins* 51.

9. *Spectator* III:379 (No. 367 (1 May 1712)).

10. "En ce temps … chacun par coustume, | Si tost qu'il sçait parler met la main à la plume, | Veut des livres escrire, & le papier broüiller." Montchrestien, *Les Tragédies* (1601 edn.) sig. avii^r.

11. Saint-Amant, *Œuvres* II:32–70 ("Le Poéte crotté"). "La scène est à Paris chez le Libraire Camusat, Rue Saint-Jacques." Saint-Evremond, *La Comédie des Académistes* 174 (circulated in manuscript in 1637, published in 1650, often attributed to the joint authorship of Saint-Evremond and the Count d'Etelan, as in this edition); and see

Helgerson, *Self-Crowned* 31, on this and on the relative prestige of labels such as poet, author, and writer. On the period's identification of dramatic "poems" as plays, see Masten, *Textual* 198 n. 53. On the various terms in France and their history, see Viala, *Naissance* 270–9.

12. Skelton, *John Skelton* 314 (*Garlande of Laurell* (1523), l. 65).
13. Beaumont and Fletcher, *Comedies* sig. b2ᵛ–b3ʳ.
14. Jonson, *Ben Jonson* V:19 (dedication for *Volpone*).
15. Ravenscroft, *Anatomist* sig. a1ᵛ (prologue by Peter Motteux).
16. Beaumont, *Poems* sig. A2ʳ (epistle by Laurence Blaikock).
17. Rochester, *Valentinian* (1685) sig. c3ᵛ (prologue).
18. "Les Muses maintenant vilement profanées | De tant d'indignes mains." Montchrestien, *Les Tragédies* (1601 edn.) sig. a4ᵛ.
19. If the distinction between ancients and moderns was not new to the 16th century, it became especially important to the early modern constitution of the canon. For a discussion of print and the canon, see Levine, *Battle*; on the relationship between dramatic adaptation (on the stage and in print) and literary canonization in England between the 1660s and 1760s, see Dobson, *Making*.
20. Beaumont and Fletcher, *Comedies* sig. e2ʳ.
21. Beaumont and Fletcher, *Comedies* sig. c3ʳ ("To the desert of the Author in his most Ingenious Pieces"); and see Masten, *Textual* 142.
22. The phrase was coined by J. W. Saunders (Saunders, "Stigma") and has been picked up by many commentators on 17th-century print culture (see e.g. Traister, "Reluctant"; and Wall, *Imprint* 17, on the manipulation of the "stigma of print" to reinforce class and gender authority).
23. Sidney, *Apology* 132.
24. "Publier [une pièce], c'est l'avilir." Corneille, *Oeuvres complètes* I:4 (preface to *Mélite*).
25. "Je sçai qu'un noble Esprit peut, sans honte et sans crime, | Tirer de son travail un tribut legitime: | Mais je ne puis souffrir ces Auteurs renommez, | Qui dégoûtéz de gloire, et d'argent affamez, | Mettent leur Apollon aux gages d'un Libraire, | Et font d'un Art divin un métier mercenaire." Boileau, *Oeuvres* 183 (*L'art poétique*, chant IV).
26. "Ce commerce qui, se fait avec les Libraires et les Comédiens, gâte tous les jours de bonnes plumes. On ne voit quasi plus personne qui travaille purement pour sa propre gloire, et l'argent fait faire la plus grande partie de tous les livres que vous voyez." Guéret, *Promenade* 76–7.
27. "L'art de composer est devenu … un métier pour gagner sa vie." *Sur la contestation entre les libraires de Paris et ceux de Lyon*; qtd. Picard, *La Carrière* 202.
28. Marston, *Workes* sig. A3ʳ–A3ᵛ (dedication).
29. Beaumont and Fletcher, *Comedies* sig. d1ᵛ ("Upon the report of the printing of the Dramaticall Poems of Master *John Fletcher*").
30. Cartwright, *Comedies* π4ʳ.
31. Killigrew, *Comedies* sig. [*2]ʳ.
32. Randolph, *Poems* 60 (Richard West, "To the pious Memory of my deare Brother-in-law, M. Thomas Randolph").
33. Walsh, *Dialogue* 97.
34. Ford, *Perkin Warbeck* 4 ("To his Worthy Friend, Master John Ford" (1634)).
35. Ford, *Works* I:3–4.
36. Webster, *Complete* I:107.
37. Daniel, *Complete* III:305–6.

38. "Nous mettons en dignité nos bestises quand nous les mettons en moule." Montaigne, *Œuvres* 1059 (*Essais* Bk. 3, Ch. 13); trans. Montaigne, *Essays* 363.

39. "Il se Déifiait d'autorité privée, ... il faisait même imprimer les sentiments avantageux qu'il a de soi." Scudéry, "Observations sur *Le Cid*" in Corneille, *Oeuvres complètes* I:783.

40. "Parecerá culpable especie de jactancia sacar a luz estos mal limados borradores, que ... tuvo por tantos años a la censura retirados; ... no sólo no es jactancia nacida de proprio amor, sino violencia de ajeno agravio ocasionada, pues, no contenta la codicia con haber impreso tantos hurtados escritos míos como andan sin mi permiso adocenados y tantos como sin ser míos andan impresos con mi nombre, ha salido ahora con un libro intitulado *Quinta parte de comedias de Calderón*, con tantas falsedades." Calderón, *Obras* III:41 (prologue, *Autos*).

41. "C'est contre mon inclination que mes libraires vous font ce présent. ... Et certes, j'aurais laissé périr entièrement ceux-ci, si je n'eusse reconnu que le bruit qu'ont fait les derniers obligeait déjà quelques curieux à la recherche des autres, et pourrait être cause qu'un imprimeur, faisant sans mon aveu ce que je ne voulais pas consentir, ajouterait mille fautes aux miennes." Corneille, *Oeuvres complètes* II:187.

42. Lord, ed., *Poems* I:356 ("Session of the Poets").

43. "Quel besoin si pressant avez-vous de rimer? | Et qui diantre vous pousse à vous faire imprimer? | Si l'on peut pardonner l'essor d'un mauvais livre, | Ce n'est qu'aux malheureux qui composent pour vivre. | ... N'allez point quitter, de quoi que l'on vous somme, | Le nom que dans la cour vous avez d'honnête homme, | Pour prendre, de la main d'un avide imprimeur, | Celui de ridicule et misérable auteur." Molière, *Œuvres complètes* II:157–8 (*Le Misanthrope* I.ii); trans. Molière, *Misanthrope* 38–9.

44. "AUTEUR. ... Se dit de tous ceux qui ont mis en lumiere quelque livre. Maintenant on ne le dit que de ceux qui en ont fait imprimer." Furetière, *Dictionaire* (1694 edn.) 114; and see the discussion in Chartier, *L'Ordre* 49–50.

45. "Si l'on m'avait donné du temps ... j'aurais tenté la libéralité par une épître dédicatoire bien fleurie, j'aurais tâché de faire une belle et docte préface." Molière, *Œuvres complètes* I:264 (preface to *Les Précieuses ridicules*).

46. "VADIUS: Je te défie en vers, prose, grec, et latin. TRISSOTIN: Hé bien, nous nous verrons seul à seul chez Barbin." Molière, *Œuvres complètes* II:1039 (III.iii).

47. Gray, *Complete* 39 ("Elegy Written in a Country Church Yard" l. 59).

48. Vanbrugh, *Complete* I:13 (first prologue to *The Relapse*).

49. Beaumont and Fletcher, *Comedies* sig. A4^r–A4^v (Shirley, "To the Reader"). Shirley is actually praising the Beaumont and Fletcher folio here in writing that the "Presse," which was "thought too pregnant before," will now be looked on as a "Benefactor to Englishmen."

50. Wright, *Passions of the Minde*; qtd. Roach, *Player's* 32.

51. "Imprimeurs affamez ... mettent tout sous la presse." Chappuzeau, *Le cercle* 76 (*L'academie des femmes* II.iii).

52. Wycherley, *Complete* 298 (*Country Wife* III.ii).

53. Randolph, *Jealous Lovers* (1632) sig. ¶¶2^r.

54. Beaumont and Fletcher, *Comedies* sig. b1^v ("On Mr. John Fletcher's Workes").

55. Randolph, *Poems* 52–3 ("Upon Mr Randolph's Poëms, collected and published after his Death").

56. For extended discussions of the representation of commerce and the market-place in English drama 1550–1750, see Agnew, *Worlds*; and, for a discussion of economic circu-

lation and "credit" as tropes for the literary and linguistic in the late 17th and 18th
centuries generally, see my "Bank"; Sherman, *Finance*; and Hammond, *Professional*.

57. Buckingham, *Rehearsal* 22 (III.i).
58. Crowne, *Comedies* 314 (IV.i.9–13).
59. Sprat, *History* 44.
60. Blackmore, *Satyr* 10–11.
61. See, for instance, Behn, *Works* VII:296 (prologue to *Widow Ranter*); Fielding, *Author's*
    26, 32 (II.i.48–9; II.vi.42); and Foote, *Dramatic* I (*Patron* 37).
62. Fielding, *Author's* 31 (II.vi.10).
63. Congreve, *Complete* 295 (*Love for Love* IV.i.739–40).
64. Steele, *Tatler* I:307–8 (no. 43, 19 July 1709); qtd. Rosenthal, *Playwrights* 168.
65. *Hortense*: "Tu sçais [que] nous nous voyons dedans une saison, | Où d'écrire chacun [a]
    la demangeaison, | Qu'il ne manque non plus pour produire un ouvrage | D'Imprimeurs
    affamez, qui sans craindre la cage | Mettent tout sous la presse, et soûs l'espoir du gain |
    Le debitent bien-tost hautement." *Guillot*: "En effet, quand je passe au Palais, on
    m'enyvre, | Le beau Livre, Monsieur; Monsieur, le nouveau Livre." Chappuzeau, *Le
    Cercle* 76 (*L'academie des femmes* II.iv.425, 427–34).
66. Rochester, *Valentinian* sig. a1ʳ–a1ᵛ. See, similarly, the unsigned poem, "Upon Mr.
    Randolph's Poems. Collected and published after his death" in Randolph, *Poems* 51–4.
67. Jonson, *Ben Jonson* VIII:391 ("To the memory of my beloved, The Author Mr. William
    Shakespeare").
68. Wycherley, *Complete* 298 (*Country Wife* III.ii).
69. Racine observes that if the actors install themselves at Pantin, near the dépôts d'ordures,
    this would at least be "un digne théâtre pour les œuvres de M. Pradon." Boileau replies
    that the actors, "y auront une commodité, c'est que, quand le souffleur aura oublié
    d'apporter la copie [des] ouvrages [de Pradon], il en trouvera infailliblement une bonne
    partie dans les précieux dépôts qu'on apporte tous les matins en cet endroit." Letters
    of 24 and 28 Aug. 1687 in Racine, *Oeuvres* (1865 edn.) VI:599, 603–4.
70. Dryden, *Works* II:56–7 (*Mac Flecknoe* ll. 100–3).
71. Buckingham, *Rehearsal* 15 (II.i).
72. Beaumont and Fletcher, *Comedies* sig. A3ᵛ.
73. Fielding, *Tragedy* 80. Fielding is parodying the language of the topos, although it is not
    "the Author" (an imaginary Elizabethan) using the piracy as an excuse to print but the
    imaginary editor "Scriblerus Secundus."
74. Sheridan, *Dramatic* I:367 (*School for Scandal* I.i).
75. Fielding, *Author's* 45 (III.i.135–7).
76. Pope, *Poems* V:300 (*Dunciad* [B] Bk. 2, ll. 103–8). See, similarly, Swift's analogy between
    the critic and the man who makes his way through the "Ordure" of the streets—"not
    that he is curious to observe the Colour and Complexion of the Ordure, or take its
    Dimensions, much less to be padling in, or tasting it" (Swift, *Prose* I:56 (*Tale of a Tub*
    Sect. III)).
77. Foote, *Dramatic* I [*Patron* 19].
78. See, for instance, Pope, on the Goddess Dulness' realm near "Rag-Fair": "Here in one
    bed two shiv'ring sisters lye, | The cave of Poverty and Poetry" (Pope, *Poems* V:64
    (*Dunciad* [A] Bk. I, ll. 31–2)); or the Beggar in Gay's *Beggar's Opera*: "If Poverty be
    a title to Poetry, I am sure no-body can dispute mine" (Gay, *Poetical* 487).
79. Fielding, *Author's* 8 (I.i.5–6).
80. Congreve, *Complete* 219 (*Love for Love* I.i.108–12).

81. Foote, *Dramatic* I [*Patron* 20].
82. "E poetessa? ... Come le donne si danno a far canzoni, i mariti cominciano andar grevi dinanzi." Aretino, *Tutte* 72 (*Il Marescalco* V.ii). For a discussion of Renaissance attitudes, see Sanders, *Gender* 169–80.
83. Gould, *Works* II:17 ("The Poetess" (1688)). For discussions of the identification of poetry and prostitution during the period, see Pearson, *Prostituted*; and Gallagher, *Nobody's* 1–48 (on Behn).
84. Lovelace, *Poems* 200. For further examples, see Pearson, *Prostituted* 9–10.
85. Centlivre, *Plays* III [*Platonick Lady* sig. A2ʳ–A2ᵛ].
86. See Chapter 4 and Chapter 6 on being "a man in print"; and, on anonymity and gender during the period, Gallagher, *Nobody's*.
87. Charke, *Narrative* 11–12.
88. Behn, *Works* V:468, 460, 505 (II.i.95, I.ii.74–5, IV.v.618–19).

11. WHO OWNS THE PLAY? PIRATE, PLAGIARIST, IMITATOR, THIEF

1. Behn, *Works* V:521.
2. The editor of Behn's *Works*, Janet Todd, reads "the Proprieter" as Killigrew (Behn, *Works* V:570). But Behn refers to a "Proprieter" from whom the "*Book-sellers*" (presumably John Amery, the eventual publisher of *The Rover*) feared trouble—hence the necessity of the Post-script inserted as a half-sheet some time during the printing of the first issue of the play. If Killigrew thought the performance of *The Rover* violated the King's Company's performance rights in *Thomaso*, he might have made trouble for the Duke's Company. But there is no record of this in the eight-month lag between the first performance (on approximately 25 March 1677) and publication (on 26 November 1677), and, since Behn does not mention any objection on Killigrew's part, it seems unlikely that he made a fuss. The "Proprieter" most likely to have made the *booksellers* fear trouble from *publication* was Henry Herringman, owner of the publishing rights in *Thomaso*, which he had published in 1663. On the three different issues of the first edition of the play in 1677—some copies of the second issue adding the phrase "especially of our Sex," and the third issue adding the author's name—see Todd's notes (Behn, *Works* V:449).
3. Historians give many explanations for the fact that the privilege and copyright system emerged with print (the first appearing in Wurzburg in 1479, the second in Venice in 1486), most important, probably, the fact that print required an initial investment in machinery and an initial print run, which was recouped only with the sale of books (unlike manuscript copying, in which a given manuscript was often ordered individually and paid for in advance). Printers needed to protect their investments. Systems of privilege, press licensing, and copyright, however, worked quite differently in different countries at different times, and, like all legal and trade systems, were highly sensitive to political change. For fuller discussions of these matters, see Armstrong, *Before*; Loewenstein, "*Idem*"; Feather, *Publishing*; Rose, *Authors* (for the 18th century); and for a European historical survey and overview from the perspective of legal theory, Saunders, *Authorship* (especially 1–121). I discuss significant norms and trends in dramatic and theatrical copyright in Chapters 1–3. For helpful studies of the impact of 17th- and early 18th-century conceptions of literary property on the English drama, see Kewes, *Authorship* and Rosenthal, *Playwrights*. Here, I use the word "privilege"

(instead of the modern term, copyright) to indicate the general commercial right across Europe, although the terms varied, the commercial and political rights could overlap, and "privilege" came to carry distinctly political connotations in the 17th century, when governments on the Continent began to use privileges to regulate both the commercial market and the contents of books.

4. For instance, a 1512 Latin translation of the farce *Pierre Pathelin* (featuring the farcical lawyer Pathelin) was covered by Guillaume Eustace's privilege for juridical works (Armstrong, *Before* 187). Thomas Creede held the rights to plays on Henry V by virtue of his ownership of the old *The Famous Victories of Henrye the Fifth* (published in 1598), so when Millington and Busby wanted to publish Shakespeare's *Henry V* in 1600 they had to acquire the rights from Creede (Blayney, "Publication" 399, and see generally his discussion of the Stationers' Company's conferral of rights in a book's subject-matter rather than its words). On the privileging of Aldus's typeface designs, see Loewenstein, "*Idem*" 215–21.

5. In England from 1586 on, privileges were granted only to members of the Stationers' Company. On the Star Chamber decree granting an internally regulated monopoly of printing rights to the Stationers' Company, see Arber, *Transcript* II:784–5. There was nothing formally like the Stationers' Company monopoly anywhere else in Europe and, as Philip Gaskell writes, in the 16th and 17th centuries "the books trades of France, the Low Countries, Germany, and Italy … were relatively free of gild [if not of political] control" (*New* 171). But privileges were rarely granted to anyone but printers and publishers from the 15th through the 17th centuries, and in France by the early 17th century, "unless an author were a printer member of the guild, he was not allowed to print or sell his own works" (Pottinger, *French* 44).

6. "Parquoy il desireroit que autre que luy … ne puissent Imprimer vendre ne distribuer ledit livre jusques a quelque temps apres quil sera de par luy imprime. A ce que lesdictz frais et mises puissent estre recovers. … Pour ce est il que nous … Voulons le dit suppliant estre remunere de ses peines labeurs et vacations." Gréban [?], *Le Premier* I, sig. +2ʳ.

7. Beaumont and Fletcher, *Dramatic* II:334 ("Printer to the Reader").

8. For a general discussion and examples of early author-held privileges, see Brown, *Poets* (esp. 17–59); and Loewenstein, "*Idem*" 211–12 (offering a 1486 example of what was only ambiguously an author-held copyright and the unambiguous 1492 example). Armstrong mentions no instances of dramatist-held copyrights during the period she covers (1498–1526), noting in any case that, in France, privileges were only rarely granted to plays during the period; "it may have been considered, at this period, that performance in itself constituted publication, and that a play once performed was therefore usually ineligible for a privilege" (Armstrong, *Before* 187).

9. Gringore, *Folles Entreprises* sig. h3ᵛ; trans. Brown, *Poets* 35 (identifying this as the first French vernacular author privilege).

10. See Westfall, *Patrons* 151.

11. "Be it known unto all men by these presents that I Richard Jones … have delivered to … Edward Alleyn all … such share, part, and portion of playing apparel, play books, instruments and other commodities whatsoever … to have, hold, and enjoy" (contract of 3 Jan. 1589, qtd. Bentley, *Profession* 85, and see the other examples 82–7).

12. Hardy must write plays "propres au theatre," and "ne … ra … bailler aulcuns [origi]naulx ny coppie des pieces." Semi-legible contract reproduced in Deierkauf-Holsboer, *Vie* 213–14. See Chapter 1 for similar contracts specifically requiring Hardy to hand over the originals to the troupe.

13. See the Lord Chamberlain's letters to the Stationers' Company in 1637 and 1641, reprinted in Boswell and Chambers, ed., "Dramatic" 384; and Chambers, "Plays" 367.

14. Chambers, "Plays" 368.

15. See Arber, ed., *Transcript* III:37; Greenstreet, "Whitefriars" 276; Jackson, ed., *Records* 110 (fol. 56ᵃ); and the discussion in Chapter 1.

16. Boswell and Chambers, ed., "Dramatic" 384.

17. "Ainsi Lecteur, l'insuportable avarice de certains Libraires faisât passer ce poëme … sous la presse, à mon déçeu, tout incorrect, force ma resolution, reduit à choisir de deux maux le moindre … à souffrir imprimer ce que je desiroy plutost supprimer, & apres quelque reveuë te le donner un peu mieux poly." Hardy, *Theatre* VI sig. aiiiiʳ (*Les Chastes et Loyales Amours*).

18. "Guardan muy vario artificio en disponer acaecimientos, y emplean … aventajadas coplas. Es libro ingenioso para leccion entretenida, y muy digno su Autor de la licencia que pide, para comunicarle a este Reyno." Castro, *Primera parte* sig. ¶2ʳ.

19. Corneille has the right to "imprimer, vendre & distribuer" the plays "par tout nostre Royaume" because "depuis les premieres impressions ledit Sieur Corneille auroit corrigé beaucoup de choses esdites Piéces, qu'il desireroit maintenant faire imprimer avec lesdiites corrections, pour l'interest de sa reputation, pourquoy il luy conviendroit faire beaucoup de frais." Corneille, *Le Théâtre de P. Corneille* (1664 edn.) sig. ééiiʳ–ééiiᵛ. There is an earlier privilege granted to Corneille for three plays in the third part of the *Oeuvres de Corneille* (1652, privilege granted 30 April 1653), and a note that he is ceding this privilege to Augustin Courbé in the 1656 edition, but no mention of the grounds for the privilege.

20. "Il s'est fait quantitée de fautes qui blessent la réputation de l'auteur; ce qui l'a obligé de revoir et corriger tous ses ouvrages pour les donner au public dans leur dernière perfection. Mais comme il lui faut faire une grande dépense tant pour l'Impression que pour les Figures qu'il faut graver, il craint que quelques envieux de son travail ne lui fassent contrefaire par concurrence, de même que l'on a déjà fait de plusieurs de sesdites pièces, ce qui l'empêcheroit de retirer les frais qu'il auroit faits et lui causeroit une perte très considérable, s'il ne lui étoit pourvu de nos lettres sur ce nécessaires." Reproduced in Molière, *Œuvres de Molière* (1893 edn.) 40 (privilege of 1671).

21. Heywood, *Apology* (1612) sig. G4ᵛ ("To my approved good Friend, Mr. *Nicholas Okes*"); Heywood, *Dramatic* I:191 (*If You Know Not Me*). For a discussion of attacks on pirates as central to the early modern construction of the printing revolution, see Johns, *Nature*, esp. 324–79.

22. George Wither's *Schollers Purgatory* (*c.*1625) tentatively proffers the notion of authors' rights as natural rights: "A worshipfull Lawyer was lately pleased on [behalf of the booksellers] to say, that the benifite arisinge from the sale of bookes, was their ancient, and lawfull birthright. But … unlesse he can prove, the Author hath sould them his birthright (as often he doth, for lesse then a messe of pottage) since [the Author] is the elder brother, the right first … falleth unto him. … I hope, all Authors shalbe excused, and unblameworthy, if having their proper rightes incroched upon, they seeke repossession by the royall power." Wither, *Schollers* 31 (and see similarly 120).

23. Jonson, *Ben Jonson* IV:351 (preface).

24. *Englands Helicon* sig. A4ʳ ("To the Reader").

25. Jonson, *Ben Jonson* VIII:44 (Epigram 56). See Loewenstein's discussion ("Printing" 184) of Jonson's borrowing of Martial's metaphoric extension of the Latin term "plagiarius" ("kidnapper"), and its introduction into English in *The Poetaster* (1601). See

also White, *Plagiarism* 120–202 (for the emergence of plagiarism as a concept); and Orgel, "Renaissance" (for a vivid summary of positions in the 17th and 18th centuries, and parallel changes in the visual arts). On early anti-plagiarism laws in Italy (and their evasion by means of the substitution of new beginnings and endings in works), see Richardson, *Print* 74.

26. Cartwright, *Comedies* π4ʳ.

27. It is worth noting the conjunction of these changes with Hobbes's famous philosophical definition of the "author" as owner (in contradistinction to the "actor"): "Of persons artificial [persons in the legal sense], some have their words and actions *owned* by those whom they represent. And then the person is the *actor*; and he that owneth his words and actions, is the AUTHOR." Hobbes, *Leviathan* 105 (Pt. 1, Ch. 16).

28. On the author as "actor," see the discussion in Chapter 6, citing Chenu, "Auctor." And see Minnis, *Medieval Theory* 10–12 (and throughout): writings or sayings were (for most, prior to the 15th or 16th century) "authentic" only if attributed to genuine *auctores* (who were to be distinguished from mere *actores*, those who practised the technical skill of writing); necessarily few in number and quasimythical, modern writers could not hope to be counted among the *auctores*.

29. On the use of commonplace books generally, see Murray, *Theatrical* 47; Burke, *Popular* 145; and Chartier, "Publishing" (lecture 3, "Stage and the Page" 8–12). On German compendia, see Benjamin, *Origin* 91. On the use of formulae in the popular drama (well into the 19th century), see Burke, *Popular* 134–5, 116–48. On the table books used by spectators to copy lines from plays, see Maguire, *Shakespearean* 100–1.

30. "Et maintenant Garnier, sçavant et copieux, | Tragique a surmonté les nouveaux et les vieux." Vauquelin de la Fresnaye, *L'Art* 121 (Bk. 2, l. 1053–4) (not published until 1605); qtd. Reiss, *Tragedy* 43.

31. Warner, trans., *Menaecmi* sig. A3ʳ.

32. "Conciosia cosa che il poeta non possa comporre una favola composta da alcun poeta, percioché o sarebbe istoria o furto." Castelvetro, *Poetica* I:95 (Pt. 2, Sect. 1); trans. Castelvetro, *Castelvetro* 42 (trans. modified).

33. Jonson, *Ben Jonson* VIII:639 (*Timber*).

34. It is "establit pour maxime indubitable, que l'invention est la principale partie, et du Poete et du Poeme." Gasté, ed., *La Querelle* 73 ("Observations sur Le Cid" (1637)).

35. "Vous m'avez voulu faire passer pour simple Traducteur, sous ombre de soixante et douze vers que vous marquez sur un ouvrage de deux mille, et que ceux qui s'y connais-sent n'appelleront jamais de simples traductions." Corneille, *Oeuvres complètes* I:801 ("Lettre apologétique"). And see Corneille's comments on the inclusion of the notes in the 1648 edition in Corneille, *Oeuvres complètes* II:189.

36. "De sorte que le Sujet du *Cid* étant d'un Auteur Espagnol, si l'invention en était bonne, la gloire en appartiendrait à Guilhem de Castro." Scudéry, "Observations sur *Le Cid*" in Corneille, *Oeuvres complètes* I:784.

37. "Vous avez déclamé contre moi, pour avoir tu le nom de l'Auteur Espagnol, bien que vous ne l'ayez appris que de moi, et que vous sachiez fort bien que je ne l'ai celé à per-sonne, et que même j'en ai porté l'original en sa langue à Mgr le Cardinal, votre Maître et le mien." Corneille, *Oeuvres complètes* I:801 ("Lettre apologétique").

38. See, for instance, Massinger's prologue for his 1641 revision of Fletcher's *Wandering Lovers* in Beaumont and Fletcher, *Dramatic* X:526; and Molière's Trissotin in *Les femmes savantes*: "fripier d'écrits, impudent plagiaire" (Molière, *Œuvres complètes* II:1038 (III.iii)).

39. Rochester, *Valentinian* sig. a1ᵛ (unsigned preface).

40. Beaumont and Fletcher, *Comedies* sig. d2ᵛ (William Cartwright, "Upon the report of the printing of the Dramaticall Poems of Master *John Fletcher*").

41. Beaumont and Fletcher, *Comedies* sig. b1ᵛ ("On Mr. John Fletcher's Workes").

42. Randolph, *Poems* 63 ("To the pious Memory of my deare Brother-in-Law, Mr. Thomas Randolph").

43. Killigrew, *Prisoners* sig. A2ʳ–A3ʳ ("To his Most Honour'd Uncle").

44. For the negative connotation, see, for instance, Bellinda's description of Lady Fancyfull as "a Ridiculous Original" in Vanbrugh's *Provoked Wife* (Vanbrugh, *Complete* I:119 (I.i)); or Voltaire's *Les originaux ou Monsieur du Cap-Vert* (1732). For the positive aesthetics articulated later in the century, see, for instance, Edward Young's *Conjectures on Original Composition* (1759); Edward Cappell's *Reflections on Originality in Authors* (1766); and William Duff's *An Essay on Original Genius* (1767).

45. Jonson, *Every Man Out of His Humor* (1601 and 1616 edns.) (title pages). Beaumont and Fletcher, *Comedies*, title page, sig. A3ʳ (and see the discussion in Chapter 6).

46. Rochester, *Valentinian* sig. a2ʳ, A4ᵛ.

47. Buckingham, *Rehearsal* 3, 12, 14 (I.i, II.i).

48. Vanbrugh, *Complete* I:37 (*Relapse* II.i).

49. Johnson, *Dictionary* sig. 18B1ʳ ("Natural").

50. Swift, *Prose* I:150 ("Battle of the Books").

51. Dryden, *Works* II:56–9 (ll. 99–100, 104, 183–4).

52. Buckingham, *Rehearsal* 3–5 (I.i). See, for an early example, "The ladies" in Jonson's *Cynthia's Revels* who "could wish, you *Poets* … would not so penuriously gleane wit, from … common stages," but who equally wish that the "*Poets*" "would leave to … way-lay all the stale *apothegmes*, or olde bookes, they can heare of (in print, or otherwise) to farce their *Scenes* withall" (Jonson, *Ben Jonson* IV:41). Similarly, Jonson's Poet-Ape can "Buy the reversion of old playes," taking advantage of the free circulation of old literary material (Jonson, *Ben Jonson* VIII:45 (Epigram 56)).

53. "AUTEUR s. m. Qui a creé ou produit quelque chose. On le dit par excellence de la premiere Cause qui est Dieu. … L'*Auteur* est celui qui n'a pas pris son ouvrage d'un autre. … AUTEUR. se dit en particulier de ceux qui sont les premiers Inventeurs de quelque chose." Furetière, *Dictionaire* 114.

54. Dryden, *Works* XIII:225, 228 (*Troilus and Cressida* (1679)). See the extensive discussions of Dryden as a pivotal figure in Kewes, *Authorship* 54–63 (and throughout), Rosenthal, *Playwrights* 46–57 (discussing this passage among others), and Hammond, *Professional* 96–104. See also Kewes's discussion of the importance of Gerard Langbaine in the constitution of English notions of dramatic property (*Authorship* 97–129).

55. Dryden, *Works* I:141; qtd. Rosenthal, *Playwrights* 56–7.

56. Shakespeare, *Works of Shakespeare* (Pope edn., 1725) I: pp. ii–iii.

57. Pope, *Poems* V:279 (*Dunciad* [B] Bk. I, ll. 127–33).

58. Fielding, *Author's Farce* 32–3 (II.vi).

59. Dennis, *Critical* II:191–2.

60. Pix, *Plays* I [*Deceiver Deceived* sig. A3ʳ].

61. Centlivre, *Plays* II:27 [*Love at a Venture* III.i].

62. Ibid. III:267 [*A Bickerstaff's Burying* sig. A4ᵛ].

63. Arthur Murphy, *Old Maid* π2ʳ ("Advertisement").

64. "*M. Baliveau*: Mais les beautés de l'art ne sont pas infinies. | Tu m'avoueras du moins que

ces rares génies, | Outre le don qui fut leur principal appui, | Moissonnoient à leur aise, où l'on glane aujourd'hui. | *Damis:* Ils ont dit, il est vrai, presque tout ce qu'on pense. | Leurs écrits sont des vols qu'ils nous ont faits d'avance; | Mais le remède est simple: il faut faire comme eux; | Ils nous ont dérobés; dérobons nos neveux; | Et tarissant la source où puise un beau délire, | A tous nos successeurs ne laissons rien à dire. | Un démon triomphant m'élève à cet emploi. | Malheur aux Écrivains qui viendront après moi!" Piron, *Œuvres* II:345 (*La Métromanie* III.vii).

65. Murphy, *Plays* I:104 ("To M. De Voltaire," appended to *The Orphan of China*).
66. Johnson, *Rambler* 394–5, 399 (No. 143 (30 July 1751)). See Lessing's simpler distinction (drawing on Aristotle) between the imitation of dramatic "subjects" and "treatments," word-for-word copying from the legitimate use of the "common stock" of literary topoi: "Nicht ebenderselbe Stoff, sagt Aristoteles, sondern ebendieselbe Verwicklung und Auflösung machen, daß zwei oder mehrere Stücke für ebendieselben Stücke zu halten sind." Lessing, *Werke* IV:462 (*Hamburgische Dramaturgie* No. 50, 20 Oct. 1767).
67. Kenrick, *Widow'd* 51–2 (III.iii). For an earlier use of the phrase "literary property" (in a 1707 petition by stationers for protection of their copies), see Feather, *History* 74.
68. See Brown, "Field" 388–9 and, on Beaumarchais's sense of dramatic property as non-material personal powers or "droits honoraires," see Brown, "After" 485–91. It is worth noting that 1777 is the year in which a series of royal decrees granted authors privileges in their works in perpetuity. On the legal status of literary property in the decades just before and after the Revolution and the conceptions of literary property that lay behind claims like Beaumarchais's, see Boncompain, *Auteurs* 119–44, Hesse, "Enlightenment" 125–7 (on Beaumarchais's agitation for dramatic copyright), and throughout (on the 1777 decrees and the shift at the Revolution from the old regime of privileges to a new regime of property).
69. The "propriétaires naturels, les auteurs, en vertu duquel ceux-ci, moyennant des clauses convenues, leur auroient concédé le droit exclusif à eux et à leurs successeurs, de représenter leurs ouvrages." La Harpe, *Adresse* 30 (and 32, explaining that the words "propriété" and "privilège" are mutually exclusive).

12. MAKING IT PUBLIC

1. "Wir kündigen dem Publico die vielleicht unerwartete Hoffnung an, das deutsche Schauspiel in Hamburg zu einer Würde zu erheben, wohin es unter andern Umständen niemals gelangen wird. ... So lange man die Dichter der Nation nicht zu National-stücken anzufeuern gewohnt ist ... so lange wird man umsonst das deutsche Schauspiel aus seiner Kindheit hervor treten sehen. ... Eine kleine Gesellschaft gutdenkender Bürger" intends "das deutsche Theater zu derjenigen Zeit, die alsdann in den öffentlichen Blättern bekannt gemacht werden soll, mit aller der Vollkommenheit zu eröffnen." *Vorläufige Nachricht von der auf Ostern 1767 vorzunehmenden Veränderung des Hamburgischen Theaters*, reproduced in Löwen, *Johann Friedrich Löwens* 85–6; trans. Brandt, ed., *German* 198–9.
2. The classic study, Jürgen Habermas's *Strukturwandel der Öffentlichkeit* (1962), argues that the emergence of a bourgeois "public sphere" of critical public debate by private individuals was essentially an 18th-century historical development, arising first in Great Britain at the turn of the 18th century (Habermas, *Structural* 57). Habermas's historical

claims have been challenged by those who point to a significant public sphere earlier than the 18th century and one not necessarily bourgeois in character, but the central argument remains the basis for much continuing historical work. For both challenges and elaborations, see the essays in Backscheider and Dykstal, ed., *Intersections* (on the continuing inseparability of public and private); Calhoun, ed., *Habermas*; Meehan, ed., *Feminists* (especially the essays by Landes and Fleming); McDowell, *Women* (on lower- and middle-class women's participation in the public sphere through print); Merlin, *Public* (on the formation of the "public" in 17th-century France via the concept of the "Res Publica"); and Landes, *Women*.

3. See Habermas, *Structural* 181, 58; and see 8–11, 59–73 (and throughout) for the distinction between medieval or baroque theatricality and the bourgeois medium of print. See also Chartier, *Cultural* 16–17, 33 (on the shift from the age of baroque politics to the bourgeois public); and Landes, *Women* 18–21, 49–61 (on the shift from theatricality to print and on the bourgeois repositioning of women in the public sphere through print). Ravel, *Contested*, convincingly challenges the developmental argument, focusing on the centrality of theatre to the constitution of the 18th-century "public" (see esp. 2–7).

4. The *Mystere des Actes des Apostres* is "publiez et mis en lumiere non seulement ... en plain theatre ... mais aussi par edition publicque des livres Imprimez." Gréban [?], *Le premier* (1537 edn.) I, sig. +2ᵛ.

5. "A qui doy-je plus justement presenter de mes poëmes qu'à vous, Monseigneur, qui les avez le premier de tous favorisez, leur donnant hardiesse de sortir en public" (Garnier, *Two Tragedies* 105).

6. "Comedien und Tragedien *publicè* und öffentlich zu *agiren* und *recitiren*." "Also hat man ihnen hierinnen willfahren und diese *Comodien* und *Tragedien* ihnen zum bestten in öffentlichen Druck geben wollen." Green and Browne, eds., *Engelische* sig. A2ʳ, A3ᵛ.

7. "Le Soleil [et Melpomène] part[ent] ... pour aller publier ensemble la même chose au reste de l'Univers." Corneille, *Oeuvres complètes* II:462 ("Prologue"). Shakespeare, *Complete* 744 (*Troilus and Cressida* (V.ii.121)). See the discussions of these passages in McKenzie, "Speech-Manuscript-Print"; and Murray, *Theatrical* 77.

8. Valleran le Conte's troupe brags that it performs "jeux convenables au teatre tant en publicque que particullier" (contract of association, excerpted in Deierkauf-Holsboer, *Vie* 209), comparable to the English public and private theatres. See, similarly, the distinction by the printer of Jean de Schelandre's *Tyr et Sidon*(1628) between productions proper to public theatres and those proper to private ones: he has asked the author to revise the play for "une co[m]pagnie privée," "ceste piece ayant esté composée propremēt à l'usage d'un theatre public, où les acteurs sont privilegiez de dire plusieurs choses qui seroient trouvées ou trop hardies, ou mal-seantes aux personnes plus retenuës que les Comediens ordinaires." Schelandre, *Tyr* sig. i2ʳ.

9. On the Renaissance usage of "private" (in its German, English, and French forms) as indicating "not holding public office or official position" ("exclusion from the sphere of state apparatus") and "public" as referring by contrast to the state, see Habermas, *Structural* 11. Identifying a developing value for privacy with print, Cecile Jagodzinski writes that privacy, in its older usage, "carried the suggestion of individual, rather than public, interest, of a person acting in an unofficial, rather than an official, capacity ...; of privilege or elitism ...; of secrecy or concealment" (*Privacy* 2); and see the related discussion in Merlin, *Public*.

10. "S'il m'estoit possible de les dégager totalement du public, ce me seroit un grand con-

tentement. ... Mais il ne reste plus en ma main." Montchrestien, *Les Tragédies* (1604 edn.) sig. a2ᵛ.

11. See, for instance, the address to the "Peuple Francoys" in Estienne Dolet, *La Maniere* (1540) 11–12 (he is publishing his book for "l'utilité de la chose publicque").

12. Hardy, *Theatre* VI sig. aiiiʳ (*Les Chastes et Loyales Amours*, "Epistre").

13. Heywood, *Dramatic* II:259 (writing of *The Fair Maid of the West* Parts I and II (1631)).

14. Jonson, *Ben Jonson* IV:322 ("Apologeticall Dialogue" ll. 164–72).

15. Milton, *Complete* 86 (*Mask*, preface). A small print run for one's genteel friends might, similarly, be "private," opposed to a larger print run for the masses, as for Samuel Daniel, who writes of his *Collection of the History of England* (1613) that, if he lives, "after this private impression, which is but of a few coppies for my friends, I will amend what is amisse in the publique" (Daniel, *Complete* V:294).

16. Qtd. Middleton, *Game of Chess* (1980 ed.) 44 (dedication to William Hammond).

17. Gould, *Poems* 157 (*Play-house* (1685)).

18. Cavendish, *Plays* (1668) sig. A1ʳ; qtd. Rosenthal, *Playwrights* 69.

19. Shakespeare's folio, for Jonson, will reach "all Scenes of *Europe*." Jonson, *Ben Jonson* VIII:391 ("To the memory of my beloved, the Author Mr. William Shakespeare"). Guidubaldo Bonarelli's *Opere* (1640) has been "in diverse parti dell'Europa publicate con le Stampe" (sig. *4ʳ). The notion that printing meant offering a work "to the world" was current even in the 16th century. See, for instance, Berni's *Opere burlesche* (1555), "hoggi ... publicate al mondo" (sig. 3ʳ, publisher's dedication); and Aretino's *Quattro Comedie* being published (writes the printer) "per mezzo della mia stampa, a te, & al mondo tutto" (Aretino, *Quattro* (1588) sig. Ee3ʳ); and the ironic address "To the World" in Dekker's *Satiromastix* (1602) (Dekker, *Dramatic* I:309–10).

20. Beaumont and Fletcher, *Comedies* sig. c2ᵛ ("To the *Manes* of the celebrated Poets and Fellow-writers, *Francis Beaumont* and *John Fletcher*").

21. Ravenscroft, *Anatomist* (1697) π2ᵛ (dedication). See, later, Susanna Centlivre's "Universal Address" to the "numerous Crowd" in the printed edition of *The Platonick Lady* (Centlivre, *Plays* III [*Platonick Lady* sig. A2ʳ]); and Oliver Goldsmith's comment that "for one who has seen [a single play] acted, hundreds will be readers." Goldsmith, *Collected* I:324 (*Enquiry into the Present State of Polite Learning*).

22. On challenges to classic aristocratic patronage of poetry in the Renaissance (and for a general discussion of the role of manuscript and print circulation in literary patronage relationships), see Marotti, *Manuscript* esp. 293, 322–4, discussing the early challenge to the literary institution of patronage (founded on a culture of printed dedications) from writers earning independent incomes from print and from readers who, increasingly, could consider themselves "patrons" in the modern sense of the word. Joseph Loewenstein notes that "by late in the sixteenth century, some English authors were in fact writing solely for compensation by publishers (or by acting companies) ... not patrons" ("*Idem*" 223 n. 43). For general discussions of the development of the literary patronage system, see Lucas, "Growth"; the essays in Lytle and Orgel, eds., *Patronage*; and Griffin, *Literary* (showing the system's persistence throughout the 18th century).

23. Massinger, *Plays* II:197.

24. See the notes on Montauron in Corneille, *Oeuvres complètes* I:1598–9; and the discussion in Brown, "Field" 49.

25. "Autrefois, les auteurs donnaient de l'argent aux libraires pour contribuer aux frais d'impression de leurs ouvrages, et cet argent leur venait des pensions et des gratifications du Roi et de ses ministres qui les engageaient ... à travailler pour le public. ...

Aujourd'hui, l'usage est contraire et, soit qu'il doive son origine au besoin ou à l'avarice de quelques auteurs … on s'y est … accoutumé." *Sur la contestation entre les libraires de Paris et ceux de Lyon*; qtd. Picard, *La Carrière* 202. A character in Charles Sorel's novel *La Jeunesse de Francion* (1626) earlier notes a general cultural shift away from patronage towards booksellers' payments in his stage poet's ironic commentary on the new system as a means by which patrons can avoid their obligations, just as aristocrats avoid paying their servants by allowing them to demand tips from others: "Mais quoi! trouvez-vous ceci indécent, de se faire donner une récompense par les libraires pour notre labeur? … Apprenez que, s'il y a eu autrefois de la honte à ceci, elle est maintenant toute levée, puisqu'il y a des marquis qui nous ont frayé le chemin; et quoi qu'ils fissent donner l'argent à leurs valets de chambre [ceci] les exemptait de payer les gages de leurs serviteurs." Sorel, *La Jeunesse* 188.

26. Gildon, *New Rehearsal, or Bays the Younger* (1714); qtd. Rosenthal, *Playwrights* 171. Gildon's claim reflected, to an extent, reality for 18th-century writers. Although the dedication of the printed play to a well-chosen patron could still, when successful, match playhouse takings, and although valuable pensions and patronage positions were still highly desirable, dedication became less attractive with the increase in plays printed, and the demand for patrons higher than the supply. Even early in the century, takings from the playhouse and printing at least matched and often were far larger than patronage receipts (normally in England, from five to twenty guineas for a play in the first quarter of the 18th century, in France from about 150 to 300 *livres* (Collins, *Authorship* 181; Viala, *Naissance* 75)). Steele dedicated *The Conscious Lovers* to the King in 1722, and received 500 guineas from him. From the playhouse, he made £329 5s. 0d. off three third-night benefits and, as a patentee, received his share of £300 more, along with £40 from Tonson for the play's publication. When Cibber dedicated *The Non-Juror* to the King in 1717–18, he received £200 from him. His playhouse takings of £1,000 dwarfed this sum, and he received £105 as well for the publication of the play. (For these examples, see Kenny, "Publication" 311. For patronage payments during the 17th century, see Helgerson, *Self-Crowned* 75 ff.).

27. Molière, *Suitte d'Estampes … Dediée au Public … Tres respectable et redoutable juge"* (and see Ravel, *Contested* 37 (fig. 5) ; and below). Goldsmith, *Collected* II:344 (*Citizen of the World*, letter 84). See similarly Elizabeth Inchbald's comment that "our best patrons" are "the purchasers of our labour" (Boaden, *Memoirs of Mrs Inchbald* II:108–9).

28. See, for instance, Fielding, *Historical* (1737) 4; and *Theatrical Museum* (1776) sig. A2ʳ (editor's dedication to "the Public").

29. Goldoni, *Tutte* I:504 (Pt. 3, Ch. 15); trans. Goldoni, *Memoirs* 413–14.

30. Foote, *Dramatic* II [*Patron* 8–9].

31. Foote, *Dramatic* II [*Patron* vi].

32. "Le Public" and "Sultan-Public." Piron, *Œuvres* IV:150, V:266 (*Les Chimères* and *Les Huit Mariannes*); and see Ravel, "La Reine" 402.

33. "Qu'un seul crie *bravo*! sans examen la salle entière le repète. … En sortant du spectacle, on se répand dans Paris … D'où venez-vous? Quelle pièce donnait-on? Qui jouait?" Clairon, *Mémoires* (1799 edn.) 87 ("Portrait du Mlle Dumesnil"); trans. Clairon, *Memoirs* (1800 edn.) I:138–9 (trans. modified).

34. On audience voting, see, for instance, Goldsmith's review of John Home's *Douglas* (Goldsmith, *Collected* I:10 (*Monthly Review* for May 1757)). On the immense political power of theatrical gatherings during this period, see, for instance, Maslan, "Resisting"; Ravel, *Contested*. On the "publick voice," see the discussion (for the 17th century) in

Merlin, *Public* 204–17; and, for 18th-century examples, see Johnson's "Drury Lane Prologue" (1747), "The stage but echoes back the publick voice" (Johnson, *Poems* 89); Lessing's *Hamburgische Dramaturgie* (1767), describing "das Publikum", "Seine Stimme soll nie geringschätzig verhöret werden" (Lessing, *Werke* IV:232, Ankündigung); and Goldoni's *Mémoires*, noting that his play on Tasso "fut placée par la voix publique dans le rang … des plus heureuses de mes productions" (Goldoni, *Tutte* I:386; *Mémoires* Pt. 2, Ch. 32).

35. Johnson, *Poems* 89 ("Drury Lane Prologue" (1747)). While similarly noting that audiences determined the shape of the drama, Rousseau is explicit about the political implications of the audience's role as theatrical legislature. Insisting that "les loix n'ont nul accés au theatre" and that therefore theatre cannot properly be regulated by the state, he explains that, "au lieu de faire la loi au public, le theatre la reçoit de lui": "Rien [n'est] plus indépendant du pouvoir suprême que le jugement du public," which could not be ruled by the decrees of the sovereign. Rousseau, *Œuvres complètes* V:21, 63 (*Lettre à D'Alembert* (1758)).

36. "Tirez le Rideau si vous en voulez voir davantage"; reproduced in Jomaron, ed., *Théâtre* 86.

37. Sheridan, *Dramatic* I:367 (I.i).

38. See, for instance, Charles Gildon's usage in his *Post-Boy Robb'd of His Mail* (1705–6), "I shall send you some Accounts at present, which the publick Papers will not furnish you withal" (Gildon, *Post-Boy* II:342, letter XLII); William Adam's letter to John Palmer, Comptroller General of the Post Office (1791), on "the public prints" (reproduced in Jordan, *Mrs. Jordan* 13); or throughout the *Journal de Paris* ("les papiers publics").

39. Sheridan, *Dramatic* II:514 (*Critic* I.ii) (echoing Touchstone's rhetoric of lying in *As You Like It* (V.iv.88–94): Shakespeare, *Complete* 651).

40. Cibber, *Ximena* sig. A3^r–A4^r.

41. Dryden, *Works* XIII:20.

42. Dryden, *Works* XVI:84. See the discussion of this prologue in Stallybrass and White, *Politics* 84–90, in which they identify it with the "bourgeois … re-territorialization" of domains, discourses, and states of mind after the Restoration that helped establish British rule both domestically and in the empire.

43. Home, *Plays* [*Story of the Tragedy of Agis* 6–7].

44. "L'opinion se forma instantanément et comme par un mouvement électrique, elle se manifesta par de longs et nombreux applaudissemens." Talma, *Mémoires* pp. li–lii; trans. Talma, *Reflexions* 32.

45. "N'y ayant point de femmes … le goût du *parterre* en est moins délicat, mais aussi moins capricieux, & sur-tout plus mâle & plus ferme. … Si le *parterre* … ne captivoit pas l'opinion publique, & ne la réduisoit pas à l'unité en la ramenant à la sienne, il y auroit le plus souvent autant de jugemens divers qu'il y a de loges au spectacle, & que de long-tems le succès d'une pièce ne seroit unanimement ni absolument décidé." *Encyclopédie* supplément IV:241–2 ("Parterre" (1777)); and see the discussion of this passage (and the discussion of the reduction of the parterre's "heterogenity") in Ravel, *Contested* 214–17.

46. "Denn Sie glauben nicht, wie streng der Herr ist, dem wir zu gefallen suchen müssen; ich meine unser Publikum." Lessing, *Werke* IV:422–3 (*Hamburgische Dramaturgie* No. 41). If some challenge the "suffrages momentanés du public," "le public assemblé n'en est pas moins le seul juge des ouvrages." Beaumarchais, *Œuvres* 121 ("Essai sur le genre

dramatique sérieux"). For the public as "tribunal," see, for instance, Voltaire, *Les Oeuvres* (1968 edn.) L:353 (*L'Écossaise* (1760)).

47. "Je n'ai voulu combattre en rien le goût du public: c'est pour lui et non pour moi que j'écris; ce sont ses sentiments et non les miens que je dois suivre." Voltaire, *Œuvres complètes* (1877–85 edn.) II(1):164; qtd. Ravel, "La Reine" 399. On the public's determination of the "fate" of plays, see Arthur Murphy's preface to his *Plays* (1786), "The works here collected have been all, at different times, before the public. Their fate has been long ago decided"; his published letter "To M. De Voltaire" (appended to his version of *The Orphan of China* (1759)), "Whether I was partially attached to them [my own preconceived notions], or whether my reasonings upon your fable were just, you, sir, and the public, will determine" (Murphy, *Plays* I: pp. v, 103); and Goldoni's comment on his play *Le Bourru bienfaisant*, "Les suffrages du Public ont prouvé ... que les Comédiens avoient jugé avec connoissance" (Goldoni, *Tutte* I:505; *Mémoires* Pt. 3, Ch. 15).

48. The public is "éclairé," but "ce public si respectable" can become "une bête brute ou féroce." Clairon, *Mémoires* (1799 edn.) 41, 202 ("Extérieur," "Seconde Époche"); trans. Clairon, *Memoirs* (1800 edn.) I:64–5, II:81–2 (trans. modified).

49. Home, *Plays* [*Story of the Tragedy of Agis* 14–15]. Goya, *Capricios* 116 ("El sueño de la razon produce monstruos" (plate 43)).

50. Hill, *Actor* 3–4.

51. "Es ist rühmlich, sich von seinem eigenen Geschmacke Rechenschaft zu geben suchen. Aber den Gründen, durch die man ihn rechtfertigen will, eine Allgemeinheit erteilen, die, wenn es seine Richtigkeit damit hätte, ihn zu dem einzigen wahren Geschmacke machen müßte, heißt aus den Grenzen des forschenden Liebhabers herausgehen, und sich zu einem eigensinnigen Gesetzgeber aufwerfen. Der angeführte französische Schriftsteller fängt mit einem bescheidenen, 'Uns wäre lieber gewesen' an, und geht zu so allgemein verbindenden Aussprüchen fort, daß man glauben sollte, dieses *uns* sei aus dem Munde der Kritik selbst gekommen. Der wahre Kunstrichter folgert keine Regeln aus seinem Geschmacke, sondern hat seinen Geschmack nach den Regeln gebildet, welche die Natur der Sache erfodert." Lessing, *Werke* IV:317 (*Hamburgische Dramaturgie*, No. 19); trans. Lessing, *Hamburg* 51.

52. "Nur daß sich nicht jeder kleine Kritikaster für das Publikum halte." Lessing, *Werke* IV:232 (*Hamburgische Dramaturgie*, Ankündigung); trans. Lessing, *Hamburg* 2.

53. See, for instance, Clairon's comments: Clairon, *Mémoires* (1799 edn.) 234 ("Voyage de Bordeaux").

54. Sheridan, *Dramatic* II:499–500 (*Critic* I.i).

55. Murphy, *Plays* I: pp. x–xi (preface). See also Gozzi on "I Signori Giornalisti, i Signori Vetturali Postiglioni Letterari, e i Signori animaleschi Romanzieri, i quali si divertono a condannare senza facoltà, e senza ministri, che obbediscano alle loro condanne"; and "I miei ipocondriaci scrittori di fogli volanti." Gozzi, *Opere* I:107, 108 (preface to *Il Corvo*).

56. Sheridan, *Dramatic* II:511 (I.ii). For a similar passage on the manipulation of political news in the public prints, see Sheridan, *Dramatic* II:517–18 (*Critic* I.ii); and, on Sheridan's own practice of puffing, see O'Toole, *Traitor's* 98–9.

57. Addison, *The Drummer* p. xv (Steele's dedication).

58. *Enquiry into the Present State of Polite Learning in Europe* (1759) and Goldsmith's review of Home's *Douglas* (*Monthly Review*, for May 1757) in Goldsmith, *Collected* I:325, 100.

59. "Cette ridicule queue de poisson n'est pas mon ouvrage. C'est celui (& j'ose me flatter que le Public voudra bien ne pas l'oublier) de la cabale qui a troublé ses plaisirs. Il retrouvera toujours, dans le Recueil de mes Ouvrages, la situation fortement Comique ... mais

s'il veut qu'on la lui rendre au Théâtre, c'est à lui seul de se faire Justice." *Journal de Paris* 28 (27 June 1782) 729; qtd. Ravel, "Printed" 8 (and see his discussion).

60. Foote, *Dramatic* I [*Patron* 59–60].

61. Ibid. I [*Taste* viii].

62. "'Le dieu des cabales est irrité'. … *Enfants! un sacrifice est ici nécessaire*." "Je ne reconnais plus d'autre juge que vous, sans excepter messieurs les spectateurs, qui, ne jugeant qu'en premier ressort, voient souvent leur sentence infirmée à votre tribunal." Beaumarchais, *Œuvres* 281, 270 ("Lettre modérée sur la chute et la critique du 'Barbier de Séville'").

63. Home, *Plays* [*Alfred* p. v] (1778).

64. Kenrick, *Widow'd* 51–2 (III.iii).

65. On the "impartial medium" of print, see, for instance, *The Dramatic Censor* (1770) I, sig. A4ʳ (unsigned preface).

66. "On a vu s'établir une nouvelle espèce de tribune, d'où se communiquaient des impressions moins vives, mais plus profondes; d'où l'on exerçait un empire moins tyrannique sur les passions, mais en obtenant sur la raison une puissance plus sûre et plus durable; où tout l'avantage est pour la vérité, puisque l'art n'a perdu sur les moyens de séduire qu'en gagnant sur ceux d'éclairer. Il s'est formé une opinion publique, puissante par le nombre de ceux qui la partagent; énergique, parce que les motifs qui la déterminaient agissaient à la fois sur tous les esprits. Ainsi, l'on a vu s'élever, en faveur de la raison et de la justice, un tribunal indépendant de toutes les puissances, auquel il était difficile de rien cacher et impossible de se soustraire." Condorcet, *Esquisse* 178 ("Huitieme periode"); and see the discussion in Chartier, *Forms* 9–10.

67. I have drawn, here, on the discussion of Rutlidge's *Les Comédiens* and *Le Bureau d'Esprit* (both 1776), and of similar comments in Louis-Sébastien Mercier's unperformed *Virginie* (1767), Antoine Renou's *Térée et Philomèle* (1773), and Andebez de Mongaubet's unperformed *Abimélech* (1776), in Brown, "Field" 178, 187, 218–19, 297–8. On Rutlidge's identity and the authorship of these plays (often attributed to Mercier), see Rutlidge, *Les Comédiens* (1999 edn.) 9–14, 33–5.

68. *Herald; or, Patriot Proclaimer* No. 28 (23 Mar. 1758); qtd. Goldsmith, *Collected* I:325–6.

69. Goldsmith, *Collected* I:323, 330 (*Enquiry into the Present State of Polite Learning in Europe*).

70. See, for instance, La Harpe, *Adresse* 32, 38; and see the discussions of free-market rhetoric in Brown, "Field" 565–7, 419; and (in the 19th century) Stephens, *Profession* 144. This argument was importantly exploited not only by dramatists but also by minor theatrical managers and booksellers who wished to strengthen their claims to works monopolized by established theatres and publishers. See the discussions of changes in English copyright law that fortified the position of minor booksellers by limiting perpetual copyright and hence allowing books more readily to enter the public domain in Feather, *Publishing* 93–6, and Rose, *Authors*; and, on the "public domain" in the law of literary property in France immediately before and after the Revolution, see Hesse, "Enlightenment" (esp. 113, 119 on the agitation for "public access" after the Revolution).

71. The pamphlet, *Mémoire à consulter et consultation pour le Sieur Palissot de Montenoy* (1775), was by Palissot's lawyer, François de Neufchâteau, in advocacy of Palissot's suit against the Comédie for its failure to perform *Les Courtisanes* (see Brown, "Field" 264–5).

72. "Nous tenons encore de la même main quantité de bons manuscrits. … Nous vous les

rendrons successivement, parce que nous croyons fermement qu'ils vous appartiennent, & que nous n'avons point la fatuité de penser, comme on faisait autrefois, qu'une troupe d'histrions, qui est à vos gages, puisse vous disputer l'héritage des Corneilles & des Racines, & de tant d'autres illustres morts." Rutlidge, *Les Comédiens* 6–7; and see Brown, "Field" 293–4. The notion of culture as public property was extended to a number of arenas: theatrical performances, for instance, could sometimes be public property, and the comedians themselves, argued Jean de La Harpe in his 1790 petition to the Assemblée Nationale, were the *property* of the public: "Ils étoient véritablement les comédiens du public, puisque c'étoit le public qui les faisoit vivre" (La Harpe, *Adresse* 13–14).

73. On the public as "the nation," see, for instance, Cailhava d'Estendoux' *Sur l'art de la comédie* (1772) (qtd. Brown, "Field" 533); and Goethe's Wilhelm Meister, who is inspired to write his plays for the "lechzenden Publikum meines Vaterlandes" (Goethe, *Gedenkausgabe* VII:206 (Bk. 3, Ch. 11)).

74. Marie-Joseph Chenier, for instance, could proclaim that the new theatre was to produce "pièces vraiment nationales" on the brink of the Revolution (Chenier, *Œuvres* IV:460 ("Discours pour la rentrée du théâtre de la Nation, 1790")), pointing to the power of theatre to create and uncreate nations. The Viennese national theatre (the Burgtheater), founded in 1776, could be understood as *the* German national theatre by its supporters: "Die Deutschen haben nun ein Nationaltheater, und ihr Kayser hat es gegründet. Welch entzückender, herrlicher Gedanke für jeden, der empfinden kann, daß er ein Deutscher ist!" (*Theater-Journal* (1777) II:110). On the theatre's role as servant of the nation, see, for instance, La Harpe, *Adresse* (throughout); Holcroft's preface to *Seduction* (1787) (*Plays* I:i–xii). For a variety of discussions of theatrical nationalism and national theatre projects (including proposals for a renamed or alternative French national theatre), see Carlson, *Theatre*; Krebs, "La Naissance"; and Kruger, *National* (esp. 85–6 on the relationship between the Enlightenment project of theatrical-aesthetic public education and national theatres).

75. "Wir setzen die großen Vortheile zum voraus, die eine Nationalbühne dem ganzen Volke verschaffen kann." Löwen, *Johann Friedrich Löwens* 85; trans. Brandt, ed., *German* 198 (trans. modified).

76. The parterre "acquitte la dette de la nation." What comes from "ces hommes assemblés; c'est l'éruption d'un volcan; les acclamations ne forment qu'une seule voix." Mercier, *Tableau* (1788) XII:131; qtd. Ravel, *Contested* 191. On the equation of the pit or parterre, "the public," and "the people," see Ravel, "La Reine" 398.

77. The members of the "Republic of Letters," drawing on the cultural stores of the nation, were at once understood as the nation's cultural representatives (just as the political deputies in the new republics served as the representatives of the public) and as giving back to the public its own cultural products: they contributed to the property of the nation, its "national treasures," its "culture." Foote's Sir Thomas Lofty can jump easily from his desire to offer his play as "an acquisition to the republic of letters" to his explanation that he writes for "love of my country" (Foote, *Dramatic* I [*Patron* 37, 48]). Murphy can evoke Voltaire's membership in a broader "Republic of Letters" in an attempt to shame him out of his nationalist derogation of the English: "'we are ferocious,'" quotes Murphy with indignation, "we are islanders …; we fall behind other nations in point of taste …; in short, barbarism still prevails among us" (Murphy, *Plays* I:99–100 (*Orphan of China*, "To M. De Voltaire")). For a few 18th-century examples, see Préville and Dazincourt, *Mémoires* 173; Goldoni, *Tutte* I:514 (*Mémoires* Pt. 3,

Ch. 17); and Murphy, *Plays* I:99–100. For a general discussion of the reconstitution of the Republic of Letters in the age of print, see Eisenstein, *Printing* 136–9.

78. Foote, *Dramatic* I [*Patron* v–vi].

79. "Erigir un monumento á la gloria de nuestra patria" (Calderón de la Barca, *Comedias* II:411; qtd. Gies, *Theatre* 90). Examples of national theatre histories include John Downes's *Roscius Anglicanus* (1708); the Parfaict brothers' 15-volume *Histoire du théâtre francois* (1735–49); or Signorelli's (to name just a few). For a discussion of the "triumphalist narrative" of French theatrical history that emerged in the 1730s and continued to be reiterated in the 1770s, see Ravel, *Contested* 199 (quoting Voltaire's comment that "of all the arts cultivated in France, the theater is the one, by common consent of all foreigners, which most honors our fatherland").

80. Shakespeare, *Mr William Shakespeare* (1768 edn.) I:a3ʳ–a3ᵛ (dedication); qtd. Dobson, *Making* 8.

81. Shakespeare, *Mr William Shakespeare* (1768 edn.) I, sig. a3ʳ–a3ᵛ (dedication); qtd. Dobson, *Making* 8.

82. "La plupart des Auteurs Dramatiques n'ont malheureusement travaillé jusqu'ici que pour un très-petit nombre d'hommes" instead of "le gros de la nation." "Travaillant pour ma nation ... [je] parle à cette multitude, où repose une foule d'ames neuves & sensibles." Mercier, *Théâtre* I:6; and see the discussion in Brown, "Field" 190.

83. Murphy, *Plays* IV: pp. v–vi. Afraid that there were some ("the dregs of the barrel") who wished to spread "the horrors of French Anarchy ... into this kingdom," Murphy claims to be writing a play that he hopes will "recall the minds of men to the origin and antiquity of the Constitution, under which the people have enjoyed their rights, their property, and their liberty" for so long. "It is well known, that an inundation of French Jacobins, whom their *o'ercloy'd country vomited forth* to propagate their detestable principles, infested every part of London" (Murphy, *Plays* IV: pp. xxvi, xi).

84. "Cette immense foule, avide des pures émotions de l'art, qui inonde chaque soir les théâtres de Paris. Cette voix haute et puissante du peuple." Hugo, *Théâtre* I:1148–9 (preface to *Hernani*).

85. "Die Schrift hat das lebendige Wort verdrängt, das Volk selbst, die sinnlich lebendige Masse, ist, wo sie nicht als rohe Gewalt wirkt, zum Staat, folglich zu einem abgezogenen Begriff geworden. ... Der Dichter muß ... die Götter wieder aufstellen, er muß alles Unmittelbare, das durch die künstliche Einrichtung des wirklichen Lebens aufgehoben ist, wieder herstellen," and throw aside whatever hinders "die Erscheinung ... seines ursprünglichen Charakters." Schiller, *Schillers Werke* X:12 ("Über den Gebrauch des Chors"); trans. Schiller, *Works* IV:229 (trans. modified).

13. SCENIC PICTURES

1. "Pour faciliter les positions théâtrales aux acteurs de province ou de société ... on a fait imprimer, au commencement de chaque scène, le nom des personnages, dans l'order où les Comédiens-Français se sont placés, de la droite à la gauche, au regard des spectateurs. Cette attention de tout indiquer peut paraître minutieuse aux indifférents, mais elle est agréable à ceux qui se destinent au théâtre ou qui en font leur amusement, surtout s'ils savent avec quel soin les Comédiens-Français, les plus consommés dans leur art, se consultent et varient leurs positions théâtrales aux répétitions, jusqu'à ce qu'ils aient rencontré les plus favorables, qui sont alors consacrées, pour eux et leurs successeurs, dans

le manuscrit déposé à leur bibliothèque. ... Si le drame, par cette façon de l'écrire, perd un peu de sa chaleur à la lecture, il y gagnera beaucoup de vérité à la représentation." Beaumarchais, *Œuvres* 201 ("Avertissement" for *Les Deux amis*).

2. "Pour faciliter les jeux du théâtre, on a eu l'attention d'écrire au commencement de chaque scène le nom des personnages dans l'ordre où le spectateur les voit. S'ils font quelque mouvement grave dans la scène, il est désigné par un nouvel ordre de noms, écrit en marge à l'instant qu'il arrive." "LA COMTESSE, agitée de deux sentiments contraires, ne doit montrer qu'une sensibilité réprimé, ou une colère très modérée; rien surtout qui dégrade aux yeux du spectateur son caractère aimable et vertueux. ... Son vêtement du premier, second et quatrième acte est une lévite [long gown of the Levites] commode, et nul ornement sur la tête: elle est chez elle et censée incommodée. ..." Beaumarchais, *Œuvres* 378, 380 ("Placement des acteurs"; "Caractères et habillements de la pièce," *La Folle journée*). And see *Les Deux amis*: "Le seul mouvement du milieu des scènes reste abandonné à l'intelligence des acteurs" (Beaumarchais, *Œuvres* 201 ("Avertissement")); and the lists of "Habillement des personnages" and "Les habits des acteurs ..." in *Eugénie* and *Le Barbier de Séville* (Beaumarchais, *Œuvres* 141–2, 289–90).

3. "Pour faciliter l'aménagement de la scène et l'exécution de cette comédie." Beaumarchais, *Œuvres* 1372 (quoting a 1785 Paris piracy labelled "Nouvelle édition").

4. "Un salon à la française du meilleur goût." Beaumarchais, *Œuvres* 143, 197 (I.i, V.ix).

5. "Mélac ... en léger habit du matin. ..." "Un andante ... qui complète l'illusion du petit concert que le spectacle représente." Beaumarchais, *Œuvres* 202 (I.i).

6. "*La comtesse, assise, tient le papier pour suivre. Suzanne est derrière son fauteuil, et prélude en regardant la musique pardessus sa maîtresse. Le petit page est devant elle, les yeux baissés. Ce tableau est juste la belle estampe d'après VanLoo, appelée* La Conversation espagnole.* [marginal note:] *Chérubin. La Comtesse. Suzanne." Beaumarchais, *Œuvres* 406 (II.iv). For details on the reception of the print and painting and a compelling reading of Beaumarchais's use of the print, see Meisel, *Realizations* 108–10.

7. See, for instance, the discussion of the prefaces to Charles Johnson's *Force of Friendship* and *Love in a Chest* in *London Stage* II(i): p. cxx; George Colman the younger's chorus at the end of *New Hay* 31; and Grimm's comments ("Il ne reste plus, ce semble, qu'un pas à faire vers la barbarie, à un peuple qui déserte ce spectacle pour courir en foule aux farces plates et indécentes des histrions italiens et de l'opéra comique" (Grimm, *Correspondance* I:33, 15 July 1753)).

8. Wilkinson, *Memoirs* III:119. On the *parades*, see Larthomas, *Le Théâtre* 66; and Martin *at al.*, eds., *Histoire* II:221.

9. See Lessing's discussion in the *Hamburgische Dramaturgie* (No. 18) (protesting against this purge and claiming that, in any case, Harlequin was indestructible: Lessing, *Werke* IV:312–14); and Van Cleve, *Harlequin*.

10. "Le seul titre de *Théâtre de la Foire* emporte une idée de bas et de grossier, qui prévient contre le livre. Pouquoi vouloir en éterniser le souvenir? On ne peut trop tôt perdre la mémoire. ... Il n'est pas facile de trouver un milieu entre le haut et le bas; de raser la terre, pour ainsi dire, sans la toucher." Preface to the *Le Théâtre de la Foire*, reproduced in Truchet, ed., *Théâtre* I:161–2.

11. Cibber, *Apology* 279 (Ch. 15).

12. Weaver, *Loves* (title page); and see Weaver, *Essay* (1712) for a more extended discussion.

13. See Goodden, *Actio* 6.

14. *Lettre écrite à un ami sur les danseurs de corde et sur les pantomimes qui ont paru autrefois chez les Grecs et chez les Romains et à Paris en 1738* (1739); and see Bourdelot and Bonnet, *His-*

toire générale de la danse sacrée et profane (1732); and Boulenger de Rivery, *Recherches historiques sur quelques anciens spectacles, et particulièrement sur les mimes et sur les pantomimes* (1751) (cited Goodden, *Actio* 99).

15. Steele, *Plays* 299 (preface to *Conscious Lovers*).

16. "Les prestiges du Théâtre subjuguent les yeux, les oreilles, l'esprit & le cœur … Son Art est par cette raison un de ceux auxquels il appartient le plus de nous faire éprouver un plaisir complet. Notre imagination est presque toûjours obligée de suppléer à l'impuissance des autres Arts imitateurs de la nature. Celui du Comédien n'exige de nous … aucun supplément." Rémond de Sainte-Albine, *Le Comédien* 14–15.

17. "Retire-toi, froid moraliste, emporte ton gros livre; que signifie l'ensilage de tes maximes seches, auprès du peintre éloquent qui montre le tableau armé de toutes ses couleurs? … Hommes, approchez, voyez, touchez, palpez. … vous pleurez! Oui, sans doute." Mercier, *Théâtre* 10–11.

18. Hill, *Actor* 232.

19. "Le geste est une des premières expressions du sentiment données à l'homme par la nature … le langage primitif de l'univers au berceau. … Le geste sera toujours la langue de toutes les nations: on l'entend dans tous les climats." Dubroca, *Principes* (1802) 378 (leçon 25).

20. See Cannone, *Philosophies* 7 (and throughout for a general discussion of music as a universal language in the later 18th century).

21. "Tous ces sons [de la Musique] … ont une force merveilleuse pour nous émouvoir, parce qu'ils sont les signes des passions, institués par la nature dont ils ont reçu leur énergie." Du Bos, *Réflexions* I:467 (Sect. 45); qtd. Murray, *Theatrical* 209–10.

22. "Elle imite ces sons antérieurs à tout langage, & que la nature avoit donnés elle-même aux hommes pour être les signes de leur tristesse & de leur joye." Mably, *Lettres* (1741) 74–5.

23. Kirkman, *Memoirs* (1799) I:366 (lecture copied from Macklin's papers).

24. "Dans le fond est une colline riante, dont la pente douce, dirigée vers la droite, s'étend jusqu'au bord de la mer." Pixérécourt, *Robinson Crusoé* 3 (I.i). For discussions of Robinson Crusoe narratives during the period, I am indebted to Jean Pascal Le Goff.

25. *Vendredi.* "Moi bien dire que père à moi être bon, aussi, li bien aimé dans tribu, parce que li savoir beaucoup choses." *Iglou.* "Quelques relations de commerce entre ceux de ma nation et les Colons de la Trinité, m'ont mis à même de connaître et de pratiquer quelques-uns des usages d'Europe: c'est pour cela qu'il m'ont nommé leur chef." Pixérécourt, *Robinson Crusoé* 13 (I.vi). For a Robinson Crusoe pantomime, see, for instance, the description of Sheridan's (Sheridan, *Dramatic* II:784–7).

26. "Vendredi cherche à leur faire comprendre, en pantomime, que les matelots ont découvert la caverne, qu'ils sont cachés dans le caveau, qu'ils sont dix, qu'il n'y a pas moyen de leur résister, et qu'il n'ont d'autre parti à prendre que de fuir sans bruit. Diégo lui fait signe de venir avec eux, il témoigne qu'il ira les rejoindre dès qu'il le pourra sans être vu." Pixérécourt, *Robinson Crusoé* 53–4 (II.xi).

27. Lessing, *Werke* VI:7–187 (especially Ch. 4 of *Laokoon* (*Werke* IV:28–40) on Sophocles' *Philoctetus*).

28. "La peinture, la bonne peinture, les grands tableaux, voilà vos modèles." Imagine that "le spectateur est au théâtre comme devant une toile où des tableaux divers se succéderaient. … Appliquez les lois de la composition pittoresque … et vous verrez que ce sont les mêmes." Diderot, *Œuvres* V:81; IV:1342 (letter to Marie-Jeanne de Heurles de Laboras de Mézières; "De la poésie dramatique").

29. Murphy, *Desert* (1760 edn.) 1 (I.i). Since the engraving was copied from the illustration that serves as the frontispiece for Collet de Messine's *L'Isle desert* (1758), it is unlikely that it represents an actual production of Murphy's *Desert Island*, though it is perfectly possible that the Drury Lane production of Murphy's play was influenced by the similar illustration in Collet de Messine's.

30. *Schulmeister* (re "Die Malerschauspiele"): "Ihr Charakter besteht darin, daß alles, was in ihnen vorkommt, malerisch ist." Grabbe, *Werke* I:228 (*Scherz, Satire, Ironie und tiefere Bedeutung* (written *c*.1822) I.iii); trans. Grabbe, *Jest* 17–18 (trans. modified).

31. Cibber, *Harlot's* 3; Colman, *Ut Pictura* 17. See the discussion of both plays in Meisel, *Realizations* 99–106, and Meisel's comment that, with a few significant exceptions, 18th- and 19th-century pictorial allusion in the theatre "uses contemporary work that has achieved enough current success to have been engraved, displayed in print-shop windows, discussed and illustrated in periodicals, and sometimes pirated" (*Realizations* 93, and see 95–6).

32. "Hier muß ein verständiger Aufseher der Schaubühne sich in den Alterthümern umgesehen haben; und die Trachten aller Nationen, die er aufzuführen willens ist, in Bildern ausstudiren." "Daher ist es lächerlich, wenn einfältige Comödianten ... eine americanische Prinzeßinn mit einem Fischbeinrocke, und eine flüchtende Zaire im Oriente mit einer drey Ellen langen Schleppe; ja endlich einen alten deutschen Herrmann, Segesth u. a. m. wie ihre Todtfeinde die Römer, aber doch mit Perücken, weißen Handschuhen und kleinen Galanteriedegen aufführet, u. d. gl." Gottsched, *Ausgewählte* VI(ii):332–3 (*Von Tragödien oder Trauerspielen* (1742)); trans. Brandt, ed., *German* 101. After Garrick revived Thomas Tomkis's early 17th-century *Albumazar* in 1747 with characters "New Dress'd after the Manner of the Old English Comedy," the claim became conventional on the London stage (see the notes in Garrick, *Plays* VII:428; and Macmillan, *Drury Lane* p. xxix). See also Levacher de Charnois's "preliminary observations" in his *Recherches* 1–8.

33. "(I) On trouvera dans l'ouvrage de P. *Lafittau*, intitulé: *Mœurs des sauvages Américains*, 2 vol. in-4°, fig. des détails très-circonstanciés et du plus grand intérêt sur la danse et les jeux des Caraïbes, lorsqu'ils mettent à mort un prisonnier, de même que sur la danse du calumet que je place à la fin du troisième acte." Pixérécourt, *Robinson Crusoé* 10n. (I.v).

34. On De Loutherbourg's use of Montfaucon, see Nicoll, *Garrick* 169. For "accuracy," see, for instance, James Boaden's lament that the 1808 Covent Garden fire had destroyed treasures "unrivalled for ... accuracy" because they had been "accumulated by unwearied research" in the Covent Garden library. Boaden, *Memoirs of the Life of John Philip Kemble* II:459.

35. "'Ich billige, daß Sie eine Minerva darin anbringen wollen, und ich denke beizeiten darauf, wie die Göttin zu kleiden ist, damit man nicht gegen das Kostüm verstößt. Ich lasse deswegen aus meiner Bibliothek alle Bücher herbeibringen, worin sich das Bild derselben befindet.' In eben dem Augenblicke traten einige Bedienten mit großen Körben voll Bücher allerlei Formats in den Saal. Montfaucon, die Sammlungen antiker Statuen, Gemmen und Münzen, alle Arten mythologischer Schriften wurden aufgeschlagen und die Figuren verglichen. Aber auch daran war es noch nicht genug! Des Grafen vortreffliches Gedächtnis stellte ihm alle Minerven vor, die etwa noch auf Titelkupfern, Vignetten oder sonst vorkommen mochten. Es mußte deshalb ein Buch nach dem andern aus der Bibliothek herbei geschafft werden, so daß der Graf zuletzt in einem Haufen von Büchern saß. Endlich ... rief er mit Lachen aus: 'Ich wollte wetten, daß nun keine Minerva mehr in der ganzen Bibliothek sei.' ... Auf seinen Reisen hatte

er ... viele Kupfer und Zeichnungen mitgebracht." Goethe, *Gedenkausgabe* VII:182–4; trans. Goethe, *Wilhelm Meister* 99–100 (Bk. 3, Ch. 7) (punctuation added; trans. modified).

36. Hugo, *Théâtre* I:428.
37. Maturin, *Bertram* (1816) 49 (IV.i).
38. Kemble, *Smiles* 87–8 (V.v).
39. Qtd. Shattuck, ed., *William Charles Macready's* 11 (emphasis added).
40. Baillie, *Dramatic* 234–5n. (preface to *Plays on the Passions*, Third Vol. (1812)). See, similarly, Dion Boucicault's characterization of the stage as "a picture frame, in which is exhibited that kind of panorama where the picture being unrolled is made to move, passing before the spectator with scenic continuity"; and the Bancrofts' decision to get rid of the forestage at the Haymarket towards the end of the 19th century and instead encircle the scenic space with "a rich and elaborate gold border, about two feet broad, after the pattern of a picture frame, [which] is continued all round the proscenium, and carried even below the actors' feet," qtd. Meisel, *Realizations* 51, 44 (and see his discussion).
41. See the discussion of baroque prototypes in Chapter 9. On the banishing of spectators from the stages of the Comédie-Française in 1759 and Drury Lane in 1762, the enlargement of theatres at the turn of the century, and improvements in lighting, see Larthomas, *Le Théâtre* 25–7; *Revels* VI:4, 7, 80; and *London Stage* V(i): pp. xliii–xlv. See also the discussion in Nicoll, *Garrick* 119 and Meisel, *Realizations* 33, 170 of the "Eidophusikon" which De Loutherbourg invented around 1782 (a brightly lit box in which he would create miniature theatrical shows for a small audience), which offered a prototype of the spectacle sequestered in a box from audience intervention—the unified and untouchable scenic image created in various forms in theatrical experiments and innovations over the course of the century.
42. "Ne pensez non plus au spectateur que s'il n'existait pas. Imaginez sur le bord du théâtre un grand mur qui vous sépare du parterre; jouez comme si la toile ne se levait pas." Diderot, *Œuvres* IV:1310 ("De la poésie dramatique," Ch. 11). Michael Fried (*Absorption*) has famously described, in this context, the phenomenon of "absorption" in 18th-century painting, which accompanied the developing ideology of absorption in the theatre: the fiction that there was no viewer or painter; the idealizing of figures fully engrossed in the theatrical or painted scene; the hypothesizing of an "ontologically impermeable" border around the scene.
43. Colman, *Polly Honeycombe* (title page); Schiller, *Schillers Werke* III:5 ("eine dramatische Geschichte"). See the suggestive account of the theatrical as model and metaphor for the 18th- and 19th-century novel in Marshall, *Figure* and, for a more extensive exploration of the exchange between theatre and novel in the 19th century, see Meisel, *Realizations*.
44. Haines, *My Poll* 49–50 (III.i).
45. Holcroft, *Tale* 10–16 (I.i).
46. "Ceçi tuera cela! Le livre tuera l'édifice." Hugo, *Œuvres* I:618 (*Notre Dame* Bk. 5, Ch. 2).
47. "Iglou, Vendredi et les autres Caraïbes ne sont pas noirs, mais seulement olivâtres ou légèrement basanés. Cette observation est importante, et je desire que l'on y ait égard partout où l'on montera la pièce." Pixérécourt, *Robinson Crusoé* sig. A1ᵛ (I.i).
48. "Nous signalons ces nuances aux comédiens qui n'auraient pas pu étudier la manière dont ces rôles sont représentés à Paris." Hugo, *Théâtre* I:1770 ("Notes d'*Hernani*").
49. Baillie, *Dramatic* 190n.
50. "Actus I. 1) Hohes Felsenufer des Vierwaldstädtersees, der See macht eine Bucht ins Land, über den See hinweg sieht man die grünen Matten, Dörfer und Höfe von

Schwytz deutlich im Sonnenschein liegen. Dahinter (zur Linken des Zuschauers) der Hakenberg mit seinen zwei Spitzen von einer Wolkenkappe umgeben. Noch weiter hinten und zur rechten (des Zuschauers) schimmern blaugrün die Glarischen Eisgebirge. An den Felsen, welche die Coulissen bilden, sind steile Wege, mit Geländern, auch Leitern, an denen man die Jäger und Hirten, im Verlauf der Handlung herabsteigen sieht. Der Mahler hat also das Kühne, Grosse, Gefährliche der Schweitzergebirge darzustellen. Ein Theil des Sees muss beweglich sein, weil er im Sturme gezeigt wird." Schiller, *Schillers Werke* XXXII:89–90; trans. Brandt, ed., *German* 98.

51. Maturin, *Bertram* 82, 88–91 (V.iii).

52. "Une fête de nuit au Louvre. Salles magnifiques pleines d'hommes et de femmes en parure. Flambeaux, musique, danses, éclats de rire.—Des valets portent des plats d'or et des vaisselles d'émail; des groupes de seigneurs et de dames passent et repassent. ... —Dans l'architecture, dans les ameublements, dans les vêtements, le goût de la Renaissance. ... LE ROI, *comme l'a peint Titien.* ... *Les seigneurs, superbement vêtus. Triboulet, dans son costume de fou, comme l'a peint Boniface.*" Hugo, *Théâtre* I:1337, 1340 (I.i).

53. "Les Français ont *le droit de publier.* ... Le théâtre n'est qu'un moyen de publication comme la presse, comme la gravure, comme la lithographie. ... La suppression ministérielle d'une pièce de théâtre attente à la liberté par la censure, à la propriété par la confiscation." Hugo, *Théâtre* I:1323–4. The Louvre had been officially opened as an art museum for the "people" in 1793, when the 1789 revolution was collapsing. In setting the play in the Louvre, Hugo is suggesting that he is giving the people *his* version of post-revolutionary art, after the similar collapse of the 1830 revolution into the autocratic July Monarchy, with Paris in a state of siege. On Hugo's visit to Chambord, see Thierry and Mélèze's notes in Hugo, *Théâtre* I:1786.

54. "La suppression d'une pièce de théâtre [est] une propriété violemment dérobée au théâtre et à l'auteur [qui] attente à la liberté [et] la propriété." Hugo, *Théâtre* I:1323–4.

55. Shaw, *Complete* I:38 (preface to *Plays Unpleasant* (1898)).

14. ACTOR/AUTHOR

1. Charke, *Narrative* 19 (17–20 for the story of her childhood prank). For clarification of biographical details, I am indebted to Morgan, *Well-Known* and the essays in Baruth, ed., *Introducing* (especially Folkenflik, "Images" 142–3 on Charke as "the perfect Representative of my Sire").

2. Cibber, *Dramatic* IV:109. Cibber is writing, here, actually, not of *An Apology for the Life of Colley Cibber* (1740) but of his hope that the memory of Ann Oldfield's performance in *The Provoked Husband* will prolong the life of the printed play, but these lines struck contemporaries as exemplifying what they viewed as his absurd pretensions.

3. Charke, *Narrative* p. vi.

4. Ibid., p. vii ("The Author to Herself").

5. Ibid., 23, 56–7, 59 (and note the capitalization of compliments and warnings to herself throughout the dedication).

6. Cibber, *Apology* 6 (Ch. 1).

7. See Patterson, *First* 15 on the late 18th-century playing cards and tobacco tins featuring Franz Brockmann, after his success as Hamlet.

8. "Nous ... rappell[ons] le langage simple, touchant, & noble de mademoiselle Lecou-

vreur. ... Sa voix n'étoit point harmonieuse, elle sut la rendre pathétique; ... ses yeux s'embellissoient par les larmes, & ses traits par l'expression du sentiment." *Encyclopédie* IV:681–2.

9. *Nouvelle biographie theatrale, ou Les acteurs, actrices, chanteurs, chanteuses, danseurs, danseuses, vus dans leurs boudoirs, à la scene et dans le monde* (1826).

10. Shaw, *Complete* I:124 (preface to *Mrs Warren's Profession*).

11. Austin, *Chironomia* 279 (Ch. 10).

12. Chiari, *La commediante in fortuna, o sia Memorie di madama N. N. scritte da lei medesima* (1755) (translated into English as *Rosara* in 1771). For Charke's equation of her own autobiography with that of Stevens, see Charke, *Narrative* vi.

13. Qtd. Jordan, *Mrs. Jordan* 3 (30 Nov. 1791). See also Clarence's letter: "I understand there is just published a book in defence of Mrs. Billington with anecdotes of Daly the Irish Manager, in which Mrs. Jordan is, and infamously, scandalized," he writes, asking his agent to sue the editor for libel. Jordan, *Mrs. Jordan* 18 (Feb. 1792). For discussions of actresses' memoirs and journalism during the period, I am indebted to Engel, "Staging."

14. Weaver, *Anatomical* (1721) 145.

15. Lang, *Dissertatio* 42 (Ch. 7); trans. Brandt, ed., *German* 59–60. On Le Brun, see Goodden, *Actio* 153 (in the context of her extensive discussion of the relationship between 18th-century theories of acting and the visual arts).

16. For a discussion of the proliferation of English acting manuals in the later 18th century, see Roach, *Player's*, esp. 58–159 (an "information explosion" (114)). On the dozens of Spanish acting manuals published in the 19th century, see Gies, *Theatre* 35.

17. Austin, *Chironomia* (facing p. 490) (Ch. 21); sig. 7G^r ("Table of References").

18. Lang, *Dissertatio ... de arte comica*; Talma, *Réflexions sur ... l'art théatral*; Roetscher, *Die Kunst der dramatischen Darstellung*. Renaissance commentaries identified acting as an "arte and facultye," in the sense of "trade," "profession," or "qualitie" (see Chambers, *Elizabethan* I:309), but the actor's profession, however, had only a marginally legal status until the late 18th century, formally legalized in England only in 1788, and in France only after the Revolution (see Nicoll, *Garrick* 65; and Lagrave, "Privilèges" 273). The public honours granted to the most prominent 18th-century actors is indicative of a significant shift. The professionalization of acting through such institutions as the École Royale de Déclamation (founded in Paris in 1786) also played an important role in changing the public and legal status of acting as a profession. It was worthy of observation, in 1790, that (as Millin de Grandmaison commented in *Sur la liberte du theatre* (1790)) the profession of acting was no longer felt to be *a priori* reprehensible (Goodden, *Actio* 168).

19. "Un des grands malheurs de notre art, c'est qu'il meurt ... avec nous, tandis que tous les autres artistes laissent des monumens dans leurs ouvrages; le talent de l'acteur, quand il a quitté la scène, n'existe plus que dans le souvenir de ceux qui l'ont vu et entendu." Talma, *Mémoires* iii–iv; trans. Talma, *Reflexions* 7.

20. "Corneille & Racine nous restent, Baron & la Lecouvreur ne sont plus; leurs leçons étoient écrites ... dans le vague de l'air, leur exemple s'est évanoüi avec eux." *Encyclopédie* IV:682 ("Déclamation théâtrale").

21. Cibber, *Apology* 60 (Ch. 4).

22. Lloyd, *Actor* 19–20.

23. "Cette considération [that the actor's art "meurt ... avec nous"] doit donner plus de prix aux écrits, aux réflexions, aux leçons que les grands acteurs ont laissés." Talma, *Mémoires* iv; trans. Talma, *Reflexions* 8.

24. Clairon, *Memoirs* (1800 edn.) I: p. xx.

25. "Combien il seroit à desirer qu'il existât un dépôt où seroient consignés les grands effets de la déclamation théâtrale, et où chaque acteur reconnu pour modèle, iroit, après avoir recueilli les justes applaudissemens du public, tracer lui-même l'histoire de son ame, de ses intentions et de ses moyens, au moments où il a excité le plus grand enthousiasme! C'est dans ce dépôt … que les jeunes acteurs pourroient puiser l'idée de ces mouvemens sublimes, qui transportent toute une assemblée, et sont le triomphe de la belle déclamation." Dubroca, *Principes* (leçon 37) 502.

26. "Les bras s'elevent à la hauteur de la poitrine et sont écartés d'environ un pied. … La tête est inclinée en avant, l'œil est baissé, les mains sont rapprochées et se joigent lorsque la prière devient plus instante; le corps dans cette attitude reste immobile après qu'on a supplié, il en attend l'effet." Dorfeuille [P.-P. Gobet], *Les Éléments de l'art du comédien*; trans. Goodden, *Actio* 71 (trans. modified).

27. Lang, *Dissertatio* 49–50 (Ch. 8); trans. Brandt, ed., *German* 60.

28. Hogarth, *Analysis* (1753) 149 (Ch. 17).

29. Austin, *Chironomia* 277 (Ch. 10); and see the discussion in Goodden, *Actio* 144.

30. Parkes, *Pause* 91.

31. "Rond du bras fait en tiers"; "Figure preste à faire le piroëté." Rameau, *Le Maître* (plate facing p. 244).

32. "La déclamation notée ne seroit autre chose que les tons & les mouvemens de la prononciation écrite en notes. … Quant au moyen d'écrire en notes la déclamation … il ne sçauroit être aussi difficile … qu'il l'étoit de trouver l'art d'écrire en notes les pas & les figures d'une entrée de ballet dansée par huit personnes. … Il n'est pas plus difficile d'apprendre par des notes quels gestes il faut faire, que d'apprendre par des notes quels pas, quelles figures il faut former." Du Bos, *Réflexions* III:165–6, III:254 (Sect. 9, 14).

33. Hill, *Actor* 232.

34. "S'il étoit possible de tracer les figures des gestes sur le papier … vous verriez qu'il n'existe pas une seule affection de l'ame … à laquelle ne réponde un geste particulier." Dubroca, *Principes* 379 (leçon 25).

35. Since "il est … naturel à des hommes, qui parlent une langue dont la prononciation approche beaucoup du chant, d'avoir un geste plus varié," it becomes clear that the ancients "leur aient prescrit des règles, et … trouvé le secret de les écrire en notes. … Les gestes étant réduits en art, et notés, il fut facile de les asservir au mouvement et à la mesure de la déclamation." Condillac, *Oeuvres* I:303–5 (*Essai sur l'origine des connoissances humaines* (1746) §§31–2).

36. Engel, *Ideen* 9–11 (letter 1).

37. Austin, *Chironomia* 274–6, 286 (Ch. 10).

38. Ibid. 284 (Ch. 10).

39. Ibid. 286 (Ch. 10).

40. Ibid. 284 (Ch. 10).

41. Hazlitt, *Complete* IV:155.

42. Fielding, *Author's Farce* 18 (I.vi.24–32).

43. Gottsched "legte seinen Fluch auf das extemporieren; er ließ den Harlekin feierlich vom Theater vertreiben, welches selbst die größte Harlekinade war, die jemals gespielt worden." Lessing, *Werke* V:71 ("Briefe, die neueste Literatur betreffend," Letter 17 (1759)); trans. Herzfeld-Sander, ed., *Essays* 2). On the actual banning of the improvised drama in Vienna in 1770, see Brandt, ed., *German* 85.

44. Cibber, *Apology* 161 (Ch. 8).

45. "Les pièces que l'on jouoit étoient à l'in-promptu. ... Il falloit que tous les acteurs eussent beaucoup d'esprit, une imagination vive et fertile" *Calendrier historique des théâtres de l'Opéra et des Comédies françoise et italienne et des Foires*; qtd. Campardon, ed., *Les Comédiens* I: pp. xix–xx.

46. "On ne doit pas s'attendre à trouver dans ce Livre des Comedies entieres, puisque les Pieces Italiennes ne sçauroient s'imprimer." Gherardi, *Le Theatre* (1695 edn.) sig. *4ʳ.

47. "Je m'approchois, tout doucement, vers la liberté d'écrire mes Pieces en entier." Goldoni, *Tutte* I:193 (*Mémoires* Pt. 1, Ch. 42); trans. Goldoni, *Memoirs* 191.

48. "*Truf.* Si pianterà in un'attidudine d'un tragico recitante, e comincierà in tuono grave: *Mentre il popolo.* Troncherà il racconto, chiederà in grazia di non esser interrotto, perchè un Poeta gli ha data in iscritto la narrazione in versi, acciò possa farsi dell'onore, e che spera di averla a memoria. ... Si rimette in una cari[c]ata serietà, e con enfasi tragica recita la seguente narrazione, gestendo accademicamente ... | Mentre il popolo attento, ed affollato, | Nel magnifico Tempio aspettatore. ... | ... Ma che? ... mesti auguri ... | ... Cento cani, e cento, ch'eran sparsi | Per l'ampia mole urlar di voci orrende. ... | (*si ras-ciuga il sudore*). ... | *Truf.* Dice di essere stanco di parlare in versi." Gozzi, *Opere* I:162–3 (*Il Corvo* III.vii); trans. Gozzi, *Five* 52–3 (trans. modified). In the preface to *Il Corvo*, Gozzi writes that the play, like his others, "ha alcune scenette disegnate col solo argo-mento, e coll'intenzione. Chiunque vorrà ... sostener le maschere, e la Commedia improvvisa dell'arte, farà ciò, che feci io." Gozzi, *Opere* I:108. In fact, only one of Gozzi's *fiabe* (out of the ten *fiabe teatrali* in his 1772 *Opere*) is written not in dialogue but as an "Analisi Riflessiva."

49. Described in Goodden, *Actio* 94 (citing *La Pantomimanie* in the *Répertoire du Théâtre sans Prétension*, held by the Bibliothèque historique de la Ville de Paris).

50. "Nessuno potrà scrivere la parte d'un Truffaldino in prosa, non che in versi, e il Sacchi è uno di quegli eccellenti Truffaldini da eseguir l'intenzione, scritta da un Poeta in una scena improvvisa, in modo da superar ogni Poeta, che volesse scriverla." Gozzi, *Opere* I:108 (preface to *Il Corvo*); trans. Gozzi, *Five* 22–3.

51. The actor's art depends on "la sensibilité unie à l'intelligence, qui s'opère en secret chez l'acteur comme chez le poète." Talma, *Mémoires* p. lxvi; trans. Talma, *Reflexions* 40–1.

52. Hill, *Actor* 139.

53. "Vous partagez entre Racine et vous | De notre encens le tribut légitime." Levesque de la Ravaillère, *Essai* (1729) 11.

54. Hill, *Actor* 271, 265, 32–3, 40–1.

55. Hill, *Actor* 188–9.

56. "La passion ne marche pas comme la grammaire. ... D'ordinaire elle respecte peu les points et les virgules, et les franchit ou les déplace au gré de son désordre et de ses emportemens." Talma, *Mémoires* pp. lvii–lviii; trans. Talma, *Reflexions* 36.

57. On "pointing," see Worthen, *Idea* 71.

58. Jordan, *Mrs. Jordan* 59 (9 Oct. 1804).

59. Hill, *Actor* 265, 22–3, 90–1.

60. Hill and Popple, *Prompter* 82 (no. 64, 20 June 1735).

61. Garrick, *Letters* II:436 (letter 345, 12 Dec. 1764). The admonition was, apparently, nec-essary, since not only did not all actors read masterpieces, but many did not even read the plays they were acting. Goethe still had to require full read-throughs at the Weimar theatre throughout his tenure as director in order to be sure that his actors would be familiar with the entire play (Patterson, *First* 75). It was widely rumoured that Hannah

Pritchard, the most famous Lady Macbeth of the 1750s and 1760s, had never read the play, but knew only her part (Nicoll, *Garrick* 158).

62. Hill, *Actor* 95–7 (recommending, above all, Milton).

63. "Il doit l'approfondir, se la rendre familière jusque dans les plus petits détails." Clairon, *Mémoires* (1799 edn.) 27 ("Force"); trans. Clairon, *Memoirs* (1800 edn.) I:42 (trans. modified).

64. "Dix volumes sur cet art divin ne feraient pas un comédien." Préville and Dazincourt, *Mémoires* 178.

65. "Si jamais il m'est arrivé d'avoir l'air vraiment naturel, c'est que mes recherches, jointes à quelques dons heureux que m'avait fait la nature, ma'avaient conduite au comble de l'art." Clairon, *Mémoires* (1799 edn.) 30 ("Force"); trans. Clairon, *Memoirs* (1800 edn.) I:46 (trans. modified).

66. Hill, *Works* I:217 (24 Oct. 1733); qtd. Roach, *Player's* 110.

67. Hill, *Actor* 9.

68. Smollett, *Adventures* 274 (Ch. 55).

69. "L'expression des yeux et du visage est l'ame de la déclamation théâtrale; c'est-là que les passions doivent se peindre en caractères de feu." Dubroca, *Principes* 518 (leçon 39).

70. "Le masque doit toujours faire beaucoup de tort à l'action de l'Acteur, soit dans la joie, soit dans le chagrin; qu'il soit amoureux, farouche ou plaisant, c'est toujours le même *cuir* qui se montre; et il a beau gesticuler et changer de ton, il ne fera jamais connoître, par les traits du visage qui sont les interpretes du cœur, les différentes passions dont som ame est agitée. … Les passions et les sentiments n'étoient pas portés dans ce tems-là au point de délicatesse que l'on exige actuellement; on veut aujourd'hui que l'Acteur ait de l'ame, et l'ame sous le masque est comme le feu sous les cendres." Goldoni, *Tutte* I:349 (*Mémoires* Pt. 2, Ch. 24).

71. "[Die Armut] kommt—erlauben Sie mir's zu sagen, Ihr Herren Aristoteliker!—, sie kommt aus der Ähnlichkeit der handelnden Personen, *partium agentium*; die Mannig-faltigkeit der Charaktere und Psychologien ist die Fundgrube der Natur." Lenz, *Werke* II:660–1 ("Anmerkungen übers Theater"); trans. Herzfeld-Sander, ed., *Essays* 23.

72. Hill, *Actor* 279.

73. The true "comédien" is "l'homme à qui la nature aurait [donné] ce qu'elle a accordé au caméléon, je veux dire le pouvoir de se montrer sous toutes les formes." Préville and Dazincourt, *Mémoires* 178.

74. Cibber, *Apology* 161 (Ch. 8).

75. Hill, *Works* IV:361, 367 ("An Essay on the Art of Acting). "Le rôle … doit imprimer sur sa figure l'esprit de ce rôle." Préville and Dazincourt, *Mémoires* 153.

76. Hill, *Actor* 257. See Goldsmith's similar comment, in *The Bee* (1759), on Hannah Pritchard as Rowe's Jane Shore: "an actress that might act the Wapping Landlady without a bolster, pining in the character of Jane Shore, and while unwieldy with fat endeavouring to convince the audience that she is dying with hunger" (Goldsmith, *Collected* I:362).

77. Hill, *Actor* 198–9.

78. "La base de l'art théâtral … est … l'oubli spontané de soi-même." Dumesnil, *Mémoires* 53–4.

79. "Celui … dont les larmes constatent les recherches profondes" and who chooses "l'oubli de sa propre existence, est certainement un être misérable." But "l'acteur qui ne se les rend pas personnels, n'est qu'un écolier qui répète sa leçon." Clairon, *Mémoires*

(1799 edn.) 28–9 ("Force"); trans. Clairon, *Memoirs* (1800 edn.) I:44 (trans. modified).

80. Cibber, *Apology* 6 (Ch. 1).

81. "Moi-même, dans une circonstance de ma vie où j'éprouvai un chagrin profond, la passion du théâtre était telle en moi, qu'accablé d'une douleur bien réele, au milieu des larmes que je versais, je fis malgré moi une observation rapide et fugitive sur l'altération de ma voix et sur une certaine vibration spasmodique qu'elle contractait dans les pleurs; et, je le dis non sans quelque honte, je pensai machinalement à m'en servir au besoin; et en effet cette expérience sur moi-même m'a souvent été très utile." Talma, *Mémoires* pp. lxiii–lxiv; trans. Talma, *Reflexions* 39.

82. Clairon, *Mémoires* (1799 edn.) 235–6 ("Baptême").

83. "Ce premier tort m'enhardit à faire de nouveaux mensonges. ... Je me fis un plaisir de la dissimulation." Clairon, *Mémoires* (1799 edn.) 170 ("Première époque"); trans. Clairon, *Memoirs* (1800 edn.) II:30.

84. "En jouant Blanche, je me croyois toujours dans ma chambre. ... En jouant Blanche je restais toujours moi." Clairon, *Mémoires* (1799 edn.) 127 ("Blanche"); trans. Clairon, *Memoirs* (1800 edn.) I:202.

15. A THEATRE TOO MUCH WITH US

1. "The Midsummer Night's Dream" in Hazlitt, *Complete* IV:247 (and on the dating of the essay and appended paragraph, see the notes IV:399). This is an early version of Hazlitt's *Examiner* essay (21 Jan. 1816), from which I take most of the passages that follow.

2. Hazlitt, *Complete* V:276 (and see IV:247).

3. Ibid. IV:246.

4. Ibid. V:276 (and see IV:247).

5. Ibid. V:275–6. See also his comment in his essay "On Marston, Chapman, Deckar and Webster" (1820): "I do not mean to speak disrespectfully of the stage; but I think higher still of nature, and next to that, of books" (Hazlitt, *Complete* VI:246–7). And see the comments on this essay in the context of Hazlitt's relation to "romantic print culture" in Mulvihill, "William Hazlitt."

6. Hazlitt, *Complete* V:275–6.

7. "Le grotesque ... y est partout. ... Il crée le difforme et l'horrible [et] le comique et le bouffon. ... C'est lui qui sème à pleines mains dans l'air, dans l'eau, dans la terre, dans le feu, ces myriades d'êtres intermédiaires. ... Et comme il est libre et franc dans son allure! comme il fait hardiment saillir toutes ces formes bizarres que l'âge précédent avait si timidement enveloppées de langes!" Hugo, *Théâtre* I:418–19 (preface to *Cromwell*).

8. Lamb and Lamb, *Works* I:98 ("On the Tragedies of Shakspeare, Considered with Reference to Their Fitness for Stage Representation" (1811)); qtd. Meisel, *Realizations* 30. On romantic anti-theatricalism, see Barish, *Antitheatrical* 295–349, esp. 326 (on 19th-century anti-theatricalism and Romantic inwardness); and for a helpful rethinking of Romantic theatricalism and anti-theatricalism, see Carlson, *In the Theatre*.

9. For discussions, see Jacobus, " 'That Great Stage' "; and Carlson, *In the Theatre* 63–93 (on Schiller's influence on Coleridge's conception of imagination as active).

10. "Das schlimmste noch ist, daß man über der nothwendigen und lebhaften Vorstellung der Wirklichkeit, des Personals und aller übrigen Bedingungen allen poetischen Sinn abstumpft. Gott helfe mir über diese Besogne hinweg." Schiller, *Schillers Werke* XXIX:292 (letter to Goethe (23 Oct. 1798)). For the clearest articulation of Schiller's view of the theatre as an arm of the state, see Schiller's "Die Schaubühne als eine moralische Anstalt betrachtet."

11. "Sie können Ihre Zeit nicht besser anwenden, als wenn Sie sich gleich von allem losmachen, und in der Einsamkeit Ihrer alten Wohnung in die Zauberlaterne dieser unbekannten Welt sehen. Es ist sündlich, daß Sie Ihre Stunden verderben, diese Affen menschlicher auszuputzen, und diese Hunde tanzen zu lehren." Goethe, *Gedenkausgabe* VII:192; Goethe, *Wilhelm Meister* 105 (Bk. 3, Ch. 8).

12. "Besonders aber laßt genug geschehn! | Man kommt zu schaun, man will am liebsten sehn. | Wird vieles vor den Augen abgesponnen, | So daß die Menge staunend gaffen kann, | Da habt Ihr in der Breite gleich gewonnen." Goethe, *Gedenkausgabe* V:144 ("Vorspiel auf dem Theater"); trans. Goethe, *Faust* 4.

13. Inchbald, *Plays* II [*Massacre* v]. See, similarly, Schiller, in the preface to *Die Räuber* (1781): it is "sein Innhalt, ... der es von der Bühne verbannet," since "mancher Karakter auftreten mußte, der das feinere Gefühl der Tugend beleidigt, und die Zärtlichkeit unserer Sitten empört." Schiller, *Schillers Werke* III:5. The play was, of course, performed in 1782 (for a description of how shocking the première was in fact, see Patterson, *First* 37–8).

14. Holcroft, *Plays* I [*Duplicity* p. v].

15. "Einen andern Eindruck macht die Erzählung von jemands Geschrei; einen andern dieses Geschrei selbst. ... In ihm glauben wir nicht bloß einen schreienden Philoktet zu sehen und zu hören; wir hören und sehen wirklich schreien. Je näher der Schauspieler der Natur kömmt, desto empfindlicher müssen unsere Augen und Ohren beleidiget werden." Lessing, *Werke* VI:30 (Ch. 4); trans. Lessing, *Laocoön* 24 (trans. modified).

16. "Le théâtre est un point d'optique." "Il y [a] péril ... à risquer sur le théâtre des tentatives confiées jusqu'ici seulement au papier *qui souffre tout*." Hugo, *Théâtre* I:436, I:1148 (prefaces to *Cromwell* and *Hernani*).

17. Lamb and Lamb, *Works* I:108, 110–11 ("On the Tragedies of Shakespeare").

18. See, for instance, Pixérécourt's *Robinson Crusoé*, which closes with a tableau centred on the passing of the peacepipe, a tableau in which Spaniards, Caribbean savages, and Englishmen are happily united (Pixérécourt, *Robinson Crusoé* 64); and similarly Simon Favart's *L'Anglois a Bordeaux* (1763), written to celebrate the peace after a series of French colonial losses to the British, which concludes with a dance of many nations "caractérisés par des habits pittoresques" after which "toutes les nations s'embrassent" (Favart, *Oeuvres* I:138). For a discussion of the politics of this play, see Ravel, *Contested* 196–7.

19. "L'art [du théâtre est] un de ceux auxquels il appartient le plus de nous faire éprouver un plaisir complet. Notre imagination est presque toûjours obligée de suppléer à l'impuissance des autres Arts imitateurs de la nature. Celui du Comédien n'exige de nous par lui-meme aucun supplément." Rémond de Sainte-Albine, *Le Comédien* 15.

20. "C'est moi, qui fais le tableau." *Journal de Paris* (28 Messidor an VI (1798)) 1250; qtd. Goodden, *Actio* 43.

21. *Lettre écrite a un ami* (1739) 7; cited Goodden, *Actio* 73.

22. *La Pantomimanie*, in the *Répertoire du Théâtre sans Prétention*, 1798–1805 (Bibliothèque historique de la Ville de Paris); qtd. Goodden, *Actio* 94.

23. "La sensibilité … nous aide … à y ajouter quelquefois les nuances qui leur manquent, ou que les vers ne peuvent exprimer, à compléter enfin [l']expression." Talma, *Mémoires* p. xxxi; trans. Talma, *Reflexions* 19.

24. "Je me tenais opiniâtrement les oreilles bouchées, tant que l'action et le jeu de l'acteur me paraissaient d'accord avec le discours que je me rappelais. Je n'écoutais que quand j'étais dérouté par les gestes, ou que je croyais l'être." Diderot, *Œuvres* IV:21 ("Lettre sur les sourds et muets").

25. Hazlitt, *Complete* V:276. On theatrical unfreedom and the reader's freedom, see, for instance, Alfred de Vigny's comment that in the theatre, one can "s'adresser à trois mille hommes assemblés, sans qu'ils puissent en aucune façon éviter d'entendre ce que l'on a à leur dire. Un lecteur a bien des ressources contre vous, comme, par exemple, de jeter le livre au feu ou par la fenêtre: … mais contre le spectateur, on est bien plus fort; une fois entré, il est pris comme dans une souricière, et il est bien difficile qu'il sorte. … Dans cet état de contraction, d'étouffement et de suffocation, il faut qu'il écoute." Vigny, *Œuvres* I:397 (letter prefaced to *Le More de Venise*); trans. Daniels, ed., *Revolution* 214.

26. Hazlitt, *Complete* V:276.

27. For attacks on the unities on these grounds, see, for instance, Johnson on Shakespeare: "Surely he that imagines [himself at Alexandria … and that he lives in the days of Antony and Cleopatra] may imagine more. He that can take the stage at one time for the palace of the Ptolemies, may take it in half an hour for the promontory of Actium. Delusion, if delusion be admitted, has no certain limitation" (Johnson, *Johnson* 76–7). And see Hugo, describing "un de ces promoteurs irréfléchis de la nature absolue, de la nature vue hors de l'art," at a performance of *The Cid*: "Qu'est cela? dira-t-il au premier mot. Le Cid parle en vers! Il n'est pas *naturel* de parler en vers.—Comment voulez-vous donc qu'il parle?—En prose.—Soit.—Un instant après:—Quoi, reprendra-t-il s'il est conséquent, … De quel droit cet acteur, qui s'appelle Pierre ou Jacques, prend-il le nom de Cid? Cela est *faux.*—Il n'y a aucune raison pour qu'il n'exige pas ensuite qu'on substitue le soleil à cette rampe, des arbres *réels*, des maisons *réelles* à ces menteuses coulisses." Hugo, *Théâtre* I:435–6 (preface to *Cromwell*).

28. "La peinture intérieure," contrasting this to "cette imitation grossière des choses créés" in "cet immense cabinet" that is the museum. *Journal de Paris* (14 Pluviose an V (1797)) 537–8; qtd. Goodden, *Actio* 42.

29. "Découvriroit-on … l'intérieur de nos maisons, cet intérieur, qui est à un empire ce que les entrailles sont au corps humain." Mercier, *Théâtre* 103 (Ch. 8). For an interesting discussion of the parallel representation of the "unseen" spaces of the body in medical literature and painting, see Stafford, *Body*.

30. Hazlitt, *Complete* VI:247 ("On Marston, Chapman, Deckar and Webster").

31. Coleridge, *Collected* V(2):268–9 (written *c.*1818–19: see the discussion in this edition of the caution with which the source, Coleridge's *Literary Remains*, compiled by Henry Nelson Coleridge from a variety of sources, should be treated).

32. Coleridge, *Literary* II:206.

33. Lamb and Lamb, *Works* II:143 ("On the Artificial Comedy of the Last Century" (1822)).

34. Hazlitt, *Complete* V:276.

35. "Cette action *Pantomime* [est] la pierre de touche de l'Acteur" because of "ces phrases coupées, ces sens suspendus, ces soupirs, ces sons à peine articulés." Noverre, *Lettres* 474 (letter 15).

36. "On sent souvent ce qu'on ne peut exprimer; une ame fière ou sensible a des élans de grandeur, des nuances de finesse, de délicatesse aux-quelles je ne sais point de nom; on les exprime par un regard, un geste, par la modulation dans l'organe, par des temps: ces riens peignent souvent mieux que la parole." Clairon, *Mémoires* (1799 edn.) 72 ("Langue, Géographie, Belles-Lettres"); trans. Clairon, *Memoirs* (1800 edn.) I:114–15 (trans. modified).

37. Keats, *Poems* 372 ("Ode on a Grecian Urn" ll. 11–12).

38. "Maguelonne et Saltabadil sont tous deux dans la salle inférieure. L'orage a éclaté depuis quelques instants. Il couvre tout de pluie et d'éclairs. ... Tous deux gardent quelque temps le silence. ... On voit paraître, au fond, Blanche ... Elle s'avance lentement vers la masure, tandis que Saltabadil boit, et que Maguelonne, dans le grenier, considère avec sa lampe le roi endormi." Hugo, *Théâtre* I:1456–7 (IV.iv).

39. "Geheimnisvoll am lichten Tag, | Läßt sich Natur des Schleiers nicht berauben." Goethe, *Gedenkausgabe* V:164 ("Nacht" ll. 672–3); trans. Goethe, *Faust* 20.

40. "Beschränkt von diesem Bücherhauf, | Den Würme nagen." Goethe, *Gedenkausgabe* V:156 (*Nacht* ll. 402–5); trans. Goethe, *Faust* 14. See, in this context, the suggestive reading in Kittler, *Discourse* 3–27.

41. "Erhabner Geist, du. ... | Gabst mir die herrliche Natur zum Königreich, | Kraft, sie zu fühlen, zu genießen ... | Vergönnest mir, in ihre tiefe Brust | Wie in den Busen eines Freunds, zu schauen. ... | Und wenn der Sturm im Walde braust und knarrt ... | Dann führst du mich zur sichern Höhle, zeigst | Mich dann mir selbst, und meiner eignen Brust | Geheime, tiefe Wunder öffnen sich." Goethe, *Gedenkausgabe* V:244 ("Wald und Hohle" ll. 3217–34); trans. Goethe, *Faust* 83.

42. "Eine Einheit des Orts und der Zeit" has been adopted "nach dem gemeinsten empirischen Sinn auf der Schaubühne eingeführt, als ob hier ein anderer Ort wäre als der bloß ideale Raum, und eine andere Zeit als bloß die stetige Folge der Handlung." Schiller, *Schillers Werke* X:10 ("Über den Gebrauch des Chors"); trans. Schiller, *Works* IV:227. And, on the function of the theatre in serving as a bridge between sense and understanding, see Schiller's "Die Schaubühne als eine moralische Anstalt betrachtet"; and, generally, Schiller's *Briefe über die äesthetische Erziehung des Menschen* (1795).

43. "Was blos die Sinne reizt" is "nur Stoff und rohes Element in einem Dichterwerk." Schiller, *Schillers Werke* X:12 ("Über den Gebrauch des Chors"); trans. Schiller, *Works* IV:230.

44. "Wirklich ... frei zu *machen*, und dieses dadurch, daß sie eine Kraft in ihm erweckt, übt und ausbildet, die sinnliche Welt, die sonst nur als ein roher Stoff auf uns lastet, als eine blinde Macht auf uns drückt, in eine objektive Ferne zu rücken, in ein freies Werk unsers Geistes zu verwandeln, und das Materielle durch Ideen zu beherrschen." Schiller, *Schillers Werke* X:8–9 ("Über den Gebrauch des Chors"); trans. Schiller, *Works* IV:225.

45. The Chorus becomes, for Schiller, an important emblem of the theatre's translation of individual sensible experience into a more general spiritual idea: "Der Chor ist selbst kein Individuum, sondern ein allgemeiner Begriff, aber dieser Begriff repräsentiert sich durch eine sinnlich mächtige Masse, welche durch ihre ausfüllende Gegenwart den Sinnen imponiert. ... Und er thut es von der ganzen sinnlichen Macht des Rhythmus

und der Musik in Tönen und Bewegungen begleitet." Schiller, *Schillers Werke* X:13 ("Über den Gebrauch des Chors"); trans. Schiller, *Works* IV:230.

46. The drama "fordert deshalb, damit das ganze Kunstwerk zu wahrhafter Lebendigkeit komme, die vollständige szenische Aufführung desselben." "Weil es seinem Inhalte wie seiner Form nach sich zur vollendetsten Totalität ausbildet [muß es], als die höchste Stufe der Poesie und der Kunst überhaupt angesehen werden." Hegel, *Werke* XV:474 (*Aesthetics* Pt. 3, Sect. 3, Ch. 3, C-III, Intro.); trans. Hegel, *Hegel* 172 (trans. modified). "Endlich geht die Poesie auch zur Rede innerhalb einer in sich beschlossenen *Handlung* fort, die sich ebenso objektiv darstellt, als sie das Innere dieser objektiven Wirklichkeit äußert und deshalb mit Musik und Gebärde, Mimik, Tanz usf. verschwistert werden kann." Hegel, *Werke* XIV:262 (*Aesthetics* Pt. 3, Intro.); trans. Hegel, *Hegel* 67 (trans. modified).

47. "Der *lebendige* Mensch [ist] selbst das Material der Äußerung. Denn einerseits soll im Drama der Charakter, was er in seinem Inneren trägt, als das Seinige wie in der Lyrik aussprechen; andererseits aber gibt er sich wirksam in seinem wirklichen Dasein als ganzes Subjekt gegen andere kund und ist dabei tätig nach außen, wodurch sich unmittelbar die Gebärde anschließt." Objectivity and subjectivity united "ist der Geist in seiner Totalität und gibt als *Handlung* die Form und den Inhalt der *dramatischen* Poesie ab." Hegel, *Werke* XV:324 (*Aesthetics* Pt. 3, Intro.); trans. Hegel, *Hegel* 147 (trans. augmented).

48. Wagner, *Sämtliche* III:67 ("Das Kunstwerk der Zukunft" Sect. II.2). "Ehe diese epischen Gesänge zum Gegenstande solcher literarischen Sorge geworden waren, hatten sie aber in dem Volke, durch Stimme und Gebärde unterstützt, als leiblich dargestellte Kunstwerke geblüht." Wagner, *Sämtliche* III:104 (Sect. II.5); trans. Wagner, *Richard Wagner's* I:135 (cf. Wagner, *Sämtliche* III:67 on poetry, music, and dance as a trinity).

49. "Die Lyrik des Orpheus hätte die wilden Tiere sicher nicht zu schweigender, ruhiger sich lagernder Andacht vermocht, wenn der Sänger ihnen etwa bloß gedruckte Gedichte zu lesen gegeben hätte: ihren Ohren mußte die tönende Herzensstimme, ihren nur nach Fraß spähenden Augen der anmutig und kühn sich bewegende menschliche Leib *der* Art erst imponieren, daß sie unwillkürlich in diesem Menschen nicht mehr nur ein Objekt ihres Magens, nicht nur einen fressenswerten, sondern auch hörens- und sehenswerten Gegenstand erkannten, ehe sie fähig wurden, seinen moralischen Sentenzen Aufmerksamkeit zu schenken." Wagner, *Sämtliche* III:103 ("Das Kunstwerk der Zukunft" Sect. II.5); trans. Wagner, *Richard Wagner's* I:134.

50. "Denn während jene Professoren und Literaturforscher im fürstlichen Schlosse an der Konstruktion eines *literarischen* Homeros arbeiten … brachte *Thespis* bereits seinen Karren nach Athen geschleppt, stellte ihn an den Mauern der Hofburg auf, rüstete die *Bühne, betrat* sie, aus dem Chore des Volkes herausschreitend." Wagner, *Sämtliche* III:104 ("Das Kunstwerk der Zukunft" Sect. II.5); trans. Wagner, *Richard Wagner's* I:135.

51. "Als die nationale Volksgenossenschaft sich selbst zersplitterte, als das gemeinsame Band ihrer Religion und ureigenen Sitte von den sophistischen Radelstichen des egoistisch sich zersetzenden athenischen Geistes zerstochen und zerstückt wurde,— … da bemächtigten sich die Professoren und Doktoren der ehrbaren Literatenzunft des in Trümmer zerfallenden Gebäudes, schleppten Balken und Steine beiseit, um an ihnen zu forschen, zu tombinieren und zu meditieren. Aristophanisch lachend ließ das Vok den gelehrten Insekten den Abgang seines Verzehrten, … während jene auf alexandrinischen Oberhofbefehl Literaturgeschichte zusammenstoppelten. … Das winterliche

Geäste der Sprache, ledig des sommerlichen Schmuckes des lebendigen Laubes der Töne, verkrüppelte sich zu den dürren, lautlosen Zeichen der *Schrift*: statt dem Ohre teilte stumm sie sich nun dem *Auge* mit; die Dichterweise ward zur *Schreibart*,—zum *Schreibstil* der Geisteshauch des Dichters." Wagner, *Sämtliche* III:105–6 ("Das Kunstwerk der Zukunft" Sect. II.5); trans. Wagner, *Richard Wagner's* I:136–7.

52. "Der *Luxus* ist … egoistisch." "Der Egoismus": "Der Trieb, sich aus der Gemeinsamkeit zu lösen, für sich, ganz im Besonderen frei, selbständig sein zu wollen." Wagner, *Sämtliche* III:49, 70 ("Das Kunstwerk der Zukunft" Sect. I.3, II.2); trans. Wagner, *Richard Wagner's* I:76, 98.

53. "Wo die Dichtkunst für sich das Alleinige sein wollte, wie im rezitierten Schauspiele, da nahm sie die Musik in ihren Dienst zu Nebenzwecken." Wagner, *Sämtliche Schriften* III:119 ("Das Kunstwerk der Zukunft" Sect. II.6); trans. Wagner, *Richard Wagner's* I:151.

54. With "Kommunismus," "das Volk," "all[e] d[ie]jenigen, welche *eine gemeinschaftliche Not empfinden*," "kein Unterschidenes, Besonderes mehr s[ind]." Wagner, *Sämtliche Schriften* III:48, 50–1 ("Das Kunstwerk der Zukunft" Sect. I.3); trans. Wagner, *Richard Wagner's* I:75, 77–8.

55. "Denn im Kunstwerk werden wir eins sein,—Träger und Weiser der Notwendigkeit, Wissende des Unbewußten, Wollende des Unwillkürlichen, Zeugen der Natur,—*glückliche* Menschen." Wagner, *Sämtliche Schriften* III:50 ("Das Kunstwerk der Zukunft" Sect. I.3); trans. Wagner, *Richard Wagner's* I:77.

56. "Die verschiedenen Künste *in ihrer Wirkung auf das Gemüth* einander immer ähnlicher werden. Die Musik in ihrer höchsten Veredlung muß Gestalt werden; und mit der ruhigen Macht der Antike auf uns wirken; die bildende Kunst in ihrer höchsten Vollendung muß Musik werden und uns durch unmittelbare sinnliche Gegenwart rühren; die Poesie, in ihrer vollkommensten Ausbildung muß uns, wie die Tonkunst, mächtig fassen, zugleich aber, wie die Plastik, mit ruhiger Klarheit umgeben," giving each "einen mehr allgemeinen Charakter." Schiller, *Schillers Werke* XX:381 (*Briefe über die ästhetische Erziehung* (1795), no. 22); trans. Schiller, *Works* IX:78.

57. "Derselbe Sinn, der den Bildhauer leitete im Begreifen und Wiedergeben der menschlichen Gestalt, leitet den *Darsteller*. … Dasselbe Auge, das den Historienmaler in Zeichnung und Farbe, bei Anordnung der Gewänder und Aufstellung der Gruppen, das Schöne, Anmutige und Charakteristische finden ließ, ordnet nun die Fülle *wirklicher menschlicher Erscheinung*," prefiguring "den tragischen Darsteller der Zukunft in Stein und auf Leinwand." Wagner, *Sämtliche Schriften* III:155 ("Das Kunstwerk der Zukunft" Sect. IV.1); trans. Wagner, *Richard Wagner's* I:188–9.

58. "In dem sie [Poesie] nämlich weder für die sinnliche Anschauung arbeitet wie die bildenden Künste noch für die bloß ideelle Empfindung wie die Musik, sondern ihre im Innern gestalteten Bedeutungen des Geistes nur für die geistige Vorstellung und Anschauung selber machen will, so behält für sie das *Material*, durch welches sie sich kundgibt, nur noch den Wert eines wenn auch künstlerisch behandelten *Mittels* für die Äußerung des Geistes an den Geist und gilt nicht als ein sinnliches Dasein, in welchem der geistige Gehalt eine ihm entsprechende Realität zu finden imstande sei." Hegel, *Werke* XIV:261 (Pt. 3, Intro.) (Hegel, *Hegel* 66, for the corresponding passage).

59. "Eine unselig falschverstandene Freiheit ist nun aber die des in der Vereinzelung, in der Einsamkeit frei sein Wollenden." Wagner, *Sämtliche* III:70 ("Das Kunstwerk der Zukunft" Sect. II.2); trans. Wagner, *Richard Wagner's* I:98.

60. "[Der Chor] erhielt die Bestimmung, auch noch das, was in dem Zuschauer vorging, die Bewegung des Gemüths, die Theilnahme, die Reflexion, ihm vorweg zu nehmen, ihn auch in dieser Rücksicht nicht frei zu lassen, und dadurch ganz durch die Kunst zu fesseln." Schelling, *Schellings* III (supplement):357 (*Zur Philosophie der Kunst*, 1804 revision); trans. Schelling, *Philosophy* 259.

61. "Nur soweit der Genius im Actus der künstlerischen Zeugung mit jenem Urkünstler der Welt verschmilzt, weiss er etwas über das ewige Wesen der Kunst; denn in jenem Zustande ist er, wunderbarer Weise, dem unheimlichen Bild des Mährchens gleich, das die Augen drehn un sich selber anschaun kann; jetzt ist er zugleich Subject und Object, zugleich Dichter, Schauspieler und Zuschauer." Nietzsche, *Werke* III(1):43–4; trans. Nietzsche, *Birth* 52.

EPILOGUE

1. "C'était la mort d'Isolde. ... Les deux jeunes gens, fort émus, pénétrèrent dans le salon. Le rythmicien brûlait du désir d'accompagner lui-même cette voix incomparable. Au centre du salon, sur un guéridon, un phonographe ouvrait largement son horrible pavillon. ... Puis deux voix s'élevèrent: 'O sink hernieder Nacht der Liebe' (*Tristan*, acte II). Notre rythmicien pâlissait, [mais] il se saisit de la partition qui reposait sur le piano, l'ouvrit à la page, [et], l'oreille penchée dans le pavillon sonore, il accompagna les deux voix. ... Notre ami s'affermissait toujours plus dans son jeu, il ne suivait pas les chanteurs: leur identité à tous trois était consommée. ... Dans le corridor il n'eut pas un instant l'idée que ce pût être autre chose qu'une voix émise par un corps *vivant*. ... Quand il vit le phonographe, il ressentit un coup qui l'étourdit. ... Deux sentiments le dominèrent complètement: Ou bien il ne pouvait pas supporter sa souffrance plus longtemps et il allait jeter [la machine] par la fenêtre; ou bien ... Ou bien quoi? ... Son corps frémissait d'indignation et d'un besoin d'agir; mais comment faire? ... Il fallait à tout prix *animer* cette enregistration monstrueuse, ou bien s'y soustraire. ... Seul avec 'eux', notre rythmicien ... commença, la tête couchée dans l'appareil. De temps en temps, il parlait doucement aux chanteurs. ... On aurait pu surprendre les mots tels que: 'Ah, c'est ainsi que tu l'entends, oui, je comprends, j'y prendrai garde, sois-en sûr!' Ou encore simplement: 'Oui! ... oui! ...'. ... Il fallait payer ainsi son tribut à l'instrument infâme. ... Les mécanisations de cette catégorie—cinéma, phonographe, ou toute autre combinaison de même sorte ... —posent à la nouvelle Présence un problème ...: acceptons-nous ce viol ou le désavouons-nous? ... Désavouer la mécanisation n'est possible à personne." Appia, *Œuvres* IV:173 (on his *L'Œuvre d'art vivant* and mechanization), IV:174–8 ("Mécanisation"). For the rest of the fragment from *Tristan und Isolde* ("... gieb Vergessen, | daß ich lebe"), see Wagner, *Sämtliche* VII:44.

2. See Brewster and Jacobs, *Theatre* 27 (on *Pluck* and train wrecks); Brockett and Findlay, *Century* 12 (on horse races and treadmills); Campardon, *Les spectacles de la foire: théâtres, acteurs, sauteurs et danseurs de corde, monstres, géants, nains, animaux curieux ou savants, marionnettes, automates, figures de cire et jeux mécaniques* (1877); Garelick, "Electric" on Loie Fuller; and Meisel, *Realizations* and Rhode, *History* 3–27 on Dioramas, Panopticans, and light boxes in general.

3. Appelbaum, ed., *Scenes* p. ix.

4. Rhode, *History* 3–27 (and, for additional items on this list, I am grateful to Philippe Willems).

5. "Il libro, mezzo assolutamente passatista di conservare e comunicare il pensiero, [e] destinato a scomparire ... statico compagno dei sedentari." Futurist films "rompono i limiti della letteratura." Marinetti, *Teoria* 138, 141; trans. Kirby, *Futurist* 212, 214 ("La cinematografia futurista" (1916), written collectively by Marinetti, Bruno Corra, Emilio Settimelli, Arnaldo Ginna, Giacomo Balla, and Remo Chiti).

6. "Il Teatro di Varietà ... collabora alla distruzione futurista dei capolavori immortali." Marinetti, *Teoria* 86 ("Il Teatro di Varietà"); trans. Kirby, *Futurist* 183.

7. "Nato con noi dall'elettricità, non ha fortunatamente, tradizione alcuna, né maestri, né dogmi, e si nutre di attualità veloce." Marinetti, *Teoria* 81 ("Il Teatro di Varietà"); trans. Kirby, *Futurist* 179.

8. "On doit en finir avec cette superstition des textes et de la poésie *écrite*." "Le théâtre tel que nous le concevons en Occident a partie liée avec le texte." "On peut brûler la bibliothèque d'Alexandrie. Au-dessus et en dehors des papyrus, il y a des forces." "Que les poètes morts laissent la place aux autres." "Ce langage de la mise en scène considéré comme le langage théâtral pur." "Cris, plaintes, apparitions, surprises, coups de théâtre de toutes sortes, beauté magique des costumes pris à certains modèles rituels." Artaud, *Œuvres* IV:76, 66–7, 11, 90 ("Théâtre oriental et théâtre occidental"; "En finir avec les chefs-d'œuvre"; preface; "Le théâtre de la cruauté"); trans. Artaud, *Theater* 78, 68–9, 10, 93.

9. Carter, *New* (1925) 238.

10. Shaw, *Bernard Shaw* 18–19 ("What the Films May Do to the Drama" (1915)).

11. For English examples, see *Revels* VII:37.

12. "Ce n'est pas le Cirque que nous avons chassé de cette salle, c'est le cinéma. Notre réussite est la première revanche du théâtre sur son adversaire[!]" Qtd. Blanchart, *Firmin Gémier* 228.

13. "Perchè il Cinematografo trionfa? ... Esso vince perchè è veloce, perchè si muove e si trasforma rapidamente." Depero, *Fortunato Depero* 59 ("Appunti sul teatro"); trans. Kirby, *Futurist* 209.

14. "On comprend que l'élite s'en détourne [du théâtre] et que le gros de la foule aille chercher au cinéma, au music-hall ou au cirque, des satisfactions violentes." Artaud, *Œuvres* IV:82 ("Le théâtre de la cruauté"); trans. Artaud, *Theater* 84. See, similarly, Meyerhold's comments on the general cultural view that there had been "a victory for the cinema over the theatre" in Meyerhold, *Meyerhold* 254–5, 262.

15. "Sostituendo la rivista (sempre pedantesca), il dramma (sempre previsto) e uccidendo il libro (sempre tedioso e opprimente). ... Preferiamo ... il cinematografo ... i mobili avvisi luminosi." Marinetti, *Teoria* 139; trans. Kirby, *Futurist* 212 ("La cinematografia futurista").

16. "Il Teatro ... utilizza oggi il cinematografo, che lo arricchisce d'un numero incalcolabile di visioni e di spettacoli irrealizzabili (battaglie, tumulti, corse, circuiti d'automobili e d'aeroplani. ... Il *meraviglioso futurista* [è] prodotto dal meccanismo moderno." Marinetti, *Teoria* 81–2 ("Il Teatro di Varietà"); trans. Kirby, *Futurist* 179–80.

17. Meyerhold, *Meyerhold* 254–6 ("The Reconstruction of the Theatre" (1930)).

18. Shaw, *Bernard Shaw* 19, 17, 71 ("What the Films May Do to the Drama" (1915); "Shaw Asserts Theatre Is Lost" (1930)). See, similarly, "A Theatrical Revolution" (1912), "The Living Talkies" (1929), and "Relation of the Cinema to the Theatre" (1932): Shaw, *Bernard Shaw* 4–5, 59–62, 79–81.

19. Beckett, *Krapp's* 28.

20. "Palcoscenico ... ampliata in tutti i sensi elettrici e meccanici." Depero, *Fortunato Depero* 58 ("Appunti sul teatro"); trans. Kirby, *Futurist* 207.

21. "Une foule que les catastrophes de chemins de fer font trembler, qui connaît les tremblements de terre, la peste, la révolution, la guerre," "le rythme épileptique et grossier de ce temps." Artaud, *Œuvres* IV:73 ("En finir avec les chefs-d'œuvre"); trans. Artaud, 75.

Works Cited

ADDISON, JOSEPH. *The Drummer; or, the Haunted-House*. 2nd edn. London: John Darby, 1722.

AGNEW, JEAN-CHRISTOPHE. *Worlds Apart: The Market and the Theater in Anglo-American Thought, 1550–1750*. Cambridge: Cambridge UP, 1986.

AGRICOLA, JOHANN. *Tragedia Johannis Huss*. Wittenberg: George Rhaw, 1537.

AITKEN, GEORGE A. *The Life of Richard Steele*. 2 vols. London: Wm. Isbister, 1889.

ALBERTI, LEON BATTISTA. *On the Art of Building in Ten Books*. Trans. Joseph Rykwert, Neil Leach, and Robert Tavernor. Cambridge, Mass.: MIT, 1988.

—— *L'architettura . . . Testo latino e traduzione*. Ed. Giovanni Orlandi and Paolo Portoghesi. Trans. Giovanni Orlandi. 2 vols. Milan: Polifilo, 1966.

ALBRIGHT, EVELYN MAY. *Dramatic Publication in England, 1580–1640: A Study of Conditions Affecting Content and Form of Drama*. London: Oxford UP, 1927.

—— "'To Be Staied.'" *PMLA* 30: 3 (1915): 451–501.

ALEMÁN, MATEO. *The Roghe: or The Second Part of the Life of Guzman de Alfarache*. London: Edward Blount, 1623.

ALTICK, RICHARD D. *The English Common Reader: A Social History of the Mass Reading Public, 1800–1900*. 2nd edn. Columbus: Ohio State UP, 1998.

ANDERSON, MICHAEL. "The Changing Scene: Plays and Playhouses in the Italian Renaissance." J. R. Mulryne and Margaret Shewring, eds. *Theatre of the English and Italian Renaissance*. London: Macmillan, 1991. 3–20.

ANDREINI, FRANCESCO. *Le bravure del Capitano Spavento; Divise in molti ragionamenti in forma di dialogo*. Venice: Giacomo Antonio Somasco, 1607.

ANDREINI, ISABELLA. *Mirtilla pastorale d'Isabella Andreini comica gelosa*. Verona: Girolamo Discepolo, 1588.

ANDREWS, RICHARD. *Scripts and Scenarios*. Cambridge: Cambridge UP, 1993.

—— "Written Texts and Performed Texts in Italian Renaissance Comedy." J. R. Dashwood and J. E. Everson, eds. *Writers and Performers in Italian Drama from the Time of Dante to Pirandello*. Lewiston, NY: Edwin Mellen, 1991. 75–94.

APPELBAUM, STANLEY, ed. *Scenes from the Nineteenth-Century Stage in Advertising Woodcuts*. New York: Dover, 1977.

APPIA, ADOLPHE. *Œuvres complètes*. Ed. Marie L. Bablet-Hahn. 4 vols. [Lausanne]: Age d'homme, 1983–91.

ARBER, EDWARD, ed. *A Transcript of the Registers of the Company of Stationers of London; 1554–1640 A.D.* 5 vols. London: n.p., 1875–94.

ARCHER, STANLEY. "The Epistle Dedicatory in Restoration Drama." *Restoration and Eighteenth-Century Theatre Research* 10:1 (1971): 8–13.

ARCHER, WILLIAM. *The Old Drama and the New: An Essay in Re-Valuation*. Boston: Small, Maynard, 1923.

ARETINO, PIETRO. *Tutte le opere di Pietro Aretino: Teatro*. Ed. Giorgio Petrocchi. Milan: Arnoldo Mondadori, 1971.

—— *Quattro comedie del divino Pietro Aretino*. London: J. Wolfe, 1588.

Ariosto, Lodovico. *La Cassaria . . . Da Lui Medesimo Riformata, Et Ridotta In Versi.* Venice: Gabriel Giolito de'Ferrari, 1560.

Aristophanes. *Aristophanis comoediae novem.* Venice: Aldo Manuzio, 1498.

Aristotle. *The Poetics of Aristotle: Translation and Commentary.* Trans. Stephen Halliwell. Chapel Hill: U of North Carolina P, 1987.

Armin, Robert. *History of the Two Maids of More-Clacke.* London: Thomas Archer, 1609.

Armour, Peter. "Comedy and the Origins of Italian Theatre around the Time of Dante." J. R. Dashwood and J. E. Everson, eds. *Writers and Performers in Italian Drama from the Time of Dante to Pirandello.* Lewiston, NY: Edwin Mellen, 1991. 1–31.

Armstrong, Elizabeth. *Before Copyright: The French Book-Privilege System 1498–1526.* Cambridge: Cambridge UP, 1990.

Arnaud, Charles. *Étude sur la vie et les oeuvres de l'Abbé d'Aubignac et sur les théories dramatiques au XVIIᵉ siècle.* Paris: Alphonse Picard, 1887.

Artaud, Antonin. *Œuvres complètes.* 22 vols. 2nd edn. Paris: Gallimard, 1978.

——— *The Theater and its Double.* Trans. Mary Caroline Richards. New York: Grove, 1958.

Aubrun, C. V. *La Comédie espagnole (1600–1680).* Paris: PUF, 1966.

Austin, Gilbert. *Chironomia; or a Treatise on Rhetorical Delivery.* London: T. Cadell and W. Davies, 1806.

Avenel, George d'. *Les Revenus d'un intellectuel de 1200 à 1913.* Paris: Flammarion, 1922.

Averroës. "The Middle Commentary of Averroës of Cordova on the *Poetics* of Aristotle." Trans. O. B. Hardison, Jr. *Classical and Medieval Literary Criticism: Translations and Interpretations.* Ed. Alex Preminger *et al.* New York: Frederick Ungar, 1974. 349–382.

Ayrer, Jakob. *Ayrers Dramen.* Ed. Adelbert von Keller. 5 vols. Stuttgart: Litterarischer Vereins, 1865.

——— *Opus Thaeatricum.* Nuremberg: Balthasar Scherffen, 1618.

Ayres Victoria, Henrique. *Tragedia da vingança que foy feita sobre a morte del rey Agamenon.* Lisbon: Germão Galharde, 1555.

Backscheider, Paula R., and Timothy Dykstal, eds. *The Intersections of the Public and Private Spheres in Early Modern England.* London: F. Cass, 1996.

Bacon, Francis. *The Works of Francis Bacon.* Ed. James Spedding *et al.* 15 vols. New York: Hurd & Houghton, 1963–4.

Baillie, Joanna. *The Dramatic and Poetical Works of Joanna Baillie.* 2nd edn. London: Longman, Brown, Green, and Longmans, 1851.

Baker, Donald C. "When is a Text a Play? Reflections upon What Certain Late Medieval Dramatic Texts Can Tell Us." *Contexts for Early English Drama.* Ed. Marianne G. Briscoe and John C. Coldewey. Bloomington: Indiana UP, 1989. 20–41.

Bale, John. *A Tragedie or Enterlude, Manifesting the Chiefe Promises of God vnto Man.* London: John Charlewoode for Stephen Peele, 1577.

Balmas, Enea, and Michel Dassonville, eds. *La tragédie à l'époque d'Henri II et de Charles IX. Théâtre français de la Renaissance.* 7 vols. Florence: Leo S. Olschki, 1986– .

Barish, Jonas. *The Antitheatrical Prejudice.* Berkeley: U of California P, 1981.

Barker, Nicolas. "Manuscript into Print." *Crisis in Editing: Texts of the English Renaissance.* Ed. Randall McLeod. New York: AMS, 1994. 1–18.

Barrera y Leirado, Cayetano Alberto de la. *Catálogo bibliográfico y biográfico del teatro antiguo español desde sus orígenes hasta mediados del siglo XVIII.* Madrid: M. Rivadeneyra, 1860. London: Tamesis, 1968.

Baruth, Philip E., ed. *Introducing Charlotte Charke: Actress, Author, Enigma.* Urbana: U of Illinois P, 1998.

BASKERVILLE, C. R. "A Prompt Copy of *A Looking Glass for London and England*," *Modern Philology* 30 (1932): 29–51.

BASORE, JOHN WILLIAM. *The Scholia on Hypokrisis in the Commentary of Donatus*. Baltimore: J. H. Furst, 1908.

BEAUJOYEULX, BALTASAR DE. *Le Balet comique de la royne 1581*. Trans. Carol and Lander MacClintock. [Leawood, Kan.]: American Institute of Musicology, 1971.

—— *Balet comique de la royne*. Paris: Adrian le Roy, Robert Ballard & Mamert Patisson, 1582.

BEAUMARCHAIS, PIERRE-AUGUSTIN-CARON DE. *Avis aux Personnes qui ont des Ecrits particuliers des Pièces fugitives ou des Lettres de M. de Voltaire*. [Kehl: Société littéraire-typographique], 1780.

—— *La Folle Journée, ou Le Mariage de Figaro*. [Kehl]: Société littéraire-typographique, 1785.

—— *Œuvres*. Ed. Jacqueline Larthomas. Paris: Gallimard, 1988.

BEAUMONT, FRANCIS. *Poems: By Francis Beaumont, Gent. . . .* London: Laurence Blaiklock, 1653.

——and JOHN FLETCHER. *Comedies and Tragedies*. London: Humphrey Robinson and Humphrey Moseley, 1647.

—— *The Works of Mr. Francis Beaumont, and Mr. John Fletcher*. 7 vols. London: Jacob Tonson, 1711.

—— *The Dramatic Works in the Beaumont and Fletcher Canon*. Ed. Fredson Bowers. 10 vols. New York: Cambridge UP, 1966–96.

BECKETT, SAMUEL. *Krapp's Last Tape and Other Dramatic Pieces*. New York: Grove, 1958.

BEHN, APHRA. *The Works of Aphra Behn*. Ed. Janet Todd. 7 vols. Columbus: Ohio State UP, 1992.

—— *The Rover, or, The Banish't Cavaliers*. London: John Amery, 1677.

BEIJER, AGNE, and P. L. DUCHARTRE, eds. *Recueil de plusieurs fragments des premières comédies italiennes qui ont esté représentées en France soul le règne de Henry III: Recueil dit de Fossard*. Paris: Duchartre et Van Buggenhoudt, 1928.

BELLOY, PIERRE-LAURENT DE. *Le Siége de Calais*. Paris: la Veuve Duchesne, 1769.

Bell's British Theatre. 20 vols. London: John Bell, 1776–8.

BENGESCO, GEORGES. *Voltaire: Bibliographie de ses oeuvres*. 3 vols. Paris: Emile Perrin, 1882–5.

BENJAMIN, WALTER. *The Origin of German Tragic Drama*. Trans. John Osborne. London: Verso, 1977.

BENNETT, H. S. *English Books and Readers*. 3 vols. Cambridge: Cambridge UP, 1989.

BENTLEY, ERIC, ed. *The Genius of the Italian Theater*. New York: New American Library, 1964.

BENTLEY, GERALD EADES. *The Profession of Dramatist in Shakespeare's Time 1590–1642*. Princeton: Princeton UP, 1971.

BEOLCO, ANGELO. *Due dialogi di Ruzzante in lingua rustica, sententiosi, arguti, et ridiculosissimi*. Venice: Stefano de Aleβi, all Libraria dal Cavalletto, 1551.

—— *Teatro*. Ed. Ludovico Zorzi. Giulio Einaudi, 1967.

—— *Tutte le opere del famosissimo Ruzante*. Venice: G. Greco, 1584.

BERGMAN, HANNAH E. "Calderón en Sevilla: Apuntes bibliográficos: Investigación en curso." Alfred González, Marshall R. Nason, and Mary Elizabeth Brooks, eds. *Estudios sobre el Siglo de Oro en homenaje a Raymond R. MacCurdy*. Albuquerque: U of New Mexico, Dept. of Modern and Classical Languages, 1983: 125–33.

——and SZILVIA E. SZMUK. *A Catalogue of Comedias Sueltas in the New York Public Library*. London: Grant & Cutler, 1980.

BERNARD, JOHN. *Retrospections of the Stage.* Ed. William Bayle Baernard. 2 vols. London: H. Colburn and R. Bentley, 1830.

BERNI, FRANCESCO. *Il primo libro del l'opere Burlesche, di M. Francesco Berni.* Florence: Giunti, 1552.

BEVINGTON, DAVID. *From 'Mankind' to Marlowe: Growth of Structure in the Popular Drama of Tudor England.* Cambridge: Harvard UP, 1962.

—— *Medieval Drama.* Boston: Houghton Mifflin, 1975.

BEYS, CHARLES. *Les Illustres fous. Johns Hopkins Studies in Romance Literatures and Languages* 42 (1942): 53–174.

BÈZE, THEODORE DE. *Abraham sacrifiant.* Lausanne: Conrad Badius, 1550.

BIBLIOTHÈQUE NATIONALE. *Comédies de Térence: reproduction des 151 dessins du manuscrit Latin 7899 de la Bibliothèque Nationale.* Paris: Imprimerie Berthaud Frères, [1907].

BIDERMANN, JAKOB. *Ludi theatrales sacri, sive, Opera comica posthuma.* 2 vols. in 1. Munich: Joannis Wagner, 1666.

BIRRELL, T. A. "The Influence of Seventeenth-Century Publishers on the Presentation of English Literature." *Historical and Editorial Studies in Medieval and Early Modern English.* Ed. Mary-Jo Arn and Hanneke Wirjes, with Hans Jansen. Groningen: Wolters Noordhoff, 1985. 163–73.

BLACKMORE, Sir RICHARD. *A Satyr Against Wit.* London: Samuel Crouch, 1700.

BLAGDEN, CYPRIAN. *The Stationers' Company.* Cambridge, Mass.: Harvard UP, 1960.

BLAKE, N. F. "Manuscript to Print." Jeremy Griffiths and Derek Pearsall, eds. *Production and Publishing in Britain, 1375–1475.* Cambridge: Cambridge UP, 1989. 403–32.

BLANCHART, PAUL. *Firmin Gémier.* Paris: L'Arche, 1954.

BLANK, PAULA. *Broken English: Dialects and the Politics of Language in Renaissance Writings.* London: Routledge, 1996.

BLAYNEY, PETER W. M. "The Publication of Playbooks." John D. Cox and David Scott Kastan, eds. *A New History of Early English Drama.* New York: Columbia UP, 1997. 383–422.

—— "Shakespeare's Fight With What Pirates?" Unpublished typescript.

BLUMENTHAL, ARTHUR R. *Italian Renaissance Festival Designs.* Madison: Elvehjem Art Center, University of Wisconsin-Madison, 1973.

—— *Theater Art of the Medici.* Hanover, NH: Dartmouth College Museum and Galleries, 1980.

BOADEN, JAMES. *Memoirs of the Life of John Philip Kemble, Esq.* 2 vols. London: Longman, 1825.

—— *Memoirs of Mrs. Inchbald.* London: R. Bentley, 1833.

BOAS, F. S. *University Drama in the Tudor Age.* Oxford, Clarendon: 1914.

BOCCACCIO, GIOVANNI. *Boccaccio In Defence of Poetry: Genealogiae Deorum Gentilium Liber XIV.* Ed. Jeremiah Reedy. Toronto: Centre for Medieval Studies, 1978.

BODLEY, THOMAS. *Letters of Sir Thomas Bodley to Thomas James First Keeper of the Bodleian Library.* Ed. G. W. Wheeler. Oxford: Clarendon, 1926.

BOGGESS, WILLIAM F. "Aristotle's Poetics in the Fourteenth Century." *Studies in Philology* 67 (1970): 278–94.

BOILEAU DESPRÉAUX, NICOLAS. *Oeuvres complètes.* Ed. Françoise Escal. Paris: Gallimard, 1966.

BONARELLI, GUIDUBALDO. *Filli di Sciro.* Venice: Bernardo Giunti and Giovanni Batista Ciotti, 1609.

—— *Opere del Co: Guid'Ubaldo Bonarelli della Rovere.* Rome: Ludovico Grignani, 1640.

BONCOMPAIN, JACQUES. *Auteurs et comédiens au XVIIIe siècle.* Paris: Libraire Académique Perrin, 1976.

——"Les deux cent ans de la Société des auteurs." *Revue d'histoire du théâtre* 29 (1977): 57–70.

BONINO, GUIDO DAVICO, ed. *Il teatro italiano.* 6 vols. Torino: Einaudi, 1977.

BONNASSIES, JULES. *Les Auteurs dramatiques et les théâtres de province au XVIIe et XVIIIe siècles.* Paris: Léon Willem, 1875.

BOOTH, MICHAEL R. *Theatre in the Victorian Age.* Cambridge: Cambridge UP, 1991.

BOST, HUBERT. *Babel: Du texte au symbole.* Geneva: Labor et Fides, 1985.

BOSWELL, ELEANORE. *The Restoration Court Stage (1660–1702) With a Particular Account of the Production of Calisto.* Cambridge, Mass.: Harvard UP, 1932.

——and E. K. CHAMBERS, eds. "Dramatic Records: The Lord Chamberlain's Office." *Collections* (Malone Society) II.3 (1931): 321–416.

BOWERS, FREDSON. *Essays in Bibliography, Text, and Editing.* Charlottesville: UP of Virginia, 1975.

BOYER, MILDRED VINSON. *The Texas Collection of "Comedias Sueltas": A Descriptive Bibliography.* Boston: G. K. Hall, 1978.

BRADEN, GORDON. *Renaissance Tragedy and the Senecan Tradition: Anger's Privilege.* New Haven: Yale UP, 1985.

BRANDT, GEORGE W., ed. *German and Dutch Theatre, 1600–1848.* Cambridge: Cambridge UP, 1993.

BRENNER, CLARENCE D. *Bibliographical List of Plays in French 1700–89.* Berkeley: U of California, Berkeley: 1947.

BRETTLE, ROBERT E. "Bibliographical Notes on Some Marston Quartos and Early Collected Editions." *The Library* (4th ser.) 8:3 (Dec. 1927): 336–48.

BREWSTER, BEN, and LEA JACOBS. *Theatre to Cinema: Stage Pictorialism and the Early Feature Film.* Oxford: Oxford UP, 1997.

BROCKETT, OSCAR G., and ROBERT R. FINDLAY. *Century of Innovation: A History of European and American Theatre and Drama Since 1870.* Englewood Cliffs, NJ: Prentice Hall, 1973.

BROME, RICHARD. *The Antipodes.* Ed. Ann Haaker. Lincoln: U Nebraska P, 1966.

BROOKS, DOUGLAS A. *From Playhouse to Printing House: Drama and Authorship in Early Modern England.* Cambridge: Cambridge UP, 2000.

BROWN, CYNTHIA J. "The Confrontation Between Printer and Author in Early Sixteenth-Century France: Another Example of Michel Le Noir's Unethical Printing Practices," *Bibliothèque d'humanisme et renaissance* 53 (1991): 105–18.

——*Poets, Patrons, and Printers: Crisis of Authority in Late Medieval France.* Ithaca, NY: Cornell UP, 1995.

BROWN, FREDERICK. *Theater and Revolution: The Culture of the French Stage.* New York: Viking, 1980.

BROWN, GREGORY S. "After the Fall: The *Chute* of a Play, *Droits d'auteur*, and Literary Property in the Old Regime," *French Historical Studies* 22:4 (Fall 1999): 465–91.

——"A Field of Honor: The Cultural Politics of Playwrighting in Eighteenth-Century France." Diss. Columbia U, 1997.

BRUNO, GIORDANO. *Opere italiane.* Ed. Giovanni Gentile and Vincenzo Spampanato. 3 vols. Bari: G. Laterza, 1923–7.

BRYLINGER, NICHOLAS. *Comoediae ac tragoediae aliquot ex novo et vetere testamento desumptae.* Basel: Nicolaum Brylingerum, 1540.

BUCHANAN, MILTON A. "Notes on Calderón: The Vera Tassis Edition; The Text of *La Vida es Sueño*," *Modern Language Notes* 22:5 (1907): 148–50.

Buch und Sammler: Private und öffentliche Bibliotheken im 18. Jahrhundert. Heidelberg: n.p. 1979.

BUCKINGHAM, GEORGE VILLIERS, Duke of. *The Rehearsal.* 3rd edn. London: Thomas Dring, 1675.

BUCKLEY, MATTHEW STEFAN. "The Illusion of Politics: The French Revolution and the Emergence of Modern Drama." Diss. Columbia U, 1999.

BÜHLER, CURT F. *The Fifteenth-Century Book.* Philadelphia: U of Pennsylvania P, 1960.

BULWER, JOHN. *Chirologia: or, The Natural Language of the Hand.* London: Thomas Harper and R. Whitaker, 1644.

—— *Chirologia: or, The Natural Language of the Hand, and Chironomia: or, The Art of Manual Rhetoric.* Ed. James W. Cleary. Carbondale: Southern Illinois UP, 1974.

BUNCH, WILLIAM A. *Jean Mairet.* Boston: G. K. Hall, 1975.

BURKE, PETER. *Popular Culture in Early Modern Europe.* New York: Harper, 1978.

BURLING, WILLIAM J. "British Plays, 1697–1737: Premieres, Datings, Attributions, and Publication Information." *Studies in Bibliography* 43 (1990): 164–82.

BUTLER, MARTIN. *Theatre and Crisis 1632–1642.* Cambridge: Cambridge UP, 1984.

CAIN, JULIEN, ROBERT ESCARPIT, and HENRI-JEAN MARTIN, eds. *Le Livre français: 1972 Année internationale du Livre.* Paris: Imprimerie Nationale, 1972.

CALDERÓN DE LA BARCA, PEDRO. *Comedias escogidas de Don Pedro Calderón de la Barca.* [Ed. Agustín Durán.] 4 vols. Madrid: Ortega y Compania, 1826–33.

—— *Los cabellos de Absalon de Don Pedro Calderon de la Barca.* [Madrid]: n.p. [*c*.1680].

—— *La Hija del Ayre, Parte Primera.* [Madrid]: n.p. [*c*.1680].

—— *Obras completas: Autos sacramentales.* Ed. Angel Valbuena Prat. Madrid: Aguilar, 1952.

—— *Primera Parte de Comedias de don Pedro Calderón de la Barca.* Ed. A. Valbuena Briones. 2 vols. Madrid: Consejo superior de investigaciones científicas, 1974–81.

—— *Verdadera quinta parte de comedias de Don Pedro Calderon de la Barca.* Madrid: Francisco Sanz, 1682.

CALDICOTT, C. E. J. *La Carrière de Molière entre protecteurs et éditeurs.* Amsterdam: Rodopi, 1998.

CALHOUN, CRAIG, ed. *Habermas and the Public Sphere.* Cambridge, Mass.: MIT, 1992.

CALLOT, JACQUES. *Callot's Etchings.* Ed. Howard Daniel. New York: Dover, 1974.

CALRO ASENSIO, PEDRO. *La Escala de la Fortuna.* Madrid: L. Cordon, 1848.

CAMPARDON, EMILE, ed. *Les Comédiens du roi de la troupe italienne pendant les deux dernier siècles: documents inédits recueillis aux Archives Nationales.* 2 vols. Paris: Berger-Levrault, 1880.

—— *Les Spectacles de la foire.* Paris: Berger-Levrault, 1877.

CANNONE, BELINDA. *Philosophies de la musique 1752–1789.* Paris: Amateurs de livres/ Klincksieck, 1990.

CAREW, RICHARD. *The Survey of Cornwall Written by Richard Carew of Antonie, Esquire.* London: John Jaggard, 1602.

CARLSON, JULIE A. *In the Theatre of Romanticism: Coleridge, Nationalism, Women.* Cambridge: Cambridge UP, 1994.

CARLSON, MARVIN. *Places of Performance: The Semiotics of Theatre Architecture.* Ithaca, NY: Cornell UP, 1989.

—— *The Theatre of the French Revolution.* Ithaca, NY: Cornell UP, 1966.

—— *Theories of Theatre.* Ithaca, NY: Cornell UP, 1984.

CARO, ANNIBAL. *Gli Straccioni*. Borsellino, ed. *Commedie del cinquecento*. 2 vols. Milan: Feltrinelli, 1967. II:193–279.

CARTER, HUNTLY. *The New Spirit in the European Theatre, 1914–1924; A Comparative Study of the Changes Effected by the War and Revolution*. London: E. Benn, 1925.

CARTWRIGHT, WILLIAM. *Comedies, Tragi-comedies, With other Poems*. London: Humphrey Moseley, 1651.

CASEY, EDWARD S. *Remembering: A Phenomenological Study*. Bloomington: Indiana UP, 1987.

CASTELLANI, CASTELLANO. *Rappresentatione del figliuolo prodigo*. Florence: Zanobi da la Barba, [*c.*1500].

CASTELVETRO, LODOVICO. *Poetica d'Aristotele Vulgarizata e Sposta*. 2 vols. Ed. Wether Romani. Rome: Laterza, 1979.

——*Castelvetro on the Art of Poetry: An Abridged Translation of Lodovico Castelvetro's Poetica d'Aristotele Vulgarizzata e Sposta*. Ed. and trans. Andrew Bongiorno. Binghamton: Medieval and Renaissance Texts and Studies, 1984.

CASTRO, GUILLÉN DE. *El curioso impertinente*. Ed. Christiane Faliu-Lacourt and María Luisa Lobato. Kassel: Reichenberger, 1991.

——*Primera parte de las comedias de Don Guillen de Castro*. Valencia: Felipe Mey, 1621.

CATACH, NINA, *L'Orthographe française à l'époque de la Renaissance (auteurs, imprimeurs, ateliers d'imprimerie)*. Geneva: Droz, 1968.

CAVE, TERENCE. *The Cornucopian Text: Problems of Writing in the French Renaissance*. Oxford: Clarendon, 1979.

CAVENDISH, MARGARET. *Plays, Never before Printed*. London: A. Maxwell, 1668.

CAWLEY, A. C., and MARTIN STEVENS, eds. *The Towneley Cycle: A Facsimile of Huntington MS HM1*. Leeds: U of Leeds School of English, 1976.

CECCHI, GIOVANMARIA. *Comedie di M. Gianmaria Cecchi Fiorentino*. Venice: Bernardo Giunti, 1585.

CENTLIVRE, SUSANNA. *The Plays of Susanna Centlivre*. Ed. Richard Frushell. 3 vols. Garland: New York, 1982.

CERTEAU, MICHEL DE. *L'Écriture de l'histoire*. Paris: Gallimard, 1975.

CERVANTES SAAVEDRA, MIGUEL DE. *Obras completas de Miguel de Cervantes*. 4 vols. Genoa and Madrid: Biblioteca Castro, 1993.

——*Ocho comedias y ocho entremeses nuevos*. Madrid: J. de Villarroel, 1615. Madrid: R.A.F., 1923.

CHAMBERS, D. S., and F. QUIVIGER, eds. *Italian Academies of the Sixteenth Century*. London: Warburg Institute, 1995.

CHAMBERS, E. K. *The Elizabethan Stage*. 4 vols. Oxford: Clarendon, 1923.

——*The Mediaeval Stage*. 2 vols. 1903. Oxford: Oxford UP, 1963.

——"Plays of the King's Men in 1641." *Collections* (Malone Society) I:4–5 (1911): 364–9.

CHAPMAN, GEORGE. *The Plays of George Chapman*. Eds. Allan Holaday and Michael Kiernan. 2 vols. Urbana: U of Illinois P, 1970.

CHAPPUIS, GABRIEL. *Les Mondes celestes, terrestres, et infernaux*. Lyon: Barthelemy Honorati, 1583.

CHAPPUZEAU, SAMUEL. *Le Cercle des femmes et L'Academie des femmes*. Ed. Joan Crow. Exeter: U of Exeter, 1983.

——*Le Théatre François*. Ed. Georges Monval. Paris: Jules Bonnassies, 1875.

CHARKE, CHARLOTTE. *A Narrative of the Life of Mrs. Charlotte Charke*. 2nd edn. London: W. Reeve, A. Dodd, and E. Cook, 1755.

CHARTIER, ROGER. "Book Markets and Reading in France at the End of the Old Regime."

Publishing and Readership in Revolutionary France and America. Westport, Conn.: Greenwood, 1993. 117–36.

—— *The Cultural Origins of the French Revolution*. Trans. Lydia G. Cochrane. Durham, NC: Duke UP, 1991.

—— "Culture as Appropriation: Popular Cultural Uses in Early Modern France." Steven L. Kaplan, ed. *Understanding Popular Culture: Europe from the Middle Ages to the Nineteenth Century*. Berlin: Mouton, 1984. 229–53.

—— *Forms and Meanings: Texts, Performances, and Audiences from Codex to Computer*. Philadelphia: U of Pennsylvania P, 1995.

—— *L'Ordre des livres: lecteurs, auteurs, bibliothèques en Europe entre XVIᵉ et XVIIIᵉ siècle*. Aix-en-Provence: Alinea, 1992.

—— "Publishing Drama in Early Modern Europe." [Panizzi Lectures, British Library, 1998]. Unpublished typescript.

—— "Texts, Printing, Readings." *The New Cultural History*. Ed. Lynn Hunt. Berkeley: U of California P, 1989: 154–75.

CHAUCER, GEOFFREY. *The Complete Works of Geoffrey Chaucer*. Ed. Walter W. Skeat. 7 vols. Oxford: Clarendon, 1972.

CHAYTOR, H. J. *From Script to Print: An Introduction to Medieval Vernacular Literature*. 1945. London: Sidgwick & Jackson, 1966.

CHENIER, MARIE-JOSEPH. *Œuvres*. 5 vols. Paris: Guillaume, 1824–6.

CHENU, M.-D. "Auctor, actor, autor." *Bulletin du Cange—Archivum Latinitatis Medii Aevi* 3 (1927): 81–6.

Chester Mystery Cycle. Ed. R. M. Lumiansky and David Mills. London: Oxford UP, 1974.

CHETTLE, HENRIE, and WILLIAM KEMP. *Kind-Hartes Dreame (1592); Nine Daies Wonder (1600)*. Ed. G. B. Harrison. New York: Barnes & Noble, 1966.

CHONÉ, PAULETTE, ed. *Jacques Callot 1592–1635*. Paris: Editions de la Réunion des musées nationaux, 1992.

CHRISMAN, MIRIAM USHER. *Lay Culture, Learned Culture: Books and Social Change in Strasbourg, 1480–1599*. New Haven: Yale UP, 1982.

CIBBER, COLLEY. *An Apology for the Life of Colley Cibber*. Ed. B. R. S. Fone. Ann Arbor: U of Michigan P, 1968.

—— *The Dramatic Works of Colley Cibber, Esq.* 5 vols. London: J. Rivington *et al.*, 1777. New York: AMS, 1966.

—— *The Tragical History of King Richard III*. London: B. Lintott and A. Bettesworth [1700].

—— *Ximena; or, the Heroick Daughter*. London: B. Lintot, A. Bettesworth, and W. Chetwood, 1719.

CIBBER, THEOPHILUS. *The Harlot's Progress: or, the Ridotto Al Fresco*. London: for the benefit of Richard Cross, 1733.

CLAIR, COLIN. *A History of Printing in Britain*. New York: Oxford UP, 1966.

CLAIRON, HYPPOLITE. *Mémoires d'Hyppolite Clairon, et réflexions sur l'art dramatique*. Paris: F. Buisson [1799].

—— *Memoirs of Hyppolite Clairon, the Celebrated French Actress: with Reflections upon the Dramatic Art*. 2 vols. London: G. G. and J. Robinson, 1800.

CLANCHY, M. T. *From Memory to Written Record: England 1066–1307*. London: Edward Arnold, 1979.

CLAVERET, JEAN. *Le Ravissement de Proserpine*. Paris: Antoine de Sommaville, 1640.

CLUBB, LOUISE GEORGE. *Italian Drama in Shakespeare's Time*. New Haven: Yale UP, 1989.

CLUBB, LOUISE GEORGE. *Italian Plays in the Folger Library (1500–1700): A Bibliography with Introduction*. Florence: Leo S. Olschki, 1968.

COHEN, GUSTAVE. *Le Théâtre en France au moyen age*. 2 vols. Paris: Rider, 1928–31.

COLERIDGE, SAMUEL TAYLOR. *Collected Works*. 11 vols. Princeton: Princeton UP, 1969– .

——*Literary Remains*. Ed. Henry Nelson Coleridge. New York: Harper, 1853.

COLLINS, A. S. *Authorship in the Days of Johnson: Being a Study of the Relation between Author, Patron, Publisher and Public 1726–1780*. 1927. Clifton: Augustus M. Kelley, 1973.

COLMAN, GEORGE. *New Hay at the Old Market; An Occasional Drama in One Act*. London: W. Woodfall for T. Cadell and W. Davies, 1795.

——*Polly Honeycombe*. London: T. Becket and T. Davies, 1760.

——*Ut Pictura Poesis!* London: T. Cadell, 1789.

CONDORCET, MARIE-JEAN-ANTOINE, MARQUIS DE. *Esquisse d'un tableau historique des progrès de l'esprit humain*. Ed. Monique and François Hincker. Paris: Editions Sociales, 1966.

CONDILLAC, ETIENNE BONNOT DE. *Oeuvres complètes*. 23 vols. Paris: C. Houel, 1798.

CONGREVE, WILLIAM. *The Complete Plays of William Congreve*. Ed. Herbert Davis. Chicago: U of Chicago P, 1967.

——*Letters and Documents*. Ed. John C. Hodges. London: Macmillan, 1964.

——*The Works of Mr. William Congreve*. 3 vols. London: Jacob Tonson, 1710.

COOKE, JOHN. *Greene's Tu Quoque or, The Cittie Gallant*. Ed. Alan J. Berman. New York: Garland, 1984.

CORBETT, MARGERY, and RONALD LIGHTBOWN. *The Comely Frontispiece: The Emblematic Title-Page in England 1550–1660*. London: Routledge, 1979.

CORNEILLE, PIERRE. *La Mort de Pompée Tragedie*. Paris: Antoine de Sommaville and Augustin Courbé, 1644.

——*Œuvres de Corneille*. 2 vols. Rouen: Augustin Courbé, 1648.

——*Le Theatre de P. Corneille*. 3 vols. Paris: Augustin Courbé and Guillaume de Luyne, 1660.

——*Le Theatre de P. Corneille. Reveu et corrigé par l'autheur*. 2 vols. Paris: Thomas Jolly *et al.*, 1663.

——*Le Theatre de P. Corneille. Reveu et corrigé par l'autheur*. 4 vols. Paris: Thomas Jolly *et al.*, 1664.

——*Oeuvres complètes*. Ed. Georges Couton. 3 vols. Paris: Gallimard, 1980.

——*Oeuvres de P. et Th. Corneille précédées de la vie de P. Corneille par Fontanelle et des discours sur la poésie dramatique*. Paris: Furne, 1844.

COUTON, GEORGES. *Richelieu et le théâtre*. Lyon: Presses Universitaires de Lyon, 1986.

COX, JOHN D., and DAVID SCOTT KASTAN, eds. *A New History of Early English Drama*. New York: Columbia UP, 1997.

CRAWFORD, J. P. WICKERSHAM. *Spanish Drama before Lope de Vega. With a Bibliographical Supplement by W. T. McCready*. Philadelphia: U of Pennsylvania P, 1967.

CREMANTE, RENZO, ed. *Teatro del cinquecento*. Milan: R. Ricciardi, 1988.

CRESSY, DAVID. *Literacy and the Social Order: Reading and Writing in Tudor and Stuart England*. Cambridge: Cambridge UP, 1980.

CROWNE, JOHN. *The Comedies of John Crowne*. Ed. B. J. McMullin. New York: Garland, 1984.

CRUCIANI, FABRIZIO. *Teatro nel Rinascimento, Roma 1450–1550*. Rome: Bulzoni, 1983.

CRUICKSHANK, DON W. "The Editing of Spanish Golden-Age Plays from Early Printed Versions." *Editing the Comedia*. Eds. Frank P. Casa and Michael D. McGaha. *Michigan Romance Studies* 5 (1985): 52–103.

——"'Literature' and the Book Trade in Golden-Age Spain." *Modern Language Review* 73 (1978): 799–824.

——"On the Stage, on the Page: Some Developments in Spanish Drama, 1681–1833." Unpublished typescript.

CURTIUS, ERNST ROBERT. *European Literature in the Latin Middle Ages*. Trans. Willard R. Trask. Princeton: Princeton UP, 1973.

CYRANO DE BERGERAC, SAVINIEN DE. *Œuvres complètes*. Ed. Jacques Prévot. Paris: Librarie Belin, 1977.

D'AUBIGNAC, FRANÇOIS HÉDELIN, ABBÉ. *Pratique du théâtre*. Ed. Pierre Martino. Alger: Jules Carbonel, 1927.

——*The Whole Art of the Stage*. London: William Cadman *et al.*, 1684.

DANIEL, SAMUEL. *The Complete Works in Verse and Prose*. Ed. Alexander B. Grosart. 5 vols. London: Hazell, Watson & Viney, 1885.

DANIELS, BARRY, ed. *Revolution in the Theatre: French Romantic Theories of Drama*. Westport, CT.: Greenwood Press, 1983.

DASHWOOD, J. R., and J. E. EVERSON, eds. *Writers and Performers in Italian Drama from the Time of Dante to Pirandello*. Lewiston, NY: Edwin Mellen, 1991.

DAUMIER, HONORÉ. *Les Cent et un Robert Macaire*. 2 vols. Paris: Galerie Vero-Dodat, 1839.

DAVENANT, WILLIAM. *The Dramatic Works of Sir William D'Avenant*. 5 vols. Edinburgh: William Paterson, 1872–4.

——*Works*. London: Henry Herringman, 1673.

DAVENPORT, ROBERT. *The Works of Robert Davenport*. Ed. A. H. Bullen. London: Hansard, 1890.

DAVIDSON, ADELE. "'Some by Stenography'? Stationers, Shorthand, and the Early Shakespearean Quartos," *Papers of the Bibliographical Society of America* 90:4 (Dec. 1996): 417–49.

DAVIDSON, CLIFFORD, ed. *The Iconography of Heaven*. Kalamazoo, Mich.: Medieval Institute, 1994.

DAVIS, NATHALIE ZEMON. *Society and Culture in Early Modern France: Eight Essays*. Stanford, Calif.: Stanford UP, 1975.

DAY, JOHN. *Humour Out of Breath. Nero & Other Plays*. Eds. Herbert P. Horne, Havelock Ellis *et al.* London: T. Fisher Unwin, [*c*.1927].

DE GRAZIA, MARGRETA. *Shakespeare Verbatim: The Reproduction of Authenticity and the 1790 Apparatus*. Oxford: Clarendon, 1991.

DE VIVRE, GÉRARD. *Comedie de la fidelité nuptiale*. Antwerp: Henry Heyndricx, 1577.

DEE, JOHN. *John Dee's Library Catalogue*. Ed. Julian Roberts and Andrew G. Watson. London: Bibliographical Society, 1990.

DEIERKAUF-HOLSBOER, S. WILMA. *Le Théâtre de l'Hotel de Bourgogne II 1635–1680*. Paris: A.-G. Nizet, 1970.

——*L'Histoire de la mise en scène dans le théâtre français de 1600 à 1657*. Paris: E. Droz, 1933.

——*Vie d'Alexandre Hardy: poète du roi 1572–1632: 47 Documents inédits*. Nouvelle édition revue et augmentée. Paris: A. G. Nizet, 1972.

DEKKER, THOMAS. *The Dramatic Works of Thomas Dekker*. Ed. Fredson Bowers. 4 vols. Cambridge: University P, 1953–61.

——*The Magnificent Entertainment*. London: E. Allde for Tho. Man the younger, 1604.

——*Troia-Nova Triumphans*. London: Nicholas Okes, 1612.

DENNIS, JOHN. *The Critical Works of John Dennis*. Ed. Edward Niles Hooker. 2 vols. Baltimore: Johns Hopkins, 1939.

DEPERO, FORTUNATO. *Fortunato Depero*. Turin: Galleria d'Arte Martano, 1969.

DERRIDA, JACQUES. *De la grammatologie*. Paris: Éditions de Minuit, 1967.

DES MASURES, LOUIS. *David Combattant.* Enea Balmas and Michel Dassonville, eds. *La Tragédie à l'époque d'Henri II et de Charles IX. Théâtre français de la Renaissance.* 7 vols. Florence: Leo S. Olschki, 1986– . II:251–305.

DIBDIN, THOMAS. *The Reminiscences of Thomas Dibdin.* 2 vols. London: Henry Colburn, 1837.

DIDEROT, DENIS. *Œuvres.* Ed. Laurent Versini. 5 vols. Paris: Robert Lafont, 1994.

DÍEZ BORQUE, JOSÉ MARÍA. *Sociedad y teatro en la España de Lope de Vega.* Barcelona: Antoni Bosch, 1978.

The Digby Plays: Facsimiles of the Plays in Bodley MSS Digby 133 and e Museo 160. Ed. Donald C. Baker and J. L. Murphy. Leeds: U of Leeds, School of English, 1976.

DOBSON, E. J. *English Pronunciation 1500–1700.* 2 vols. 2nd edn. Oxford: Clarendon, 1968.

DOBSON, MICHAEL. *The Making of the National Poet: Shakespeare, Adaptation and Authorship, 1660–1769.* Oxford: Clarendon, 1992.

DOGLIO, FEDERICO, ed. *Il teatro tragico italiano: storia e testi del teatro tragico in Italia.* Bologna: Guanda, 1960.

DOLCE, LODOVICO. *Marianna.* Renzo Cremante, ed. *Teatro del cinquecento.* Milan: R. Ricciardi, 1988. 743–877.

DOLET, ESTIENNE. *La Maniere de Bien traduire d'une langue en autre. D'advantage de la poinctuation de la Langue Françoyse, plus des accents d'ycelle.* Lyon: Estienne Dolet, 1540.

DOVIZI, BERNARDO, DA BIBBIENA. *Calandra, comedia di Bernardo Diuitio da Bibiena intitolata la Calandra.* [Venice, 1530].

——*Cõmedia elegantissima ĩ prosa nuovamẽte cõposta p Mesß Bernardo da Bibiena. Intitulata Calandria.* Siena: Giovani di Alixãdro, 1521.

DOWNES, JOHN. *Roscius Anglicanus.* Ed. Judith Milhous and Robert D. Hume. London: Society for Theatre Research, 1987.

The Dramatic Censor; or, Critical Companion. 2 vols. London: J. Bell and C. Etherington, 1770.

DRYDEN, JOHN. *The Works of John Dryden.* Ed. Edward Niles Hooker, H. T. Swedenberg, Jr., *et al.* 20 vols. Berkeley: U of California P, 1956– .

DU BELLAY, JOACHIM. *La Défense et illustration de la langue française par Joachim du Bellay.* Ed. Louis Humbert. Paris: Garnier, 1930.

DU BOS, JEAN BAPTISTE. *Réflexions critiques sur la poësie et sur la peinture.* 7th edn. 3 vols. Paris: Pissot, 1770. Geneva: Slatkine, 1967.

DUBROCA, LOUIS. *Principes raisonnés sur l'art de lire a haute voix.* Paris: Louis Dubroca, 1802.

DUFF, WILLIAM. *An Essay on Original Genius; and its Various Modes of Exertion in Philosophy and the Fine Arts, Particularly Poetry.* London: Edward and Charles Dilly, 1767.

DU MÉRIL, ÉDÉLESTAND. *Histoire de la comédie.* 2 vols. Paris: Librairie Académique, 1864.

DUMESNIL, MARIE FRANÇOISE. *Mémoires de Mlle Dumesnil, en réponse aux Mémoires d'Hippolyte Clairon.* Paris: L. Tenré, 1823.

DUTHIE, G. I. *Elizabethan Shorthand and the First Quarto of "King Lear."* Oxford: Blackwell, 1949.

EAVES, T. C. DUNCAN, and BEN D. KIMPEL. "The Text of Congreve's *Love for Love.*" *The Library* 30:4 (Dec. 1975): 334–6.

EDEN, KATHY. *Poetic and Legal Fiction in the Aristotelian Tradition.* Princeton: Princeton UP, 1986.

EISENSTEIN, ELIZABETH L. "From Scriptoria to Printing Shops: Evolution and Revolution in the Fifteenth-Century Book Trade." Kenneth E. Carpenter, ed. *Books and Society in History.* New York: R. R. Bowker, 1983. 29–42.

——*The Printing Press as an Agent of Change: Communications and Cultural Transformations in Early-Modern Europe.* 2 vols. Cambridge: Cambridge UP, 1979.

ELIOT, GEORGE. *Daniel Deronda*. Ed. Barbara Hardy. Middlesex: Penguin, 1967.

ELIOT, SIMON. *Some Patterns and Trends in British Publishing*. London: Bibliographical Society, 1994.

ELSKY, MARTIN. *Authorizing Words: Speech, Writing, and Print in the English Renaissance*. Ithaca, NY: Cornell UP, 1989.

ENCINA, JUAN DEL. *Cancionero de todas las obras de Juan del Enzina: con otras cosas nuevamente añadidas*. Salamanca: Hans Gysser, 1509.

—— *Obra completa*. Ed. Miguel Ángel Pérez Priego. Madrid: Biblioteca Castro, 1996.

Encyclopédie, ou Dictionnaire raisonné des sciences, des arts et des métiers. 28 vols. Paris: Briasson, 1751–80.

ENDERS, JODY. *Rhetoric and the Origins of Medieval Drama*. Ithaca, NY: Cornell UP, 1992.

ENGEL, JOHANN JAKOB. *Ideen zu einer Mimik*. 2 vols. Berlin: August Mylius, 1785.

ENGEL, LAURA. "Staging Identities: The Memoirs and Portraits of Eighteenth-Century British Actresses." Unpublished typescript.

Englands Helicon. London: J. R. for John Flasket, 1600.

ENRÍQUEZ DE GUZMÁN, FELICIANA. *The Dramatic Works of Feliciana Enríquez de Guzmán*. Ed. Louis C. Pérez. Valencia: Albatros Hispanofila, 1988.

ENTRAMBASAGUAS Y PEÑA, JOAQUÍN. *Una Guerra literaria del siglo de oro: Lope de Vega y los preceptistas aristotélicos*. Madrid: Tipografía des Archivos, 1932.

ERASMUS, DESIDERIUS. *Collected Works of Erasmus*. 86 vols. Toronto: U Toronto P, 1978– .

—— *Das Theür und Künstlich Büchlin Morie Encomion das ist. Ein Lob der Thorhait*. Ulm: Hans Varnir, [*c*.1510–50?].

EUCLID. *The Elements of Geometrie of the most auncient Philosopher Euclide of Megara*. Trans. H. Billingsley. Preface by John Dee. London: John Daye, 1570.

Everyman. London: Rycharde Pynson, [*c*.1510–19].

Everyman. Ed. A. C. Cawley. Manchester: Manchester UP, 1961.

FABIAN, BERNHARD, and MARIE-LUISE SPIECKERMANN. "The House of Weidmann and English Books." John L. Flood and William A. Kelly, eds. *The German Book 1450–1750: Studies Presented to David L. Paisey in his Retirement*. London: British Library, 1995. 299–317.

FAIVRE, BERNARD. "La 'Profession de comédie.'" Jomaron, ed. *Le Théâtre en France du moyen age à 1789*. Paris: Armand Colin, 1988. 111–28.

—— "Le Théâtre de la grand-place." Jacqueline de Jomaron, ed. *Le Théâtre en France du moyen age à 1789*. Paris: Armand Colin, 1988. 41–88.

FARGET, PIERRE. *Le Miroir de la vie humaine*. Lyon: N. Philippi and M. Reinhardi, 1482.

FARQUHAR, GEORGE. *The Works of George Farquhar*. Ed. Shirley Strum Kenny. 2 vols. Oxford: Clarendon, 1988.

FAVART, CHARLES-SIMON. *Mémoires et correspondance littéraires, dramatiques et anecdotiques*. Paris: L. Collin, 1808.

—— *Oeuvres choisies de Favart*. 3 vols. Paris: Didot, 1813.

FEATHER, JOHN. *A History of British Publishing*. London: Croom Helm, 1988.

—— *The Provincial Book Trade in Eighteenth-Century England*. Cambridge: Cambridge UP, 1985.

—— *Publishing, Piracy and Politics: An Historical Study of Copyright in Britain*. London: Mansell, 1994.

FEBVRE, LUCIEN and HENRI-JEAN MARTIN. *L'Apparition du livre*. Paris: Éditions A. Michel, 1958.

—— *The Coming of the Book: The Impact of Printing 1450–1800*. Ed. Geoffrey Nowell-Smith and David Wootton. Trans. David Gerard. London: Verso, 1984.

FÉLIBIEN, ANDRÉ, sieur des Avaux et de Javercy. *Relation de la feste de Versailles du 18. juillet mil six cens soixante-huit*. Paris: L'Imprimerie royale, 1679.

FIELDING, HENRY. *The Author's Farce*. Ed. Charles B. Woods. Lincoln: U of Nebraska P, 1966.

—— *The Historical Register For the Year 1736 and Euridice Hissed*. Ed. William W. Appleton. Lincoln: U of Nebraska P, 1967.

—— *The Tragedy of Tragedies or the Life and Death of Tom Thumb the Great With the Annotations of H. Scriblerus Secundus*. Ed. James T. Hillhouse. New Haven: Yale UP, 1918.

FILMER, EDWARD. *The Unnatural Brother*. London: J. Orme for Richard Wilkin, 1697.

FINDLEN, PAULA. "The Museum: Its Classical Etymology and Renaissance Genealogy." *Journal of the History of Collections* I.1 (1989): 59–78.

FINNEGAN, RUTH. *Oral Poetry: Its Nature, Significance and Social Context*. Bloomington: Indiana UP, 1977.

—— *Oral Traditions and the Verbal Arts: A Guide to Research Practices*. London and New York: Routledge, 1992.

FITZBALL, EDWARD. *Thirty-Five Years of a Dramatic Author's Life*. 2 vols. London: T. C. Newby, 1859.

FLETCHER, IFAN KYRLE. "British Playbills Before 1718." *Theatre Notebook* 17 (1962–3): 48–50.

Flor de las comedias de España, de diferentes Autores: Quinta parte. Ed. Francisco de Avila. Alcala: Antonio Sanchez, 1615.

FOAKES, R. A. *Illustrations of the English Stage 1580–1642*. Stanford, Calif.: Stanford UP, 1985.

FOOTE, SAMUEL. *The Dramatic Works of Samuel Foote, Esq*. London: J. F. and C. Rivington *et al.*, 1788.

FORD, JOHN. *The Fancies*. Ed. Dominick J. Hart. New York: Garland, 1985.

—— *The Golden Meane*. 2nd edn. London: Jeffery Chorlton, 1614.

—— *Perkin Warbeck*. Ed. Donald K. Anderson, Jr. Lincoln: U Nebraska P, 1965.

—— *The Works of John Ford*. Ed. William Gifford and Alexander Dyce. Revised edn. 3 vols. London: James Toovey, 1869.

FORSETT, EDWARD. *Pedantius*. London: Robert Mylbourn, 1631.

—— *Pedantius*. Ed. E. F. J. Tucker. Hildesheim: Georg Olms, 1989.

FOUCAULT, MICHEL. *The Order of Things: An Archaeology of the Human Sciences*. London: Tavistock, 1970.

FOXE, JOHN. *The Acts and Monuments of John Foxe: A New and Complete Edition*. Ed. Stephen Reed Cattley. 8 vols. London: R. B. Seeley and W. Burnside, 1837–41.

FRANCHI, SAVERIO. *Drammaturgia romana: Repertorio bibliografico cronologico dei testi drammatici pubblicati a Roma e nel Lazio: Secolo XVII*. Rome: Edizioni di storia e letteratura, 1988.

FRANK, GRACE. *The Medieval French Drama*. Oxford: Clarendon, 1954.

FRANKO, MARK. *Dance as Text: Ideologies of the Baroque Body*. Cambridge: Cambridge UP, 1993.

FREEHAFER, JOHN. "Formation of the London Patent Companies." *Theatre Notebook* 20 (1965): 6–30.

FRENZEL, HERBERT A. *Geschichte des Theaters: Daten und Dokumente 1470–1890*. Munich: Deutscher Taschenbuch, 1979.

FRIED, MICHAEL. *Absorption and Theatricality: Painting and Beholder in the Age of Diderot*. Chicago: U of Chicago P, 1980.

FRONING, RICHARD. *Das Drama des Mittelalters*. 3 vols. Stuttgart: Union Deutsche Verlagsgesellschaft, [1891–2].

FUCHS, MAX. *La Vie théâtrale en Province au XVIII siècle*. Paris: CNRS, 1986.

FULWELL, ULPIAN. *Like Will to Like. Two Moral Interludes.* Oxford: Malone Society, 1991.

FUMAROLI, MARC. *L'Age de l'éloquence: Rhétorique et 'res literaria' de la Renaissance au seuil de l'époque classique.* Geneva: Droz, 1980.

FURET, FRANÇOIS, and JACQUES OZOUF. *Reading and Writing: Literacy in France from Calvin to Jules Ferry.* Cambridge: Cambridge UP, 1982.

FURETIÈRE, ANTOINE. *Dictionaire universel.* Revised edn. The Hague: Arnout and Reinier Leers, 1694.

FURTTENBACH, JOSEPH. *Architectura Recreationis.* Augsburg: Johann Schultes, 1640.

——[*Mannhaffter Kunstspiegel*]. *Joseph Furtenbachs deß Aeltern Mannhaffter Kunst-Spiegel.* Augspurg: Johann Schultes, 1663.

GADAMER, HANS GEORG. *Wahrheit und Methode.* Tübingen: Mohr, 1965.

——*Truth and Method.* Trans. Joel Weinsheimer and Donald G. Marshall. 2nd edn. New York: Crossroad, 1991.

GADOL, JOAN. *Leon Battista Alberti: Universal Man of the Early Renaissance.* Chicago: U Chicago P, 1969.

GAILLARD, ANTOINE. *La Carline.* Paris: J. Corrozet, 1626.

GALLAGHER, CATHERINE. *Nobody's Story: The Vanishing Acts of Women Writers in the Marketplace, 1670–1820.* Berkeley: U of California P, 1994.

GALLUCCIO, GIOVANNI PAOLO. *Theatrum mundi, et temporis.* Venice: I. B. Somascum, 1588.

Gammer Gurton's Needle. London: Thomas Colwell, 1575.

GARELICK, RHONDA K. "Electric Salome: Loie Fuller at the Exposition Universelle of 1900." J. Ellen Gainor, ed. *Imperialism and Theatre: Essays on World Theatre, Drama and Performance.* London: Routledge, 1995. 85–103.

GARNIER, ROBERT. *Les Tragedies de Rob. Garnier.* Paris: Robert Estienne, 1582.

——*Two Tragedies: Hippolyte and Marc Antoine.* Ed. Christine M. Hill and Mary G. Morrison. London: Athlone, 1975.

GARRICK, DAVID. *The Letters of David Garrick.* Ed. David M. Little, George M. Kahrl, and Phoebe deK. Wilson. 3 vols. Cambridge: Belknap Press, 1963.

——*The Plays of David Garrick.* Ed. Harry William Pedicord and Frederick Louis Bergmann. 7 vols. Carbondale: Southern Illinois UP, 1980–2.

GASKELL, PHILIP. *A New Introduction to Bibliography.* Winchester: St Paul's Bibliographies, 1995.

GASTÉ, ARMAND, ed. *La Querelle du Cid: Pièces et Pamphlets.* Paris: H. Welter, 1899.

GAY, JOHN. *Poetical Works.* Ed. G. C. Faber. New York: Russell & Russell, 1926.

——ALEXANDER POPE, and JOHN ARBUTHNOT. *Three Hours After Marriage.* Ed. Richard Morton and William Peterson. Painesville, Oh.: Lake Erie College P, 1961.

GENEST, JOHN. *Some Account of the English Stage.* 10 vols. Bath: H. E. Carrington, 1832.

GENGENBACH, PAMPHILUS. *Die [Zehn] alter dyser welt.* Basel: P. Gengenbach, [1516?].

GHERARDI, EVARISTO. *Le Theatre italien.* Amsterdam: Adrian Braakman, 1695.

——*Le Theatre italien de Gherardi.* 6 vols. Paris: Jean-Bapt. Cusson et Pierre Witte, 1700.

GIAMBULLARI, PIER FRANCESCO. *Apparato et feste nelle noze dello illustrissimo Signor Duca di Firenze, & della Duchessa sua Consorte.* Florence: Benedetto Giunta, 1539.

GIES, DAVID THATCHER. *The Theatre in Nineteenth-Century Spain.* Cambridge: Cambridge UP, 1994.

GILCHRIST, ALEXANDER. *Life of William Etty.* 2 vols. London: David Bogue, 1855.

GILDON, CHARLES. *A New Rehearsal, or Bays the Younger.* London: J. Roberts, 1714.

——*The Post-Boy Robb'd of His Mail.* 2 vols. London: John Sprint, 1706.

GIRALDI CINTIO, GIOVANNI BATTISTA. *Scritti critici.* Ed. Camillo Guerrieri Crocetti. Milan: Marzorati, 1973.

GIRALDI CINZIO, GIOVANNI BATTISTA. *Orbecche, tragedia . . . Di Nuovo corretta secondo l'originale dell'autore, e ristampata.* Venice: G. Giolito, 1572.

GOETHE, JOHANN WOLFGANG VON. *Faust I and II.* Trans. Stuart Atkins. Boston: Suhrkamp/ Insel, 1983.

—— *Faust, Tragédie de M. de Goethe.* Trans. Albert Stapfer. Paris: Motte, 1828.

—— *Gedenkausgabe der Werke, Briefe und Gespräche.* 25 vols. Ed. Ernst Beutler. Zürich: Artemis, 1950–60.

—— *Elective Affinities.* Trans. R. J. Hollingdale. London: Penguin, 1971.

—— *Wilhelm Meister's Apprenticeship.* Ed. and trans. Eric A. Blackall and Victor Lange. New York: Suhrkamp, 1983.

GOFF, FREDERICK RICHMOND. *Incunabula in American Libraries: A Third Census of Fifteenth-Century Books Recorded in North American Collections.* New York: Bibliographical Society of America, 1964.

GOLDBERG, JONATHAN. *Writing Matter: From the Hands of the English Renaissance.* Stanford, Calif.: Stanford UP, 1990.

GOLDONI, CARLO. *Delle commedie di Carlo Goldoni avvocato veneto.* 17 vols. Venice: Giambatista Pasquali, 1761.

—— *Memoirs of Carlo Goldoni Written by Himself.* Ed. William A. Drake. Trans. John Black. New York: Knopf, 1926.

—— *Tutte le opere.* Ed. Giuseppe Ortolani. 14 vols. Milan: Mondadori, 1935–56.

GOLDSMITH, OLIVER. *Collected Works.* Ed. Arthur Friedman. 5 vols. Oxford: Clarendon, 1966.

GOODDEN, ANGELICA. *Actio and Persuasion: Dramatic Performance in Eighteenth-Century France.* Oxford: Clarendon, 1986.

GORDON, D. J. "Poet and Architect: The Intellectual Setting of the Quarrel between Ben Jonson and Inigo Jones." *The Renaissance Imagination.* Ed. Stephen Orgel. Berkeley: U of California P, 1975. 77–101.

GORDON, MEL. *Lazzi: The Comic Routines of the Commedia dell'Arte.* New York: Performing Arts Journal Publications, 1983.

GOSSON, STEPHEN. *Playes Confuted in Five Actions.* Ed. Arthur Freeman. New York: Garland, 1972. [London: Thomas Gosson, 1582]

—— *The Schoole of Abuse.* London: Thomas Woodcocke, 1579.

GOTTSCHED, JOHANN CHRISTOPH. *Ausgewählte Werke.* Eds. Joachim Birke and Brigitte Birke. 12 vols. Berlin: Walter de Gruyter, 1968– .

GOULD, ROBERT. *Poems Chiefly consisting of Satyrs and Satyrical Epistles.* London: privately printed, 1689.

—— *The Works of Mr. Robert Gould.* 2 vols. London: W. Lewis, 1709.

GOYA, FRANCISCO. *Capricios: Their Hidden Truth.* Ed. Oto Bihalji-Merin. New York: Harcourt, 1980.

GOZZI, CARLO. *Five Tales for the Theatre.* Eds. and trans. Albert Bermel and Ted Emery. Chicago: U of Chicago P, 1989.

—— *Opere edite ed inedite del Co: Carlo Gozzi.* 14 vols. Venice: Giacomo Zanardi, 1801–2.

GRABBE, CHRISTIAN DIETRICH. *Werke und Briefe.* Ed. Albert Bergmann. 6 vols. Emsdetten: Lechte, 1960– .

—— *Jest, Satire, Irony and Deeper Significance.* Trans. Maurice Edwards. New York: Frederick Ungar, 1966.

GRAFTON, ANTHONY, and LISA JARDINE. *From Humanism to the Humanities: Education and the Liberal Arts in Fifteenth- and Sixteenth-Century Europe.* London: Duckworth, 1986.

GRAY, CHARLES HAROLD. *Theatrical Criticism in London to 1795*. New York: Columbia UP, 1931.

GRAY, THOMAS. *Complete Poems of Thomas Gray*. Ed. H. W. Starr and J. R. Hendrickson. Oxford: Clarendon, 1965.

GRÉBAN, ARNOUL. *Le Mystère de la passion*. Ed. Gaston Paris and Gaston Raynaud. Paris: F. Vieweg, 1878.

—— and JEAN MICHEL. *Le Mistere de la passion de nostre saulveur et redempteur Jesuchrist*. Paris: Michel le Noir, [1512].

GRÉBAN, SIMON [?]. *Le Premier [Second] Volume des Catholicques oeuvres et Actes des Apostres*. 3 vols in 2. Paris: Arnoul et Charles les Angeliers, 1541.

—— *Le premier volume du triumphant Mystere des Actes des Apostres: translate fidelement a la verite historiale*. 2 vols. Paris: Arnoul and Charles les Angeliers, 1537.

GREEN, JOHN [pseud.], and ROBERT BROWNE, eds. *Engelische Comedien und Tragedien*. Frankfurt: n.p., 1620.

GREENE, ROBERT. *Friar Bacon and Friar Bungay*. London: E. Allde, 1630.

GREENFIELD, CONCETTA CARESTIA. *Humanist and Scholastic Poetics, 1250–1500*. Lewisburg: Bucknell UP, 1981.

GREENSTREET, JAMES. "The Whitefriars Theatre in the Time of Shakspere [*sic*]." *Transactions of the New Shakspere Society* 1st ser. III (1887–92): 269–84.

GREG, W. W. *A Bibliography of English Printed Drama to the Restoration*. 4 vols. London, 1939–59.

—— *Dramatic Documents from the Elizabethan Playhouses*. 2 vols. 1931. Oxford, 1969.

—— "On Certain False Dates in Shakespearian Quartos." *Library* 9:34 (Apr. 1908): 112–31.

—— "Prompt Copies, Private Transcripts, and the 'Playhouse Scrivener.'" *Library* 4:6 (1926): 148–56.

—— *The Shakespeare First Folio: Its Bibliographical and Textual History*. Oxford: Clarendon, 1955.

GRÉVIN, JACQUES. *Théatre complet et poésies choisies*. Ed. Lucien Pinvert. Paris: Garnier, 1922.

GRIFFIN, DUSTIN. *Literary Patronage in England, 1650–1800*. Cambridge: Cambridge UP, 1996.

GRIFFITHS, RICHARD. *The Dramatic Technique of Antoine de Montchrestien: Rhetoric and Style in French Renaissance Tragedy*. Oxford: Clarendon, 1970.

GRIMM, FRIEDRICH MELCHIOR. *Correspondance littéraire, philosophe et critique de Grimm et de Diderot depuis 1753 jusqu'en 1790*. Paris: Furne, 1829–31.

GRINGORE, PIERRE. *Les Folles Entreprises*. Paris: Pierre Le Dru, 1505.

GRYPHIUS, ANDREAS. *Großmütiger Rechtsgelehrter oder Sterbender Aemilius Paulus Papinianus: Trauerspiel*. Ed. Ilse-Marie Barth. 1965. Stuttgart: Reclam, 1973.

GUÉRET, GABRIEL. *La Promenade de Saint-Cloud*. Geneva: Slatkine, 1968.

GURR, ANDREW. *Playgoing in Shakespeare's London*. 2nd edn. Cambridge: Cambridge UP, 1996.

—— *The Shakespearean Stage 1574–1642*. 3rd edn. Cambridge: Cambridge UP, 1992.

HAAKER, ANN. "The Plague, the Theater, and the Poet." *Renaissance Drama* I (1968): 283–306.

HABERMAS, JÜRGEN. *The Structural Transformation of the Public Sphere: An Inquiry into a Category of Bourgeois Society*. Trans. Thomas Burger and Frederick Lawrence. Cambridge, Mass.: MIT, 1989.

HACKEL, HEIDI BRAYMAN. "'Rowme' of Its Own: Printed Drama in Early Libraries." John D. Cox and David Scott Kastan, eds. *A New History of Early English Drama*. New York: Columbia UP, 1997. 113–30.

HAIGHT, ANNE LYON. *Hroswitha of Gandersheim: Her Life, Times, and Works.* New York: Hroswitha Club, 1965.

HAINES, JOHN THOMAS. *My Poll and My Partner Joe.* London: John Cumberland, [1835].

HALL, H. GASTON. "Ponctuation et dramaturgie chez Molière." Roger Laufer, ed. *La Bibliographie matérielle.* Paris: CNRS, 1983. 125–41.

HAMMOND, ANTHONY. "The Noisy Comma: Searching for the Signal in Renaissance Dramatic Texts." *Crisis in Editing: Texts of the English Renaissance.* Ed. Randall McLeod. New York: AMS, 1994. 203–49.

HAMMOND, BREAN S. *Professional Imaginative Writing in England, 1670–1740, 'Hackney for Bread'.* Oxford: Clarendon, 1997.

HARBAGE, ALFRED. *Annals of English Drama 975–1700: An Analytical Record of all Plays . . . Chronologically Arranged.* 3rd edn. Rev. Sylvia Stoler Wagonheim. London: Routledge, 1989.

HARDIN, JAMES, ed. *German Baroque Writers, 1661–1730.* Detroit: Gale Research, 1996.

HARDISON, O. B. "Medieval Literary Criticism: General Introduction." Alex Preminger *et al.*, eds. *Classical and Medieval Literary Criticism: Translations and Interpretations.* New York: Frederick Ungar, 1974.

HARDY, ALEXANDRE. *Le Theatre d'Alexandre Hardy, Parisien.* 6 vols. Paris: Jacques Quesnel, 1626–8.

HARINGTON, Sir JOHN. *Nugae Antiquae: Being a Miscellaneous Collection of Original Papers in Prose and Verse; Written During the Reigns of Henry VIII, Edward VI, Queen Mary, Elizabeth, and King James.* Ed. Thomas Park. 2 vols. London: J. Wright, 1804.

HARRISON, ANN TUKEY, ed. *The Danse Macabre of Women.* Kent, Oh.: Kent State UP, 1994.

HARSDÖRFFER, GEORG PHILIPP. *Frauenzimmer Gesprächspiele.* Ed. Irmgard Böttcher. 6 vols. 1644–6. Tübingen: Max Niemeyer, 1968.

HART, JOHN. *An Orthographie.* London: William Seres, 1569.

HAZLITT, WILLIAM. *The Complete Works of William Hazlitt.* Ed. P. P. Howe. 21 vols. London: J. M. Dent, 1931.

HEGEL, GEORG WILHELM FRIEDRICH. *Hegel: On the Arts. Selections from G. W. F. Hegel's Aesthetics of the Philosophy of Fine Art.* Trans. Henry Paolucci. New York: Frederick Ungar, 1979.

—— *Werke.* Ed. Eva Moldenhauer and Kurt Markus Michel. 20 vols. Frankfurt: Suhrkamp, 1969–71.

HELGERSON, RICHARD. *Self-Crowned Laureates: Spenser, Jonson, Milton and the Literary System.* Berkeley: U of California P, 1983.

HEMMINGS, F. W. J. *The Theatre Industry in Nineteenth-Century France.* Cambridge: Cambridge UP, 1993.

HENSLOWE, PHILIP. *Henslowe's Diary.* Ed. W. W. Greg. 2 vols. London: A. H. Bullen, 1904–8.

HERBERT, Sir HENRY. *The Control and Censorship of Caroline Drama: The Records of Sir Henry Herbert, Master of the Revels 1623–73.* Ed. N. W. Bawcutt. Oxford: Clarendon, 1996.

HERMANNUS ALEMANNUS. *Rhetorica, cum Alpharabii declaratione, Poetica, cum lbinrosdin determinatione.* Venice: Philipum Venetu, 1481.

HERRMANN, MAX. *Forschungen zur deutschen Theatergeschichte des Mittelalters und der Renaissance.* Berlin: Weidmann, 1914.

HERZEL, ROGER W. "The Decor of Molière's Stage: The Testimony of Brissart and Chauveau." *PMLA* 93 (1978): 925–54.

—— "Racine, Laurent, and the *Palais à Volonté.*" *PMLA* 108 (1993): 1064–82.

HERZFELD-SANDER, MARGARET, ed. *Essays on German Theater.* New York: Continuum, 1985.

HESSE, CARLA. "Enlightenment Epistemology and the Laws of Authorship in Revolutionary France, 1777–1793." *Representations* 30 (1990): 109–37.

HESSE, EVERETT W. "The Publication of Calderón's Plays in the Seventeenth Century." *Philological Quarterly* 27 (Jan. 1948): 37–51.

HEWITT, BARNARD, ed. *The Renaissance Stage: Documents of Serlio, Sabbattini and Furttenbach.* Coral Gables: U of Miami P, 1958.

HEYWOOD, THOMAS. *An Apology for Actors* (1612). Ed. Richard H. Perkinson. New York: Scholars' Facsimile Reprints, 1941.

—— *The Dramatic Works of Thomas Heywood.* 6 vols. London: John Pearson, 1874.

—— *The English Traveller.* London: Robert Raworth, 1633.

—— *If You Know Not Me You Know Nobody, Part I.* Ed. Madeleine Doran. Malone Society Reprints 1934. Oxford: Oxford UP, 1935.

—— *The Rape of Lucrece.* London: John Raworth for Nathaniel Butler, 1638.

HILL, AARON. *The Works of the Late Aaron Hill, Esq.* 4 vols. London: Printed for the Benefit of the Family, 1753.

—— and WILLIAM POPPLE. *The Prompter: A Theatrical Paper* (1734–6). Ed. William W. Appleton and Kalman A. Burnim. New York: Benjamin Blom, 1966.

HILL, JOHN. *The Actor: or, a Treatise on the Art of Playing.* London: R. Griffiths, 1755.

HIRSCH, RUDOLF. "Classics in the Vulgar Tongues Printed During the Initial Fifty Years, 1471–1520," *Papers of the Bibliographical Society of America* 81 (1987): 249–337.

—— *The Printed Word: Its Impact and Diffusion.* London: Variorum Reprints, 1978.

—— *Printing, Selling and Reading 1450–1550.* Wiesbaden: O. Harrossowitz, 1974.

HOBBES, THOMAS. *Leviathan Or the Matter, Forme and Power of a Commonwealth.* Ed. Michael Oakeshott. Oxford: Basil Blackwell, 1946.

HOGARTH, WILLIAM. *The Analysis of Beauty with the Rejected Passages from the Manuscript Drafts and Autobiographical Notes.* Ed. Joseph Burke. Oxford: Clarendon, 1955.

HOLCROFT, THOMAS. *The Life of Thomas Holcroft.* London: Constable, 1925.

—— *The Plays of Thomas Holcroft.* Ed. Joseph Rosenblum. 2 vols. New York: Garland, 1980.

—— *A Tale of Mystery.* London: R. Phillips, 1802.

HOLLANDER, JOHN. *The Figure of Echo.* Berkeley: U of California P, 1981.

HOLROYD, MICHAEL. *Bernard Shaw.* 5 vols. New York: Random House, 1988–9.

HOME, JOHN. *The Plays of John Home.* Ed. James S. Malek. New York: Garland, 1980.

HONIGMANN, E. A. J. *Stability of Shakespeare's Text.* London: E. Arnold, 1965.

HORTIS, ATTILIO. *Studi sulle opere latine del Boccaccio con particolare riguardo alla storia della erudizione nel medio evo e alle letterature straniere.* Trieste: J. Dase, 1879.

HOWARD, EDWARD. *The Usurper.* London: Henry Herringman, 1668.

HOWARD-HILL, T. H. "The Evolution of the Form of Plays in English During the Renaissance," *Renaissance Quarterly* 43:1 (Spring 1990): 112–45.

—— "Shakespeare's Earliest Editor, Ralph Crane." *Shakespeare Survey* 44 (1992): 113–29.

HOWARTH, WILLIAM D., ed. *French Theatre in the Neo-Classical Era, 1550–1789.* Cambridge: Cambridge UP, 1997.

HOWE, ALAN. "Alexandre Hardy, His Printers and His Patron: On an Unknown 'Privilège' for His 'Théâtre.'" *Seventeenth-Century French Studies* 8 (1986): 132–42.

HUDSON, NICHOLAS. *Writing and European Thought 1600–1830.* Cambridge: Cambridge UP, 1994.

HUGH OF ST VICTOR. *Didascalicon: De Studio Legendi: A Critical Text.* Ed. Charles Henry Buttimer. Washington: Catholic UP, 1939.

HUGH OF ST VICTOR. *The Didascalicon of Hugh of St. Victor: A Medieval Guide to the Arts.* Trans. Jerome Taylor. New York: Columbia UP, 1961.

HUGO, VICTOR. *Œuvres complètes.* Ed. Jacques Seebacher *et al.* 16 vols. Paris: R. Laffont, 1985–90.

——*Théâtre complet.* 2 vols. Ed. J.-J. Thierry and Josette Mélèze. Paris: Gallimard, 1963–4.

——*Théatre de Victor Hugo.* Paris: J. Hetzel, 18– .

HUME, ROBERT D. *Henry Fielding and the London Theatre 1728–1737.* Oxford: Clarendon, 1988.

——"Securing a Repertory: Plays on the London Stage 1660–5." *Poetry and Drama, 1570–1700: Essays in Honour of Harold F. Brooks.* London: Methuen, 1981: 156–72.

INCHBALD, ELIZABETH. *The Plays of Elizabeth Inchbald.* Ed. Paula R. Backscheider. 2 vols. New York: Garland, 1980.

INGARDEN, ROMAN. *The Literary Work of Art: An Investigation on the Borderlines of Ontology, Logic and Theory of Literature With an Appendix on the Functions of Language in the Theater.* Trans. George G. Grabowicz. Evanston, Ill.: Northwestern UP, 1973.

INGRAM, R. W. *John Marston.* Boston: G. K. Hall, 1978.

JACKSON, MacD. P. "Fluctuating Variation: Author, Annotator, or Actor?" Gary Taylor and Michael Warren, eds. *The Division of the Kingdoms: Shakespeare's Two Versions of* King Lear. Oxford: Clarendon, 1983. 313–49.

JACKSON, WILLIAM A., ed. *Records of the Court of the Stationers' Company 1602 to 1640.* London: Bibliographical Society, 1957.

JACOBUS, MARY. "'That Great Stage Where Senators Perform': *Macbeth* and the Politics of Romantic Theatre." *Studies in Romanticism* 22 (1983): 353–87.

JACQUOT, JEAN. "Le Théâtre du monde de Shakespeare à Calderón." *Revue de littérature comparée* 31 (1957): 341–72.

JAGODZINSKI, CECILE M. *Privacy and Print: Reading and Writing in Seventeenth-Century England.* Charlottesville: UP of Virginia, 1999.

JARVIS, SIMON. *Scholars and Gentlemen: Shakespearian Textual Criticism and Representations of Scholarly Labour, 1725–1765.* Oxford: Clarendon, 1995.

JAYNE, SEARS. *Library Catalogues of the English Renaissance.* Surrey: St Paul's Bibliographies, 1983.

JOHN OF SALISBURY. *Le Policratique de Jean de Salisbury, 1372, livres i–iii.* Trans. Denis Foulechat. 1372. Ed. Charles Brucker. Geneva: Librairie Droz, 1994.

JOHNS, ADRIAN. *The Nature of the Book: Print and Knowledge in the Making.* Chicago: U of Chicago P, 1998.

JOHNSON, CHRISTOPHER. *System and Writing in the Philosophy of Jacques Derrida.* Cambridge: Cambridge UP, 1993.

JOHNSON, ROBERT CARL. "Stage Directions in the Tudor Interlude." *Theatre Notebook* 26 (1971–2): 36–42.

JOHNSON, SAMUEL. *A Dictionary of the English Language.* London: J. and P. Knapton *et al.*, 1755.

——*Johnson on Shakespeare.* Ed. Arthur Sherbo. Vols. 7–8 of *The Yale Edition of the Works of Samuel Johnson.* New Haven: Yale UP, 1968.

——*Poems.* Ed. E. L. McAdam, Jr. and George Milne. Vol. 6 of *The Yale Edition of the Works of Samuel Johnson.* New Haven: Yale UP, 1964.

——*The Rambler.* Ed. W. J. Bates and Albrecht Strauss. Vols. 3–5 of *The Yale Edition of the Works of Samuel Johnson.* New Haven: Yale UP, 1969.

JOMARON, JACQUELINE DE, ed. *Le Théâtre en France du moyen age à 1789.* Paris: Armand Colin, 1988.

JONSON, BEN. *Ben Jonson.* Ed. C. H. Herford and Percy Simpson. 22 vols. Oxford: Clarendon, 1925–52.

—— *The Comicall Satyre of Every Man Out of His Humor.* London: Nicholas Linge, 1600.

—— *The Workes of Benjamin Jonson.* London: Will Stansby, 1616.

JORDAN, DOROTHY. *Mrs. Jordan and Her Family being the Unpublished Correspondence of Mrs. Jordan and the Duke of Clarence, later William IV.* Ed. A. Aspinall. London: Arthur Baker, 1951.

JORGENS, ELISE BICKFORD. "The Singer's Voice in Elizabethan Drama." *Renaissance Rereadings: Intertext and Context.* Ed. Maryanne Cline Horowitz, Anne J. Cruz, and Wendy A. Furman. Urbana: U of Illinois P, 1988. 33–47.

JOWETT, JOHN. "'Fall before this Book': The 1605 Quarto of Sejanus." *Text: Transactions of the Society for Textual Scholarship* 4 (1988): 279–85.

Joyeuse farce, à trois personnages, d'un curia qui trompa par finesse la femme d'un laboureur. Lyon: n.p. 1595.

KASTAN, DAVID SCOTT. "From Manuscript to Print: or, Making a Good Impression." *Shakespeare and the Book.* Cambridge: Cambridge UP, 2000 (forthcoming).

—— "The Mechanics of Culture: Editing Shakespeare Today." *Shakespeare Studies* 24 (1996): 30–7.

—— *Shakespeare after Theory.* New York: Routledge, 1999.

KATZ, RUTH. *Divining the Powers of Music: Aesthetic Theory and the Origins of Opera.* New York: Pendragon, 1986.

KEATS, JOHN. *The Poems of John Keats.* Ed. Jack Stillinger. Cambridge, Mass.: Belknap, 1978.

KEMBLE, JOHN PHILIP. *John Philip Kemble Promptbooks.* Ed. Charles H. Shattuck. 11 vols. Charlottesville: UP of Virginia for the Folger Shakespeare Library, 1974.

KEMBLE, MARIE THÉRÈSE DE CAMP. *Smiles and Tears; or, The Widow's Stratagem.* London: John Miller, 1815.

KENNY, SHIRLEY STRUM. "The Publication of Plays." *The London Theatre World, 1660–1800.* Ed. Robert D. Hume. Carbondale: Southern Illinois UP, 1980. 309–36.

KENRICK, WILLIAM. *The Widow'd Wife.* London: T. Davies *et al.*, 1767.

KERNODLE, GEORGE R. *From Art to Theatre: Form and Convention in the Renaissance.* Chicago: U of Chicago P, 1970.

KEWES, PAULINA. *Authorship and Appropriation: Writing for the Stage in England, 1660–1710.* Oxford: Clarendon, 1998.

KIEFER, FREDERICK. *Writing on the Renaissance Stage: Written Words, Printed Pages, Metaphoric Books.* Newark: U of Delaware P, 1996.

KILLIGREW, THOMAS. *Comedies, and Tragedies.* London: Henry Herringman, 1664.

—— *The Prisoners.* London: Andrew Crooke, 1640.

KINDERMANN, HEINZ. *Theatergeschichte Europas.* 10 vols. Salzburg: Otto Müller, 1957–74.

KING, JOHN N. *English Reformation Literature: The Tudor Origins of the Protestant Tradition.* Princeton: Princeton UP, 1982.

KIRBY, MICHEL and VICTORIA NES. *Futurist Performance.* New York: PAJ, 1986.

KIRKMAN, JAMES THOMAS. *Memoirs of the Life of Charles Macklin, Esq.* London: Lackington, Allen, 1799.

KIRSOP, WALLACE. "Le Théâtre français du XVIIᵉ siècle ou la bibliographie matérielle mise à l'épreuve." *La Bibliographie matérielle.* Ed. Roger Laufer. Paris: CNRS, 1983. 87–101.

KIRSOP, WALLACE. "Les Mécanismes éditoriaux." Henri-Jean Martin *et al.*, eds. *Histoire de l'édition française*. Paris: Promodis, 1982–6. II:21–33.

——."Nouveautés: théâtre et roman." Henri-Jean Martin *et al.*, eds. *Histoire de l'édition française*. Paris: Promodis, 1982–6. II:218–29.

KITTLER, FRIEDRICH. *Discourse Networks 1800/1900*. Trans. Michael Metteer and Chris Cullens. Stanford, Calif.: Stanford UP, 1990.

KNAPP, ROBERT. *Shakespeare: The Theater and the Book*. Princeton: Princeton UP, 1989.

KNOWLSON, JAMES R. "The Idea of Gesture as a Universal Language in the XVIIth and XVIIIth Centuries." *Journal of the History of Ideas* 26:4 (1965): 495–508.

KNUTSON, ROSLYN L. "The Repertory." John O. Cox and David Scott Kastan, eds. *A New History of Early English Drama*. New York: Columbia UP, 1997. 461–80.

KRAKOVITCH, ODILE. "Le Théâtre sous la Restauration et la monarchie de Juillet: lecture et spectacle." Alain Vaillant, ed. *Mesure(s) du livre*. Paris: Bibliothèque Nationale, 1992. 147–64.

KRAUTHEIMER, RICHARD. "Alberti and Vitruvius." *Acts of the Twentieth International Congress of the History of Art* 2 (1961): 65–72.

KREBS, ROLAND. "La Naissance des théâtres nationaux en Europe." *Études Germaniques* 39:4 (1984): 414–18.

KRELL, DAVID FARRELL. *Of Memory, Reminiscence, and Writing: On the Verge*. Bloomington: Indiana UP, 1990.

KRISTELLER, PAUL OSCAR. "The Modern System of the Arts." *Renaissance Thought and the Arts: Collected Essays*. Expanded edn. Princeton: Princeton UP, 1990.

KROLL, RICHARD W. F. *The Material Word: Literate Culture in the Restoration and Early Eighteenth Century*. Baltimore: Johns Hopkins UP, 1991.

KRUGER, LOREN. *The National Stage: Theatre and Cultural Legitimation in England, France, and America*. Chicago: U of Chicago P, 1992.

KYD, THOMAS. *The Spanish Tragedie*. London: Edward White [1592].

——*Spanish Tragedy*. London: W. White and T. Langley, 1615.

LA CALPRENÈDE, GAUTIER DE COSTES. *La Mort de Mithridate*. Jacques Scherer, ed. *Théâtre du XVIIᵉ siècle*. Paris: Gallimard, 1975. II:143–201.

LA CHESNAYE, NICOLAS DE. *La Condamnation de banquet*. Ed. Jelle Koopmans and Paul Verhuyck. Geneva: Librairie Droz, 1991.

LACROIX, PAUL. *Bibliographie Moliéresque*. 2nd edn. Paris: Auguste Fontaine, 1875.

La Danse macabre des femmes. Paris: Guyot Marchant, 1491.

La Festa di sancta Felicita hebrea quando fu martyrizata con septe figliuoli. [Florence: Bartolomeo de'Libri, *c*.1490].

LAFITAU, JOSEPH-FRANÇOIS. *Mœurs des sauvages ameriquains, comparées aux mœurs des premiers temps*. 4 vols. Paris: Saugrain the Elder and Charles-Estienne Hochereau, 1724.

LA GRANGE, CHARLES VARLET, SIEUR DE. *Le Registre de La Grange 1659–1685*. Ed. Bert Edward Young and Grace Philputt Young. 2 vols. Paris: E. Droz, 1947.

LAGRAVE, HENRI. "Privilèges et libertés." Jacqueline de Jomaron ed. *Le Théâtre en France du moyen age à 1789*. Paris: Armand Collin, 1988. 237–94.

——*Le Théâtre et le public à Paris de 1715 à 1750*. Paris: C. Klincksiek, 1972.

LA HARPE, JEAN-FRANÇOIS DE. *Adresse des auteurs dramatiques a l'assemblé nationale, Prononcée par M. de la Harpe, dans la Séance du mardi soir 24 Août*. [Paris]: n.p., [1790].

LA MESNARDIÈRE, JULES DE. *La Poétique*. Paris: Antoine de Sommaville, 1639.

LAMB, CHARLES and MARY. *Works of Charles and Mary Lamb*. Ed. E. V. Lucas. London: Methuen, 1903–5.

LANCASTER, HENRY CARRINGTON. *A History of French Dramatic Literature in the Seventeenth Century*. 9 vols. Baltimore: Johns Hopkins, 1929–42.

LANDAU, SIDNEY I. *Dictionaries: The Art and Craft of Lexicography*. New York: Charles Scribner's Sons, 1984.

LANDES, JOAN B. *Women and the Public Sphere in the Age of the French Revolution*. Ithaca, NY: Cornell UP, 1988.

LANG, FRANCISCUS. *Dissertatio de actione scenica, cum Figuris eandem explicantibus, et Observationibus quibusdam de Arte Comica*. Munich: Mariæ Magdalenæ Riedlin, 1727.

LANGHANS, EDWARD A. *Eighteenth Century British and Irish Promptbooks: A Descriptive Bibliography*. New York: Greenwood, 1987.

—— *Restoration Promptbooks*. Carbondale: Southern Illinois UP, 1981.

La Passion Nostre Seigneur. Ed. Edward Joseph Gallagher. Chapel Hill: U of North Carolina P, 1976.

LA PÉRUSE, JEAN DE. *La Medee*. Poitiers: Marnez and Guillaume Bouchet, 1555.

—— *La Médée*. Enea Balmas and Michel Dassonville, eds. *La tragédie à l'époque d'Henri II et de Charles IX. Théâtre français de la Renaissance*. Florence: Leo S. Olschki, 1986. I:119–73.

LARIVEY, PIERRE DE. *Les Six premiers comedies facecieuses*. Paris: Abel l'Angelier, 1579.

—— *The Widow*. Trans. Catherine E. Campbell. Ottawa, Ont.: Dovehouse, 1992.

LARTHOMAS, PIERRE. *Le Théâtre en France au XVIIIe siècle*. Paris: PUG, 1980.

LA TAILLE, JEAN DE. *Saül le furieux*. Enea Balmas and Michel Dassonville, eds. *La tragédie à l'époque d'Henri II et de Charles ix. Théâtre français de la Renaissance*. Florence: Leo S. Olschki, 1986– . IV:178–267.

LAUFER, ROGER. "L'Espace visuel du livre ancien." Henri-Jean Martin *et al*. eds., *Histoire de l'édition française*. Paris: Promodis, 1982. I:479–97.

LAWRENSON, T. E. *The French Stage and Playhouse in the XVIIth Century: A Study in the Advent of the Italian Order*. 2nd edn. (revised and enlarged). New York: AMS, 1986.

—— and HELEN PURKIS. "Les Éditions illustrées de Térence dans l'histoire du théâtre." *Le Lieu théâtral à la Renaissance*. Ed. J. Jacquot. Paris, 1964. 1–23.

LAZARD, MADELEINE. *Le Théâtre en France au XVIe siècle*. Paris: PUF, 1980.

LEA, K. M. *Italian Popular Comedy: A Study in the Commedia dell'Arte, 1560–1620 with special reference to the English stage*. 2 vols. Oxford: Clarendon, 1934.

LEACROFT, RICHARD. *The Development of the English Playhouse: An Illustrated Survey of Theatre Building in England From Medieval to Modern Times*. London: Methuen, 1973.

LEBÈGUE, RAYMOND. "Le Répertoire d'une troupe française à la fin du XVIe siècle." *Revue d'histoire du théâtre*. I–II (1948): 9–24.

LE BRUN, CHARLES. *Caracteres des passions Gravés sur les desseins de l'Illustre Monsr le Brun. Par S. le Clerc*. Paris: N. Langlois, [1696].

LEE, FREDERICK GEORGE. "Oxfordshire Christmas Miracle Play." *Notes and Queries* (5th ser.) 2:52 (Dec. 1874): 503–5.

LE FAUCHER, MICHEL. *Traicté de l'action de l'orateur*. Paris: Augustin Courbé, [1676].

Le Livre de conduite du régisseur et Le compte des dépenses pour le Mystère de la passion, joué à Mons en 1501. Ed. Gustave Cohen. Paris: H. Champion, 1925.

Le Mystère de la passion de Jésus-Christ, par personnages. Paris, Anthoine Vérard [1490?].

LENZ, JAKOB MICHAEL REINHOLD. *Werke und Briefe in drei Banden*. Ed. Sigrid Damm. Munich: Hanser, 1987.

LERER, SETH. *Chaucer and His Readers: Imagining the Author in Late-Medieval England.* Princeton: Princeton UP, 1993.

LE SAGE, ALAIN RENÉ, and D'ORNEVAL. *Le Théâtre de la foire, ou l'opera comique.* 10 vols. Amsterdam: L'Honoré and Chatelain, 1722–36.

Les Plaisants devis des suppots du Seigneur de la Coquille recités publiquement le vingt-uniesme feburier 1580. Lyon: Par les trois suppots, [1580?].

LESSING, GOTTHOLD EPHRAIM. *Hamburg Dramaturgy.* Trans. Victor Lange. New York: Dover Publications, 1962.

——*Laocoön: An Essay on the Limits of Painting and Poetry.* Trans. Edward Allen McCormick. Baltimore: Johns Hopkins UP, 1984.

——*Werke.* Ed. Herbert G. Göpfert *et al.* 8 vols. Munich: Carl Hanser, 1970–9.

Le Tres excellẽt & sainct mystere du vieil testament par personnages. Paris: Symon Colinet, 1542.

Lettre écrite a un ami sur les danseurs de corde, et sur les Pantomimes *qui ont paru autrefois chez les Grecs & chez les Romain, & à Paris en 1738.* Paris: La V[euve] Valleyre, 1739.

LEVACHER DE CHARNOIS, JEAN CHARLES. *Recherches sur les costumes et sur les théatres de toutes les nations, tant anciennes que modernes.* Paris: M. Drouhin, 1790.

LEVESQUE DE LA RAVAILLÈRE, PIERRE-ALEXANDRE. *Essai de comparaison entre la declamation et la poesie dramatique.* Paris: la Veuve Pissot and Jean-François Tabair, 1729.

LEVINE, JOSEPH M. *The Battle of the Books: History and Literature in the Augustan Age.* Ithaca, NY: Cornell UP, 1991.

——*Humanism and History: Origins of Modern English Historiography.* Ithaca, NY: Cornell UP, 1987.

LEWICKA, HALINA, and TERESA JAROSZEWSKA. *Bibliographie du theatre profane français des XVe et XVIe siècles: supplement.* Paris: CNRS, 1988.

LICHTENBERG, GEORG CHRISTOPH. *Lichtenberg's Visits to England.* Ed. Margaret L. Mare and W. H. Quarrell. Oxford: Clarendon, 1938.

LLOYD, ROBERT. *The Actor.* London: R. and J. Dodsley, 1760.

LOEWENSTEIN, JOSEPH F. "*Idem*: Italics and the Genetics of Authorship." *The Journal of Medieval and Renaissance Studies* 20:2 (Fall 1990): 205–24.

——"Printing and 'The Multitudinous Presse': The Contentious Texts of Jonson's Masques." *Ben Jonson's 1616 Folio.* Ed. Jennifer Brady and W. H. Herendeen. Newark: U of Delaware P, 1991.

——"The Script in the Marketplace." *Representations* 12 (1985): 101–14.

LOHENSTEIN, DANIEL CASPER VON. *Daniel Caspers Cleopatra, Trauer-Spiel.* Breslau: Esaieae Fellgibels, 1661.

The London Stage, 1660–1800: A Calendar of Plays. 5 vols. in 11. Carbondale: Southern Illinois UP, 1960–79.

LONG, WILLIAM B. "'Precious Few': English Manuscript Playbooks." *A Companion to Shakespeare.* Ed. David Scott Kastan. Oxford: Blackwell, 1999: 414–33.

LOPEZ DE YANGUAS, HERNAN. *Farsa del mundo y moral del actor d'la Real que es Fernan Lopez de Yanguas.* N.p.: n.p., 1524.

LORD, GEORGE DE F., ed., *Poems on Affairs of State.* 7 vols. New Haven: Yale UP, 1963–75.

LORDI, R. J. "Proofreading of *The Revenge of Bussy D'Ambois.*" *English Language Notes* 10:2 (Mar. 1973): 188–97.

LOVE, HAROLD. *Scribal Publication in Seventeenth-Century England.* Oxford: Clarendon, 1993.

LOVELACE, RICHARD. *The Poems of Richard Lovelace.* Ed. C. H. Wilkinson. Oxford: Clarendon Press, 1930.

LÖWEN, JOHANN FRIEDRICH. *Johann Friedrich Löwens Geschichte des deutschen Theaters (1766) und Flugschriften über das Hamburger Nationaltheater (1766 und 1767)*. Ed. Heinrich Stümcke. Berlin: Ernst Frensdorff, [1905].

LOWRY, MARTIN. *Nicholas Jenson and the Rise of Venetian Publishing in Renaissance Europe.* Oxford: Basil Blackwell, 1991.

—— *The World of Aldus Manutius: Business and Scholarship in Renaissance Venice.* Ithaca, NY: Cornell UP, 1979.

LUCAS, PETER J. "The Growth and Development of English Literary Patronage in the Late Middle Ages and Early Renaissance." *The Library* 6th ser. 4 (1982): 219–48.

LUNEL, ERNEST. *Le Théâtre et la Révolution.* Paris: H. Daragon, 1911.

LUPTON, THOMAS. *All for Money.* London: Roger Warde and Richard Mundee, 1578.

—— *London and the Country Carbonadoed and Quartered into Severall Characters.* London: Nicholas Okes, 1632.

LUTZ, CORA. *Essays on Manuscripts and Rare Books.* Hamden, Conn: Archon, 1975.

LYLY, JOHN. *Campaspe.* Ed. G. K. Hunter. New York: Manchester UP, 1991.

LYTLE, GUY FITCH, and STEPHEN ORGEL, eds. *Patronage in the Renaissance.* Princeton: Princeton UP, 1981.

MABLY, GABRIEL BONNOT DE. *Lettres à Madame la Marquise de P*** sur l'opéra.* Paris: Didot, 1741. New York: AMS, 1979.

McCOLLEY, DIANE KELSEY. *Poetry and Music in Seventeenth-Century England.* Cambridge: Cambridge UP, 1997.

McDOWELL, PAULA. *The Women of Grub Street: Press, Politics, and Gender in the London Literary Marketplace 1678–1730.* Oxford: Clarendon, 1998.

MACHIAVELLI, NICCOLÒ. *Tutte le opere.* Ed. Mario Martelli. 3rd edn. Florence: Sansoni, 1989.

McKENDRICK, MELVEENA. *Theatre in Spain 1490–1700.* Cambridge: Cambridge UP, 1989.

McKENZIE, D. F. "Speech-Manuscript-Print." *New Directions in Textual Studies.* Ed. Dave Oliphant and Robin Bradford. Austin, TX: Harry Ransom Humanities Research Center, 1990. 87–109.

—— "When Congreve Made a Scene," *Transactions of the Cambridge Bibliographical Society* 7 (1979): 338–42.

—— "Typography and Meaning: The Case of William Congreve." *Wolfenbütteler Schriften zur Geschichte des Buchwesens* 4 (1980): 81–125.

McKEON, MICHAEL. *The Origins of the English Novel 1600–1740.* Baltimore: Johns Hopkins UP, 1987.

McKERROW, R. B. "Edward Allde as a Typical Trade Printer." *The Library* 4th ser. 10 (1929): 121–62.

McMAHON, A. PHILIP. "Seven Questions on Aristotelian Definitions of Tragedy and Comedy." *Harvard Studies in Classical Philology* 40 (1929): 97–198.

MACMILLAN, DOUGALD. *Drury Lane Calendar 1747–1776.* Oxford: Clarendon, 1938.

McMILLIN, SCOTT. *The Elizabethan Theatre and the Book of Sir Thomas More.* Ithaca, NY: Cornell UP, 1987.

The Macro Plays: The Castle of Perseverance; Wisdom; Mankind. Ed. David Bevington. Washington, DC: Folger Facsimiles, 1972.

MADURELL MARIMÓN, JOSÉ MARIALL, and JORGE RUBIÓ BALAGUER, eds. *Documentos para la historia de la imprenta y libreria en Barcelona (1474–1553).* Barcelona: Gremios de Editores, de Libreros y de Maestros impresores, 1955.

MAGAGNATO, LICISCO. *Teatri italiani del cinquecento.* Venice: N. Pozza, 1954.

MAGUIRE, LAURIE E. *Shakespearean Suspect Texts: The "Bad" Quartos and Their Contexts.* Cambridge: Cambridge UP, 1996.

—— and THOMAS L. BERGER, eds. *Textual Formations and Reformations.* Newark: U of Delaware P, 1998.

MAHELOT, LAURENT. *Le Mémoire de Mahelot, Laurent et d'autres décorateurs de l'Hôtel de Bourgogne et de la Comédie-Française au XVIIe siècle.* Ed. Henry Carrington Lancaster. Paris: Edouard Champion, 1920.

MAIRET, JEAN. *La Silvanire.* Jacques Scherer, ed. *Théâtre du XVIIe siècle.* Paris: Gallimard, 1975. I:492–593.

—— *La Sophonisbe.* Jacques Scherer, ed. *Théâtre du XVIIe siècle.* Paris: Gallimard, 1975. I:669–729.

Maistre Pierre Pathelin. Paris: Pierre Levet, 1489.

MALLET, DAVID, and JAMES THOMPSON. *Alfred: A Masque. The Songs, chorusses &c.* London: T. Beckett, 1773.

MANGINI, NICOLA. *Alle origini del teatro moderno e altri saggi.* Modena: Mucchi, 1989.

MARCUS, LEAH S. *Unediting the Renaissance: Shakespeare, Marlowe, Milton.* London: Routledge, 1996.

MARESCHAL, ANDRÉ. *Le Railleur ou la satire du temps, comédie.* Ed. Giovanni Dotoli. Bologna: R Pàtron, 1971.

MARINETTI, FILIPPO T. *Teoria e invenzione futurista.* Ed. Luciano De Maria. Milan: Arnoldo Mondadori, 1968.

MARITI, LUCIANO. *La commedia ridicolosa: comici di professione, dilettanti, editoria teatrale nel Seicento: Storia e testi.* Rome: Bulzoni, 1978.

MARIVAUX, PIERRE CARLET DE CHAMBLAIN DE. *Théâtre complet.* Ed. Marcel Arland. Paris: Gallimard, 1949.

MARLOWE, CHRISTOPHER. *The Complete Works of Christopher Marlowe.* Ed. Fredson Bowers. 2nd edn. 2 vols. Cambridge: Cambridge UP, 1981.

MAROTTI, ARTHUR. *Manuscript, Print, and the English Lyric.* Ithaca, NY: Cornell UP, 1995.

MARSHALL, DAVID. *The Figure of Theater: Shaftesbury, Defoe, Adam Smith, and George Eliot.* New York: Columbia UP, 1986.

MARSTON, JOHN. *Parasitaster, or the Fawne.* 2nd edn. London: William Cotton, 1606.

—— *The Plays of John Marston.* Ed. H. Harvey Wood. 3 vols. London: Oliver and Boyd, 1934.

—— *The Workes of Mr. John Marston.* London: William Sheares, 1633.

MARTIN, HENRI-JEAN. *The French Book: Religion, Absolutism, and Readership, 1585–1715.* Trans. Paul Saenger and Nadine Saenger. Baltimore: Johns Hopkins UP, 1996.

—— *Le Livre francais sous l'ancien régime.* Paris: Promodis, 1987.

—— ROGER CHARTIER, and JEAN-PIERRE VIVET, eds. *Histoire de l'édition française.* 4 vols. Paris: Promodis, 1982–6.

Mary Magdalen. The Late Medieval Religious Plays of Bodleian Mss Digby 133 and E Museo 160. Ed. Donald C. Baker, John L. Murphy, and Louis B. Hall, Jr. Oxford: Oxford UP, 1982. 24–95.

MASSINGER, PHILIP. *The Plays and Poems of Philip Massinger.* Ed. Philip Edwards and Colin Gibson. 5 vols. Oxford: Oxford UP, 1976.

—— THOMAS MIDDLETON, and WILLIAM ROWLEY. *The Old Law.* London: E. Archer, 1656.

MASLAN, SUSAN. "Resisting Representation: Theater and Democracy in Revolutionary France," *Representations* 52 (Fall 1995): 27–51.

MASTEN, JEFFREY. "Pressing Subjects: Or, The Secret Lives of Shakespeare's Compositors."

Language Machines: Technologies of Literary and Cultural Production. Ed. Jeffrey Masten, Peter Stallybras, and Nancy Vickers. London: Routledge, 1997. 75–107.

——*Textual Intercourse: Collaboration, Authorship, and Sexualities in Renaissance Drama.* Cambridge: Cambridge UP, 1997.

MATHUR, OM PRAKASH. *The Closet Drama of the Romantic Revival.* Salzburg Studies in English Literature 35. Salzburg: Institut für Englische Sprache und Literatur, 1978.

MATURIN, CHARLES. *Bertram; or, The Castle of St. Aldobrand.* Oxford: Woodstock Books, 1992.

MAURITIUS, GEORG. *Comoedia von allerley Ständen.* Leipzig: Abraham Lamberg, 1606.

MEDWALL, HENRY. *The Plays of Henry Medwall.* Ed. Alan H. Nelson. London: D. S. Brewer, 1980.

MEEHAN, JOHANNA, ed. *Feminists Read Habermas: Gendering the Subject of Discourse.* New York: Routledge, 1995.

MEISEL, MARTIN. *Realizations: Narrative, Pictorial, and Theatrical Arts in Nineteenth-Century England.* Princeton UP, 1983.

MÉLÈSE, PIERRE. *Le Théâtre et le public à Paris sous Louis XIV 1659–1715.* Paris: Droz, 1934.

MERBURY, FRANCIS. *The Marriage Between Wit and Wisdom.* 1579. Oxford: Malone Reprints, 1971.

MERCIER, LOUIS-SÉBASTIEN. *Du théâtre, ou nouvel essai sur l'art dramatique.* Amsterdam: E. van Harrevelt, 1773.

——*Tableau de Paris.* 12 vols. Amsterdam: n.p., 1783–9.

——*Théâtre complet.* 4 vols. Amsterdam: B. Vlam, 1778–84.

MEREDITH, PETER. "Scribes, texts and performance." Paula Neuss, ed. *Aspects of Early English Drama.* Cambridge: D. S. Brewer, 1983. 14–29.

——and JOHN E. TAILBY, eds. *The Staging of Religious Drama in Europe in the Later Middle Ages: Texts and Documents in English Translation.* Trans. Raffaella Ferrari, *et al.* Kalamazoo, Mich: Medieval Institute, 1983.

MERLAND, M. A. "Tirage et vente des livres à la fin du XVIIIᵉ siècle. Des documents chiffrés." *Revue française d'histoire du livre* 5 (1972): 87–112.

MERLIN, HÉLÈNE. *Public et littérature en France au XVIIᵉ siècle.* Paris: Les Belles Lettres, 1994.

MESCHONNIC, HENRI. *Des mots et des mondes: Dictionnaires, encyclopédies, grammaires, nomenclatures.* Paris: Hatier, 1991.

MEYER, REINHART. *Bibliographia dramatica et dramaticorum.* 6 vols. Tübingen: Max Niemeyer, 1986–93.

MEYERHOLD, VSEVOLOD EMILEVICH. *Meyerhold on Theatre.* Trans. and ed. Edward Braun. New York: Hill & Wang, 1969.

MICHEL, PAUL-HENRI. "The French Book in the XIXth Century (1801–1870)." André Lejard, ed. *The Art of the French Book from Early Manuscripts to the Present Time.* London: Paul Elek, 1947. 87–112.

MIDDLETON, THOMAS. *A Game at Chæss as it was Acted nine days together at the Globe.* London: n.p., 1625.

——*A Game of Chess.* Ed. Milton Arthur Buettner. Salzburg: Institut für Anglistik und Amerikanistik, 1980.

——*The Works of Thomas Middleton.* Ed. A. H. Bullen. 8 vols. London: J. C. Nimmo, 1885. New York: AMS, 1964.

MILET, JACQUES. *L'Istoire de la destruction de Troye la grant.* Paris: Jehan Bonhomme, 1484.

MILHOUS, JUDITH, and ROBERT D. HUME. "Dating Play Premières from Publication Data, 1660–1700." *Harvard Library Bulletin* 22 (1974): 374–405.

MILLS, A. D. "Chester's Mystery Cycle and the Mystery of the Past." *Transactions of the Historic Society of Lancashire and Cheshire* 137 (1988): 13.

MILTON, JOHN. *Complete Poems and Major Prose*. Ed. Merritt Y. Hughes. Indianapolis: Odyssey, 1957.

MINNIS, ALASTAIR J. *Medieval Theory of Authorship*. 2nd edn. Philadelphia: U of Pennsylvania P, 1988.

MINNIS, ALASTAIR J., and A. B. SCOTT, eds. *Medieval Literary Theory and Criticism c.1100–c.1375*. Oxford: Clarendon, 1988.

The Minor. A Comedy, In Two Acts. London: W. Lowndes, S. Bladon and W. Nicoll, 1788.

MINTURNO, ANTONIO SEBASTIANO. *L'arte poetica*. Venice: Andrea Valuassori, 1564. Munich: Wilhelm Fink, 1971.

MOLIÈRE [JEAN BAPTISTE POQUELIN]. *Les Oeuvres de Monsieur de Moliere*. 8 vols. Paris: Denys Thierry, Claude Barbin et Pierre Trabouillet, 1682.

—— *The Misanthrope and Tartuffe*. Trans. Richard Wilbur. New York: Harcourt, 1954.

—— *Œuvres complètes*. 2 vols. Ed. Georges Couton. Paris: Gallimard, 1971.

—— *Œuvres de Molière*. Ed. Eugène Despois. Paris: Hachette, 1893–1900.

MOLINA, TIRSO DE [Gabriel Tellez]. *Obras completas de Tirso de Molina: Prosa y verso*. Ed. Pilar Palomo and Isabel Prieto. 3 vols. Madrid: Turner, 1994–7.

MOLLIER, JEAN-YVES. *L'Argent et les lettres: histoire du capitalisme d'édition, 1880–1920*. Paris: Fayard, 1988.

MONTAIGNE, MICHEL DE. *Œuvres complètes*. Eds. Albert Thibaudet and Maurice Rat. Paris: Gallimard, 1962.

—— *Essays*. Trans. J. M. Cohen. London: Penguin, 1958.

MONTCHRESTIEN, ANTOINE DE. *Les Tragédies d'Ant. de Montchrestien, sieur de Vasteuille*. Rouen: Jean Petit, 1601.

—— *Les Tragédies d'Anthoine de Montchrestien*. Nyport: J. Vaultier, 1606.

—— *Les Tragédies de Montchrestien*. Ed. L. Petit de Julleville. Paris: Plon, 1891.

MONTEVERDI, CLAUDIO. *Tutte le opere di Claudio Monteverdi*. Ed. G. Francesco Malipiero. 17 vols. Venice: Fondazione Giorgio Cini, 1926–66.

MORGAN, FIDELIS. *The Well-Known Troublemaker: A Life of Charlotte Charke*. London: Faber & Faber, 1988.

MORLEY, S. G., and C. BRUERTON. "How Many *Comedias* Did Lope de Vega Write?" *Hispania* 19 (1936): 217–34.

—— *Chronology of Lope de Vega's Comedias*. New York: MLA, 1940.

MORYSON, FYNES. *Shakespeare's Europe: Unpublished Chapters of Fynes Moryson's Itinerary Being a Survey of the Condition of Europe at the end of the 16th Century*. Ed. Charles Hughes. London: Sherratt & Hughes, 1903.

MOTTEUX, PETER. *The Novelty. Every Act a Play*. London: Rich. Parker and Peter Buck, 1697.

MOWAT, BARBARA A. "The Theater and Literary Culture." John D. Cox and David Scott Kastan, eds. *A New History of Early English Drama*. New York: Columbia UP, 1997. 213–230.

MOXON, JOSEPH. *Mechanick Exercises on the Whole Art of Printing (1683–4)*. Ed. Herbert Davis and Harry Carter. London: Oxford UP, 1958.

MULCASTER, RICHARD. *Mulcaster's Elementarie*. 1582. Ed. E. T. Campagnac. London: Clarendon, 1925.

MULLANEY, STEVEN. *The Place of the Stage: License, Play, and Power in Renaissance England*. Chicago: U of Chicago P, 1988.

MULRYNE, J. R., and MARGARET SHEWRING, eds. *Theatre of the English and Italian Renaissance*. London: Macmillan, 1991.

MULVIHILL, JAMES. "William Hazlitt and the 'Impressions' of Print Culture." *Keats-Shelley Journal* 40 (1991): 127–45.

MUMBY, FRANK ARTHUR, and IAN NORRIE. *Publishing and Bookselling*. London: Jonathan Cape, 1974.

MUNDAY, ANTHONY. *John A Kent and John A Cumber*. Ed. Muriel St Clare Byrne. Oxford: Malone Reprints, 1923.

MURPHY, ARTHUR. *The Desert Island, a Dramatic Poem, in Three Acts*. London: Paul Vaillant, 1760.

—— *The Old Maid*. London: P. Vaillant, 1761.

—— *The Plays of Arthur Murphy*. Ed. Richard B. Schwartz. 4 vols. New York: Garland, 1979.

MURRAY, TIMOTHY. *Theatrical Legitimation: Allegories of Genius in Seventeenth-Century England and France*. New York: Oxford UP, 1987.

MYERS, ROBIN. "Writing for Booksellers in the Early Nineteenth Century: A Case Study." Robin Meyers and Michael Harris, eds. *Author/Publisher Relations During the Eighteenth and Nineteenth Centuries*. Oxford: Oxford Polytechnic, 1983. 119–55.

NABBES, THOMAS. *Playes, Maskes, Epigrams, Elegies, and Epithalamiums Collected into one Volume*. London: I. Dawson, 1639.

—— *The Works of Thomas Nabbes*. Ed. A. H. Bullen. 2 vols. London: Wyman, 1887.

NAGLER, ALOIS. *Theatre Festivals of the Medici, 1539–1637*. Trans. George Hickenlooper. New Haven: Yale UP, 1964.

NAOGEORG, THOMAS. *Pammachius*. N.p: n.p, [1539].

The National Union Catalog: Pre-1956 Imprints. Chicago: Mansell, 1968.

NEUBAUER, JOHN. *The Emancipation of Music from Language: Departure from Mimesis in Eighteenth-Century Aesthetics*. New Haven: Yale UP, 1986.

NEWTON, RICHARD C. "Jonson and the (Re-)Invention of the Book." Claude J. Summers and Ted-Larry Pebworth, eds. *Classic and Cavalier: Essays on Jonson and the Sons of Ben*. Pittsburgh: U of Pittsburgh P, 1982. 31–55.

NICASTRO, GUIDO. *Metastasio e il teatro del primo settecento*. Rome: Laterza, 1973.

NICOLAISEN, W. F. H., ed. *Oral Tradition in the Middle Ages*. Binghamton, NY: Medieval and Renaissance Texts and Studies, 1995.

NICOLL, ALLARDYCE. *The Development of the Theatre: A Study of Theatrical Art from the Beginnings to the Present Day*. 4th edn. New York: Harcourt, 1958.

—— *The Garrick Stage: Theatres and Audience in the Eighteenth Century*. Athens: U of Georgia P, 1980.

—— *A History of English Drama 1660–1900*. 5 vols. 1923. 4th edn. Cambridge: University P, 1952.

—— *Stuart Masques and the Renaissance Stage*. New York: Arno, 1980.

NIETZSCHE, FRIEDRICH. *The Birth of Tragedy and The Case of Wagner*. Trans. Walter Kaufmann. New York: Vintage, 1967.

—— *Werke: Kritische Gesamtausgabe*. Eds. Giorgio Colli and Mazzino Montinari. 8 vols. Berlin: Walter de Gruyter, 1967– .

Non-Cycle Plays and Fragments. Ed. Norman Davis. London: Oxford UP, 1970.

Non-Cycle Plays and the Winchester Dialogues. Ed. Norman Davis. Leeds: U of Leeds School of English, 1979.

NORRIS, EDWIN. *The Ancient Cornish Drama*. 2 vols. Oxford: Oxford UP, 1859.

Nouvelle biographie theatrale Paris: A. Beraud, 1826.

NOVERRE, JEAN GEORGES. *Lettres sur la danse, et sur les ballets*. Stuttgart: A. Delaroche, 1760. New York: Broude Brothers, 1967.

The N-Town Plays: A Facsimile of British Library MS Cotton Vespasian D VIII. Ed. Peter Meredith and Stanley J. Kahrl. Leeds: U of Leeds School of English, 1977.

OBIZZI, PIO ENEA. *L'Ermiona del Sʳ Marchese Pio Enea Obizzi*. Padua: Paolo Frambotto, 1638.

OLSON, GLENDING. *Literature as Recreation in the Later Middle Ages*. Ithaca, NY: Cornell UP, 1982.

ONG, WALTER J. *Ramus, Method, and the Decay of Dialogue*. Cambridge: Harvard UP, 1958.

OOSTING, J. THOMAS. *Andrea Palladio's Teatro Olimpico*. Ann Arbor: UMI, 1981.

OPPORINUS, JOHANNES, ed. *Dramata Sacra Comoediae atque tragoediae*. Basel: Ionnis Oporini, 1547.

ORGEL, STEPHEN. "Acting Scripts, Performing Texts." *Crisis in Editing: Texts of the English Renaissance*. Ed. Randall McLeod. New York: AMS, 1994. 251–94.

—— "The Authentic Shakespeare." *Representations* 21 (Winter 1988): 1–25.

—— *The Jonsonian Masque*. Cambridge, Mass.: Harvard UP, 1965.

—— "Poetics of Spectacle." *New Literary History* 2 (1971): 367–89.

—— "The Renaissance Artist as Plagiarist." *ELH* 48 (3): 476–95.

—— "What is a Text?" David Scott Kastan and Peter Stallybrass, eds. *Staging the Renaissance: Reinterpretations of Elizabethan and Jacobean Drama*. New York: Routledge, 1991. 83–7.

ORIEL, CHARLES. *Writing and Inscription in Golden Age Drama*. West Lafayette, Ind.: Purdue UP, 1992.

ORME, NICHOLAS. *Education and Society in Medieval and Renaissance England*. London: Hambledon, 1989.

ORTELIUS, ABRAHAM. *Theatrum oder Schawplatz des erdbodems warin die Landttafeil der gantzen weldt*. Antwerp: Gielis von Diest, 1573.

O'TOOLE, FINTAN. *The Traitor's Kiss: The Life of Richard Brinsley Sheridan, 1751–1816*. New York: Farrar, Straus & Giroux, 1998.

OXBERRY, WILLIAM, ed. *The New English Drama*. 22 vols. London: W. Simpkin and R. Marshall, 1818–25.

PARFAICT, FRANÇOIS, and CLAUDE. *Histoire du theatre françois depuis son origine jusqu'à présent*. 15 vols. Paris: P. G. Le Mercier et Saillant, 1746.

PARKES, M. B. *Pause and Effect: An Introduction to the History of Punctuation in the West*. Berkeley: U of California P, 1993.

—— *Scribes, Scripts and Readers: Studies in the Communication, Presentation and Dissemination of Medieval Texts*. London: Hambledon, 1991.

PASK, KEVIN. *The Emergence of the English Author: Scripting the Life of the Poet in Early Modern England*. Cambridge: Cambridge UP, 1996.

PASTA, RENATO. "Towards a Social History of Ideas: The Book and Booktrade in Eighteenth-Century Italy." Hans Erich Bodeker, ed. *Histoires du livre: Nouvelles orientations*. Paris: IMEC, 1995. 101–38.

PATTERSON, MICHAEL. *The First German Theatre: Schiller, Goethe, Kleist and Büchner in Performance*. London: Routledge, 1990.

PEARSALL, DEREK. *John Lydgate*. London: Routledge & Kegan Paul, 1970.

PEARSON, JACQUELINE. *The Prostituted Muse: Images of Women and Women Dramatists, 1642–1737*. New York: St Martin's, 1988.

PELETIER DU MANS, JACQUES. *Dialogue de lOrtografe e Prononciacion Françoese (1555)*. Ed. Lambert C. Porter. Geneva: Droz, 1966.

—— *L'Art poëtique de Jacques Peletier du Mans*. Ed. André Boulanger. Paris: Société d'édition, 1930.

PEREIRE, ALFRED. *Le Journal des débats politiques et littéraires 1814–1914*. Paris: Edouard Champion, 1914.

PETERS, JULIE STONE. "The Bank, the Press, and the 'Return of Nature': On Currency, Credit, and Literary Property in the 1690s." John Brewer and Susan Staves, eds. *Early Modern Conceptions of Property*. London: Routledge, 1995. 365–88.

—— *Congreve, the Drama, and the Printed Word*. Stanford, Calif.: Stanford UP, 1990.

—— "Orality, Literacy, and Print Revisited." *Time, Memory, and the Verbal Arts*. Ed. Dennis L. Weeks and Jane Hoogestraat. Gainsville: U of Florida P, 1988: 27–50.

PETIT DE JULLEVILLE, LOUIS. *Les Mystères*. Vol. 1 of *Histoire du théâtre en France*. 4 vols. In 5. Paris: Hachette, 1880–6.

PETRUCCI, ARMANDO. "Scrittura, alfabetismo ed educazione grafica nella Roma del primo cinquecento." *Scrittura e Civilta* 2 (1978): 163–207.

PICARD, RAYMOND. *La Carrière de Jean Racine*. 2nd edn. Paris: Gallimard, 1961.

PICOT, EMILE. *Bibliographie Cornélienne*. Paris: Auguste Fontaine, 1876. Naarden: Anton W. Van Bekhoven, 1967.

—— *Catalogue des livres composant la bibliothèque de feu M. le baron James de Rothschild*. 5 vols. Paris: D. Morgand, 1884–1920.

PIERI, MARZIA. *La nascita del teatro moderno in Italia tra XV e XVI secolo*. Torino: Bollati Boringhieri, 1989.

PINERO, ARTHUR WING. *The Collected Letters of Sir Arthur Wing Pinero*. Ed. J. P. Wearing. Minneapolis: U of Minnesota P, 1974.

—— *The Times*. London: Heinemann, 1891.

PIPONNIER, FRANÇOISE, and PERRINE MANE. *Se vêtir au Moyen Âge*. Paris: Adam Biro, 1995.

PIRON, ALEXIS. *Œuvres completes*. 7 vols. Paris: M. Lambert, 1776.

PIRROTTA, NINO, and ELENA POVOLEDO. *Music and Theatre from Poliziano to Monteverdi*. Trans. Karen Eales. Cambridge: Cambridge UP, 1982.

PIX, MARY, and CATHERINE TROTTER. *The Plays of Mary Pix and Catherine Trotter*. Ed. Edna L. Steeves. 2 vols. New York: Garland, 1982.

PIXÉRÉCOURT, R. C. GUILBERT DE. *Robinson Crusoé*. Paris: Barba, 1805.

PLANCHÉ, JAMES ROBINSON. *The Recollections and Reflections of J. R. Planché (Somerset Herald). A Professional Autobiography*. 2 vols. London: Tinsley Brothers, 1872.

PLANT, MARJORIE. *The English Book Trade: An Economic History of the Making and Sale of Books*. London: George Allen & Unwin, 1939.

PLATO. *The Collected Dialogues of Plato*. Trans. Edith Hamilton and Huntington Cairns. Princeton: Princeton UP, 1961.

POCOCK, ISAAC. *Robinson Crusoe: or The Bold Buccaniers*. London: John Cumberland, *c.*1817.

POLLARD, ALFRED W. *Shakespeare's Fight with the Pirates and the Problems of the Transmission of his Text*. London: Alexander Moring, 1917.

—— *Shakespeare's Folios & Quartos*. New York: Methuen, 1909.

—— and G. R. REDGRAVE. *A Short-Title Catalogue of Books Printed in England, Scotland, and Ireland, and of English Books Printed Abroad, 1475–1640*. 2nd edn. Rev. W. A. Jackson *et al.* 3 vols. London: Bibliographical Society, 1976–91.

POPE, ALEXANDER. *The Poems of Alexander Pope*. Ed. John Butt. 11 vols. 1951–69. New York: Routledge, 1993.

PORTA, GIAMBATTISTA DELLA. *Le commedie*. Ed. Vincenzo Spampanato. Bari: G. Laterza & figli, 1910–1911.

POTTINGER, DAVID T. *The French Book Trade in the Ancien Regime 1500–1791*. Cambridge, Mass.: Harvard UP, 1958.

PRÉVILLE, PIERRE-LOUIS DUBUS, and JOSEPH-JEAN-BAPTISTE ALBOUIS DAZINCOURT. *Mémoires de Préville et de Dazincourt*. [Ed. Henri-Alexis Cahaisse.] Paris: Baudoin, 1823.

PRICE, OWEN. *The Vocal Organ*. Oxford: Amos Curteyne, 1665.

The Prodigal Son, a fragment of an interlude printed c.1530. Collections (Malone Society) I. 1 (1907): 27–30.

PRYNNE, WILLIAM. *Histriomastix*. London, E. A. and W. I. for Michael Sparke, 1633. Ed. Arthur Freeman. New York: Garland, 1974.

PULCI, ANTONIA. *La rapresentatione di santa Domitilla*. Florence: n.p., 1594.

—— *La rappresentatione di santa Guglielma*. Florence: n.p., 1554.

PULCI, BERNARDO and ANTONIA. *Rappresentazioni sacre di s. Eustachio, s. Apollonia, l'angelo Raffaello e Tobia, la regina stella*. Florence: Antonio Miscomini, [*c.*1485].

PUTTENHAM, GEORGE. *The Arte of English Poesie (1589)*. Ed. Gladys Doidge Willcock and Alice Walker. Cambridge: Cambridge UP, 1936.

RACAN, HONORAT DE BUEIL, Seigneur de. *Les Bergeries*. Jacques Scherer, ed. *Théâtre du XVIIᵉ Siècle*. Paris: Gallimard, 1975. I:287–391.

RACINE, JEAN. *Oeuvres*. Ed. Paul Mesnard. Paris: Hachette, 1865.

—— *Oeuvres complètes*. Ed. Raymond Picard. 2 vols. Paris: Gallimard, 1950.

RADCLIFF-ULMSTEAD, DOUGLAS. *The Birth of Modern Comedy in Renaissance Italy*. Chicago: U Chicago P, 1969.

RAMEAU, PIERRE. *Le Maître à danser*. Paris: Jean Villette, 1725.

RANDOLPH, THOMAS. *The Jealous Lovers*. Cambridge: U of Cambridge, 1632.

—— *The Poems and Amyntas of Thomas Randolph*. Ed. John Jay Parry. New Haven: Yale UP, 1917.

RAPPAPORT, STEVE LEE. *Worlds within Worlds : Structures of Life in Sixteenth-Century London*. Cambridge: Cambridge UP, 1989.

Rappresentatione di sco' Grisante e Daria. N.p.: Francescho di Giovanni Benvenuto, 1516.

RASMUSEEN, B. H. *The Transition from Manuscript to Printed Book*. London: Oxford UP, 1962.

RASTALL, RICHARD. *The Notation of Western Music: An Introduction*. London: M. Dent, 1983.

RASTELL, JOHN [?]. *Gentleness and Nobility*. Ed. A. C. Partridge and F. P. Wilson. Oxford: Malone Society, 1950.

—— *Time and Narrative*. Trans. Kathleen McLaughliss and David Pellauer. 2 vols. Chicago: U of Chicago P, 1984.

—— [*The Nature of the Four Elements*]. *A new interlude and a mery of the nature of the.iiii. elements*. London: John Rastell, 1519.

—— *The Nature of the Four Elements*. London: T. C. & E. C. Jack, 1908.

RAVEL, JEFFREY S. *The Contested Parterre: Public Theater and French Political Culture, 1680–1791*. Ithaca, NY: Cornell UP, 1999.

—— "The Printed Word and Audience Behavior in Eighteenth-Century France." Unpublished typescript.

—— "'La Reine Boit!': Print, Performance, and Theater Publics in France, 1724–1725." *Eighteenth-Century Studies* 29:4 (1996): 391–411.

RAVENSCROFT, EDWARD. *The Anatomist: or, the Sham Doctor*. London: R. Baldwin, 1697.

—— *Titus Andronicus, or the Rape of Lavinia*. London: J. Hindmarsh, 1687.

Recueil faict au vray de la chevauchee de l'asne, faicte en la ville de Lyon. Lyon: Guillaume Testefort, 1566.

REED, A. W. *Early Tudor Drama: Medwall, the Rastells, Heywood and the More Circle*. London: Methuen, 1926.

REICHARD, HEINRICH. *Theater-Kalender, auf das Jahr 1781*. Gotha: Carl Wilhelm Ettinger, 1781.

REISS, TIMOTHY. *Tragedy and Truth: Studies in the Development of a Renaissance and Neoclassical Discourse*. New Haven: Yale UP, 1980.

RÉMOND DE, SAINTE-ALBINE, PIERRE. *Le Comédien. Ouvrage divisé en deux parties*. Paris: Vincent, fils, 1749.

RENNERT, HUGO A. "Bibliography of the Dramatic Works of Lope de Vega Carpio Based Upon the Catalogue of John Rutter Chorley." *Revue hispanique* 33:83 (1915): 1–282.

——*Life of Lope de Vega*. 1904. New York: B. Blom, 1968.

——*The Spanish Stage in the Time of Lope de Vega*. New York: Hispanic Society of America, 1910.

RENOU, ANTOINE. *Téréé et Philomele*. Amsterdam: Delalain, 1773.

RESTORI, ANTONIO. *Saggi di Bibliografia teatrale spagnuola*. Geneva: Leo S. Olschki, 1927.

REUCHLIN, JOHANN. *Ioanis Reuchlin Phorcensis Scenica Progymnasmata*. Leipzig: Valentinus Schuman, [1503?].

The Revels History of Drama in English. Eds. Clifford Leech and T. W. Craik. 7 vols. London: Metheun, 1975–1980.

REYNOLDS, FREDERICK. *Fortune's Fool*. London: T. N. Longman, 1796.

RHODE, ERIC. *A History of the Cinema from its Origins to 1970*. New York: Da Capo, 1976.

RHODES, DENNIS E. "The Printer of Ariosto's Early Plays." *Italian Studies* 18 (1963): 13–18.

——"La Publication des comédies de Térence au XVᵉ siècle." Pierre Aquilon, Henri-Jean Martin and François Dupuigrenet Desrousilles, eds. *Le Livre dans l'Europe de la renaissance*. Paris: Promodis, 1988. 285–96.

RICCOBONI, LUIGI. *An Historical and Critical Account of the Theatres in Europe*. London: T. Waller and R. Dodsley, 1741.

RICHARDS, KENNETH and LAURA. *Commedia dell'Arte: A Documentary History*. Oxford: Basil Blackwell, 1990.

RICHARDSON, BRIAN. *Print Culture in Renaissance Italy: The Editor and the Vernacular Text, 1470–1600*. Cambridge: Cambridge UP, 1994.

RICOEUR, PAUL. *Du texte à l'action*. Paris: Seuil, 1986.

RIVAUDEAU, ANDRÉ DE. *Les Oeuvres poétiques d'André de Rivaudeau*. Ed. C. Mourain de Sourdeval. Paris: A. Aubry, 1859.

ROACH, JOSEPH R. *The Player's Passion: Studies in the Science of Acting*. Newark: U of Delaware P, 1985.

ROBBINS, EDWIN W. *Dramatic Characterization in Printed Commentaries on Terence 1473–1600*. Urbana: U of Illinois P, 1951.

ROBERTSON, JAN, and D. J. GORDON, eds. *A Calendar of Dramatic Records in the Books of the Livery Companies of London 1485–1640. Collections* (Malone Society) III. Oxford: Oxford UP, 1954.

ROBINSON, ROBERT. *The Art of Pronuntiation*. 1617. *Phonetic Writings of Robert Robinson*. Ed. E. J. Dobson. New York: Oxford UP, 1957.

ROBORTELLO, FRANCISCO. [*DeArte*] *Francisci Robortelli . . . in librum Aristotelis de Arte poetica explicatoiones*. Florence: L. Torrentini, 1548.

ROCHESTER, JOHN WILMOT, Earl of. *Valentinian*. London: Timothy Goodwin, 1685.

ROCHON DE CHABANNES, MARC ANTOINE JACQUES. *Le Jaloux*. Bordeaux: Phillipot, 1788.

ROGERS, PAT. *Grub Street: Studies in a Subculture*. London: Methuen, 1972.

ROJAS FERNANDO DE. *Celestina: tragicomedia de Calisto et Melibea*. Venice: Gregorio de Gregorii, 1525.

ROJAS FERNANDO DE. *Celestina: tragicomedia de Calisto y Melibea*. Ed. Miguel Marciales. 2 vols. Urbana: U of Illinois P, 1985.

——*Celestine en laquelle est traicte des deceptions des serviteurs envers leurs maistres*. Paris: Galliot du Pre, 1527.

——*Celestine or the Tragick-Comedie of Calisto and Melibea*. Trans. James Mabbe. Ed. Guadalupe Martinez LaCalle. London: Tamesis, 1972.

——*Comedia de Calisto y Melibea*. Seville: Stanislas Polonus, 1501.

RONSARD, PIERRE DE. *Œuvres complètes*. Ed. Gustave Cohen. 2 vols. Paris: Gallimard, 1950.

ROSA, GUY. "'Quot libras in duce?' L'édition des œuvres de Victor Hugo 1870–1885." *Mesure(s) du livre: Colloque organisé par la Bibliothèque Nationale et la Société des études romantiques*. Ed. Alain Vaillant. Paris: Bibliothèque Nationale, 1992. 223–56.

ROSE, MARK. *Authors and Owners: The Invention of Copyright*. Cambridge, Mass.: Harvard UP, 1993.

ROSENFELD, SYBIL. "Dramatic Advertisements in the Burney Newspapers 1660–1700." *PMLA* 51 (1936): 123–52.

——*The Georgian Theatre of Richmond, Yorkshire, and Its Circuit*. London: Society for Theatre Research, 1984.

——*A Short History of Scene Design in Great Britain*. Oxford: Basil Blackwell, 1973.

ROSENTHAL, LAURA J. *Playwrights and Plagiarists in Early Modern England: Gender, Authorship, Literary Property*. Ithaca, NY: Cornell UP, 1996.

ROTROU, JEAN. *La Bague de l'oubli*. Jacques Scherer, ed. *Théatre du XVIIᵉ siècle*. Paris: Gallimard, 1975. I:731–91.

ROUSSEAU, JEAN-JACQUES. *Œuvres complètes*. Ed. Bernard Gagnebin and Marcel Raymond. 5 vols. Paris: Gallimard, 1959.

ROWLEY, WILLIAM, THOMAS DEKKER, and JOHN FORD. *The Witch of Edmonton*. London: J. Cottrel for Edward Blackmore, 1658.

RUEDA, LOPE DE. *Las Cuatro Comedias: Eufemia, Armelina, Los Engañados, Medora*. Ed. Alfredo Hermenegildo. Madrid: Taurus, 1985.

RUGGLE, GEORGE. *Ignoramus*. Trans. R. C. London: W. Gilbertson, 1662.

RUNNALS, GRAHAM A. "An Actor's Role in a French Morality Play," *French Studies* 42:4 (Oct. 1988): 398–407.

——*Études sur les mystères*. Paris: Honoré Champion, 1998.

RUTLIDGE, JEAN-JACQUES. *Les Comédiens, ou le Foyer*. Paris: Successeurs de la V[eu]ve Duchesne, 2440 [1776].

——*Les Comédiens ou le foyer. Le Bureau d'esprit. Le Train de Paris ou les Bourgeois du Temps*. Ed. Pierre Peyronnet. Paris: Honoré Champion, 1999.

RYMER, THOMAS. *The Critical Works of Thomas Rymer*. Ed. Curt A. Zimansky. New Haven: Yale UP, 1956.

SABBATTINI, NICOLA. *Pratica di Fabricar Scene e Machine ne' Teatri*. Ravenna: Camerali, 1638.

SACHS, HANS. *Eygentliche Beschreibung aller Stände auff Erden*. Frankfurt: Sigmund Feyerabents, 1568.

——*Eyn gesprech vö den Scheinwercke der Gaystlichen, und jren gelübdten, damit sy züuerlesterung des blüts Christi vermaynen selig züwerden*. Nuremberg: H. Höltzel, 1524.

——*[Gedicht]. Sehr herrliche schöne und warrhaffte Gedicht, Geistlich und Weltlich, Allerley Art*. 5 vols. Nuremberg: C. Heusller, 1558–79.

SACKVILLE, THOMAS, and THOMAS NORTON. *Gorboduc or Ferrex and Porrex*. Ed. Irby B. Cauthen, Jr. Lincoln: U of Nebraska P, 1970.

SAEGER, JAMES P., and CHRISTOPHER J. FASSLER. "The London Professional Theater,

1576–1642: A Catalogue and Analysis of the Extant Printed Plays." *Research Opportunities in Renaissance Drama* 34 (1995): 63–109.

SAENGER, PAUL. "Books of Hours and the Reading Habits of the Later Middle Ages." Roger Chartier, ed. *The Culture of Print: Power and the Uses of Print in Early Modern Europe.* Trans. Lydia G. Cochrane. Cambridge: Polity, 1989.

——"Silent Reading: Its Impact on Late Medieval Script and Society." *Viator* 13 (1982): 367–414.

——and MICHAEL HEINLEN. "Incunable Description and Its Implication for the Analysis of Fifteenth-Century Reading Habits." Sandra Hindman, ed. *Printing the Written Word: The Social History of Books, circa 1450–1520.* Ithaca, NY: Cornell UP, 1991. 225–58.

SAINT-AMANT, MARC ANTOINE GÉRARD, sieur de. *Œuvres.* Ed. Jean Lagny. 5 vols. Paris: Marcel Didier, 1967.

SAINT-EVREMOND, CHARLES DE MARGUETEL DE SAINT-DENIS. *La Comédie des Académistes et Les Académiciens.* Ed. Paolo Carile. Milan: Cisalpino-Goliardica, 1976.

——*Œuvres en prose.* Ed. René Ternois. 4 vols. Paris: Didier, 1962–69.

SAINTE-BEUVE, CHARLES AUGUSTIN. *Œuvres.* 2 vols. Ed. Maxime Leroy. Paris: Gallimard, 1949–56.

SAMPSON, H. GRANT. "Some Bibliographical Evidence Concerning Restoration Attitudes Towards Drama." *Journal of the Rutgers University Libraries* 38:2 (Dec. 1976): 98–108.

SANCHEZ, JOSÉ. *Academias literarias del siglo de oro español.* Madrid: Biblioteca Romanica Hispanica, 1961.

SANDERS, EVE RACHELE. *Gender and Literacy on Stage in Early Modern England.* Cambridge: Cambridge UP, 1998.

SAUNDERS, DAVID. *Authorship and Copyright.* London: Routledge, 1992.

SAUNDERS, J. W. *The Profession of English Letters.* London: Routledge, 1964.

——"The Stigma of Print: A Note on the Social Bases of Tudor Poetry," *Essays in Criticism* 1 (1951): 139–64.

SAVERIO, FRANCHI. *Drammaturgia Romana.* Rome: Edizioni di storia e letteratura, 1988.

SCALA, FLAMINIO. *Il teatro delle favole rappresentative.* Ed. Ferruccio Marotti. 2 vols. Milan: Edizioni Il Polifilo, 1976.

——*Scenarios of the Commedia dell'Arte: Flaminio Scala's Il teatro delle favole rappresentative.* Trans. Henry F. Salerno. New York: New York UP, 1967.

SCALIGER, JULIUS CAESAR. *Poetices libri septem. Sieben Bücher über die Dichtkunst.* Ed. Luc Deitz. 4 vols. Stuttgart: Bad Cannstatt, 1994–8.

——*Select Translations from Scaliger's Poetics.* Trans. Frederick Morgan Padelford. New York: Holt, 1905.

SCHELANDRE, JEAN DE. *Tyr et Sidon Tragicomedie Divisee en deux journees.* Paris: Robert Estienne, 1628.

SCHELLING, FRIEDRICH. *The Philosophy of Art.* Trans. Douglas W. Scott. Minneapolis: U of Minnesota P, 1989.

——*Schellings Werke.* Ed. Manfred Schröter. 6 vols. Munich: C. H. Beck and R. Oldenbourg, 1956–62.

SCHERER, JACQUES. *La Dramaturgie classique en France.* Paris: Nizet, [1950].

——ed. *Théâtre du XVIIᵉ siècle.* 3 vols. Paris: Gallimard, 1975.

SCHEVILL, RUDOLPH. *Dramatic Art of Lope de Vega.* New York: Russel & Russell, 1964.

SCHILLER, FRIEDRICH. *Schillers Werke: Nationalausgabe.* 43 vols. Ed. Julius Petersen and Gerhard Fricke. Weimar: Hermann Böhlaus Nachfolger, 1943– .

SCHILLER, FRIEDRICH. *Works of Friedrich Von Schiller*. Trans. Theodore Martin *et al.* 10 vols. in 5. New York: Aldus, 1902.

SCHINKEL, KARL FRIEDRICH. *Sammlung von Theater-Decorationen*. Revised edn. Potsdam: Ferdinand Riegel, 1849.

SCHÖNE, GÜNTER. *Die Entwicklung der Perspektivbühne von Serlio bis Galli-Bibiena nach den Perspektivbüchern theatergeschichtliche Forschungen*. Leipzig: Leopold Voss, 1933.

SCOTT, VIRGINIA. *The Commedia dell'Arte in Paris 1644–1697*. Charlottesville: UP of Virginia, 1990.

SCUDÉRY, GEORGES DE. *La Comédie des comédiens*. Ed. Joan Crow. Exeter: U of Exeter P, 1975.

—— *La Comédie des comédiens*. Paris: Augustin Courbé, 1635.

SEBILLET, THOMAS. *Art poétique françoys*. Ed. Félix Gaiffe. Paris: Société Nouvelle de Librarie et d'édition, 1910.

SENECA, LUCIUS ANNAEUS. *Lucii ānei Senece . . . decem tragediae*. [Paris: Jean Petit, 1512].

—— *Tragoediae Senecae*. Venice: Joannes Rivius, 1505.

SERLIO, SEBASTIANO. *The First [-fifth] booke of architecture*. London: R. Peake, 1611.

—— *I sette libri dell'architettura*. 2 vols. Venice: Arnaldo Forni, 1584.

—— *Tutte le opere d'architettura*. Venice: Giacomo de'Franceschi, 1619.

SHADWELL, THOMAS. *The Lancashire-Witches, and Tegue o Dibelly the Irish-Priest*. London: John Starkey, 1682.

SHAKESPEARE, WILLIAM. *The Complete Works*. Ed. Stanley Wells and Gary Taylor. Oxford: Clarendon, 1988.

—— *The Dramatic Works of William Shakespeare*. Ed. Isaac Reed *et al.* 10 vols. New York: H. Durell, 1817–18.

—— *The History of King Henry the Fourth as Revised by Sir Edward Dering*. Ed. George Walton Williams and G. Blakemore Evans. Charlottesville: UP of Virginia, 1974.

—— *King Henry IV*. London: R. W., 1700.

—— *King Henry IV Part 2*. Ed. A. R. Humphreys. London: Methuen, 1966.

—— *Love's Labour's Lost*. Ed. Richard David. 5th edn. London: Methuen, 1956.

—— *Mr. William Shakespeare: His Comedies, Histories, and Tragedies*. Ed. Edward Capell. 10 vols. London: J. and R. Tonson, [1768].

—— *Mr. William Shakespeares Comedies, Histories, & Tragedies*. London: Isaac Jaggard and Edward Blount, 1623.

—— *The Plays and Poems of William Shakspeare, with the Corrections and Illustrations of Various Commentators*. Ed. Edmond Malone. 21 vols. London: F. C. and J. Rivington *et al.*, 1821.

—— *Titus Andronicus*. Ed. J. C. Maxwell. 3rd edn. London: Methuen, 1961.

—— *The Tragedy of Hamlet Prince of Denmark*. London: J. Martyn and H. Herringman, 1676.

—— *Romeo and Juliet*. Ed. Brian Gibbons. London: Methuen, 1980.

—— *The Works of Mr. William Shakespear*. Ed. Nicholas Rowe. 6 vols. London: Jacob Tonson, 1709.

—— *The Works of Shakespeare*. Ed. Alexander Pope. 6 vols. London: Jacob Tonson, 1725.

SHAPIRO, BARBARA J. *Probability and Certainty in Seventeenth-Century England: A Study of the Relationships Between Natural Science, Religion, History, Law, and Literature*. Princeton: Princeton UP, 1983.

SHARPHAM, EDWARD. *A Critical Old Spelling Edition of the Works of Edward Sharpham*. Ed. Christopher Gordon Petter. New York: Garland, 1986.

SHATTUCK, CHARLES H. *The Shakespeare Promptbooks: A Descriptive Catalogue*. Urbana: U of Illinois P, 1965.

——ed. *William Charles Macready's King John: A Facsimile Prompt-Book*. Urbana: U of Illinois P, 1962.

SHAW, GEORGE BERNARD. *Bernard Shaw on Cinema*. Ed. Bernard F. Dukore. Carbondale: Southern Illinois UP, 1997.

——*Collected Letters 1874–1897*. Ed. Dan Laurence. 2 vols. New York: Dodd, Mead, 1965–72.

——*The Complete Prefaces*. Ed. Dan H. Laurence and Daniel J. Leary. 3 vols. London: Penguin, 1993.

——*Shaw on Theatre*. Ed. E. J. West. New York: Hill & Wang, 1958.

SHERGOLD, N. D. *A History of the Spanish Stage from Medieval Times Until the End of the Seventeenth Century*. Oxford: Clarendon, 1967.

SHERIDAN, RICHARD BRINSLEY. *The Dramatic Works of Richard Brinsley Sheridan*. Ed. Cecil Price. 2 vols. Oxford: Clarendon, 1973.

SHERMAN, SANDRA. *Finance and Fictionality in the Early Eighteenth Century: Accounting for Defoe*. Cambridge: Cambridge UP, 1996.

SHIRLEY, JAMES. *The Bird in a Cage*. London: B. Alsop and T. Fawcet for W. Cooke, 1633.

——*The Triumph of Peace*. London: John Norton for William Cooke, 1633.

SIDNEY, PHILIP. *An Apology for Poetry or The Defence of Poesy*. Ed. Geoffrey Shepherd. London: Thomas Nelson, 1965.

SIMÓN DÍAZ, JOSÉ. *Bibliografía de la literatura hispánica*. 2nd edn. Madrid: Consejo superior de Investigaciones Científicas, Istituto "Miguel de Cervantes" de Filología Hispánica, 1960–84.

SIMPSON, PERCY. *Proof-Reading in the Sixteenth, Seventeenth and Eighteenth Centuries*. London: Oxford UP, 1935.

SISSON, C. J. "Shakespeare Quartos as Prompt-Copies," *Review of English Studies* 18 (1942): 135–40.

SKELTON, JOHN. *John Skelton, The Complete English Poems*. Ed. John Scattergood. New Haven: Yale UP, 1983.

——*Magnificence. A goodly Interlude and a mery, devysed and made by mayster Skelton poet laureate, late deceasyd*. [London: J. Rastell, *c*.1530–3].

SLIGHTS, WILLIAM W. E. "Bodies of Text and Textualized Bodies in *Sejanus* and *Coriolanus*." *Medieval and Renaissance Drama in England* 5 (1990): 181–93.

SMITH, PAUL JULIAN. *Writing in the Margin: Spanish Literature of the Golden Age*. Oxford: Clarendon, 1988.

SMITH, JOAN SUMNER. "The Italian Sources of Inigo Jones's Style." *Burlington Magazine* 94:592 (July 1952): 200–7.

SMOLLETT, TOBIAS. *The Adventures of Peregrine Pickle*. Ed. James L. Clifford. London: Oxford UP, 1964.

SNYDER, JON R. *Writing the Scene of Speaking: Theories of Dialogue in the Late Italian Renaissance*. Stanford, Calif.: Stanford UP, 1989.

SOREL, CHARLES. *La Jeunesse de Francion*. Paris: Brossard, 1922.

SOUFAS, TERESA SCOTT, ed. *Women's Acts: Plays by Women Dramatists of Spain's Golden Age*. Louisville: UP of Kentucky, 1997.

SOUTHEY, ROBERT. *New Letters*. Ed. Kenneth Clarke. 2 vols. New York: Columbia UP, 1965.

SPANGENBERG, WOHLFARTH. *Jeremia. Eine Geistliche Tragœdia*. Strasbourg: Tobias Jobin, 1603.

The Spectator. Ed. Donald F. Bond. 5 vols. Oxford: Clarendon, 1965.

SPENSER, EDMUND. *The Faerie Queene*. Ed. Thomas P. Roche, Jr. New Haven: Yale UP, 1981.

SPRAT, THOMAS. *History of the Royal Society*. London: T. R. for J. Martyn, 1667. Eds. Jackson I. Cope and Harold W. Jones. St. Louis: Washington U, 1958.

STAFFORD, BARBARA. *Body Criticism: Imaging the Unseen in Enlightenment Art and Medicine*. Cambridge, Mass.: MIT, 1991.

STALLYBRASS, PETER, and ALLON WHITE. *The Politics and Poetics of Transgression*. Ithaca, NY: Cornell UP, 1986.

STATES, BERT O. *Great Reckonings in Little Rooms*. Berkeley: U of California P, 1985.

STEELE, RICHARD. *The Plays of Richard Steele*. Ed. Shirley Strum Kenny. Oxford: Clarendon, 1971.

—— *The Tatler*. Ed. Donald F. Bond. 3 vols. Oxford: Clarendon, 1987.

STEINBERG, S. H. *Five Hundred Years of Printing*. Middlesex: Penguin, 1955.

STEPHENS, JOHN RUSSELL. *The Profession of the Playwright: British Theatre 1800–1990*. Cambridge: Cambridge UP, 1992.

STOCK, BRIAN. *The Implications of Literacy: Written Language and Models of Interpretation in the Eleventh and Twelfth Centuries*. Princeton: Princeton UP, 1983.

—— *Listening for the Text: On the Uses of the Past*. Baltimore: Johns Hopkins UP, 1990.

STOCKWOOD, JOHN. *A Sermon Preached at Paules Crosse on Barthelmew Day*. London: George Byshop, [1578].

STONE, GEORGE WINCHESTER, Jr. "The Making of the Repertory." Robert D. Hume, ed. *The London Theatre World, 1660–1800*. Carbondale: Southern Illinois UP, 1980. 181–209.

STRATMAN, CARL J. *Dramatic Play Lists: 1591–1963*. New York: New York Public Library, 1966.

STREET, BRIAN V. ed. *Cross-Cultural Approaches to Literacy*. Cambridge: Cambridge UP, 1993.

—— *Literacy in Theory and Practice*. Cambridge: Cambridge UP, 1984.

STRONG, ROY. *Splendour at Court: Renaissance Spectacle and Illusion*. London: Weidenfeld and Nicholson, 1973.

STURGESS, K. M. "The Early Quartos of Heywood's *A Woman Killed with Kindness*." *Library* 5th ser. 25:2 (June 1970): 93–104.

SUÁREZ DE FIGUEROA, CHRISTOVAL. *Plaza Universal de Todas Ciencias y Artes*. Madrid: Luis Sanchez, 1615.

SUMMERS, MONTAGUE. *The Restoration Theatre*. New York: Macmillan, 1934.

SUTHERLAND, JAMES R. " 'Polly' Among the Pirates," *Modern Language Review* 37 (1942): 291–303.

SWIFT, JONATHAN. *The Prose Works of Jonathan Swift*. Ed. Herbert Davis. 14 vols. Oxford: Basil Blackwell, 1951–68.

TALMA, FRANÇOIS-JOSEPH [and HENRI-LOUIS LEKAIN]. *Mémoires de Lekain, précédés de Réflexions sur cet acteur, et sur l'art théatral*. Paris: Étienne Ledoux, 1825.

—— *Reflexions on the Actor's Art*. New York: Dramatic Museum of Columbia U, 1915.

TASSO, TORQUATO. *Tasso's Dialogues: A Selection, with the Discourse on the Art of the Dialogue*. Trans. Carnes Lord and Dain A. Trafton. Berkeley: U of California P, 1982.

TATARKIEWICZ, W. "Theatrica, the Science of Entertainment." *Journal of the History of Ideas* 26 (1965): 263–72.

TATE, NAHUM. *The History of King Lear*. London: E. Flesher, 1681.

TAYLOR, GARY. "Monopolies, Show Trials, Disaster, and Invasion: *King Lear* and Censorship." Gary Taylor and Michael Warren, eds. *The Division of the Kingdoms: Shakespeare's Two Versions of* King Lear. Oxford: Clarendon, 1983. 75–120.

——and Michael Warren, eds. *The Division of the Kingdoms: Shakespeare's Two Versions of* King Lear. Oxford: Clarendon, 1983.

TAYLOR, STEVEN M. "Typography and Thalia: Printing's Contribution to the Comic in Fifteenth- and Sixteenth-Century France." *Fifteenth-Century Studies* (1985) 11: 111–20.

TCHEMERZINE, AVENIR. *Bibliographie d'éditions originales et rare d'auteurs français des XVᵉ, XVIᵉ, XVIIᵉ et XVIIIᵉ siècles*. 5 vols. Paris: Marcel Plée, 1932. Paris: Hermann, 1977.

TERENCE. *Comedie*. Venice: Jacob da Borgo Francho, 1538.

—— *Comoediae*. Venice: Jacobus Rubeus, 1476.

—— *Comoediae*. Ed. J. Badius Ascensius. Lyon: Johann Trechsel, 1493.

—— *Eunuchus*. Trans. Hans Neidhart. Ulm: Conrad Dinckmut, 1486.

—— *Les Sis comedies de Terence*. Antwerp: Jean Waesberghe, 1566.

—— *P. Terentii comoediae sex*. Paris: Robert Stephanus, 1529.

—— *Sechs Comoedien Publij Terentij Aphri*. Frankfurt: Christian Egenolffs Erben, 1568.

—— *Terence in English*. Trans. Richard Bernard. Cambridge: John Legate, 1598.

—— *Terenti cũ Directorio vocabulorũ Sententiarũ artis Comice*. Strasbourg: Johann Grüninger, 1496.

—— *Terentius comico carmine*. Strasbourg: Johann Grüninger, 1503.

Theater-Journal für Deutschland. Gotha: Carl Wilhelm Ettinger, 1777.

Theatre Miscellany: Six Pieces connected with the Seventeenth-Century Stage. Oxford: Basil Blackwell, 1953.

The Theatrical Museum. London: E. Johnstone, 1776.

Thēterlude of Youth. London: John Waley, [1550s].

THOMAS, DIANA M. *The Royal Company of Printers and Booksellers of Spain: 1763–1794*. Troy, NY: Whitston, 1984.

THOMAS, KEITH. "The Meaning of Literacy in Early Modern England." *The Written Word: Literacy in Transition*. Ed. Gerd Baumann. Oxford: Clarendon, 1986. 97–131.

THOMPSON, ANN, and JOHN O. THOMPSON. *Shakespeare: Meaning and Metaphor*. Sussex: Harvester, 1987.

The Three Parnassus Plays (1598–1601). Ed. J. B. Leishman. London: Ivor Nicholson & Watson, 1949.

THUAU, ÉTIENNE. *Raison d'état et pensée politique a l'époque de Richelieu*. Paris: Armand Colin, 1966.

TICKNOR, GEORGE. *History of Spanish Literature*. 6th edn. 3 vols. 1891. New York: Gordian, 1965.

TIGERSTEDT, E. N. "Observations on the Reception of the Aristotelian *Poetics* in the Latin West." *Studies in the Renaissance* 15 (1968): 7–24.

TOMALIN, CLAIRE. *Mrs. Jordan's Profession: The Story of a Great Actress and a Future King*. London, Viking, 1994.

Tom Tyler and his Wife. London: [Francis Kirkman], 1661.

TORRES NAHARRO, BARTOLOMÉ. *Propalladia and Other Works*. Ed. Joseph E. Gillet. Vol. 2 of *Collected Plays*. Bryn Mawr, Pa.: George Banta, 1946.

TOSCANI, BERNARD. "Antonia Pulci (?1452–?)." *Italian Women Writers: A Bio-Bibliographical Sourcebook*. Ed. Rinaldina Russell. Westport, Conn.: Greenwood, 1994. 344–52.

The Towneley Cycle: A Facsimile of Huntington MS HMI. Ed. A. C. Cawley and Martin Stevens. Leeds: U. of Leeds School of English, 1976.

TOWNSHEND, AURELIAN. *Aurelian Townshend's Poems and Masks*. Ed. E. K. Chambers. London: Clarendon, 1912.

TRAISTER, DANIEL. "Reluctant Virgins: The Stigma of Print Revisited." *Colby Quarterly* 26:2 (June 1990): 75–86.

TRIBBLE, EVELYN B. *Margins and Marginality: The Printed Page in Early Modern England.* Charlottesville: UP of Virginia, 1993.

TRISSINO, GIOVANNI GIORGIO. *La quinta e la sesta divisione.* Venice: Andrea Arrivabene, 1562. Ed. Bernhard Fabian. Munich: Wilhelm Fink, 1969.

——*La poetica.* Venice: n.p. 1529. Ed. Bernhard Fabian. Munich: Wilhelm Fink, 1969.

——*Sophonisba.* Ed. Gilles Corrozet. Trans. Mellin de Saint-Gelais. Paris: P. Danfrie et R. Breton, 1559.

——[Type-specimen of chancery italic, Ludovico degli Arrighi's type designs] [Vicenza: Tolomeo Janiculo, 1529].

TROTT, DAVID. "A Dramaturgy of the Unofficial Stage: The Non-Texts of Louis Fuzelier." *L'Age du théâtre en France/The Age of Theatre in France.* Ed. David Trott and Nicole Boursier. Edmonton, AB: Academic Printing and Publishing, 1988. 209–18.

TROVATO, PAOLO. *Con ogni diligenza corretto: la stampa e le revisioni editoirali dei testi letterari italiani (1470–1570).* Bologna: Il Mulino, 1991.

TRUCHET, JACQUES, ed. *Théâtre du XVIII⁰ siècle.* 2 vols. Paris: Gallimard, 1972.

URKOWITZ, STEVEN. "The Base Shall to th'Legitimate: The Growth of an Editorial Tradition." Gary Taylor and Michael Warren, eds. *The Division of the Kingdoms: Shakespeare's Two Versions of* King Lear. Oxford: Clarendon, 1983. 23–43.

VAN CLEVE, JOHN WALTER. *Harlequin Besieged: The Reception of Comedy in Germany during the Early Enlightenment.* Bern: Peter Lang, 1980.

VAN HOOF, HENRI. *Petite histoire des dictionnaires.* Louvain: Peeters, 1994.

VANBRUGH, JOHN. *The Complete Works of Sir John Vanbrugh.* Ed. Bonamy Dobrée. 4 vols. London: Nonesuch, 1927.

VAUQUELIN DE LA FRESNAYE, JEAN. *L'Art poétique de Vauquelin de la Fresnaye.* Ed. Georges Pellissier. Paris: Garnier, 1885.

VEGA CARPIO, LOPE FÉLIX DE. *Decima septima parte de las comedias de Lope de Vega Carpio.* Madrid: Fernando Correa, 1621.

——*Doze comedias de Lope de Vega, Sacadas de sus originales por el mismo.* Madrid: Alonso Martin, 1617.

——*El arte nuevo de hacer comedias. La discreta enamorada.* 4th edn. Madrid: Espasa-Calpe, S. A., 1973.

——*Fuente Ovejuna.* Ed. Maria Grazia Profeti. Barcelona: Planeta, 1981.

——*La Dorotea.* Trans. Alan S. Trueblood and Edwin Honig. Cambridge, Mass.: Harvard UP, 1985.

——*The New Art of Writing Plays.* Trans. William T. Brewster. New York: Dramatic Museum of Columbia U, 1914.

——*Obras completas de Lope de Vega.* Ed. Manuel Arroyo Stephens and Domingo Yndurain. 18 vols. Madrid: Biblioteca Castro, 1993–8.

——*Trezena parte de las comedias de Lope de Vega Carpio.* Madrid: Alonso Martin, 1620.

VIALA, ALAIN. *Naissance de l'écrivain: sociologie de la littérature à l'âge classique.* Paris: Editions de minuit, 1985.

VIGNOLA, GIACOMO BAROZZIO DA. *Le due regole della prospettiva pratica di M. Iacomo Barozzi da Bignola.* Rome: Francesco Zannetti, 1583.

VIGNY, ALFRED DE. *Œuvres complètes.* Eds. François Germain and André Jarry. 2 vols. Paris: Gallimard, 1986.

VINCE, RONALD W. *Ancient and Medieval Theatre.* Westport, Conn.: Greenwood, 1984.

——*Neoclassical Theatre: A Historiographical Handbook.* New York: Greenwood, 1988.

VIPERANO, GIOVANNI ANTONIO. *De poetica libri tres.* 1579. Münich: Wilhelm Fink, 1967.

—— *On Poetry*. Ed. Philip Rollinson. Cambridge: James Clarke, 1987.

VITRUVIUS. *I dieci libri dell'architettura di M. Vitruvio*. Trans. Daniel Barbaro. Venice: Francesco de'Franceschi Senes & Giovanni Chrieger Alemano Compagni, 1567.

VOET, LEON. *The Golden Compasses: a History and Evaluation of the Printing and Publishing Activities of the Officina Plantiniana at Antwerp*. 2 vols. Amsterdam: Van Gend, 1969–72.

VOLTAIRE, FRANÇOIS MARIE AROUET DE. *Les Oeuvres complètes de Voltaire*. Ed. Theodore Besterman *et al*. 135 vols. Geneva: Institut et Musée Voltaire, 1968–77.

—— *Œuvres complètes*. 52 vols. Paris: Garnier, 1877–85.

—— *Pièces inédites de Voltaire, imprimées d'après les manuscrits originaux*. Paris: Didot, 1820.

WAGNER, RICHARD. *Richard Wagner's Prose Works*. Trans. William Ashton Ellis. 8 vols. London: Kegan Paul, 1895.

—— *Sämtliche Schriften und Dichtungen*. 6th edn. 16 vols. Leipzig: Breitkopf & Härtel, 1912.

WALKER, GREG. *The Politics of Performance in Early Renaissance Drama*. Cambridge: Cambridge UP, 1998.

WALL, WENDY. *Imprint of Gender*. Ithaca, NY: Cornell UP, 1993.

WALLER, EDMUND. *The Maid's Tragedy Altered. With some other Pieces*. London: Jacob Tonson, 1690.

WALSH, WILLIAM. *A Dialogue Concerning Women, Being a Defence of the Sex*. London: R. Bentley and J. Tonson, 1691.

WAQUET, FRANÇOISE. "Book Subscriptions in Early Eighteenth-Century Italy." *Publishing History* 33 (1993): 77–88.

WARNER, RALPH E. "The First and Second Editions of Calderón's *Cuarta Parte*." *Hispanic Review* 16 (1948): 209–37.

WARNER, WILLIAM, trans. *Menaecmi*. London: Tho. Creede to be sold by William Barley, 1595.

[*Wealth and Health*] *The Interlude of Wealth and Health*. Oxford: Oxford UP, 1963.

WEAVER, JOHN. *Anatomical and Mechanical Lectures Upon Dancing*. London: J. Brotherton, 1721.

—— *An Essay Towards a History of Dancing*. London: Jacob Tonson, 1712.

—— *The Loves of Mars and Venus*. London: W. Mears, 1717.

—— *The Complete Works of John Webster*. Ed. F. L. Lucas. 4 vols. London: Chatto & Windus, 1927.

WEINBERG, BERNARD. *Critical Prefaces of the French Renaissance*. Evanston, Ill.: Northwestern UP, 1950.

—— *A History of Literary Criticism in the Italian Renaissance*. 2 vols. Chicago: U of Chicago P, 1961.

—— "Robortello on the *Poetics*." *Critics and Criticism: Ancient and Modern*. Ed. R. S. Crane. Chicago: U of Chicago P, 1952. 319–48.

WERKMEISTER, LUCYLE. *A Newspaper History of England 1792–1793*. Lincoln, NB: U of Nebraska P, 1967.

WESTFALL, SUZANNE R. *Patrons and Performance: Early Tudor Household Revels*. Oxford: Clarendon, 1990.

WESTON, KARL E. "The Illustrated Terence Manuscripts." *Harvard Studies in Classical Philology* 14 (1903): 37–54.

WHITE, HAROLD OGDEN. *Plagiarism and Imitation During the English Renaissance*. Cambridge, Mass.: Harvard UP, 1935.

WHITE, PAUL WHITFIELD. *Theatre and Reformation: Protestantism, Patronage, and Playing in Tudor England*. Cambridge: Cambridge UP, 1993.

WICKHAM, GLYNNE. *Early English Stages 1300–1660.* 3 vols. London: Routledge & Kegan Paul, 1980–1.

—— *The Medieval Theatre.* 1974. 3rd edn. Cambridge: Cambridge UP, 1987.

WIKANDER, MATTHEW H. *The Play of Truth & State: Historical Drama From Shakespeare to Brecht.* Baltimore: Johns Hopkins UP, 1986.

WILDE, OSCAR. *The Letters of Oscar Wilde.* Ed. Rupert Hart-Davis. New York: Harcourt, Brace & World, 1962.

WILES, R. M. *Serial Publication in England before 1750.* Cambridge: University Press, 1957.

WILHELM, JACQUES. "The French Book in the XVIIth and XVIIIth Centuries." André Lejard, ed. *The Art of the French Book from Early Manuscripts to the Present Time.* London: Paul Elek, n.d. 69–86.

WILKINSON, TATE. *Memoirs of His Own Life.* 4 vols. York: Wilson, Spence and Mawman, 1790.

WILLIAMS, GORDON. *Shakespeare, Sex and the Print Revolution.* London: Athlone, 1996.

WILLISON, IAN. "Editorial Theory and Practice and the History of the Book." *Library Chronicle of the University of Texas* 20:1–2 (1990): 110–25.

WILSHIRE, BRUCE. *Role Playing and Identity: The Limits of Theatre as Metaphor.* Bloomington: Indiana UP, 1982.

WILSON, F. P. *The English Drama 1485–1585.* Ed. G. K. Hunter. Oxford: Clarendon, 1968.

WILSON, MARGARET. *Tirso de Molina.* New York: Twayne, 1977.

WILSON, THOMAS. *The Arte of Rhetorique.* London: R. Graftonus, 1553.

WIMPHELING, JAKOB. *Stilpho Jacobi Vympfelingii Sletstatini.* [Speier: Conrad Hist, 1495.]

WINN, JAMES ANDERSON. *John Dryden and His World.* New Haven: Yale UP, 1987.

—— *Unsuspected Eloquence: A History of the Relations between Poetry and Music.* New Haven: Yale UP, 1981.

WITHER, GEORGE. *The Schollers Purgatory.* [London]: n.p., [c.1625].

WITTMANN, REINHARD. *Geschichte des deutschen Buchhandels: Ein Überblick.* Munich: C. H. Beck, 1991.

WOODES, NATHANIEL. *An Excellent New Commedie, Intituled: The Conflict of Conscience.* London: Richard Bradocke, 1581.

WORDSWORTH, WILLIAM. *The Borderers.* Ed. Robert Osborn. Ithaca: Cornell UP, 1982.

WORTHEN, WILLIAM B. *The Idea of the Actor: Drama and the Ethics of Performance.* Princeton: Princeton UP, 1984.

WOUDHUYSEN, H. R. *Sir Philip Sidney and the Circulation of Manuscripts 1558–1640.* Oxford: Clarendon, 1996.

WRIGHT, LOUIS B. "The Reading of Plays during the Puritan Revolution." *Huntington Library Bulletin* 6 (1934): 72–108.

WYCHERLEY, WILLIAM. *The Complete Plays of William Wycherley.* Ed. Gerald Weales. New York: New York UP, 1967.

WYCLIFFE JOHN, et al., trans. *The Holy Bible.* Ed. Josiah Forshall and Frederic Madden. 4 vols. Oxford: Oxford UP, 1850.

WYNNE, SHIRLEY. "Reviving the Gesture Sign: Bringing the Dance Back Alive." *The Stage and the Page: London's 'Whole Show' in the Eighteenth-Century Theatre.* Ed. George Winchester Stone, Jr. Berkeley: U of California P, 1981. 193–208.

YATES, FRANCES A. *The Art of Memory.* London: Routledge and Kegan Paul, 1966.

—— *The French Academies of the Sixteenth Century.* London: Routledge, 1988.

—— *Theatre of the World.* Chicago: U of Chicago P, 1969.

The York Play: A Facsimile of British Library MS Additional 35290. Eds. Richard Beadle and Peter Meredith. Leeds: U of Leeds School of English, 1983.

Young, Edward. *Edward Young's Conjectures on Original Composition*. Ed. Edith J. Morley. Manchester: Manchester UP, 1918.

Young, Bert Edward, and Grace Philputt Young. "'Une Nouvelle édition des oeuvres de feu Monsieur de Molière.'" Charles Varlet, Sieur de La Grange, *Le Registre de La Grange 1659–1685*. Ed. Bert Edward Young and Grace Philputt Young. 2 vols. Paris: E. Droz, 1947. 137–63.

Zola, Émile. *Œuvres complètes*. Ed. Henri Mitterand. 15 vols. Paris: Cercle du Livre Précieux, 1966.

Index